Selling Today

Creating Customer Value

10th Edition

Selling Today

Creating Customer Value

Gerald L. Manning
Des Moines Area Community College

Barry L. Reece
Virginia Polytechnic Institute and State University

Upper Saddle River, New Jersey, 07458

Library of Congress Cataloging-in-Publication Data

Manning, Gerald L.
Selling today : creating customer value / Gerald L. Manning, Barry L. Reece.—10th ed.
p. cm.
Includes bibliographical references and index.
ISBN 0-13-186683-4
1. Selling. I. Reece, Barry L. II. Title.

HF5438.25.M35 2007
658.85—dc22

2005052712

VP/Editorial Director: Jeff Shelstad
Acquisitions Editor: Katie Stevens
Project Manager: Melissa Pellerano
Editorial Assistant: Christine Ietto
Media Project Manager: Peter Snell
Marketing Manager: Ashaki Charles
Marketing Assistant: Joanna Sabella
Associate Director: Judy Leale
Managing Editor: Renata Butera
Production Editor: Suzanne Grappi
Permissions Coordinator: Charles Morris
Manufacturing Buyer: Diane Peirano
Design/Composition Manager: Christy Mahon
Composition Liaison: Suzanne Duda
Art Director: Janet Slowik
Interior Design: Liz Harasymczuk
Cover Design: Liz Harasymczuk
Cover Illustration/Photo: IT Stock Int'l/eStock Photo
Illustrator (Interior): ElectraGraphics, Inc
Director, Image Resource Center: Melinda Reo
Manager, Rights and Permissions: Zina Arabia
Manager, Visual Research: Beth Brenzel
Manager, Cover Visual Research & Permissions: Karen Sanatar
Image Permission Coordinator: Joanne Dippel
Photo Researcher: Teri Stratford
Composition/Full-Service Project Management: Preparé, Inc.
Printer/Binder: Courier/Kendalville
Typeface: 10.5/12 AGaramond

Credits and acknowledgments borrowed from other sources and reproduced, with permission, in this textbook appear on appropriate page within text.

Pearson Education Ltd.
Pearson Education Singapore, Pte. Ltd
Pearson Education, Canada, Ltd
Pearson Education—Japan
Pearson Education Australia PTY, Limited
Pearson Education North Asia Ltd
Pearson Educación de Mexico, S.A. de C.V.
Pearson Education Malaysia, Pte. Ltd

10 9 8 7 6 5 4
ISBN 0-13-186683-4

We wish to dedicate this book to our wives
whose patience and support make our work possible.

Beth Hall Manning and Vera Marie Reece

Brief Contents

PART | 6

Management of Self and Others

Contents

PREFACE

Salespeople and selling teams are currently in the process of redefining their roles and adopting new selling frameworks. These changes, reflected in the tenth edition of *Selling Today,* are driven by rapidly changing market conditions and heightened customer's expectations. Today's more demanding customers expect the salesperson to create and communicate a consistent and convincing concept of value at every step of the selling process. The creation and delivery of value is an expanded theme of this new edition.

The goal of each revision of *Selling Today: Creating Customer Value* is to develop the most practical and applied text available. The revision process begins with a thorough review of several hundred articles, books, and research reports. The authors also study popular sales training programs such as Conceptual Selling, SPIN Selling, Integrity Selling and Solution Selling. These training programs are used by major corporations such as Microsoft, Marriott, Principal Financial Group, Wells Fargo Bank, UPS, SAS Institute and Xerox Corporation. Of course, numerous reviews by current adopters influence decisions made during the revision process.

BUILDING ON TRADITIONAL STRENGTHS

Selling Today: Creating Customer Value has been successful because the authors continue to build on strengths that have been enthusiastically praised by instructors and students. Previous editions of *Selling Today* have chronicled the evolution of consultative selling, strategic selling, partnering, customer relationship management (CRM) and value-added selling. This edition provides new material on each of these important concepts.

1. ***The four broad strategic areas of personal selling,*** introduced in Chapter 1, serve as a catalyst for skill development and professional growth throughout the textbook. Success in selling depends heavily on the student's ability to develop relationship, product, customer, and presentation strategies. Salespeople who have achieved long-term success in personal selling have mastered the skills needed in each of these four strategic areas.
2. ***The partnering era is described in detail.*** A series of partnering principles is presented in selected chapters. Strategic alliances, the highest form of partnering, are discussed in detail.
3. ***Value-added selling strategies*** are presented throughout the text. Salespeople today are guided by a new principle of personal selling: **Partnerships are established and maintained only when the salesperson creates customer value.** Customers have fundamentally changed their expectations. They want to partner with salespeople who can create value, not just communicate it. Value creation involves a series of improvements in the sales process that enhance the customer's experience.

4. ***Real-world examples,*** a hallmark of our previous editions and continued in this edition, build the reader's interest and promote understanding of major topics and concepts. Examples have been obtained from a range of progressive organizations, large and small, such as Whirlpool Corporation, UPS, Mutual of Omaha, Baxter Healthcare, Marriott Hotels, and Nordstrom.

5. ***A three-dimensional approach to the study of ethical decision making.*** One dimension is a chapter on ethics (Chapter 5) titled "Ethics: The Foundation for Relationships in Selling," which provides a contemporary examination of ethical considerations in selling. The second dimension involves the discussion of ethical issues in selected chapters throughout the text. The authors believe that ethics in selling is so important that it cannot be covered in a single chapter. The third dimension is an exciting business game entitled, ***Gray Issues—Ethical Decision Making in Personal Selling***. Participation in this game provides students with an introduction to a range of real-life ethical dilemmas, and it stimulates in-depth thinking about the ethical consequences of their decisions and actions. Students play the game to learn without having to play for keeps.

6. ***The Knowing—Doing Gap,*** common in personal selling classes, is closed by having students participate in the comprehensive role-play/ simulation featured in Appendix 3. Students assume the role of a new sales trainee employed by the Park Inn International Convention Center. Serving as an excellent capstone experience, students develop the critical skills needed to apply relationship, product, customer and presentation strategies. New to the tenth edition are three professionally produced videos that demonstrate important skills presented in the text. Role-plays utilizing Appendix 3 follow each video and provide student practice in mastering skills.

7. Each chapter features the following boxed inserts:
   - **Selling Is Everyone's Business.** These real-world examples explain how selling skills affect the success of persons who do not consider themselves salespeople.
   - **Global Business Etiquette.** These brief inserts provide practical tips on how to build global relationships. Each insert focuses on a different country.
   - **Customer Relationship Management with Technology.** These application exercises help the student learn how to use technology to add value to the sales process.

8. **Our unique companion text, *Selling-Today: Creating Value with Computers*** has been completely revised and expanded. The new edition emphasizes how customer value can be added to the sales process through the use of computers and CRM software. E-mail etiquette, signature lines, and the use of Word to develop professional letterheads, resumes, and application letters are new to this edition. This technology, plus electronic sales proposals, PowerPoint and Excel, and ACT! Contact Management software are presented and supported with application exercises. The companion

Selling Is Everyone's Business

LIFE AFTER ENRON

Cary and Rachel Bryant, husband and wife, believed they had a bright future at Enron Corporation. Then the company filed for bankruptcy and they were terminated on the same day. Cary and Rachel immediately started sending out résumés and making phone calls. However, no one returned their calls. Finally, they decided to stop and reevaluate their careers. They decided that returning to the high-pressure corporate world was not a good idea. Cary decided to start a contracting company. In order to build his business he started making cold calls on people in the neighborhood. He often called on homeowners whose homes looked like they needed repair. His business began to grow and today Bryant Contractors (www.bryantcontractors.com) is doing well. Meanwhile, Rachel decided to begin selling a line of skin-care products she had developed prior to working for Enron. In the years ahead, Cary and Rachel will rely on their personal selling skills to grow their businesses.[b]

text can be used for in-class assignments or learning experiences outside of class. Students can use this supplement on their own for further practice and application. **Instructors: Request Value Package ISBN: 0-13-186683-4** on your book order and your students will receive the *Selling Today: Creating Value with Computers* companion text shrink wrapped with this textbook at no additional cost.

STAYING ON THE CUTTING EDGE—NEW TO THIS EDITION

Today, business as usual is not an option. The restructuring of America from an industrial economy to an information economy has hastened the transformation of personal selling. The tenth edition of *Selling Today: Creating Customer Value* describes how sales professionals must cope with new forces shaping the world of sales and marketing. The most significant changes in the new edition include:

- ***New Professional Sales Training Video Program*** New to the tenth edition are three professional videos produced by Art Bauer, award winning video producer and founder of American Media. These videos, based on research conducted for the 10th edition, describe the behaviors of high performance salespeople as they prepare for and proceed through typical sales presentations. Specifically designed for classroom use, the three 7–10 minute videos begin with an introduction by Gerald Manning, coauthor of *Selling Today*. These introductions tie together the video content and concepts presented in the text. Students observe salespeople working with customers in a modern business setting. Each video presents important issues that spark student discussion. The capstone experience at the conclusion of each video is a role-play exercise designed to help students apply important concepts.
- ***Expanded coverage of how value creation*** is achieved when selling to different types of customers. *Transactional buyers,* for example, are usually aware of their needs and knowledgeable regarding the product they intend to purchase. They are often very focused on price. *Consultative buyers*, on the other hand, often lack needs awareness or need help evaluating possible solutions. Each of these customers will require different selling strategies. Throughout the tenth edition of *Selling Today* the reader will grow in their ability to understand and apply value creation strategies in a variety of selling situations.
- ***New role-play application exercises at the end of each part.*** These new role plays are designed to reinforce the key concepts in each of the first five parts of the text. They also provide opportunities for skill development. Of special interest to professors and students is the new "user friendly" format that greatly increases the comfort level of everyone involved in the role play.

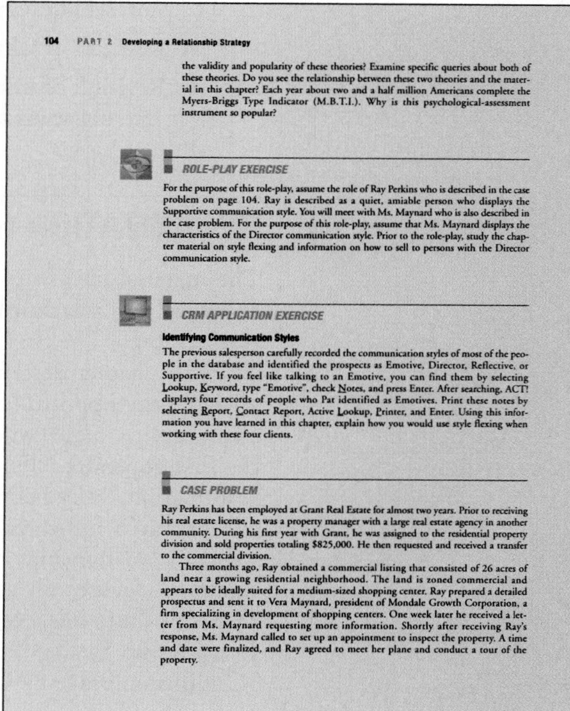

104 PART 2 Developing a Relationship Strategy

the validity and popularity of these theories? Examine specific queries about both of these theories. Do you see the relationship between these two theories and the material in this chapter? Each year about two and a half million Americans complete the Myers-Briggs Type Indicator (M.B.T.I.). Why is this psychological-assessment instrument so popular?

ROLE-PLAY EXERCISE

For the purpose of this role-play, assume the role of Ray Perkins who is described in the case problem on page 104. Ray is described as a quiet, amiable person who displays the Supportive communication style. You will meet with Ms. Maynard who is also described in the case problem. For the purpose of this role-play, assume that Ms. Maynard displays the characteristics of the Director communication style. Prior to the role-play, study the chapter material on style flexing and information on how to sell to persons with the Director communication style.

CRM APPLICATION EXERCISE

Identifying Communication Styles

The previous salesperson carefully recorded the communication styles of most of the people in the database and identified the prospects as Emotive, Director, Reflective, or Supportive. If you feel like talking to an Emotive, you can find them by selecting Lookup, Keyword, type "Emotive", check Notes, and press Enter. After searching, ACT! displays four records of people who Pat identified as Emotives. Print these notes by selecting Report, Contact Report, Active Lookup, Printer, and Enter. Using this information you have learned in this chapter, explain how you would use style flexing when working with these four clients.

CASE PROBLEM

Ray Perkins has been employed at Grant Real Estate for almost two years. Prior to receiving his real estate license, he was a property manager with a large real estate agency in another community. During his first year with Grant, he was assigned to the residential property division and sold properties totaling $825,000. He then requested and received a transfer to the commercial division.

Three months ago, Ray obtained a commercial listing that consisted of 26 acres of land near a growing residential neighborhood. The land is zoned commercial and appears to be ideally suited for a medium-sized shopping center. Ray prepared a detailed prospectus and sent it to Vera Maynard, president of Mondale Growth Corporation, a firm specializing in development of shopping centers. One week later he received a letter from Ms. Maynard requesting more information. Shortly after receiving Ray's response, Ms. Maynard called to set up an appointment to inspect the property. A time and date were finalized, and Ray agreed to meet her plane and conduct a tour of the property.

- **New coverage and new sections.** These major new topics, models, and concepts have been added to the tenth edition of *Selling Today.*
  - A review of sales training programs offered by commercial vendors (Chapter 2).
  - Tailoring the relationship strategy to transactional, consultative and strategic alliance customers (Chapter 3).
  - Description of Mutual of Omaha's "Values for Success" program (Chapter 5).
  - How the meaning of trust changes with the type of sale (Chapter 5).
  - Tailoring the product strategy to the needs of transactional, consultative and strategic alliance buyers (Chapter 6).
  - The use of return on investment (ROI) selling appeals (Chapter 6).
  - The importance of linking specific benefits to a need expressed by the buyer (Chapter 6).
  - Value creation investments for transactional, consultative, and strategic alliance buyers (Chapter 7).
  - Steps in the typical buying process and how to achieve alignment with the customer's buying process (Chapter 8).
  - Expanded coverage of cold calling and networking (Chapter 9).
  - How to develop presentation objectives for each stage of the buying process (Chapter 10).
  - Complete revision of material on effective use of questions to achieve need identification and need satisfaction (Chapter 11).
  - New material on listening and acknowledging the customer's response (Chapter 11).
  - Introduction of the concepts of value reinforcement and adding value with expansion selling (Chapter 15).
  - Revision of Chapter 16 to place more emphasis on opportunity management.
  - Revision of information on leadership styles and expanded information on use of external rewards (Chapter 17).

ORGANIZATION OF THIS BOOK

The material in *Selling Today* continues to be organized around **the four pillars of personal selling: relationship strategy, product strategy, customer strategy, and presentation strategy**. The first two chapters set the stage for an in-depth study of these strategies. The first chapter describes the evolution of personal selling and the second chapter gives students the opportunity to explore career opportunities in the four major employment areas: service, retail, wholesale, and manufacturing. Career-minded students will also find the first appendix, "Finding Employment: A Personalized Marketing Plan for the Age of Information," very helpful.

Research indicates that high-performance salespeople are better able to build and maintain relationships than are moderate performers. Part 2, "Developing a Relationship Strategy," focuses on several important person-to-person relationship-building practices that contribute to success in personal selling. Chapter 3 is entitled "Creating Value With a Relationship Strategy" and Chapter 4 is entitled "Communication Styles: Managing the Relationship Process." Chapter 5 examines the influence of ethics on relationships between customers and salespeople.

Part 3, "Developing a Product Strategy," examines the importance of complete and accurate product, company, and competitive knowledge in personal selling. A well-informed salesperson is in a strong position to configure value-added product solutions for complex customer's needs.

Part 4, "Developing a Customer Strategy," presents information on why and how customers buy and explains how to identify prospects. With increased knowledge of the customer, salespeople are in a better position to understand complex customer's wants and needs and create customer value.

The concept of a salesperson as advisor, consultant, and partner to buyers is stressed in Part 5, "Developing a Presentation Strategy." The traditional sales presentation that emphasizes closing as the primary objective of personal selling is abandoned in favor of need-satisfaction presentations. As in the ninth edition, the salesperson is viewed as a counselor and a consultant. Part 6 includes two chapters: "Opportunity Management: The Key to Greater Sales Productivity," and "Management of the Sales Force."

INTELECOM TELECOURSE

The tenth edition has once again been selected by INTELECOM for use in its video course entitled, *The Sales Connection.* To encourage distance learning the 26 videos present strategies and techniques of top-rated-sales oriented companies and their high-performing individual salespeople. In addition, several recognized college and university professors are featured in the videos. For more information on the availability of the INTELECOM tele-course material, including the videos, contact **www.intelecom.org.**

SELLING TODAY SUPPLEMENTS

New Classroom-Designed Video Program based on a long-standing professional relationship between the authors and Art Bauer, the tenth edition of *Selling Today* includes a breakthrough video series on the behaviors displayed by today's high performing salespeople. Applying the research that the authors have conducted for the tenth edition, these videos bring a new reading, viewing, experiencing dimension to the classroom. Completely aligned with concepts in the tenth edition of *Selling Today*, students have the opportunity to travel with salespeople as they are challenged in the market place to use modern personal selling practices. Following each video, students apply the text/video concepts with easy to implement role-play exercises presented in the text.

The first video **"Questions-Discovering and Confirming Customer Problems"** introduces the viewer to the use of Survey and Confirmation questions. These questions are introduced and explained with examples in the text. The video demonstrates how these two types of questions are used in a strategic/consultative sales setting to reveal the customer's problems and assure a mutual understanding of them. The second video **"Questions-Discovering Customer Pain and**

Pleasure" introduces the viewer to the use of Probing and Need-Satisfaction questions. Probing questions reveal the consequences or pain your customer may be experiencing. Need-Satisfaction questions are a turning point in the strategic/consultative presentation and they reveal the pleasure or satisfaction your customer will experience from your solution. **"Questions-Getting It Right"** is the third video in this series and it dramatically describes how a sales representative updates selling strategies with these newly acquired skills to make a successful presentation to a very challenging customer. Classroom designed discussion and role-play opportunities for each video in the series are presented in the text and the Instructor's manual.

Selling-Today: Creating value With Computers is an 82 page companion text available for professors to use in class or for students to study on their own. This supplement introduces the reader to the technology that is available to sales and marketing personnel including Customer Relationship Management software, Web-based prospect lists, product configuration software, presentation software, electronic data interchange software, and travel planning software. It is written as a self-study guide that can be used in the classroom with 36 application exercises or as an out-of-class personal enrichment activity.

ACT! Contact Management Software New to the 10th edition is a CD-ROM that includes the number one selling ACT! Contact Management software. The ACT! software will include a preloaded prospect data base of 20 customers who are in various stages of the buying process. Users will complete exercises provided in the text that involve the sales process for $1.2 million in sales. Student completing these self-instructional exercises will be familiar with the functionality of the ACT! software, plus they will have "hands on" application experience of CRM with the buying and selling processes.

Instructor's Manual includes detailed presentation outlines, answers to review questions, hand-outs for the ethics game, suggested responses to learning activities, hand-outs for CRM exercises, easy-to-follow instructions on how to use the role-play/simulation included in the text, descriptions of the accompanying videos, written term projects, a Telecourse guide, transparency masters, and suggestions for organizing a sales course.

Test Bank includes true/false, multiple choice, matching, completion, and short answer questions. The correct answer and textbook page reference for each question is provided.

Ten chapter/case problem videos. Ten videos from the *The Sales Connection* telecourse provide custom support for the chapter material and case problems found at the end of key chapters in the text. The selected chapters come alive with video footage filmed in real sales settings, with real salespeople. Salespeople and their companies represented include Amgen, Body Glove International, Universal Studios, Alta Dena Dairy, and other companies. The 27 minute videos also provide an introduction to several careers in selling.

Sales Connection Telecourse Study Guide (ISBN 0-13-186661-3): Published through Prentice Hall's partnership with INTELECOM. Contact your Prentice Hall representative for the package ISBN.

Companion Website (www.prenhall.com/manning) offers students valuable resources, including an Internet Study Guide for review purposes, as well as materials for use with the ACT! Contact Management Software that accompanies the textbook.

Instructor's Resource CD-ROM with PowerPoint presentation, Instructor's Manual, Test Bank, and **Computerized Test Bank.** These resources can also be accessed via the Instructor's Resource Center online at **www.prenhall.com/manning**.

THE SEARCH FOR WISDOM IN THE AGE OF INFORMATION

The search for the fundamentals of personal selling has become more difficult in the age of information. The glut of information (information explosion) threatens our ability to identify what is true, right, or lasting. The search for knowledge begins with a review of information, and wisdom is gleaned from knowledge (see model below). Books continue to be one of the best sources of wisdom. Many new books, and several classics, were used as references for the tenth edition of *Selling Today.* A sample of the more than 40 books used to prepare this edition follows.

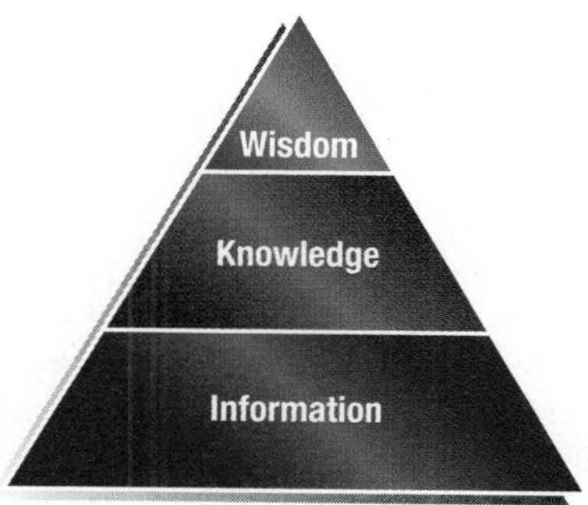

First Impressions—What You Don't Know About How Others See You by Ann Demarais and Valerie White
The New Solution Selling by Keith M. Eades
SPIN Selling Fieldbook by Neil Rackham
The Sedona Method by Hale Dwoskin
The Success Principles by Jack Canfield
A Whole New Mind by Daniel H. Pink
Re-Imagine! Business Excellence in a Disruptive Age by Tom Peters
The New Conceptual Selling by Stephen E. Heiman and Diane Sanchez
Value-Added Selling by Tom Reilly
Hug Your Customers by Jack Mitchell
Blur: The Speed of Change in the Connected Economy by Stan Davis and Christopher Meyer
Strategic Selling by Robert B. Miller and Stephen E. Heiman
Working with Emotional Intelligence by Daniel Goleman
Psycho-Cybernetics by Maxwell Maltz
The Double Win by Denis Waitley
Zero-Resistance Selling by Maxwell Maltz, Dan S. Kennedy, William T. Brooks, Matt Oechsli, Jeff Paul and Pamela Yellen
SPIN Selling by Neil Rackham
The Power of 5 by Harold H. Bloomfield and Robert K. Cooper
The New Professional Image by Susan Bixler and Nancy Nix-Rice
Complete Business Etiquette Handbook by Barbara Pachter and Marjorie Brody
The 7 Habits of Highly Effective People by Stephen R. Covey
Integrity Selling for the 21st Century by Ron Willingham

Changing the Game: The New Way to Sell by Larry Wilson
Business @ The Speed of Thought by Bill Gates
Consultative Selling by Mack Hanan
The 10 Natural Laws of Successful Time and Life Management by Hyrum W. Smith
Personal Styles and Effective Performance by David W. Merrill and Roger H. Reid
The Versatile Salesperson by Roger Wenschlag
Megatrends and Megatrends 2000 by John Naisbitt
Rethinking the Sales Force by Neil Rackham and John R. DeVincentis
The Agenda by Michael Hammer
Hope Is Not a Strategy by Rick Page

ACKNOWLEDGMENTS

Many people have made contributions to the tenth edition of *Selling Today: Creating Customer Value.* We are very grateful to our CRM technology associate Jack Linge who contributed significantly to the development of the CRM Insights, Application Exercises, CRM Case Studies and our key supplement, *Selling Today: Creating Value with Computers.* Throughout the years the text has been improved as a result of numerous helpful comments and recommendations. We extend special appreciation to the following reviewers:

Jurgita Baltrusaitye
University of Illinois at Chicago
De'Arno De'Armond
West Texas A&M University
Lynnea Mallalieu
University of North Carolina—Wilmington
Ron Pimentel
California State University—Bakersfield
Quenton Pullman
Nashville Technical Community College
Joan Weiss
Bucks County Community College
Stanley "Martin" Welc
Saddleback College
Stacia Wert-Gray
University of Central Oklahoma
Scott Widmier
University of Akron
Douglas A. Cords
California State University, Fresno
David Grypp
Milwaukee Area Technical College
Kathy Illing
Greenville Technical College
Russ Movritsem
Brigham Young University
Quenton Pulliam
Nashville State Technical Institute
Larry P. Butts
Southwest Tennessee Community College
Patricia W. Clarke
Boston College
Nicholas A. Santarone
Penn State University, Abington
Karl Sooder
University of Central Florida
C. David Shepherd
Kennesaw State University
Jon Hawes
Akron University
Robert Bochrath
Gateway Technical Institute
Jim Boespflug
Arapahoe Community College
Jerry Boles
Western Kentucky University
Jim Boles
Georgia State University
Duane Brickner
South Mountain Community College
Don Brumlow
St. John's College
Murray Brunton
Central Ohio Technical College
William R. Christensen
Community College of Denver (North Campus)
Larry Davis
Youngstown State University
Lynn Dawson
Louisiana Technical University—Ruston
Dayle Dietz
North Dakota State School of Science

Casey Donoho
Northern Arizona University
Wendal Ferguson
Richland College
Dean Flowers
Waukesha County Technical College
Victoria Griffis
University of South Florida
Donald Hackett
Wichita State University
Jon Hawes
The University of Akron
Ken Hodge, Marketing Manager
Nordson
Norm Humble
Kirkwood Community College
Michael Johnson
Chippewa Valley Tech College
Richard Jones
Marshall University
Katy Kemp
Middle Tennessee State University
Wesley Koch
Illinois Central College
Stephen Koernig
University of Illinois—Chicago
Wilburn Lane
Lambuth University
R. Dale Lounsburg
Emporia State College
George H. Lucas, Jr.
Texas A & M University
Alice Lupinacci
University of Texas at Arlington
Leslie E. Martin
University of Wisconsin, Whitewater
Jack Maroun
Herkimer County Community College
Tammy McCullough
Eastern Michigan University
Bob McMahon
Appalachian State University
Darrel Millard
Kirkwood Community College
Ron Milliaman
Western Kentucky University
Irene Mittlemark
Kingsborough Community College
Rita Mix
Our Lady of the Lake University—Dallas
Mark Mulder
Grand Rapids Junior College
Gordon Myron
Lucent Technologies
John Odell
Marketing Catalysts
Jim Parr
Louisiana State University
James Randall
Georgia Southern University
Stan Salzman
American River College
Donald T. Sedik
William Rainey Harper College
Robert E. Smiley
Indiana State University, Terra Haute
C. Phillip Smith
John C. Calhoun, State Community College, Alabama
Robert Thompson *Indiana State University*
Rae Verity
Southern Alberta Institute of Technology
Curtis W. Youngman
Salt Lake Community College
Donald A. Zimmerman
University of Akron

Finally, we thank the book team at Prentice Hall: Katie Stevens, Melissa Pellerano, Christine Ietto, Ashaki Charles, Suzanne Grappi, Judy Leale, Renata Butera, and Janet Slowik.

ABOUT THE AUTHORS

Dr. Barry L. Reece

Virginia Polytechnic Institute and State University

Dr. Reece has devoted more than three decades to teaching, researching, consulting, and to the development of training programs in the areas of sales, leadership, human relations, and management. He has conducted over 600 seminars and workshops for public and private sector organizations. He has written extensively in the areas of sales, supervision, communications, and management. Dr. Reece was named "Trainer of the Year" by the Valleys of Virginia Chapter of the American Society for Training and Development and was awarded the "Excellence in Teaching Award" by the College of Human Sciences and Education at Virginia Polytechnic Institute and State University.

Dr. Reece has contributed to numerous journals and is author or co-author of thirty books including *Business, Human Relations—Principles and Practices, Supervision and Leadership in Action,* and *Effective Human Relations—Personal and Organizational Applications.* He has served as a consultant to Lowe's Companies, Inc., Wachovia, WLR Foods, Kinney Shoe Corporation, Carilion Health System, and numerous other profit and not-for-profit organizations.

Gerald L. Manning

Des Moines Area Community College

Mr. Manning served as chair of the Marketing/Management Department for more than 30 years. In addition to his administrative duties, he has served as lead instructor in sales and sales management. The classroom has provided him with an opportunity to study the merits of various experimental learning approaches such as role-plays, simulations, games, and interactive demonstrations. *Partnership Selling: A Role-Play/Simulation for Selling Today,* included in the tenth edition, was developed and tested in the classroom by Mr. Manning. He has also applied numerous personal selling principles and practices in the real world as owner of a real estate development and management company.

Mr. Manning has served as a sales and marketing consultant to senior management and owners of over 500 businesses, including several national companies. He appears regularly as a speaker at national sales conferences. Mr. Manning has received the "Outstanding Instructor of the Year" award given annually by his college.

Keeping Current in a Changing World

Throughout the past decade, Professors Manning and Reece have relied on three strategies to keep current in the dynamic field of personal selling. First, both are actively involved in sales training and consulting. Frequent interaction with salespeople and sales managers provides valuable insight regarding contemporary issues and developments in the field of personal selling. A second major strategy involves extensive research and development activities. The major focus of these activities has been factors that contribute to high-performance salespeople. The third major strategy involves completion of training and development programs offered by America's most respected sales training companies. Professors Manning and Reece have completed seminars and workshops offered by Wilson Learning Corporation, Forum Corporation, Franklin-Covey, Sedona Training Associates, Association for Humanistic Psychology, and several other organizations.

An Investment in the Future

Charles Schwab, the great industrialist and entrepreneur, said, "We are all salespeople every day of our lives, selling our ideas and enthusiasm to those with whom we come in contact." As authors, we suggest that you retain this book for future reference. Periodic review of the ideas in this text will help you daily in areas such as:

- interacting more effectively with others
- interviewing for new jobs in the future
- understanding and training salespeople who work for you or with you
- selling new ideas to senior management, co-workers, or employees you might be supervising
- selling products or services that you represent as a salesperson

We wish you much success and happiness in applying your knowledge of personal selling.

Gerald L. Manning Barry L. Reece

Every employee at Federal Express must be sales oriented and each manager must be an outstanding individual salesperson.

Federal Express

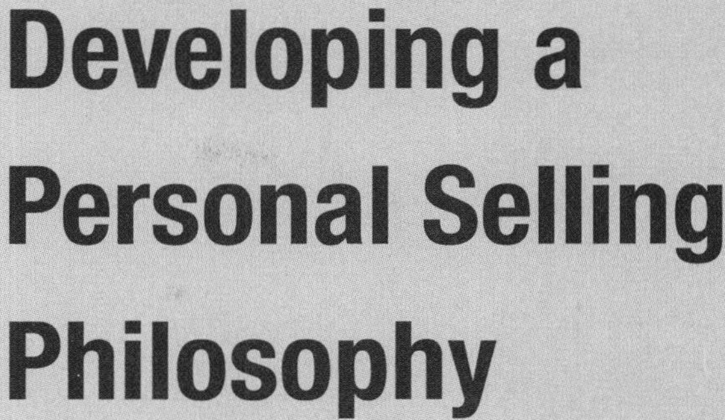

Developing a Personal Selling Philosophy

➥ The two chapters that make up Part 1 establish a foundation for the entire textbook. Chapter 1 introduces the major themes that connect all of the chapters. Chapter 2 describes personal selling career opportunities.

Chapter Preview

When you finish reading this chapter, you should be able to

1 Describe the contributions of personal selling to the information economy

2 Define personal selling and discuss personal selling as an extension of the marketing concept

3 Describe the evolution of consultative selling from the marketing era to the present

4 Define strategic selling and name the four broad strategic areas in the strategic/consultative selling model

5 Describe the evolution of partnering and discuss how it relates to the quality improvement process

6 Explain how value-added selling strategies enhance personal selling

CHAPTER 1

Personal Selling and the Marketing Concept

Kim Fernandez, Director of Natural Food Sales at Alta Dena Certified Dairy (*www.altadenadairy.com*), uses the consultative selling approach exclusively. She takes pride in her ability to look through the eyes of her retail and wholesale customers and answer the question, "What can I do to help them improve sales of natural dairy foods?" Although she is employed by Alta Dena, her first obligation is to her customers.

Alta Dena Dairy, founded in 1945, was a pioneer in the national food industry. A few years later Alta Dena earned "Certified Dairy" status, which means its milk meets special requirements for safety, nutrition, and production standards. Over the years the product line has expanded to include a variety of milk drinks, yogurts, cheeses, eggs, and other all-natural dairy products.[1]

In 1980 Amgen (*www.amgen.com*) was a pharmaceutical company with nothing to sell. Over the years the research and development (R&D) staff began to develop life-saving medical products. At that point Amgen began to recruit and train a team of professional salespeople. Deborah Karish was one of the first salespeople hired to call on doctors, pharmacists, and other health professionals. Karish found that one of her greatest challenges was winning acceptance of Amgen and its new line of medical products. Prospects were accustomed to buying products from well-established pharmaceutical companies. Karish also had to sell herself. Health care professionals needed assurance that she was qualified to give accurate information on the applications of complex medical products. Today Amgen is the world's largest independent biotechnology company.[2]

STRATEGIC/CONSULTATIVE SELLING MODEL

Strategic step	*Prescription*
Develop a Personal Selling Philosophy	☐ Adopt Marketing Concept ☐ Value Personal Selling ☐ Become a Problem Solver/Partner

FIGURE 1.1

Today, salespeople use a strategic plan based on a personal philosophy that emphasizes adopting the marketing concept, valuing personal selling, and becoming a problem solver/partner.

Kim Fernandez and Deborah Karish represent just two of the many careers in personal selling. Today, sales offer a broad range of career opportunities requiring a wide variety of skills and expertise. Success in sales requires a strong commitment to the roles of consultant and problem solver. Salespeople like Fernandez and Karish seek to become an extension of the client's business—a true partner. They are constantly searching for ways to create value for the customer.

A highly competitive one-world market exists for products ranging from consulting services to automobiles. To stay competitive, many salespeople need to adopt a global perspective. A sales representative employed by United Parcel Service, for example, must compete with Federal Express, DHL Worldwide Express, and Emery Worldwide for the opportunity to serve customers throughout the world.

PERSONAL SELLING—A DEFINITION AND A PHILOSOPHY

Personal selling involves person-to-person communication with a prospect. It is a process of developing relationships; discovering needs; matching the appropriate products with these needs; and communicating benefits through informing, reminding, or persuading. The term **product** should be broadly interpreted to encompass information, services, ideas, and issues. Increasingly, personal selling is viewed as a process that adds value. In an ideal situation the salesperson diagnoses the customer's needs and custom fits the product to meet these needs.

Preparation for a career in personal selling begins with the development of a personal philosophy or set of beliefs that provides guidance. To some degree this philosophy is like the rudder that steers a ship. Without a rudder the ship's direction is unpredictable. Without a personal philosophy the salesperson's behavior also is unpredictable.

The development of a **personal selling philosophy** involves three prescriptions: adopt the marketing concept, value personal selling, and assume the role of a problem solver or partner in helping customers make buying decisions (Fig. 1.1). These three prescriptions for success in personal selling are presented here as part of the Strategic/Consultative Selling Model. This model is expanded in future chapters to include additional strategic steps in the selling process.

PERSONAL SELLING IN THE AGE OF INFORMATION

The restructuring of America from an industrial economy to an information economy began in the 1950s (Fig. 1.2). John Naisbitt, author of the popular book *Megatrends*, noted that during this period our economy began shifting from an emphasis on industrial activity to an emphasis on information processing. He recognized that industrial America was giving way to a new society where most of us would work with information instead of producing goods.[3] We live in an age in which the effective exchange of information is the foundation of most economic transactions. Today we are in the latter stages of the age of

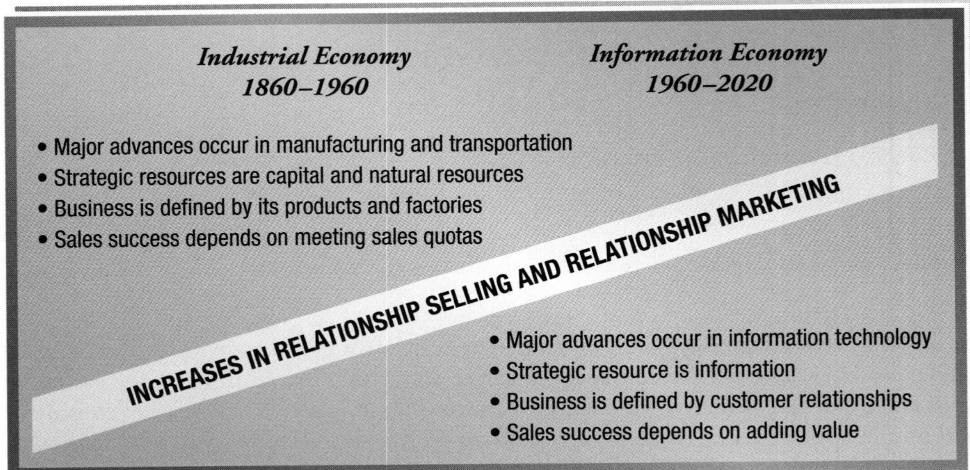

FIGURE | 1.2

The age of information has greatly influenced personal selling. Today, salespeople use a variety of information technology tools to gather and process information of value to the customer. They recognize that information is a strategic resource and relationship skills are needed to build a conduit of trust for information acceptance.

information, and the implications for personal selling are profound. We will describe the four major developments that have shaped the information economy and discuss the implications for personal selling.

Major Advances in Information Technology

The information age has spawned the information technology revolution. Salespeople and other players in the information age use personal computers, e-mail, instant messaging, mobile phones, and other forms of technology to obtain and process information. The explosive growth of electronic commerce and other Internet activities has changed the way in which computers are used. Stan Davis, futurist and co-author of *Blur: The Speed of Change in the Connected Economy*, says that we now use the computer less for data crunching and more for connecting. These connections involve people to people, machine to machine, product to service, organization to organization, and all these in combination.[4] Without these connections, information age workers cannot do their jobs. People who work extensively with information, such as salespeople, need these connections to conduct their information gathering and information management responsibilities.

Strategic Resource Is Information

Advances in information technology have increased the speed at which we acquire, process, and disseminate information. David Shenk, author of *Data Smog: Surviving the Information Glut*, notes that we have moved from a state of information scarcity to one of information overload.[5] The information age is dynamic, but it also can be disorienting. In an era of limitless data, informed salespeople are expected to help us decide which information has value and which information should be ignored. Customers who have less time to adjust to new products and circumstances value this assistance.

Business Is Defined by Customer Relationships

Michael Hammer, consultant and author of *The Agenda*, says the *real* new economy is the customer economy. As scarcity gave way to abundance, as supply exceeded demand, and as customers became better informed, we have seen a power shift. Customers have taken more control of their own destinities.[6]

On the surface, the major focus of the age of information seems to be the accumulation of more and more information and the never-ending search for new forms of information technology. It's easy to overlook the importance of the human element. Humans, not computers, have the ability to think, feel, and create ideas. It is no coincidence that relationship selling and relationship marketing, which emphasize long-term, mutually satisfying buyer–seller relationships, began to gain support at the beginning of the information age. Personal selling provides a counterbalancing human response to the impersonal nature of technology.

Michael Hammer is credited with popularizing the concept of reengineering the corporation. The driving factors behind reengineering are lower costs, better quality, better use of information and improved customer satisfaction. Salespeople can play an important role in this management practice.

Sales Success Depends on Adding Value

Value-added selling can be defined as a series of creative improvements within the sales process that enhance the customer experience. Salespeople can create value by developing a quality relationship, carefully identifying the customer needs, and then configuring and presenting the best possible product solution. Value is also created when the salesperson provides excellent service after the sale. Neil Rackman, author of *Rethinking the Sales Force*, and other experts in sales and marketing say that success no longer depends on merely communicating the value of products and services. Success in personal selling rests on the critical ability to create value for customers.

The value added by salespeople today is increasingly derived from intangibles such as the quality of the advice offered and the level of trust that underlies the relationship between the customer and the salesperson. The value of these intangibles can erode with shocking speed when the customer feels deceived or discovers that the competition is able to add more value to the sales process.[7]

"One question: If this is the Information Age, how come nobody knows anything?"

PERSONAL SELLING AS AN EXTENSION OF THE MARKETING CONCEPT

A careful examination of personal selling practices during the past 40 years reveals some positive developments. We have seen the evolution of personal selling from an era that emphasized *pushing or peddling products* to an era that emphasizes *partnering.* Throughout this period we have seen the emergence of new thinking patterns concerning every aspect of sales and sales management. Today, salespeople are no longer the flamboyant product "pitchmen" of the past. Instead they are increasingly becoming diagnosticians of customers' needs and problems. A growing number of salespeople recognize that the quality of the partnerships they create is as important as the quality of the products they sell.

Evolution of the Marketing Concept

What is the **marketing concept**? When a business firm moves from a product orientation to a company-wide consumer orientation, we say that it has adopted the marketing concept. This concept springs from the belief that the firm should dedicate all of its policies, planning, and operations to the satisfaction of the customer.

The era of marketing and the age of information began in the early 1950s (Table 1.1). A General Electric executive is credited with making one of the earliest formal statements indicating corporate interest in the marketing concept. In a paper heralding a new management philosophy, he observed that the principal marketing function of a company is to determine what the customer wants and then develop the appropriate product or service. This view contrasted with the prevailing practice of that period, which was to develop products and then build customer interest in those products.[8]

The foundation for the marketing concept is a business philosophy that leaves no doubt in the mind of every employee that customer satisfaction is of primary importance. All energies are directed toward satisfying the customer. As Peter Drucker once observed, "The customers define the business."

Although the marketing concept is a very basic business fundamental, some companies ignore it and suffer the consequences. Ford Motor Company was a leader in quality control during the 1980s and early 1990s but then seemed to shift its focus to other areas. The result was a drop in J. D. Power and Associates quality rankings and a drop in sales. Ford also failed to stay in touch with consumer taste.[9]

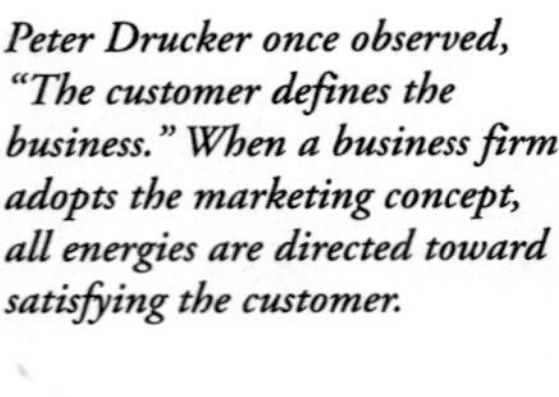

Peter Drucker once observed, "The customer defines the business." When a business firm adopts the marketing concept, all energies are directed toward satisfying the customer.

Business firms vary in terms of how strongly they support the marketing concept. Some firms have gone the extra mile to satisfy the needs and wants of their customers:

- UPS founder Jim Casey adopted the marketing concept when the company was first established. He described the firm's customer focus this way: "Our real, primary objective is to serve—to render perfect service to our stores and their customers. If we keep that objective constantly in mind, our reward in money can be beyond our fondest dreams."[10]

TABLE 1.1 EVOLUTION OF PERSONAL SELLING (1950 TO PRESENT)

SALES AND MARKETING EMPHASIS	SELLING EMPHASIS
Marketing Era Begins (Early 1950s) Organizations determine needs and wants of target markets and adapt themselves to delivering desired satisfaction; product orientation is replaced by a customer orientation	• More organizations recognize that the salesperson is in a position to collect product, market, and service information concerning the buyer's needs
Consultative Selling Era (Late 1960s to early 1970s) Salespeople are becoming diagnosticians of customer's needs as well as consultants offering well-considered recommendations; mass markets are breaking into target markets	• Buyer needs are identified through two-way communication • Information giving and negotiation tactics replace manipulation
Strategic Selling Era (Early 1980s) The evolution of a more complex selling environment and greater emphasis on market niches create the need for greater structure and more emphasis on planning	• Strategy is given as much attention as selling tactics • Product positioning is given more attention
Partnering Era (1990 to the present) Salespeople are encouraged to think of everything they say or do in the context of their long-term, high-quality partnership with individual customers; sales force automation provides specific customer information	• Customer supplants the product as the driving force in sales • Greater emphasis on strategies that create customer value

- Marriott Hotels uses a blend of "high tech" and "high touch" to build customer goodwill and repeat business. Each of the 8,500 sales representatives can sell the services of 10 motel brands in Marriott's portfolio. The customer with a small meeting budget might be encouraged to consider a Fairfield Inn property. The customer seeking luxury accommodations might be introduced to a Ritz-Carlton hotel (acquired a few years ago). All reservations go through the same system, so if one Marriott hotel is full, the sales representative can cross-sell rooms in another Marriott hotel in the same city.[11]

Marketing Concept Yields Marketing Mix

Once the marketing concept becomes an integral part of a firm's philosophy, its management seeks to develop a network of marketing activities that maximize customer satisfaction and ensure profitability. The combination of elements making up a program based on the marketing concept is known as the **marketing mix** (Fig. 1.3). The marketing mix is a set of controllable, tactical marketing tools that consists of everything the firm can do to influence the demand for its product. The many possibilities can be organized into four groups of variables: *product, price, place,* and *promotion.*[12]

FIGURE | 1.3

Each of the elements that make up the marketing mix must be executed effectively for a marketing program to achieve the desired results.

One of the four P's shown in Figure 1.3—promotion—can be further subdivided into advertising, public relations, sales promotion, and personal selling. When a company adopts the marketing concept, it must determine how some combination of these elements can result in maximum customer satisfaction.

Important Role of Personal Selling

Every marketer must decide how much time and money to invest in each of the four areas of the marketing mix. The decision must be objective; no one can afford to invest money in a marketing strategy that does not provide a good return on money invested. *Personal selling is often the major promotional method used—whether measured by people employed, by total expenditures, or by expenses as a percentage of sales.* One way to assess the magnitude of personal selling is to study employment data for the 500 largest sales forces in America. These companies employ several million salespeople and these salespeople produce over $4.5 trillion dollars in sales. Each salesperson supports, on average, 10.4 other jobs within the company.[13]

Firms make large investments in personal selling in response to several major trends: Products and services are becoming increasingly sophisticated and complex; competition has greatly increased in most product areas; and demand for quality, value, and service by customers has risen sharply. In response to these trends, personal selling has evolved to a new level of professionalism. Since the beginning of the information age, personal selling has evolved through three distinct developmental periods: the consultative selling era, the strategic selling era, and the partnering era.

EVOLUTION OF CONSULTATIVE SELLING

Consultative selling, which emerged in the late 1960s and early 1970s, is an extension of the marketing concept (see Table 1.1). This approach emphasizes need identification, which is achieved through effective communication between the salesperson and the customer. The salesperson establishes two-way communication by asking appropriate questions and listening carefully to the customer's responses. The salesperson assumes the role of consultant and offers well-considered recommendations. Negotiation replaces manipulation as the salesperson sets the stage for a long-term partnership. Salespeople who have adopted consultative selling possess a keen ability to listen, define the customer's problems, and offer one or more solutions.

Although consultative selling is emphasized throughout this text, it is helpful to understand the role of transactional selling in our economy. **Transactional selling** is a sales process that most effectively matches the needs of the value-conscious buyer who is primarily interested in price and convenience. Many transactional buyers are well aware of their needs and may already know a great deal about the products or services they intend to purchase. Because the transaction-based buyer tends to focus primarily on low price, some marketers are adopting lower-cost selling channels. Low-cost transaction selling strategies include telesales, direct mail, and the Internet. This approach to selling is usually used by marketers who do not see the need to spend very much time on customer need assessment, problem solving, relationship building, or sales follow-up.[14]

Some companies use both consultative and transactional selling approaches. Dell Computer Corporation, well known for its transactional sales methods, maintains the Preferred Account Division which uses consultative selling practices to achieve its objectives.[15]

Service, retail, manufacturing, and wholesale firms that embrace the marketing concept already have adopted or are currently adopting consultative selling practices. The major features of consultative selling are as follows:

1. The customer is seen as a *person to be served*, not a prospect to be sold. Consultative salespeople believe their function is to help the buyer make an intelligent decision. They use a four-step process that includes need discovery, selection of a solution, a need–satisfaction presentation, and servicing the sale (Fig. 1.4). These customer-centered strategies are fully developed and explained in Chapters 10 to 15.
2. The consultative salesperson, unlike the peddler of an earlier era, does not try to overpower the customer with a high-pressure sales presentation. Instead the buyer's needs are identified through *two-way* communication. The salesperson conducts precall research and asks questions during the sales call in an attempt to learn as much as possible about the person's needs and perceptions.

Dell Computer is known primarily for its e-commerce transactional selling methods. However, it employs consultative selling methods at its Dell Direct Stores and within its Preferred Accounts Division.

FIGURE 1.4

The Consultative Sales Presentation Guide

This contemporary presentation guide emphasizes the customer as a person to be served.

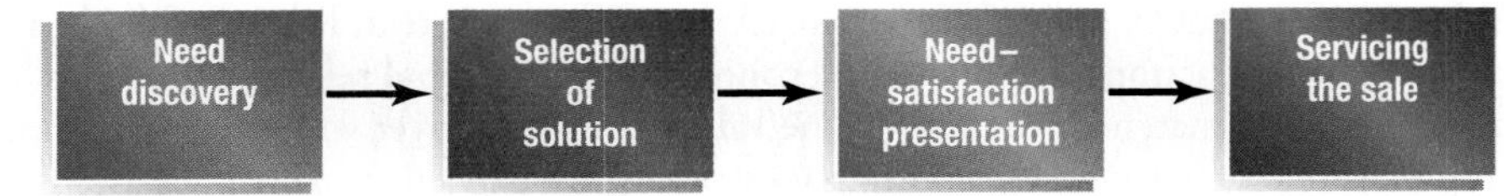

3. Consultative selling emphasizes *information giving, problem solving, and negotiation instead of manipulation.* This approach leads to a more trusting relationship between buyer and seller. Helping the buyer make an informed and intelligent buying decision adds value to the sales process.
4. Consultative selling emphasizes *service* after the sale. Theodore Levitt, author-consultant, recognizes that the relationship between a seller and a buyer seldom ends when a sale is made. In an increasing number of transactions the relationship actually intensifies because the customer has higher expectations after the sale. The personalized service provided after the sale may include making credit arrangements, supervising product delivery and installation, servicing warranties, and following up on complaints.

At first glance, it may appear that consultative selling practices can be easily mastered. The truth is, consultative selling is a complex process that puts great demands on sales personnel. This approach to personal selling requires an understanding of concepts and principles borrowed from the fields of psychology, communications, and sociology. It takes a great deal of personal commitment and self-discipline to become a sales consultant/adviser.

EVOLUTION OF STRATEGIC SELLING

Strategic selling began receiving considerable attention during the 1980s (see Table 1.1). During this period we witnessed the beginning of several trends that resulted in a more complex selling environment. These trends, which include increased global competition,

Sales success in the new economy requires us to think of ourselves as a problem solver/partner throughout the sales process.

Global Business Etiquette

STRATEGIES FOR BUILDING GLOBAL RELATIONSHIPS

The authors of *Complete Business Etiquette Handbook* state, "The key to being successful in international business revolves around knowing where you've come from as well as where you are headed." Keep in mind these tips when hosting an international visitor or visiting another country.

- Be respectful and nonjudgmental about the cultural differences you encounter. Try to react positively to unusual experiences.
- Understand your own viewpoint. International travel provides an opportunity to examine your own beliefs, values, and habits.
- Be flexible and patient. If you are too rigid or set in your ways, international travel will be difficult.
- Know enough about the etiquette in the country you plan to visit so you do not unwittingly offend its customs.[a]

broader and more diverse product lines, more decision makers involved in major purchases, and greater demand for specific, custom-made solutions, continue to influence personal selling and sales training in the age of information.

As companies face increased levels of complexity in the marketplace, they must give more attention to strategic planning. The strategic planning done by salespeople is often influenced by the information included in their company's strategic market plan. **Strategic planning** is the managerial process that matches the firm's resources to its market opportunities. It takes into consideration the various functional areas of the business that must be coordinated such as financial assets, workforce, production capabilities, and marketing.[16] Almost every aspect of strategic planning directly or indirectly influences sales and marketing.

The strategic plan should be a guide for a strategic selling plan. This plan includes strategies that you use to position yourself with the customer before the sales call even begins. The authors of *Strategic Selling* point out that there is a difference between a *tactic* and a *strategy*.[17] **Tactics** are techniques, practices, or methods you use when you are face-to-face with a customer. Examples are the use of questions to identify needs, presentation skills, and various types of closes. These and other tactics are discussed in Chapters 10 and 15.

A **strategy**, on the other hand, is a prerequisite to tactical success. If you develop the correct strategies, you are more likely to make your sales presentation to the right person, at the right time, and in a manner most likely to achieve positive results.

A selling strategy is a carefully conceived plan that is needed to accomplish a sales objective. Let's assume you are a sales representative employed by a pharmaceutical company. In an ideal situation, you want to establish a dialogue with the physician and learn about the types of patients she sees, diseases she treats, and challenges facing her practice. However, you do not want to call on busy doctors who may have no use for the drugs offered by your company. A strategy might include a careful study of the entire physician population in your territory. This analysis will help you identify those who need information about the drugs your company offers.[18] With this information you can select the most appropriate selling tactic (method), which might be to present samples to doctors who are not currently prescribing your drug.

Strategic planning sets the stage for a value-added form of consultative selling that is more structured, more focused, and more efficient. The result is better time allocation, more precise problem solving, and a greater chance that there will be a good match between your product and the customer's needs.

Many companies have discovered that specialized sales training is an effective strategy. When Microsoft wanted to build a stronger partnership with its customers, all of its

Salespeople who build partnering relationships are rewarded with repeat business and referrals. These relationships require a strategic approach to selling.

5,000 sales professionals completed the Solution Selling sales training course. This training, based on concepts presented in *The New Solution Selling*, by Keith Eades, helped Microsoft salespeople create greater value for its customers.[19]

Strategic/Consultative Selling Model

When you study a value-added approach to personal selling that combines strategic planning, consultative selling practices, and partnering principles, you experience a mental exercise that is similar to solving a jigsaw puzzle. You are given many pieces of information that ultimately must form a complete picture. Putting the parts together isn't nearly as difficult if you can see the total picture at the beginning. Therefore, a single model has been developed to serve as a source of reference throughout the entire text. Figure 1.5 shows this model.

The Strategic/Consultative Selling Model features five steps, and each step is based on three prescriptions. The first step involves the development of a personal selling philosophy (see page 5). Each of the other four steps relates to a broad strategic area of personal selling. Each step makes an important and unique contribution to the selling/buying process.

Developing a Relationship Strategy

Success in selling depends heavily on the salesperson's ability to develop, manage, and enhance interpersonal relations with the customer. People seldom buy products or services from someone they dislike or distrust. Harvey B. Mackay, founder of Mackay Envelope Corporation, says, "People don't care how much you know until they know how much you care." Most customers are more apt to openly discuss their needs and wants with a salesperson with whom they feel comfortable.

A **relationship strategy** is a well-thought-out plan for establishing, building, and maintaining quality relationships. This type of plan is essential for success in today's marketplace, which is characterized by vigorous competition, look-alike products, and customer loyalty dependent on quality relationships as well as quality products. The relationship strategy must encompass every aspect of selling from the first contact with a prospect to servicing the sale once this prospect becomes an established customer. The primary goal of the relationship strategy is to create

STRATEGIC/CONSULTATIVE SELLING MODEL*

Strategic step	*Prescription*
Develop a Personal Selling Philosophy	☐ Adopt Marketing Concept ☐ Value Personal Selling ☐ Become a Problem Solver/Partner
Develop a Relationship Strategy	☐ Adopt Win-Win Philosophy ☐ Project Professional Image ☐ Maintain High Ethical Standards
Develop a Product Strategy	☐ Become a Product Expert ☐ Sell Benefits ☐ Configure Value-Added Solutions
Develop a Customer Strategy	☐ Understand the Buying Process ☐ Understand Buyer Behavior ☐ Develop Prospect Base
Develop a Presentation Strategy	☐ Prepare Objectives ☐ Develop Presentation Plan ☐ Provide Outstanding Service

*Strategic/consultative selling evolved in response to increased competition, more complex products, increased emphasis on customer needs, and growing importance of long-term relationships.

Place	Promotion
Product	Price

FIGURE | 1.5

The Strategic/Consultative Selling Model is an extension of the marketing concept.

rapport, trust, and mutual respect, which ensures a long-term partnership. To establish this type of relationship, salespeople must adopt a win-win philosophy; that is, if the customer wins, I win; project a professional image; and maintain high ethical standards (see Fig. 1.5). Chapters 3, 4 and 5 provide important information on development of the relationship strategy.

Some people think that the concept of *relationships* is too soft and too emotional for a business application; these people think that it's too difficult to think about relationships in strategic terms. In fact, this is not the case at all. Every salesperson can and should formulate a strategic plan that builds and enhances relationships.

Developing a Product Strategy

Products and services represent problem-solving tools. The **product strategy** is a plan that helps salespeople make correct decisions concerning the selection and positioning of products to meet identified customer needs. The three prescriptions for the product strategy are *become a product expert, sell benefits*, and *configure value-added solutions*. The development of a product strategy begins with a thorough study of one's product (see Fig. 1.5) using a feature–benefit analysis approach. Product features such as technical superiority, reliability, fashionableness, design integrity, or guaranteed availability should be converted to benefits that appeal to the customer. Today's high-performance salespeople strive to become product experts. Chapter 6 focuses on company, product, and competition knowledge needed by salespeople.

Product knowledge is not the only important element of a product strategy. In fact, salespeople who are too focused on selling products often fail to identify complete solutions to the customer's problem. Stephen Covey, author of the best selling book, *The 7 Habits of Highly Effective People*, says "Diagnose before you prescribe." If the salesperson does not deeply engage the customer and fails to diagnose the problem correctly, chances are the solution recommended may not be the best one.[20]

The development of a product strategy often requires thoughtful decision making. Today's more knowledgeable customers seek a cluster of satisfactions that arise from the product itself, from the manufacturer or distributor of the product,and from the salesperson. The "new" product that customers are buying today is the sum total of the satisfactions that emerge from all three sources. The cluster of satisfactions concept is discussed in more detail in Chapter 7.

Selling Is Everyone's Business

SALES SUCCESS PAVES THE WAY FOR HISPANIC ENTREPRENEUR

At age 19 Rosado Shaw wanted to be a salesperson, but the company she worked for wouldn't let her sell. She had recently dropped out of elite Wellesley College and took a job with a company that makes umbrellas and tote bags. One day she took a sick day and called on the marketing staff at the Museum of Natural History. The result of this impromptu sales call was a $140,000 order. She then went to the president of the company and asked him, "Are you going to let me sell now, or what?" After two years in sales, Shaw moved to a rival firm, Umbrellas Plus, and acquired more experience. Years later she purchased controlling interest in the company and turned it into a $10 million enterprise.[b]

Entrepreneur Rosado Shaw.

Developing a Customer Strategy

Patricia Seybold, CEO and founder of the Patricia Seybold Group, and best-selling business author of The Customer Revolution, *says we are in the midst of a profound revolution—the customer revolution.*

Patricia Seybold, author of *The Customer Revolution,* says we are in the midst of a profound revolution—the customer revolution. And it's bigger than the Internet revolution:

> Customers have taken control of our companies' destinies. Customers are transforming our industries. And customers' loyalty—or lack thereof—has become increasingly important. ...[21]

Customers have become increasingly sophisticated in their buying strategies. More and more, they have come to expect value-added products and services and long-term commitments. Selling to today's customers starts with getting on the customers' agenda and carefully identifying their needs, wants, and buying conditions.

A **customer strategy** is a carefully conceived plan that results in maximum responsiveness to the customer's needs. This strategy is based on the fact that success in personal selling depends, in no small measure, on the salesperson's ability to learn as much as possible about the prospect. It involves the collection and analysis of specific information on each customer. When developing a customer strategy, the salesperson should develop an understanding of the customer's buying process, understand buyer behavior, and develop a prospect base. The first two parts of the customer strategy are introduced in Chapter 8. Suggestions concerning ways to develop a solid prospect base are discussed in Chapter 9.

Many of the most progressive companies in the United States have well-established customer strategies. Baxter Healthcare, a company based in Deerfield, Illinois, provides a good example of a marketer that has adopted a unique customer strategy. Baxter's salespeople are encouraged to continuously collect information from those who use their products, or prospective customers in the medical field, and then use this information to refine existing products or develop new products (Fig. 1.6). A Baxter publication entitled *Doing Business with Baxter* states, "We enhance our business relationships by listening to feedback from our customers and considering new and innovative ways to provide service and information."[22]

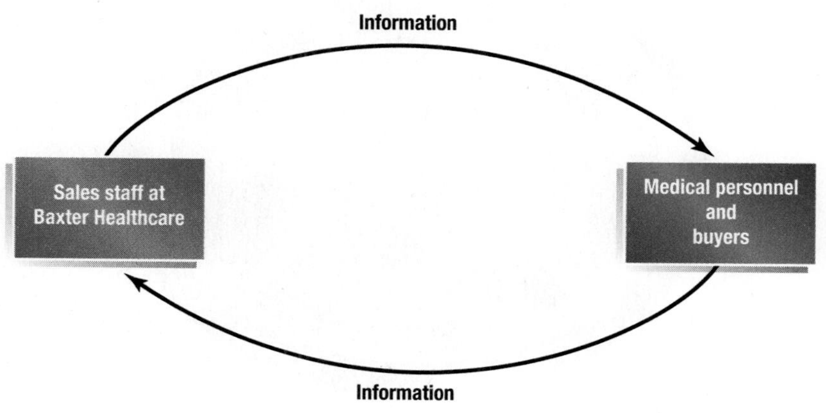

FIGURE | 1.6

Baxter's customer strategy loop illustrates how salespeople obtain information on ways to better serve their customers.

Developing a Presentation Strategy

Typical salespeople spend about 30 percent of their time in actual face-to-face selling situations. However, the sales presentation is a critical part of the selling process. The **presentation strategy** is a well-developed plan that includes preparing the sales presentation objectives, preparing a presentation plan that is needed to meet these objectives, and renewing one's commitment to provide outstanding customer service (see Fig. 1.5).

The presentation strategy usually involves developing one or more objectives for each sales call. For example, a salesperson might update personal information about the customer, provide information on a new product, and close a sale during one sales call. Multiple-objective sales presentations, which are becoming more common, are discussed in Chapter 10.

Presale presentation plans give salespeople the opportunity to consider those activities that take place during the sales presentation. For example, a salesperson might preplan a demonstration of product features to use when meeting with the customer. Presale planning ensures that salespeople are well organized during the sales presentation and prepared to offer outstanding service.

Interrelationship of Basic Strategies

The major strategies that form the Strategic/Consultative Selling Model are by no means independent. The relationship, product, and customer strategies all influence development of the presentation strategy (Fig. 1.7). For example, one relationship-building practice might be developed for use during the initial face-to-face meeting with the customer and another for possible use during the negotiation of buyer resistance. Another relationship-building method might be developed for use after the sale is closed. The discovery of customer needs (part of the customer strategy) greatly influences planning for the sales presentation.

Electronic Commerce, CRM, and the Complex Sale

Electronic business or e-business involves the use of intranets, extranets, and the Internet to conduct a company's business. Customer relationship management (CRM) software is an important element of electronic business.[23] Most organizations involved in sales and marketing use electronic business to support a variety of business activities.

FIGURE | 1.7

The major strategies that form the Strategic/Consultative Selling Model are by no means independent of one another. The focus of each strategy is to satisfy customer needs and build quality partnerships.

A complex sale will almost always require the use of several forms of information technology to gather and distribute information to customers. These tools, described in selected chapters, include electronic product catalogs, product configurators, and sales proposal writers (Chapter 6), contact management systems (see ACT! references throughout the book), PowerPoint and Excel spreadsheet software (Chapter 12), Internet applications (references throughout the book), and electronic mapping software (Chapter 16). **Electronic commerce**, a more specific form of e-business, refers to buying and selling activities conducted on the Internet.

EVOLUTION OF PARTNERING

Partnering became a buzzword in the 1990s and in the 2000s it became a business reality.[24] Partnering has been driven by several economic forces. One is the demise of the product solution in several industries. When products of one company are nearly identical to the competition, the product strategy becomes less important than the relationship, customer, and presentation strategies. By contrast, some partnerships grow out of the need for customized products or services. Many manufacturers have formed partnerships with companies that offer flexibility in terms of product configuration, scheduling of deliveries, or some other factor.

Today's customer wants a quality product *and* a quality relationship. Salespeople willing to abandon short-term thinking and invest the time and energy needed to develop a high-quality, long-term relationship with customers are greatly rewarded. A strong partnership serves as a barrier to competing salespeople who want to sell to your accounts. Salespeople who are able to build partnerships enjoy more repeat business and referrals. Keeping existing customers happy makes a great deal of sense from an economic point of view. Experts in the field of sales and marketing know that it costs four to five times more to get a new customer than to keep an existing one. Therefore, even small increases in customer retention can result in major increases in profits.[25]

Partnering is a strategically developed, long-term relationship that solves the customer's problems. A successful long-term partnership is achieved when the salesperson is able to skillfully apply the four major strategies and, thus, add value in various ways (Fig. 1.8). Successful sales professionals stay close to the customer and constantly search for new ways to add value.

The salespeople at Mackay Envelope Corporation achieve this goal by making sure they know more about their customers than the competitors know. Salespeople who

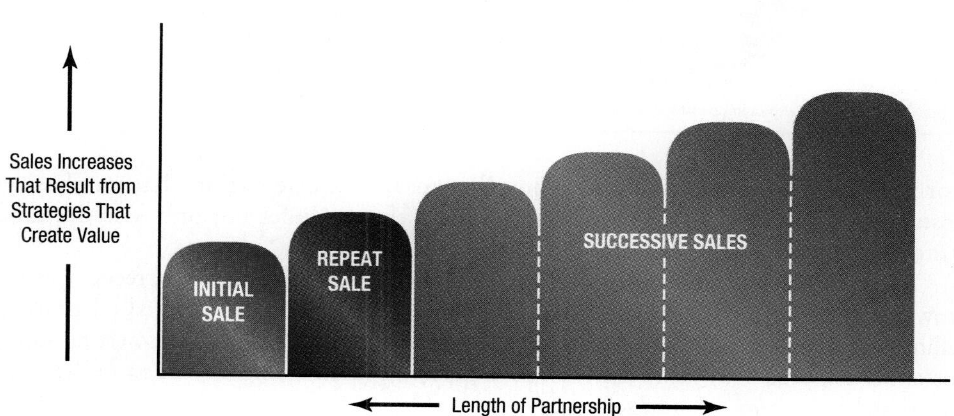

FIGURE 1.8

Partnering is a strategically developed, long-term relationship that solves the customer's problems. A successful partnering effort results in repeat sales and referrals that expand the prospect base. The strength of the partnership increases each time the salesperson uses value-added selling strategies.

National account managers at Campbell's work closely with sales teams that call on culinary accounts. They add value by helping these customers improve their menu. These improvements add value and help build long-term partnerships.

work for Xerox Corporation are responding to a sales orientation that emphasizes postsale service. Bonuses are based on a formula that includes not only sales but also customer satisfaction.

The term **relationship selling**, popularized over the past several years, recognizes the growing importance of partnerships in selling. Salespeople who have adopted relationship selling work hard to build and nourish long-term partnerships. They rely on a personal, customized approach to each customer. This approach stands in stark contrast to the more traditional *transaction-oriented* selling.

Cushman & Wakefield understands that in today's global market customers want a partnership that emphasizes a quality product and a quality relationship. Trust is a key element of a strong partnership.

Strategic Alliances—The Highest Form of Partnering

Throughout the past decade we have seen the growth of a new form of partnership that often is described as a **strategic alliance**. The goal of strategic alliances is to achieve a marketplace advantage by teaming up with another company whose products or services fit well with your own.[26] Alliances often are formed by companies that have similar business interests and, thus, gain a mutual competitive advantage. It is not uncommon for a company to form several alliances. Corning, a maker of glass products, has formed partnerships with several companies that need innovative glass technology. For example, Corning formed an alliance with Samsung, a Korean manufacturer of television screens. RadioShack has formed strategic alliances with several leading consumer electronics manufacturers. This move helped the company avoid the costs of starting new divisions.[27]

Strategic alliances have created a new selling environment. The first step in building an alliance is to learn as much as possible about the proposed partner. This study takes place long before face-to-face contact. Alliances that are formed between companies that vary greatly in such areas as customer focus, financial stability, or ethical values will likely fail.[28] The second step is to meet with the proposed partner and explore mutual benefits of the alliance. At this

Customer Relationship Management with Technology

INTRODUCING CRM

Today, many sales professionals use computers to help them better perform the tasks associated with successful personal selling. Various software programs are used, including e-mail, electronic spreadsheets, word processors, configuration systems, presentation packages, fax managers, and customer relationship management (CRM) systems. A basic CRM system consists of a database containing information about the people with whom a salesperson maintains relationships, such as customers, prospects, coworkers, and suppliers. For your use with the CRM studies in this text, a basic Windows-based CRM system is included on the CD that came with your book. You can learn the fundamentals of CRM with this software, including searching for customer and product-related information, managing time and priorities, communicating, forecasting sales, and estimating your commissions. (See the exercise, Introducing CRM Software, on p. 27)

point the salesperson (or account manager) is selling advice, assistance, and counsel, not specific products. Building win-win alliances requires the highest form of consultative selling. Very often, the salesperson is working with a company team made up of persons from such areas as research and development (R&D), finance, and distribution. Presentations and proposals usually focus on profit impact and other strategic alliance benefits.

Partnering Is Enhanced with High Ethical Standards

In the field of selling there are certain pressures that can influence the ethical conduct of salespeople, and poor ethical decisions can weaken or destroy partnerships. To illustrate, let us assume a competitor makes exaggerated claims about a product. Do you counteract by promising more than your product can deliver? What action do you take when there is a time management problem and you must choose between servicing past sales and making new sales? What if a superior urges you to use a strategy that you consider unethical? These and other pressures must be dealt with everyday.

Although pressures exist in every selling position, most salespeople are able to draw the line between ethical and unethical behavior. This is especially true of those who have taken a long-range view of sales work that emphasizes building partnerships. These people know that the best way to ensure repeat business is to deal honestly and fairly with every customer. Most customers today are reaching out for a partner they can trust.

Although Chapter 5 is devoted entirely to ethical considerations in personal selling, it should be noted that ethics is a major theme of the text. The topic of ethics has been interwoven throughout several chapters. The authors believe that ethical decisions must be made everyday in the life of a salesperson, so this important topic cannot be covered in a single chapter.

Partnering Is Enhanced with Customer Relationship Management

Many companies have adopted some form of customer relationship management. **Customer relationship management (CRM)**, sometimes referred to as *sales automation*, is the process of building and maintaining strong customer relationships by providing customer value.[29] A modern CRM program relies on a variety of technologies to improve communications in a sales organization and enhance customer responsiveness. A variety of CRM applications will be discussed throughout the text.

VALUE CREATION—THE NEW SELLING IMPERATIVE

We have defined value-added selling as a series of creative improvements within the sales process that enhance the customer experience. The *information economy* will reward those salespeople who have the skills, the knowledge, and the motivation to determine how to create value at every step of the sales process.

To better understand value-added selling it helps to reflect on the roles assumed by other professionals such as management consultants, fee-based financial planners, lawyers, doctors, and psychologists. The value they bring to a relationship is based on the intangible information they possess. They create value by establishing a dialogue with the patient or client and becoming thoroughly familiar with the client's problem. Traditional selling has too often emphasized communicating only the value that lies in the product or service. The focus of the sales call has too often been the product, not creating value for the customer.[30]

When the customer is not aware of the value added by the salesperson, the focus of the sale may shift to price. Successful salespeople determine what drives a customer's behavior beyond price. In today's rapidly changing marketplace the perception of value often shifts.

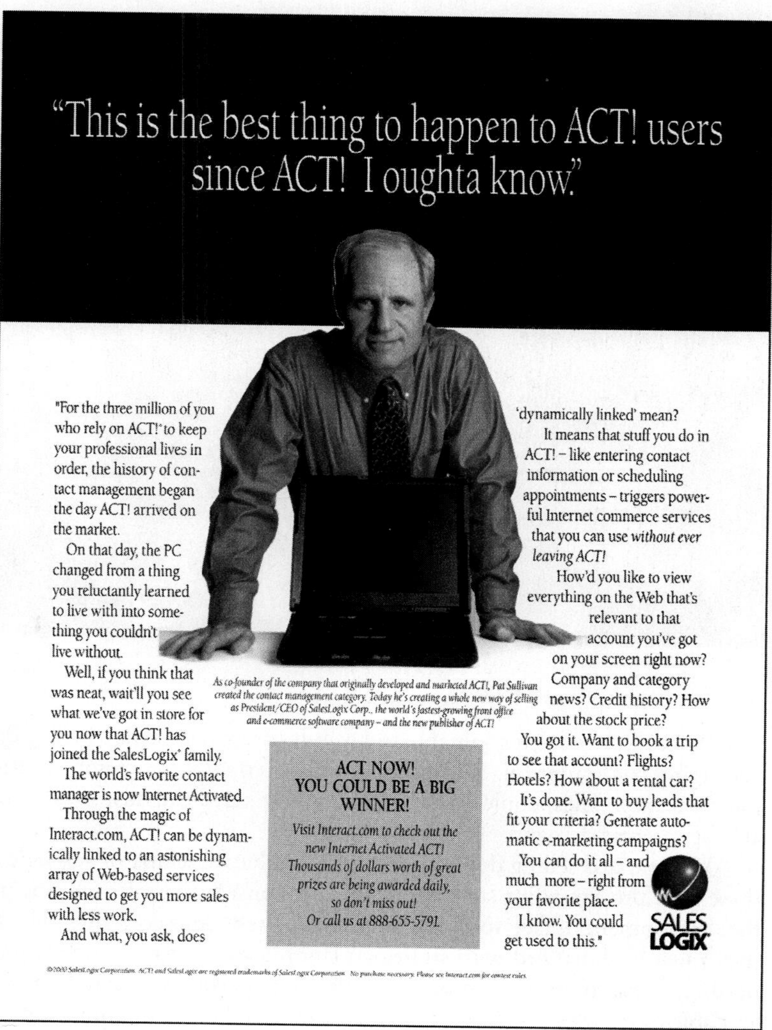

The ACT! contact management program has been improved with a new technology called Internet Activated. This new technology, available to the 3 million ACT! users, links the salesperson to an array of Web-based services.

Value-added selling consists of a series of creative ways to improve and enhance the customer experience. Wisconsin Cheese offers its sales organization value-adding ideas and supports them with strategic tools and programs.

Low price may be what's valuable today, but tomorrow it may be fast delivery or a different packaging configuration. Sensing value shifts is one of the major benefits of staying close to the customer. Salespeople who can effectively solve the customer's problems will prosper and be in great demand.

Value-added selling does not replace consultative selling or strategic selling—it builds on these time-proven selling strategies. The early consultative sales training programs emphasized the development of face-to-face selling skills. These skills continue to be important today, but they must be enhanced with strategic planning and a strong commitment to building partnerships. Customers want to partner with a salesperson who is well organized, well informed, and able to use strategic thinking to add value when meeting their complex needs.

Summary

As the global economy has shifted from one of excess demand to one of excess supply, competition has increased, both from organizations within the United States and from those in foreign countries. Vigorous sales promotion, including personal selling, are key factors in stimulating global demand for products.

Personal selling is the process of developing customer relationships, discovering customer needs, matching the appropriate products with those needs, and communicating benefits through a need satisfaction presentation. (A *product* can be information, a service, an idea, an issue, or an item.) The *marketing concept* is the belief that a firm should dedicate all its policies, planning, and operations to the satisfaction of the customer.

The *marketing era* that began in the United States in the 1950s looked first at customer needs and wants and then created goods and services to meet those needs and wants. (During the industrial age, the emphasis first was on creating products and then on building customer interest in those products.) *Consultative selling* emerged in the late 1960s and early 1970s as an approach that emphasizes the identification of customer needs through effective communication between the salesperson and the customer. *Strategic selling* evolved in the 1980s and involves the preparation of a carefully conceived plan to accomplish sales objectives. In the 1990s, the evolution of *partnering* began. This approach involves providing customers with a quality product *and* a high-quality, long-term relationship.

Strategic selling is based on a company's *strategic market plan*, which takes into consideration the coordination of all the major functional areas of the business—production, marketing, finance, and personnel. The four broad strategic areas in the Strategic/Consultative Selling Model (after development of a personal selling philosophy) are developing a relationship strategy, developing a product strategy, developing a customer strategy, and developing a presentation strategy.

Value-added selling has emerged as a major response to the customer economy. This approach to personal selling is defined as a series of creative improvements that enhance the customer's experience.

Ethical considerations are particularly important in the field of personal selling because the salesperson represents his company to the buyer. The salesperson may encounter pressures to "bend" principles of honesty, so it is necessary to consider and develop ethical principles that serve as the guidelines for one's entire career.

KEY TERMS

Personal selling
Product
Personal selling philosophy
Marketing concept
Marketing mix
Consultative selling
Transactional selling
Customer relationship management
Strategic planning
Tactics
Strategy
Relationship strategy
Product strategy
Customer strategy
Presentation strategy
Information economy
Electronic commerce
Relationship selling
Partnering
Strategic alliance
Value-added selling
Customer economy
Electronic business

REVIEW QUESTIONS

1. Explain how personal selling can help solve the problem of information overload.
2. According to the Strategic/Consultative Selling Model (see Fig. 1.1), what are the three prescriptions for developing a successful personal selling philosophy?
3. Why is peddling or "pushing products" inconsistent with the marketing concept?
4. What is consultative selling? Give examples.
5. Diagram and label the four-step Consultative Sales Presentation Guide.
6. List and briefly explain the four broad strategic areas that make up the selling process.
7. Briefly describe the evolution of partnering. Discuss the forces that contributed to this approach to selling.
8. Provide a brief description of value-added selling. What economic forces have motivated companies to adopt value-added selling?
9. Briefly describe why some organizations are developing strategic alliances.
10. Explain why the ethical conduct of salespeople has become so important today.

APPLICATION EXERCISES

1. Assume that you are an experienced professional salesperson. A professor who teaches at a nearby university has asked you to speak to a consumer economics class about the benefits of personal selling to customers. Make an outline of what to say.
2. A friend of yours has invented a unique and useful new product. This friend, an engineer by profession, understands little about marketing and selling this new product. She does understand, however, that "nothing happens until somebody sells the product." She has asked you to describe the general factors that need to be considered when you market a product. Prepare an answer to her question.
3. Sharon Alverez has been teaching college biology courses. She is offered a position selling pharmaceutical products. This position requires that she call on doctors and pharmacists to explain her product line. Describe the similarities and the differences between personal selling and teaching.

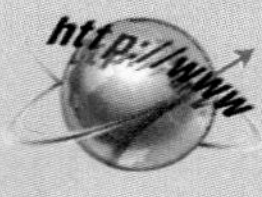

4. To learn more about an industry-based sales training program, access *www.wilsonlearning.com*. Click on the "Sales Effectiveness" link and examine the content of the various sales courses offered.

ROLE-PLAY EXERCISE

The purpose of this role-play is to provide you with an opportunity to engage in a basic need identification exercise. You will be meeting with someone (a class member) who is preparing for an important job interview and needs a pen and/or pencil. Prior to the meeting, make a list of the questions you will ask. Then pair off with the class member and ask your questions. Be sure to take notes. At the end of the interview, be prepared to recommend the most appropriate pen and/or pencil.

CRM APPLICATION EXERCISE

Introducing CRM Software

The CRM system that is included on the CD that came with this book is a demonstration version of the best selling software called ACT!. This version of ACT! includes a database of information about prospective customers for a company selling network systems. In the case study and exercises ahead, you assume the role of a salesperson who is selling these network systems. The emphasis in these exercises is customer relationship management. No prior experience or prior knowledge of networking systems is required to complete these exercises.

ACT! is a database program, which means that it uses records and fields. Records are the screens that contain information about each person. Fields are the boxes on the records for entering and displaying data, such as the name of the person (e.g., Bradley Able). ACT! also is known as a contact management program because it maintains a record for each contact (person). Some CRM systems offer a separate record for each organization.

You can experiment with ACT! without concern about damaging the program. To get acquainted with the ACT! version of CRM, click on the various menu items and icons and observe the functions that are available to you. Experimenting with this software gives you a feel for the potential power of using technology to enhance your sales career. Test ACT!'s report capabilities by printing a phone list: Select Report and Phone; in the Prepare Report box, choose Active Group, and Printer; then print the list.

As you experiment with ACT!, you can obtain help at any time by pressing the F1 function key. (See the Learning CRM Software exercise in Chapter 2.)

VIDEO CASE PROBLEM

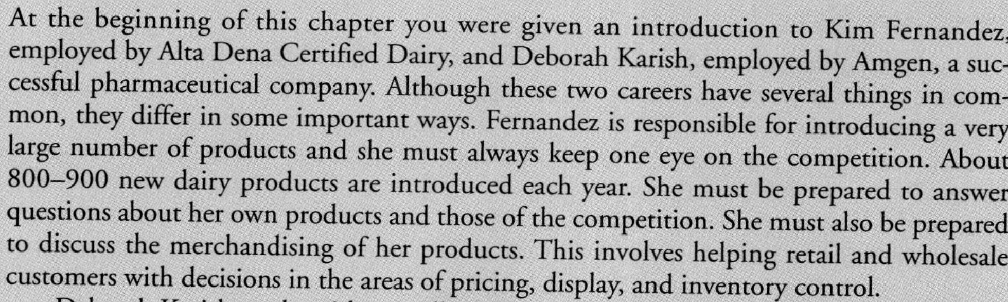

At the beginning of this chapter you were given an introduction to Kim Fernandez, employed by Alta Dena Certified Dairy, and Deborah Karish, employed by Amgen, a successful pharmaceutical company. Although these two careers have several things in common, they differ in some important ways. Fernandez is responsible for introducing a very large number of products and she must always keep one eye on the competition. About 800–900 new dairy products are introduced each year. She must be prepared to answer questions about her own products and those of the competition. She must also be prepared to discuss the merchandising of her products. This involves helping retail and wholesale customers with decisions in the areas of pricing, display, and inventory control.

Deborah Karish works with a small number of pharmaceutical products, but each one is complex. She must be able to explain how each of her drugs will interact with other drugs the patient is taking. Karish must also be familiar with dosage requirements of each drug. In some cases she must seek help from the pharmaceutical staff employed by Amgen. Medical personnel ask tough questions because human lives are involved.

Fernandez, Karish, and every other professional salesperson are constantly involved in learning. We now know that the principles of selling can be learned and applied by people whose personal characteristics are quite different. Most successful salespeople spend considerable time acquiring product knowledge, keeping up to date in their industry, and learning more about their customers. In the pharmaceutical industry, salespeople often earn the Certified Medical Representative (CMR) designation. This lengthy program of study covers courses in four concentrations: science and medicine; disease management; business and health care; and pharmacy management.

Karish and Fernandez realize the importance of a relationship strategy that is built upon a win-win philosophy. In addition to building a strong relationship with the customer, they must be able to work effectively with others who directly or indirectly influence the sale. Kim Fernandez realizes that the employees who stock and price her products in retail stores are very important. She must also build rapport with management personnel. In a hospital setting, the purchase and use of Amgen products will be influenced by doctors and pharmacists. The salesperson who is honest, accountable, and sincerely concerned about the customer's welfare brings added value to the sales. (See chapter opener on page 4 for more information.)

Questions

1. Does it appear that Alta Dena Certified Dairy and Amgen have adopted the three prescriptions of a personal selling philosophy? (See Strategic/Consultative Selling Model.) Explain.
2. What prescriptions of the relationship strategy (see Strategic/Consultative Selling Model) have been adopted by Kim Fernandez and Deborah Karish?
3. Value-added selling is defined as a series of creative improvements in the sales process that enhance the customer's experience. Describe the various ways that Kim Fernandez and Deborah Karish can create value for their customers.
4. Let's assume you are considering a career in personal selling. Which of these two careers do you find more appealing? Explain.

PARTNERSHIP SELLING: ROLE-PLAY/SIMULATION

[If your instructor has chosen to use the *Partnership Selling Role-Play/Simulation* exercise that accompanies this text, these boxes alert you to your Role-Play/Simulation assignments. Your instructor will also provide you with needed information.]

Preview the role-play/simulation materials in Appendix 3. These materials are produced by the Park Inn International Hotel and Convention Center, and you will be using them in your role as a new salesperson (and, at times, as the customer) for the hotel and its convention services.

The role-play exercises begin in Chapter 6, as you begin to create your product strategy. However, in anticipation of the role-play, you can begin to imagine yourself in the role of an actual salesperson. Start to think about how you can develop your personal selling philosophy. What are some ethical guidelines that you may wish to adopt for yourself? (Ethics is also the subject of Chapter 5, "Ethics—The Foundation for Relationships in Selling.") What skills do you need to develop to become a partner with your prospective customers? (Refer to the position description in Part I of Appendix 3.)

The Park Inn has implemented a quality improvement process. How does this affect your role as a sales representative? (Refer to the Total Quality Customer Service Glossary in Part I of Appendix 3.)

CHAPTER 2

Chapter Preview

When you finish reading this chapter, you should be able to

1. Describe how personal selling skills contribute to work performed by knowledge workers

2. Discuss the rewarding aspects of personal selling careers

3. Describe the opportunities for women and minorities in the field of personal selling

4. Discuss the characteristics of selling positions in four major employment settings: service, retailing, wholesaling, and manufacturing

5. Identify the four major sources of sales training

Personal Selling Opportunities in the Age of Information

Job seekers who visit Monster.com or CareerBuilder.com are usually surprised to discover that sales careers represent one of the largest job posting categories. Many thousands of entry-level sales positions are listed every day. The next big surprise comes when they discover the great variety of companies that hire salespeople. Some companies, such as Marriott and United Parce Service (UPS), are well known throughout the nation. Other companies, such as SpeechPhone, LLC and World Golf Hospitality, Inc., may be unfamiliar to the job seeker. SpeechPhone, LLC, founded in 2002, sells call forwarding, message retrieval, and other phone services. World Golf Hospitality, Inc., founded in 1992, plans corporate-travel events and meetings that typically involve golf. The company has created travel programs for major events including the Masters, the Ryder Cup, and the U.S. Open tournaments.[1]

In recent years, the labor market has become a place of churning dislocation caused by the heavy volume of mergers, acquisitions, business closings, bankruptcies, and downsizings. Personal selling careers have become an attractive employment option to the thousands of professionals who walk away from—or are pushed out of—corporate jobs.

PERSONAL SELLING IN THE AGE OF INFORMATION

The late Stanley Marcus, chairman emeritus of the prestigious Neiman Marcus retail company, said, "Sooner or later in business, everybody has to sell something to somebody." He noted that even if you are not in sales, you must know how to sell a product, a service, an idea, or yourself.[2] Marcus's views have garnered a great deal of support among observers of the information age. Today's workforce is made up of millions of knowledge workers who succeed only when they add value to information. The new economy is about the growing value of knowledge, making it the most important ingredient of what people buy and sell.[3] One way to add value to information is to collect it, organize it, clarify it, and present it in a convincing manner. This skill, used every day by professional salespeople, is invaluable in a world that is overloaded with information.

As noted in Chapter 1, relationships began to become more important at the beginning of the information age. In many cases, information does not have value unless people interact effectively. A salesperson may possess information concerning an important new technology, but that information has no value until it is communicated effectively to an investor, a customer, or someone else who can benefit from knowing more about his product. A bank loan officer may have the resources needed to assist a prospective homeowner reach her dream, but in the absence of a good relationship, communications may break down.

Today, personal selling skills contribute in a major way to four groups of knowledge workers who usually do not consider themselves salespeople:

- Customer service representatives
- Professionals (accountants, consultants, lawyers, etc.)
- Entrepreneurs
- Managerial personnel

Customer Service Representatives

The assignment of selling duties to employees with customer service responsibilities has become quite common today. The term **customer service representative** (CSR) is used to describe people who process reservations, accept orders by phone or other means, deliver products, handle customer complaints, provide technical assistance, and assist full-time sales representatives. Some companies are teaming CSRs and salespeople. After the sale is closed, the CSR helps process paperwork, check on delivery of the product, and engage in other customer follow-up duties. Some examples of companies that are moving customer service representatives into the proactive role of selling are:

> *Item*: Nick Nicholson, CEO of Ecology Group, a $40 million recycling and waste-management company in Columbus, Ohio, believes that each of his employees should possess selling skills. All his staff members receive sales training. To illustrate how sales training makes a difference, he points to a member of his accounting staff who received a call from a customer concerning an overbilling problem. In the process of clarifying the problem, the staff member identified an opportunity to expand the Ecology Group's agreement with the client. This involved extending service to more locations.[4]
>
> *Item*: A growing number of employees in the financial services industry are completing the Sales Skills Mastery sales training and certification program. Tellers, commercial lenders, and other customer service employees at First National Bank in Montevideo, Minnesota, have completed this self-paced course. Kathy Gilkey, vice president of sales and marketing at the bank, says, "If you don't have a strong sales and service program in place, you're not as effective in helping your clients." Dyana Herrig, branch manager with AmeriCU Credit Union, agrees. All of her employees are encouraged to sell services that will benefit members.[5]

The new economy's workforce is made up of millions of knowledge workers who succeed only when they add value to information. Today's salesperson collects information, organizes it, clarifies it, and presents it in a convincing manner, thereby adding value.

Assigning sales duties to customer service representatives makes sense when you consider the number of contacts customers have with CSRs. When a customer seeks assistance with a problem or makes a reservation, the CSR learns more about the customer and often provides the customer with needed information. Customer needs often surface as both parties exchange information. It is important to keep in mind the advice offered by the authors of *Selling the Invisible*: "Every act is a marketing act. Make every employee a marketing person."[6]

Professionals

Today's professional workers include lawyers, designers, programmers, engineers, consultants, dietitians, counselors, doctors, accountants, and many other specialized knowledge workers. Our labor force includes nearly 20 million professional service providers, persons who need many of the skills used by professional salespeople. Clients who purchase professional services are usually more interested in the person who delivers the service than in the firm that employs the professional. They seek expert diagnosticians who are truly interested in their needs. The professional must display good communication skills and be able to build a relationship built on trust.

Technical skills are not enough in the information age. Many employers expect the professional to bring in new business in addition to keeping current customers satisfied. Employers often screen professional applicants to determine their customer focus and ability to interact well with people.

Many firms are providing their professional staff with sales training. The accounting firm Ernst & Young sets aside several days each year to train its professional staff in personal selling. The National Law Firm Marketing Association recently featured Neil Rackham, author of *Spin Selling*, as keynote speaker at its national conference. The Wicker Corporation, a manufacturer of equipment for the plastics industry, has initiated a program

Selling Is Everyone's Business

SELLING PHILANTHROPY TO THE "CYBER-STINGY"

As president of the Community Foundation Silicon Valley, Peter Hero is selling the concept of philanthropy to high-tech millionaires. Although Silicon Valley is home to several thousand millionaires, his job is not easy. Many of the wealthy residents are very young and they don't spend much time thinking about leaving behind a lasting civic legacy. And many of those who are skilled at generating wealth don't have a clue when it comes to giving it away. Yet the foundation is growing and large grants are being given to education programs, social-service agencies, and neighborhood groups. Thanks to Peter Hero, philanthropy is becoming another growth industry in Silicon Valley.[a]

Peter Hero, president of Community Foundation Silicon Valley.

designed to motivate its researchers, engineers, and manufacturing staff members to get involved in sales. Faced with increased competition and more cost-conscious customers, a growing number of law, accounting, engineering, and architectural firms are discovering the merits of personal selling as an auxiliary activity.[7]

While many professional service firms are trying to train their employees to sell, others have been hiring professional salespeople to assist or team up with their service professionals. A common approach is to use a team selling approach that involves a salesperson and a service professional who has received training in the area of team selling.[8]

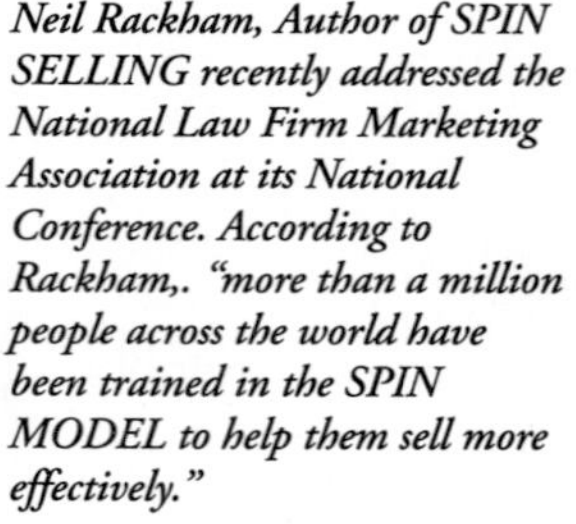

Neil Rackham, Author of SPIN SELLING recently addressed the National Law Firm Marketing Association at its National Conference. According to Rackham,. "more than a million people across the world have been trained in the SPIN MODEL to help them sell more effectively."

Entrepreneurs

Thousands of new businesses are started each year in the United States. As noted previously, people who want to start a new business frequently need to sell their plan to investors and others who can help get the firm established. Once the firm is open, owners rely on personal selling to build their businesses.

James Koch, chief executive officer of the Boston Beer Company (brewer of Samuel Adams beer), makes a strong case for personal selling. Like most new companies, his started with no customers. To get the new company established in 1985, he assumed the role of salesperson and set a goal of establishing one new account each week.

Today Koch continues to spend time on the street, visiting convenience stores, supermarkets, and taverns. Competition from popular craft beers such as Fat Tire and Magic Hat, and imports such as Stella Artois and Beck, present a major challenge. He's also trying to get the attention of young men who think of Samuel Adams as their father's beer. He readily admits that selling his beer is the most rewarding part of his job. Koch could have sold his company to a megabrewer long ago, but that option is not appealing to this wealthy entrepreneur who loves to sell.[9]

Managerial Personnel

Brian Tracy, noted author and consultant, reminds us that everyone must be able to sell their ideas and sell themselves.

People working in managerial occupations represent another large group of knowledge workers. They are given such titles as executive, manager, or administrator. Leaders are constantly involved in capturing, processing, and communicating information. Some of the most valuable information is acquired from customers. This helps explain the rapid growth in what is being described as "executive selling." Chief executive officers and other executives often accompany salespeople on sales calls to learn more about customer needs and in some cases to assist with presentations. Manny Fernandez of the Gartner Group, a technology consulting firm based in Stamford, Connecticut, spends more than half his time traveling on sales calls.[10] Leaders also must articulate their ideas in a persuasive manner and win support for their vision. Brian Tracy, author of *The 100 Absolutely Unbreakable Laws of Business Success*, says, "People who cannot present their ideas or sell themselves effectively have very little influence and are not highly respected."[11]

Increasingly, work in the information economy is understood as an expression of thought. At a time when people change their careers eight or more times during their lives, selling skills represent important transferable employment skills.

YOUR FUTURE IN PERSONAL SELLING

The 500 largest sales forces in America employ 17.5 million salespeople.[12] These companies will seek to recruit 500,000 college graduates. A large number of additional salespeople are employed by smaller companies. In addition, the number of sales positions is increasing in most industrialized countries. A close examination of these positions reveals that there is no single "selling" occupation. Our labor force includes hundreds of different selling careers and chances are there are positions that match your interests, talents, and ambitions. The diversity within selling becomes apparent as you study the career options discussed in this chapter.

Although many college students ultimately become salespeople, often it's not their first career choice. Students tend to view sales as dynamic and active but believe a selling career requires them to engage in deceitful or dishonest practices. The good news is that old stereotypes about sales are gradually going by the wayside. Students who study the careers of highly successful salespeople discover that ethical sales practices represent the key to long-term success.

A professional selling position encompasses a wide range of tasks (Fig. 2.1), and, therefore, salespeople must possess a variety of skills. A salesperson representing Federal Express (FedEX) makes numerous sales calls each day in an attempt to establish new accounts and provide service to established accounts. There is a wide range of potential customers who can use FedEX delivery services. A salesperson working for a Caterpillar construction equipment dealer may make only two or three sales calls per day. The products offered by the dealer are expensive and are not purchased frequently.

Just as selling occupations differ, so do the titles by which salespeople are known. Their titles reflect, in part, the variety of duties they perform. A survey of current job announcements indicates that companies are using such titles as these:

Account Executive	Sales Consultant
Account Representative	Client Development Manager
Sales Account Manager	Sales Associate
Relationship Manager	Marketing Representative
District Representative	Territory Manager

Two factors have contributed to the creation of new titles. First, we have seen a shift from "selling" to "consulting." When salespeople assume a consulting role, the value of the relationship exceeds the value of the transaction. Second, the new titles reflect a difference in education and skill sets needed for the position.[13]

Salespeople, regardless of title, play an important role in sustaining the growth and profitability of organizations of all sizes (Table 2.1). They also support the employment of many nonselling employees.

FIGURE 2.1

How Salespeople Spend Their Time During an Average 46-Hour Workweek (Approximate)

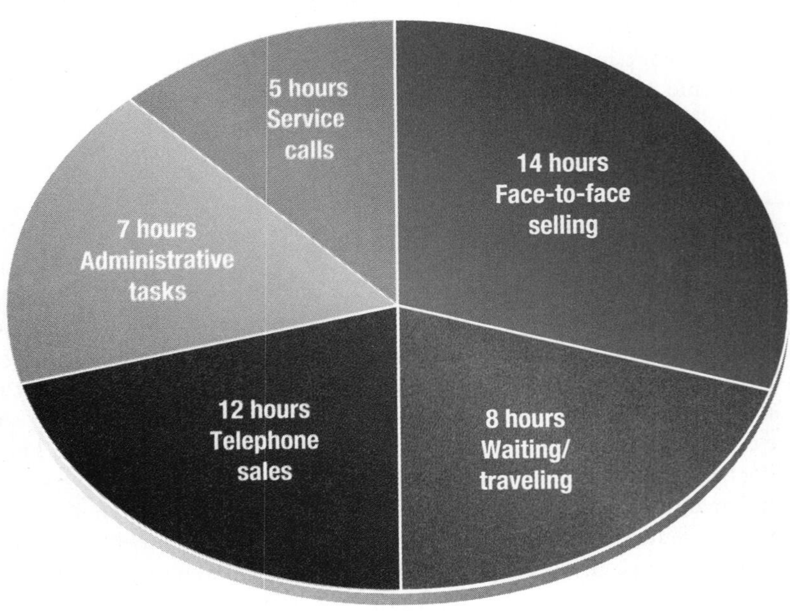

TABLE | 2.1 SELECTED LARGE U.S. SALES FORCES

COMPANY	CATEGORY	U.S. SALESPEOPLE
PepsiCo	Food, Beverage	36,000
Marriott	Hospitality	8,500
Interstate Bakeries	Food, Beverage	10,000
Microsoft	Computer and Office Equipment	16,000
Schering-Plough	Medical Products	10,975
IBM	Computer and Office Equipment	10,000
Johnson & Johnson	Medical Products	8,500
American Express	Financial	23,406
Merrill Lynch	Financial	14,471
Citigroup	Financial	12,442
Hartford Financial Services	Insurance	100,000
Clear Channel Communications	Communications	11,000
Torchmark	Insurance	49,000
Humana	Insurance	37,800

Source: "The Major Sales Forces in America," *Selling Power*, October 2005, pp. 58–78.

Rewarding Aspects of Selling Careers

From a personal and economic standpoint, selling can be a rewarding career. Careers in selling offer financial rewards, recognition, security, and opportunities for advancement to a degree that is unique, when compared with other occupations.

Above-Average Income

Studies dealing with incomes in the business community indicate that salespeople earn significantly higher incomes than most other workers. Some salespeople actually earn more than their sales managers and other executives within the organization. This high level of compensation (whether from base salary, bonus, or incentives) is justified for good performance. Table 2.2 provides a summary of the 2005 compensation survey by *Sales & Marketing Management* magazine. Executive and sales force compensation continues to climb despite uncertain economic conditions.[14]

TABLE | 2.2 EXECUTIVE AND SALES FORCE COMPENSATION

	TOTAL COMPENSATION	BASE SALARY	BONUS PLUS COMMISSIONS
Executive	$145,978	$96,774	$49,204
Top Performer	$155,055	$88,443	$66,612
Mid-level Performer	$ 93,499	$59,389	$34,110
Low-level Performer	$ 64,990	$45,624	$19,366
Average for All Reps	$110,206	$70,553	$39,653

Source: Christine Galea, "The 2005 Compensation Survey," *Sales & Marketing Management*, May 2005, p.25.

In recent years we have seen new ways to report compensation for salespeople. The Hay's Group, working with C&C Market Research Inc., developed a reporting method that tracks earnings for different types of sales approaches. Research indicates that salespeople involved in transactional sales earned the lowest compensation. Sales personnel involved in value-added sales earned the highest level of compensation. These highly paid salespeople created improvements in the sales process that enhanced the customer experience.[15]

Above-Average Psychic Income

Two major psychological needs common to all people are recognition and security. **Psychic income**, which consists of factors that provide psychological rewards, helps satisfy these important needs and motivates us to achieve higher levels of performance. The need for recognition has been established in numerous studies that have examined human motivation. Workers from all employment areas indicate that recognition for work well done is an important morale-building factor.

In selling, recognition occurs more frequently and with greater intensity than it does in most other occupations. Because selling contributes so visibly to the success of most business firms, the accomplishments of sales personnel seldom go unrecognized.

Most people want to achieve some measure of security in their work. Selling is one of those occupations that usually provides job security during both good and bad times.

Opportunity for Advancement

Each year, thousands of openings appear in the ranks of supervision and management. Because salespeople work in positions of high visibility, they are in an excellent position to be chosen for advancement to positions of greater responsibility. The top executives of many of today's companies began their careers in the ranks of the sales force.

Of course, not all salespeople can become presidents of large corporations, but in the middle-management ranks there are numerous interesting and high-paying positions in which experience in selling is a prime requisite for advancement. Information on careers in sales management is presented in Chapter 17.

Opportunities for Women

Prodded by a growing awareness that gender is not a barrier to success in selling, business firms are recruiting qualified women in growing numbers. The percentage of women in the sales force has increased considerably. Although women are still relative newcomers to industrial sales, they have enjoyed expanded career opportunities in such areas as real estate, insurance, advertising services, investments, and travel services. A growing number of women are turning to sales employment because it offers excellent economic rewards and in many cases a flexible work schedule. Flexible schedules are very appealing to women who want to balance career and family.

At Pitney Bowes, the nation's largest provider of corporate mail services, about 24 percent of the top employees are women. Many of the top salespeople are women who were formerly teachers.[16]

Opportunities for Minorities

From a historical perspective, the field of selling has not provided equal opportunity to minorities. In the past, it was not easy for a member of a minority group to obtain a sales position. Today the picture has changed, and more firms are actively recruiting

Selling in Action

OPPORTUNITIES FOR WOMEN IN SALES

In a world that is beginning to value diversity, we are seeing growing opportunities for women in sales. However, some misinformation concerning women in sales still exists. Four common myths follow:

Myth: *Women will not relocate or stick around long enough to repay the firm's hiring and training expenses.* Today, working women make up nearly half of the workforce and they have made significant gains in a wide range of traditionally male-dominated areas. About 50 percent of the working women contribute more than half of their family's income. Most of the women in this group need to work, want to work, and seek rewarding career opportunities.

Myth: *Women earn significantly less in sales than their male counterparts.* Although a pay gap between men and women exists in the field of sales, it is relatively small compared with the earnings gap for women who work full-time in the workforce as a whole.

Myth: *Buyers are less accepting of female salespeople.* In the field of personal selling, perceived expertise, likability, and trustworthiness can have a major influence on purchase decisions. Women who project these qualities seldom face rejection based on gender.

Myth: *Women face special problems when assigned to selling positions in foreign countries.* The truth is recent research suggests that businesswomen often enjoy a significant edge over their male counterparts when given overseas assignments.[b]

employees from minority groups. Although state and federal equal opportunity legislation can be credited, in part, for bringing about changes in hiring practices, many firms now view the recruitment and training of minority employees as simply good business. Minority salespeople have become top producers in many organizations.

Opportunities for minorities exist in a variety of selling careers.

In recent years, several trade journal reports have highlighted the underrepresentation of minority employees in sales. Many companies recognize that shifting population demographics require a reexamination of hiring practices. The biggest population gains have been made by women, minorities, and immigrants. Many companies realize the need for a diverse sales force that can gain access to the diverse clientele that make up certain market segments.[17] This philosophical shift should open the doors for our growing population of minorities.

EMPLOYMENT SETTINGS IN SELLING TODAY

Careers in the field of selling may be classified in several ways. One of the broadest differentiations is based on whether the product is tangible or intangible. Tangibles are physical goods such as furniture, homes, and data processing equipment. Intangibles are nonphysical products or services such as stocks and bonds, insurance, and consulting services. This chapter classifies selling careers according to the type of employer. We explore the following four major employment settings and identify some of the unique characteristics of each:

Selling a service
Selling for a retailer
Selling for a wholesaler
Selling for a manufacturer

Selling a Service

What do Ernst & Young, Unisys, Radisson Hotels, Mayflower Transit, and Manpower have in common? Each of these companies is selling services. In recent years the number of consumer and business dollars spent on services in our society has steadily increased. Nearly 80 percent of the U.S. labor force is now employed in the service sector. The growth rate for service companies continues to be much higher than the growth rate for companies that are product-led.[18] Customers feel the need for assistance from a knowledgeable salesperson when making purchases in such areas as insurance, real estate, vacation planning, business security, and advertising.

We will look briefly at some of the career opportunities in the service field.

Financial Services

At the present time, there are over 1 million sales jobs in the securities and financial services field, and employment is expected to increase. Banks, brokerage firms, and other businesses are branching out, selling a broader range of financial planning and investment services.

Radio, Television, and Internet Advertising

Revenue from advertising supports the radio and television broadcasting industry, and to a lesser degree, the Internet. Every station must employ a force of salespeople whose job is to call on current and prospective advertisers. Each client's needs are unique and meeting them makes the work of a media sales representative interesting. Additionally, there is a creative side to media sales, for members of the sales staff often help develop commercials.

Newspaper Advertising

There are several thousand daily and weekly newspapers in this country. Each newspaper is supported by both local and national advertisers and each newspaper must sell advertising space to stay in business. Many business firms rely heavily on media sales personnel for help in developing effective advertising campaigns.

Hotel, Motel, and Convention Center Services

Each year thousands of seminars, conferences, and business meetings are held throughout the United States. Most of these events are hosted by hotels, motels, or convention centers. By diversifying their markets and upscaling their services these marketers are catering to business clients in many new and exciting ways. The salespeople employed by these firms play an important role in attracting meetings. They sell room space, food, beverages, and other services needed for a successful meeting. (See the job description of a Convention Center salesperson in Part I of Appendix 3.)

Real Estate

Buying a home is a monumental undertaking. It is usually the single largest expenditure in the average consumer's lifetime. The purchase of commercial property by individual investors or business firms also is a major economic decision. Therefore, the 800,000 people who sell real estate assume an important responsibility.[19] Busy real estate salespeople often hire sales associates who help hold open houses or perform other duties.

Insurance

Selling insurance always has been one of the most rewarding careers in sales. Common forms of insurance sold include fire, liability, life, health, automobile, casualty, and homeowners. There are two broad groups of insurance salespeople. One group is employed by major companies such as Allstate, Prudential, Travelers, State Farm, and Mutual of Omaha. The second group is made up of independent insurance agents who serve as representatives for a number of various companies. The typical independent agency offers a broad line of personal and business insurance services.

Banking

The banking industry is very competitive today. Most banks have a sales promotion program, and personal selling is one of their key strategies. An increasing number of bank officers and customer service representatives are involved in personal selling activities. They develop new accounts and service established accounts. Bank personnel are completing sales training courses in record numbers these days.

Business Services

The heavy volume of new businesses and the expansion of existing businesses has increased the demand for business services provided by outside contractors. Some of the business services purchased today are computer programming, training, printing, credit reporting, payroll, and recruiting.

Global Business Etiquette

MAJOR FAUX PAS RESULTS IN LOST SALE

Selling overseas (or to foreigners visiting the United States) demands a high degree of cultural sensitivity. Steve Waterhouse, affiliated with Waterhouse Group of Scarborough, Maine, learned this lesson the hard way. He had been courting a Tokyo-based meeting planning company for six months. Finally, he arranged a meeting with the company's representative who was attending a national convention in the United States. She handed her business card to him in the traditional Japanese way, extending the card while holding onto both corners. Waterhouse says, "I took the card and scribbled a note on the back of it." This behavior shocked the woman. "I might as well have spit in her face," Waterhouse says. Although he quickly offered a sincere apology, the damage was done. His breach of etiquette resulted in the loss of a $100,000 sale. He didn't realize that in Japan the business card is examined carefully at the time it is offered because it provides all of the information needed to assess the person's status (title, position, etc.) in the business community.[c]

The list of careers involving the sales of services is much longer. We have not explored the expanding fields of home and business security, travel and recreation, pest control, and transportation. As the demand for services increases, so do the employment opportunities for salespeople.

Selling for a Retailer

The sales staff at Julian's men's shop in Chapel Hill, North Carolina, takes pride in their work. After all, Julian's is a legend not only in Chapel Hill but also throughout the Southeast. This family-owned business, founded in 1942, is located near the University of North Carolina (UNC) campus. The store sells custom-order suits to UNC alumni who live all over the South. Some buy private-label suits created by the founder's son, Alexander Julian, who is a noted fashion designer.[20]

The 1440 member sales staff employed by Asbury Automotive Group, the nation's fifth-largest automotive dealership group, also takes pride in their work. Many of the salespeople working at Asbury dealerships were recruited at college and university job fairs. Some are management trainees who will sell cars for 8 to 15 months, earning a salary plus bonus that pays $45,000 to $60,000 per year. Then they are trained and certified to work in the finance and insurance department. The next position in the promotion ladder is new or used car sales manager. Sales managers earn $100,000 to $150,000 per year. The final promotion opportunity is general manager of the dealership.[21]

The **retail salesperson** usually engages in full-time professional selling and is paid well for her contributions to the business. Products sold at the retail level range from exotic foreign automobiles to fine furniture. A partial list of retail products that usually require personal selling skills follows:

Automobiles	Recreational vehicles
Musical instruments	Television and radio receivers
Photographic equipment	Furniture/decorating supplies
Fashion apparel	Tires and related accessories
Major appliances	Computers

Well-trained retail salespeople can add value to the traditional shopping experience.

Today, traditional retailers are facing new competition from online retailers. Consumers are spending billions of dollars on Internet purchases, a clear sign that electronic commerce is here to stay. Traditional retailers must offer customers more than products. Wendy Liebmann, president of WSL Strategic Retail, a retail consulting firm, says, "In order to get someone to come into the store, retailers really need to create a compelling environment; a combination of product, value, and experience."[22] Well-trained salespeople can add value to the traditional shopping experience.

Selling for a Wholesaler

More than a million wholesale salespeople are employed in the United States. Wholesalers play an important role in making channels of distribution efficient. A full-service wholesaler offers a wide variety of services to its customers, including maintaining inventories, gathering and interpreting market information, extending credit, distributing goods, and providing promotional activities. Wholesalers employ two kinds of salespeople: "inside" and "outside."

Inside Salesperson

The **inside salesperson** relies almost totally on telephone orders and follows a strict timetable of customer contact. Because of the escalating cost of personal selling, selling by telephone is growing in popularity. This selling method has become so popular that some companies are taking their salespeople off the road and bringing them back to headquarters, where they are retrained to sell by telephone. The Internet is often used to support the work of inside salespeople.

Outside Salesperson

The duties of an **outside salesperson** vary from one wholesale firm to another. Some specialize in a single area such as electronics or small appliances, whereas others sell a wide range of product lines. The typical outside salesperson must have knowledge of many products and be able to serve as a consultant to the customer. For example, a sales representative for a pharmaceutical wholesaler calling on retail stores needs to be familiar with advertising and display techniques, store layout, and other merchandising strategies. Most important, this person must be completely familiar with the customer's operation.

Selling for a Manufacturer

Alan Mayer, Regional Account Executive for Dell Computer, enjoys working on complex sales. He likes the challenge of devising a solution for customers who truly need the help of a consultative salesperson. He recalls a large sale to a New York City–based company that needed a financial software solution. Mayer says he had to use all of his personal selling skills and rely on Dell's product strength to configure a solution and close the sale.[23]

Manufacturers employ sales and sales support personnel in many different capacities. Field salespeople, sales engineers, and detail salespeople are outside salespeople who interact face-to-face with prospects and customers. Inside salespeople rely primarily on the telephone to identify prospects and engage in other selling activities.

Field Salesperson

A **field salesperson** sells to new customers and increases sales to current ones. These salespeople must be able to recognize buyer needs and prescribe the best product or service to meet these needs. Field salespeople who provide excellent service find their customers to be a good source of leads for new prospects.

Sales Engineer

A **sales engineer** must have detailed and precise technical knowledge and the ability to discuss the technical aspects of his products. Expertise in identifying, analyzing, and solving customer problems is of critical importance. The sales representatives at Zeks Compressed Air Solutions in West Chester, Pennsylvania, use the title "application engineer." Although their primary responsibility is selling, they must be technically proficient in product applications.[24]

Detail Salesperson

The primary goal of a **detail salesperson** (sometimes referred to as a missionary salesperson) is to develop goodwill and stimulate demand for the manufacturer's products. This person is usually not compensated on the basis of the orders obtained but receives recognition for increasing the sale of goods indirectly. A salesperson employed by Pfizer is involved in detail sales work when she calls on physicians to influence them to prescribe a medication available from Pfizer.[25] The detail salesperson calls on wholesale, retail, and other customers to help improve their marketing. In a typical day this salesperson may help train a sales staff or offer advice to a firm that is planning an advertising campaign. Detail salespeople also collect valuable information concerning customer acceptance of products. They must be able to offer sound advice in such diverse areas as credit policies, pricing, display, store layout, and storage.

Customer Relationship Management with Technology

LEARNING CRM SOFTWARE

Many salespeople are at first apprehensive about using computers; yet research shows a high degree of acceptance, with this comment often heard, "I don't know how I got along without it."

Following the instructions in this text's customer relationship management (CRM) application exercises and case study gives you a good understanding of basic CRM. This knowledge can be valuable as you enter today's selling environment. Many sales organizations are using CRM and your understanding of the basics can help you learn more rapidly any system in use by your potential employers. Some people, after following these instructions, list their use of CRM on their résumés.

Many users of CRM enter information about friends and family into their databases and use it to enhance all their relationships. CRM helps people remember the status of relationships, steps to take, and pending events, such as anniversaries and birthdays. (See the exercise, Learning CRM Software, on p. 49 for more information.)

Inside Salesperson

As face-to-face sales costs increase, some manufacturers have developed an inside sales force. At IBM, about 15 percent of the sales force never leave the office. They make calls to smaller customers, take orders, and in some cases provide support to field salespeople.[26] Some marketers are finding that only the initial sale of the product requires face-to-face contact. Inside salespeople can handle repeat contacts.

The Telemarketing Sales Channel

Telemarketing is a channel in which the sales process is conducted by telephone. Telemarketing serves two general purposes—sales and service. In the business-to-business market, the inside sales team may include technical support people who provide technical information and answer the customer's questions. In some cases, sales assistants provide clerical backup for outside salespeople. They may confirm appointments, conduct credit checks, and follow up on deliveries.[27] Business-to-business marketers sometimes use the telephone to maintain contact with smaller customers. This approach is much less expensive than a face-to-face sales call.

As noted previously, IBM is now using telemarketing to find, qualify, and sell to certain types of prospects. It is now selling e-business solutions to small and midsize businesses, a market segment that was often ignored in the past. About 1,200 sales representatives now generate 30 percent of IBM's revenues by presenting solutions to this segment.

Climax Portable Machine Tools, a relatively small company, is using telemarketing to sell its products throughout the nation. The Climax telemarketing team, made up of five sales engineers, contact about 30 prospects a day. They rely on leads generated by ads and direct mail. After every phone call, the prospect's computer file is updated. If a prospect says he just returned from a fishing trip, this information is recorded and used to personalize the next call to that person. The first mailing to a prospect includes the sales engineer's business card with his or her picture on it.[28]

LEARNING TO SELL

"Are salespeople made or are they born?" This classic question seems to imply that some people are born with certain qualities that give them a special advantage in the selling field. This is not true. The principles of selling can be learned and applied by people whose personal characteristics are quite different.

In the past few decades, sales training has been expanded on four fronts. These four sources of training are corporate-sponsored training, training provided by commercial vendors, certification studies, and courses provided by colleges and universities.

Corporate Sponsored Training

Hundreds of business Organizations, such as Apple Computer, IBM, Maytag, Western Electric, and Zenith, have established training programs. These large corporations spend millions of dollars each year to develop their salespeople. *Training* magazine, which conducts annual analysis of employer-provided training in U.S. organizations, indicates that salespeople are among the most intensively trained employee groups. A new salesperson, preparing for a consultative selling position, may spend a few months to a year or more in training. For many salespeople, the training is as close as their laptop computer. Lucent Technologies, for example, uses Web-based training for about one third of its training courses.[29]

Training Provided by Commerical Vendors

The programs designed by firms specializing in the development of sales personnel are a second source of sales training. Some of the most popular courses are offered by Wilson Learning Corporation, Miller Heiman Inc., Dale Carnegie Training, and AchieveGlobal. (See Table 2.3) The legendary Professional Selling Skills (PSS) course, developed in the late 1960s by Gene Keluche, is still offered by AchieveGlobal. This carefully designed course, once owned by Xerox, has been completed by millions of salespeople.[30]

Certification Programs

The trend toward increased professionalism in personal selling has been the stimulus for a third type of training and education initiative. Many salespeople are returning to the classroom to earn certification in a sales or sales-related area. In the pharmaceutical industry many salespeople earn the Certified Medical Representative (CMR) designation. The CMR curriculum includes nearly 40 courses that are delivered to more than 9,000 students. The National Automobile Dealers Association sponsors the Code of Conduct Certification program for automotive sales representatives. Both of these certification programs require extensive study of modules and the completion of rigorous examinations. Sales & Marketing Executives–International offers the Certified Sales Executive (CSE) designation to sales professionals who meet the highest standards of education, experience, and ethical conduct.

Some companies have developed their own sales training certification programs. The Pitney Bowes Certified Postal Consultant (CPC) program is designed to improve the level of assistance given to customers who want to upgrade their mail process. It is available to members of the 4,000-person Pitney Bowes sales force who sell both products (postage meters) and services. Freightliner developed a certification program for its 1,800-member sales force. The various courses include topics ranging from product knowledge to truck-selling skills.[31]

College and University Courses

The fourth source of sales training is personal selling courses offered by colleges and universities throughout the United States. A large majority of the nation's undergraduate business schools offer this course, and it is attracting more interest among business

TABLE 2.3 SALES TRAINING OFFERED BY COMMERCIAL VENDORS

Training programs provided by commercial vendors are very popular. This table introduces a few of the well established sales training programs offered throughout America.

COMPANY	TRAINING PROGRAMS	DESCRIPTION
Sales Performance International www.spisales.com	• Solution Selling • Opportunity Selling	Provides sales training based on concepts explained in *The New Solution* Selling by Keith Eades.
Integrity Systems, Inc. www.integritysystems.com	• Integrity Selling • The Customer	Provides sales training based on concepts explained in *Integrity Selling for the 21st Century* by Ron Willingham.
Huthwaite, Inc. www.huthwaite.com	• Spin Selling Certificate • Creating Client Value	Provides sales training based on concepts in *The Spin Selling Fieldbook* by Neil Rackham.
Miller Heiman, Inc. www.millerheiman.com	• Strategic Selling • Conceptual Selling	Provides sales training based on concepts presented in *Strategic Selling* and *The New Conceptual Selling.*
Achieve Global www.achieveglobal.com	• Professional Selling Skills (PSS) • Professional Sales Coaching	Provides the original Xerox *Professional Selling Skills* (PSS) sales training. *Course content* has been updated.
Wilson Learning Worldwide www.wilsonlearning.com	• The Versatile Salesperson	Provides updated sales training based on the original Larry Wilson *Counselor Selling* Training Program.
Dale Carnegie Training, Inc. www.dalecarnegie.com	• Sales Advantage • How to Sell Like a Pro	One of the largest international training companies providing sales training using many of the concepts presented in the Dale Carnegie books, such as *How to Win Friends and Influence People.*

majors. Some two- and four-year colleges have developed extensive education programs for students interested in a sales career. Cardinal Stritch College offers a Sales Certificate Program that includes a five-course sequence. Weber State University, located at Ogden, Utah, offers a bachelor of science degree in technical sales. The University of Akron, the University of Houston, Western Carolina University, Ball State University, Baylor University, the College of St. Catherine, William Paterson University, Hillsdale College, Kennesaw State University, and the University of Memphis offer undergraduate programs for students who are preparing for a career in personal selling.

For over 35 years, the Certified Medical Representatives Institute has been empowering sales representatives who call on medical professionals. The CMR Certification program is designed to increase sales performance.

Summary

Today's workforce is made up of millions of *knowledge workers* who succeed only when they add value to information. The new economy rewards salespeople and other knowledge workers who collect, organize, clarify, and present information in a convincing manner. Selling skills contribute in a major way to four groups of knowledge workers who usually do not consider themselves salespeople: customer service representatives, professionals (accountants, consultants, lawyers, etc.), entrepreneurs, and managerial personnel.

Selling careers offer many rewards not found in other occupations. Income, both monetary and psychic, is above average, and there are many opportunities for advancement. Salespeople enjoy job security, mobility, and independence. Opportunities in selling for members of minority groups and for women are growing. In addition, selling is very interesting work, because a salesperson is constantly in contact with people. The redundant adage "no two people are alike" reminds us that sales work is never dull or routine.

The text describes each of the four major career options in the field of personal selling. We provide a brief introduction to the variety of employment opportunities in service, retail, wholesale, and manufacturer's sales. Keep in mind that each category features a wide range of selling positions, varying in terms of educational requirements, earning potential, and type of customer served. The discussion and examples should help you discover which kind of sales career best suits your talents and interests.

KEY TERMS

Representative Customer Service
Psychic Income
Retail Salesperson
Inside Salesperson
Outside Salesperson
Telemarketing
Field Salesperson
Sales Engineer
Detail Salesperson

REVIEW QUESTIONS

1. List and describe the four employment settings for people who are considering a selling career.
2. Explain the meaning of *psychic income*.
3. Explain why personal selling is an important auxiliary skill needed by lawyers, engineers, accountants, and other professionals.
4. What future is there in selling for women and minorities?
5. Develop a list of retail products that require well-developed personal selling skills.
6. Some salespeople have an opportunity to earn certification in a sales or sales-related area. How can a salesperson benefit from certification?
7. Explain why high-performance value-added salespeople earn much more than high-performance transactional salespeople.
8. List three titles commonly used to describe manufacturing salespeople. Describe the duties of each.
9. Develop a list of eight selling career opportunities in the service field.
10. List and briefly describe the four major sources of sales training.

APPLICATION EXERCISES

1. Examine a magazine or newspaper ad for a new product or service that you have never seen before. Evaluate its chances for receiving wide customer acceptance. Does this product require a large amount of personal selling effort? What types of salespeople (service, manufacturing, wholesale, or retail) are involved in selling this product?

2. For each of the following job classifications, list the name of at least one person you know in that field:

   a. Full-time retail salesperson
   b. Full-time wholesale salesperson
   c. Full-time manufacturer's salesperson
   d. Full-time person who sells a service

   Interview one of the people you have listed, asking the following questions concerning her duties and responsibilities:

   a. What is your immediate supervisor's title?
   b. What would be a general description of your position?
   c. What specific duties and responsibilities do you have?
   d. What is the compensation plan and salary range for a position like yours?

   Write a job description from this information.

3. Shelly Jones, a vice president and partner in the Chicago office of the consulting firm Korn/Ferry International, has looked into the future and he sees some new challenges for salespeople. He recently shared the following predictions with *Selling* magazine:

   a. Salespeople will spend more time extending the range of applications or finding new markets for the products they sell.
   b. The selling function will be less pitching your product and more integrating your product into the business equation of your client. Understanding the business environment in which your client operates will be critical.
   c. In the future you will have to be a financial engineer for your client. You need to understand how your client makes money and be able to explain how your product or service contributes to profitable operation of the client's firm.

   Interview a salesperson who is involved in business-to-business selling, a manufacturer's representative, for example, and determine if this person agrees with the views of Shelly Jones.

4. There are many information sources on selling careers and career opportunities on the Internet. Two examples include Monster.com and CareerBuilder.com. *Search the Internet for information on selling careers.*

   Use your search engine to find career information on a pharmaceutical representative, a field sales engineer, and a retail salesperson.

ROLE-PLAY EXERCISE

This role-play will give you experience in selling your knowledge, skills, and experience to a prospective employer. You will be meeting with a class member who will assume the role of an employer who is developing a new sales team. Prior to this interview, reflect on the courses you have completed, work experience, and other life experiences that may have value in the eyes of the employer. You may also want to reflect on any volunteer work you have completed and leadership roles you have held. Be prepared to discuss the personal selling skills you are developing in this course.

CRM APPLICATION EXERCISE

Learning CRM Software

After downloading and launching the CD Rom supplied with yout book, you will become acquainted with the layout and features of the ACT! program. Start by pressing the F1 function key that displays the contents of the help file. Clicking on the first entry, ACT! Screens, shows information about the program's three main screens: Contact Screens (records with information about people), Word Processing Screens, and the Query Screen. Print the ACT! Screens page by selecting File, Print Topic. At the bottom of this page is a row of icons, a small version of the tool bar icons found on the main contact screen. Click on each of these icons for an explanation of its function.

Next select the underlined link, The Contact Screens, to learn about the two screens that are available to view information about a contact (person). At the top of this screen, click on the link labeled Status Area to read a description of the information found along the side of the contact screens. Here you learn to determine the number of records in the database; how to use the card index icon to navigate; and how to discover whether there are notes, history information, or activities scheduled for this contact.

Browse through the help screens to learn more about the structure and functions of this CRM software.

CASE PROBLEM

Ronald McMains is 23 years old and works for Metropolitan Financial Bank in the information services department. He was employed part-time while attending college and decided to accept a full-time position after graduation.

The position in information services offers an opportunity to learn a great deal about banking, a secure income, a good insurance and retirement program, two weeks of vacation a year, and 15 days of sick leave a year if needed. There also will be opportunities to move into supervision within the next couple of years because the company is expanding rapidly.

Ron has been thinking about changing jobs and has been described by his friends as an opportunist—a person who seeks out opportunities and takes advantage of them. He sees himself the same way and someday hopes to earn well above the average income.

Ron has been interviewing for several positions. One company has offered him a position that involves calling on potential dealers for a new line of fiberglass power boats. The manufacturer has a patent on an improved fiberglassing technique that is setting new standards for boat strength. The boat has proved to be a success and has sold extraordinarily well in the five territories that the company already has opened. Letters are coming from dealers all over the country expressing an interest in taking on a dealership. The company has decided to open up new territories in the southern half of Wisconsin and northern half of Illinois. The latter is the territory they have offered to Ron.

The specific responsibilities of the position include calling on marinas and boat dealers in the territory and setting up the better ones as distributors of the new line of boats. Ron would evaluate each potential distributorship and would select and appoint the new distributors. The company's excellent training program would teach Ron how to help each new dealer set up a promotional program to sell the boats.

The company has offered Ron a commission program that includes a "draw against commission" form of compensation. In this type of program, a drawing account enables the salesperson to receive a set amount either weekly or monthly that is later subtracted from earned commissions. Ron's draw would equal his present salary, including his overtime pay. Ron's commissions would be based on the number of boats his dealers sold. The company expects this territory to be one of the best; and if Ron is successful, his income could be well into the $50,000 to $60,000 range within the second year, if not sooner.

Ron would have to relocate about 100 miles from where he now lives. The company has offered relocation expenses to cover the cost of the entire move. Ron realizes he would be away from home on the average of one night a week, and this poses no problems. The company will cover all of Ron's travel and lodging expenses and will provide him with a new car.

Questions

1. List the pros and cons of this job opportunity.
2. On the basis of the information given, should Ron accept the new job? Why or why not?

PART 1 Role Play Exercise

DEVELOPING A PERSONAL SELLING PHILOSOPHY

Scenario

You are currently working part time at the Dell Direct Store located in Three Rivers Mall. You are a full-time student majoring in marketing at Vista College. The manager of your store wants you to identify potential customers on your campus and sell Dell notebook computers to those who have a need for this product.

Customer Profile

Melissa Tores is a full-time commuter student who lives with her parents and shares one computer with her mom. Each morning she drives about 20 miles to the campus (one way) and spends most of the day attending classes, working in the library, and visiting with friends. She currently spends about two hours each evening on the computer at home.

Salesperson Profile

Paul Windom started working at the Dell Direct Store shortly after graduating from high school. The store manager was impressed with Paul's computer expertise and his friendly manner. Although Paul is able to sell any type of computer, he tends to specialize in notebook computers which are ideal for college studends who have mobile computing needs. Paul's personal computer is a new Dell notebook, which replaced his desktop computer.

Product

Paul Windom sells several different notebook computers that vary in price from $795 to $1,649. Each notebook is equipped with specific, easily accessible ports to interact with a variety of external components. All of his notebooks offer both productivity and entertainment applications. Services offered by Dell include helpful assistance via telephone or online tutorials at *support.dell.com*. Dell's warranty provides for service and support at no extra charge.

Instructions

For this role play activity you will assume the role of Paul Windom. You will meet with Melissa Torres and determine her interest and need for a notebook computer. Prior to meeting with Ms. Torres, preplan your relationship strategy, product strategy, customer strategy, and presentation strategy. Chapter 1 provides a description of each strategic area. Be prepared to close the sale if you feel the customer will benefit from this purchase.

All selling is ultimately relationship selling. This is especially true in complex sales where the relationship continues after the sale.

Brian Tracy, Author, *The 100 Absolutely Unbreakable Laws of Business Success*

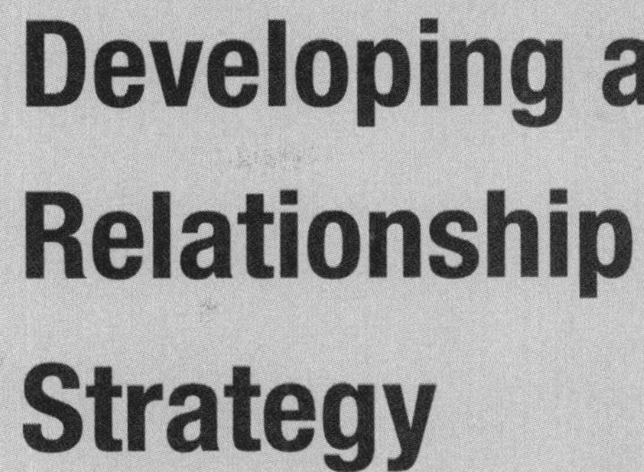

PART 2 Developing a Relationship Strategy

High performance salespeople are generally better able to build and maintain relationships than moderate performers. Part 2 includes three chapters that focus on person-to-person relationship building strategies. Chapter 3 explains how to create value with a relationship strategy. Chapter 4 introduces communication style bias and explains how to build strong interpersonal relationships with style flexing. The influence of ethical decisions on relationships in selling is discussed in Chapter 5.

Chapter Preview

When you finish reading this chapter, you should be able to

1 Explain the importance of developing a relationship strategy

2 List the four key groups with which the salesperson needs to develop relationship strategies

3 Discuss how self-image forms the foundation for building long-term selling relationships

4 Describe the importance of a win-win relationship

5 Identify and describe the major nonverbal factors that shape our sales image

6 Describe conversational strategies that help us establish relationships

7 Explain how to establish a self-improvement plan based on personal development strategies

CHAPTER 3

Creating Value with a Relationship Strategy

The salespeople who work for Fred Sands Realtors (*www.fredsands.com*) understand the importance of developing relationship strategies. This successful company, with offices throughout the United States and in many parts of the world, strives to build a long-term partnership with each customer. Sandra Khadra, vice president of marketing at Fred Sands Realtors, encourages salespeople to begin building rapport during the first contact. She, like most other real estate professionals, knows that rapport with home buyers and home sellers is of critical importance. Khadra teaches salespeople the basics of creating a professional image and stresses the importance of empathy with the customer. She knows that when you sincerely care about the welfare of the customer, you add value to the sale.[1]

Helping people buy a home requires a multitude of skills. You must assume the roles of financial adviser, educator, and counselor. Above all, you must listen closely to everything that prospects say to accurately identify their wants and needs.

DEVELOPING A RELATIONSHIP STRATEGY

Developing and applying the wide range of interpersonal skills needed in today's complex sales environment can be challenging. Daniel Goleman, author of the best-selling books, *Emotional Intelligence* and

Working with Emotional Intelligence, notes that there are many forms of intelligence that influence our actions throughout life. One of these, **emotional intelligence**, refers to the capacity for monitoring our own feelings and those of others, for motivating ourselves, and for managing emotions well in ourselves and in our relationships. People with a high level of emotional intelligence display many of the qualities needed in sales work: self-confidence, trustworthiness, adaptability, initiative, optimism, empathy, and well-developed social skills.[2]

Daniel Goleman, author of Emotional Intelligence, *says that IQ tends to be stable throughout life, but the competencies that determine our emotional intelligence (EQ) can be learned and improved on.*

Goleman and other researchers state that there are widespread exceptions to the rule that IQ predicts success. In the field of personal selling and most other business occupations, emotional intelligence is a much greater predictor of success.[3] The good news is that emotional intelligence can be enhanced with a variety of self-development activities, many of which are discussed in this chapter.

Information age selling involves three major relationship challenges. The first major challenge is building new relationships. Salespeople who can quickly build rapport with new prospects have a much greater chance of achieving success in personal selling. The second major challenge is transforming relationships from the personal level to the business level. Once rapport is established, the salesperson is in a stronger position to begin the need identification process. The third major challenge is the management of relationships. To achieve a high level of success, salespeople have to manage a multitude of different relationships."[4] Salespeople must develop relationship management strategies that focus on four key groups. These groups are discussed later in this chapter.

In this chapter we introduce the win-win philosophy and discuss the importance of projecting a professional image. Chapter 4 explains how an understanding of communication styles can help us better manage the relationship process. Chapter 5 focuses on the importance of maintaining high ethical standards to build long-term relationships with the customer (Fig. 3.1).

STRATEGIC/CONSULTATIVE SELLING MODEL

Strategic step	*Prescription*
Develop a Personal Selling Philosophy	☑ Adopt Marketing Concept ☑ Value Personal Selling ☑ Become a Problem Solver/Partner
Develop a Relationship Strategy	☐ Adopt Win-Win Philosophy ☐ Project Professional Image ☐ Maintain High Ethical Standards

FIGURE | 3.1

Every salesperson should have an ongoing goal of developing a relationship strategy that adds value to the sale.

Customers perceive that value is added when they feel comfortable with the relationship they have with the salesperson.

Relationships Add Value

Ron Willingham, author of *Integrity Selling For The 21st Century*, says there is a relationship between the salesperson's achievement drive and their view of personal selling. Salespeople who feel a professional responsibility to create as much value for customers as possible exhibit more energy, a stronger work ethic, and a greater eagerness to ask customers for decisions.[5]

The manner in which salespeople establish, build, and manage relationships is not an incidental aspect of personal selling; in the information age it is the key to success. In the information economy, business is defined by customer relationships and sales success depends on adding value (see Fig. 1.2). We have defined value-added selling as *a series of creative improvements in the sales process that enhance the customer experience.*

Customers perceive that value is added when they feel comfortable with the relationship they have with a salesperson. A good relationship causes customers to feel that, if a problem arises, they will receive a just and fair solution. A good relationship creates a clearer channel of communication about issues that might surface during each step of the sales process. Len Rodman, CEO of Black & Veatch, a large engineering and construction company, recalls a problem operation on the West Coast. Earnings were minimal and the person in charge could not sell to high-tier clients. He put a salesperson in charge whose strength was building relationships. Within an 18-month period that region became one of the most profitable.[6]

The salesperson who is honest, accountable, and sincerely concerned about the customer's welfare brings added value to the sale. These characteristics give the salesperson a competitive advantage—an advantage that is becoming increasingly important in a world of "look-alike" products and similar prices.

Partnering—The Highest-Quality Selling Relationship

Salespeople today are encouraged to think of everything they say or do in the context of their relationship with the customer. They should constantly strive to build a long-term partnership. In a marketplace characterized by increased levels of competition and greater product complexity, we see the need to adopt a relationship strategy that emphasizes the "lifetime" customer. High-quality relationships result in repeat business and those important referrals. A growing number of salespeople recognize that the quality of partnerships they create is as important as the quality of the products they sell. Today's customer wants a quality product *and* a quality relationship. One example of this trend is the J. D. Power and Associates customer satisfaction studies. For example, the Domestic Hotel Guest Satisfaction Study measures guest satisfaction among frequent business travelers. J. D. Power conducts customer satisfaction research in several different industries.[7]

In Chapter 1 we defined patnering as a strategically developed, high-quality, long-term relationship that focuses on solving the customer's buying problems.[8] This definition is used in the sales training video entitled "Partnering—The Heart of Selling Today." Traditional industrial age sales training programs emphasized the importance of creating a good first impression and then "pushing" your product. Partnering emphasizes building a

Today's customer wants a quality product and a quality relationship. This means that salespeople can create value with a well developed relationship strategy.

strong relationship during every aspect of the sale and working hard to maintain a quality relationship with the customer after the sale. Today, personal selling must be viewed as a process, not an event.[9]

Larry Wilson, noted author and founder of Wilson Learning Worldwide, identifies partnering as one of the most important strategic thought processes needed by salespeople. He points out that the salesperson who is selling a "one-shot" solution

Selling Is Everyone's Business

SELLING HIP CHAIRS

Gregg Buchbinder is chairman of Emeco Ltd., a small company in Pennsylvania that manufactures modern chairs. One of the company's newest products is a sleek, six-and-a-half-pound aluminum chair called the Superlight. This chair was created by renowned architect Frank Gehry. When Buchbinder acquired Emeco from his father in 1998, he dreamed of becoming a producer of hip home furnishings. The problem was that Emeco was unfamiliar to most of the architects and designers he wanted to do business with. So Buchbinder hit the streets of SoHo, knocking on shop doors with a copy of a magazine that showed his modern aluminum chairs. He also visited trade shows in search of new prospects. Today revenues have reached about $10 million and Buchbinder is optimistic about the future.[a]

cannot compete against the one who has developed and nurtured a long-term, mutually beneficial partnership. Wilson believes there are three keys to a partnering relationship:

- The relationship is built on shared values. If your client believes that you both share the same ideas and values, it goes a long way toward creating a powerful relationship.
- Everyone needs to clearly understand the purpose of the partnership and be committed to the vision. Both the salesperson and the client must agree on what they are trying to do together.
- The role of the salesperson must move from selling to supporting. The salesperson in a partnership is actively concerned with the growth, health, and satisfaction of the company to which she is selling.[10]

Brakebush wants every relationship to be long-term, so this family owned business offers customers a broad range of products and unique flavor profiles. When these products are properly matched to the restaurant's menu, value is created.

Customer Relationship Management with Technology

COMMUNICATING THROUGH CRM

Customer relationship management (CRM) software can be used to enhance the quality of your relationships. A good example is the software's ability to improve communications between you and your contacts. With the ACT! software, for example, you can quickly prepare and send a letter, a fax, or an e-mail to one or more people with records in the database. Recipients of your appointment confirmations, information verifications, company or product news, or brief personal notes recognize and appreciate your effort to keep them informed. The written word conveys consideration and helps avoid misunderstandings and miscommunications. CRM empowers you to easily use the written word to advance your relationship building. (See the exercise, Preparing Letters with CRM, on p. 78 for more information.)

Salespeople willing to abandon short-term thinking and invest the time and energy needed to develop a high-quality, long-term relationship with customers are rewarded with greater earnings and the satisfaction of working with repeat customers. Sales resulting from referrals also increase.

Relationship Strategies Focus on Four Key Groups

Establishing and maintaining a partnering-type relationship internally as well as one with the customers is a vital aspect of selling. High-performance sales personnel build strong relationships with four groups (Fig. 3.2):

1. *Customers.* As noted previously, a major key to success in selling is the ability to establish working relationships with customers in which mutual support, trust, and goals are nurtured over time. Salespeople who maintain regular contact with their customers and develop sound business relationships based on mutual trust are able to drive up sales productivity according to research conducted by the American Productivity and Quality Center.[11]

   Cisco Systems is one of many companies that now measure themselves by the quality of their relationships with their customers. Salespeople earn their bonuses in large part based on customer satisfaction instead of gross sales or profit.[12]

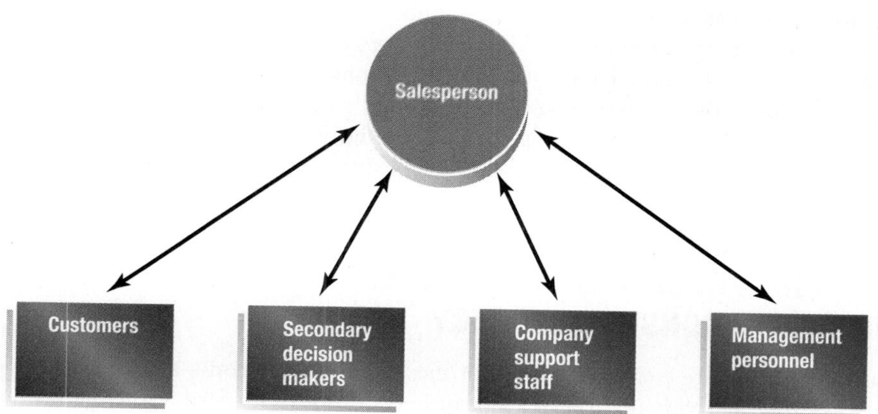

FIGURE | 3.2

An effective relationship strategy helps high-performing salespeople to build and maintain win-win relationships with a wide range of key groups.

2. *Secondary decision makers.* High-performance salespeople understand the importance of building relationships with the people who work with customers. In many selling situations, the first person the salesperson meets is a receptionist, a secretary, or an assistant to the primary decision maker. These persons often can facilitate a meeting with the prospect. Also, the prospect may involve other people in making the buying decision. For example, the decision to buy new office furniture may be made by a team of persons including the buyer and persons who will actually use the furniture.
3. *Company support staff.* The maintenance of relationships internally is a vital aspect of selling. Support staff may include persons working in the areas of market research, product service, credit, training, or shipping. Influencing these people to change their priorities, interrupt their schedules, accept new responsibilities, or fulfill any other request for special attention is a major part of the salesperson's job. At UPS, the drivers are the eyes and ears of the sales force. The most successful UPS salespeople nurture a relationship with the drivers in their sales territory.[13]
4. *Management personnel.* Sales personnel usually work under the direct supervision of a sales manager, a department head, or some other member of the firm's management team. Maintaining a good relationship with this person is very important.

Tailoring the Relationship Strategy

Ideally, the relationship strategy should be tailored to the type of customer you are working with. Chapter 1 provided a description of the three most common types of selling situations: transactional selling, consultative selling, and strategic alliance selling. Transactional buyers are usually aware of their needs and often stay focused on such issues as price, convenience, and delivery schedules. They usually know a great deal about the products or services they wish to purchase. In the transactional sale, the relationship strategy is often secondary.

In the consultative sale, however, the impact of relationships on the sale is quite important. A consultative sale emphasizes need identification which is achieved through effective communication and a relationship built upon mutual trust and respect. The consultative salesperson must display a keen ability to listen, define the customer's problem, and offer one or more solutions. The opportunity to uncover hidden needs and create custom solutions is greatly enhanced by a well-conceived relationship strategy.[14]

In terms of relationship building, strategic alliance selling is often the most challenging. Very often the salesperson is working with a company team made up of people from such areas as research and development (R & D), finance, and distribution. The salesperson must build a good working relationship with each team member. Forming an alliance with another company involves building relationships with several representatives of that buying organization.

We will revisit these three types of selling situations later in Chapter 5 when we discuss the trust factor. In the meantime, keep in mind that customers almost never buy products from someone whom they dislike. A salesperson who is not viewed as being helpful and trustworthy will not succeed in any type of selling situation.

THOUGHT PROCESSES THAT ENHANCE YOUR RELATIONSHIP STRATEGY

Industrial age folklore created the myth of the "born" salesperson—a dynamic, outgoing, highly assertive individual. Experience acquired during the information age has taught us that many other factors determine sales success. Key among these factors are a positive self-image and the ability to relate to others in effective and productive ways. With the aid of knowledge drawn from the behavioral sciences, we can develop the relationship strategies needed in a wide range of selling situations.

Self-Image—An Important Dimension of the Relationship Strategy

Self-image is shaped by the ideas, attitudes, feelings, and other thoughts you have about yourself that influence the way you relate to others. Psychologists have found that once we form a thought process about ourselves, it serves to edit all incoming information and influence our actions. This process can set the limits of our accomplishments, defining what we can and cannot do. Realizing the power of self-image is an important breakthrough in our understanding of the factors that influence us.

A pioneer in the area of self-image psychology was the late Dr. Maxwell Maltz, author of *Psycho-Cybernetics* and other books devoted to this topic. We are indebted to him for two important discoveries that help us understand better the "why" of human behavior:

1. *Feelings and behavior are consistent with the self-image.* The individual who feels like a "failure" is likely to find some way to fail. There is a definite relationship between self-image and accomplishments at work. A positive self-image helps generate the energy needed to get things done.
2. *The self-image can be changed.* Numerous case histories show that you are never too young or too old to change your self-image and thereby achieve new accomplishments.[15]

Phillip McGraw, author of *Self Matters*, says we often sabotage our own success by adopting limiting beliefs. These are the specific things we think about that cause us to conclude that we are not capable of achieving success. These beliefs restrict our thinking and our actions.[16]

How can you develop a more positive self-image? How can you get rid of self-destructive ways of thinking? Bringing your present self-image out into the open is the first step in understanding who you are, what you can do, and where you are going. Improving your self-image does not happen overnight, but it can happen. A few practical approaches are summarized as follows:

1. *Focus on the future and stop being overly concerned with past mistakes or failures.* We should learn from past errors, but we should not be immobilized by them.

Global Business Etiquette

PATIENCE AND SENSITIVITY HELP CLINCH THE DEAL

Going global? If so, pack plenty of sensitivity and patience. And be prepared to emphasize value-added selling. Too often Americans rely on the "time is money" belief and they take shortcuts in some key areas. For example, they do not spend enough time learning about the culture of the country they are visiting. Also, they often fail to take the time needed to build a relationship with the client. Assaf Kedem, a representative of U.S.-based Intercomp, recalls having lunch with two prospects in Germany. For three hours the German executives asked questions about America and talked about their favorite foods and interests. Business was never discussed. Kedem viewed that long lunch as an important first step in building a relationship that will last for years.[b]

Stephen Covey, author of Seven Habits of Highly Successful People, *says the ability to build effective, long-term relationships is based on character strength, not quick-fix techniques.*

2. *Develop expertise in selected areas.* By developing "expert power" you not only improve your self-image but also increase the value of your contributions to your employer and your customers.
3. *Learn to develop a positive mental attitude.* To develop a more positive outlook, read books and listen to audiotapes that describe ways to develop a positive mental attitude.

Consider materials developed by Jack Canfield Stephen Covey, Brian Tracy, Dale Carnegie, and Phillip McGraw.

Later in this chapter you will learn how to develop and initiate a plan for self-improvement. If you want to improve your self-image, consider adopting this plan.

The Win-Win Philosophy

As noted in Chapter 1, the marketing concept is a philosophy that leaves no doubt in the mind of every employee that customer satisfaction is of primary importance. Salespeople, working closely with customers, are in the best position to monitor customer satisfaction.

Adopting the win-win philosophy is the first step in developing a relationship strategy. Stephen Heiman and Diane Sanchez, authors of *The New Conceptual Selling,* describe the "win-win" approach as follows:

> In Win-Win selling, both the buyer and seller come out of the sale understanding that their respective best interests have been served—in other words, that they've both won. It is our firm conviction, based on thousands of selling situations, that over the long run the only sellers who can count on remaining successful are the ones who are committed to this Win-Win philosophy.[17]

The win-win strategy is based on such irrefutable logic that it is difficult to understand why any other approach would be used. The starting point to the development of a win-win philosophy is to compare the behaviors of persons who have adopted the win-lose approach with the behaviors of persons who have adopted the win-win approach (Fig. 3.3).

Character and Integrity

Shoshana Zuboff, contributing columnist for *Fast Company* magazine, sees widespread acceptance of wrong as normal. She points to acceptance in some industries of the belief that "It's not wrong because everyone is doing it."[18] Employees working for prominent companies such as Merck, WorldCom, Putman Investments, Tyco, and Edward D. Jones & Company have been involved in ethical lapses.[19] Most white collar crime is committed by persons who lack character and integrity.

Character is composed of personal standards, including honesty, integrity, and moral strength. It is a quality that is highly respected in the field of personal selling. **Integrity** is the basic ingredient of character that is exhibited when you achieve congruence between

Win-Lose People
- See a problem in every solution
- Fix the blame
- Let life happen to them
- Live in the past
- Make promises they never keep

Win-Win People
- Help others solve their problems
- Fix what caused the problem
- Make life a joyous happening for others and themselves
- Learn from the past, live in the present, and set goals for the future
- Make commitments to themselves and to others and keep them both

FIGURE | 3.3

The starting point to developing a win-win relationship strategy is to compare behaviors of win-lose salespeople with those of salespeople who have adopted the win-win approach.

(Adapted from a list of losers, winners, and double winners in *The Double Win* by Denis Waitley.)

what you know, what you say, and what you do.[20] In a world of uncertainty and rapid change, integrity has become a valuable character trait. Salespeople with integrity can be trusted to do what they say they will do. One way to achieve trustworthiness in personal selling is to avoid deceiving or misleading the customer. More is said about this topic in Chapter 5, which examines the ethical conduct of salespeople.

VERBAL AND NONVERBAL STRATEGIES THAT ADD VALUE TO YOUR RELATIONSHIPS

The first contact between a salesperson and a prospect is very important. During the first few minutes—or seconds in most cases—the prospect and the salesperson form impressions of each other that either facilitate or distract from the sales call. Malcolm Gladwell, author of the best selling book *Blink*, says that when two people meet for the first time, both will make very superficial, rapid judgments about the other person. This decision-making process, he argues, usually happens subconsciously in a split second (in the blink of an eye).[21]

Every salesperson projects an image to prospective customers, and this image influences how a customer feels about the sales representative. The image you project is the sum total of many verbal and nonverbal factors. The quality of your voice, the clothing you wear, your posture, your manners, and your communication style represent some of the factors that contribute to the formation of your image. We discuss several forms of verbal and nonverbal communication in this chapter. Communication style is examined in Chapter 4.

Nonverbal Messages

When we attempt to communicate with another person, we use both verbal and nonverbal communications. **Nonverbal messages** are "messages without words" or "silent messages." These are the messages (other than spoken or written words) that we communicate through facial expressions, voice tone, gestures, appearance, posture, and other nonverbal means.[22]

Research indicates that when two people communicate, nonverbal messages convey much more impact than verbal messages. Words play a surprisingly small part in the communication process. Every spoken message has a vocal element, coming not from *what* we say but from *how* we say it. The voice communicates in many ways: through tone, volume, and speed of delivery. A salesperson wishing to communicate enthusiasm needs to use a voice that is charged with energy.

The manner in which salespeople establish, build, and maintain relationships is an important aspect of the relationship strategy.

As we attempt to read nonverbal communication, it is important to remember that no *one* signal carries much meaning. If the person you meet for the first time displays a weak grip during the handshake, don't let this one signal shape your first impression. Such factors as posture, eye contact, gestures, clothing, and facial expression must all be regarded together.[23]

Nonverbal messages can reinforce or contradict the spoken word. When your verbal message and body language are consistent, they tend to give others the impression that you can be trusted and that what you say reflects what you truly believe. When there is a discrepancy between your verbal and nonverbal messages, you are less apt to be trusted.[24]

Entrance and Carriage

As noted earlier, the first impression we make is very important. The moment a salesperson walks into a client's office, the client begins making judgments. Susan Bixler, author of *The Professional Image* and *Professional Presence*, makes this comment:

> All of us make entrances throughout our business day as we enter offices, conference rooms, or meeting halls. And every time we do, someone is watching us, appraising us, sizing us up, and gauging our appearance, even our intelligence, often within the space of a few seconds.[25]

Bixler says that the key to making a successful entrance is simply believing—and projecting—that you have a reason to be there and have something important to offer the client. You can communicate confidence with a strong stride, a good posture, and a friendly smile. A confident manner communicates to the client the message, "This meeting will be beneficial to you."

Shaking Hands

An inadequate handshake is like dandruff: No one mentions it, but everyone notices it. Today, the handshake is an important symbol of respect and in most business settings it is the proper greeting.[26]

STEP-BY-STEP TO SUCCESS

To achieve personal change, Gary Coxe suggests you follow these steps:

Focus on the big picture. "When you look at the big picture, realize that the defeat is only a small dot in your life," he says. Acknowledging it's only a small part of your life will help you find the strength and courage to get on your feet again and move forward.

Change your thinking. Get your beliefs back. The wrong mentality never achieves success—it's a positive attitude that will get you there.

Set goals and have a clear vision of what they are. Define what exactly you want. If the goal is fuzzy, you won't be able to see the end result.

Open doors. Make your own opportunities and you will notice that more and more will happen. "It's cool and fun to see all these new opportunities in front of you," Coxe comments. "You just have to do things and see how great they really are."

Meet people who are supportive of your dreams. They will give you the motivation and courage to move forward with your life.

Recognize that success is a journey, not a destination. Failure leads to success.

Courtesy of Gary Coxe.

Gary Coxe, a 37 year-old millionaire, has been described by Selling Power *magazine as a "salesman extraordinaire". His* Step by Step Plan *offers guidance to anyone in personal selling.*

In the field of selling, the handshake is usually the *first* and frequently the *only* physical contact one makes during a sales call. The handshake can communicate warmth, genuine concern for the prospect, and an image of strength. It also can communicate aloofness, indifference, and weakness to the customer. The message we communicate with a handshake is determined by a combination of five factors:

1. *Eye contact during handshake.* Eyes transmit more information than any other part of the body, so maintaining eye contact throughout the handshaking process is important when two people greet each other.

2. *Degree of firmness.* Generally speaking, a firm handshake communicates a caring attitude, while a weak grip (the dead-fish handshake) communicates indifference.
3. *Depth of interlock.* A full, deep grip communicates friendship to the other person.
4. *Duration of grip.* There are no specific guidelines to tell us what the ideal duration of a grip should be. However, by extending the duration of the handshake we can often communicate a greater degree of interest and concern for the other person. Do not pump up and down more than once or twice.
5. *Degree of dryness of hands.* A moist palm not only is uncomfortable to handle but also can communicate the impression that you are quite nervous. Some people have a physiological problem that causes clammy hands and should keep a handkerchief within reach to remove excess moisture. A clammy hand is likely to repel most customers.[27]

The best time to present your name is when you extend your hand. When you introduce yourself, state your name clearly and then listen carefully to be certain you hear the customer's name. To ensure that you remember the customer's name, repeat it. In some cases you need to check to be sure you are pronouncing it properly.[28]

Facial Expressions

If you want to identify the inner feelings of another person, watch facial expressions closely. The face is a remarkable communicator, capable of accurately signaling emotion in a split second and capable of concealing emotion equally well. We can often determine if the customer's face is registering surprise, pleasure, or skepticism (see Fig. 3.4). Facial expressions are largely universal so people around the world tend to "read" faces in a similar way. It is worth noting that the smile is the most recognized facial signal in the world and it can have a great deal of influence on others. George Rotter, professor of psychology at Montclair University, says, "Smiles are an enormous controller of how people perceive you." People tend to trust a smiling face.[29] Get in the habit of offering a sincere smile each time you meet with a prospect.

Eye Contact

When the customer is talking, eye contact is one of the best ways to say, "I'm listening." If you are looking across the room or at papers in your briefcase, the customer will assume you are not listening. However, prolonged eye contact can send the wrong message. A prolonged direct stare can be threatening. To avoid the prolonged stare, take fleeting glances at your notes. As the customer speaks, nod occasionally to indicate agreement or interest.[30]

FIGURE | 3.4

Our subtle facial gestures are continuously sending messages to others.

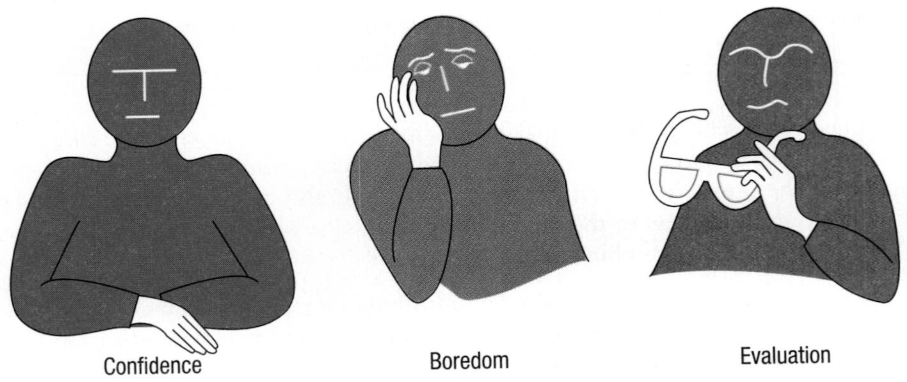

Effect of Appearance on Relationships

We form opinions about people based on a pattern of immediate impressions conveyed by appearance. The clothing we wear, the length and style of our hair, the fragrances we use, and the jewelry we display all combine to make a statement about us to others—a statement of primary importance to anyone involved in selling.

We all have certain views, or **unconscious expectations**, concerning appropriate dress. In sales work we should try to anticipate the expectations of our clientele. The clothing worn by salespeople does make a difference in terms of customer acceptance because it communicates powerful messages. The clothing we wear can influence our credibility and likability. Martin Siewert, a member of the business development team for Axiom Management Consulting, has adopted a flexible approach to dress. His company's policy favors an informal dress code, so he usually wears casual clothing at work unless he is meeting with a client. When he calls on customers, most of whom are *Fortune* 500 companies, he wears a suit and tie. "I want to show that I respect their culture," he says.[31]

Most image consultants agree that there is no single "dress for success" look. The appropriate wardrobe varies from one city or region to another and from company to company. However, there are some general guidelines that we should follow in selecting clothing for sales work. Three key words should govern our decisions: simplicity, appropriateness, and quality.

Simplicity

The color of clothing, as well as design, communicates a message to the customer. Some colors are showy and convey an air of casualness. In a business setting we want to be taken seriously, so flashy colors should usually be avoided.

Appropriateness

Selecting appropriate clothing for sales work can be a challenge. We must carefully consider the clients we serve and decide what may be acceptable to them. Many salespeople are guided by the type of products they sell and the desired image projected by their employers. Deciding what constitutes appropriate attire in today's business casual world begins with an understanding of what it means to "dress down." **Business casual** is clothing that allows you to feel comfortable but looks neat and professional. Pay close attention to the clothing your clients wear.[32] If a client is wearing a nice sport coat, a collared long-sleeved shirt, and dress slacks, don't wear khaki trousers and a short-sleeve polo shirt. In recent years, the casual dress trend has reversed at many companies, and workplace dress codes have become more formal.[33]

Quality

The quality of our wardrobe also influences the image we project to customers. A salesperson's wardrobe should be regarded as an investment, with each item carefully selected to look and fit well. Susan Bixler says, "If you want respect, you have to dress as well as or better than your industry standards."[34]

Visual Integrity

Visual presence must have a certain amount of integrity and consistency. The images you project are made up of many factors, and lack of attention to important details can negate your effort to create a good impression. Too much jewelry, a shirt that does not fit well, or unshined shoes can detract from the professional look you want to project. People often are extra alert when meeting someone new and this heightened consciousness makes every detail count.[35]

Spending an afternoon with a customer on the golf course is part of the relationship strategy of this salesperson. Many companies support this approach to building and maintaining relationships.

Keep in mind that customer contact often takes place in several settings. The first meeting with a customer may take place in her office, but the second meeting may be on the golf course. And the third meeting may take place at a nice restaurant. The clothing you wear in each of these settings is important.

Effect of Voice Quality on Relationships

As noted previously, every spoken message has a vocal element. What we hear is greatly influenced by the speaker's tone of voice, vocal clarity, and verbal expressiveness. On the telephone, voice quality is even more important because the other person cannot see your facial expressions, hand gestures, and other body movements. You cannot trade in your current voice for a new one. However, you can make your voice more pleasing to others. How?

Consider these suggestions:

1. *Do not talk too fast or too slowly.* Rapid speech often causes customers to become defensive. They raise psychological barriers because a "rapid-fire monologue" is associated with high-pressure sales methods. Many salespeople could improve their verbal presentation by talking more slowly. The slower presentation allows others to follow, and it allows the speaker time to think ahead—to consider the situation and make judgments. Another good tip is to vary the speed of your speech, leaving spaces between thoughts. Crowding too many thoughts together may confuse the listener.[36]
2. *Avoid a speech pattern that is dull and colorless.* The worst kind of voice has no color and no feeling. Enthusiasm is a critical element of an effective sales presentation. It also is contagious. Your enthusiasm for the product is transmitted to the customer. Your tone of voice mirrors your emotional state and physical well-being. When you are feeling good and enjoying a positive mental state, your voice naturally sounds upbeat, energetic, and enthusiastic. However, the normal stresses and strains of life can be reflected in your voice. Sometimes you have to manipulate your tone of voice to communicate

greater warmth and enthusiasm. Before you make that important phone call or meet with a prospect, reflect on your state of mind. To drain tension from your voice, inhale and tense every muscle. Hold for a count of 5, and then exhale for a count of 10. If you want to sound warm and friendly, smile while speaking.[37]

3. *Avoid bad speech habits.* Kristy Pinand, a youthful-looking 23-year old, routinely used "teen speak." For example, she described a recent promotion as "so cool." Her supervisor felt she not only looked young, but sounded very young, and this image could potentially hurt her ability to win the respect of clients. She urged Ms. Pinand to select her words more carefully. Ms. Pinand heeded the constructive advice and now rehearses her remarks aloud before she calls a client.[38]

   Some speech habits can make us sound poorly educated and inarticulate. At age 22, Mike White learned that his east Tennessee accent and colorful backwoods speech patterns created problems at work. He recognized that his southern drawl was a "turnoff" to some of the image-conscious people he worked with. One day his sales manager asked him if he had his racquetball equipment with him, and White replied, "Yeah, I brung it." Fortunately, White's supervisor was willing to tactfully correct his grammatical problems and help him communicate with greater clarity. Today, Mike White is CEO of a successful company and a frequent speaker at trade shows.[39]

Effect of Manners on Your Relationships

The study of manners (sometimes called etiquette or protocol) reveals a number of ways to enhance your relationship strategy. Salespeople who possess knowledge of the rules of etiquette can perform their daily work with greater poise and confidence. Think of manners as a universal passport to positive relationships and respect.

With practice, anyone can develop good manners without appearing to be "stiff" and at the same time win the respect and admiration of others. Space does not permit a complete review of this topic, but we cover some of the rules of etiquette that are especially important to salespeople.

1. *Avoid the temptation to address a new prospect by first name.* In a business setting, too much familiarity too quickly can cause irritation.
2. *Avoid offensive comments or stories.* Never assume that the customer's value system is the same as your own. Rough language, off-color stories, or personal views on political issues can do irreparable damage to your image.
3. *Recognize the importance of punctuality.* Ann Marie Sabath, owner of a firm that provides etiquette training for business employees, says "... we teach people that if you're early, you're on time, and if you're on time, in reality, you're late." Showing up late for an appointment will be viewed as rudeness by most clients.[40]
4. *When you invite a customer to lunch, do not discuss business before the meal is ordered unless the client initiates the subject.* Also, avoid ordering food that is not easily controlled, such as ribs, chicken, or lobster.
5. *When you use voice mail, leave a clear, concise message.* Do not speak too fast or mumble your name and number.
6. *Avoid cell phone contempt.* Turn off the cell phone ringer anytime you are with a client. Never put your phone on the table during a meal.

It has been said that good manners make other people feel better. This is true because good manners require that we place the other person's comfort ahead of our own. One of the best ways to develop rapport with a customer is to avoid behavior that might be offensive to that person.

Jay Mechling, Senior Vice-President at Morgan Stanley Dean Witter, believes that carefully selected casual dress is appropriate for certain customer contacts.

CONVERSATIONAL STRATEGIES THAT ENHANCE RELATIONSHIPS

The foundation for a long-term relationship with the customer is frequently a "get acquainted" type of conversation that takes place before any discussion of business matters. Within a few minutes it is possible to reduce the relationship tension that is so common when two people meet for the first time. This informal visit with the customer provides the salesperson with an opportunity to apply three guidelines for building strong relationships featured in *How to Win Friends and Influence People*, the classic book written by Dale Carnegie.

- *Become genuinely interested in other people.* Tim Sanders, chief solutions officer at Yahoo!, says, "How we are perceived as human beings is becoming increasingly imporant in the new economy."[41] When you become genuinely interested in the customer, you create an experience that is long remembered.
- *Be a good listener; encourage others to talk about themselves.* Stephen Covey, the noted author and consultant, recommends empathic listening. This requires listening with your ears, your eyes, and your heart.[42] We live in a culture where empathic listening is quite rare. Interrupting has become all too common as people rush to fill every gap in the conversation. Someone who has developed empathic listening skills can make a very powerful first impression.[43]
- *Talk in terms of the other person's interests.*[44] When you are initiating a conversation with a customer, don't hesitate to use small talk to get the conversation started. This may involve current events, business, or sports. Be sure to focus on topics that the customer is interested in.

The length of this conversation depends on your sense of the prospect's reaction to your greeting, how busy the prospect appears to be, and your awareness of topics of mutual interest. In developing this conversation the following three areas should be considered.

Selling in Action

Adding Value With the CARE Model

Andrew Gallan, a district sales manager for Abbott Laboratories, supervises a group of sales representatives who call on busy physicians. From many years of experience, he has discovered that what matters most to these customers is caring for them and their needs. He uses the acronym CARE to remind his sales representatives of behaviors that build long-term relationships.

Customize Every customer is unique and requires a custom tailored selling effort.

Appreciate Expressing sincere appreciation is an important strategy for building a relationship with the customer.

Respond The sales presentation should match product features with benefits to the patient base and the physician's practice.

Execute Always follow through on your commitment to provide a valued service to your customers.

Those who adopt the CARE model are more likely to become a trusted, respected, and invaluable partner to the customer.[c]

Comments on Here and Now Observations

Observant salespeople are aware of the things going on around them. These observations can be as general as unusual developments in the weather or as specific as noticing unique artifacts in the prospect's office.

Compliments

When you offer a *sincere* compliment to your prospect, you are saying, "Something about you is special." Most people react positively to compliments because they appeal to the need for self-esteem. Your admiration should not be expressed, however, in phony superlatives that seem transparent. Jack Canfield, author of *The Success Principles*, reminds us that everything we say to a customer produces an effect: "Know that you are constantly creating something—either positive of negative—with your words."[45]

Ken Viselman, Chairman of Itsy Bitsy Entertainment in New York, provides salespeople with many artifacts to talk about in his office. He states that "behind every object in his office is a story and a bit of my life". These items include an 18th century armoire, a crowded shelf of toys, and a Picasso lithograph to name only a few.

Search for Mutual Acquaintances or Interests

A frequent mode for establishing rapport with a new prospect is to find friends or interests you have in common. If you know someone with the same last name as your prospect, it may be appropriate to ask whether your friend is any relation. Anything you observe in the prospect's office or home might suggest an interest that you and your prospect share. A strong bond often develops between two persons who share the same interest or hobby. Frances Carlisle, an estate planner in New York, says her love of animals lands her many clients. Some of these clients wish to include provisions for the care of pets in their estate plans. Sometimes an unusual hobby (sky diving, mountain climbing, auto racing, etc.) is the perfect way to stand out and cultivate relationships with clients.[46]

STRATEGIES FOR SELF-IMPROVEMENT

Orson Welles, one of the most highly respected actors in this country, once said, "Every actor is very busy getting better or getting worse." To a large extent, salespeople are also "very busy getting better or getting worse." To improve, salespeople must develop an ongoing program for self-improvement (see Chapter 16). It is important to keep in mind that all improvement is self-initiated. Each of us controls the switch that allows personal growth and development to take place.

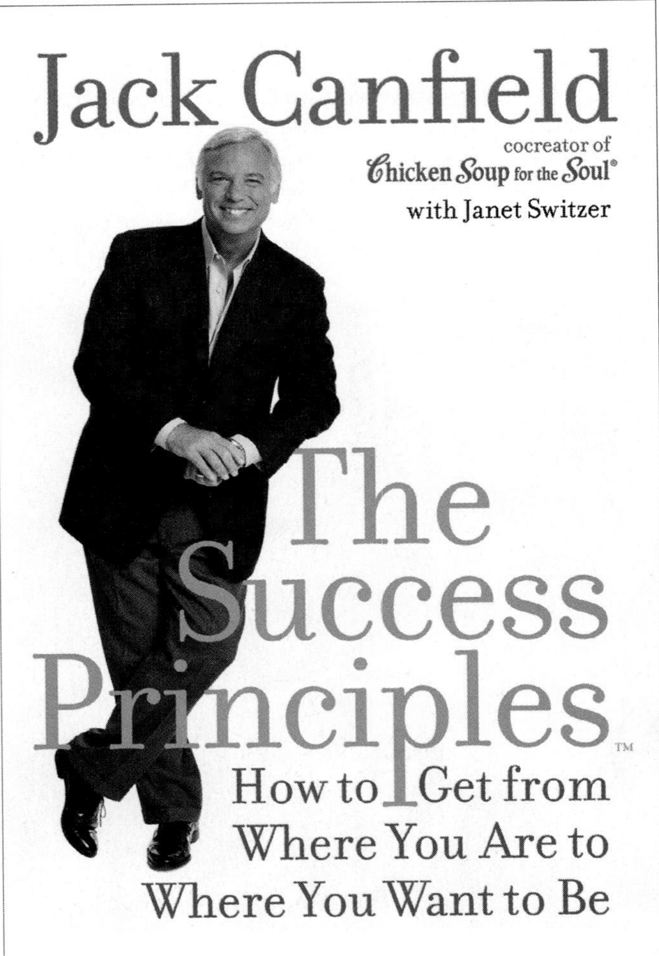

Mastering conversational strategies that enhance relationships is an important part of the skill of professional selling. Sincerity is a must. Jack Canfield, author of the best selling CHICKEN SOUP FOR THE SOUL and THE SUCCESS PRINCIPLES reminds us that everything we say to a customer produces an affect. "Know that you are constantly creating something—either positive or negative—with your words."

At the beginning of this chapter we introduced the concept of emotional intelligence. We noted that this form of intelligence can be increased with the aid of self-development activities. Would you like to develop a more positive self-image? Improve your ability to develop win-win relationships? Develop effective nonverbal communication skills? Improve your speaking voice? These relationship-building strategies can be achieved if you are willing to follow these steps:

Step one: Set goals. The goal-setting process begins with a clear, written statement that describes what you want to accomplish. If your goal is too general or vague, progress toward achieving that goal is difficult to observe. Next, you must identify the steps you will take to achieve your goal.

In the age of information, companies also need to build their Web sites around the concept of "a relationship strategy."

This salesperson has set a fitness goal. Physical fitness can be an important part of a self-improvement program.

Step two: Use visualization. To **visualize** means to form a mental image of something. The power to visualize (sometimes called guided imagery) is in a very real sense the power to create. If you really want to succeed at something, picture yourself doing it successfully. For example, spend time developing mental pictures of successful sales presentations or visualize yourself as one of the top salespeople in your organization. Once you have formed a clear mental picture of what you want to accomplish, identify the steps needed to get there and then mentally rehearse them. The visualization process needs to be repeated over and over again.[47]

Step three: Use positive self-talk. People with a strong inner critic will receive frequent negative messages that can erode their self-esteem. It helps to refute and reject those negative messages with positive self-talk. **Self-talk** takes place silently in the privacy of your mind. It is the series of personal conversations you have with yourself almost continually throughout the day. Just like statements from other people, your self-talk can dramatically affect your behavior and self-esteem.[48]

Step four: Reward your progress. When you see yourself making progress toward a goal, or achieving a goal, reward yourself. This type of reinforcement is vital when you are trying to change a behavior. There is nothing wrong with taking pride in your accomplishments.

Self-improvement efforts can result in new abilities or powers, and they give us the motivation to utilize more fully the talents we already have. As a result, our potential for success is greater.

Summary

The manner in which salespeople establish, build, and maintain relationships is a major key to success in personal selling. The key relationships in selling include management personnel, company support staff, secondary decision makers, and customers.

The concept of *partnering* is revisited and discussed in detail. Partnering emphasizes building a strong relationship during every aspect of the sale and working hard to maintain a quality relationship with the customer after the sale. Partnerships can be strengthened when salespeople use value-added relationship strategies.

An understanding of the psychology of human behavior provides a foundation for developing relationship strategies. In this chapter we discuss the link between *self-image* and success in selling. Self-imposed fears can prevent salespeople from achieving success.

We describe several factors that influence the image we project to customers. The image others have of us is shaped to a great extent by nonverbal communication. We may choose the right words to persuade a customer to place an order, but aversive factors communicated by our clothing, handshake, facial expression, tone of voice, and general manner may prejudice the customer against us and our product or service.

The various conversational strategies that enhance relationships are reviewed. Dale Carnegie's guidelines for building strong relationships are discussed.

We also discuss the importance of self-improvement. A four-step, self-improvement plan is described.

KEY TERMS

Emotional intelligence
Self-image
Character
Integrity
Nonverbal messages
Unconscious expectations
Business casual
Self-talk
Visualize

REVIEW QUESTIONS

1. List the three prescriptions that serve as the foundation for development of a relationship strategy.
2. How important are establishing, building, and maintaining relationships in the selling process? List the four groups of people with whom sales personnel must be able to work effectively.
3. Why is partnering described as the highest-quality selling relationship? Why has the building of partnerships become more important today?
4. Defend the statement, "Successful relationships depend on a positive self-image."
5. Describe the win-win approach to selling.
6. How is our self-image formed? Why is a positive self-image so important in personal selling?
7. Describe the meaning of the term **emotional intelligence**.

8. Identify three conversational methods that can be used to establish relationships.
9. Describe the meaning of nonverbal messages. Why should salespeople be concerned about these messages?
10. List and describe each step in the four-step self-improvement plan.

APPLICATION EXERCISES

1. Select four salespeople you know and ask them if they have a relationship strategy for working with customers, management personnel, secondary decision makers, and company support staff. Ask each salesperson to give you two or three specific examples of steps they have taken to build and maintain a positive relationship with their customers.

2. The partnering style of selling is emphasized throughout the book. To gain more insight into the popularity of this concept, use one of your Internet search engines to key in the words "partnering + selling." Notice the large number of documents related to this query. Click on and examine several of these documents to learn more about this approach to selling.
3. Complete the following etiquette quiz. Your instructor will provide you with answers so you can check your responses.
   - **a.** On what side should you wear your name tag?
   - **b.** Is it appropriate to drink beer from a bottle at a reception?
   - **c.** When introducing a female salesperson to a male prospect, whose name should be spoken first?
   - **d.** At the table, when should you place your napkin in your lap?
   - **e.** Is it ever proper to comb, smooth, or touch your hair while seated at a restaurant table?
4. In October, people of the Hindu religion celebrate Diwali, the festival of lights. The festival of lights is one of the most important and most beautiful Indian festivals. Rick Saulle, a pharmaceutical sales representative employed by Pifzer, knew that one of the most important physicians he called on was Indian and would celebrate Diwali. He also knew that it is commonplace to provide sweets to Indians who celebrate Diwali. Saulle visited an Indian grocery store and purchased a plate of Indian sweets to celebrate Diwali. When he presented the sweets to the physician, the response was very positive. The doctor grabbed Saulle's hand, shook it forcefully, and sincerely thanked him for honoring this important holiday.[49]

   As a nation, we serve as host to a kaleidoscope of the worlds cultures, and the trend toward greater diversity will accelerate in the years ahead. Reflect on the gift given by Mr. Saulle and then answer these questions.
   - **a.** Is it appropriate for a salesperson to give a gift to someone who is celebrating a religious holiday?
   - **b.** In addition to giving a gift, what are some other ways to recognize a religious festival or holiday?
   - **c.** List and describe three religious holidays or festivals celebrated by denominations other than Christian.
5. Move quickly through the following list of traits. Use a check mark beside those that fit your self-image. Use an *X* to mark those that do not fit. If you are unsure, indicate with a question mark.

   ——— I like myself.
   ——— People trust me.
   ——— I usually say the right thing.
   ——— I dislike myself.
   ——— I trust myself.
   ——— I often do the wrong thing.
   ——— People avoid me.
   ——— I enjoy work.

——— I waste time.
——— I put up a good front.
——— I use my talents.
——— I feel hemmed in.
——— I use time well.
——— I enjoy people.
——— I usually say the wrong thing.
——— I am discouraged about life.
——— I have not developed my talents.
——— People like to be around me.
——— I control myself.
——— I enjoy nature.
——— I am dependent on others for ideas.
——— I am involved in solving community problems.
——— I do not use my talents fully.
——— I do not like myself.
——— I do not like to be around people.

Now look at the pattern of your self-assessment.

a. Is there a pattern?
b. Is there a winner or loser pattern?
c. What traits would you like to change? (List them.)
d. Pick the trait you would like to change the most and prepare a plan to achieve this change. Your plan should include specific goal statements.

6. It is pointed out in this chapter that clothing communicates strong messages. In this exercise you become more aware of whether or not your clothes communicate the messages you want them to communicate.

a. Make a chart like the one that follows:

ITEM OF CLOTHING BEING ANALYZED	WHAT I WANT MY CLOTHES TO SAY ABOUT ME TO OTHERS	WHAT OTHERS THINK MY CLOTHING SAYS

b. In the first column, list the clothing you are now wearing, for example, dress slacks, dress shoes, and sweater; athletic shoes, jeans, and T-shirt; or suit, tie, and dress shoes.
c. In the middle column, describe the message you would like the clothes you have chosen to say. For example, "I want to be comfortable," "I want people to trust me," or "I want people to take me seriously."
d. Have somebody else fill in the third column by describing what your clothes do say about you.
e. Compare the two columns. Do your clothes communicate what you want them to? Do the same exercise for social dress, casual dress, business attire, and hairstyle.

Note: If you are currently employed, analyze the clothing you wear at work.

ROLE-PLAY EXERCISE

This is a two-part role-play exercise. Part one involves preparation for a sales call on a new prospect whom you have not met previously. The primary objective of this meeting is to get acquainted with the prospect and begin the process of building a long-term relationship. You anticipate that this prospect will become a very good customer. Review the text material on thought processes that will enhance your relationship strategy, nonverbal strategies that add value to your relationships, and conversational strategies that enhance relationships. Prepare a written outline of what you plan to say and do during the first 5 to 10 minutes of the meeting. Think of this outline as your "strategic plan." Part two involves a role-play with a class member who will play the role of the prospect. Throughout the role-play try to say and do everything that was part of your plan. At the end of the role-play, give your strategic plan outline to the prospect and request feedback on your performance.

CRM APPLICATION EXERCISE

Preparing Letters with CRM

Load the ACT! software and look up (Lookup) My Record. This screen identifies the person using the database who, in this case, was Pat Silva and now will be you. Replace Pat Silva's name with your own.

The ACT! software demonstrates how customer relationship management (CRM) programs are designed to be used by people in a hurry or without extensive typing skills. Menu choices can be made with the mouse, by typing simple key combinations, or by selecting an icon. This means that a procedure, such as preparing and printing correspondence, can be started by (1) selecting with a mouse the word Write, then the word Letter, from the menus; (2) pressing the Alt key and the W (Write) keys at the same time (Alt + W), and then the L (Letter) key; or (3) picking the Letter icon with the mouse.

A blank letter with the date, inside address, salutation, closing line, your name, and your title will appear on your screen. All you need to do is begin typing the letter. With your printer connected you can print this same letter by selecting Print from the File menu. With the File menu open, note that the right column displays key combinations, such as Ctrl + P to print.

Find the record for Brad Able by choosing Lookup, Last Name; type in the name "Able"; and press Enter. With Brad Able's record on the screen, choose the letter icon or Write and Letter from the menus. Prepare and then print a brief letter to Brad Able confirming an appointment to meet at his office next Thursday at 9:00 A.M. to discuss his training needs. Your letter should feature the win-win approach discussed in the chapter.

VIDEO CASE PROBLEM

When people buy or sell a home, they hold their realtor to high standards. After all, for most people, the home purchase represents the largest single investment they will make throughout their lifetime. The salespeople employed by Fred Sands Realtors (fredsands.com) introduced at the beginning of this chapter, understand the magnitude of the home purchase or home sale experience. They know that the customers are anxious to partner with someone who can be trusted to look after their best interests.

When new salespeople join the Fred Sands Realtors sales force, they usually come under the tutelage of Sandra Khadra, vice president of marketing. She helps salespeople form a professional image that appeals to the type of clientele served by the company. She knows that there is a direct link between the image projected by the salespeople and the success of the company. When working with salespeople, she emphasizes the following points:

- Customers notice even the little details such as the quality of stationery, notepaper, and business cards. If the business card features a photo of the salesperson, the person should be looking straight ahead, not away from the camera. This pose permits the salesperson to make eye contact with the customer.
- Salespeople at Fred Sands Realtors must be able to build rapport with a variety of personality types. Some customers are quiet, reserved, and somewhat guarded when expressing their views. Others are more impulsive and express their views openly. Salespeople are encouraged to alter their communication style to increase the comfort level of the customer. Sandra Khadra encourages salespeople to mirror the behavior of the prospect to the greatest extent possible. She says that it is always important to gauge how your communication style impacts on the prospect. A positive attitude is another important aspect of the relationship-building process at Fred Sands Realtors.

- In some cases, salespeople at Fred Sands Realtors must communicate across language and cultural barriers. Foreign-born clients are becoming more common, and this means that salespeople must gain a greater understanding and respect for cultural diversity. To impose our way of doing business on every prospect is shortsighted.
- Sandra Khadra suggests that salespeople should find out what customers value. What is the most important aspect of the home purchase or home sale? Most customers do not open up and share important information until they trust the salesperson. (See chapter opener on p. 54 for more information.)

Questions

1. Does it appear that Fred Sands Realtors supports the three prescriptions that serve as a foundation of the relationship strategy? (See Strategic/Consultative Selling Model in Figure 3.1.) Explain your answer.
2. Why should real estate salespeople spend time developing a relationship strategy? What might be some long-term benefits of this strategy?
3. Is it ever appropriate to touch your client other than with a handshake? Explain your answer.
4. What are some benefits to the salesperson who can mirror the behavior of the prospect?
5. What are some precautions to take when preparing a meeting with a foreign-born prospect?

Chapter Preview

When you finish reading this chapter, you should be able to

1. Discuss communication-style bias and how it influences the relationship process

2. Explain the benefits derived from an understanding of communication styles

3. Identify the two major dimensions of the comunication-style model

4. List and describe the four major communication styles in the communication-style model

5. Learn how to identify your preferred communication style and that of your customer

6. Learn to overcome communication-style bias and build strong selling relationships with style flexing

CHAPTER 4

Communication Styles: Managing Selling Relationships

Every year publications such as *Business Week, Fortune*, and *Fast Company* feature profiles of well-known business leaders. These articles often focus on the communication style of the executives who provide leadership in companies across America. Who can forget Al "Chainsaw" Dunlap who was described as aggressive, frank, opinionated, and impatient. He earned his nickname by ordering huge layoffs when he was the CEO responsible for restructuring companies such as Scott Paper and Sunbeam Corporation. Deborah Hopkins earned the nickname "Hurricane Debby" for the way she conducted business while holding leadership positions at Unisys, GM Europe, Boeing, and Lucent Technologies. Her demanding, ambitious, and sometimes emotional style occasionally created personality clashes. By contrast, Bill Gates is described as a quiet, reflective person who often seems preoccupied with other matters. And then there is Jeff Bezos, the founder and CEO of Amazon.com, who is often described as the happy extrovert. He seems to enjoy being with other people and often displays spontaneous, uninhibited behavior.[1]

We form impressions of people by observing their behavior. The thoughts, feelings, and actions that characterize someone are generally viewed as their **personality**.[2] Communication style is an important aspect of our personality.

We form impressions of others by observing their behavior. Jeff Bezos, founder of Amazon.com is often described as the happy extrovert who frequently displays spontaneous, uninhibited laughter. By contrast, Microsoft's Bill Gates is described as a quiet, reflective person who often seems preoccupied with other matters.

COMMUNICATION STYLES—AN INTRODUCTION TO MANAGING SELLING RELATIONSHIPS

Almost everyone has had the pleasant experience of meeting someone for the first time and developing an instant mutual rapport. There seems to be a quality about some people that makes you like them instantaneously—a basis for a mutual understanding that is difficult to explain. On the other hand, we can all recall meeting people who "turn us off" almost immediately. Why does this happen during the initial contact?

The impressions that others form about us are based on what they observe us saying and doing. They have no way of knowing our innermost thoughts and feelings, so they make decisions about us based on what they see and hear.[3] The patterns of behavior that others observe can be called **communication style**.

Communication-Style Bias

Bias in various forms is quite common in our society. In fact, local, state, and national governments have passed many laws to curb blatant forms of racial, age, and sex bias. We also observe some degree of regional bias when people from various parts of the country meet.

The most frequently occurring form of bias is not commonly understood in our society. What has been labeled **communication-style bias** is a state of mind that almost every one of us experiences from time to time, but we usually find it difficult to explain the symptoms. Communication-style bias can develop when we have contact with another person whose communication style is different from our own. For example, a purchasing agent was overheard saying, "I do not know what it is, but I just do not like that sales representative." The agent was no doubt experiencing communication-style bias but could not easily describe the feeling.

Your communication style is the "you" that is on display every day—the outer pattern of behavior that others see. If your style is very different from the other person's, it may be difficult for the two of you to develop a rapport. All of us have had the experience of saying or doing something that was perfectly acceptable to a friend or co-worker and being surprised when the same behavior irritated someone else. However, aside from admitting that this happens, most of us are unable to draw meaningful conclusions from these experiences to help us perform more effectively with people in the future.[4]

In recent years, thousands of sales professionals have learned to manage their selling relationships more effectively through the study of communication styles. Books, such as *People Styles at Work* by Robert Bolton and Dorothy Grover Bolton, and *The Versatile Salesperson* by Roger Wenschlag, serve as good references. Many training companies offer seminars that provide enrollees with a practical understanding of communication-style theory and practice. Wilson Learning offers a program entitled *The Versatile Salesperson*. This program helps salespeople develop the interpersonal skills necessary to work effectively with customers whose communication style is different than their own. Over seven million people worldwide have completed Wilson Learning programs that focus on communication styles.[5] The term **adaptive** selling is sometimes used to describe training programs that encourage salespeople to adjust their communication style to accommodate the communication style of the customer.

Communication-Style Principles

The theory of behavioral- or communication-style bias is based on a number of underlying principles. A review of these principles can be beneficial before we examine specific styles.

1. *Individual differences exist and are important.* It is quite obvious that we all differ in terms of physical characteristics such as height, shoe size, facial features, and body build, but the most interesting differences are those patterns of behavior that are unique to each of us. Voice patterns, eye movement, facial expression, and posture are some of the components of our communication style. Additional characteristics are discussed later in this chapter. Research by the Swiss psychoanalyst Carl Jung and others has helped us understand the importance of individual differences.
2. *A communication style is a way of thinking and behaving.* It is not an ability but, instead, a preferred way of using abilities one has. This distinction is very important. An ability refers to how well someone can do something. A style refers to how someone likes to do something.[6]
3. *Individual style differences tend to be stable.* Our communication style is based on a combination of hereditary and environmental factors. Our style is somewhat original at the time of birth; it takes on additional individuality during the first three to five years of life. By the time we enter elementary school, the teacher should be able to identify our preferred communication style. This style tends to remain fairly constant throughout life.
4. *There is a finite number of styles.* Most people display one of several clusters of similar behaviors, and this allows us to identify a small number of behavioral categories. By combining a series of descriptors we can develop a single "label" that describes a person's most preferred communication style.
5. *To create the most productive relationships, it is necessary to get in sync with the communication style of the people you work with.*[7] Differences between people can be a source of friction unless you develop the ability to recognize and respond to the other person's style.

Group sales presentations can be very challenging because in most cases you are attempting to relate to several different communication styles.

The ability to identify another person's communication style, and to know how and when to adapt your own preferred style to it, can afford you a crucial advantage in dealing with people. Differences between people can be a source of friction. The ability to "speak the other person's language" is an important relationship-management skill.[8]

Improving Your Relationship-Management Skills

Anyone who is considering a career in selling can benefit greatly from the study of communication styles. These concepts provide a practical method of classifying people according to communication styles and give the salesperson a distinct advantage in the marketplace. A salesperson who understands communication-style classification methods and learns how to apply them can avoid common mistakes that threaten interpersonal relations with customers. Awareness of these methods greatly reduces the possibility of tension arising during the sales call.

The first major goal of this chapter is to help you better understand your own most preferred communication style. The second goal is to help you develop greater understanding and appreciation for styles that are different from your own. The third goal is to help you manage your selling relationships more effectively by learning to adapt your style to fit the communication style of the customer. This practice is called "style flexing."

COMMUNICATION-STYLE MODEL

This section introduces you to the four basic communication styles. One of these will surface as your most preferred style. The communication-style model that defines these styles is based on two important dimensions of human behavior: dominance and sociability. We look at the dominance continuum first.

Selling Is Everyone's Business

PERSONAL SELLING FILLS THE SEATS

Mark Cuban, owner of the NBA Dallas Mavericks, has been described as "probably the most involved owner in day-to-day activities that the pro basketball league has ever seen." When he bought the team, it had not been in the playoffs for 10 years. His mission, of course, was not only to improve the team's on-court performance but also to dramatically increase its revenue from season ticket sales and sponsorships. Within one week, he added 30 new salespeople to the team's five-member sales force. Cuban says, "I think the key to any business is to be able to connect with customers and prove to them that you can give better value than the next guy. We take things into our own hands by selling and talking directly to customers." In one year, paid attendance increased 60 percent; season ticket sales increased 25 percent; sponsorship revenue increased 30 percent; and the Mavericks made the playoffs.[a]

Mark Cuban, owner of the NBA Dallas Mavericks.

Dominance Continuum

Dominance can be defined as the tendency to control or prevail over others.[9] Dominant people tend to be quite competitive. They also tend to offer opinions readily and be decisive and determined. Each of us falls somewhere on the dominance continuum illustrated by Figure 4.1.

A person classified as being high in dominance is generally a "take charge" type of person who makes a position clear to others. A person classified as being low in dominance is usually more reserved, unassertive, and easygoing. Dominance has been recognized as a universal behavioral characteristic. David W. Johnson developed the Interpersonal Pattern Exercise to help people achieve greater interpersonal effectiveness. He believes that people fall into two dominance categories:

1. *Low dominance.* These people have a tendency to be quite cooperative and let others control things. They tend to be low in assertiveness.
2. *High dominance.* These people tend to like to control things and frequently initiate demands. They are more aggressive in dealing with others.[10]

FIGURE 4.1

The first step in determining your most preferred communication style is to identify where you are on the dominance continuum.

Low ▬▬▬▬▬▬ High

TABLE 4.1 DOMINANCE INDICATOR

Rate yourself on each scale by placing a check mark on the continuum at the point that represents how you perceive yourself.

I PERCEIVE MYSELF AS SOMEWHAT						
Cooperative						Competitive
Submissive						Authoritarian
Accommodating						Domineering
Hesitant						Decisive
Reserved						Outgoing
Compromising						Insistent
Cautious						Risk taking
Patient						Hurried
Complacent						Influential
Quiet						Talkative
Shy						Bold
Supportive						Demanding
Relaxed						Tense
Restrained						Assertive

The first step in determining your most preferred communication style is to identify where you fall on the dominance continuum. Do you tend to rank low or high on this scale? To answer this question, complete the Dominance Indicator form in Table 4.1. Rate yourself on each scale by placing a check mark on the continuum at the point that represents how you perceive yourself. If most of your check marks fall to the right of center, you are someone who is high in dominance. If most of your check marks fall to the left of center, you are someone who is low in dominance. Is there any best place to be on the dominance continuum? The answer is no. Successful salespeople can be found at all points along the continuum.

Sociability Continuum

Sociability reflects the amount of control we exert over our emotional expressiveness.[11] People who are high in sociability tend to express their feelings freely, while people who are low in this dimension tend to control their feelings. Each of us falls somewhere on the sociability continuum illustrated in Figure 4.2.

Sociability is also a universal behavioral characteristic. It can be defined as the tendency to seek and enjoy interaction with others. Therefore, high sociability is an indication of a person's preference to interact with other people. Low sociability is an indicator of a person's desire to work in an environment where the person has more time alone instead of having to make conversation with others. The person who is classified as being low in the area of sociability is more reserved and formal in social relationships.

The second step in determining your most preferred communication style is to identify where you fall on the sociability continuum. To answer this question, complete the Sociability Indicator form shown in Table 4.2. Rate yourself on each scale by placing

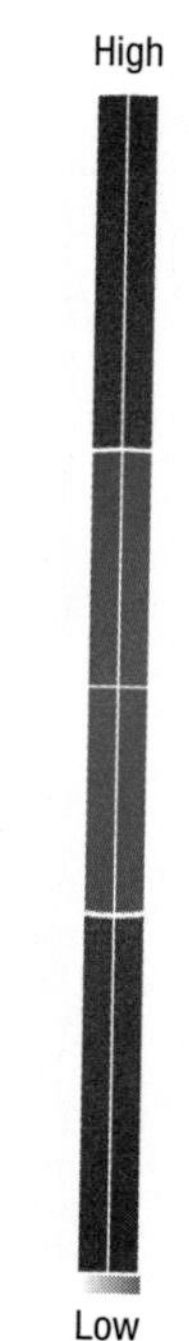

FIGURE 4.2

The second step in determining your most preferred communication style is to identify where you are on the sociability continuum.

TABLE 4.2 SOCIABILITY INDICATOR

Rate yourself on each scale by placing a check mark on the continuum at the point that represents how you perceive yourself.

I PERCEIVE MYSELF AS SOMEWHAT		
Disciplined	⊢—⊢—⊢—⊢—⊢	Easygoing
Controlled	⊢—⊢—⊢—⊢—⊢	Expressive
Serious	⊢—⊢—⊢—⊢—⊢	Lighthearted
Methodical	⊢—⊢—⊢—⊢—⊢	Unstructured
Calculating	⊢—⊢—⊢—⊢—⊢	Spontaneous
Guarded	⊢—⊢—⊢—⊢—⊢	Open
Stalwart	⊢—⊢—⊢—⊢—⊢	Humorous
Aloof	⊢—⊢—⊢—⊢—⊢	Friendly
Formal	⊢—⊢—⊢—⊢—⊢	Casual
Reserved	⊢—⊢—⊢—⊢—⊢	Attention seeking
Cautious	⊢—⊢—⊢—⊢—⊢	Carefree
Conforming	⊢—⊢—⊢—⊢—⊢	Unconventional
Reticent	⊢—⊢—⊢—⊢—⊢	Dramatic
Restrained	⊢—⊢—⊢—⊢—⊢	Impulsive

a check mark on the continuum at the point that represents how you perceive yourself. If most of your check marks fall to the right of center, you are someone who is high in sociability. If most of your check marks fall to the left of center, you are someone who is low in sociability. Keep in mind that there is no best place to be. Successful salespeople can be found at all points along this continuum.

As you reflect on your dominance and sociability ratings, keep in mind that self-ratings can be misleading. Many people do not see themselves in the same way that others see them. Friends and co-workers who frequently observe your behaviors may be in a better position to identify your communication style.

With the aid of the dominance and sociability continuums we are now prepared to discuss a relatively simple communication-style classification plan that has practical application in the field of selling. We describe the four basic styles: Emotive, Director, Reflective, and Supportive.

Four Styles of Communication

By combining the two dimensions of human behavior, dominance and sociability, we can form a partial outline of the communication-style model (Fig. 4.3). Dominance is represented by the horizontal axis, and sociability is represented by the vertical axis. Once the two dimensions of human behavior are combined, the framework for communication-style classification is established.

Emotive Style

The upper right-hand quadrant of Figure 4.4 defines a style that combines high sociability and high dominance. We call this the **Emotive style**. Emotive people like Al Roker and Jay Leno usually stand out in a crowd. They are expressive and willing

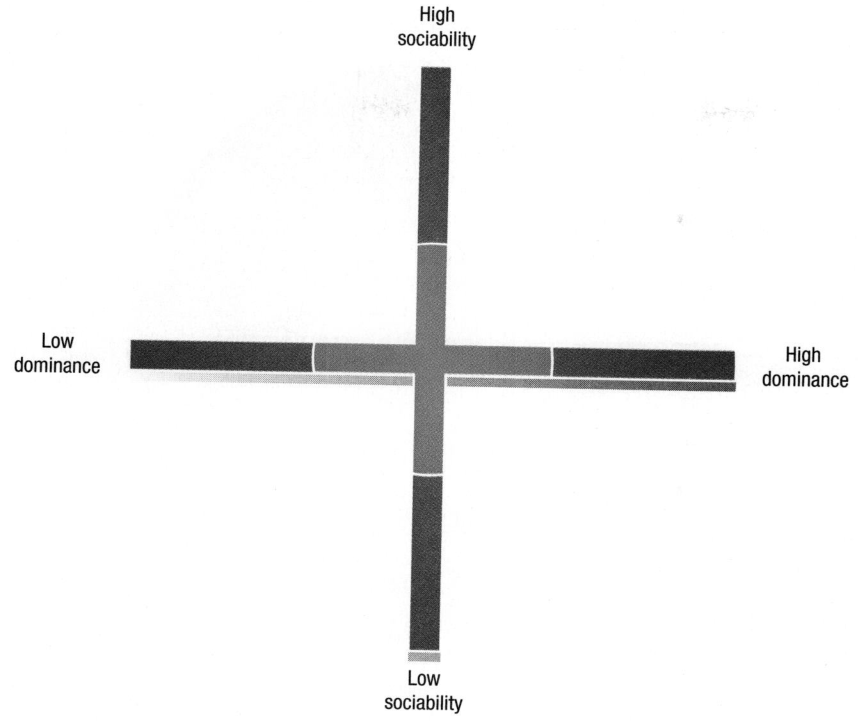

FIGURE | 4.3

When the dominance and sociability dimensions of human behavior are combined, the framework for communication-style classification is established.

to spend time maintaining and enjoying a large number of relationships.[12] Oprah Winfrey, the well-known television personality, and talk show host David Letterman provide excellent models of the Emotive communication style. Rosie O'Donnell provides still another example. They are outspoken, enthusiastic, and stimulating. Robin Williams, the popular actor, and Richard Branson, the founder of Virgin Atlantic Airways, also project the Emotive communication style. The Emotive person wants to create a social relationship quickly and usually feels more comfortable in an informal atmosphere. Some of the verbal and nonverbal clues that identify the Emotive person follow:

1. *Appears quite active.* This person gives the appearance of being busy. A person who combines high dominance and high sociability is often restless. The Emotive person is likely to express feelings with vigorous movements of the hands and a rapid speech pattern.
2. *Takes the social initiative in most cases.* Emotives tend to be extroverts. When two people meet for the first time, the Emotive person is more apt to initiate and maintain the conversation as well as to initiate the handshake. Emotives rate high in both directness and openness.
3. *Likes to encourage informality.* The Emotive person moves to a "first name" basis as soon as possible (too soon in some cases). Even the way this person sits in a chair communicates a preference for a relaxed, informal social setting.
4. *Expresses emotional opinions.* Emotive people generally do not hide their feelings. They often express opinions dramatically and impulsively.

FIGURE | 4.4

The Emotive style combines high sociability and high dominance.

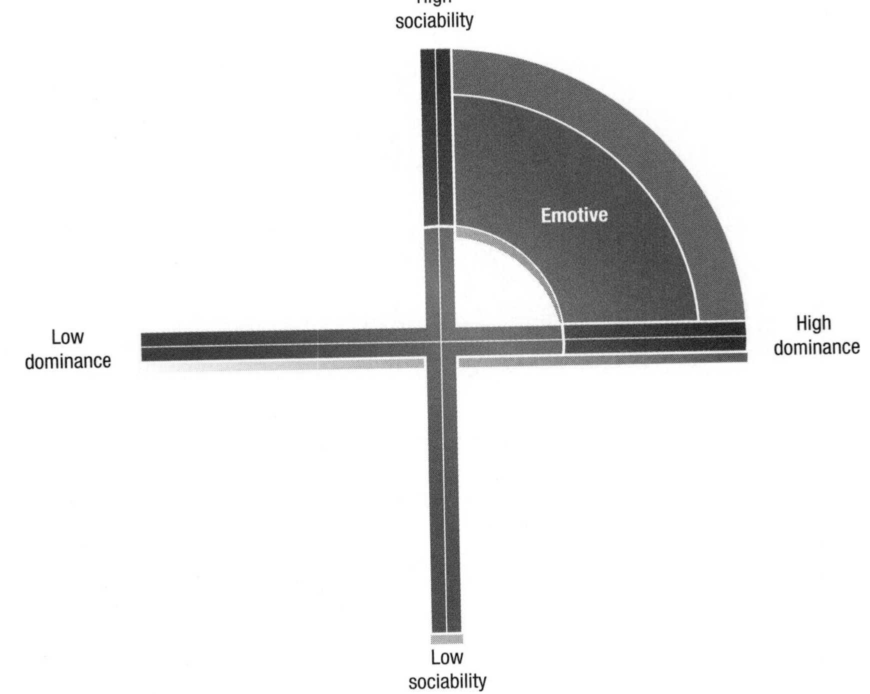

Emotive people like Oprah Winfrey are enthusiastic, outspoken, and stimulating. By contrast, persons who display the Reflective style like Tiger Woods are more reserve and tend not to express dramatic opinions.

KEY WORDS FOR THE EMOTIVE STYLE

Sociable	Emotional	Personable
Spontaneous	Unstructured	Persuasive
Zestful	Excitable	Dynamic
Stimulating		

Director Style

The lower right-hand quadrant defines a style that combines high dominance and low sociability. We will call this the **Director style** (Fig. 4.5).

To understand the nature of people who display the Director communication style, picture in your mind's eye the director of a Hollywood film. The person you see is giving orders in a loud voice and is generally in charge of every facet of the operation. Everyone on the set knows this person is in charge. Although the common stereotyped image of the Hollywood film director is probably exaggerated, this example is helpful as you attempt to become familiar with the Director style.

Persons who display the Director style such as Martha Stewart and Vice President Dick Cheney, like to take charge and maintain control. Persons who display the Director style are generally viewed as determined, bold and serious.

Martha Stewart (television personality), Jessie Ventura, former governor of Minnesota, and Vice

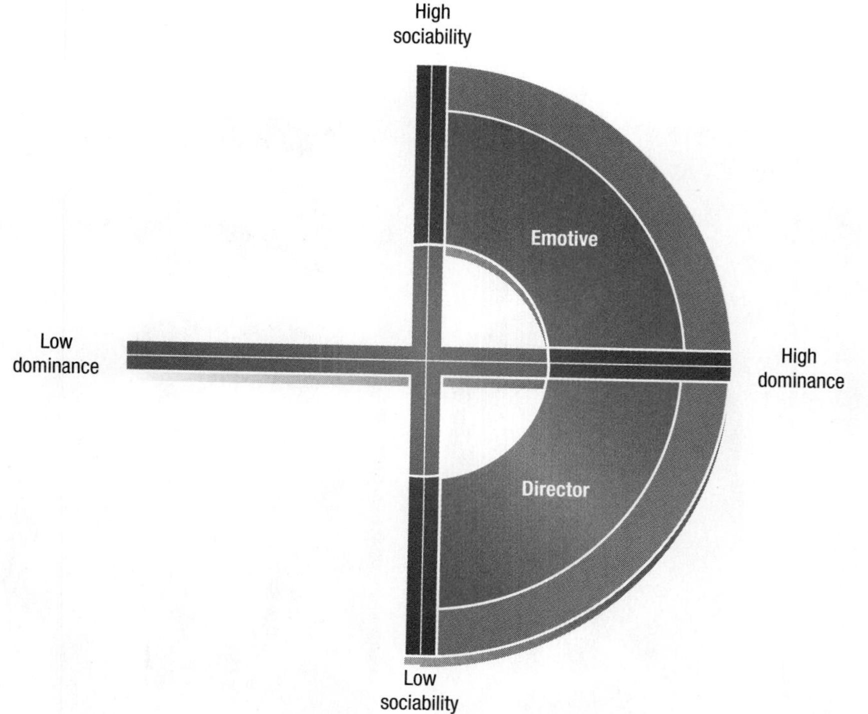

FIGURE | 4.5

The Director style combines high dominance and low sociability.

President Dick Cheney project the Director style. These people have been described as frank, demanding, assertive, and determined.

In the field of selling you will encounter a number of customers who are Directors. How can you identify these people? What verbal and nonverbal clues can we observe? A few of the behaviors displayed by Directors follow:

1. *Appears to be quite busy.* The Director generally does not like to waste time and wants to get right to the point. General Norman Schwarzkopf and Judge Judy Sheindlin of the *Judge Judy* television show display this behavior.
2. *May give the impression of not listening.* In most cases the Director feels more comfortable talking than listening.
3. *Displays a serious attitude.* A person who is low in sociability usually communicates a lack of warmth and is apt to be quite businesslike and impersonal. Mike Wallace, one of the stars on the popular *60 Minutes* television show, seldom smiles or displays warmth.
4. *Likes to maintain control.* The person who is high on the Dominance continuum likes to maintain control. During meetings the Director often seeks to control the agenda.[13]

KEY WORDS FOR THE DIRECTOR STYLE

Aggressive	Serious	Opinionated
Intense	Determined	Impatient
Demanding	Frank	Bold
Pushy		

Business Week *identifies Steven Reinemund, CEO, and Indra Nooyi, President of Pepsico, as the "odd couple". Indra (born and raised in India) is a free spirited strategist while Steven is a spit-and-polish detail man. Individuals with different communication styles can work well together if they possess communication-style flexibility.*

John Abbott Photography

Reflective Style

The lower left-hand quadrant of the communication-style model features a combination of low dominance and low sociability (Fig. 4.6). People who regularly display this behavior are classified as having the **Reflective style**.

The Reflective person tends to examine all the facts carefully before arriving at a decision. Like a cautious scientist, this individual wants to gather all available information and weigh it carefully before taking a position. The reflective type is usually a stickler for detail.[14] The late physicist, Albert Einstein, fits the description. Dr. Joyce Brothers (psychologist), former U.S. President Jimmy Carter, and Alan Greenspan (former Chairman of the Federal Reserve) also display the characteristics of the Reflective type.

The Reflective communication style combines low dominance and low sociability; therefore, people with this classification tend to be reserved and cautious. Some additional behaviors that characterize this style follow:

1. *Controls emotional expression.* Reflective people tend to curb emotional expression and are less likely to display warmth openly.
2. *Displays a preference for orderliness.* The Reflective person enjoys a highly structured environment and generally feels frustration when confronted with unexpected events.
3. *Tends to express measured opinions.* The Reflective individual usually does not express dramatic opinions. This communication style is characterized by disciplined, businesslike actions.
4. *Seems difficult to get to know.* The Reflective person tends to be somewhat formal in social relationships and therefore is viewed as aloof by many people.

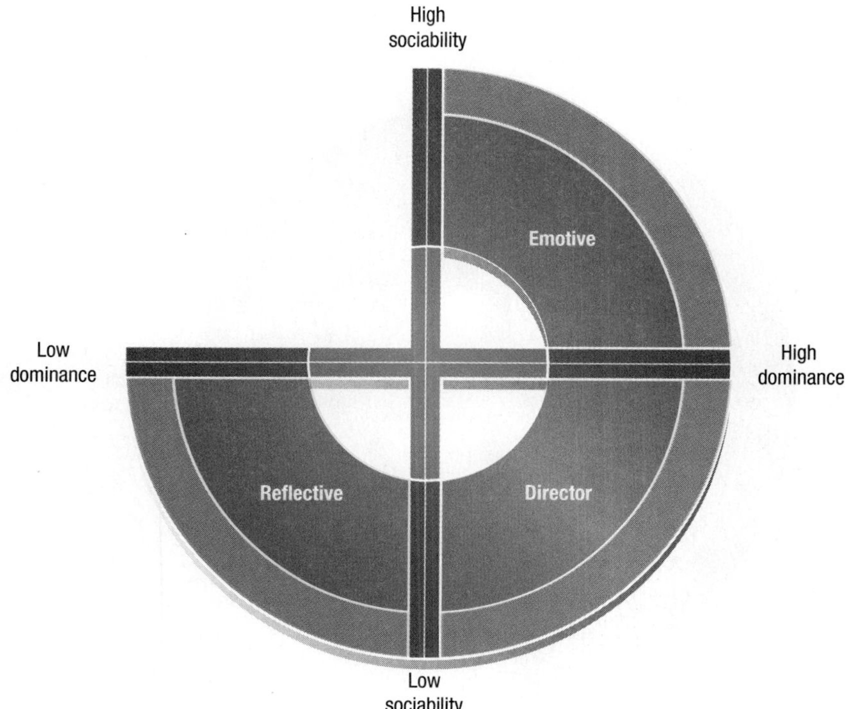

FIGURE 4.6

The Reflective style combines low dominance and low sociability.

In a selling situation, the Reflective customer does not want to move too fast. This person wants the facts presented in an orderly and unemotional manner and does not want to waste a lot of time socializing.

KEY WORDS FOR THE REFLECTIVE STYLE

Precise	Aloof	Serious
Deliberate	Scientific	Industrious
Questioning	Preoccupied	Stuffy
Disciplined		

Supportive Style

The upper left-hand quadrant shows a combination of low dominance and high sociability (Fig. 4.7). This communication style is called the **Supportive style** because these people find it easy to listen and usually do not express their views in a forceful manner. Former U.S. President Gerald Ford and the late Princess Diana; and entertainers Meryl Streep, Kevin Costner, Mary Tyler Moore, and Julia Roberts display the characteristics of the Supportive style.

Low visibility generally characterizes the lifestyle of Supportive people. They complete their tasks in a quiet, unassuming manner and seldom draw attention to what they have accomplished. In terms of assertiveness, persons with the Supportive style rank quite low. Someone who ranks high on the dominance continuum might view the

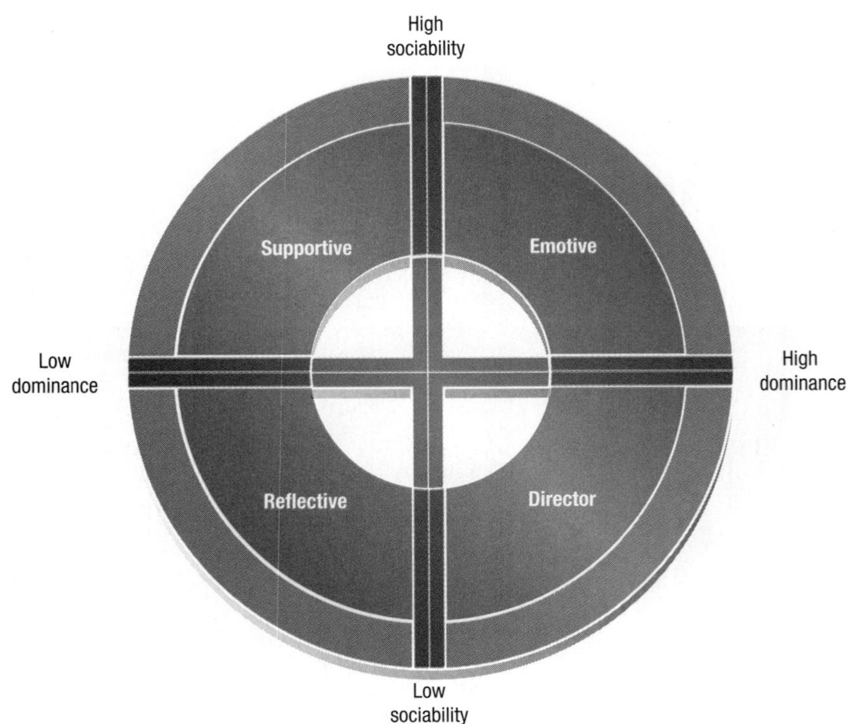

FIGURE | 4.7

The Supportive style combines low dominance and high sociability.

Supportive individual as being too easygoing. Other behaviors that commonly characterize the Supportive person follow:

1. *Gives the appearance of being quiet and reserved.* People with the Supportive behavioral style can easily display their feelings, but not in the assertive manner common to the Emotive individual.
2. *Listens attentively to other people.* In selling, good listening skills can be a real asset. This talent comes naturally to the Supportive person.
3. *Tends to avoid the use of power.* Whereas the Director may rely on power to accomplish tasks, the Supportive person is more likely to rely on friendly persuasion.
4. *Makes decisions in a thoughtful and deliberate manner.* The Supportive person usually takes longer to make a decision.

The late Princess Diana and Former President Gerald Ford display the characteristics of the supportive style. Persons with the supportive style are generally observed as warm, patient, and easygoing.

KEY WORDS FOR THE SUPPORTIVE STYLE

Lighthearted	Docile	Relaxed
Reserved	Patient	Compliant
Passive	Sensitive	Softhearted
Warm		

The nonverbal gestures displayed by this customer indicate a preference for the Reflective communication style. Persons who display the Reflective style are often observed as precise, industrious, and deliberate.

FIGURE | 4.8

The four basic communication styles have been used in a wide range of training programs. For comparison purposes the approximate equivalents to the four communication styles discussed in this chapter are listed.

Supportive (Manning/Reece) Amiable (Wilson Learning) Supportive-Giving (Stuart Atkins Inc.) Relater (People Smarts) Steadiness (Personal Profile System) Supportive (Disc Behavioral Style)	Emotive (Manning/Reece) Expressive (Wilson Learning) Adapting-Dealing (Stuart Atkins Inc.) Socializer (People Smarts) Influencing (Personal Profile System) Influencing (Disc Behavioral Style)
Reflective (Manning/Reece) Analytical (Wilson Learning) Conserving-Holding (Stuart Atkins Inc.) Thinker (People Smarts) Cautiousness/Compliance (Personal Profile System) Conscientious (Disc Behavioral Style)	Director (Manning/Reece) Driver (Wilson Learning) Controlling-Taking (Stuart Atkins Inc.) Director (People Smarts) Dominance (Personal Profile System) Dominance (Disc Behavioral Style)

Popularity of the Four-Style Model

We are endlessly fascinated by ourselves, and this helps explain the growing popularity of the four-style model presented in this chapter. To satisfy this insatiable appetite for information, many training and development companies offer training programs that present the four social or communication styles. Figure 4.8 features the approximate equivalents of the four styles presented in this chapter.

Determining Your Communication Style

You now have enough information to identify your own communication style. If your location on the dominance continuum is right of center and your position on the sociability continuum is below the center mark, you fall into the Director quadrant. If your location on the dominance continuum is left of center and your position on the sociability continuum is above the center mark, then your most preferred style is Supportive. Likewise, low dominance matched with low sociability forms the Reflective communication style, and high dominance matched with high sociability forms the Emotive style.

Of course, all of us display some characteristics of the Emotive, Director, Reflective, and Supportive communication styles. However, one of the four styles is usually predominant and readily detectable.[15]

Some people who study the communication-style model for the first time may initially experience feelings of frustration. They find it hard to believe that one's behavioral style tends to remain quite uniform throughout life. People often say, "I am a different person each day!" It is certainly true that we sometimes feel different from day to day, but our most preferred style tends to remain stable.

The Supportive person might say, "I sometimes get very upset and tell people what I am thinking. I can be a Director when I want to be!" There is no argument here. Just because you have a preferred communication style does not mean you never display the behavioral characteristics of another style. Some people use different styles in different contexts and in different relationships.[16] Reflective people sometimes display Emotive behavior, and Emotive people sometimes display Reflective behavior. We are saying that each person has one most preferred and habitually used communication style.

MINIMIZING COMMUNICATION-STYLE BIAS

Salespeople often make the mistake of focusing too much on the content of their sales presentation and not enough on how they deliver their message.[17] Communication-style bias is a barrier to success in selling. This form of bias is a common problem in sales work simply because salespeople deal with people from all four quadrants. You cannot select potential customers on the basis of their communication style. You must be able to develop a rapport with people from each of the four quadrants. When people of different styles work together but don't adjust to one another, serious problems can develop.[18]

How Communication-Style Bias Develops

To illustrate how communication-style bias develops in a sales situation, let us observe a sales call involving two people with different communication styles. Mary Wheeler entered the office of Dick Harrington with a feeling of optimism. She was sure that her product would save Mr. Harrington's company several hundred dollars a month. She had done her homework and was 99 percent certain that the sale would be closed. Thirty minutes after meeting Mr. Harrington she was walking out of his office without the order. What went wrong?

Mary Wheeler is an "all business" type who is a Director in terms of communication style. Her sales calls are typically fast paced and focused. She entered the office of Mr. Harrington, a new prospect, and immediately began to talk business. Mr. Harrington interrupted to ask if she wanted coffee. She declined the offer and continued her sales presentation. Mr. Harrington asked Mary if she enjoyed selling. After a quick glance at her watch, she responded by saying that selling was a rewarding career and then quickly returned to her sales presentation.

Mr. Harrington's communication style is Supportive. He feels uncomfortable doing business with strangers and likes slow-paced interactions with people. He felt tension when Mary failed to establish a social relationship. He also felt she was moving at a pace that was too fast. If she had spent a few minutes socializing with Mr. Harrington, his preferred approach to communication would have become apparent. The "all business" approach she used would be more appropriate for the Director or Reflective communication style.

Selling in Action

CLOSING THE SALE WITH STYLE FLEXING

Rich Goldberg, CEO of Warm Thoughts Communications, a New Jersey–based marketing communications company, sensed he was about to lose an important client. He met with his staff, and together they created a profile based on their knowledge of the client's communication style. It soon became apparent that there was a mismatch between the client and the salesperson who called on that person. The customer was low in sociability but high in dominance. The customer was also described as someone who needed facts and figures. The salesperson was working on relationship building, and this approach was agitating the client. Goldberg counseled his staff to keep conversations with this customer brief, use facts and figures frequently, and clearly spell out the company's commitment to the client.[b]

A salesperson who is highly adaptable can usually build a rapport with customers regardless of their communication style. Style flexibility is a sales strategy that can be learned.

Achieving Interpersonal Versatility

Personal selling has become more customer-focused than ever before, so every effort should be made to reduce the tension between the salesperson and customer. Dr. David Merrill, one of the early pioneers in the development of communication style instruments and training programs, uses the term **versatility** to describe our ability to minimize communication style bias.[19] Roger Wenschlag, author of *The Versatile Salesperson*, describes versatility as "the degree to which a salesperson is perceived as developing and maintaining buyer comfort throughout the sales process." *Adapting* to the customer's preferred communication style can enhance sales performance.[20]

Adaptive selling, is another term used to describe how salespeople use communication styles and versatility to manage their selling relationships. Roger Wenschlag, author of THE VERSATILE SALESPERSON describes versatility as "the degree to which a salesperson is perceived as developing and maintaining buyer comfort throughout the sales process." He goes on to state "that adapting *to the customer's preferred communication style can enhance sales performance."*

Mature and Immature Behavior

There is a mature and an immature side to each behavioral style. Let us examine the Emotive style to illustrate this point. People with this style are open, personable individuals who seem genuinely friendly. The natural enthusiasm displayed by the mature Emotive is refreshing. On the other hand, an Emotive person who is too talkative and too emotional may have difficulty building rapport with some customers; this is the immature side of the Emotive communication style.

You recall that we use the words *industrious* and *precise* to describe the Reflective style. These are words that apply to the mature side of the Reflective person. We also use the words *aloof* and *stuffy*. These words describe the immature side of the Reflective. The good news is that we all have the potential for developing the mature side of our communication style.

Customer Relationship Management with Technology

BEING PREPARED

Customer relationship management (CRM) software empowers a salesperson with information essential to continue a relationship. The software can be used to record, retain, and produce personal information including such factors as marital status, names and ages of children, and individual preferences. Before placing a call, the salesperson might review the database information to refresh her memory about the prospect. This can be especially helpful when preparing to talk with someone with a specific communication style. (See the exercise, Identifying Communication Styles, on p. 104 for more information.)

Strength–Weakness Paradox

It is a fact of life that your greatest strength can become your greatest weakness. If your most preferred style is Reflective, people are likely to respect your well-disciplined approach to life as one of your strengths. However, this strength can become a weakness if it is exaggerated. The Reflective person can be too serious, too questioning, and too inflexible. Robert Haas, former chairman of Levi Strauss & Company, is known for extraordinary (some say obsessive) attention to detail. Those who work with him say an offhand conversation can sound like a lecture. This Reflective, however, has the ability to flex his style. Levi's employees are fiercely loyal to Haas and describe him as compassionate to a fault.[21]

People with the Director style are open and frank. They express their true feelings in a direct manner. In most cases we appreciate candor, but we do not like to be around people who are too straightforward or too blunt in expressing their views. Steven Ballmer, CEO of Microsoft, was known as a very demanding executive during his early years with the company. His explosive temper was legendary and he often put the fear of God into his staff members. He once needed throat surgery because he yelled so much. Later he became more diplomatic and less domineering.[22] When people come across as *opinionated*, they tend to antagonize others. We should avoid pushing our strengths to the point of unproductive excess.[23]

To illustrate how strengths become weaknesses in excess, let us add more detail to our communication-style model. Note that it now features three zones that radiate out from the center (Fig. 4.9). These dimensions might be thought of as intensity zones.

Zone one People who fall within this zone display their unique behavioral characteristics with less intensity than those in zone two. The Emotive person, for example, is moderately high on the dominance continuum and moderately high on the sociability continuum. As you might expect, zone one communication styles are more difficult to identify because there is less intensity in both dimensions (dominance and sociability).

In his early years Steve Balmer, CEO of Microsoft, pushed his directive strengths to the point of excess. His explosive temper was legendary. In recent years, he has displayed greater adaptability and versatility, and is now observed as being more diplomatic and less domineering.

FIGURE | 4.9

The completed communication-style model provides important insights needed to manage the relationship process in selling.

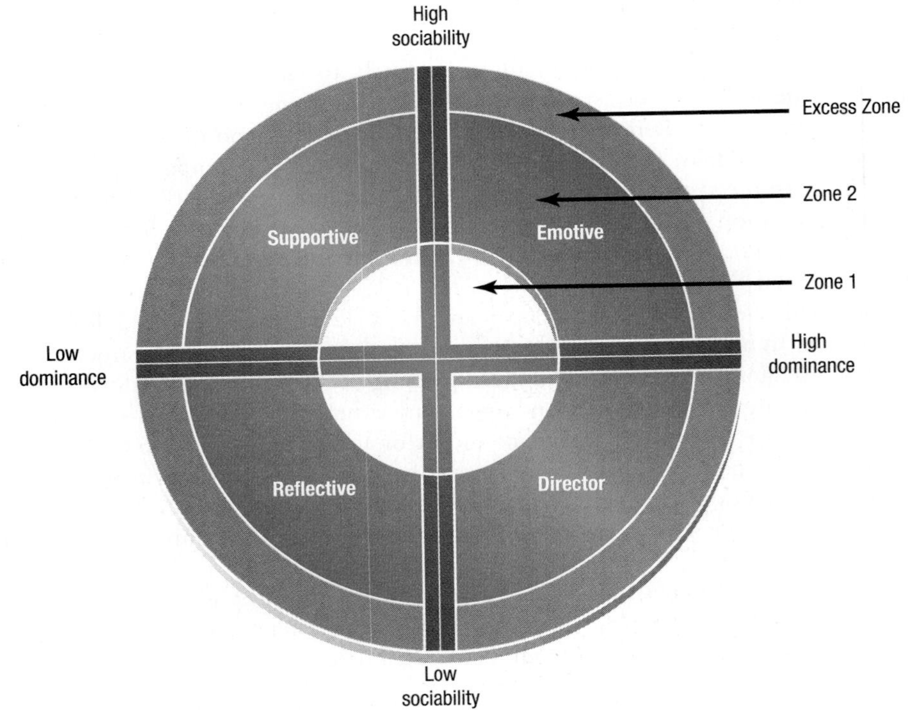

Zone two Persons who fall within this zone display their unique behavioral characteristics with greater intensity than persons in zone one. The zone two Reflective, for example, falls within the lowest quartile of the dominance continuum and the lowest quartile of the sociability continuum.

The boundary line that separates zone one and zone two should not be seen as a permanent barrier restricting change in intensity. Under certain circumstances we should abandon our most preferred style temporarily. A deliberate move from zone one to zone two, or vice versa, is called style flexing.

Excess zone The excess zone is characterized by a high degree of intensity and rigidity. When people allow themselves to drift into this zone, they become very inflexible, which is often interpreted by others as a form of bias toward their style. In addition, the strengths of the inflexible person become weaknesses. Extreme intensity in any quadrant is bound to threaten interpersonal relations.

We are apt to move into the excess zone and exaggerate our style characteristics under stressful conditions. Stress tends to bring out the worst in many people. Some of the behaviors that salespeople and customers may display when they are in the excess zone follow:

Emotive style

Expresses highly emotional opinions
Stops listening to the other person
Tries too hard to promote own point of view
Becomes outspoken to the point of being offensive

The excess zone is characterized by a high degree of intensity and rigidity. We are more apt to move into the excess zone under very stressful conditions.

Director style	Gets impatient with the other person Becomes dictatorial and bossy Does not admit being wrong Becomes extremely competitive
Reflective style	Becomes stiff and formal Is unwilling to make a decision Avoids displaying any type of emotion Is overly interested in detail
Supportive style	Agrees with everyone Is unable to take a strong stand Becomes overly anxious to win approval of others Tries to comfort everyone

Global Business Etiquette

DOING BUSINESS IN CANADA

Canada and the United States share a continent, a border, an auto racing series (CART), and a hockey league. Yet, it would be a mistake to assume that business practices are the same in both countries. Canada is a more formal country than the United States and businesspersons are less likely to be on a first-name basis. Jan Yager, author of *Business Protocol*, says, "The worst faux pas an American doing business with a Canadian might commit is to say to a Canadian, 'You and I, we Americans ...'." Canadians are proud of their country and do not think of themselves as Americans. Although Canada is bilingual and most businesspeople speak English, some provinces such as Quebec are French speaking. Carry business cards printed in both English and French.[C]

ACHIEVING VERSATILITY THROUGH STYLE FLEXING

Style flexing is the deliberate attempt to adjust one's communication style to accommodate the needs of the other person. You are attempting to communicate with the other person on her own "channel." Ron Willingham, in his book *Integrity Selling*, reminds us, "People are more apt to buy from you when they perceive you view the world as they view the world." [24] In a selling situation you should try to determine the customer's most preferred style and flex your own accordingly. If your preferred communication style is Director, and your customer is a Supportive, try to be more personal and warmer in your presentation. Once you know the customer's style, flexing your style can make the difference between a presentation that falters, and one that exceeds your expectations.[25] Style sensitivity and flexing add value to the sales process.

Throughout the preapproach, you should learn as much as possible about the customer and try to determine his style. Once you are in the presence of the customer, do not become preoccupied analyzing the person's style. If you are trying hard to analyze the person's style, you may not listen closely enough to what she is trying to tell you. If you are truly tuned into the customer, you can absorb many clues that help you determine her style. After the sales call, analyze the communication and record your findings. Use this information to plan your next contact with the customer.[26] Listen closely to the customer's tone of voice. A Supportive person sounds warm and friendly. The Reflective customer's voice is more likely to be controlled and deliberate. Pay particular attention to gestures. The Emotive individual uses his hands to communicate thoughts and ideas. The Director also uses gestures to communicate but is more controlled and less spontaneous. The Reflective person appears more relaxed, less intense. The Emotive individual is an open, impulsive communicator, while the Reflective person is quite cautious. The Supportive type is personal and friendly, while the Reflective person may seem difficult to get to know. To avoid relationship tension, consider the following suggestions for each of the four styles.

Selling to Emotives

If you are attempting to sell products to an Emotive person, keep in mind the need to move at a pace that holds the attention of the prospect. Be enthusiastic and avoid an approach that is too stiff and formal. Take time to establish goodwill and build relationships. Do not place too much emphasis on the facts and details. To deal effectively with Emotive people, plan actions that provide support for their opinions, ideas, and dreams.[27] Plan to ask questions concerning their opinions and ideas, but be prepared to help them get "back on track" if they move too far away from the topic. Maintain good eye contact and, above all, be a good listener.

Selling to Directors

The key to relating to Directors is to keep the relationship as businesslike as possible. Developing a strong personal relationship is not a high priority for Directors. In other words, friendship is not usually a condition for a good working relationship. Your goal is to be as efficient, time disciplined, and well organized as possible and to provide appropriate facts, figures, and success probabilities. Most Directors are goal-oriented people, so try to identify their primary objectives and then determine ways to support and help with these objectives. Early in the sales presentation, ask specific questions and carefully note responses. Look for specific points you can respond to when it is time to present your proposals.

Selling to Reflectives

The Reflective person responds in a positive way to a thoughtful, well-organized approach. Arrive at meetings on time and be well prepared. In most cases it is not necessary to spend a great deal of time building a social relationship. Reflective people appreciate a no-nonsense, businesslike approach to personal selling. Use specific questions that show clear direction. Once you have information concerning the prospect's needs, present your proposal in a slow, deliberate way. Provide as much documentation as possible. Do not be in too big a hurry to close the sale. Never pressure the Reflective person to make quick decisions.

Selling to Supportives

Take time to build a social relationship with the Supportive person. Spend time learning about the matters that are important in this individual's life—family, hobbies, and major interests. Listen carefully to personal opinions and feelings. Supportive individuals like to conduct business with sales personnel who are professional but friendly. Therefore, study their feelings and emotional needs as well as their technical and business needs. Throughout the presentation, provide personal assurances and support for their views. If you disagree with a Supportive person, curb the desire to disagree too assertively; Supportive people tend to dislike interpersonal conflict. Give them the time to comprehend your proposal. Patience is important.

As you develop your communication-style identification skills and become more adept at style flexing, you are better able to manage the relationship process. With these skills you should be able to open more accounts, sell more to established customers, and more effectively meet the pressures of competition. Most important, your customers will view you as a person better able to understand and meet their needs.

Word of Caution

It is tempting to put a label on someone and then assume the label tells you everything you need to know about that person. If you want to build an effective partnering type of relationship with a prospect, you must acquire additional information about that person. Stuart Atkins, a respected authority on communication styles and author of *The Name of Your Game*, says we should be careful not to use labels that make people feel boxed in, typecast, or judged. He believes we should not classify *people*; we should classify their *strengths* and *preferences* to act one way or another under certain circumstances.[28] You also must be careful not to let the label you place on yourself become the justification for your own inflexible behavior. Try not to let the label justify or reinforce why you are unable or unwilling to communicate effectively with others.

Summary

The primary objective of this chapter is to introduce *communication-style bias* and examine the implications of this concept for salespeople. Many sales are lost because salespeople fail to communicate effectively with the prospect. Communication-style bias contributes to this problem. Every salesperson who is willing to develop style sensitivity and engage in appropriate *style flexing* can minimize one of the most common barriers to success in selling.

The communication-style model is based on two continuums that assess two major aspects of human behavior: *dominance* and *sociability*. By combining them as horizontal and vertical continuums we create quadrants that define four styles of communication. We have called these the *Emotive*, *Director*, *Reflective*, and *Supportive styles*. With practice in observation you should be able to increase your sensitivity to other people's styles. Practice in self-awareness and self-control gives you the ability to flex your own style and helps others to feel at ease.

KEY TERMS

Communication style
Communication-style bias
Dominance
Adaptive selling
Sociability
Emotive style
Director style
Reflective style
Supportive style
Style flexing

REVIEW QUESTIONS

1. What is the meaning of the term communication style?
2. Describe the five major principles that support communication-style theory.
3. What are the benefits to the salesperson who understands communication styles?
4. What two dimensions of human behavior are used to identify communication style?
5. Describe the person who tends to be high in sociability.
6. What are the four communication styles? Develop a brief description of each of the styles.
7. What is the reaction of most people who study communication styles for the first time? Why does this reaction surface?
8. Define style flexing. How can style flexing improve sales productivity?
9. Explain the statement, "Your greatest strength can become your greatest weakness."
10. What suggestions would you give a salesperson who is planning to meet with a new prospect who displays the reflective communication style?

APPLICATION EXERCISES

1. Oprah Winfrey has been referred to as one of America's best talk show hosts.

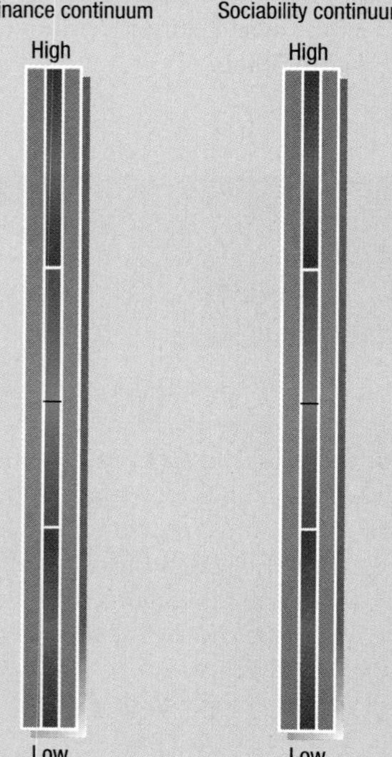

a. On the dominance continuum, mark where you think she belongs.
b. On the sociability continuum, mark where you believe she belongs.
c. Using the two continuums to form the communication-style model, what is Oprah Winfrey's communication style? Does Oprah Winfrey possess style flexibility? Explain this in terms of (i) the different styles of guests on her program and (ii) her apparent popularity with millions of people.
d. Describe Oprah Winfrey's personality using statements and terms from this chapter.
e. Have you ever observed Oprah Winfrey slipping into her excess zone? Explain.

2. Many salespeople, after being introduced to communication-style concepts attempt to categorize each of their customers. They report that their relationships become mutually more enjoyable and productive. Select four people whom you know quite well (supervisor, subordinate, customer, teacher, friend, or members of your sports team). Using the two behavioral continuums in this chapter, determine these people's communication styles. Using your own descriptive terminology in conjunction with terminology in this chapter, develop a descriptive behavioral profile of each of these people. Explain how this information can improve your relationship with each of these people.

3. Self-awareness is important in personal selling. As we get to know ourselves, we can identify barriers to acceptance by others. Once you have identified your most preferred communication style, you have taken a big step in the direction of self-awareness. If you have not yet determined your most preferred communication style, take a few minutes to complete the Dominance Indicator form (see Table 4.1) and the Sociability Indicator form (see Table 4.2). Follow the instructions provided on pp. 85–86. We have noted that self-ratings can sometimes be misleading because some people lack a high degree of self-awareness. They do not see themselves as others see them. Consider asking four or five people, co-workers for example, to assess your communication style using Tables 4.1 and 4.2. Then compare these ratings with your self-rating.

4. To develop your observation skills and your ability to identify communication styles, watch two or three television shows and attempt to identify the style of individuals portrayed on the screen. To develop your listening and observation skills, try this three-step approach:

   a. Cover the screen with a towel or newspaper and try to identify the style of one or two persons, using voice only.
   b. Turn down the volume, uncover the screen, and attempt to identify the style of the same persons, using visual messages only.
   c. Turn up the volume and make another attempt to identify the communication style of the persons portrayed on the screen. This time the identification process should be easier because you will be using sight and sound.

   These practice sessions will help you learn how to interpret the nonverbal messages that are so important in identifying another person's communication style. When you select TV shows, avoid situation comedies that often feature persons displaying exaggerated styles. You may want to watch a talk show or a news program that features interviews.

5. Myers-Briggs Personality Types and Jungian Personality Types are two very popular descriptions of the concepts in this chapter. Using your search engine, access the Internet sites that refer to these concepts. Type in "Jungian" + personality profiles to access the Jungian personality types. To access the Myers-Briggs types, type in "Myers-Briggs" + personality profiles. Does the number of queries indicate anything about

the validity and popularity of these theories? Examine specific queries about both of these theories. Do you see the relationship between these two theories and the material in this chapter? Each year about two and a half million Americans complete the Myers-Briggs Type Indicator (M.B.T.I.). Why is this psychological-assessment instrument so popular?

ROLE-PLAY EXERCISE

For the purpose of this role-play, assume the role of Ray Perkins who is described in the case problem on page 104. Ray is described as a quiet, amiable person who displays the Supportive communication style. You will meet with Ms. Maynard who is also described in the case problem. For the purpose of this role-play, assume that Ms. Maynard displays the characteristics of the Director communication style. Prior to the role-play, study the chapter material on style flexing and information on how to sell to persons with the Director communication style.

CRM APPLICATION EXERCISE

Identifying Communication Styles

The previous salesperson carefully recorded the communication styles of most of the people in the database and identified the prospects as Emotive, Director, Reflective, or Supportive. If you feel like talking to an Emotive, you can find them by selecting Lookup, Keyword, type "Emotive", check Notes, and press Enter. After searching, ACT! displays four records of people who Pat identified as Emotives. Print these notes by selecting Report, Contact Report, Active Lookup, Printer, and Enter. Using this information you have learned in this chapter, explain how you would use style flexing when working with these four clients.

CASE PROBLEM

Ray Perkins has been employed at Grant Real Estate for almost two years. Prior to receiving his real estate license, he was a property manager with a large real estate agency in another community. During his first year with Grant, he was assigned to the residential property division and sold properties totaling $825,000. He then requested and received a transfer to the commercial division.

Three months ago, Ray obtained a commercial listing that consisted of 26 acres of land near a growing residential neighborhood. The land is zoned commercial and appears to be ideally suited for a medium-sized shopping center. Ray prepared a detailed prospectus and sent it to Vera Maynard, president of Mondale Growth Corporation, a firm specializing in development of shopping centers. One week later he received a letter from Ms. Maynard requesting more information. Shortly after receiving Ray's response, Ms. Maynard called to set up an appointment to inspect the property. A time and date were finalized, and Ray agreed to meet her plane and conduct a tour of the property.

Ray is a quiet, amiable person who displays the Supportive communication style. Friends say that they like to spend time with him because he is a good listener.

Questions

1. If Ms. Maynard displays the characteristics of the Director communication style, how should Ray conduct himself during the meeting? Be specific as you describe those behaviors that would be admired by Ms. Maynard.
2. If Ms. Maynard wants to build a rapport with Ray Perkins, what behavior should she display?
3. It is not a good idea to put a label on someone and then assume the label tells us everything about the person. As Ray attempts to build a rapport with Ms. Maynard, what other personal characteristics should he try to identify?

Chapter Preview

When you finish reading this chapter, you should be able to

1. Discuss the influence of ethical decisions on relationships in selling
2. Describe the factors that influence the ethical conduct of sales personnel
3. Compare legal versus ethical standards
4. Discuss the influence of company policies and practices on the ethical conduct of salespeople
5. Explain how role models influence the ethical conduct of sales personnel
6. Explain how values influence behavior
7. Discuss guidelines for developing a personal code of ethics

CHAPTER 5

Ethics: The Foundation for Relationships in Selling

Edward D. Jones & Company, founded in 1871, has worked hard over the years to establish a corporate culture that rewards honest, ethical behavior at every level of the company. The St. Louis-based company has nearly 10,000 sales offices nationwide, making it the largest network of brokerage outlets in the United States. In late 2003, Edward Jones took out advertisements in newspapers across the nation, criticizing the "anything goes" approach that led to abuses in the mutual fund industry. One year later, the company agreed to pay a $75 million penalty to settle charges by the Securities and Exchange Commission (SEC) that it improperly encouraged its brokers to steer customers to seven "preferred" mutual fund groups. The investors were not told that Edward Jones was secretly paid hundreds of millions of dollars in compensation from the seven mutual fund companies. Brokers were awarded points toward trips to Caribbean and European resorts for selling customers mutual funds from the firms who were making cash payments to Edward Jones.[1]

One should not be too quick to find fault with Edward Jones' brokers who steered customers toward the "preferred" mutual funds. The practice of making payments to brokerage firms, called "revenue sharing," is common in the industry. Most brokers never considered what they were doing to be questionable. They know that any violation of the moral contract the company has with customers can risk the loss of goodwill built up over many years. In the interest of full disclosure, Edward Jones' brokers now report any revenue sharing to customers who purchase mutual funds.[2]

MAKING ETHICAL DECISIONS

Business ethics comprise principles and standards that guide behavior in the world of business. They help translate your values into appropriate and effective behaviors in your day-to-day life. Whether a specific behavior is right or wrong, ethical or unethical, is often determined by company leaders, customers, investors, the legal system, and the community.[3] Of course, the views of various stakeholders may be in conflict. Kickbacks and secret payoffs may be acceptable practices to the vice president of sales and marketing, yet may be viewed as unethical by members of the sales force, the board of directors, investors, and the general public.

There is no one uniform code of ethics for all salespeople. However, a large number of business organizations, professional associations, and certification agencies have established written codes. For example, the National Association of Sales Professionals (NASP) states that members must abide by its Standards of Professional Conduct[4] (Fig. 5.1).

Today, we recognize that character and integrity strongly influence relationships in personal selling. As noted in the previous chapter, character is composed of your personal standards of behavior, including your honesty and integrity. Your character is based on your internal values and the resulting judgments you make about what is right and what is wrong. The ethical decisions you make reflect your character strength.

We are indebted to Stephen Covey, author of *The Seven Habits of Highly Effective People*, for helping us better understand the relationship between character strength and success in personal selling. In his best-selling book, Covey says that there are basic principles that must be integrated into our character. One example is to always do what you say you are going to do. "As we make and keep commitments, even small commitments, we begin to establish an inner integrity that gives us the awareness of self-control and courage and strength to accept more of the responsibility for our own lives."[5] Fulfilling your commitments builds trust, and trust is the most important precondition of partnering.

NASP Standards of Professional Conduct

1. **Ethics and Professionalism:** I will act with the highest degree of professionalism, ethics, and integrity.
2. **Representation of Facts:** I will fairly represent the benefits of my products and services.
3. **Confidentiality:** I will keep information about my customers confidential.
4. **Conflicts of Interest:** I will disclose potential conflicts of interest to all relevant parties and, whenever possible, resolve conflicts before they become a problem.
5. **Responsibility to Clients:** I will act in the best interest of my clients, striving to present products and services that satisfy my customers' needs.
6. **Responsibility to Employer:** I will represent my employer in a professional manner and respect my employer's proprietary information.
7. **Responsibility to NASP Members:** I will share my lessons of experience with fellow NASP members and promote the interests of NASP.
8. **Responsibility to the Community:** I will serve as a model of good citizenship and be vigilant to the effects of my products and services on my community.
9. **Continuing Education:** I will maintain an ongoing program of professional development.
10. **Laws:** I will observe and obey all laws that affect my products, services, and profession.

FIGURE 5.1

This code of ethics serves as a foundation for a relationship strategy by members of the National Association of Sales Professionals (NASP).

Character Development

Colleges and universities are beginning to play a more active role in character development. Courses that focus on ethics are becoming quite common. When a new ethics course was developed at the University of Virginia, the faculty indicated that the purpose of the course is not to point out what is right and what is wrong. The course is designed to help students understand the consequences of their actions when they face an ethical dilemma.[6]

Despite a growing interest in business ethics, unethical behavior has become all too common. A survey conducted by *Newsweek* suggests that the current generation of workers may be more tolerant of deception. Many of those involved in the survey did not view lying and cheating as unacceptable.[7] Employees who are involved in unethical behavior often report that they were under pressure to act unethically or illegally on the job.

The Erosion of Character

As the past decade unfolded, many large, inflexible corporations were transformed into smaller, more nimble competitors. New economy thinking prevailed as business firms, large and small, worked hard to become lean, innovative, and profitable. We witnessed an almost unrelenting emphasis on earnings that was driven, in some cases, by executive greed. It was during this period that some of America's most respected companies began to cross the ethical divide.[8]

A company cannot enjoy long-term success unless its employees are honest, ethical, and uncompromising about values and principles. Yet many employees engage in dishonest practices that erode character. The collapse of Enron, the largest U.S. corporation ever to file for bankruptcy, can be traced to a culture that emphasized risk taking, personal ambition over teamwork, and earnings growth at any cost. The new economy depends on innovation and aggressive development of markets, but actions that weaken the moral contract with employees, customers, and shareholders can bring serious consequences. Let's examine some "half-truths" that have influenced the erosion of character in a business setting.

- *We are only in it for ourselves.* Some critics of today's moral climate feel that the current moral decline began when society's focus shifted from "what is right" to "what is right for me." In personal selling, this point of view can quickly subtract rather than add value to a relationship with the customer. Fortunately, there are many salespeople for whom integrity and self-respect are basic values. Darryl Ashley, a pharmaceutical representative for Eli Lilly Company, suspected that a pharmacist (a customer) was diluting chemotherapy drugs in order to increase profit margins. Ashley shared his suspicions with one of the cancer doctors who was purchasing the drug from the pharmacist. Tests indicated that the drug had been diluted.[9]
- *Corporations exist to maximize shareholder value.* In the past, corporations were more often viewed as *economic* and *social* institutions—organizations that served a balanced group of stakeholders. In recent years analysts, stock traders, CEOs, and the media have too often focused on a single standard of performance—share price.[10] Marjorie Kelly, editor of *Business Ethics*, says, "Managing a company solely for maximum share price can destroy both share price and the entire company."[11]

  Pressure to increase "numbers" led to sales abuses at WorldCom Incorporated. Some salespeople double-booked accounts in order to make their quota and collect increased commissions. The false reporting was identified by an internal company probe and the guilty sales representatives were fired.[12]

Selling in Action

HONESTY FROM A QUARTERBACK'S PERSPECTIVE

Jack Kemp, former National Football League quarterback, believes that sports can teach important moral lessons. Some of these lessons can be applied in personal selling. This is what he says about honesty:

> The importance of honesty colors all the rest of life. Why is truth so important? It is because respect, relationships, and unity all depend on truth. If you cannot be honest with people, you cannot have healthy relationships.

Kemp found that honesty was the foundation for harmony among team members. He says, "Without truth, I couldn't trust my teammates and they couldn't trust me."[a]

Each year *Fortune* publishes a list of the 100 best companies to work for in America. It is encouraging to note that most of these companies still say that employees represent their most important asset and the customer is still "king."

- *Companies need to be lean and mean.*[13] Downsizing has become a common practice even when the economy is strong. After the layoffs, companies must deal with serious problems of low morale and mistrust of management. Those employees who remain after a company reduces its ranks often feel demoralized, overworked, and fearful. The stress of long hours and a faster pace can result in quality losses and bad service

Character strength builds as we display loyalty, mutual commitment, and the pursuit of long-term goals. These are the qualities needed to build strong buyer-seller relationships.

Selling Is Everyone's Business

LIFE AFTER ENRON

Cary and Rachel Bryant, husband and wife, believed they had a bright future at Enron Corporation. Then the company filed for bankruptcy and they were terminated on the same day. Cary and Rachel immediately started sending out résumés and making phone calls. However, no one returned their calls. Finally, they decided to stop and reevaluate their careers. They decided that returning to the high-pressure corporate world was not a good idea. Cary decided to start a contracting company. In order to build his business he started making cold calls on people in the neighborhood. He often called on homeowners whose homes looked like they needed repair. His business began to grow and today Bryant Contractors (www.bryantcontractors.com) is doing well. Meanwhile, Rachel decided to begin selling a line of skin-care products she had developed prior to working for Enron. In the years ahead, Cary and Rachel will rely on their personal selling skills to grow their businesses.[b]

that alienate customers. Richard Sennett, author of *The Corrosion of Character*, says that the decline of character strength can be traced to conditions that have grown out of our fast-paced, high-stress, information-driven economy. He states that character strength builds in a climate that encourages loyalty, mutual commitment, and the pursuit of long-term goals.[14] These are the qualities needed to build strong buyer–seller relationships.

Today, many business firms are struggling to align their values, ethics, and principles with the expectations of their salespeople and their customers. The process of negotiating ethical standards and practices must be ongoing. Citigroup Incorporated, the world's largest financial services firm, is working hard to move beyond regulatory scandals. Charles Prince, Citigroup CEO, wants the company to better balance its "delivering-the-numbers" culture with a long-term attention to reputation. He readily admits that ". . . at times, our actions have put at risk our most precious commodity—the trust of our clients, the patience of our employees, and the faith of our shareholders."[15]

FACTORS INFLUENCING THE ETHICS OF SALESPEOPLE

In the field of personal selling, the temptation to maximize short-term gains by some type of unethical conduct is always present. Salespeople are especially vulnerable to moral corruption because they are subject to many temptations. A few examples follow:

The competition is using exaggerated claims to increase the sale of its product. Should you counteract this action by using exaggerated claims of your own to build a stronger case for your product?

You have visited the buyer twice, and each time the person displayed a great deal of interest in your product. During the last visit the buyer hinted that the order might be signed if you could provide a small gift. Your company has a long-standing policy that gifts are not to be given under any circumstances. What do you do?

Your sales manager is under great pressure to increase sales. At a recent meeting of the entire sales staff, this person said, "We have to hit our numbers no matter what it takes!" Does this emotional appeal change your way of dealing with customers?

During a recent business trip you met an old friend and decided to have dinner together. At the end of the meal you paid for the entire bill and left a generous tip. Do you now put these non-business-related expenses on your expense account?

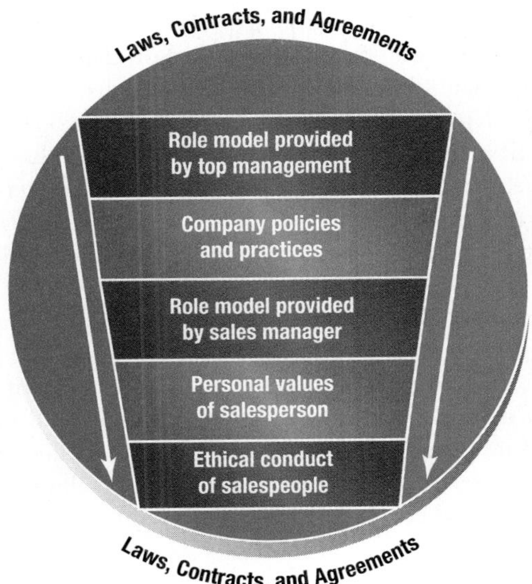

FIGURE | 5.2

Factors Determining the Ethical Behavior of Salespeople

These ethical dilemmas arise frequently in the field of selling. How do salespeople respond? Some ignore company policy, cast aside personal standards of conduct, and yield to the pressure. However, a surprising number of salespeople are able to resist. They are aided by a series of factors that help them distinguish right from wrong. Figure 5.2 outlines the forces that can help them deal honestly and openly with prospects at all times. Next we discuss each of these factors.

Top Management as Role Model

Ethical standards tend to filter down from the top of an organization. Employees look to company leaders for guidance. The organization's moral tone, as established by management personnel, is the most important single determinant of employee ethics. At Citigroup

Global Business Etiquette

DOING BUSINESS IN CHINA

China has entered the World Trade Organization and the leaders have promised to tear down the barriers that have frustrated foreign business representatives. This country provides a huge market for foreign brands. However, doing business in China begins with a careful study of Chinese business customs.

- Patience is critical when doing business in China. Avoid taking the initiative until you fully understand the rules.
- Business entertaining is frequently done banquet style. If you host a banquet, plan your menu carefully because foods have different meanings. You will be in complete control and no one will eat or drink until you give the signal. Toasting is a ritual in China.
- Chinese businesspeople do not make deals quickly. They prefer to spend time building relationships that will last for years. Harmony is important.
- When making introductions, the oldest and highest-ranking person is introduced first. Chinese bow slightly when greeting another person and the handshake follows.
- Gift giving is a complex process in China. Gifts should be given after all business transactions have been completed. Avoid gifts that suggest death in the Chinese culture: clocks, knife openers, and handkerchiefs, for example.[c]

Incorporated, Charles Prince is the person who must put ethics concerns on the front burner and make sure that the employees stay focused on that priority.[16]

In recent years, top management has often been guided by advice from professional service firms such as McKinsey & Company, Arthur Anderson, and Merrill Lynch and Company. Too often these firms are recommending strategies that result in quick, short-term gains. Alan M. Webber, who has been studying professional service firms for 20 years, notes, "They want the money right now." He says, "... to make the most money, you actually have to believe in the product or service you offer and care for the customers or clients whom you serve."[17]

Minnesota Life Insurance Company has been able to steer clear of scandal for more than 100 years by adopting a values-based management philosophy that rewards integrity and honesty. Success at the management level requires commitment to the company's core values. Managers must demonstrate their ability to infuse ethical values in their subordinates. The Minnesota Life Insurance Company mission and values statement includes the following statement on integrity: "We keep our promises. In all our activities, we adhere to the highest standards of ethical conduct."[18]

Company Policies and Practices

Company policies and practices can have a major impact on the ethical conduct of salespeople. Many employees do not have well-developed moral sensitivity and, therefore, need the guidance of ethics policies. These policies should cover distributor relations, customer service, pricing, product development, and related areas.[19]

Developing policy statements forces a firm to "take a stand" on various business practices. Distinguishing right from wrong can be a healthy activity for any organization. The outcome is a more clear-cut philosophy of how to conduct business transactions. Furthermore, the efforts of salespeople can be compromised by the unethical actions of their companies. Selling products for a company that condones unethical practices is very difficult for the salesperson who maintains high ethical standards.[20]

Mutual of Omaha Executives provide its employees with a carefully worded document entitled "Values for Success." Several of these values form the foundation for a corporate culture that encourages ethical behavior:[21]

- **Openness and Trust** We encourage an open sharing of ideas and information, displaying a fundamental respect for each other as well as our cultural diversity.
- **Honesty and Integrity** We are honest and ethical with others, maintaining the highest standards of personal and professional conduct.
- **Customer-Focus** We never lose sight of our customers, and constantly challenge ourselves to meet their requirements even better.

Most marketing companies provide salespeople with guidelines in such areas as sharing confidential information, reciprocity, bribery, gift giving, entertainment, and business defamation.

Sharing Confidential Information

Personal selling, by its very nature, promotes close working relationships. Customers often turn to salespeople for advice. They disclose confidential information freely to someone they trust. It is important that salespeople preserve the confidentiality of the information they receive.

It is not unusual for a customer to disclose information that may be of great value to a competitor. This might include the development of new products, plans to expand into new markets, or anticipated changes in personnel. A salesperson may be tempted to share

Salepeople representing The St. Paul Property and Liability Insurance Company (www.stpaul.com) can be proud of the firm's record of high ratings.

confidential information with a representative of a competing firm. This breach of confidence might be seen as a means of gaining favor. In most cases this action backfires. The person who receives the confidential information quickly loses respect for the salesperson. A gossipy salesperson seldom develops a trusting relationship with a customer.

Reciprocity

Reciprocity is a mutual exchange of benefits, as when a firm buys products from its own customers. Some business firms actually maintain a policy of reciprocity. For example, the manufacturer of commercial sheets and blankets may purchase hotel services from firms that use its products.

Source: *The New Yorker,* May 3, 2005, p. 48.

"Now we'll all close our eyes and cover our ears, and the person who took the four hundred and twenty-eight million dollars will put it back."

Is there anything wrong with the "you scratch my back and I'll scratch yours" approach to doing business? The answer is sometimes yes. In some cases, the use of reciprocity borders on commercial blackmail. Salespeople have been known to approach firms that supply their company and encourage them to buy out of obligation. Reciprocity agreements are illegal when one company pressures another company to join in the agreement.

A business relationship based on reciprocity has other drawbacks. There is the ever-present temptation to take such customers for granted. A customer who buys out of obligation may take a backseat to customers who were won in the open market.

Bribery

The book, *Arrogance and Accords: The Inside Story of the Honda Scandal,* describes one of the largest commercial corruption cases in U.S. history. Over a 15-year period, Honda officials received more than $50 million in cash and gifts from dealers anxious to obtain fast-selling Honda cars and profitable franchises. Eighteen former Honda executives were convicted of obtaining kickbacks; most went to prison.[22]

In some cases, a bribe is wrong from a legal standpoint. In almost all cases, the bribe is wrong from an ethical point of view. However, bribery does exist, and a salesperson must be prepared to cope with it. It helps to have a well-established company policy to use as a reference point.

Salespeople who sell products in foreign markets need to know that giving bribes is viewed as an acceptable business practice in some cultures. However, bribes or payoffs may violate the U.S. Foreign Corrupt Practices Act (FCPA). Lucent Technologies Incorporated dismissed two high ranking executives in China after it found potential violations of the FCPA.[23]

Gift Giving

Gift giving is a common practice in America. However, some companies do maintain a "no gift" policy. Many companies report that their policy is either no gifts or nothing of real value. Some gifts, such as advertising novelties, planning calendars, or a meal, are of limited value and cannot be construed as a bribe or payoff.

There are some gray areas that separate a gift from a bribe. Most people agree that a token of insignificant price, such as a pen imprinted with a company logo or a desk calendar, is appropriate. These types of gifts are meant to foster goodwill. A bribe, on the other hand, is an attempt to influence the person receiving the gift.

Personal selling, by its nature, promotes close working relationships. It is important that salespeople preserve the confidentiality of information they receive. Violation of this ethical responsibility will quickly erode a relationship with the customer.

Are there right and wrong ways to handle gift giving? The answer is yes. The following guidelines are helpful to any salesperson who is considering giving gifts to customers:

1. Do not give gifts before doing business with a customer. Do not use the gift as a substitute for effective selling methods.
2. Never convey the impression you are "buying" the customer's business with gifts. When this happens, the gift becomes nothing more than a bribe.
3. When gift giving is done correctly, the customer clearly views it as symbolic of your appreciation—a "no strings attached" goodwill gesture.
4. Be sure the gift is not a violation of the policies of your firm or of your customer's firm. Some firms do not allow employees to accept gifts at all. Other firms place a dollar limit on a gift's value.

In summary, if you have second thoughts about giving a gift, do not do it. When you are sure some token is appropriate, keep it simple and thoughtful.

Entertainment

Entertainment is a widespread practice in the field of selling and may be viewed as a bribe by some people. The line dividing gifts, bribes, and entertainment is often quite arbitrary.

Salespeople must frequently decide how to handle entertaining. A few industries see entertainment as part of the approach used to obtain new accounts. This is especially true when competing products are nearly identical. A good example is the cardboard box industry. These products vary little in price and quality. To win an account may involve knowing whom to entertain and how to entertain.

Entertainment is a highly individualized process. One prospect might enjoy a professional football game, while another would be impressed most by a quiet meal at a good restaurant. The key is to get to know your prospect's preferences. How does the person spend leisure time? How much time can the person spare for entertainment? You need to answer these and other questions before you invest time and money in entertainment.

Business Defamation

Salespeople frequently compare their product's qualities and characteristics with those of a competitor during the sales presentation. If such comparisons are inaccurate, are misleading, or slander a company's business reputation, such conduct is illegal. Competitors have sued hundreds of companies and manufacturer's representatives for making slanderous statements while selling.

What constitutes business defamation? Steven M. Sack, coauthor of *The Salesperson's Legal Guide*, provides the following examples:

1. *Business slander.* This arises when an unfair and untrue oral statement is made about a competitor. The statement becomes actionable when it is communicated to a third party and can be interpreted as damaging the competitor's business reputation or the personal reputation of an individual in that business.
2. *Business libel.* This may be incurred when an unfair and untrue statement is made about a competitor in writing. The statement becomes actionable when it is communicated to a third party and can be interpreted as damaging the company.
3. *Product disparagement.* This occurs when false or deceptive comparisons or distorted claims are made concerning a competitor's product, services or property.[24]

Use of the Internet

Use of the Internet offers salespeople many advantages, but it can also create a number of ethical dilemmas. For example, e-mail abuse has become a modern-day problem because some employees forget that their employer owns the e-mail system. E-mail messages that contain inflammatory or abusive content, embarrassing gossip, or breaches of confidentiality can lead to legal liabilities. A growing number of companies are developing policies that define permissible uses of their e-mail system.[25]

Some resourceful salespeople have created their own Web sites to alert, attract, or support clients. The rise of these "extranets" has created some problems because they often function outside of the company's jurisdiction. What should top management do if a top salesperson encourages her customers to participate in a special Web auction for a backlogged product? What if the salesperson makes exaggerated claims about a new product? Every marketing firm needs to carefully monitor the development and use of extranets.[26]

The effectiveness of company policies as a deterrent to unethical behavior depends on two factors. The first is the firm's attitude toward employees who violate these policies. If violations are routinely ignored, the policy's effect soon erodes. Second, policies that influence personal selling need the support of the entire sales staff. Salespeople should have some voice in policy decisions; they are more apt to support policies they have helped develop.

Sales Manager as Role Model

The salesperson's actions often mirror the sales manager's behavior and expectations. This is not surprising when you consider the relationship between salespeople and their supervisors. They look to their supervisors for guidance and direction. The sales manager is generally the company's closest point of contact with the sales staff. This person is usually viewed as the chief spokesperson for top management.

Sales managers generally provide new salespeople with their first orientation to company operations. They are responsible for interpreting company policy. On a continuing basis, the sales manager monitors the salesperson's work and provides important feedback concerning conduct. If a salesperson violates company policy, it is usually the sales manager who is responsible for administering reprimands. If the moral fiber of a sales force begins to break down, the sales manager must shoulder a great deal of responsibility.

Sales managers influence the ethical behavior of salespeople by virtue of what they say and what they do.

Sales managers influence the ethical behavior of salespeople by virtue of what they say and what they do. From time to time, managers must review their expectations of ethical behavior. Salespeople are under continuous pressure to abandon their personal ethical standards to achieve sales goals. Values such as integrity and honesty must receive ongoing support from the sales manager. The role of the sales manager will be discussed in more detail in Chapter 17.

Salesperson's Personal Values

Ann Kilpatrick, a sales representative in the transportation industry, encountered an unexpected experience when entertaining a potential client. The client said, "Let's go to Johnny's." She was not familiar with Johnny's, but on arrival discovered it was a raunchy bar. Kilpatrick related that she sat there for five minutes and then said, "This is not what I was expecting. This is a sleazy place. Let's go somewhere else where we can talk." She was not willing to compromise her personal values to win a new account.[27]

Values represent the ultimate reasons people have for acting as they do. Values are your deep personal beliefs and preferences that influence your behavior. To discover what really motivates you, carefully examine what you value.[28] Values serve as a foundation for our attitudes, and our attitudes serve as a foundation for our behavior (Fig. 5.3). We do not adopt or discard values quickly. In fact, the development and refinement of values is a lifelong process.

Customers have a very negative view of salespeople who lack integrity. Yet, the temptation to lie about a product's features or benefits grows when you are trying to meet sales quotas. John Craig, a pharmacist at Hancock Drugs in Scottsburg, Indiana, describes a meeting with a pushy sales representative employed by a pharmaceutical company.

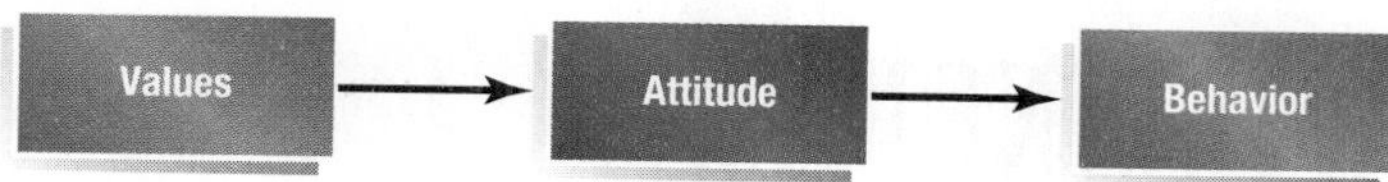

FIGURE 5.3

The Relationship of Values, Attitudes, and Behavior

The salesperson emphasized the wonders of a powerful, expensive painkiller but failed to describe its side effects. Craig said, "He was very pushy at the beginning," and this behavior revealed a character flaw.[29]

Values Conflict

Values help us establish our own personal standards concerning what is right and what is wrong. Ron Willingham, author of *Integrity Selling for the 21st century*, says, "Selling success is more an issue of who you are than what you know."[30] A salesperson's ethics and values contribute more to sales success than do techniques or strategies. Some salespeople discover a values conflict between themselves and their employer. If you view your employer's instructions or influence as improper, you have three choices:

1. Ignore the influence of your values and engage in the unethical behavior. The end result is likely to be a loss of self-respect and a feeling of guilt. When salespeople experience conflicts between their actions and values, they also feel a loss of confidence and energy.[31] Positive energy is the result of creating value for the customer. Negative energy is experienced when salespeople fail to honor and embrace their ethical values.
2. Voice strong opposition to the practice that is in conflict with your value system. Take a stand and state your beliefs. When ethical infractions occur, it's best to bring them up internally and try to influence decisions made by your peers or superiors. In some cases, doing the right thing may not be popular with others. Price Pritchett, the author of *The Ethics of Excellence*, says, "Not everybody will be on your side in your struggle to do the right thing."[32]
3. Refuse to compromise your values and be prepared to deal with the consequences. This may mean leaving the job. It also may mean that you will be fired.

Ron Willingham says a salesperson's ethics and values contribute more to sales success than do techniques and strategies.

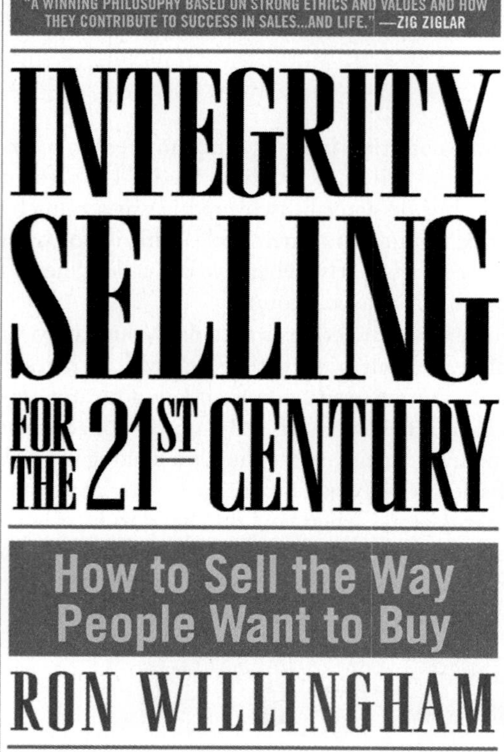

Salespeople face ethical problems and decisions every day. In this respect they are no different from the doctor, the lawyer, the teacher, or any other professional. Ideally, they make decisions on the basis of the values they hold.

Laws, Contracts, and Agreements

Take another look at Figure 5.2 (page 111) and you notice that all of the key elements, personnel and policies, are influenced by laws, contracts, and agreements. Everyone involved in sales and marketing is guided by legal as well as ethical standards. We live in a society in which the legal system plays a key role in preventing people from engaging in unethical behavior.

Laws

The specific obligations imposed by government on the way business operates take the form of *statutes*, laws passed by Congress or state legislatures. Some of the most common laws deal with price competition, credit reporting, debt collection practices, contract enforcement, and land sales disclosure. The Uniform Commercial Code (UCC) is a major law influencing sales throughout the United States (see Table 5.1). The UCC is a legal guide to a wide range of transactions between the seller and the buyer. This law has been adopted throughout the United States and, therefore, has implications for most salespeople.

A majority of the states have passed legislation that establishes a cooling-off period during which the consumer may void a contract to purchase goods or services. Although the provisions of **cooling-off laws** vary from state to state, their primary purpose is to give

TABLE | 5.1 UNIFORM COMMERCIAL CODE DEFINES LEGAL SIDE OF SELLING

Any list of the major developments in American law would have near its top the adoption of the Uniform Commercial Code (UCC), a body of statutes that replaces several areas of business law formerly covered individually by each state's common law of contracts.

The Uniform Commercial Code (UCC) is the source of the major laws influencing sales throughout the United States. Several areas featured in the UCC focus directly on the seller–buyer relationship. Some of the primary areas follow:

1. *Definition of a sale.* The code defines the legal dimensions of a sale. It clearly states that salespeople have the authority to legally obligate the company they represent.
2. *Warranties and guarantees.* The code distinguishes between express warranties and implied warranties. Express warranties are those that are described by the express language of the seller. Implied warranties are the obligations imposed by law on the seller that are not assumed in express language.
3. *Salesperson and reseller.* In many cases, the salesperson has resellers as customers or prospects. Salespeople must be aware of their employer's obligations to the reseller.
4. *Financing of sales.* Often salespeople work for firms that are directly involved in financing products or services or in arranging such financing from outside sources. A salesperson needs to be familiar with the legal aspects of these credit arrangements.
5. *Product consignment.* In some cases, goods are delivered to the buyer, but the title remains with the seller. This type of transaction can become complicated if the goods have a limited life span. Depreciation may occur with the passing of time. Salespeople should be familiar with the company's rights in cases in which goods are sold on consignment.

customers an opportunity to reconsider a buying decision made under a salesperson's persuasive influence. Many laws are designed to deal specifically with sales made in the consumer's home. For example, the Federal Trade Commission (FTC) established the National Do Not Call Registry in an attempt to reduce the number of telemarketing calls.

Contracts and Agreements

The word *contract* may bring to mind the familiar multipage, single-spaced documents that no ordinary person seems able to understand. In fact, contracts can be oral or written. A **contract** is simply a promise or promises that the courts will enforce. Oral contracts are enforceable, but written contracts are preferable. They reduce the possibility of disagreement and the courts give them great weight in a lawsuit. A written contract can consist of a sales slip, a notation on a check, or any other writing that evidences the promises that the parties made.[33]

Salespeople are sometimes the legal representatives of their company and, therefore, must be careful when signing written contracts. They often oversee contracts with customers, suppliers, and resellers. Salespeople also frequently sign employment contracts at the time they are hired. Most of these agreements include a noncompete clause. One of the most common clauses, a noncompete clause prohibits salespeople from joining a competing firm for a year after they leave. Most clauses are legally binding even when an employee's position is cut. Employers see employment contracts as an effective way to protect intellectual property, customer lists, and other resources an employee might take to a competing firm.[34]

Many companies are learning that resolving legal disputes can be very costly and time consuming. Resolving a dispute in the courts can sometimes take several years. A serious effort to prevent unethical activities can prevent costly litigation.

Ethics Beyond the Letter of the Law

Too often people confuse ethical standards with legal standards. They believe that if you are not breaking the law, then you are acting in an ethical manner.[35] A salesperson's ethical sense must extend beyond the legal definition of what is right and wrong. To view ethics only in terms of what is legally proper encourages the question, "What can I get by with?" A salesperson must develop a personal code of ethics that extends beyond the letter of the law.

A PERSONAL CODE OF ETHICS THAT ADDS VALUE

Many people considering a career in selling are troubled by the thought that they may be pressured into compromising their personal standards of right and wrong. These fears may be justified. The authors of *The Ethical Edge*, a book that examines organizations that have faced moral crises, contend that business firms have given too little thought to the issue of helping employees to function ethically within organizations.[36] Many salespeople wonder if their own ethical philosophy can survive in the business world. These are some of their questions:

"Can a profitable business and good ethics coexist?"

"Are there still business firms that value adherence to high ethical standards?"

"Is honesty still a valued personal trait in the business community?"

It is becoming more difficult to provide a concise yes or no answer to these questions. We read about the unethical use of gifts and bribes by corporate officials. Investigations of the Medicaid program turned up overbilling and other unethical behaviors by

Customer Relationship Management with Technology

EXERCISING CARE WITH CRM DATA

Customer relationship management systems enable you to collect information about people with whom you maintain relationships, including the taking of notes. It is a good practice to record more than basic transaction information, such as personal details about your customers. Reviewing your observations about the customers' behavior and your recording of their statements can help you understand them and their needs. Rereading their comments about ethical issues can assist you in assessing the value of maintaining a business relationship with them.

To be fair, it is important to record only the facts concerning your observations, not necessarily your conclusions. Information in an electronic database can last a long time and, for reasons such as litigation or company acquisitions, can be "mobile." This means that others may form an opinion about your customer, based on your recorded observations, with potential detrimental consequences for your customer. Because the customer may not be aware of the existence of the information in your database, that person does not have a fair opportunity to correct any erroneous conclusions. Another reason to carefully record only the facts is the possibility that the information may be read by the customer. For example, there are instances in which a customer later joined the sales organization and gained access to the customer relationship management (CRM) system.

Most CRM systems contain scheduling functions, which means that you can set aside time on your calendar to attend meetings, make phone calls, and perform tasks. The scheduling tools usually include alarms, which remind you that a deadline is approaching. The disciplined use of these features can help you get tasks done on time. Taking advantage of the system's reminder tools can be especially important when it involves fulfilling your commitments. The system can help you build trust by reminding you to always do what you said you would do. (See the exercise, Preparing Mailing Labels with CRM, on p. 125 for more information.)

doctors, pharmacists, and nursing home operators. Reports from colleges and universities indicate that cheating is becoming more common. Even some of our most respected political leaders have been guilty of tax fraud, accepting illegal campaign contributions, and accepting payments for questionable favors. We are tempted to ask, "Is everybody doing it?"

In the field of athletic competition, the participants rely heavily on a written set of rules. The referee or umpire is ever present to detect rule violations and assess a penalty. In the field of personal selling, there is no universal code of ethics. However, some general guidelines can serve as a foundation for a personal code of business ethics.

1. *Personal selling must be viewed as an exchange of value.* Salespeople who maintain a value focus are searching for ways to create value for their prospects or customers. This value may take the form of increased productivity, greater profit, enjoyment, or security. The value focus motivates the salesperson to carefully identify the prospects' wants and needs.[37] Salespeople who accept this ethical guideline view personal selling as something you do *for* customers, not something you do *to* customers. The role of the salesperson is to diagnose buyer needs and determine if value can be created. Always be prepared to add value.
2. *Relationship comes first, task second.* Sharon Drew Morgan, author of *Selling with Integrity*, says that you can't sell a product unless there is a level of comfort between you and the prospect. She encourages salespeople to take the time to create a level of comfort, rapport, and collaboration that encourages open communication.[38] Placing task before relationship is based on the belief that the salesperson knows more than

Personal selling must be viewed as an exchange of value. Salespeople who accept this ethical guideline view personal selling as something you do for customers, not something you do to customers.

the customer. Morgan reminds us, "The buyer has the answers, the seller has the questions."[39] These answers surface only when the buyer–seller relationship is characterized by rapport and trust.

3. *Be honest with yourself and with others.* To achieve excellence in terms of ethical practices, you have to believe that everything you do counts. Tom Peters in *Thriving on Chaos* said, "Integrity may be about little things as much as or more than big ones."[40] Integrity is about accuracy in completing your expense account. There is always the temptation to inflate the expense report for personal gain. Integrity is also about avoiding the temptation to stretch the truth, to exaggerate, or to withhold information. Paul Ekman, author of *Telling Lies*, says that withholding important information is one of the primary ways of lying.[41] A complete and informative sales presentation may include information concerning the product's limitations. If you let your character and integrity be revealed in the little things, others can see you as one who acts ethically in all things. Any violation of honesty, however small, dilutes your ethical strength, leaving you weaker for the big challenges you will face sooner or later.[42]

The Trust Factor

Everyone involved in personal selling must work hard to build relationships based on trust. When the customer and the salesperson trust each other, they will usually find ways to form a productive partnership. Although trust is an essential element of every sale, the meaning of trust changes with the type of sale.[43]

- *Trust in Transactional Sales.* The primary customer focus in this type of sale is trust in the product. Is the product reliable? Is the product priced as low as possible? Can the product be delivered in a timely fashion? The transactional buyer may purchase a product from a salesperson they do not feel totally comfortable with if it meets their purchase criteria.
- *Trust in Consultative Sales.* In a consultative sale, the customer focus shifts from the product to the person who sells the product. The consultative buyer is thinking,

"Can I trust this salesperson to identify my problem and offer me one or more solutions?" Customers involved in a consultative sale usually do not separate the product from the person selling it. They want to do business with a salesperson who displays such positive qualities as warmth, empathy, genuineness, competence, and integrity.

- *Trust in Strategic Alliance Sales.* The strategic alliance buyer wants to do business with an institution that can be trusted. This buyer looks beyond the well-qualified salesperson and assesses the entire organization. A strategic alliance customer will not feel comfortable partnering with a company whose values differ greatly from their own. Ethical accountability will greatly influence the way an alliance partner is judged and valued.

Trust exists when we strongly believe in the integrity, ability, and character of a person or an organization. Although trust is an intangible, it is at the very core of all meaningful relationships. Trust is quickly lost and slowly won.[44]

Summary

At the beginning of this chapter we noted that business ethics comprise principles and standards that guide behavior in the world of business. Ethics are not legally constituted guidelines. To consider only what is legally right and wrong limits our perception of ethical conduct. Laws alone do not bring a halt to unethical selling practices.

Salespeople can benefit from the stabilizing influence of good role models. Although top management personnel are usually far removed from day-to-day selling activities, they can have a major impact on salespeople's conduct. Dishonesty at the top of an organization causes an erosion of ethical standards at the lower echelons. Sales managers provide another important role model. They interpret company policies and help establish guidelines for acceptable and unacceptable selling practices.

Company policies and practices can have a strong influence on the ethical conduct of salespeople. These policies often help salespeople cope with ethical conflicts.

Finally, salespeople must establish their own standards of personal conduct. They must decide how best to serve their company and build strong partnerships with their customers. The pressure to compromise one's ethical standards surfaces almost daily. The temptation to take the easy road to achieve short-term gains is always present. The primary deterrent is a strong sense of right and wrong. Three general guidelines that can serve as a foundation for a personal code of ethics are presented. We also explained that the meaning of trust changes with the type of sale.

We strongly support the premise that bad ethics is bad business and unethical sales practices will ultimately destroy relationships with customers. Anyone who relies on unethical sales practices cannot survive in the selling field very long. These practices undermine the company's reputation and ultimately reduce profits.

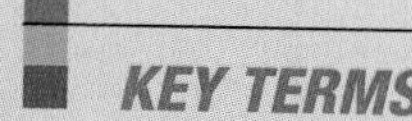

KEY TERMS

Business ethics
Reciprocity
Values
Cooling-off laws
Contract

REVIEW QUESTIONS

1. What is the definition of *business ethics* Why is this topic receiving so much attention today?
2. Carefully review the Standards of Professional Conduct developed by the National Association of Sales Professionals (NASP). Select the three standards you feel would present the greatest challenge to salespeople. Explain your answer.
3. How does business slander differ from business libel?
4. What major factors help influence salespeople's ethical conduct?
5. What is the Uniform Commercial Code? Why is it needed?
6. Why must a salesperson's ethical sense extend beyond the legal definition of what is right and wrong?
7. Explain why the sales manager plays such an important role in influencing the ethical behavior of salespeople.
8. A company policy on ethics should cover several major areas. What are they?
9. Is it ever appropriate to give gifts to customers? Explain.
10. List and describe three guidelines used as a foundation of a self-imposed code of business ethics.

APPLICATION EXERCISES

1. You find that you have significantly overcharged one of your clients. The error was discovered when you received payment. It is unlikely that the customer or your company will become aware of the overcharge. Because of this error, the company realized a higher net profit on the sale. Your commissions are based on this profit. What, if anything, will you do about the overcharge?

2. Access the National Association of Sales Professionals Web site at www.nasp.com. Click on the sales certification link and examine the steps to becoming a certified sales professional. Also click on the Registry of Accredited Salespeople and the Directory of Members. Examine the backgrounds of several members of the NASP. Reviewing the Standards of Professional Conduct printed in this chapter, discuss your views on the impact professional certification has on the ethical behavior of salespeople. Do you think the designation CPSP would affect the impression a customer might have of a salesperson?
3. You work for a supplier of medical equipment. Your sales manager informs you that he wants you to capture a certain hospital account. He also tells you to put on your expense account anything it costs to secure the firm as a client. When you ask him to be more specific, he tells you to use your own judgment. Up to this time you have never questioned your sales manager's personal code of ethics. Make a list of the items you believe can be legitimately charged to the company on your expense account.
4. For some time your strongest competitor has been making untrue derogatory statements about your product and about your company. You know for a fact that her product is not as good as yours. Yet hers has a higher price. Several of your best customers have confronted you with these charges. Describe how you plan to answer them.
5. Sales managers must approve expense reports turned in by members of the sales force. Assume the role of sales manager for a sales force that includes 12 salespeople who

travel frequently and average about two overnight trips each week. Recently you noticed that the expense reports turned in by two of your salespeople seem quite high. You suspect that these salespeople are padding their expense reports. What steps should you take to determine if cheating is occurring? How can a sales manager prevent the padding of expense reports?

ROLE-PLAY EXERCISE

This morning you met with a customer who has purchased office supplies from you for almost three years. You are quite surprised when she says, "I am prepared to place a $10,500 order, but you must match an offer I received from a competitor." She then explains that the competitor is offering *new* customers a seven-day trip to Disney World in Orlando if they place an order over $10,000. All expenses will be paid. What would you do?

Prepare to role-play your response with another student. Review the material in this chapter, paying special attention to ways you can add value and build long-term relationships with ethical decision making.

CRM APPLICATION EXERCISE

Preparing Mailing Labels with CRM

Access the ACT! software and select Report, Other. From the list of mailing label formats, choose avry5160, and press OK. In the Prepare Report window, pick Active Group and Document and press OK. The mailing information for each contact will be displayed on the screen. Select File, Print and print this list.

A friend of yours is a salesperson with a firm that installs the cables used to connect network components, a service that your company does not offer. Your friend wants to know if you will share the customer list that you printed. What should be your response?

CASE PROBLEM

Dana Davis dropped into the store's receiving department of Regina Steel Fabricators, one of the company's oldest and best accounts. Dana had been called by Tyler Hensman, their senior purchasing person, to inspect the last shipment of structural tubing sold them. According to Tyler, when the tubing was sheared to the lengths required, the shear had dimpled the ends of the tubes, and the dimples had not been removed as requested. The tubes were, therefore, not perfectly round, and the casters that were to fit into the ends would not do so without considerable effort. Davis was puzzled by the quality control problem. The company has a long-standing policy of not shipping a product to a customer unless it has passed inspection by the quality control staff.

Dana arrived just after lunch, and while waiting for Gary Anderson, the store's supervisor, noticed that there was a large shipment of stainless steel bolts and nuts sitting in the store's receiving area. They were marked type 304 stainless steel, one of the cheaper grades. Dana was curious because a price quotation had been given to Tyler Hensman the previous week on the same material in type 316 stainless steel, a much more expensive grade.

Dana Davis approached a young clerk who was working in the receiving area. "Where did that shipment come from?"

"Quality Distribution," the young man replied, without looking directly at Dana.

"What was the cost of the material?" Dana inquired.

"Don't know. My copy of the order doesn't show a cost, nor does the packing slip that came in the shipment," the young man said as he shrugged his shoulders.

"Is it supposed to be type 304 or type 316?" Dana persisted.

"It just says stainless steel bolts and nuts on my copy of the purchase order," replied the clerk. "And the packing slip just says stainless steel as well. There's no mention of type of stainless. If you want to find out more, you'll have to contact Tyler Hensman in our purchasing department. This order was placed by him."

Dana Davis was getting more curious about the shipment from Quality Distribution. Upon returning to the office, Dana decided to call Tyler Hensman and ask for the order. A decision was made not to mention what was seen in the store's receiving area. "Tyler, I'm calling about that price quotation I gave you last week for 316 stainless steel bolts and nuts. Will you give us an order?"

"Sorry. I placed the order with Quality Distribution last week because their price was better," Tyler replied. "You'll have to sharpen your pencil if you want our business."

Dana Davis knew there was no way Quality Distribution could compete on price because it was basically a small jobber firm that really wasn't in the stainless steel business. But Dana didn't want to say that to Tyler Hensman. "How much sharper?"

"Just a bit, but you know it wouldn't be honest for me to tell you," Tyler laughed.

After they talked for a few more minutes Dana Davis promised to check pricing options and determine if the next price could be more competitive. After hanging up the phone, Dana sat at his desk, staring at the wall. Davis realized a careful approach was needed. There was something wrong and the issue needed to be resolved quickly. This was an important long-term account for American Steel, and the company couldn't afford to lose it.

Questions

1. Has Dana Davis's behavior been ethical? Why or why not?
2. Has Tyler Hensman's behavior been ethical? Why or why not?
3. What should Dana Davis do?

DEVELOPING A RELATIONSHIP STRATEGY

Scenario

You are an experienced sales representative employed by American Steel Processing, a company that has been in business for over 25 years. American is an ISO 9002–certified manufacturing company that has earned many accolades, including three consecutive J. D. Power & Associates awards for customer satisfaction. Over the years the company has invested heavily in automation technology as a means of ensuring consistent manufacturing quality. The American Steel processing sales force understands that the company will not be the lowest bidder in most sales situations because the highest quality can never be obtained at the lowest price.

Customer Profile

Tyler Hensman has held the position of senior purchasing agent at Regina Steel Fabricators for several years. Throughout this period of time Tyler has negotiated over a dozen purchase agreements with Dana Davis, senior account representative with American Steel Processing. Tyler takes pride in purchasing quality steel products at the best price.

Salesperson Profile

Dana Davis began working for American Steel Processing Company about four years ago. After completion of an extensive sales training program, Dana was assigned to a territory in central Ohio. After three successful years, Dana Davis was promoted to senior account representative.

Product

American Steel Processing sells a wide range of steel products. Many of the orders filled are for high stress steel beams, stainless steel bolts and nuts, and structural tubing used in commercial building construction. Most orders specify a certain quality of steel.

Instructions

For this role play you will assume the role of Dana Davis, senior account representative employed by American Steel Processing Company. To prepare for the role play you should carefully read the case problem at the end of Chapter 5. This information will help you understand the issues that need to be addressed during the role play. During the early stages of the role play you will want to obtain more information from the customer and resolve any misunderstandings. You want to obtain the order for type 316 stainless steel bolts and nuts, and maintain a good relationship with this important customer. Keep in mind that ethical decisions can greatly influence the relationship between a salesperson and the customer. Reflect on the important information covered in Chapter 5 prior to meeting with Tyler Hensman.

Service is not a competitive edge, it is <u>The</u> competitive edge. People do not buy just products; they also buy expectations. One expectation is that the item they buy will produce the benefits the seller promised. Another is that if it doesn't, the seller will make good on the promise.

Karl Albrecht and Ron Zemke, *Service America: Doing Business in the New Economy*

Developing a Product Strategy

➥ Part III examines the important role of complete and accurate product, company, and competitive knowledge in personal selling. Lack of knowledge in these areas impairs the salesperson's ability to configure value-added solutions. Part III also describes several value-added selling strategies.

Chapter Preview

When you finish this chapter, you should be able to

1. Explain the importance of developing a product strategy
2. Describe product configuration
3. Identify reasons why salespeople and customers benefit from thorough product knowledge
4. Discuss the most important kinds of product and company information that salespeople use in creating product solutions
5. Describe how knowledge of competition improves personal selling
6. List major sources of product information
7. Explain the difference between product features and buyer benefits
8. Demonstrate how to translate product features into buyer benefits

CHAPTER 6

Creating Product Solutions

Thousands of people decide each year to start their own business. Some want independence, some look for large profits, and others hope to have some effect on society's ills. Some of these risk-takers are prospects for Cart Works, a company that manages free-standing retail booths (often called kiosks) that operate in shopping malls. Many mall managers have incorporated kiosks to create the busy and happy atmosphere of an open marketplace.

Every would-be entrepreneur has choices. Some prefer to start a business on their own, make all the decisions, and reap all the rewards. Others prefer a franchise-type arrangement that includes help with major decisions. Cart Works is searching for people who do not want to go it alone. The company has conducted careful research to determine the best merchandise mix for certain types of malls. The company also provides training for persons who own and operate a kiosk. Cart Works representatives are involved in two types of personal selling. They are selling the Cart Works concept to would-be entrepreneurs and mall managers. The kiosks cannot operate in a mall without approval. The prospective entrepreneur and the mall manager are seeking specific kinds of product and company information.[1]

DEVELOPING A PRODUCT SOLUTION THAT ADDS VALUE

As noted in Chapter 1, a product strategy helps salespeople make correct decisions concerning the selection and positioning of products to meet identified customer needs. The **product strategy** is a well-conceived plan that emphasizes

According to Keith Eades, author of THE NEW SOLUTION SELLING, a solution is a mutually shared answer to a recognized customer problem. It is more encompassing than a specific product, and it provides measurable results. Eades states that more than 500,000 individuals worldwide have been trained in solution selling. Solution Selling forms the core of Microsoft's selling processes.

becoming a product expert, selling specific benefits, and configuring value-added solutions (Figure 6.1). Configuring value-added solutions is discussed in detail in Chapter 7.

Selling Solutions

A **solution** is a mutually shared answer to a recognized customer problem. In many selling situations, a solution is more encompassing than a specific product. It often provides measurable results such as greater productivity, increased profits, or less employee turnover. Selling a solution, versus selling a specific product, usually requires a greater effort to define and diagnose the customer's problem.[2]

Most salespeople have adopted a broad definition of the term *product*. It is broadly interpreted to encompass information, services, ideas, tangible products, or some combination of these that satisfy the customer's needs, with the right solution.[3] Let's look at the sales process at two firms:

- Trilogy, an Austin, Texas–based company, creates configuration software for large manufacturers such as Boeing and Hewlett-Packard. These two companies sell products with a great many variants. Boeing, for example, can use a wide range of components to assemble a plane that matches the customer's highly

FIGURE | 6.1

Developing a product strategy enables the salesperson to custom fit products or services to the customer's needs.

STRATEGIC/CONSULTATIVE SELLING MODEL

Strategic step	*Prescription*
Develop a Personal Selling Philosophy	☑ Adopt Marketing Concept ☑ Value Personal Selling ☑ Become a Problem Solver/Partner
Develop a Relationship Strategy	☑ Adopt Win-Win Philosophy ☑ Project Professional Image ☑ Maintain High Ethical Standards
Develop a Product Strategy	☐ Become a Product Expert ☐ Sell Specific Benefits ☐ Configure Value-Added Solutions

specific preferences. With the aid of Trilogy software, Boeing sales representatives, using a laptop computer, can translate a customer's specific needs into a workable specification.[4]

- Sunflower Travel Corporation based in Wichita, Kansas, creates specialized vacation packages for individuals and groups. A package might include airline tickets, hotel reservations, and accommodations on a cruise line. The sales staff at Sunflower have the knowledge to plan a highly customized trip.[5]

From the customer's point of view, salespeople employed by Trilogy and Sunflower are selling primarily information and expertise. The problem-solving ability these salespeople provide the customer is viewed as the product. When you sell a complex product, it is knowledge and expertise that creates value.

Tailoring the Product Strategy

A product strategy should be tailored to the customer's buying needs (see Figure 6.2). Transactional buyers are usually well aware of their needs. Most of these customers have conducted their own research and have a good understanding of the product that will meet their needs. The office manager who frequently buys a large amount of copy paper knows that this standard item can be purchased from several vendors. The quality of the paper usually does not vary from one vendor to another.

The consultative buyer may lack needs awareness and will usually welcome need clarification. This customer will want help evaluating possible solutions and usually needs a customized product solution. The customized solution appeals to the customers desire for choices that are tailored to their needs. Developing a product strategy for the strategic alliance customer usually

FIGURE | 6.2

Tailoring the Product Strategy

Adapted from Neil Rackham and John R. DeVincentis, *Rethinking the Sales Force* (New York: McGraw-Hill, 1999), p. 79.

PRODUCT CHARACTERISTICS

Transactional	*Consultative*	*Strategic Alliance*
• Standard or generic items • Well understood • Easily substitutable	• Hidden features • Differentiated choices • Customizable	• High cost importance • Limited substitutability

Salespeople employed by a distributor (wholesaler) that carries Tabasco can become a "recipe expert" by taking advantage of support services offered by the manufacturer. Tabasco's product strategy is to team up with salespeople who call on restaurants and other customers. Salespeople can add value by introducing the "flavor solutions" recipes.

offers the greatest challenge. Study of the proposed alliance partner can be very time consuming, but the rewards of a successful alliance may be substantial. In some cases, the company that wishes to form an alliance with a new customer must be prepared to make a large investment in capital-intensive technology and additional personnel.[6]

Explosion of Product Options

The domestic and global markets are overflowing with a vast array of goods and services. In some industries, the number of new products introduced each year is mind-boggling. Consumer-product makers, for example, churn out more than 30,000 new products each year. Want to buy a product in the securities and financial services field? In the segment of mutual funds alone, you can choose from more than 7,000 products.[7]

For the customer, this much variety creates a "good news–bad news" situation. The good news is that almost all buyers have a choice when it comes to purchasing a product or service. People like to compare various options. The bad news is that so many choices often complicate the buying process. One of the most important roles of the salesperson is to simplify the customer's study of the product choices. Later in this chapter we discuss how product features (information) can add value when converted into specific benefits (knowledge) that can help the buyer make an intelligent buying decision.

Creating Solutions with Product Configuration

The challenge facing both customers and salespeople in this era of information overload is deciding which product applications, or combination of applications, can solve the buying problem. If the customer has complex buying needs, then the salesperson may have to bring together many parts of the company's product mix to develop a custom-fitted solution. The product selection process is often referred to as **product configuration**. Salespeople representing Cisco Systems are often involved in the sale of new products to new and established customers. They use Cybrant Solutions Architect software to quickly identify solutions. The software helps salespeople ask prospects the right questions to discover their needs and then configures a solution that best meets those needs.[8]

Product configuration is no less important in retail situations where the salesperson is selling a complex product. Assembling a professional wardrobe, preparing an interior design for a home or office, or putting together an automobile lease plan involves product configuration.

Many companies use product configuration software because it develops customized product solutions quickly and accurately. It incorporates product selection criteria and associates them directly with customer requirements. Members of the sales force can use the

Selling Is Everyone's Business

SELLING MOTHERHOOD

Cynthia Cunningham and Shelley Murray worked 60-hour workweeks to achieve success as BankBoston branch managers. They wanted more time with their children, but the long hours created a major barrier to motherhood. Then they came up with a novel plan: package themselves and share one job. Once the plan was developed, the selling began. They wrote a letter that described their accomplishments, attached a résumé, and delivered the package to several senior executives. Eventually they met with more than a dozen executives and finally hit pay dirt. They began sharing a vice president–level job that involved teaching branch personnel and small businesses how to sell their services to customers. Cynthia and Shelley now work 20 to 25 hours each week at what has since become Fleet Bank.[a]

Cynthia Cunningham and Shelley Murray.

Busch solves complex buying problems and adds value by bringing together many parts of their company's product mix. They also ensure the highest level of service support. Busch is a ISO 9001 Registered Company.

sales configurator to identify product options, prices, delivery schedules, and other parts of the product mix while working interactively with the customer. Most of today's product configuration software can be integrated with contact management software programs such as ACT! and Siebel. In addition to improving the quality of the sales proposal, this software reduces the time-consuming process of manually preparing written proposals.

Preparing Written Proposals

Written proposals are frequently part of the salesperson's product strategy. It is only natural that some buyers want the proposed solution put in writing. *Written proposals* can be defined as a specific plan of action based on the facts, assumptions, and supporting documentation

This salesperson is making a follow-up call to determine if the customer needs any additional information regarding the written proposal, which was sent earlier.

included in the sales presentation.[9] A well-written proposal adds value to the product solution and can set you apart from the competition. It offers the buyer reassurance that you will deliver what has been promised. Written proposals, which are often accompanied by a sales letter, vary in terms of format and content. Many government agencies, and some large companies, issue a Request For Proposal (RFP) that specifies the format of the proposal. Most proposals include the following parts:

Budget and overview. Tell the prospect the cost of the solution you have prescribed. Be specific as you describe the product or service features to be provided and specify the price. When you confirm pricing with a proposal, misunderstandings and mistakes can be avoided.

Objective. The objective should be expressed in terms of benefits. A tangible objective might be to "reduce payroll expense by 10 percent." An intangible objective might be stated as "increased business security offered by a company with a reputation for dependability." Focus on specific benefits that relate directly to the customer's needs.

Strategy. Briefly describe how you will meet your objective. How will you fulfill the obligations you have described in your proposal? In some cases this section of your proposal includes specific language: "Your account will be assigned to Susan Murray, our senior lease representative."

Schedule. Establish a time frame for meeting your objective. This might involve the confirmation of dates with regard to acquisition, shipping, or installation.

Rationale. With a mixture of logic and emotion present your rationale for taking action now. Once again, the emphasis should be on benefits, not features.[10]

Some written proposals follow a specific format developed by the company. The length of a proposal can vary from a single page to dozens of pages for a complex product.

The proposal should be printed on quality paper and free of any errors in spelling, grammar, or punctuation. Before completing the proposal, review the content one more time to be sure you have addressed all the customer's concerns. Bob Kantin, author of *Sales Proposals Kit*

Selling in Action

WRITING EFFECTIVE SALES LETTERS

Sales letters are increasingly being used by salespeople to describe features and benefits, position products, build relationships, and provide assurances to customers. Sales letters also are used in conjunction with prospecting plans. There are several standard rules that apply to all written sales letters. These include:

1. Sales letters should follow the standard visual format of a business letter. They should contain in the following order either a letterhead or the sender's address, date, inside address (the same as on the outside of the envelope), salutation, body of letter, complimentary close, typed name and handwritten signature of sender, and a notation of enclosures (if there are any).
2. Placement of the letter on paper should provide a balanced white space border area surrounding the entire letter. Three to five blank lines should separate the date and inside address; a single blank line should separate the inside address and the salutation, salutation and opening paragraph of the letter, and each paragraph. A single blank line should separate the last paragraph and the complimentary close. Single spacing should generally be used within the paragraphs.
3. Proper business punctuation includes a colon after the salutation and comma after the complimentary close.
4. Most sales letters include at least three paragraphs. The first paragraph should indicate why you are writing the letter; the second should be a summary of the benefits proposed; and the third paragraph should state what the next action step will be for the salesperson, the customer, or both.
5. Proper grammar and spelling must be used throughout the entire letter. Business letters provide an opportunity to build a stronger relationship with the customer and close the sale. Improper placement, punctuation, spelling errors, or weak content convey a negative impression to the reader and may result in a lost sale.
6. The use of the personal pronoun "I" should be minimized in a sales letter. To keep the letter focused on the customer's needs, the pronouns "you" and "your" should appear throughout the body of the letter.

for Dummies, says the proposal is really the first "product" that the customer receives from you, so be sure it is perfect.[11] Neil Rackham, noted author and sales consultant, says to address your proposal to the "invisible" customer. Very often the proposal will be reviewed by individuals the salesperson has never met. And these are often the people who will make or break the deal.[12]

The remainder of this chapter is divided into five major sections. The first two sections examine the kinds of product information and company information required by the salesperson. The third section describes the type of information about the competition that is helpful to salespeople. Sources of information are covered in the fourth section, and the fifth section describes how product features can be translated into buyer benefits.

BECOMING A PRODUCT EXPERT

One of the major challenges facing salespeople is winning the customer's trust. A survey reported in *Sales & Marketing Management* ranked product knowledge as the number-one characteristic of salespeople who are able to build trust.[13] Ideally, a salesperson possesses product knowledge that meets and exceeds customer expectations. Tom Peters says that when it comes to product knowledge, remember: "More, more, more. And, more important: Deeper, deeper, deeper." In summary: "He or she who has the largest appetite for Deep Knowledge wins."[14] This section reviews some of the most common product information categories: (1) product development and quality improvement processes,

(2) performance data and specifications, (3) maintenance and service contracts, and (4) price and delivery. Each is important as a potential source of knowledge concerning the product or service.

Product Development and Quality Improvement Processes

Companies spend large amounts of money in the development of their products. In **product development**, the original idea for a product or service is tested, modified, and retested several times before it is offered to the customer. Each of the modifications is made with the thought of improving the product. Salespeople should be familiar with product development history. Often this information sets the stage for stronger sales appeals.

Patagonia, a company that makes high-quality sports and outdoor equipment and clothing, uses a unique product development process. Patagonia hires many expert kayakers, skiers, climbers, and fishermen who under actual conditions help develop and test the company's products. In the outdoor recreation market, Patagonia wins high praise for its many product innovations.[15]

Quality improvement continues to be an important long-term business strategy for most successful companies. Salespeople need to identify quality improvement processes that provide a competitive advantage and to be prepared to discuss this information during the sales presentation. Gulfstream Aircraft Company, Ritz-Carlton Hotels, Toyota, and Sea Ray Boats provide examples of companies that have implemented important quality controls. **Quality control**, which involves measuring products and services against established standards, is one dimension of the typical quality improvement process.

Sea Ray Boats, a quality leader in the pleasure boat industry, worked hard to become an ISO 9002 certified builder. This certification, from the International Organization for Standardization (ISO), assures a high level of quality in the manufacturing process. The company is the industry leader in robotic applications, a means of ensuring consistent quality from boat to boat. Sea Ray Boats has also earned two consecutive J. D. Power & Associates awards for customer satisfaction.[16]

Performance Data and Specifications

Most potential buyers are interested in performance data and specifications. Some typical questions that might be raised by prospects are:

"What is the frequency response for this stereo loudspeaker?"

"What is the anticipated rate of return on this mutual fund?"

"What is the energy consumption rating for this appliance?"

"Are all your hotel and conference center rooms accessible to persons with physical disabilities?"

A salesperson must be prepared to address these types of questions in the written sales proposal and the sales presentation. Performance data are especially critical in cases in which the customer is attempting to compare the merits of one product with another.

To become familiar with the performance of Whirlpool appliances, salespeople literally "live" the brand. The company rented and redesigned an eight-bedroom farmhouse near corporate headquarters and outfitted it with Whirlpool dishwashers, refrigerators, washers, dryers, and microwaves. Salespeople, in groups of eight, live at the house for two months and use all of the appliances. Whirlpool engineers visit the home and present information on design, performance data, and specifications. A recent graduate of the training program says, "I have a confidence level that's making a difference in my client contacts."[17]

Sea Ray Boats, a quality leader in the pleasure boat industry, worked hard to become an ISO 9002 certified builder. Sea Ray has also earned two consecutive J. D. Power and Associates awards for customer satisfaction. High performing salespeople are familiar with these important product knowledge achievements and able to communicate the benefits to prospective boat buyers.

A Tradition of Forward Thinking

For over 45 years, Sea Ray has used forward thinking to design some of the best built, most technologically advanced boats in the industry. We are proud to have received the J.D. Power and Associates Award for Express Cruisers three times in a row, and the NMMA Award for highest satisfaction in sport boats.

To depict our heritage, and our future, we commissioned nationally known illustrator Ted Wright to create this exciting montage.

To receive a copy of this print, register at www.searay.com. Those registered will receive a 17" x 11" reproduction of the original art. Supplies are limited so register on-line today.

NMMA Award for Highest Satisfaction in Sport Boats, (17 - 29 Feet)

The Standard of Excellence™

"Highest in Customer Satisfaction with Express Cruisers (24 - 33 Feet), Three Times in a Row"

J.D. Power and Associates 2002-2003, 2005 Boat Competitive Information Studies℠. 2005 study based on responses from a total of 12,530 owners of 2003 and 2004 model year boats registered between March 1, 2003 and May 31, 2004. Includes mostly sterndrive-powered family cruisers from 24 to 33 feet with cabins that include sleeping, galley/cooking and head/toilet facilities. www.jdpower.com

Maintenance and Service Contracts

Prospects often want information concerning maintenance and care requirements for the products they purchase. The salesperson who can quickly and accurately provide this information has the edge. Proper maintenance usually extends the life of the product, so this information should be provided at the time of the sale.

Today, many salespeople are developing customized service agreements that incorporate the customer's special priorities, feelings, and needs. They work hard to acquire a real understanding of the customer's specific service criteria. If call return expectations are very important to the customer, the frequency and quantity of product-related visits per week or month can be included in the service contract. Customized service agreements add value to the sale and help protect your business from the competition.[18]

BOC converts their product data and specifications into benefits. A product strategy with emphasis on selling benefits adds value because time starved customers quickly understand how the product meets and possibly exceeds their needs. Note how BOC has quantified their benefits.

Pricing and Delivery

Potential buyers expect salespeople to be well versed in price and delivery policies and be in a position to set prices and plan deliveries. If a salesperson has pricing authority, buyers perceive the person as someone with whom they can really talk business. The ability to set prices puts the salesperson in a stronger position.[19]

Decision-making authority in the area of pricing gives the salesperson *more power and responsibility*. If the salesperson negotiates a price that is too low, the company may lose money on the sale. Price objections represent one of the most common barriers to closing a sale, so salespeople need to be well prepared in this area.

In most situations, the price quotation should be accompanied by information that creates value in the mind of the customer. The process of determining whether or not the proposal adds value is often called **quantifying the solution**. When the purchase represents

TABLE 6.1 QUANTIFYING THE SOLUTION WITH COST–BENEFIT ANALYSIS

Quantifying the solution often involves a carefully prepared cost–benefit analysis. This example compares the higher-priced Phoenix semitruck trailer with the lower-priced FB model, which is a competing product.

COST SAVINGS OF THE PHOENIX VERSUS FB MODEL FOR A 10-YEAR PERIOD (ALL PRICES ARE APPROXIMATE)

	Cost Savings
• Stainless steel bulkhead (savings on sandblasting and painting)	$ 425.00
• Stainless steel rear door frame (savings on painting)	425.00
• Air ride suspension (better fuel mileage, longer tire life, longer brake life)	3,750.00
• Hardwood or aluminum scuff (savings from freight damages and replacement of scuff)	1,000.00
• LED lights (last longer; approximate savings: $50 per year × 10 years)	500.00
• Light protectors (save $50 per year on replacement × 10 years)	500.00
• Threshold plate (saves damage to entry of trailer)	200.00
• Internal rail reinforcement (saves damage to lower rail and back panels)	500.00
• Stainless steel screws for light attachment (savings on replacement cost)	200.00
• Domestic oak premium floor—$1\frac{3}{8}$ (should last 10 years under normal conditions)	1,000.00
• Doors—aluminum inner and outer skin, outside white finish, inside mill finish, fastened by five aluminum hinges (savings over life of trailer)	750.00
• Five-year warranty in addition to standard warranty covers bulkhead rust, LED lights, floor, scuff liner, glad hands, rear frame, mudflap assembly, and threshold plate (Phoenix provides a higher trade-in value)	1,500.00
Total approximate savings of Phoenix over 10-year period (all the preceding is standard equipment on a Phoenix; this trailer will sell for $23,500; an FB standard trailer would sell for $19,500)	$10,750.00
Less additional initial cost of Phoenix over FB standard	4,000.00
Overall cost savings of Phoenix over FB trailer	$ 6,750.00

a major buying decision, such as the purchase of a new computer system, quantifying the solution is important. One way to quantify the solution is to conduct a cost-benefit analysis to determine the actual cost of the purchase and savings the buyer can anticipate from the investment (Table 6.1).

Another way to quantify the solution is to calculate return on investment (ROI). As products and services become more complex and more expensive, customers are more likely to look at the financial reasons for buying. This is especially true in business-to-business selling. Salespeople who can develop a sales proposal that contains specific information on return on investment are more likely to get a favorable response from key decision makers. Chief financial officers, for example, are more inclined to approve an expensive purchase if it results in a good return on investment.[20]

Performing accurate ROI calculations often requires the collection of detailed financial information. You may need to help the prospect collect information within the company to build a case for the purchase. BAX Global offers customers multi-modal shipping solutions. It has the capabilities to employ more than one mode of transportation for a customer. In order to develop a customized solution for the customer, the sales representative must collect a great deal of financial and nonfinancial data from the prospect. Transportation modes (trucks, airplanes, railroads, etc.) vary in terms of cost, speed, dependability, frequency, and other criteria, so preparation of the sales proposal can be a complicated process.[21]

The use of ROI selling appeals requires more work upfront, but it often leads to shorter sales cycles. The salesperson who is not well schooled in financial issues, and cannot compute and supply price information accurately, may be at a serious disadvantage. In Chapter 7, we discuss how to position products according to price.

KNOW YOUR COMPANY

We should never underestimate information about the company itself as a strong appeal that can be used during the sales presentation. This is especially true when the customer is considering a strategic alliance. Before teaming up with another company, the strategic alliance buyer will want to learn a great deal about the firm the salesperson represents. In many cases, you are selling your company as much or more than you are selling a product.

Some companies such as Microsoft, Four Seasons Hotels, and American Express have what might be called "brand power." These companies, and the products offered to consumers, are quite well known. However, if you are selling loudspeakers made by Klipsch or financial services offered by Van Kampen Equity, you may find it necessary to spend considerable time providing information about the company. In this section we examine the types of information needed in most selling situations.

A quick response to a customer's questions about product configurations or pricing can serve as a product strategy improvement within the sales process. This salesperson is adding value by using her notebook computer and cellphone to access and quickly communicate information.

Company Culture and Organization

Many salespeople take special pride in the company they work for. Salespeople employed by Cisco Systems feel good about the company's high ranking on *Fortune* magazine's list of the 100 best companies to work for. Employees receive bonuses for exceptional performance. Marriott International, another member of the *Fortune* list, works hard to reward employee excellence at all levels.[22]

Every organization has its own unique culture. **Organizational culture** is a collection of beliefs, behaviors, and work patterns held in common by people employed by a specific firm. Most organizations over a period of time tend to take on distinct norms and practices. At GEAR for Sports, employees are guided by a statement of values that communicates what is held important by the company (Figure 6.3). Research indicates that the customer orientation of a firm's salespeople is influenced by the organization's culture. A supportive culture that encourages salespeople to offer tailor-made solutions to buyer problems sets the stage for long-term partnerships.[23]

Many prospects use the past performance of a company to evaluate the quality of the current product offering. If the company has enjoyed success in the past, there is good reason to believe that the future will be bright.

Company Support for Product

Progressive marketers support the products they sell. In some cases, product support takes the form of sales tools that can be used in preparation for a sales call or during a sales call.

GEAR For Sports® Vision

Guided by our GEAR values, we strive to be the leader in quality and delivery of our customer's image through marketing innovative sportswear, accessories and services.

GEAR Values

GEAR For Sports' business is predicated on respect for, and attention to, all of our customers, business partners, employees, government and community. We value:

Customers
by exceeding their expectations.

Excellence
by taking pride and responsibility in everything we do.

Employees
by demonstrating respect and consideration for each other.

Teamwork
by fostering trust and recognition among all stakeholders.

Professionalism
by exhibiting integrity and proficiency.

Innovation
by embracing creativity and change.

Social Responsibility
by caring for and sharing with each other and our community.

FIGURE 6.3

At GEAR for Sports, the employees are guided by a statement of values that communicates what is held important by the company. Shared values are especially important when the sales process involves development of strategic partnerships.

The company culture at Bar-S is clearly communicated in this introduction to the company legends and history.

BAR-S LEGENDS & HISTORY

Technical Innovation - A Competitive Advantage

Bar-S strives for excellence in everything that we do. There is no exception when it comes to technology. It was early in the development of the Company that management recognized the competitive advantage that technology could bring them. Despite a relatively small staff (just a couple of years ago we were down to a staff of 3) the Company is an information systems technology leader in the processed meat industry.

UCC 128 – At a time when we only had four IS employees we participated with the Uniform Code Council (UCC) in a grocery industry pilot program to develop a standard bar coding system for shipping containers. This system came to be known as the UCC128. We participated in this pilot program with companies like Oscar Mayer and IBP. Despite our small IS staff, Bar-S was the first processed meat company to implement the UCC128 bar code system throughout all of its warehousing and shipping systems.

E-FORMS – Over the past couple of years we have converted hundreds of forms we use on a regular basis to an electronic format. These forms are now available through our Subscription List application. Based on a recent article that specifically mentioned companies converting from paper to electronic forms, we are significantly ahead of most companies in our efforts.

EDI – In 1995, our customers began requiring Electronic Data Interchange (EDI) to receive orders and send invoices. In response, the Company took a very proactive stance with their EDI program. Within 12 months Bar-S not only met our customers' EDI demands, we started seeking out customers to participate in expanding our EDI program.

SFA – In August of 1997 we started to develop a state of the art sales force automation system. By August of 1998 the system had been deployed to the entire sales force. The system includes several productivity enhancing software applications and communication software that allows information to be shared with both teammates and customers. We think the SFA system is state of the art.

VISION – In 1999 the Company was selected as a recipient of the "Vision Award". The award was sponsored by The American Institute of CPA's, and Anderson Consulting. This award is only presented to three companies that "demonstrate excellence in business performance reporting systems", and the use of information systems technology.

The technical accomplishments of our Company have also been recognized in trade publications. Some of the IS staff have even been asked to present the technical successes of our Company as case studies at non-competitor trade show speaking engagements. ■

Hunter Douglas, a manufacturer of window fashions, has developed a Dealer Merchandising Portfolio. A dealer sales representative can select and order sample books, brochures, videos, in-store display material, and many other items.[24]

Company support after the sale is also very important. Olin Mathieson, a major chemical corporation, regularly checks with customers to get their reaction to services and keep real needs in perspective. Jagemann Stamping Company, a tool-and-die firm in Manitowoc, Wisconsin, often uses a sales team made up of a salesperson, an engineer, and line workers. Line workers can often answer the technical questions raised by a customer. Whenever there is a problem or defect, a small group of line workers is sent out with either a salesperson or an engineer to investigate. This involvement raises the worker's commitment to the customer.[25]

Global Business Etiquette

DOING BUSINESS IN AUSTRALIA

American and Australian businesspeople have a lot in common. Everyone in Australia speaks English and business dress is similar in both countries. However, subtle differences do exist.

- When you greet an Australian businessperson, give your full name and then firmly shake hands.
- Australians tend to be modest people who often root for the underdog. Keep information about your power and wealth to yourself.
- Although Australian businesspeople tend to be informal and friendly, they still expect you to be a good listener and be completely familiar with your product.
- Keep your presentations simple. Most Australians want you to get to the point.[b]

KNOW YOUR COMPETITION

Acquiring knowledge of your competition is another important step toward developing complete product knowledge. Salespeople who have knowledge of their competitor's strengths and weaknesses are better able to emphasize the benefits they offer and add value. Prospects often raise specific questions concerning competing firms. If you cannot provide answers or if your answers are vague, the sale may be lost.

Your Attitude Toward Your Competition

Regardless of how impressive your product is, the customer naturally seeks information about similar products sold by other companies. Therefore, you must acquire facts about competing products before the sales presentation. It has never been easier to obtain information about competing products. Check the competitor's Web site, annual reports, press releases, and marketing material. Once armed with this information, you are more confident in your ability to handle questions about the competition.

The attitude you display toward your competition is of the utmost importance. Every salesperson should develop a set of basic beliefs about the best way of dealing with competing products. A few helpful guidelines follow:

1. *In most cases, do not refer to the competition during the sales presentation.* This shifts the focus of attention to competing products, which is usually not desirable.
2. *Never discuss the competition unless you have all your facts straight.* Your credibility suffers if you make inaccurate statements. If you do not know the answer to a specific question, simply say, "I do not know."
3. *Never criticize the competition.* You may be called on to make direct comparisons between your product and competing products. In these situations, stick to the facts and avoid emotional comments about apparent or real weaknesses.
4. *Be prepared to add value.* The competition may come to your prospect with a comparative advantage in price, delivery, or some other area. Be prepared to neutralize the competitor's proposal with a value-added approach. If your competitor has slow delivery, encourage the customer to talk about why prompt delivery is important.[26]

Customers appreciate an accurate, fair, and honest presentation of the facts. They generally resent highly critical remarks about the competition. Avoid mudslinging at all costs. Fairness is a virtue that people greatly admire.

Become an Industry Expert

Salespeople need to become experts in the industry they represent. In many cases this means moving beyond the role of product specialist and becoming a business analyst. Staying current and developing an understanding of business processes takes time and may require additional education.[27] If your clients work in the banking industry, read the appropriate trade journals and become active in professional associations that serve bankers' needs.

SOURCES OF PRODUCT INFORMATION

There are several sources of product information available to salespeople. Some of the most common include: (1) product literature developed by the company, (2) sales training programs, (3) plant tours, (4) internal sales and sales support team members, (5) customers, (6) product, and (7) publications.

Product Literature, Catalogs, and Web-Based Sources

Most companies prepare materials that provide a detailed description of their product. This information is usually quite instructional, and salespeople should review it carefully. If the company markets a number of products, a sales catalog is usually developed. To save salespeople time, many companies give them computer software that provides a constantly updated, online product catalog. Advertisements, promotional brochures, and audio cassettes also can be a valuable source of product information.

Knowing, understanding, and being able to clarify information in product literature adds value within the sales process. Customers seek out the "product experts" who can assist them in making intelligent buying decisions.

Customer Relationship Management with Technology

STARTING FAST WITH CRM

New salespeople can be overwhelmed by the amount of information they need to master. This includes information about the company and its processes, products, and customers. Companies can now make learning easier with information technology. Information about the company and its processes can be stored on the company's network, on its virtual private network (VPN), or on CD-ROM disks. Computer-based training (CBT) permits new employees to learn at their own pace about products—specifications, features, benefits, uses, and selling points.

Companies can now provide salespeople with software that they can use accurately and effectively to create product solutions. Electronic configuration software allows salespeople to select the components necessary to assemble a custom-tailored solution to meet their prospects' needs. This software guides users through the product selection process while assuring that the components are compatible with one another.

Companies can deliver a rich body of customer information to new salespeople through the strong commitment to the use of customer relationship management software. The salesperson who carefully records her business and relationship contacts with customers and prospects over time accumulates a valuable store of information. A new salesperson taking over these accounts can quickly "come up to speed" with these people and their needs. (See the exercise, Finding Product Information in CRM, on p. 154 for more information.)

Mitsubishi Caterpillar Forklift America presents its basic product information online, so it's available to dealer representatives in the privacy of their homes, hotel rooms, or wherever else they bring their laptops. Each of the seven product information courses takes about an hour. To reinforce basic product knowledge, the company offers advanced instructor-led courses.[28] Some companies are using interactive distance learning (delivered via satellite) to present different types of sales training.

Plant Tours

Many companies believe that salespeople should visit the manufacturing plant and see the production process firsthand. Such tours not only provide valuable product information but also increase the salesperson's enthusiasm for the product. A new salesperson may spend several days at the plant getting acquainted with the production process. Experienced personnel within the organization also can benefit from plant tours.

Internal Sales and Sales Support Team Members

Team selling has become popular, in part, because many complex sales require the expertise of several sales and sales support personnel. Expertise in the areas of product design, finance, or transportation may be needed to develop an effective sales proposal. Pooled commissions are sometimes used to encourage team members to share information and work as a team.

Customers

Persons who actually use the product can be an important source of information. They have observed its performance under actual working conditions and can provide an objective assessment of the product's strengths and weaknesses. Some companies collect testimonials from satisfied customers and make this persuasive information available to the sales staff. Patagonia customers include mountain bikers, backcountry skiers, sailors, paddlers, and fly fisherman. The companies success lies in maintaining a close connection to persons who actually use their products.[29]

E-learning has become popular because it is inexpensive and fast, and it can be geared to the flexible schedules of salespeople. This regional sales team is receiving sales training via satellite from the company's home office.

Product

The product itself should not be overlooked as a source of valuable information. Salespeople should closely examine and, if possible, use each item they sell to become familiar with its features. Investigation, use, and careful evaluation of the product provide a salesperson with additional confidence.

Publications

Trade and technical publications such as *Supermarket Business* and *Advertising Age* provide valuable product information. Popular magazines and the business section of the newspaper also offer salespeople considerable information about their products and their competition. A number of publications such as *Consumer Reports* test products extensively and report the findings in nontechnical language for the benefit of consumers. These reports are a valuable source of information.

Word of Caution

Is it possible to be overly prepared? Can salespeople know too much about the products and services they sell? The answer to both questions is generally no. Communication problems can arise, however, if the salesperson does not accurately gauge the prospect's level of understanding. There is always the danger that a knowledgeable salesperson can overwhelm the potential buyer with facts and figures. This problem can be avoided when salespeople adopt the feature–benefit strategy.

ADDING VALUE WITH A FEATURE–BENEFIT STRATEGY

Frederick W. Smith, founder of Federal Express, first proposed the concept of overnight delivery in a paper that he wrote as an undergraduate at Yale University. The now-famous paper was given a C by his professor. Many years later, Smith said, "I don't think that we understood our real goal when we first started Federal Express. We thought that we were selling the transportation of goods; in fact, we were selling peace of mind."[30]

Throughout this chapter, we emphasize the importance of acquiring information on the features of your product, company, and competition. Now it is important to point out that successful sales presentations translate product features into benefits that meet a specific need expressed by the customer. The "peace of mind" that Frederick W. Smith mentioned is a good example of a buyer benefit. Only when a product feature is converted to a buyer benefit does it make an impact on the customer.

Distinguish between Features and Benefits

To be sure we understand the difference between a product feature and a benefit, let us define these two terms.

A **feature** is data, facts, or characteristics of your product or service. Features often relate to craftsmanship, design, durability, and economy of operation. They may reveal how the product was developed, processed, or manufactured. Product features often are described in the technical section of the written sales proposal and in the literature provided by the manufacturer.

A **benefit** is whatever provides the customer with a personal advantage or gain. It answers the question, "How will I benefit from owning or using the product?" If you mention to a prospect that a certain tire has a four-ply rating, you are talking about a product feature. If you go on to point out that this tire provides greater safety, lasts longer, and improves gas mileage, you are pointing out benefits.

General versus Specific Benefits

Neil Rackham, author of *The SPIN Selling Fieldbook*, says that a statement can only be a benefit if it meets a specific need expressed by the buyer. When you link a benefit to a buyer's expressed need, you demonstrate that you can help solve a problem that has been described by the customer. A general benefit shows how a feature can be helpful to a buyer, but it does not relate to a specific need expressed by the buyer. Here are two examples of specific benefits:

> "Our water purification system meets the exact specifications you have given us for EPA compliance."
>
> "Our XP400 model meets the safety criteria you've spelled out."

Rackham says that benefit statements linked to the customer's expressed need are especially effective in large or complex sales.[31]

Some sales training programs suggest that salespeople need to include advantages in the sales presentation. Advantages are characteristics of the product (features) that can be used or will help the buyer. Consider the following statement:

> "Prior to shipping, all of our containers are double wrapped. This means that our product is completely free of contamination when it arrives at your hospital."

Some salespeople develop an advantage statement for each important product feature. Unfortunately, these advantages are often included in the sales presentation even when the buyer has not expressed a need for this information. When this happens, the advantage can be described as a general benefit.

Successful salespeople focus on specific benefits that relate to an explicit need expressed by the customer. Less successful salespeople take the position that the best way to create value is to present as many benefits as possible. High performance salespeople work hard to discover which benefits the customer really cares about. Today's customer measures value by how well your product benefits fit their needs.[32]

DOONESBURY **by Garry Trudeau**

Jerry Vass, consultant and sales trainer, says that the buyer has three questions about the product you sell: So what, what's in it for me, and can you prove it? He cautions salespeople to avoid burying the prospect with features that, by themselves, would not answer any of these questions. Vass also believes that very few salespeople have the ability to sell benefits instead of features.[33]

Use Bridge Statements

We know that people buy benefits, not features. One of the best ways to present benefits is to use a bridge statement. A **bridge statement** is a transitional phrase that connects a statement of features with a statement of benefits. This method permits customers to connect the features of your product to the benefits they receive. A sales representative of Fleming Companies, Inc. might use bridge statements to introduce a new snack food.

> "This product is nationally advertised, *which means* you will benefit from more presold customers."
>
> "You will experience faster turnover and increased profits *because* the first order includes point-of-purchase advertising materials that focus on the Valentine's day promotion you have planned."

Some companies prefer to state the benefit first and the feature second. When this occurs, the bridge statement may be a word such as "because."

Identify Features and Benefits

A careful analysis of the product helps identify both product features and buyer benefits. Once all the important features are identified, arrange them in logical order. Then write beside each feature the most important benefit the customer can derive from that feature. Finally, prepare a series of bridge statements to connect the appropriate features and benefits. By using this three-step approach, a hotel selling conference and convention services and a manufacturer selling electric motors used to power mining equipment developed feature–benefit worksheets (Tables 6.2 and 6.3). Notice how each feature is translated into a benefit that would be important to someone purchasing these products and services. Table 6.3 reminds us that company features can be converted to benefits.

TABLE | 6.2 SELLING PRODUCT BENEFITS WITH A FEATURE–BENEFIT WORKSHEET

Salespeople employed by a hotel can enhance the sales presentation by converting features to benefits.

FEATURE	BENEFIT
Facilities	
The hotel conference rooms were recently redecorated.	This means all your meetings will be held in rooms that are attractive as well as comfortable.
All our guest rooms were completely redecorated during the past six months and most were designated as nonsmoking rooms.	This means your people will find the rooms clean and attractive. In addition, they can easily select a nonsmoking room.
Food Services	
We offer four different banquet entrees prepared by Ricardo Guido who was recently selected Executive Chef of the Year by the National Restaurant Association.	This means your conference will be enhanced by delicious meals served by a well-trained staff.
Our hotel offers 24-hour room service.	This means your people can order food or beverage at their convenience.

Avoiding Information Overload

Knowing your product has always been essential to good selling, but concentrating on product alone can be a serious mistake. Salespeople who love their products, and possess vast product knowledge, sometimes overload their customers with product data they neither need nor want. This practice is often described as a "data dump."[34] With the aid of specific types of questions (see Chapter 11), the customer's needs can be identified. Once the customer's needs are known, the salesperson can develop a customized sales presentation that includes selected features that can be converted to specific benefits.

TABLE | 6.3 SELLING COMPANY BENEFITS WITH A FEATURE–BENEFIT WORKSHEET

Here we see company features translated into customer benefits.

FEATURE	BENEFIT
Our company has . . .	***This means for you . . .***
1. The best selection of motors in the area	• Choice of the best models to interface with your current equipment • Equipment operates more efficiently
2. Certified service technicians	• Well-qualified service personnel keep your equipment in top running condition • Less downtime and higher profits

Summary

A salesperson whose product knowledge is complete and accurate is better able to satisfy customers. This is without doubt the most important justification for becoming totally familiar with the products you sell. It is simply not possible to provide maximum assistance to potential customers without this information. Additional advantages to be gained from knowing your product include greater self-confidence, increased enthusiasm, improved ability to overcome objections, development of stronger selling appeals, and the preparation of more effective *written sales proposals*.

A complete understanding of your company also yields many personal and professional benefits. The most important benefit, of course, is your ability to serve your customer most effectively. In many selling situations, customers inquire about the company's business practices. They want to know details about support personnel, product development, credit procedures, warranty plans, and product service after the sale. When salespeople are able to provide the necessary company information, they gain respect. They also close more sales.

This chapter also stresses knowing your competition. It pays to study other companies that sell similar products to determine areas where you have a competitive advantage.

Salespeople gather information from many sources. Company literature and sales training programs are among the most important. Other sources include factory tours, customers, competition, publications, the Internet, and actual experience with the product itself.

In the sales presentation and in preparing the written sales proposal, your knowledge of the product's features and your company's strengths must be presented in terms of the resulting benefits to the buyer. We distinguished between general and specific benefits. Specific benefits, linked to a customer's expressed need, are very effective.

KEY TERMS

Product strategy
Product configuration
Written proposals
Product development
Quality control
Quantifying the solution
Organizational culture
Feature
Benefit
Bridge statement
Solution

REVIEW QUESTIONS

1. Provide a brief description of the term *product strategy*.
2. Distinguish between *product features* and *buyer benefits*.
3. What is *product configuration*? Provide an example of how this practice is used in the sale of commercial stereo equipment.
4. Review the GEAR for Sports' statement of values and then identify the two items that you believe contribute the most to a salesperson's career success.
5. Define the term *organizational culture*. How might this company information enhance a sales presentation?

6. Basic beliefs underlie the salesperson's method of handling competition. What are four guidelines a salesperson should follow in developing basic beliefs in this area?
7. Explain what the customer's expectations are concerning the salesperson's attitude toward competition.
8. List and briefly describe the five parts included in most written sales proposals.
9. What are the most common sources of product information?
10. Distinguish between a general benefit and a specific benefit. Why do customers respond positively to specific benefits?

APPLICATION EXERCISES

1. Secure, if possible, a copy of a customer-oriented product sales brochure or news release that has been prepared by a marketer. Many salespeople receive such selling tools. Study this information carefully; then develop a feature–benefit analysis sheet.
2. Today many companies are automating their product configuration and proposal writing activities. Go to the Internet and find these providers of the following software: *www.qwikquote.com* (for simple sales configuration) and *www.results-online.com* (for moderately complex sales configuration). Click on each company's demonstration software and study the design of each product.

3. Select a product you are familiar with and know a great deal about. (This may be an item you have shopped for and purchased, such as a compact disc player, laptop computer, or an automobile.) Under each of the categories listed, fill in the required information about the product.
   a. Where did you buy the product? Why?
   b. Did product design influence your decision?
   c. How and where was the product manufactured?
   d. What different applications or uses are there for the product?
   e. How does the product perform? Are there any data on the product's performance? What are they?
   f. What kinds of maintenance and care does the product require? How often?
   g. Could you sell the product you have written about in categories (a) through (f)? Why or why not?

ROLE-PLAY EXERCISE

Study the convention center information in Part 1, Developing a Sales Oriented Product Strategy in Appendix 3, paying special attention to pricing on the meals and meeting rooms. Access the *www.prenhall.com/manning* Web site. Click on the sales proposal link and configure a sales proposal for your instructor (using your school name and address) who is responsible for setting up a student awards meeting. The meeting includes a banquet-style meal of chicken Wellington for 26 attendees from 5:30 P.M. to 8:00 P.M. on the last Wednesday of next month. The meal will be served at 5:45 P.M., and the awards session is scheduled from 6:45 to 8:00 P.M. in the same room. The seating should be banquet style. Present the completed proposal to another student (acting as your customer) and communicate the features and benefits of your proposal.

CRM APPLICATION EXERCISE

Finding Product Information in CRM

Providing immediate access to product information can increase a salesperson's efficiency and responsiveness to customer requests. Computers excel at the task of quickly providing information. An example can be found in the ACT! CRM case study software. Basic information about networks is available in the Reference Library, a feature of this version of ACT!. After loading the software, select View, Reference Library, to view the networking information. Print this information by selecting File, Print. While in the Reference Library, other library documents can be opened by selecting File, Open, and double-clicking on one of the files that ends with "wpd." When finished, these ACT! word processing files can be closed by selecting File, Close (Alt + F C).

VIDEO CASE PROBLEM

Cart Works manages several free-standing retail booths (often called kiosks) that operate in shopping malls. Many of the newer malls have incorporated kiosks to create the busy and happy atmosphere of an open marketplace. The design of the kiosk varies from a stationary booth to a movable cart. A typical kiosk offers a specialized product line such as greeting cards, inexpensive jewelry, T-shirts, sunglasses, candy, or snacks. A small number of kiosks can add a new dimension to the shopping atmosphere.

Cart Works is currently seeking new entrepreneurs who want to operate kiosks in shopping malls. The company offers training and help in selecting a high-traffic location in the mall. Once a location is selected, members of the Cart Works staff decide what products are most likely to be popular at that location.

Cart Works wants to expand its business to include several western states. A decision has been made to promote the Cart Works concept by placing ads in selected newspapers in large cities (e.g., Denver, Seattle, Los Angeles, etc.). These ads will briefly explain the business opportunity and invite prospects to attend an information meeting at a local hotel. A representative of Cart Works will conduct the meeting. Persons who attend the meeting will be given an overview of the company that includes the following features:

- Cart Works has conducted research to determine what type of merchandise sells best from a booth or movable cart. The company knows what type of mall shopper is most likely to buy a product from a booth or cart.
- Cart Works can provide merchandise that sells well from a booth or cart. Entrepreneurs also have the option of providing their own merchandise, which can be purchased from another vendor.
- Cart Works will provide the training needed to successfully establish and operate the business.
- Cart Works will meet with the mall manager and obtain permission to operate the business within the mall. Most malls will require a contract that outlines the business relationship. All malls charge a fee for operation of the booth or cart.

Persons who attend the meeting will be given a package of materials that explains the business opportunity. Serious prospects will be contacted after the meeting. They will be invited to meet with a Cart Works representative. (See opening chapter material on page 130.)

Questions

1. Explain how a Cart Works representative can use the three prescriptions for a product selling strategy in preparing and presenting product solutions.
2. What are the major benefits that could be incorporated into the group and individual presentations?
3. In addition to the actual product strategy, how important will company information (history, mission, past performance, product support, etc.) be in closing the sale during individual meetings with prospects?

PARTNERSHIP SELLING: A ROLE-PLAY/SIMULATION

(see Part 1 of Appendix 3)

Part I: Developing a Product Strategy

Read Employment Memorandum 1 in Appendix 3, which introduces you to your new training position with the Hotel Convention Center. You also should study the product strategy materials that follow the memo to become familiar with the company, product, and competitive knowledge you need in your new position.

Read the Customer Service/Sales Memorandum in Part I of Appendix 3 and complete the two-part customer/service assignment provided by your sales manager. In item 1, you are to configure a price/product sales proposal; and in item 2 you are to write a sales cover letter for the sales proposal. Note that the information presented in the price/product sales proposal consists of product facts/features, and the information presented in your sales cover letter should present specific benefit statements. These forms should be custom fitted to meet the specific needs of your customer, B. H. Rivera. All the product information you need is in the product strategy materials provided as enclosures and attachments to Employment Memorandum 1.

Chapter Preview

When you finish reading this chapter, you should be able to

1 Describe positioning as a product-selling strategy

2 Discuss product differentiation in personal selling

3 Explain how today's customer is redefining products

4 Describe how to sell products at various stages of the product life cycle

5 Explain how to sell your product with a price strategy

6 Explain how to sell your product with a value-added strategy

7 List and describe the four dimensions of the total product concept

CHAPTER 7

Product-Selling Strategies That Add Value

You just finished paying off your college loans and it's time to replace that old rust bucket with a new car. You have looked at the sport-compact cars available, but they all seem so small. Now you are eagerly looking at cars in the sports-sedan category. The cars in this niche offer a good blend of comfort, design, and performance. However, there are almost too many choices. *Road & Track* says there are 11 different automobiles in this group. The list price for these cars ranges from $29,000 to $40,000. The Audi A4 and Jaguar X-Type offer all-wheel drive; all the rest offer front- or rear-wheel drive. As you learn more about the choices available, it becomes clear that each manufacturer has taken steps to differentiate its product.[1]

Several years ago, automobile manufacturers from around the world began to develop and position cars for the sports-sedan segment. Research indicated that demand for these cars would increase. The result was the introduction of 11 different marques, each with its own unique characteristics. At the dealer level, the process of product differentiation continues. If you want something more than standard equipment, the salesperson can describe a variety of options that can add $7,000 to $10,000 to the price. Each car can be accessorized to meet your personal needs. The dealer can also help position this product with modern facilities, customer-friendly service policies, and a reputation for honesty and integrity.

Some automobile manufacturers see the sports-sedan category as critical to their success. At BMW, the 3 Series sports sedan accounts for nearly half of the company's sales worldwide. Sports-sedans can be very profitable because many buyers purchase expensive options such as special wheel and tire packages, anti-skid electronics, ground-effect's trim, and top-of-the line audio systems.

The Jaguar X-Type, Saab 9-5 Aero, Audi A4, and Cadillac CTS compete in the crowded sports-sedan category. Adding value depends on the salesperson's ability to provide a competitive analysis that positions the brand.

Design can play a major role in the sports-sedan market segment. BMW and Audi recently unveiled completely redesigned cars. These new cars will face off against the Infinite G35 and the Cadillac CTS, two cars noted for advanced design.[2]

Salespeople at the dealer level can play an important role in positioning the automobile for competitive advantage. They can describe the quality control process that ensures the build quality of the BMW 330i or demonstrate the sports car driving characteristics of the Lexus IS 350. Adding value depends on the salesperson's ability to provide a competitive analysis using knowledge of the manufacturer, the automobile, and the dealership.

PRODUCT POSITIONING—A PRODUCT SELLING STRATEGY

Long-term success in today's dynamic global economy requires the continuous positioning and repositioning of products. **Positioning** involves those decisions and activities intended to create and maintain a certain concept of the firm's product in the customer's mind. It requires developing a marketing strategy aimed at influencing how a particular market segment perceives a product in comparison to the competition.[3] In a market that has been flooded with various types of sport-utility vehicles (SUVs), Land Rover has been positioned as a dependable vehicle that can climb a steep, rock-covered hillside with ease. Every effort has been made to create the perception of safety, durability, and security. To give sales representatives increased confidence in the Land Rover, the company has arranged plant tours and the opportunity to observe actual testing of the Land Rover vehicles under extremely demanding conditions.

Selling Is Everyone's Business

MICHAEL DELL'S EARLY YEARS

At the age of 12, Michael Dell, CEO of Dell Computer Corporation, was displaying the characteristics of an opportunistic entrepreneur. He turned his stamp-collecting hobby into a mail-order business that netted $2,000. This money was used to purchase his first computer. He also developed his personal selling skills at an early age. At age 16, he was selling subscriptions to his hometown paper, the *Houston Post*. Later he enrolled in college but had difficulty focusing on his course work. He often cut classes in order to spend more time assembling and selling computers. When Dell's parents discovered his newest enterprise, they pressured him to stay focused on completing his degree. Dell completed the spring semester and then spent the summer expanding his business. In the month prior to the fall semester, he sold $180,000 worth of computers. He did not return to college.[a]

Michael Dell, CEO of Dell Computer Corporation.

Good positioning means that the product's name, reputation, and niche are well recognized. However, a good positioning strategy does not last forever. The positioning process must be continually modified to match the customer's changing wants and needs.[4]

Essentials of Product Positioning

Most companies use a combination of marketing and sales strategies to give their products a unique position in the marketplace. Every salesperson needs a good understanding of the fundamental practices that contribute to product positioning. The chapter begins with a brief introduction to the concept of product differentiation. This is followed by an explanation of how products have been redefined in the age of information. The remainder of the chapter is devoted to three product-selling strategies that can be used to position a product. Emphasis is placed on positioning your product with a value-added strategy. In the age of information, salespeople who cannot add value to the products they sell will diminish in number and influence.

Achieving Product Differentiation in Personal Selling

One of the basic tenets of sales and marketing is the principle of product differentiation. **Differentiation** refers to your ability to separate yourself and your product from that of your competitors. It is the key to building and maintaining a competitive advantage.[5] The competitors in virtually all industries are moving toward differentiating themselves on the basis of quality, price, convenience, economy, or some other factor. Salespeople, who are on the front line of many marketing efforts, assume an important role in the product differentiation process.

Differentiating your product helps you stand out from the crowd. It often allows you to distance yourself from the competition. In many cases, the process of differentiation creates barriers that make it difficult for the buyer to choose a competing product simply on the basis of price.[6]

A well-informed customer will usually choose the product that offers the most value. Therefore, salespeople need to position their product with a value proposition. A **value proposition** is the set of benefits and values the company promises to deliver to customers to satisfy their needs. The value proposition presented by Porsche promises driving performance and excitement.[7] Kinko's, which is now part of FedEx, is attempting to differentiate itself from Sir Speedy, AlphaGraphics, and print shops found at Office Depot, OfficeMax, and Staples. The new value proposition promises that 1200 FedEx Kinko's locations offer a breadth of services unparalleled in the industry. These new centers leverage the traditional strengths and brand awareness of FedEx and Kinko's.[8]

Nordstrom, a department store chain based in Portland, Oregon, has positioned itself with upscale merchandise and a shopping experience that includes the personal touch. Each store stocks fashion goods that reflect the lifestyle of customers in the surrounding area. Well-trained salespeople keep records on their customers' sizes and preferences so that they can let them know when an item that may be of interest to them arrives at the store. Nordstrom works hard to achieve product and service differentiation and offer customers a well-defined value proposition.

REDEFINING PRODUCTS IN THE AGE OF INFORMATION

Ted Levitt, former editor of the *Harvard Business Review*, says that products are problem-solving tools. People buy products if they fulfill a problem-solving need. Today's better-educated and more demanding customers are seeking a *cluster of satisfactions*. **Satisfactions** arise from the product itself, from the company that makes or distributes the product, and from the salesperson who sells and services the product.[9] Figure 7.1 provides a description of a three-dimensional *Product-Selling Model*. As noted in Chapter 6, many companies are attempting to transform themselves from *product selling* to *solution selling*. To develop and sell solutions, salespeople must be familiar with the satisfactions that meet the needs of each customer.

To illustrate how the cluster of satisfactions concept works in a business setting, let us examine a complex buying decision. Elaine Parker, a sales representative for Elmore Industries Incorporated, sells metals for manufacturing operations. Over a period of six months, she frequently called on a prospect that had the potential to become a valued customer. During every call, the buyer's receptionist told her they were happy with their present supplier. She refused to give up and finally the buyer agreed to see her. At first she was greeted with cool silence, so she decided to ask him some questions about his business: "How's the slow economy affecting your sales?" The buyer's answers focused on materials costs. He said his company could not raise prices nor cut quality. He wanted to lower costs, but was unsure how it could be done. Parker suggested he consider trying some new alloys that are less expensive than the standard metals he had been purchasing. As she described the new alloys, the buyer's interest began to build. She offered to make a full presentation to the buyer and his engineers at a follow-up meeting. The second meeting was a success. Soon after that meeting, Parker received

FIGURE | 7.1

Product-Selling Model

The product strategy should include a cluster of satisfactions that meets the needs of today's better-educated and more demanding customers. Drawing from this cluster, the salesperson can configure value-added solutions that meet individual customer's needs.

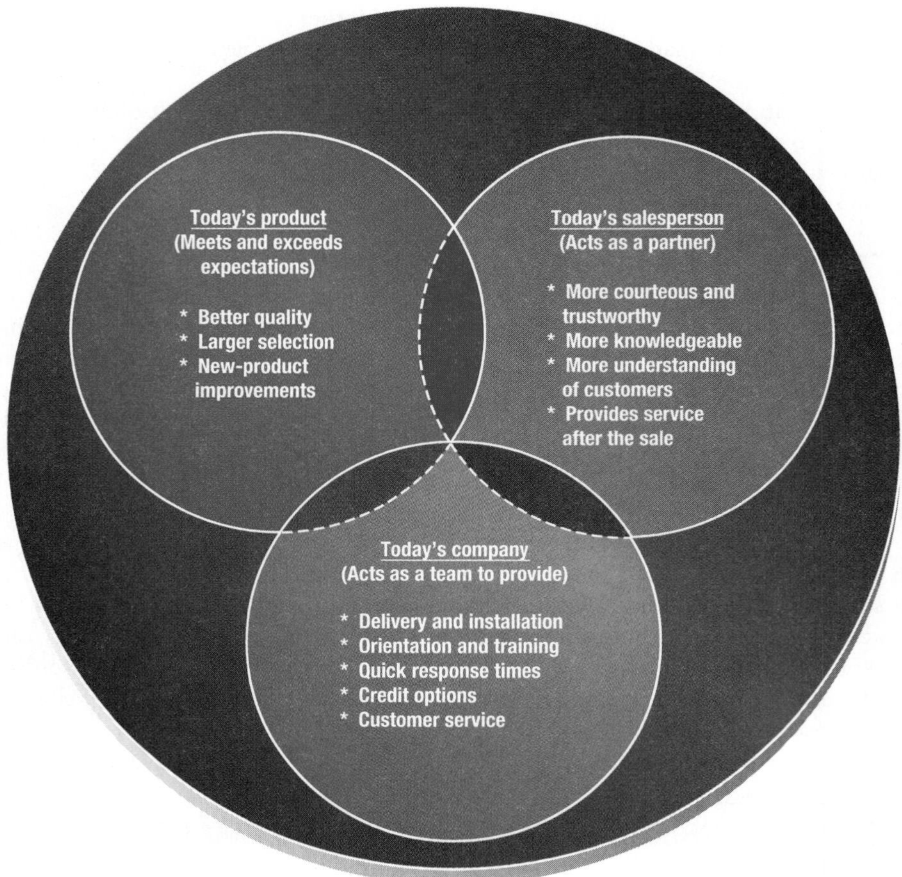

her first order from the customer. Within a year, she had become the customer's most trusted advisor on technological developments in the industry and his exclusive supplier.[10]

Elaine Parker used questions to engage the customer and identify his problem. She also provided satisfactory answers to questions raised by the customers:

Questions Related to the Product

What product is best for our type of operation?

Does the product meet our quality standards?

Given the cost of this product, will we maintain our competitive position in the marketplace?

Questions Related to the Company

Does this company provide the most advanced technology?

What is the company's reputation for quality products?

What is the company's reputation for standing behind the products it sells?

Questions Related to the Salesperson

Does this salesperson possess the knowledge and experience needed to recommend the right product?

TABLE 7.1 COMPETITIVE ANALYSIS WORKSHEET

A value-added product selling strategy is enhanced when salespeople analyze product, company, and salesperson attributes of the competition in relation to the benefits they offer. This information helps the salesperson create value within the sales process.

	MY COMPANY	COMPETITOR A	COMPETITOR B
Product Attributes			
Quality			
Durability			
Reliability			
Performance			
Packaging flexibility			
Warranty			
Brand			
Company Attributes			
Reputation			
Industry leadership			
Facilities			
Ease of doing business			
Distribution channels			
Ordering convenience			
Returns, credits, etc.			
Salesperson Attributes			
Knowledge/expertise			
Responsiveness			
Pricing authority			
Customer orientation			
Honesty/Integrity			
Follow-through			
Presentation skills			

Can the salesperson clearly communicate specific buyer benefits?

Can this salesperson serve as a trusted advisor?

Will this salesperson provide support services after the sale?

Salespeople who are knowledgeable in all areas of the Product-Selling Model are better able to position a product. Knowledge helps you achieve product differentiation, understand the competition, and prepare an effective value proposition. The competitive analysis worksheet (Table 7.1) can help you discover ways to position your product as the superior choice over your competition.

A Word of Caution

Because many of today's information age products are very complex, product differentiation must be handled with care. Salespeople are sometimes tempted to use technical lingo, real and invented, to impress the buyer. This problem often surfaces in a situation in which the salesperson is not sure how to describe the value-added features of the product. Robert Notte, technology chief for travel outfitter Backroads, says that during the telecom boom salespeople representing WorldCom (now MCI) and other firms babbled endlessly, using industry jargon that was often unintelligible. "They wanted you to be impressed," Mr. Notte says. Some customers were so intimidated they were afraid to ask questions ... or make a buying decision.[11]

PRODUCT-POSITIONING OPTIONS

Product positioning is a concept that applies to both new and existing products. Given the dynamics of most markets, it may be necessary to reposition products several times in their lives because even solid, popular products can lose market position quickly. Salespeople have assumed an important and expanding role in differentiating products. To succeed in our overcommunicated society, marketers must use a direct and personalized form of communication with customers. Advertising directed toward a mass market often fails to position a complex product.

Throughout the remainder of this chapter we discuss specific ways to use various product-positioning strategies. We explain how salespeople can (1) position new and emerging products versus well-established products, (2) position products with price strategies, and (3) position products with value-added strategies.

Selling New and Emerging Products versus Mature and Well-Established Products

In many ways, products are like human beings. They are born, grow up, mature, and grow old. In marketing, this process is known as the **product life cycle**. The product life cycle includes the stages a product goes through from the time it is first introduced to the market

Customer Relationship Management with Technology

MANAGING NEW-PRODUCT INFORMATION WITH CRM

Today salespeople are challenged to manage a steady stream of information about customers (needs) and products (solutions). From this stream of information, the sales professional must select product information that is relevant to a specific customer and deliver the information in a manner that can be understood by the customer. Customer relationship management (CRM) assists the busy salesperson by providing tools that can collect information and link it to those who need it. Most CRM systems can receive and organize information from e-mail, Web sites, and the files of reference material kept within the company's information system. Sales professionals can add value to this information by summarizing, combining, and tailoring the information to meet a customer's needs.

When new-product information is received, databases of customer data can be quickly searched to find those customers who might have an interest. The new-product information can be merged into an e-mail, fax, or letter to that customer, along with other information (benefits) that can help the customer assess its value. Later, the CRM system can display a follow-up alert, reminding the sales professional of the information that was shared with the customer. (See the exercise, Informing Customers with CRM, on page 176 for more information.)

until it is discontinued. As the product moves through its cycle, the strategies relating to competition, promotion, pricing, and other factors must be evaluated and possibly changed. The nature and extent of each stage in the product life cycle are determined by several factors, including:

1. The product's perceived advantage over available substitutes
2. The product's benefits and the importance of the needs it fulfills
3. Competitive activity, including pricing, substitute product development and improvement, and effectiveness of competing advertising and promotion
4. Changes in technology, fashion, or demographics[12]

As we attempt to develop a product-selling strategy, we must consider where the product is positioned in terms of the life cycle. The sales strategy used to sell a new and emerging product is much different from the strategy used to sell a mature, well-established product (Fig. 7.2).

Selling New and Emerging Products

Selling strategies used during the new and emerging stage (see Fig. 7.2) are designed to develop a new level of expectation, change habits, and in some cases establish a new standard of quality. The goal is to build desire for the product.

When Brother International Corporation introduced its line of Multi-Function Center (MFC) machines, the goal was to convince buyers that one machine could replace five separate machines. However, before buyers would give up their copy machine, fax machine, laser printer, and other machines, they ask some hard questions. Is a multifunction machine reliable? Does the quality match that of the current machines? Finding the best machine for each customer is challenging because Brother offers more than 10 different MFC models to choose from.

In some cases the new product is not a tangible item. Several years ago IntraLinks closed its first big sale, a $50,000 contract, with J. P. Morgan. The company got its start providing the financial services industry with the secure transmission of highly confidential

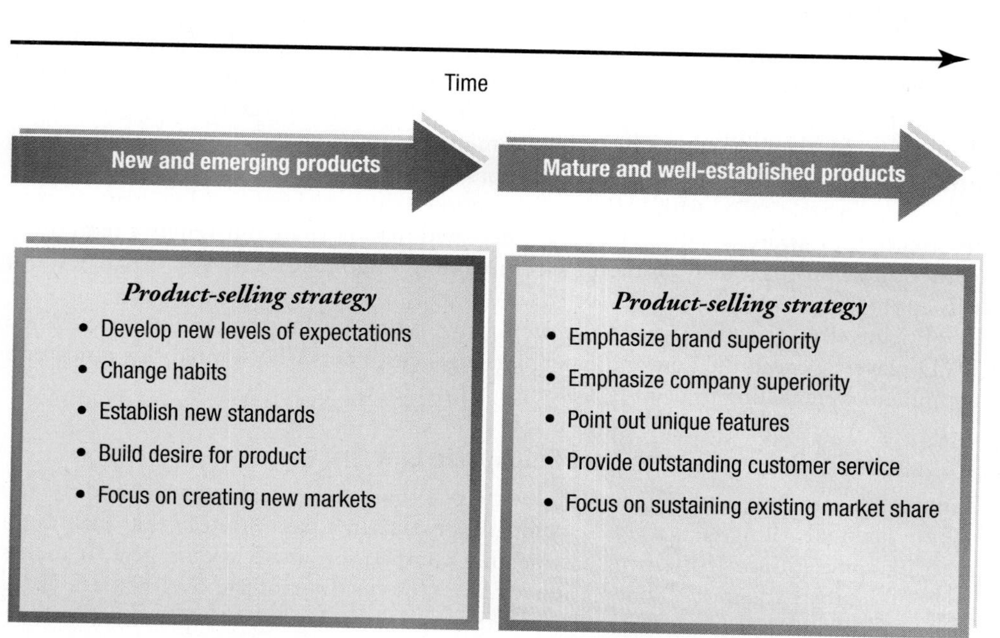

FIGURE | 7.2

Product-Selling Strategies for Positioning New and Emerging Products Versus Mature and Well-Established Products

information across the Internet. Patrick Wack and his business partners convinced J. P. Morgan and other financial firms that they did not need to rely on an army of foot messengers and FedEx trucks to deliver sensitive documents. They were not only selling a new product, they were selling a vision that included new levels of expectations. The value proposition focused on faster, more secure document transfer which, in the customer's mind, translated into improved customer service and cost savings. Today Patrick Wack is selling this document transfer concept to customers in a variety of business communities.[13]

Selling Mature and Well-Established Products

Mature and well-established products are usually characterized by intense competition as new brands enter the market. Customers who currently buy your product will become aware of competing products. With new and emerging products, salespeople may initially have little or no competition and may dominate the market; however, this condition may not last long.

New York Life Insurance Company provides its sales agents with new products almost every year. The product portfolio was recently expanded to include the Asset Preserver, which allows the policy death benefit to be accelerated, on an income tax-free basis, to pay for long-term care services. The company also developed the Universal Life Protector, which offers long-term protection at lower prices. New products offered by a market leader are quickly copied by competing insurance companies. When competing products enter the market, New York Life agents must adopt new strategies. One positioning strategy is to emphasize the company's 150 years of outstanding service to policyholders. They can also note that New York Life is a "mutual" company; it is owned by policyholders, not corporate shareholders. The objective is to create in the customer's mind the perception that New York Life is a solid company that will be strong and solvent when it's time to pay premiums.[14]

The relationship strategy is often critical in selling mature and well-established products. To maintain market share and ward off competitors, many salespeople work hard to maintain a strong relationship with the customer. At New York Life, salespeople have found that good service after the sale is one of the best selling strategies because it builds customer loyalty.

Selling Products with a Price Strategy

Price, promotion, product, and place are the four elements that make up the marketing mix. Pricing decisions must be made at each stage of the product life cycle. Therefore, setting the price can be a complex process. The first step in establishing price is to determine the firm's pricing objectives. Some firms set their prices to maximize their profits. They aim for a price as high as possible without causing a disproportionate reduction in unit sales. Other firms set a market share objective. Management may decide that the strategic advantage of an increased market share outweighs a temporary reduction in profits. Many of the new companies doing business on the Internet adopt this approach.

Pricing strategies often reflect the product's position in the product life cycle. When DVD players were in the new and emerging stage, customers who wanted this innovative equipment were willing to pay $1,000 or more for a unit.

Transactional Selling Tactics That Emphasize Low Price

Some marketers have established a positioning plan that emphasizes low price and the use of transactional selling tactics. These companies maintain a basic strategy that focuses on meeting competition. If the firm has meeting competition as its pricing goal, it makes every effort to charge prices that are identical or close to those of the competition. Once this positioning strategy has been adopted, the sales force is given several price tactics to

FMC partners with customers to test new products before they are sold.

use. Salespeople can alter (lower) the base price through the use of discounts and allowances. Discounts and allowances can take a variety of forms. A few of the more common ones follow:

Quantity discount. The quantity discount allows the buyer a lower price for purchasing in multiple units or above a specified dollar amount.

Seasonal discount. With seasonal pricing, the salesperson adjusts the price up or down during specific times to spur or acknowledge changes in demand. Off-season travel and lodging prices provide examples.

Selling in Action

HOW DO CUSTOMERS JUDGE SERVICE QUALITY?

In the growing service industry there is intense price competition. From a distance, one gets the impression that every buyer decision hinges on price alone. However, a closer examination of service purchases indicates that service quality is an important factor when it comes to developing a long-term relationship with customers.

How do customers judge service quality? Researchers at Texas A&M University have discovered valuable insights about customer perceptions of service quality. They surveyed hundreds of customers in a variety of service industries and discovered that five service-quality dimensions emerged:

1. *Tangibles:* Details the customers can see, such as the appearance of personnel and equipment.
2. *Reliability:* The ability to perform the desired service dependably, accurately, and consistently.
3. *Responsiveness:* The willingness of sales and customer service personnel to provide prompt service and help customers.
4. *Assurance:* The employees' knowledge, courtesy, and ability to convey trust and confidence.
5. *Empathy:* The provision of caring, individualized attention to customers.

Customers apparently judge the quality of each service transaction in terms of these five quality dimensions. Companies need to review these service-quality dimensions and make sure that each area measures up to customers' expectations. Salespeople should recognize that these dimensions have the potential to add value to the services they sell.[b]

Promotional allowance. A promotional allowance is a price reduction given to a customer who participates in an advertising or a sales support program. Many salespeople give supermarkets promotional allowances for advertising or displaying a manufacturer's products.

Trade or functional discounts. Channel intermediaries, such as wholesalers, often perform credit, storage, or transportation services. Trade or functional discounts cover the cost of these services.[15]

Another option available to salespeople facing a buyer with a low-price buying strategy is to "unbundle" product features. Let's assume that a price-conscious customer wants to schedule a conference that will be accompanied by a banquet-style meal. To achieve a lower price, the salesperson might suggest a cafeteria-style meal, thereby eliminating the need for servers. This product configuration involves less cost to the seller, and cost savings can be passed on to the buyer. Timken Company, a century-old bearing maker, has adopted bundling as a way to compete with other manufacturers around the world. The company now surrounds its basic products with additional components in order to provide customers with exactly what they need. These components can take the form of electronic sensors, lubrication systems, castings, or installation and maintenance. Giving customers bundling options has given Timken a big advantage over foreign competitors who often focus on the basic product. Salespeople who represent Timken have flexible pricing options.[16]

These examples represent only a small sample of the many discounts and allowances salespeople use to compete on the basis of price. Price discounting is a competitive tool available to large numbers of salespeople. Excessive focus on low prices and generous discounts, however, can have a negative impact on profits and sales commissions.

"WE HAVE QUALITY AND WE HAVE LOW PRICES... WHICH DO YOU WANT?"

Agency Sales Magazine *from the Manufacturing Agent National Association (MANA).*

Consequences of Using Low-Price Tactics

Pricing is a critical factor in the sale of many products and services. In markets where competition is extremely strong, setting a product's price may be a firm's most complicated and important decision.

The authors of *The Discipline of Market Leaders* encourage business firms to pick one of three disciplines—best price, best product, or best service—and then do whatever is necessary to outdistance the competition. However, the authors caution us not to ignore the other two disciplines: "You design your business to excel in one direction, but you also have to strive to hit the minimum in the others."[17] Prior to using low-price tactics, everyone involved in sales and marketing should answer these questions:

- *Are you selling to high- or low-involvement buyers?* Some people are emotionally involved with respected brands such as BMW, Sony, and American Express. A part of their identity depends on buying the product they consider the best. Low-involvement buyers care mostly about price.[18]
- *How important is quality in the minds of buyers?* If buyers do not fully understand the price-quality relationship, they may judge the product by its price. For a growing number of customers, long-term value is more important than short-term savings that result from low prices.
- *How important is service?* For many buyers, service is a critical factor. Even online customers, thought to be very interested in price, rate quality of service very highly. This is especially true in business-to-business sales. A survey conducted by Accenture reports that 80 percent of nearly 1,000 corporate buyers rate a strong brand and reliable customer service ahead of low prices when deciding which companies to do business with online.[19]

Influence of Electronic Commerce on Pricing

Companies large and small are racing to discover new sales and marketing opportunities on the Internet. Products ranging from personal computers to term insurance can be purchased from various Web sites. Salespeople who are involved primarily in transactional selling and add little or no value to the sales transaction often are not able to compete with online vendors. To illustrate, consider the purchase of insurance. At the present time it is possible to purchase basic term insurance online from InsureMarket.com, AccuQuote.com, and other Web sites. A well-informed buyer, willing to visit several Web sites, can select a policy with a minimum amount of risk. In the case of long-term care insurance, which can pay for health care at home or in a nursing home, the buyer needs the help of a well-trained agent. These policies are complex and the premiums are high.

Investors now have more choices than they have had in the past. Persons who need little or no assistance buying stocks can visit the E*Trade Web site or a similar online discount vendor. The person who wants help selecting a stock can turn to a broker, such as Merrill Lynch or UBS Paine Webber, that offers both full-service and online options. Full-service brokers can survive and may prosper as long as they can add value to the sales transaction. The new economy is reshaping the world of commerce and every buyer has more choices.

Selling Your Product with a Value-Added Strategy

Many progressive marketers have adopted a market plan that emphasizes *value-added strategies*. Companies can add value to their product with one or more intangibles such as better-trained salespeople, increased levels of courtesy, more dependable product deliveries, better service after the sale, and innovations that truly improve the product's value in the eyes of the customer. In today's highly competitive marketplace, these value-added benefits give the company a unique niche and a competitive edge.

To understand fully the importance of the value-added concept in selling, and how to apply it in a variety of selling situations, it helps to visualize every product as being four dimensional. The *total product* is made up of four "possible" products: the generic product, the expected product, the value-added product, and the potential product[20] (Fig. 7.3).

Generic Product

The **generic product** is the basic, substantive product you are selling. Generic product describes only the product category, for example, life insurance, rental cars, or personal computers. Every Ritz-Carlton hotel offers guest rooms, one or more full-service restaurants, meeting rooms, guest parking, and other basic services. For Yellow Freight System, a company that provides shipping services, the generic product is the truck and trailer that move the customer's freight. At the generic level, Nordstrom provides categories of goods traditional to an upscale specialty clothing retailer. The generic products at a bank are money that can be loaned to customers and basic checking account services.

The capability of delivering a generic product simply gives the marketer the right to play in the game, to compete in the marketplace.[21] Generic products, even the lowest-priced ones, often cannot compete with products that are "expected" by the customer.

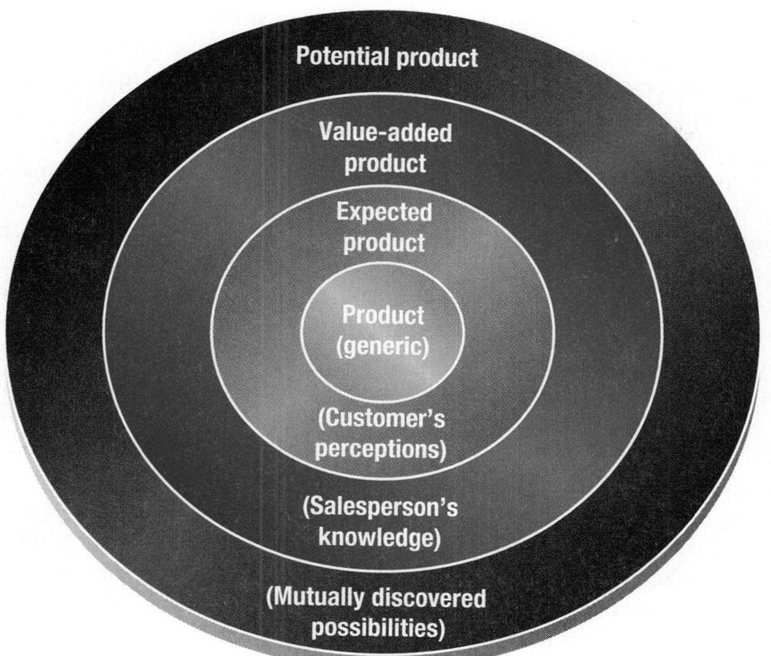

FIGURE 7.3

The Total Product Concept
An understanding of the four "possible" products is helpful when the salesperson develops a presentation for specific types of customers.

Expected Product

Every customer has minimal purchase expectations that exceed the generic product itself.[22] Ritz-Carlton must offer not only a comfortable guest room but also a clean one. Some customers expect a "super" clean room. Yellow must provide clean, well-maintained trucks *and* well-trained drivers. The **expected product** is everything that represents the customer's minimal expectations. The customer at a Nordstrom store *expects* current fashions and well-informed salespeople.

Global Business Etiquette

DOING BUSINESS IN INDIA

India is a very large country that is growing in importance in terms of international trade. Indians' customs are often dictated by their religious beliefs. In addition to the Hindus and Muslims, there are dozens of other religious groups. Study the Indian culture carefully before your first business trip to this country.

- Customs of food and drink are an important consideration when you do business in India. Avoid eating meat in the presence of Hindus because they are vegetarians and consider the cow a sacred animal. Muslims will not eat pork or drink alcoholic beverages.
- There is a very strict caste system in India so be aware of the caste of the clients with whom you are dealing and any restrictions that may apply to that caste.
- Most members of the Indian business community speak English.
- Indians tend to be careful buyers who seek quality and durability. They respect a salesperson who is caring and well informed. Personal relationships in business transactions are very important.[c]

The minimal purchase conditions vary among customers, so the salesperson must acquire information concerning the expected product that exists in the customer's mind. When the customer expects more than the generic product, the product can be sold *only* if those expectations are met. Every customer perceives the product in individualized terms, which a salesperson cannot anticipate.

To determine each customer's expectations requires the salesperson to make observations, conduct background checks, ask questions, and listen to what the customer is saying. You are attempting to discover both feelings and facts. Top salespeople encourage the customer to think more deeply about the problems they face and discover for themselves the value of a solution. They *avoid* offering solutions until the needs are clearly spelled out. If the buyer says, "The average gas mileage for our fleet of delivery trucks is only 17 miles per gallon," the salesperson might respond with this question: "How does this low mileage rate affect your profitability?" To move the customer's attention from the expected product to a value-added product, you need to keep the customer focused on solutions.[23]

Research reported in the *Harvard Business Review* indicates that it is very difficult to build customer loyalty if you are selling only the expected product. Customer satisfaction and loyalty do not always move in tandem. The customer who purchases the services of Ernst & Young Consulting may feel satisfied after the project is completed but never do business with the company again. Customer loyalty is more likely to increase when the purchase involves a value-added product.[24]

Value-Added Product

The **value-added product** exists when salespeople offer customers more than they expect. When you make a reservation at one of the Ritz-Carlton hotels and request a special amenity such as a tennis lesson, a record of this request is maintained in the computer system. If you make a reservation at another Ritz-Carlton at some future date, the agent informs you of the availability of a tennis court. The guest who buys chocolate chip cookies in the lobby gift shop in New Orleans may find a basket of them waiting in his room in Boston two weeks later. The hotel company uses modern technology to surprise and delight guests.[25]

In the mid-1990s, Yellow Freight System was a troubled long-haul carrier offering customers a generic product. Bill Zollars was hired to transform the company by adding a variety of services built around unprecedented customer service. The new services positioned the company to satisfy a broader range of transportation needs. For example, the company launched Yellow's Exact Express, its first time-definite, guaranteed service. Exact Express is now Yellow's most expensive and most profitable service. Today, Yellow Freight System salespeople are able to offer its 300,000 customers a value-added product.[26]

Potential Product

After the value-added product has been developed, the salesperson should begin to conceptualize the **potential product**. The potential product refers to what may remain to be done, that is, what is possible.[27] As the level of competition increases, especially in the case of mature products, salespeople must look to the future and explore new possibilities.

In the highly competitive food services industry, restaurant owners like to do business with a distribution sales representative (DSR) who wants to help make the business profitable. The DSR who assumes this role becomes a true partner and looks beyond the

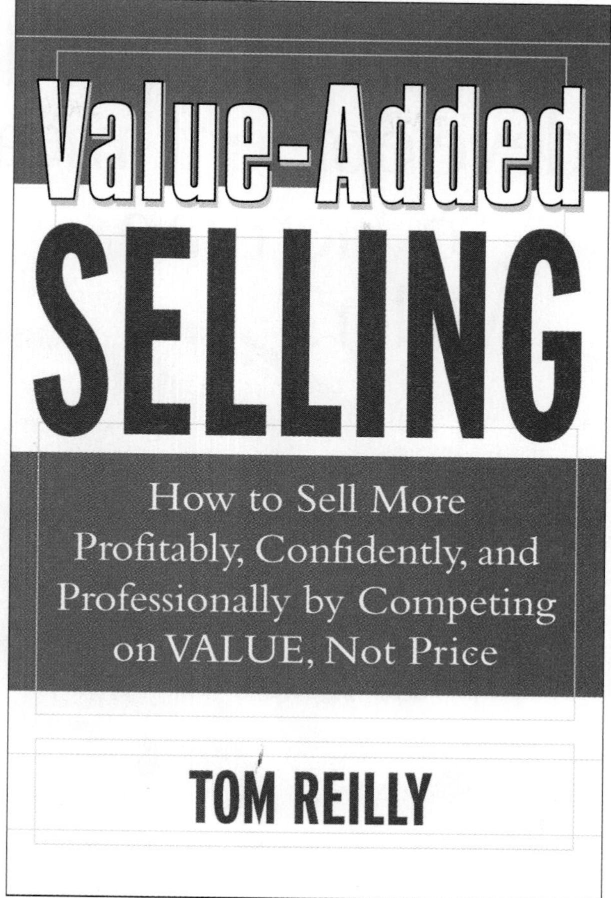

In his book VALUE ADDED SELLING, Tom Reilly states that "Value-added selling is a business philosophy. It's proactively looking for ways to enhance, augment, or enlarge your bundled package for the customer. Value added salespeople sell a three-dimensional bundle of value: the product, the company and themselves".

customer's immediate and basic needs. The potential product might be identified after a careful study of the restaurant's current menu and customer base. To deliver the potential product, a salesperson must discover and satisfy new customer needs, which requires imagination and creativity.

Steelcase Incorporated, a leading manufacturer of office furniture, has developed the "Think" chair which is 99% recyclable and can be disassembled with basic hand tools in about five minutes. This $900 chair meets a growing demand for products made of parts that can be recycled several times and manufactured in ways least harmful to the environment. Steelcase developed this "potential product" after learning that customers are increasingly seeking environmentally safe products and are sometimes willing to pay a premium for them.[28]

The potential product is more likely to be developed by salespeople who are close to their customers. Many high-performing salespeople explore product possibilities with their customers on a regular basis. Potential products are often mutually discovered during these exchanges.

Every indication points toward product-selling strategies that add value becoming more important in the future. New product life cycles are shrinking, so more companies are searching for ways to add value during the new and emerging stage. Some companies that

Herman Miller salespeople can assure customers of a custom solution with their CEO's commitment.

have experienced low profits selling low-priced products are reinventing those products. They search for product features that provide benefits customers think are worth paying for. Maytag Corporation developed the expensive environment-friendly Neptune washing machine for customers who will pay more for a washer that uses less water. Yellow Freight System created value for customers with the addition of Yellow's Exact Express and other service options.

Selling in Action

PRICING YOUR PROFESSIONAL FEES

The age of information has created many career opportunities for people who want to sell professional services. Strong demand for professional services has surfaced in such diverse fields as telecommunications, banking, computer technology, training, and health care. Dana Martin spent 18 years working in the human resources division of Allstate Insurance Company. His specialty was the design and delivery of training programs. He decided to leave the corporate environment and start his own training firm. Martin, like thousands of other professional service providers, had to decide how much to charge for his service. Before he could sell the first training program, he had to decide how much to charge. Should he price his service on an hourly basis or on a project basis? Here are some points to consider when determining fees:

- *Experience:* In the case of Dana Martin, new clients benefit from what he has learned during many years at Allstate.
- *Exclusivity:* If you are one of only a small number of people with a particular capability, you may be able to charge more. Specialists often charge higher fees than generalists.
- *Target Market:* Some markets are very price sensitive. If you are selling your services to large corporations that are used to paying high fees, you may be able to set your fees higher. If you are providing your services to small business clients, expect resistance to high fees.
- *Value:* How important is your service to the client? In the late 1990s, many companies needed help preparing their computers for transition to the year 2000. This was known as the "Y2K" problem. These firms were willing to pay high fees for this assistance. Some service providers charge higher fees because they add value in one form or another.[d]

Value Creation Investments for Transactional, Consultative, and Strategic Alliance Buyers

In most cases, value creation investments during the transactional sale are minimal. Emphasis is usually placed on finding ways to eliminate any unnecessary costs associated with the sale and avoiding delays in processing the order. Technology investments can sometimes play a big role in improving efficiencies.[29] For example, customers may be encouraged to order products online.

A considerable amount of value creation takes place in consultative sales. Higher investments in value creation are permitted because companies need to invest in developing a good understanding of the customer's needs and problems. This is especially true in large, complex sales. The opportunity to create custom tailored solutions and deliver more real benefits to the customer provides the opportunity for high margins. If your company is selling mobile autonomous robots, for example, the sales cycle will be quite long and investments will be quite high. It may take several weeks to study the applications of this product in a hospital, a manufacturing plant, or a large warehouse facility. The use of these robots may ultimately result in significant cost savings for the customer.[30]

Value creation investments in strategic alliance sales are the highest. As noted in Chapter 1, strategic alliances represent the highest form of partnering. Building an alliance is always preceded by a careful study of the proposed partner. Creating value often requires leveraging the full assets of the company, so investments go well beyond the sales force. Alliances are often developed by a team of specialists from such areas as finance, engineering, and marketing. A proposed alliance may require investments in new technology, manufacturing facilities, and warehouses.[31]

Lexus, a major success story in the automobile industry, offers the customer a value-added strategy that encompasses the product, the company, and the salesperson.

WHAT IS LEXUS?

Lexus is... Engineering sophistication and manufacturing quality.

Lexus is... Luxury and performance.

Lexus is... An image and an expectation of excellence.

Lexus is... Valuing the customer as an important individual.

Lexus is... Treating customers the way THEY want to be treated.

Lexus is... A total experience that reflects professionalism and a sincere commitment to satisfaction.

Lexus is... "Doing it right the first time".

Lexus is... Caring on a personal level.

Lexus is... Exceeding customer expectations.

And... In the eyes of the customer I AM LEXUS !!!

00-LTT-034

Summary

Success in today's dynamic global economy requires the continuous positioning and repositioning of products. Product positioning involves those decisions and activities intended to create and maintain a certain concept of the firm's product in the customer's mind. Salespeople can make an important contribution to the process of product positioning. In many cases they assume an important role in product differentiation.

We note that today's better educated customers are often seeking a cluster of satisfactions. They seek satisfactions that arise from the product itself, from the company that makes or distributes the product, and from the salesperson who sells and services the product. Lexus, a major success story in the automobile industry, offers the customer a value-added strategy that encompasses the product, the company, and the salesperson.

We introduce the major product-positioning strategies available to salespeople: positioning new and emerging products versus mature and well-established products, positioning with a price strategy, and positioning with a value-added strategy.

Part of this chapter is devoted to the total product concept. The total product is made up of four possible products. This range of possibilities includes the generic product, the expected product, the value-added product, and the potential product. Value creation investments for transactional, consultative, and strategic alliance buyers were discussed.

KEY TERMS

Positioning
Satisfactions
Product life cycle
Quantity discount
Seasonal discount
Differentiation
Promotional allowance
Trade or functional discount
Generic product
Expected product
Value-added product
Potential product
Value proposition

REVIEW QUESTIONS

1. Why has product differentiation become so important in sales and marketing?
2. According to Ted Levitt, what is the definition of a product? What satisfactions do customers want?
3. Explain what is meant by *positioning* as a product-selling strategy. What is a value proposition?
4. Why have salespeople assumed an important role in positioning products?
5. Briefly describe the influence of electronic commerce on pricing. What types of products are likely to be sold on the Internet?
6. What are the possible consequences a salesperson might experience when using low-price tactics?
7. Read the Selling in Action insight titled "How Do Customers Judge Service Quality" on page 166. How might this information help a salesperson who wants to adopt the value-added-selling strategy?
8. What are some of the common ways salespeople add value to the products they sell?
9. What are the four possible products that make up the *total product* concept?
10. Describe the difference between a generic product and a value-added product.

APPLICATION EXERCISES

1. Study catalogs from two competing industrial supply firms or two competing direct-mail catalog companies. Assume one of the represented businesses is your employer. After studying the catalogs, make a comparative analysis of your company's competitive advantages.
2. Several weeks ago Erin Neff fell in love with the Scion tC coupe. After reading about the car in a magazine she decided to visit a local Scion dealer. A test drive convinced her to place an order. What happened next was very frustrating. The salesperson, Tim Downey, immediately started recommending options she should add to the basic car: sporting wheel and tire package ($1,565), ground-effects trim ($995), performance exhaust system ($525), and a satellite radio tuner and antenna ($449). Suddenly the price of $15,950

jumped to nearly $19,000, way more than she had planned to spend. Erin returned home without placing an order. Assume the role of sales trainer and suggest ways that Tim can improve his ability to position this product so it meets the customer's needs.

3. The Ritz-Carlton hotel chain illustrates the total product concept discussed in this chapter. Research value-added information on the Ritz-Carlton chain by accessing the www.ritzcarlton.com Web site. Choose a location and click on "Conference Facilities." Click on the fact sheet and print the information presented. Circle at least five features you consider to be value-added features. Examine the room rates by clicking on accommodations. On the fact sheet you printed, record the room rate for a single- and double-occupancy room.
4. Call a local financial services representative specializing in stock, bond, or equity fund transactions. Ask what percentage of clients rely on the information given to make complex decisions on their investments. Also ask this person if customers believe that advice on custom-fitting investment programs adds value to their decision making. Find out whether financial products are getting more or less complex and what effect this will have on providing value-added service in the future.

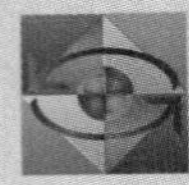

ROLE-PLAY EXERCISE

Study the Convention Center information in Part 1 of Appendix 3. Analyze this information and determine the value-added product that would appeal to a meeting planner (customer). Prepare a value proposition that summarizes the mix of key benefits on which your product is positioned. The proposition might include, for example, the free limousine service to and from the airport. Present your value proposition to another class member who will assume the role of the customer. Consider using information sheets, pictures, and other materials that will enhance your presentation.

CRM APPLICATION EXERCISE

Informing Customers with CRM

The notes in the ACT! database software contain two references to Extranets, another system offered by SimNet Systems. One account is a prospective buyer of an Extranet who needs more information. The other account has an Extranet and is willing to show it to others. The Reference Library also contains information about private virtual networks, including Extranets. Find the two accounts by selecting Lookup, Keyword; type "Extranet," check Notes, uncheck Contact, and press Enter. After searching, ACT! displays two records. An examination of the notes shows the account with an Extranet and the one with an interest. Make a note of the name of the organization now using an Extranet. Close the notes screen (File, Close) and use the Page Up or Page Down key to display the account that needs information. Select View, Reference Library to display the information about networks. Page Down to the last paragraph of that document, titled VPN. Highlight the paragraph with your mouse and select Edit, Copy. Select File, Close to close the library. Select Write, Letter, and enter the following: "You might find this of interest." Press Enter twice to begin a new paragraph. Select Edit, Paste to add the information from the Reference Library. Press Enter twice again for a new paragraph, type "If you wish, I can arrange for you to look at the Extranet in use at," and then enter the name of the person and organization using the Extranet. Select File, Print (Ctrl+P) to print the letter and File, Close to close the letter window.

CASE PROBLEM

Many of the most profitable companies have discovered that there are "riches in market niches." They have developed products and services that meet the needs of a well-defined or newly created market. Steelcase Incorporated, a leading source of information and expertise on work effectiveness, has been working hard to develop products that meet the needs of people who do most of their work in an office environment. The company's motto is "the office environment company." One of its newest products is the "Think" chair. Steelcase also developed the Personal Harbor Workspaces, a self-contained, fully equipped, and totally private podlike workstation. Steelcase sales literature describes the product as ideal for companies that are tired of waiting for the future:

> They were developed to support the individual within a highly collaborative team environment, and they work best when clustered around common work areas equipped with mobile tables, carts, benches, screens, and other Steelcase Activity Products. These "commons" are meant to be flexible spaces that enhance communication and facilitate interaction.

Steelcase realized that selling this advanced product would not be easy, so a decision was made to develop an advanced sales team to presell the Personal Harbor before its major introduction. Once the team started making sales calls, it became evident that a traditional product-oriented sales presentation would not work. The Personal Harbor was a departure from conventional office design, so many customers were perplexed. Sue Sacks, a team member, said, "People acted like we had fallen from Mars." Team members soon realized that to explain the features and benefits of the product they had to begin studying new organizational developments such as team-oriented workforces and corporate reengineering. The advanced sales team was renamed the advanced solutions team. Sales calls put more emphasis on learning about the customers' problems and identification of possible solutions. Members of the team viewed themselves as consultants who were in a position to discuss solutions to complex business problems.

The consultative approach soon began to pay off in sales. One customer, a hospital, was preparing to build a new office building and needed workstations for 400 employees. The hospital had formed a committee to make decisions concerning the purchase of office equipment. After an initial meeting between the Steelcase sales team and the hospital committee, a visit to the Steelcase headquarters in Grand Rapids, Michigan, was arranged. The hospital committee members were able to tour the plant and meet with selected Steelcase experts. With knowledge of the hospital's goals and directions, Sue Sacks was able to arrange meetings with Steelcase technical personnel who could answer specific questions. The hospital ultimately placed an order worth more than a million dollars.

Questions

1. To fulfill a problem-solving need, salespeople must often be prepared to communicate effectively with customers who are seeking a cluster of satisfactions (see Fig. 7.1). Is it likely that a customer who is considering the Personal Harbor Workspaces will seek information concerning all three dimensions of the Product-Selling Model? Explain your answer.
2. What product-selling strategies are most effective when selling a new and emerging product such as the Personal Harbor Workspaces?

3. Sue Sacks and other members of her sales team discovered that a traditional product-oriented presentation would not work when selling the Personal Harbor Workspaces. Success came only after the team adopted the consultative style of selling. Why was the product-oriented presentation ineffective?
4. Sue Sacks and other members of the advanced solutions team found that the consultative approach resulted in meetings with people higher in the customer's organization. "We get to call on a higher level of buyer," she said. Also, the team was more likely to position the product with a value-added strategy instead of a price strategy. In what ways did the advanced solutions team members add value to their product? Why was less emphasis placed on price during meetings with the customer?

DEVELOPING A PRODUCT STRATEGY

Scenario

First National Bank is a full-service bank with a reputation for excellent customer service. Personal selling efforts by tellers, loan officers and financial consultants are considered an integral part of the bank's customer service program.

Customer Profile

At age 45, Gianni Diaz is looking forward to early retirement. To supplement a company sponsored retirement program a Certificate of Deposit (CD) in the amount of $4,000 is purchased each year. The annual percentage yield earned on CDs is currently in the range of 3.75 to 4.00 percent. Diaz is not interested in stocks and bonds because these products represent high risk investments.

Salesperson Profile

Deaven Ray is a senior investment officer with First National Bank. Ray represents a wide range of financial products such as stock and bond mutual funds, blue chip stocks, diversified mutual funds, fixed annuities, money market funds, and certificates of deposit. Ray feels that Gianni Diaz may be a good candidate for an investment in fixed annuities. Diaz has agreed to meet and discuss investment options.

Product

A guaranteed-growth annuity at an annual percentage yield of 5.0 percent for a term of five years. This product, offered by General Electric Capital Assurance Company, gives the customer a guaranteed principal and a fixed rate of return. At the contract maturity date, the customer can select several payout options. This is a tax-deferred annuity which means you won't pay income taxes on earnings until you choose to withdraw the funds. You can add funds to your account throughout the contract period. You need not close the account at the end of the contract period. You can allow your money to continue to grow at the same interest rate. If funds are withdrawn prior to the end of the contract, a withdrawal charge will be assessed. The minimum single premium purchase is $5,000.

Instructions

For this role play activity you will meet with Gianni Diaz and discuss current and future financial plans. You will determine if Diaz might benefit by investing in a guaranteed growth annuity. Prior to meeting with the customer, review the following material in Chapter 6:

- Adding value with a feature-benefit strategy
- Use of bridge statements
- General versus specific benefits

Also, think about the implications of the Product-Selling Model (Figure 7.1) introduced in Chapter 7. At the beginning of the role play, use appropriate questions to acquire information regarding the customer's needs. Be prepared to recommend this product and close the sale if you feel the customer will benefit from this purchase.

"Instead of mass consumers, we're now complex individuals in search of choice, control, and influence. We want more from companies than efficiency. We want relationships that help solve our unique problems, not anonymous transactions that create more of them."

Shoshana Zuboff, Professor
Harvard Business School

PART 4

Developing a Customer Strategy

➡ With increased knowledge of the customer, the salesperson is in a better position to achieve sales goals. This part presents information on understanding the buying process, understanding buyer behavior, and developing a prospect base.

Chapter Preview

When you finish reading this chapter, you should be able to

1 Discuss the meaning of a customer strategy

2 Explain the difference between consumer and organizational buyers

3 List and describe the steps in the typical buying process

4 Discuss the buying process of the transactional, consultative, and strategic buyer

5 Understand the importance of alignment between the selling process and the customer's buying process

6 Discuss the social and psychological influences that shape customer buying decisions

CHAPTER 8

The Buying Process and Buyer Behavior

Throughout the past few years, we have seen a major power shift in the direction of the customer. Today's customers have greater access to information that lets them make more informed decisions. They are more demanding, and salespeople must work harder to meet their needs. Every sales call must begin with the customer as the central focus of attention. Tom Peters, noted author and consultant, says, we must "become one with the customer."[1] The customer focus must encompass the buying process (how people buy) and buyer behavior (why people buy).

We know that new products must satisfy the customer's needs, but identifying these needs can be very challenging. No one understands this challenge better than Kim Fernandez, Director of Natural Food Sales for Alta Dena Certified Dairy (www.altadenadairy.com). She sells a wide range of natural dairy foods to wholesalers and retailers. Almost all her products are displayed in the dairy department. In a typical supermarket, the dairy department accounts for about 9 percent of sales. Kim Fernandez is responsible for servicing existing accounts and obtaining new accounts. She also is responsible for introducing new products.[2] This is a challenging part of her work in view of the fact that 800 to 900 new dairy products are introduced each year. The proliferation of new items is an attempt to satisfy more customer needs.

Kim Fernandez must understand each customer's buying process. Prior to calling on a retail supermarket, for example, she must perform pre-call planning and research. Who makes the buying decisions for this organization?

What type of information will this person need to make a buying decision? In addition to understanding how the customer buys, she must be knowledgeable in the area of buyer behavior.

DEVELOPING A CUSTOMER STRATEGY

The greatest challenge to salespeople in the age of information is to improve responsiveness to customers. In fact, a growing number of sales professionals believe the customer has supplanted the product as the driving force in sales today. This is especially true in those situations in which the products of one company in an industry are becoming more and more similar to those of the competition. The salesperson can distinguish between similar products and services and help customers perceive important differences. The development of valuable, customer-specific services and information is the hallmark of value-added selling.

Adding Value with a Customer Strategy

A **customer strategy** is a carefully conceived plan that results in maximum customer responsiveness. One major dimension of this strategy is to achieve a better understanding of the customer's buying needs and motives. As noted in Chapter 1, information has become a strategic resource (Fig. 1.2). When salespeople take time to discover needs and motives, they are in a much better position to offer customers a value-added solution to their buying problem.

Every salesperson who wants to develop repeat business should figure out a way to collect and systematize customer information. The authors of *Reengineering the Corporation* discuss the importance of collecting information about the unique and particular needs of each customer:

> Customers—consumers and corporations alike—demand products and services designed for their unique and particular needs. There is no longer any such notion as *the* customer; there is only *this* customer, the one with whom a seller is dealing at the moment and who now has the capacity to indulge his or her own personal tastes.[3]

The first prescription for developing a customer strategy focuses on the customer's buying process (see Fig. 8.1). Buying procedures and policies can vary greatly from one buyer to another. This is especially true in business to business selling. If a salesperson fails to learn how the buyer plans to make the purchase, then there is the danger that the selling process will be out of alignment with the customer's buying process. Keith Eades, author of *The New Solution Selling*, says:

> If we haven't defined how our buyers buy, then we make assumptions that throw us out of alignment with our buyers. Misalignment with buyers is one of selling's most critical mistakes.[4]

The second prescription focuses on why customers buy. This topic will be discussed in detail later in this chapter. The third prescription for developing a customer strategy emphasizes building a strong prospect base, which is discussed in Chapter 9.

Complex Nature of Customer Behavior

The forces that motivate customers can be complex. Arch McGill, former vice president of IBM, reminds us that individual customers perceive the product in their own terms and that these terms may be "unique, idiosyncratic, human, emotional, end-of-the-day, irrational,

FIGURE | 8.1

Today, one of the greatest challenges to salespeople is to improve responsiveness to customers. A well developed customer strategy is designed to meet this challenge.

STRATEGIC/CONSULTATIVE SELLING MODEL

Strategic step	*Prescription*
Develop a Personal Selling Philosophy	☑ Adopt Marketing Concept ☑ Value Personal Selling ☑ Become a Problem Solver/Partner
Develop a Relationship Strategy	☑ Adopt Win-Win Philosophy ☑ Project Professional Image ☑ Maintain High Ethical Standards
Develop a Product Strategy	☑ Become a Product Expert ☑ Sell Benefits ☑ Configure Value-Added Solutions
Develop a Customer Strategy	☐ Understand the Buying Process ☐ Understand Buyer Behavior ☐ Develop Prospect Base

erratic terms."[5] Different people doing the same thing, for example, purchasing a personal computer (PC), may have different needs that motivate them; and each person may have several motives for a single action.

The proliferation of market research studies, public opinion polls, surveys, and reports of "averages" makes it easy to fall into the trap of thinking of the customer as a number. The customer is a person, not a statistic. Companies that fully accept this basic truth are likely to adopt a one-to-one marketing strategy. The one-to-one strategy is based on a bedrock concept: Treat different customers differently.[6]

CONSUMER VERSUS ORGANANIZATIONAL BUYERS

Consumer buyer behavior refers to the buying behavior of individuals and households who buy goods and services for personal consumption. Each year, consumers purchase many trillion dollars' worth of goods and services. **Business buyer behavior** refers to the organizations that buy goods and services for use in the production of other products and services that are sold, rented, or supplied to others.[7]

It is not uncommon for salespeople to sell products and services to both consumer and business buyers. A well-established interior decorating firm will likely work with homeowners as well as commercial clients who own hotels, restaurants, or art galleries. A salesperson employed by an automobile dealership will often sell to corporate customers who maintain a fleet of cars or trucks as well as consumers who buy vehicles for personal use.

There are some similarities between consumer markets and business markets. Both involve people who assume the role of buyer and make purchase decisions to satisfy needs. These two markets differ, however, in some important areas. Figure 8.2 provides a brief review of some of these differences. A business purchase is likely to involve more decision participants and these participants may be well-trained. Most purchasing agents spend time learning how to buy better.[8]

Consumer Buyers

- Purchases for individual or household consumption
- Decisions usually made by individuals
- Purchases often made based on brand reputation or personal recommendations with little or no product expertise
- Purchases based primarily on emotional responses to product or promotions
- Individual purchasers may make quick decisions
- Products: consumer goods and services for individual use

Organizational Buyers

- Purchases made for some purpose other than personal consumption
- Decisions frequently made by several people
- Purchases made according to precise technical specification based on product expertise
- Purchases based on primarily rational criteria
- Purchasers may engage in lengthy decision process
- Products: often complex; classified based on how organizational customers use them

FIGURE | 8.2

Differences between Consumer and Organizational Buyers

Adapted from Michael R. Solomon and Elnora W. Stuart, *Marketing: Real People, Real Choices*, 3rd edition (Upper Saddle River, NJ: Prentice Hall, 2003), p. 193.

Types of Organizational Buying Situations

There are three major types of organizational buying situations. The amount of time and effort organizational buyers spend on a purchase usually depends on the complexity of the product and how often the decision must be made.[9] At one extreme is the *straight rebuy* which is a fairly routine decision. At the other extreme is the *new-task buy* which may require extensive research. In the middle is the *modified rebuy* which will require some research.[10]

New Task Buy

A first-time purchase of a product or service is a **new-task buy**. Depending on the cost and complexity of this purchase, the buying decision may require several weeks of information gathering and the involvement of numerous decision participants. In some cases, a buying committee is formed to consider the new product's quality, price, and service provided by suppliers. Salespeople who are involved in new-task buying situations must rely heavily on consultative selling skills.

Straight Rebuy

A **straight rebuy** is a routine purchase of items needed by a business-to-business customer. Let's assume you have decided to open a new restaurant and need a steady supply of high quality cooking oil. After talking to several restaurant suppliers, and testing several oils, you select one that meets your needs. Your goal now is to simplify the buying process with the use of a straight rebuy plan. As long as the supplier meets your criteria for price, quality, service, and delivery, future purchases will be very routine. Organizations often use the straight rebuy approach for such items as cleaning supplies, copy paper, and cartridges for computer printers. Salespeople must constantly monitor every straight rebuy situation to be sure the customer is completely satisfied. A competing supplier will be quick to exploit any sign of dissatisfaction by the customer.

Modified Rebuy

The tide of change is a powerful force in the world of business. From time to time, your customers may wish to modify product specifications, change delivery schedules, or renegotiate prices. Several years ago, the American automobile manufacturers, faced with

The sales personnel at Mitchells/Richards sell high quality apparel to discriminating customers. Many of these customers are business executives who invest heavily in their business wardrobes. Salespeople at Mitchells/Richards work hard to discover the customer's needs and provide outstanding service after the sale.

greater competitive pressures from China, Korea, Japan, Germany, and other nations, turned to their suppliers and demanded price reductions. Suppliers were required to become involved in a **modified rebuy** situation or risk loss of the account. A modified rebuy often requires the involvement of several participants.

Well-trained professional salespeople work hard to provide outstanding service after the sale and anticipate changes in customer needs. Some salespeople regularly ask their customers what they value most about the existing buying situation and how can improvements be made in this area.

Building Strategic Alliances

In Chapter 1, we described strategic alliances as the highest form of partnering. Alliances are often formed by companies that have similar business interests and believe the partnership will help them gain a mutual competitive advantage. Large companies often form several alliances. Some strategic alliances take the form of systems selling. **Systems selling** appeals to buyers who prefer to purchase a packaged solution to a problem from a single seller, thus avoiding all the separate decisions involved in a complex buying situation.[11]

Several years ago, Kinko's reinvented itself as a document solutions provider for business firms of all sizes. Full-service Kinko's stores began offering the buyer networks of computers equipped with popular software, ultrafast color printers, high-speed Internet connections and, of course, a variety of document preparation services. After Kinko's was purchased by FedEx a network of 1,200 digitally connected FedEx Kinko's locations began offering a wider selection of customized, needs-based document solutions. One large financial institution consolidated the services of 13 vendors by forming an alliance with FedEx Kinko's.[12] Systems selling efforts at FedEx Kinko's has become an important strategy for winning and holding accounts.

Types of Consumer Buying Situations

As noted previously, consumer buying behavior refers to purchases of products for personal or household use. The amount of time consumers devote to a purchase decision can vary greatly depending on the cost of the product, familiarity with the product, and the importance of the item to the consumer. Few buyers invest much effort in selecting a tube of toothpaste, but the purchase of a new automobile or a home will involve extensive decision making. Consumer buying situations can fall into one of three categories depending on the degree of buyer involvement.

Habitual Buying Decisions

Habitual buying decisions usually require very little consumer involvement and brand differences are usually insignificant.[13] For frequently purchased, low-cost items such as shampoo, copy paper, or laundry detergent, consumer involvement in the decision-making process is very low. Supermarket shoppers often display habitual buying behavior as they select items.

Variety-Seeking Buying Decisions

Variety-seeking buying decisions are characterized by low customer involvement, but important perceived brand differences.[14] Brand switching is not uncommon among these buyers because they can be influenced by advertising appeals, coupons, or lower prices to try a new brand. Brand switching is usually motivated by the desire for variety rather than dissatisfaction.

Complex Buying Decisions

A complex buying decision is characterized by a high degree of involvement by the consumer. Consumers are likely to be highly involved when the product is expensive, purchased infrequently, and highly self-expressive.[15] The purchase of a vacation home, a long-term care insurance policy, an expensive boat, or a costly piece of art would require a complex buying decision. The learning process for some purchases can be very lengthy.

ACHIEVING ALIGNMENT WITH THE CUSTOMER'S BUYING PROCESS

The foundation of a successful sales effort is knowing how buyers buy. As noted previously, if we have not defined how buyers buy, then we make assumptions that throw our sales process out of alignment with the buyer's buying process.[16] Too often salespeople rely on generalizations about the buyer's decision-making process rather than acquiring specific information.

The **buying process** is a systematic series of actions, or a series of defined, repeatable steps intended to achieve a result.[17] Organizational purchasing structures and buying procedures can vary greatly from company to company, so we need to be clear on how decisions are being made within each account. In some cases, the steps in the buying process

Yerecic Label has learned that customers want essential preparation information on the food packages. To appeal to this buying motive, Yerecic has developed an easy-peel on-pack label.

have been clearly defined by the organization and this information is available to any potential supplier. However, this information may not tell us the whole story. Salespeople need to obtain answers to these types of questions:

- How urgent is my proposal to the buyer? When will a buying decision be made?
- Will any "political" factors within the organization influence how decisions are made?
- Has the money needed to purchase my product been allocated?
- Which person or persons in the buying organization will actually use or supervise the use of the product I am selling?[18]

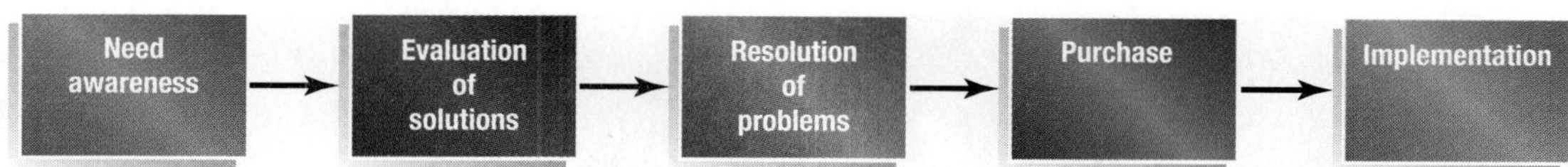

FIGURE | 8.3

Stages in the typical buying process.

Customers make buying decisions in many ways, so understanding each individual buyer's decision-making process is central to success in personal selling. Some buyers will have multiple buying processes. Buying decisions involving a *straight rebuy*, for example, will likely differ from buying decisions involving a *new-task buy*.

Steps in the Typical Buying Process

The term "process" brings to mind a set formula that applies to every situation. But buying decisions are made in different ways, so it would be inappropriate to view the buying process as a uniform pattern of decision making. However, there is a model—a form of decision making that buyers usually apply to their unique circumstances. Figure 8.3 shows the typical stages in the buying decision process: need awareness, evaluation of solutions, resolution of problems, purchase, and implementation. This model is especially helpful in understanding organizational buying decision and large consumer acquisitions. Consumers who make habitual buying decisions often skip or reverse some of these stages.[19]

Need Awareness

Need awareness is the first stage in the buying process. The buyer recognizes that something is imperfect or incomplete. The need for energy conservation technology may surface when oil prices rise to higher levels. The need for a customer service training program may become evident when customer satisfaction survey scores decline. Salespeople can create value at this stage of the buying process if they can help determine the magnitude of the customer's problem and identify a solution. For example, a sales representative may be able to help the buyer estimate the cost of poor customer service and recommend a way to improve service. Customers often need help in determining whether they have a problem large enough to justify the cost of a solution.[20]

Evaluation of Solutions

Buyers who experience need awareness usually begin searching for information that will help them evaluate possible problem solutions. They realize, at this point, that the problem they face is amenable to some type of solution. In some cases, there are several solutions that the customer needs to study. Salespeople can add value at this stage by providing useful information that helps the customer make an informed choice. In some cases, the value justification can be presented in terms of cost reduction or increased revenues. In other cases, the value justification may be an intangible such as customer satisfaction, improved security, or reduced stress. In business-to-business selling situations, value justification that can be measured is usually the most powerful.

To establish a true partnership with the customer, you need to be sure that you are offering them information that will help them achieve their objectives. If you possess a good understanding of the customer's buying process, you will know what they are trying to accomplish.[21]

There is no longer any such notion as the customer—there is only this customer, the one whom a seller is dealing with at the moment. Discovering the individual needs of this customer can be challenging.

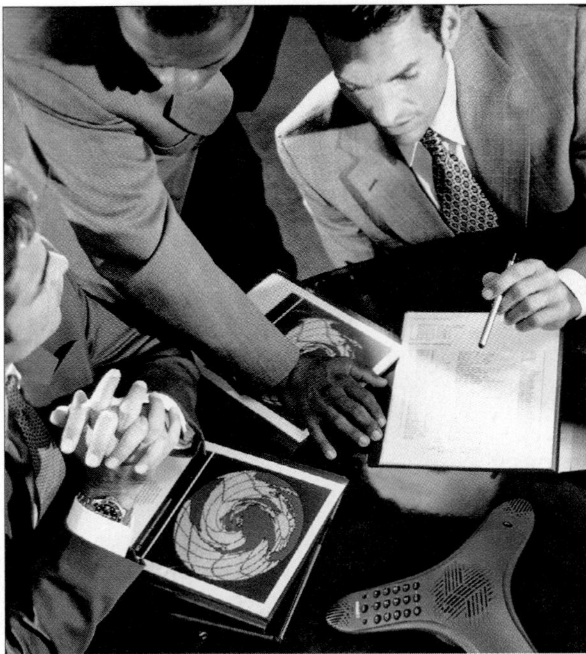

Resolution of Problems

At this stage of the buying process, the customer is aware of a need and has evaluated one or more solutions. The customer has resolved to do something. However, the customer is likely to have issues and concerns that must be resolved before moving ahead. This is especially true in the case of complex sales.[22]

Some customers will want the proposed solution put in writing. Competitors may be invited to submit written proposals. A well-written proposal is one way to add value (see Chapter 6). The customer may request specific information that can only be provided by the supplier's engineers or accountants. The customer many insist on visiting the supplier's manufacturing plant so they can see the production process firsthand. Buyers often need help overcoming obstacles that prevent them from moving to the purchase stage of the buying process.

Purchase

After all the customer's obstacles and concerns have been overcome, the purchase decision is made. Professional salespeople create value in many ways at this stage of the buying process. First, they do whatever is necessary to make sure the purchase is "hassle free." This may mean working with the customer to arrange the best financing or supervising the delivery and installation of the product. Salespeople add value by becoming a "customer advocate" within their own organizations. This may mean negotiating with various departments to expedite the order. Buyers want to work with salespeople who are able to quickly solve any order fulfillment problems.[23]

Implementation

The first sale is only the beginning of the relationship with the buyer. Repeat sales occur when the supplier has demonstrated the ability to add value in various ways after the sale. Value creation can take the form of timely delivery, superior installation, accurate invoicing, follow-up contacts by the salesperson, or something else that is important to the customer.

UNDERSTANDING THE BUYING PROCESS OF THE TRANSACTIONAL, CONSULTATIVE, AND STRATEGIC ALLIANCE BUYER

The next step in understanding the customer's buying process is to discuss three value creation selling approaches that appeal to certain types of customers. In Chapter 1, we briefly introduced transactional selling, consultative selling, and strategic alliance selling. We will now discuss how to work effectively with each type of buyer.[24]

Transactional Process Buyer

Transactional buyers are well aware of their needs and usually know a great deal about the products or services they intend to purchase. In a true transactional sale, buyers will become frustrated if the salesperson attempts to use needs assessment, problem solving, or relationship building. They are not looking for new information or advice from the salesperson. Most transactional buyers have conducted their own research and, in most cases, have decided which product best meets their needs. They don't want hand-holding and they don't want the salesperson to waste their time.[25]

How can a salesperson add value to a transactional sale? If the buyer is already aware of their needs, has evaluated solutions, and has no issues or concerns that need to be resolved, then the salesperson needs to focus on the purchase stage of the five-part buying process model (see Figure 8.3). Do whatever is necessary to facilitate a convenient and hassle-free purchase. Eliminate any unnecessary costs or delays in processing the order. The transactional buyer may quickly turn to a competitor if they experience unnecessary costs or delays.

Consultative Process Buyer

Consultative selling, a major theme of this text, was described in Chapter 1. This sales approach appeals to buyers who lack needs awareness or need help evaluating possible solutions. Some buying decisions require assistance from a consultative salesperson because the product is very complex and/or the cost of the product is very high. The purchase of a new home provides a good example in the consumer arena. Home buyers usually seek the assistance of an experienced realtor. The purchase of Internet phone-calling equipment provides a good example in the business-to-business arena. Organizations that are considering the purchase of complex Internet telephone equipment seek answers to several questions: Can we keep a portion of our traditional phone network or must we adopt an all–Internet phone system? Will the new system provide the same voice quality as our traditional system? Internet phone-calling equipment is available from several suppliers, including Avaya Incorporated and Cisco Systems Incorporated. Some customers will need help comparing the technology available from these and other suppliers.[26]

Successful consultative salespeople focus a great deal of attention on needs awareness which is step one in the buying process model (see Figure 8.3). This is where salespeople can create the most value by helping customers gain an understanding of their problems and create solutions that correct these problems.[27] Many customers seek help defining needs and solutions, but avoid dealing with a sales representative who simply wants to sell a product.

Consultative selling encompasses the concept that salespeople should conduct a systematic assessment of the prospect's situation. This usually involves collecting as much information as possible prior to the sales call and using a series of carefully worded questions to obtain the customer's point of view during the sales call. Two-way communication will provide for a mutual exchange of ideas, feelings, and perceptions.

Avaya sells to consultative process buyers who may lack needs awareness and need help evaluating possible solutions. The statement "Let us assess your network for VoIP readiness" is featured in this ad. Need assessment is a very important responsibility of every salesperson.

The consultative salesperson will help the customer evaluate solutions and help resolve any problems that surface prior to the purchase stage. Consultative salespeople also work hard to add value at the implementation stage of the sales process. This may involve supervising product delivery and installation, servicing warranties, and providing other services after the sale.

Strategic Alliance Process Buyer

As noted previously, the goal of strategic alliances is to achieve a marketplace advantage by teaming up with another company. Alliances are often formed by companies that have similar business interests and seek to gain a mutual competitive advantage. Dell Computer, for example, formed a partnership with Microsoft and Intel to provide customized e-business solutions. In the highly competitive global market, going it alone is sometimes more difficult.[28]

Step one in building an alliance is a careful study of the proposed partner. This research is often coordinated by senior management and may involve persons working in the areas of sales, marketing, finance, and distribution. At some point, representatives from both companies will meet and explore the mutual benefits of the alliance. Both parties must be prepared to explain how they will add value once the alliance is formed.

The Buyer Resolution Theory

Several theories explain how customers arrive at a buying decision. One traditional point of view is based on the assumption that a final buying decision is possible only after the prospect has answered five logical questions (see Figure 8.4). This is called the **buyer resolution theory**. One strength of this buying theory is that it focuses the salesperson's attention on five important factors that the customer is likely to consider before making a purchase. Answers to these five questions provide valuable insights about the customer's buying strategy. One important limitation of this theory is that it is often not possible to anticipate which of the five buying decisions might be most difficult for the prospect to make. If the selling process does not mesh with the buying process, a sale is less likely. There is no established sequence in which prospects make these five decisions, so a highly inflexible sales presentation would not be effective.

Buyer Resolution Theory

This view of the buying process recognizes that a purchase is made only after the prospect has made five buying, decisions involving specific affirmative responses to the following questions:

Why Should I Buy?
Realistically, it is sometimes difficult to provide prospects with an answer to this question. In many cases, salespeople fail in their attempt to help customers become aware of a need. Thus, large numbers of potential customers are not sufficiently persuaded to purchase products that provide them with genuine buyer benefits.

What Should I Buy?
If a prospect agrees that a need does exist, then you are ready to address the second buying decision. You must convince the prospect that the product being offered can satisfy the need. In most cases, the buyer can choose from several competing products.

Where Should I Buy?
As products become more complex, consumers are giving more attention to "source" decisions. In a major metropolitan area the person who wants to buy a Laserjet 3160 or a competing product can choose from several sources.

What Is a Fair Price?
Today's better educated and better informed consumers are searching for the right balance between price and value (benefits). They are better able to detect prices that are not competitive or do not correspond in their minds with the product's value.

When Should I Buy?
A sale cannot be closed until a customer has decided when to buy. In some selling situations, the customer may want to postpone the purchase because of reluctance to part with the money.

FIGURE | 8.4

The buyer resolution theory, sometimes referred to as "The 5 W's Theory", focuses attention on questions the customer may need answers to before making a purchase. "An absence of an answer to any of these will likely result in a customer objection".

UNDERSTANDING BUYER BEHAVIOR

Although every customer is unique, salespeople need an understanding of the important social and psychological influences that tend to shape customer buying decisions. We will review concepts that come from the fields of psychology, sociology, and anthropology. Figure 8.5 illustrates the many forces that influence buying decisions.

Basic Needs That Influence Buyer Behavior

Basic human needs have changed little throughout our economic history. However, the ways in which needs are fulfilled have changed greatly during the age of information.[29] The starting point for developing an understanding of the forces influencing buying decisions is a review of the individual needs that shape the customer's behavior. To gain insights into customer behavior motivated by both physiological and psychological needs, it is helpful to study the popular hierarchy of needs developed by Abraham Maslow.

Maslow's Hierarchy of Needs

According to Abraham Maslow, basic human needs are arranged in a hierarchy according to their strength (Fig. 8.6). His theory rests on the assumption that as each lower-level need is satisfied, the need at the next level demands attention.

Physiological Needs Sometimes called primary needs, **physiological needs** include the needs of food, water, sleep, and shelter. Maslow placed our physiological needs at the bottom of the pyramid because he believed that these basic needs tend to be strong in the minds of most people.

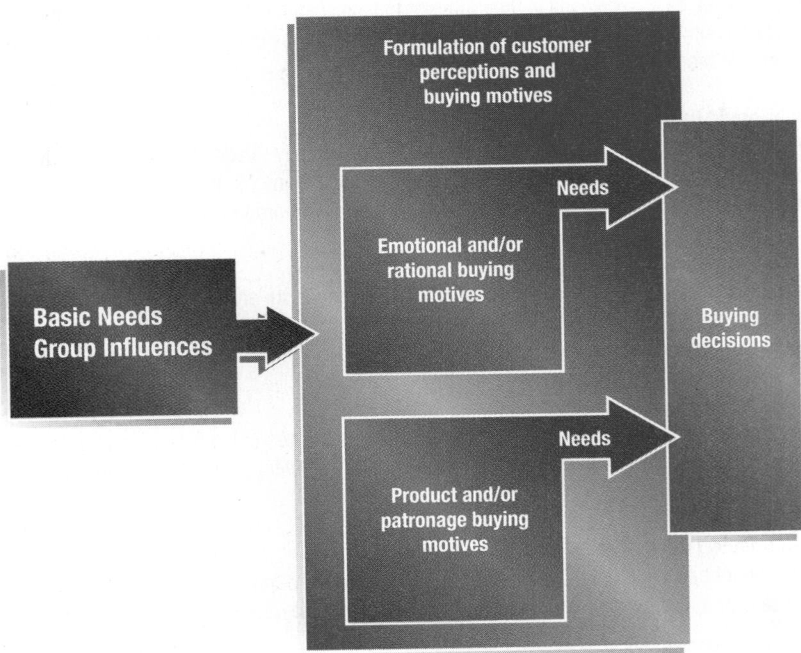

FIGURE 8.5

Developing a Customer Strategy Model

This model illustrates the many factors that influence buying decisions. It can serve as a guide for developing a highly responsive customer strategy.

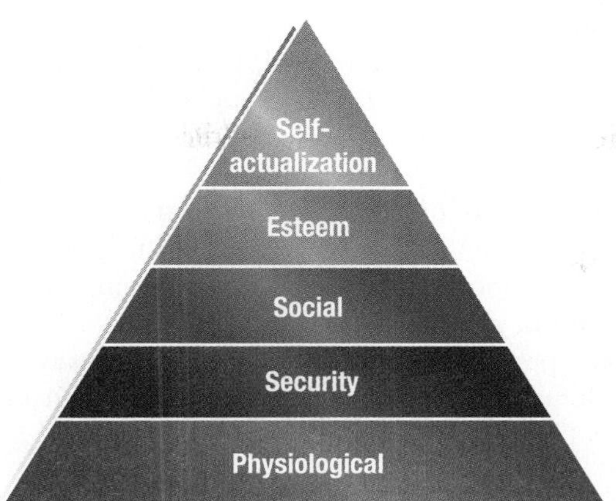

FIGURE 8.6

The forces that motivate customers to make specific buying decisions are complex. This model illustrates Maslow's hierarchy of needs.

Security Needs After physiological needs have been satisfied, the next need level that tends to dominate is safety and security. **Security needs** represent our desire to be free from danger and uncertainty. The desire to satisfy the need for safety and security often motivates people to purchase such items as medical and life insurance or a security alarm for the home or business.

Social Needs The need to belong, or **social needs**, reflects our desire for identification with a group and approval from others. These needs help explain our continuing search for friendship, companionship, and long-term business relationships.

Esteem Needs At the fourth level of Maslow's need priority model appear **esteem needs**. Esteem needs reflect our desire to feel worthy in the eyes of others. We seek a sense of personal worth and adequacy, a feeling of competence.

Selling in Action

DEVELOPING A "SEGMENT BUSTER"

The Chrysler PT Cruiser has been described as a wacky-looking cross between a 1937 Ford and a London taxicab. Some view it as part 1920s' gangster car and part 1950s' hot rod. DaimlerChrysler AG describes the car as a surefire "segment buster" that combines the room of a minivan with the flair of a sport-utility vehicle and the utility of a small car. The car is built in Mexico and sold in North America and in about 40 foreign markets.

DaimlerChrysler knows that some people will love the car and some will hate it. The PT (which stands for personal transportation) Cruiser is the company's first vehicle designed entirely through an unconventional market research process known as "archetype research." This research was conducted by a French-born medical anthropologist named G. Clotaire Rapaille. The process began with a series of free-wheeling, three-hour focus group sessions in Great Britain, France, Germany, Italy, and North America. With lights dimmed and mood music playing, participants were asked to drift back to their childhoods and jot down the memories invoked by the prototype PT Cruiser parked in the room. After the sessions, Dr. Rapaille and members of the research team pored over the stories looking for emotions sparked by the vehicle. This research led to major design changes that made the car look even more outlandish. The final design is one that thrills some and puts off others, just what the research team hoped to accomplish.[a]

Self-Actualization Needs Maslow defined the term **self-actualization** as a need for self-fulfillment, a full tapping of one's potential. It is the need to "be all that you can be," to have mastery over what you are doing. One goal of consultative selling is to help the customer experience self-actualization in terms of the relationship with the salesperson.

The five-level need priority model developed by Maslow is somewhat artificial in certain instances. At times several of our needs are interacting together within us. One example is the business lunch. Not only are you conducting business with a client but also you are satisfying your needs for food and beverages, for engaging in social activities, and perhaps for feeling important in your own eyes and—you hope—in the eyes of your customer. However, the model can provide salespeople with a practical way of understanding which need is most likely to dominate customer behavior in certain situations.

Group Influences That Influence Buying Decisions

As noted earlier, the people around us also influence our buying decisions. These **group influences** can be grouped into four major areas: (1) role influences, (2) reference groups, (3) social class, and (4) culture and subculture[30] (Fig. 8.7). Salespeople who understand these roles and influences can develop the type of insight customers view as being valuable.

Role Influence

Throughout our lives we occupy positions within groups, organizations, and institutions. Closely associated with each position is a **role**: a set of characteristics and expected social behaviors based on the expectations of others. All the roles we assume (student, member of the school board, or position held at work) influence not only our general behavior but also

FIGURE 8.7

To gain additional insights into customers' motivations, it is helpful to study the group influences that affect buying decisions.

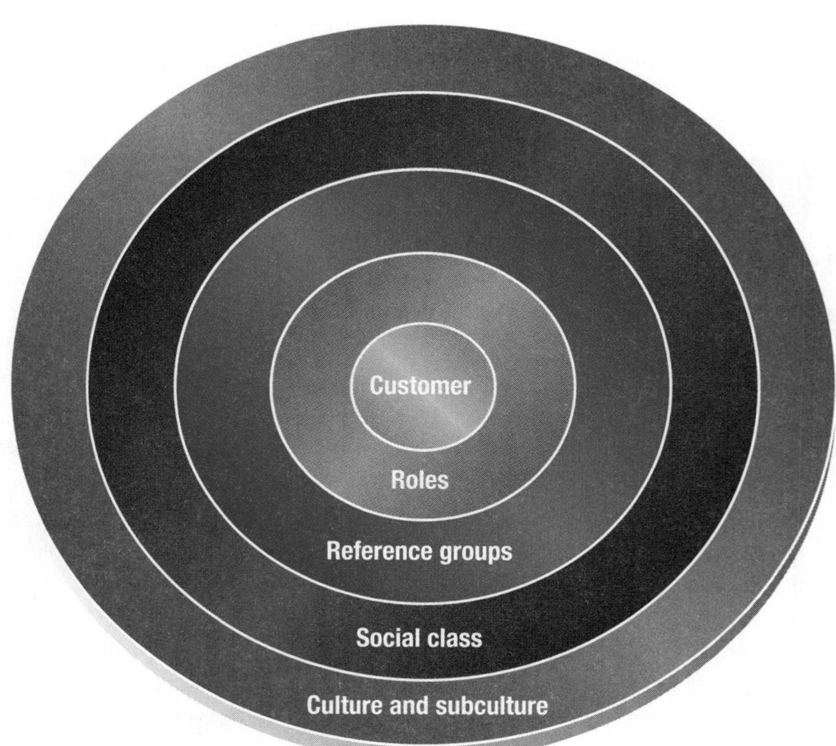

our buying behavior. In today's society, for example, a woman may assume the role of mother at home and purchasing manager at work. In the manager's role, she may feel the need to develop a conservative wardrobe, enroll in a leadership training course, or join a professional association.

Reference Group Influence

A **reference group** consists of the categories of people that you see yourself belonging to, and with which you habitually compare yourself. Members of a reference group tend to influence the values, attitudes, and behaviors of one another.[31] The reference group may act as a point of comparison and a source of information for the individual member. For example, Pi Sigma Epsilon, the national fraternity in marketing, sales management, and selling, may serve as a reference group for a college business major. In the business community, a chapter of the American Society for Training and Development, or Sales & Marketing Executives International may provide a reference group for its members. As members of a reference group we often observe other people in the group to establish our own norms, and these norms become a guide for our purchasing activity.

Social Class Influence

Social classes are society's relatively permanent and ordered divisions whose members share similar values, interests, and behavior.[32] The criteria used to rank people according to social class vary from one society to another. In some societies, land ownership allows entry into a higher social class. In other societies, education is a major key to achieving upper-class status. Social class, in most cases, is not determined by a single factor. It is determined by a combination of factors such as income, education, occupation, and accumulated wealth.

"It would never work out between us, Tom—we're from two totally different tiers of the upper middle class."

Source: *The New Yorker*, March 25, 2002.

In the Fleet Operations Division, DaimlerChrysler is marketing their team of professionals. This sales team will appeal to customers who want to work with salespeople who are accessible, responsive, and knowledgeable.

DON'T JUST SELECT FLEET VEHICLES.

SELECT FLEET SPECIALISTS.

Sedans. Minivans. Sport utilities. Trucks. Coupes. Convertibles. We have an extensive selection of exciting, stylish and versatile vehicles. But variety isn't the only reason to select DaimlerChrysler Fleet. Consider the support we provide. Our service and contact people are ready, willing and able to make your job easier. They're accessible, responsive, knowledgeable and attentive. They can answer questions, supply information and offer solutions that serve your needs.

That's why we say...

DON'T JUST SELECT A VEHICLE. SELECT A COMPANY.

Visit us online at www.fleet.chrysler.com or call 1-800-999-FLEET for more information.

Chrysler, Jeep and Dodge are registered trademarks of DaimlerChrysler. DaimlerChrysler Fleet Operations is a division of DaimlerChrysler Motors Company LLC.

Customer Relationship Management with Technology

MANAGING MULTIPLE CONTACTS WITH CRM

Salespeople often find that groups of their contacts have common interests and buying motives. Customers and prospects may be segmented into groups by buying influences, by the products they purchase, by the industries they are involved in, or by their size. Customer relationship management (CRM) software can enable the salesperson to easily link contacts together as groups and "mass-produce" information that is custom-fitted to the needs of people in a specific group. For example, each owner of a specific product may receive a telephone call, personalized letter, or report that describes the benefits of a new accessory available from the salesperson. (See the exercise, Managing Multiple Contacts with CRM, on p. 205 for more information.)

Cultural Influence

Culture can be defined as the accumulation of values, rules of behavior, forms of expression, religious beliefs, transmitted behavior patterns, and the like for a group of people who share a common language and environment. Culture tends to encourage or discourage particular behaviors and mental processes.[33] We maintain and transmit our culture chiefly through language. Culture has considerable influence on buying behavior. Today, culture is getting more attention because of the rapid increases in immigrant groups. As cultural diversity increases, companies must reexamine their sales and marketing strategies.

Within most cultures are groups whose members share value systems based on common life experiences and situations. We call such a group a **subculture**. Some subcultures, such as mature consumers, Hispanic, African American, and Generation Y (16 to 24 year-olds) make up important market segments.[34]

Perception—How Customer Needs Are Formed

Perception is the process through which sensations are interpreted, using our knowledge and experience. These sensations are received through sight, hearing, touch, taste, and smell. Buyer behavior is often influenced by perception.[35] When Volkswagen announced that it would build an ultra-luxury car selling for $70,000 many people questioned the merits of this decision. Could the maker of the Beetle and Thing compete in the market segment dominated by Lexus, Mercedes Benz, Jaguar, and BMW? Thus far sales of the Volkswagen Phaeton have been slow even though most automobile journalists view it as a true luxury car.[36] Is perception the barrier to sales growth?

We tend to screen out or modify stimuli, a process known as *selective attention*, for two reasons. First, we cannot possibly be conscious of all inputs at one time. Just the commercial messages we see and hear each day are enough to cause sensory overload. Second, we are conditioned by our social and cultural background, and our physical and psychological needs, to use selectivity.

Buyers may screen out or modify information presented by a salesperson if it conflicts with their previously learned attitudes or beliefs. The business buyer who feels the new office furniture designs that combine individual work space will only encourage impromptu employee chitchat is apt to use selective attention when the salesperson begins discussing product features. Salespeople who can anticipate this problem of selective attention should acquire as much background information as possible before meeting with the prospect. During the first meeting with the customer, the salesperson should make every effort to build a strong relationship so that the person opens up and freely discusses personal perceptions. Salespeople who do this have accepted one of the great truisms in sales and marketing: "Facts are negotiable. Perception is rock solid."

Buying Motives

Every buying decision has a motive behind it. A **buying motive** can be thought of as an aroused need, drive, or desire. This motive acts as a force that stimulates behavior intended to satisfy the aroused need. Our perceptions influence or shape this behavior. An understanding of buying motives provides the salesperson with the reasons why customers buy.

As you might expect, some buying decisions are influenced by more than one buying motive. The buyer of catering services may want food of exceptional quality

Selling Is Everyone's Business

SELLING NASCAR IN MANHATTAN

NASCAR is growing in popularity each year. This form of auto racing, with deep roots in the South, is attracting fans throughout the nation. About 40 million people consider themselves avid fans. Although NASCAR TV ratings are rising and most races are sold out, someone still needs to sell this product to team sponsors. Brett Yormark is a corporate sales representative representing NASCAR in New York City. It now costs from \$10 million to \$14 million to sponsor a top team, so he is a key member of the NASCAR sales and marketing team. Yormark faces major challenges because he is selling stock car racing to an upscale, urban crowd. Many of his prospects are corporate executives who have never seen a NASCAR race.[b]

served quickly so all her guests can eat together. This customer also may be quite price conscious. In this situation, the caterer should attempt to discover the *dominant buying motive* (DBM). The DBM may have the greatest influence on the buying decision.[37] If the customer is anxious to make a good impression on guests who have discriminating food tastes, then food quality may be the dominant buying motive.

Successful salespeople have adopted a product strategy that involves discovery of the buying motives that influence the purchase decision. In Chapter 10, we describe a need identification process that can be used to discover the customer's buying motives.

Emotional versus Rational Buying Motives

A careful study of buyer behavior reveals that people make buying decisions based on both emotional and rational buying motives. An **emotional buying motive** is one that prompts the prospect to act because of an appeal to some sentiment or passion. When customers buy expensive Harley-Davidson motorcycles, they are paying for much more than a high-flying hog. They are purchasing entry into a community of like-minded enthusiasts who share a passion for all things Harley.[38] Emotions can be powerful and often serve as the foundation of the dominant buying motive. A **rational buying motive** usually appeals to the prospect's reason or judgment based on objective thought processes. Some common rational buying motives include profit potential, quality of service, and availability of technical assistance.

Emotional Buying Motives A surprising number of purchases are guided by emotional buying motives. This is why many firms use emotional appeals. Even technology firms sometimes rely on these appeals. Panasonic, maker of the Interactive Panaboard, a product used to enhance business presentations, says this product is "the easiest way to share your big idea." Ads for Gulfstream business jets explain how the planes can save executives time and also describe the roomy interiors that offer comfort to the passengers.

CEO Glenn Sandberg understands that in the business-to-business market, exact specifications and 24-hour support appeals to those customers who are motivated by rational buying motives.

Doing business in America, or anyplace else in the world, is never purely a rational or logical process. To inspire people and move them in the right direction, you have to engage them emotionally.[39] In a world filled with look-alike products, emotional factors can have considerable influence. If two vendors have nearly identical products, then the influence of the vendors' salespeople becomes more important. The salesperson who is able to connect at a personal level has the advantage.

Rational Buying Motives A purchase based on rational buying motives is generally the result of an objective review of available information. The buyer closely examines product or service information with an attitude that is relatively free of emotion. Business buyers are most likely to be motivated by rational buying motives such as on-time delivery, financial gain, competent installation, saving of time, increased profits, or durability.

Business buyers representing large firms such as Ford Motor Company, IBM, and General Electric rely on a buying process that is more formalized than the consumer buying process. Purchases made by these companies usually call for detailed product specifications, written purchase orders, and formal approval. The business buyer and the salesperson work closely during all stages of the buying process that begins with a precise definition of the customer's problem. Salespeople who sell to business buyers spend a great deal of time gathering, interpreting, and disseminating customer-specific information.[40]

Patronage versus Product Buying Motives

Another way to help explain buyer behavior is to distinguish between patronage and product buying motives. Patronage buying motives and product buying motives are learned reasons for buying. These buying motives are important because they can stimulate repeat business and referrals.

Patronage Buying Motives A **patronage buying motive** is one that causes the prospect to buy products from one particular business. The prospect has had prior direct or indirect contact with the business and had judged this contact to be beneficial. In those situations where there is little or no appreciable difference between two products, patronage motives can be highly important. At a time when look-alike products are very common, these motives take on a new degree of importance. Some typical patronage buying motives are superior service, complete selection of products, competence of sales representatives, and ability to buy online.

Product Buying Motives A **product buying motive** is one that leads a prospect to purchase one product in preference to another. Interestingly enough, this decision is sometimes made without direct comparison between competing products. The buyer simply believes that one product is superior to another. There are numerous buying motives that trigger prospects to select one product over another. These include brand preference, quality preference, price preference, and design or engineering preference.

Global Business Etiquette

DOING BUSINESS IN FRANCE

The French people are very proud of their history, language, social systems, and customs. They expect visitors to respect the many things that make their country unique. Preparation for a business trip to France may take a little extra time.

- Learn basic French and use it often. Although most French businesspeople speak English, some will not admit it.
- Introductions should be made by someone (attorney, banker, or a friend) known to the person with whom you want to do business. French people tend to be cautious when meeting someone new.
- Be prepared to conduct business over meals at nice restaurants. A business lunch might last for two hours. The French rarely invite business guests to their homes.
- French businesspeople are reluctant to take risks, so negotiations may take a long time. Be well prepared to discuss the merits of your product but avoid the hard sell.[c]

To identify the customer scenario, the salesperson must get inside the customer's life. This can be done with appropriate questions, listening to the responses, and making observations.

Summary

The importance of developing a *customer strategy* was introduced in this chapter. This type of planning is necessary to ensure maximum customer responsiveness. Buying procedures and policies can vary greatly from one buyer to another. If a salesperson does not learn how the buyer plans to make the purchase, then there is the strong possibility that the selling process will be out of alignment with the customers buying process.

Business buyer behavior was compared to consumer buyer behavior. Three types of business buying situations were described: straight rebuy, new-task buy, and the modified rebuy. Systems selling, a common business buying strategy, was also described. Three types of consumer buying situations were defined: habitual buying decisions, variety-seeking buying decisions, and complex buying decisions. Customers make buying decisions in many ways, so it would be inappropriate to view the buying process as a uniform pattern of decision making. However, there is a common decision-making model that most buyers apply to their unique circumstances. The typical stages in the buying decision process are needs awareness, evaluation of solutions, resolution of problems, purchase, and implementation. This model is especially helpful in understanding organizational buying decisions and large consumer acquisitions. Three value-creation selling approaches that appeal to certain types of customers were discussed: the transactional process buyer, the consultative process buyer, and the strategic alliance process buyer.

We noted that buyer behavior is influenced in part by individual (physical and psychological) needs. Maslow's popular model ranks these needs. There are also a number of group influences that shape our psychological needs to various degrees. Buyer behavior is influenced by the roles we assume, reference groups, social class, and culture.

Perception was defined as the process of selecting, organizing, and interpreting information inputs to produce meaning. We use our five senses to assign meaning to these inputs. We discussed *emotional and rational buying motives*. Emotional buying motives prompt the prospect to act because of an appeal to some sentiment or passion. Rational buying motives tend to appeal to the prospect's reasoning power or judgment.

We also compared patronage and product *motives*. Patronage buying motives grow out of a strong relationship that has developed between the customer and the supplier. When competing products are quite similar, patronage motives can be very important. Product buying motives are usually in evidence when a prospect purchases one product in preference to another.

KEY TERMS

Customer strategy
Physiological needs
Security needs
Social needs
Esteem needs
Self-actualization
Group influences
Role
New-task buy
Straight rebuy
Modified rebuy
Systems selling
Habitual buying decisions
Buying process
Variety-seeking buying decisions
Buyer Resolution Theory
Reference group
Social class
Culture
Consumer buyer behavior
Business buyer behavior
Subculture
Perception
Buying motive
Emotional buying motive
Rational buying motive
Patronage buying motive
Product buying motive

REVIEW QUESTIONS

1. According to the Strategic/Consultative Selling Model, what are the three prescriptions for the development of a successful customer strategy?
2. List and describe the three most common types of organizational buying situations.
3. Describe the five major stages in the typical buying process.
4. List and describe three value creation selling approaches that appeal to various types of customers.
5. According to the buyer resolution theory, a purchase is made only after the prospect has made five buying decisions. What are they?
6. Explain how Maslow's hierarchy of needs affects buyer behavior.
7. Describe the four group influences that affect buyer behavior.
8. What is meant by the term *perception*?
9. Distinguish between emotional and rational buying motives.
10. J. D. Power, founder of J. D. Power and Associates, says, "We define quality as what the customer wants." Do you agree or disagree with his observations? Explain your answer.

APPLICATION EXERCISES

1. Select several advertisements from a trade magazine. Analyze each one and determine what rational buying motives the advertiser is appealing to. Do any of these advertisements appeal to emotional buying motives? Then select a magazine that is aimed at a

particular consumer group, for example, *Architectural Digest*, *Redbook*, or *Better Homes and Gardens*. Study the advertisements and determine what buying motives they appeal to.

2. The $70,000 Volkswagen Phaeton, which entered the U.S. market as a 2003 model, is a far cry from the Beetle. VW's new flagship model is designed to challenge the best from Lexus, Mercedes Benz, and BMW. The Phaeton, like the original Lexus LS400, will be positioned as another choice in the luxury-car market. Will potential customers accept the Phaeton as a true luxury car? Will customer perceptions play a role in the acceptance of this new model?
3. J. D. Power and Associates is a global marketing information services firm that helps businesses and consumers make better decisions through credible customer-based information. The company provides an unbiased source of marketing information based on opinions of consumers. Visit *www.jdpower.com* and become familiar with the type of information services offered.

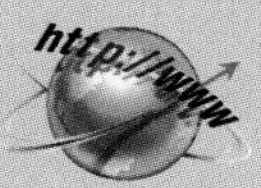

ROLE-PLAY EXERCISE

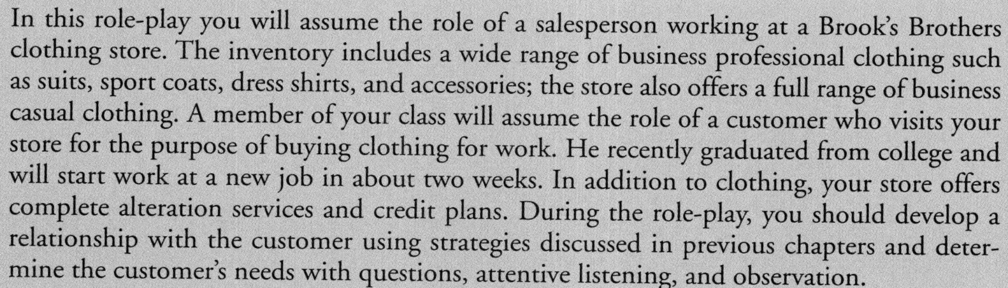

In this role-play you will assume the role of a salesperson working at a Brook's Brothers clothing store. The inventory includes a wide range of business professional clothing such as suits, sport coats, dress shirts, and accessories; the store also offers a full range of business casual clothing. A member of your class will assume the role of a customer who visits your store for the purpose of buying clothing for work. He recently graduated from college and will start work at a new job in about two weeks. In addition to clothing, your store offers complete alteration services and credit plans. During the role-play, you should develop a relationship with the customer using strategies discussed in previous chapters and determine the customer's needs with questions, attentive listening, and observation.

CRM APPLICATION EXERCISE

Managing Multiple Contacts with CRM

The ACT! database software identifies four firms involved with architecture. You can look up these firms and arrange to make contact with them. Start by selecting Lookup, Other, and, on the blank record, enter "architectural" in the Account Code field and click OK. ACT! then displays four records with architectural in that field.

For scheduling multiple telephone calls, start with the first record, Bryan Enterprises, and select the schedule call icon or select the following menu choices: Schedule, Calls. Use your mouse to select the following Monday, pick OK, select 9:00 A.M., pick OK, choose Follow up on the menu, and pick OK. On the next window, called Schedule an Activity, select the box labeled "Contact … " that displays another window called Select a Contact. On the Select a Contact window, pick the box labeled Lookup. This returns you to the Schedule an Activity window, where you can pick OK.

To confirm that a phone call was scheduled with each person in these architectural firms, select View, Task List. When the task list window appears, choose the Time Period, Future. Pick OK when finished.

For creating form letters to send to each of the four people in the four architectural firms, select Write, Edit Template, type the word "letter," and press Enter. A template with codes is displayed. Type the words, "I'll call Monday"; next select File, Save As, and type "Form"; then press Enter. Select File, Close. To prepare the four letters, select Write, Form

Letter, type "Form," and press Enter. On the next window—labeled Prepare Form Letter—choose Active Lookup and Document, and then pick OK. The first form letter is displayed on your screen. By pressing the PageDown key, you can review all four letters. Select Print (Ctrl+P) to print the four letters and File, Close to close the letter window.

VIDEO CASE PROBLEM

Kim Fernandez, director of natural food sales for Alta Dena Certified Dairy (www.altadenadairy.com), takes a great deal of pride in her efforts to win new customers for her line of natural dairy foods. As a sales representative for this national company (introduced at the beginning of this chapter), she is in a key position to meet the needs of a growing number of health-conscious consumers.

Like most professional salespeople, Kim Fernandez is continuously developing new accounts, servicing existing accounts, and introducing new products. When she calls on a large regional grocery wholesaler, such as Fleming Companies, closing the sale can be challenging. Wholesalers do not want to inventory products that do not appeal to the retail supermarkets they serve. Wholesalers want to buy products from companies that maintain the highest-quality production standards and provide outstanding service after the sale. Wholesalers also want to buy products at the lowest possible prices. The retail supermarkets (chain operated and independent) that Kim Fernandez calls on are no less demanding. They operate in a competitive environment and must offer products at the lowest possible price.

The motto, "Give the consumers what they want," could easily be adopted by the typical American supermarket. A typical store features from 10,000 to 12,000 items. Some large supermarkets feature over 20,000 different items. Thousands of new products are introduced each year, so buyers must make many difficult purchase decisions. Supermarket dairy departments have been revitalized in recent years by the growth of new items and growing demand for healthy foods. Each year from 800 to 900 new dairy products are introduced. When Alta Dena Certified Dairy introduces a new product, the sales force must work hard to win acceptance.

Kim's product line includes yogurt, butter, cottage cheese, milk, ice cream, cheese, and many other dairy products. The company makes every effort to offer only products that are of the highest quality and made with all natural ingredients. The Alta Dena research and development (R&D) laboratory is constantly searching for ways to improve existing products and develop new ones. Customers often are involved in the product development process. They are given samples and encouraged to give their impressions. The Alta Dena product development staff, along with the sales staff, work hard to determine the customer's wants and needs. Kim often takes samples of new products to supermarkets and involves the dairy department staff in a taste test. When Kim meets with a prospect, she asks several questions to determine the person's needs and buying motives. She realizes that in some cases several motives may influence the purchase decision. She also knows that buying behavior is influenced by perception, so she must probe to find out what prospects are really thinking. The prospect who believes that natural dairy products have a short shelf life may be reluctant to carry her line of products. If this perception is uncovered, then Kim knows how to respond to it.

Kim views education as a major sales tool. She often explains the quality controls used at Alta Dena plants and even invites customers to participate in plant tours. She talks about the "contented cows" that make up the Alta Dena dairy herd. She knows that education can add value to her products. Kim also knows that a long-term partnership with the customer is based on attention to details. She checks on deliveries and makes sure all complaints are handled quickly and courteously. (For more information see chapter opener on p. 182.)

Questions

1. Does it appear that Kim Fernandez has built her customer strategy on the three prescriptions featured in the Strategic/Consultative Selling Model? Explain.
2. What aspects of the need–satisfaction theory has Kim Fernandez incorporated into her approach to customers? Explain.
3. As a buyer for a large supermarket chain, would you be more influenced by rational or emotional buying motives? Explain.
4. What steps has Kim Fernandez taken to build a long-term partnership with her customers?

Chapter Preview

When you finish reading this chapter, you should be able to

1 Discuss the importance of developing a prospect base

2 Identify and assess important sources of prospects

3 Describe criteria for qualifying prospects

4 Explain common methods of organizing prospect information

5 Name some characteristics that are important to learn about customers as individuals and business representatives

6 Describe the steps in developing a prospecting and sales forecasting plan

CHAPTER 9

Developing and Qualifying a Prospect Base

Graig Phillips, a sales representative for International Dehydrated Foods, has found a "no hassle" method of maintaining contact with over 500 people with whom he works. He is using ACT! contact software (*www.act.com*). He now can maintain a detailed profile of every customer and customer support personnel. With a single keystroke on his laptop computer he can bring up detailed information on each contact. Customer service has been improved because the ACT! software reminds him when it is time to make a follow-up call. The ACT! software also makes it easy to network with other members of the sales force and his sales manager.[1]

ACT! and other software vendors such as Epicor and Siebel Systems are helping companies develop effective customer relationship management (CRM) systems. These systems are at the heart of every successful one-to-one marketing initiative. Success in selling depends on one's ability to identify prospects, gain insight into the prospect's needs, and develop an accurate picture of the prospect's value.[2]

PROSPECTING—AN INTRODUCTION

Gerhard Gschwandtner, publisher of *Selling Power*, says, "The main purpose of a salesperson is not to make sales, but to create customers."[3] Identifying potential customers is an important aspect of the customer strategy. In the terminology of personal selling this process is called **prospecting**. A potential customer, or **prospect**, is someone who meets the qualification criteria established by you or your company.

Finding prospects who can make the purchase is not as easy as it sounds. This is especially true in business-to-business sales. In many situations the salesperson must make the sales presentation to multiple decision makers. One of these decision makers might be the technical expert who wants an answer to the question: "Does the product meet the company's specifications?" Another decision maker may be the person who will actually use the product. The employee who will use the forklift truck you are selling may be involved in the purchase decision. Of course, there is often a "purse-string" decision maker who has the ultimate authority to release funds for the purchase. During periods of economic uncertainty, the decision-making process often moves upward. It is sometimes difficult to make connections with upper-level executives. One solution is to plan a joint sales call involving a higher-level executive from your company.[4]

The goal of prospecting is to build a **prospect base** made up of current customers and potential customers. Many successful companies find that current customers account for a large percentage of their sales. Every effort is made to keep these clients satisfied because they provide the repeat business that is necessary to maintain profitability.

Importance of Prospecting

Every salesperson must cope with customer attrition, that is, the inevitable loss of customers over a period of time, which can be attributed to a variety of causes. Unless new prospects are found to replace lost customers, a salesperson eventually faces a reduction in income and possible loss of employment.

To better understand the significance of prospecting, let us examine a few common causes of customer attrition.

The customer may move to a new location outside the salesperson's territory. The American population is very mobile. This cause of attrition is especially common in the retail and service areas.

A firm may go out of business or merge with another company. In some areas of business the failure rate is quite high. In recent years, we have witnessed a record number of mergers that have caused massive changes in purchasing plans.

A loyal buyer or purchasing agent may leave the position because of promotion, retirement, resignation, or serious illness. The replacement may prefer to buy from someone else.

Sales are lost to the competition. In some cases, the competition offers more value. The added value may take the form of better quality, a better price, a stronger relationship, better service, or some combination of these factors.

Some studies reveal that the average company loses 15 to 20 percent of its customers every year. Depending on the type of selling, this figure might be higher or lower. It becomes clear that many customers are lost for reasons beyond the salesperson's control. If salespeople want to keep their earnings at a stable level, they need to develop new customers.

Joe Girard, once recognized by the *Guinness Book of Records* as the world's greatest salesperson, used the "Ferris wheel" concept to illustrate the relationship between prospecting and loss of customers due to the attrition. As people get off the Ferris wheel, the operator fills their seats one at a time, moves the wheel a little, and continues this process until all the original riders have left the wheel and new ones come aboard (Fig. 9.1). In reality, of course, established customers do not come and go this fast. With the passing of time, however, many customers must be replaced.

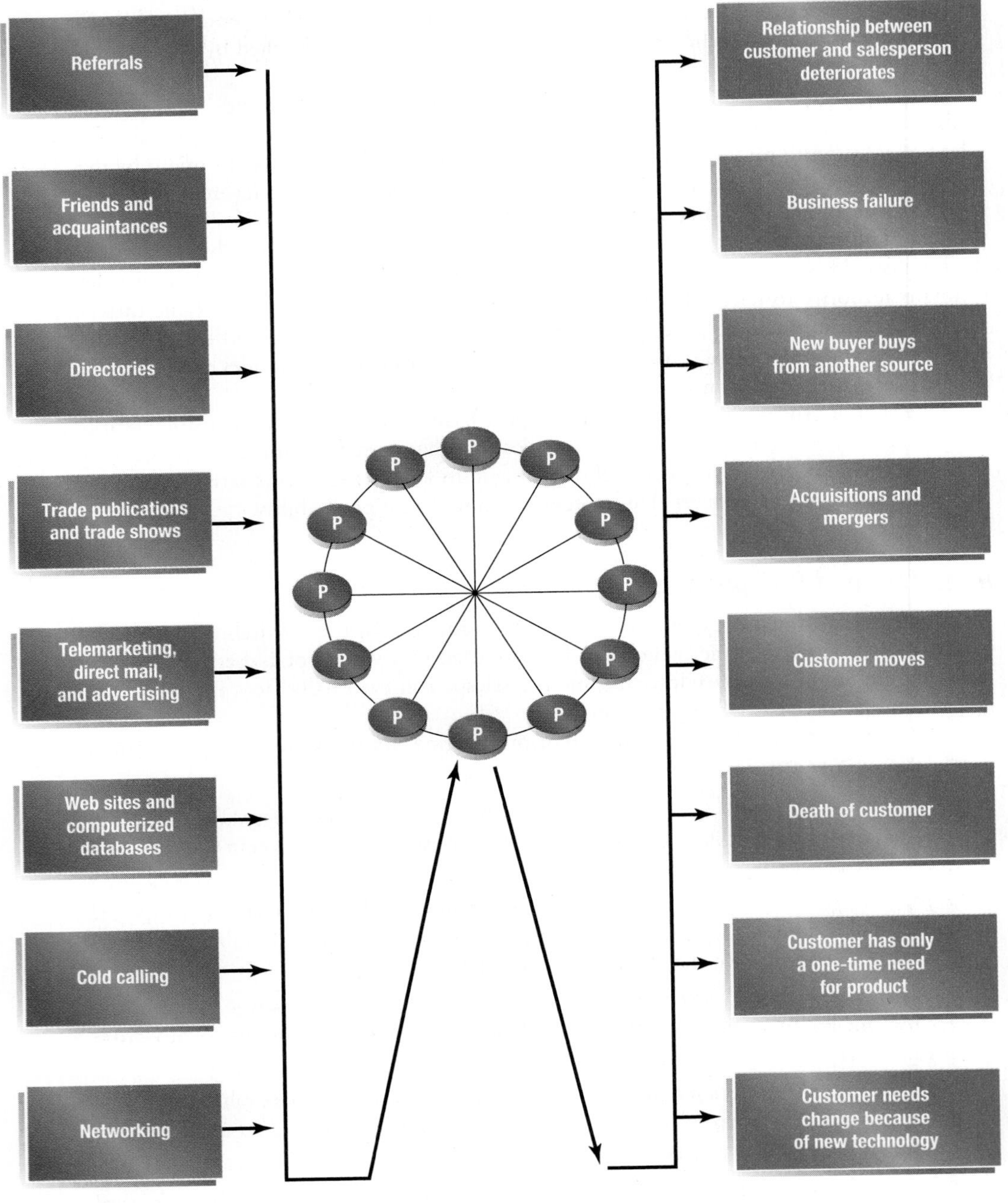

FIGURE | 9.1

The "Ferris wheel" concept, which is aimed at supplying an ongoing list of prospects, is part of world sales record holder Joe Girard's customer strategy.

PROSPECTING REQUIRES PLANNING

Prospecting should be viewed as a systematic process of locating potential customers. Some prospecting efforts can be integrated easily into a regular sales call. Progressive marketers are doing three things to improve the quality of the prospecting effort:

Developing a prospect base is an important part of the customer strategy. Hancock's CRM software can help increase the number of prospects who board the Ferris wheel, improve the quality of these prospects and shorten the sales cycle.

Spotting Your Best Prospects Is Easy,

With Hancock Information Group Generating Your Leads.

We are your direct link to potential customers — identifying what they are thinking, what motivates them and ultimately, what they will buy. Let our intuitive business-to-business sales-support team help you make better business decisions on how your marketing dollars are spent with:

- Lead generation
- Appointment setting
- Pipeline management

Find out about Hancock's award-winning, consultative approach to spotting your next sale. Call Christine Resch at 1-800-749-1556.

1-800-749-1556
Insights into the world of your prospects
www.hancockinfo.com

1. *Increase the number of people who board the Ferris wheel.* You want to see a continuous number of potential prospects board the Ferris wheel because they are the source of sales opportunities. If the number of potential prospects declines sharply, the number of sales closed also declines.
2. *Improve the quality of the prospects who board the Ferris wheel.* Companies often establish quality standards that ensure a steady supply of prospects with high profit potential. For example, some companies focus their prospecting efforts on consultative process buyers. These are prospects who often lack need awareness and need help evaluating possible solutions.

3. *Shorten the sales cycle by quickly determining which of the new prospects are qualified prospects—qualified as to need, ability to pay, and authority to purchase the product.* Gerhard Gschwandtner says, "Time is the ultimate scorekeeper in the game of selling." He points out that many salespeople do not meet their sales goals because they do not quickly qualify new prospects.[5] Later in this chapter we examine qualifying practices and discuss how to shorten the sales cycle with sales automation methods.

In most selling situations, prospecting begins with a study of the market for your product or service. When Pitney Bowes first developed the desktop postage meter, the company conducted a careful study of the market. At first glance, equipment of this nature seemed well suited only to a large business firm. With additional market analysis, the company identified many small firms that could benefit from purchasing the product.

Prospecting Plans Must Be Assessed Often

In today's dynamic, ever-changing marketplace, prospecting plans must be monitored continuously. Some prospecting techniques that worked well in the past may become ineffective because of changing market conditions. Midwest Training Institute, a firm that helps companies improve their production and sales efficiency, experienced a dramatic sales decline during the first quarter of the year. This decline came after years of steady sales increases. Joel Pecoraro, president of the company, initiated a thorough investigation and discovered that his sales staff were relying primarily on one prospecting approach that was no longer successful: The salespeople were calling established customers. Pecoraro designed an incentive program that rewarded salespeople who adopted new prospecting techniques such as attending an association meeting where the salesperson could meet potential prospects, or speaking at a meeting attended by persons who might need the services offered by Midwest Training Institute.[6]

Salespeople who view prospecting as an important key to success spend time every day on this activity. Prospecting is not thought of as a chore but as an opportunity to identify persons who can benefit from owning your product. Prospecting is viewed as a process that can take place in virtually any environment—in social situations, on an airplane, during a professional meeting, or in any situation in which people are present.

Customer Relationship Management with Technology

USING THE SAME CRM SOFTWARE AS AT&T

AT&T implemented a CRM program that resulted in major increases in productivity and improved customer service. The first stage of the automation project involved 11,000 desktop computers and the popular ACT! software (*www.act.com*). This combination of hardware and software resulted in a reported 15 to 20 percent improvement in productivity. AT&T salespeople gained easier and quicker access to account information such as the prospect's name, title, company, assistant's name, and notes concerning the account. Placing the database on a server gives all network users access to this important information.

Information in a CRM database can be reviewed prior to calling or visiting a prospect, thus ensuring a more personalized contact. Through CRM, salespeople gain a competitive edge in relating to their prospects' needs and interests.

You have the opportunity to use a demonstration version of the same software (ACT!) used by AT&T. Just as an AT&T salesperson, you are assigned a number (20) of prospect accounts and given individual and company information about each account's contact person in the database software. Your participation in the CRM case study and exercises will give you hands-on experience with the strategic development of a prospect base, using modern sales technology. You not only will be using the same software being used by thousands of salespeople but also will be working with data that are derived from authentic selling challenges. (See the CRM Case Study, Reviewing the Prospect Database, on p. 232 for more information.)

SOURCES OF PROSPECTS

Every salesperson must develop a prospecting system suited to a particular selling situation. Some of the many sources of prospects follow, and each should be carefully examined:

- Referrals
- Friends, family members, and centers of influence
- Directories
- Trade publications
- Trade shows and special events
- Telemarketing
- Direct-response advertising and sales letters
- Web site
- Computerized database
- Cold calling
- Networking
- Educational seminars
- Prospecting by nonsales employees

Referrals

The use of referrals as a prospecting approach has been used successfully in a wide range of selling situations. In most cases, referral leads result in higher close rates, larger sales, and shorter sales cycles. A **referral** is a prospect who has been recommended by a current customer or by someone who is familiar with the product. Satisfied customers, business acquaintances, and even prospects who do not buy often can recommend the names of persons who might benefit from purchasing the product.

Customers are more likely to give a referral if they perceive value in the product you sell. When you build value into your sales process, you increase the odds that the customer will give you a referral. Steve Lewis, managing partner of New England Financial, says, "Our attitude is that we can't ask for referrals until clients have perceived value in the process."[7]

Endless Chain Referrals

The endless chain approach to obtaining referrals is easy to use because it fits naturally into most sales presentations. A salesperson selling long-term health care insurance might say, "Miss Remano, whom do you know who might be interested in our insurance plan?" This open-ended question gives the person the freedom to recommend several prospects and is less likely to be answered with a no response. Be sure to use your reference's name when you contact the new prospect—"Mary Remano suggested that I call you. . . ."

Referral Letters and Cards

The referral letter method is a variation of the endless chain technique. In addition to requesting the names of prospects, the salesperson asks the customer to prepare a note or letter of introduction that can be delivered to the potential customer. The correspondence is an actual testimonial prepared by a satisfied customer. Some companies use a referral card to introduce the salesperson. The preprinted card features a place for your customer to sign the new prospect's name and his own name, and can be used as part of the sales presentation.

Within the field of personal selling, there is not complete agreement regarding the timing of the referral request. Some sales training programs encourage salespeople to request the referral immediately after closing the sale. Others point out that if you are working with a new customer, it takes time to earn the customer's trust. The customer may feel there is a risk involved in giving you referrals. Once you have built a strong, trusting relationship with the customer, referral requests are more likely to receive a positive response.[8]

Referral Organizations

Some salespeople have found that membership in a referral organization is an effective way to obtain good leads. BNI (Business Network International) is one of the largest business networking organizations with over 3,600 chapters worldwide (*www.bni.com*). BNI offers members the opportunity to share ideas, contacts and referrals.[9]

Friends, Family Members, and Centers of Influence

A person who is new in the field of selling often uses friends and family members as sources of information about potential customers. It is only natural to contact people we know. In many cases these people have contacts with a wide range of potential buyers.

The center-of-influence method involves establishing a relationship with a well-connected, influential person who is willing to provide prospecting information. This person may not make buying decisions but has influence on other people who do. To illustrate, consider the challenge facing Gary Schneider, creator of a powerful software product that would help small farmers optimize their crop selection. After spending several years developing the product, Schneider and his wife began selling the product one copy at a time. During one cold call on a major crop insurer, American Agrisurance, he met a senior researcher who immediately saw the benefits of the software product. This respected researcher is in a position to influence buying decisions at his company and to provide prospect information for other crop insurers.[10]

Directories

Directories can help salespeople search out new prospects and determine their buying potential. A list of some of the more popular national directories is provided next:

Middle Market Directory lists 14,000 firms worth between $500,000 and $1 million (available from Dun & Bradstreet *www.dnb.com*).

TrackAmerica is a database management company that offers online information on millions of U.S. businesses and consumers (*www.trackamerica.com*).

Standard & Poor's Corporation Records Service provides details on more than 11,000 companies (*www.spglobal.com*).

Thomas Register of American Manufacturers provides a listing of 60,000 manufacturers by product classifications, addresses, and capital ratings (*www.thomasregister.com*).

Polk City Directory provides detailed information on the citizens of a specific community. Polk, in business for over 125 years, publishes about 1,100 directories covering 6,500 communities in the United States and Canada (*www.citydirectory.com*).

Selling in Action

PROSPECTING WITH YOUR PARTNERS

When Megan Michael sees a new office building going up, she stops her car and makes inquiries about who is to occupy the building. As a sales representative for BKM Total Office, an office furniture supplier in San Diego, she needs to be aware of new office space. However, this approach is not her most important prospecting method. She has found the telephone to be her most effective prospecting tool. Michael speaks regularly with her customers to find out if they know companies that might need BKM's products. Architects, designers, and builders who have previously worked with Michael have proved to be good sources of referrals. The key to her prospecting success is maintaining a strong relationship with her customers. She realizes that you must be an effective partner before you can ask for help.[a]

The Encyclopedia of Associations lists more than 23,000 U.S. associations and more than 20,000 international organizations with details on membership, publications, and conferences (*www.gale.com*).

These are just a few of the better-known directories. There are hundreds of additional directories covering business and industrial firms on the regional, state, and local levels. Some directories are free, whereas others must be purchased at a nominal fee. One of the most useful free sources of information is the telephone directory. Most telephone directories have a classified (yellow pages) section that groups businesses and professions by category. Web Yellow Pages (*www.bigyellow.com*) provides more than 11 million U.S. business listings.

If you are involved in the sale of products in the international market, a valuable resource is the world traders data reports published by U.S. and Foreign Commercial Service (US & FCS), which has district offices located in several cities throughout the nation. If you want to know more about a prospective customer or agent in a foreign country, US & FCS can provide a complete profile, including background information within the local business community, payment history, creditworthiness, and overall reliability and suitability as a trade contact.

Trade Publications

Trade publications provide a status report on every major industry. If you are a sales representative employed by Super Valu Stores, Fleming Companies Inc., Sysco Corporation, or one of the other huge food wholesaling houses that supplies supermarkets, then you can benefit from a monthly review of *Progressive Grocer* magazine. Each month this trade publication reports on trends in the retail food industry, new products, problems, innovations, and related information. Trade journals such as *Women's Wear Daily, Home Furnishings, Hardware Retailer, Modern Tire Dealer*, and *Progressive Architecture* are examples of publications that might help salespeople identify prospects.

Trade Shows and Special Events

A trade show is a large exhibit of products that are, in most cases, common to one industry, such as electronics or office equipment. The prospects walk into the booth or exhibit and talk with those who represent the exhibitor. In some cases, sales personnel invite existing customers and prospects to attend trade shows so they can have an opportunity to demonstrate their newest products.

Research studies indicate that it is much easier to identify good prospects and actually close sales at a trade show. In most cases, fewer sales calls are needed to close a sale if the prospect was qualified at a trade show. Once a trade show contact is identified and judged

The Thomas Register of American Manufacturers (www.thomasregister.com) *is one source of prospects for salespeople. Thomas Register products are available on CD, DVD, and in a print edition.*

Thomas Register of American Manufacturers

Order Now And Get All Of This...

The most complete listings of North American manufacturers available with 1.5 million listings...

- 149,000 companies
- 50,000 product and service headings
- 1,700 company catalogs
- 105,000 brand and trade names
- 98,000 supplier ads for vendor comparisons

Over 50,000 pages of facts and figures organized to help you find the information you need in seconds. Who makes it? ...Who's closest? ...Who do I contact to order? ...Who do I contact to sell? ...What's their phone number and address?

You'll find the answers you need in Thomas Register — fast.

To Order Call 212–290–7277 or Fax 212–290–7365

to be a qualified lead, information regarding the lead should be carefully recorded. When a prospect enters a Xerox Corporation booth, a salesperson uses a few questions to qualify the lead and types the answers into an on-screen form. Xerox uses software developed by NewLeads to record and process data obtained from prospects who have been qualified by a salesperson working in the booth.[11]

A special event can be a baseball game, a golf tournament, a reception for a dignitary, or a charity event. Bentley Motor Cars invited a number of potential clients to the famous Le Mans 24-hour endurance race. Prospects watched the Bentley race car compete while sipping champagne. Back in America, charity events serve as a venue for cultivating wealthy clientele who can afford a Bentley automobile.[12]

Telemarketing

Telemarketing is the practice of marketing goods and services through telephone contact. It is an integral part of many modern sales and marketing campaigns. One use of telemarketing is to identify prospects. A financial services company used telemarketing to identify prospects for its customized equipment leasing packages. Leads were given to salespeople

Research shows that it is much easier to identify good prospects and actually close sales at a trade show.

for consideration. Telemarketing also can be used to quickly and inexpensively qualify prospects for follow-up. Some marketers use the telephone to verify sales leads generated by direct mail, advertisements, or some other method.

Direct-Response Advertising and Sales Letters

Many advertisements invite the reader to send for a free booklet or brochure that provides detailed information about the product or service. In the category of business-to-business marketing, advertising has strong inquiry-generating power. Some firms distribute

Bentley Motor Cars invited a number of potential clients to the famous LeMans 24-hour endurance race. This special event helped the company develop its prospect base.

Selling Is Everyone's Business

WINEMAKER APPLIES HER SALES SKILLS

Gina Gallo is a third-generation family winemaker who knows a thing or two about personal selling. She not only knows how to make the wines offered by E. & J. Gallo Winery, but she also knows how to sell them. The year she spent as a member of the sales force helped her learn about consumer's buying habits and the needs of retailers who sell Gallo wines. Gina Gallo sees some similarities between winemaking and sales. The better you understand your vineyards, the soil, and the grapes, the greater the chance you have of creating an excellent wine. The better you understand your customer's needs, the better you can relate to and fulfill those needs.[b]

Gina Gallo.

postage-free response cards (also known as bingo cards) to potential buyers. Recipients are encouraged to complete and mail the cards if they desire additional information. In some cases the name of the person making the inquiry is given to a local sales representative for further action.

Sales letters, sent via e-mail or the U.S. postal service, can be incorporated easily into a prospecting plan. The prospecting sales letter is sent to persons who are in a position to make a buying decision. Shortly after mailing the letter (three or four days) the prospect is called and asked for an appointment. The call begins with a reference to the sales letter. To make the letter stand out, some salespeople include product information. As noted in Chapter 6, all sales letters must be written with care. To get results, sales letters must quickly get the reader's attention.

Web Site

Thousands of companies and businesspeople have established Web sites on the World Wide Web. A **Web site** is a collection of Web pages maintained by a single person or organization. It is accessible to anyone with a computer and a modem. Large firms, such as Century 21, maintain Web sites that feature 20 to 30 Web pages. Web sites frequently offer prospects the opportunity to acquire product information that can help them make a buying decision. Financial services companies describe home financing and refinancing options. The Sun Microsystems Web site provides detailed descriptions of Sun's products and solutions. When someone clicks on a Web page and requests information, they will likely become a prospect. Some Web sites offer an incentive to leave contact information.

New technologies can be used to enhance your online sales message. LifeFX is working with Kodak to develop personalized e-mail messages that will include a photo of the salesperson and a verbal message in the salesperson's own voice. With this technology, a salesperson could send an e-mail to an advance list of trade-show attendees inviting them to visit her booth.[13]

Computerized Database

With the aid of electronic data processing, it is often possible to match product features with the needs of potential customers quickly and accurately. In many situations, a firm can develop its own computerized database. In other cases it is more economical to purchase the database from a company that specializes in the collection of such information. One example is infoUSA, a company that offers a whole range of lead generation and prospect selection services. infoUSA can provide lead generation information for different market segments. For example, it has compiled a national list of doctors, dentists, nurses, office managers, and other health care organizations and professionals. The company can also help you develop your own tools for the analysis and selection of prospects.[14]

With the aid of a personal computer (PC), salespeople can develop their own detailed customer files. The newer PCs provide expanded storage capacity at a lower price than in the past. This means that salespeople can accumulate a great deal of information about individual customers and use this information to personalize the selling process. For example, a PC can help an independent insurance agent maintain a comprehensive record of each policyholder. As the status of each client changes (marriage, birth of children, etc.), the record can be easily updated. With the aid of an up-to-date database, the agent can quickly identify prospects for the various existing and new policy options.

Cold Calling

With some products, cold call prospecting is an effective approach to prospect identification. In **cold calling**, the salesperson selects a group of people who may or may not be actual prospects and then calls (by phone or personal visit) on each one. For example, the sales representative for a wholesale medical supply firm might call on every hospital in a given community, assuming that each one is a potential customer. Many new salespeople must rely on the cold call method because they are less likely to get appointments through referrals.

With computers, salespeople can accumulate a great deal of information about individual customers and use this information to add value during the selling process.

Increasingly, lists of prospects are becoming available on the Internet. These lists can be used as a "combination approach" with direct mail, telemarketing, or cold calling.

Drew Lundgren
President
Mid Markets Group

Look what our customers have to say...

"*infoUSA* has consistently surpassed all competitors. *They have helped us achieve new levels of sales performance with responsive, accurate contact names and sales leads that get results!*"

-*Mason Yamashiro, CEO Alliance Communication Technologies*

Without Sales Leads There is NO Selling!

Find the right prospects, get complete information about them, and use our database marketing services to improve your revenue.

14 Million Businesses:
Select by Type of Business, Number of Employees, Sales Volume, Number of PCs, Contact Name, Credit Rating, Geography, public filings, e-mail addresses and more.

250 Million Consumers:
Select by demographics, age, income, gender, buying behavior, home value, length of residence, ailments, census data, e-mail addresses and much more. Over 70 selects.

13 Million Executives & Professionals By Title:
Businesses are nothing without people. We have the decision-makers. CEO's, Owners, Presidents, Human Resources Executives, Chairman, Attorneys, Physicians and Surgeons, Dentists, Accountants, Engineers, Architects, Controller, Purchasing Executive, Telecommunications Executive...And More!

Customer Analyzer & Prospect Builder™:
Analyze your current customers and find prospects just like them. No guesswork, no headache.

State-of-the-Art Database Marketing:
Turn your CRM solution into a powerful database tool. Clean your file. Match it. Model it. Add more information, profile your customers, merge/purge, update through NCOA and more.

infoConnect:
Integrates information about your customers or prospects; delivers timely and accurate data and data processing services; performs multiple DP work with one pass; and a new privacy feature remove opt-out names.

Databases on the Internet:
Buy sales leads and mailing lists 24/7 at www.infoUSA.com. To subscribe and get a 10% discount call Drew Lundgren.

FREE
Business Credit Ratings on 14 million businesses Just for calling!

Sales leads are dynamic, only with monthly updates do you stay ahead of the competition!

Call Drew Lundgren at 1-888-242-5512

Call: 1-888-242-5512 • Fax: 402-537-7909
5711 S. 86th Circle • Omaha, NE 68127
E-mail: drew.lundgren@infousa.com • Internet: www.infoUSA.com

Edward Jones Corporation, a financial services company, is a strong supporter of cold calling. Sales representatives knock on doors and introduce themselves with a friendly, professional message:

> "Hi, my name is Brad Ledwith, I represent the Edward Jones Corporation, and we sell financial services. We're a unique firm because we try to do all of our business face-to-face. I just wanted to stop by and let you know that I've opened up a Jones office in the area and to find out if it's OK to contact you when I have an investment idea."[15]

Sales representatives such as Brad Ledwith connect personally with members of their communities.

Successful cold calls do not happen spontaneously. Some strategic thinking and planning must precede personal visits and telephone calls. Whom do you contact? What do you say during the first few seconds? Samantha Ettus, CEO of Ettus Media Management, a New York City public relations agency, says cold calls helped her firm land some of its biggest clients. Ettus does plenty of research before she reaches for the phone. She collects all the pertinent information she can find—memberships and professional affiliations, career history, awards received, and of course information regarding the prospect's business. Then she makes the call, which is as brief and precise as possible. Immediately after the call, she sends the prospect a personalized e-mail that summarizes what her firm has to offer. Ettus views the cold call as nothing more than a way to introduce herself and her company to a prospect.[16]

Networking

One of the most complete books on networking is *Dig Your Well Before You're Thirsty* by Harvey Mackay. He says, "If I had to name the single characteristic shared by all the truly successful people I've met over a lifetime, I'd say it's the ability to create and nurture a network of contacts."[17] Networking skills are of special importance to new salespeople who cannot turn to a large group of satisfied customers for referrals and leads. Professionals (accountants, lawyers, consultants, etc.), entrepreneurs, managerial personnel, and customer service representatives also must develop networking skills. Networking skills are also of critical importance to job seekers because at any given time about 80 percent of all available jobs are not posted in the classifieds or on job boards.[18]

In simple terms, **networking** is the art of making and using contacts, or people meeting people and profiting from the connections. Although networking is one of the premier prospecting methods, some salespeople are reluctant to seek referrals in this manner. In addition, many salespeople do not use effective networking practices. Skilled networkers suggest the following guidelines for identifying good referrals:

1. *Meet as many people as you can.* Networking can take place on an airplane, at a Rotary Club meeting, at a trade show, or a professional association meeting.
2. *When you meet someone, tell the person what you do.* Give your name and describe your position in a way that explains what you do and invites conversations. Instead of saying, "I am in stocks and bonds," say, "I am a financial counselor who helps people make investment decisions." Listen more than you talk.
3. *Do not do business while networking.* It usually is not practical to conduct business while networking. Make a date to call or meet with the new contact later.
4. *Offer your business card.* The business card is especially useful when the contact attempts to tell others about your products or services.
5. *Edit your contacts and follow-up.* You cannot be involved with all your contacts, so separate the productive from the nonproductive. Send a short e-mail message to contacts you deem productive and include business information, brochures—anything that increases visibility.[19] Make sure your materials are professional. Use inexpensive contact management software, such as ACT!, to organize your contact information.

There are three types of networks salespeople should grow and nurture (Fig. 9.2). Every salesperson can be well served by networking within their own organization. You never know when someone in finance, technical support, or shipping may be needed to help solve a problem or provide you with important information. A second form of networking involves establishing contacts inside your industry. Make contact

FIGURE | 9.2

Three Types of Networks
Top performing salespeople recognize that networking can take place in three areas.

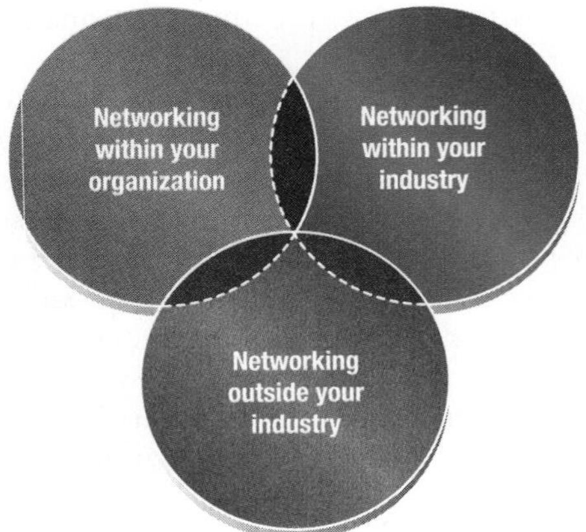

with experts in your field, top performers, leaders, successful company representatives, and even competitors. The third form of networking involves business contacts with people outside of your industry such as bankers, government officials, developers, and other people in your community. The local golf course is frequently a good place to make these contacts.[20]

Educational Seminars

Many salespeople are using educational seminars as a method of identifying prospects. Seminars provide an opportunity to showcase your product without pressuring prospects to buy. The owners of Source Digital Systems, a McLean, Virginia, firm that sells video-editing systems, attracted 128 corporate prospects to an educational seminar held next

Selling in Action

DEVELOP YOUR PROSPECT BASE WITH SEMINARS

The use of educational seminars has become an important prospecting method. You can educate prospective customers with brochures, news releases, catalogs, or your Web site, but educational seminars offer the advantage of face-to-face contact. Barbara Siskind, in her book, *Seminars to Build Your Business,* identifies 15 objectives for hosting seminars. A few of the most important ones follow:

Obtain sales leads. This is one of the most common objectives for seminars. You can obtain the names of attendees and arrange appointments for future sales calls. Seminars also may help identify actual product users, technical support people, or engineers who, although they may not be the decision maker, may influence the purchase decision.

Promote your place of business. Your place of business can become a destination for people who might otherwise not consider visiting it. You have an opportunity to create awareness of your company and develop a positive image for your entire operation and its capabilities.

Showcase and demonstrate your expertise. Seminars allow you to show a carefully targeted group of people that you really know your stuff. Salespeople can be supported by technical experts and others in the organization who can address clients' specific concerns.

Polaroid Canada advertised educational seminars across Canada where imaging specialists assisted prospective clients in exploring imaging solutions. Toronto-based Charon Systems, Incorporated, a systems integrator that deploys networks for organizations, regularly organizes seminars for 80 to 100 technology people from midsized firms. President David Fung estimates that 25 percent of prospects become clients.[c]

door to the Baltimore Orioles baseball field. While the guests enjoyed lunch, the staff demonstrated the newest video-editing technology. The group was given an opportunity to ask questions and complete a survey form. Afterward, everyone attended an Orioles–Red Sox game. Within two months the company closed six sales worth $420,000.[21] Many banks, investment firms, accounting firms, wine merchants, and consulting companies use seminars to generate new prospects. When inviting prospects, be clear about the seminar's content and always deliver what you promise.[22]

Prospecting by Nonsales Employees

Should service technicians, receptionists, bank tellers, and other nonsales personnel be involved in prospecting? In a growing number of organizations the answer is yes. Prospecting does not need to be the exclusive responsibility of the sales force. Janet Dixon, a UPS sales representative, needed help making contact with an important prospect. This person wouldn't take her calls. She talked to the UPS service provider (driver) who called on this account and requested his help. He had serviced this company for years and was like part of the family. He knew the prospect personally and persuaded her to accept a call from the salesperson.[23]

Employees do not have to work in sales to identify potential customers. However, they may not be alert to opportunities unless they are given an orientation to this role. Nonsales personnel need special training to function effectively in this role. Also, an incentive program can keep them focused on new business opportunities for the organization.

Combination Approaches

In recent years, we have seen an increase in the number of prospecting approaches used by salespeople. In many cases, success in selling depends on your ability to use a combination of the methods described in this chapter. For example, the large number of prospects identified at a trade show might be used to develop an effective telemarketing program. Prospects are called and an effort is made to set up a personal call. Prospects identified at a trade show or educational seminar might be sent a sales-oriented newsletter, a sales letter, or an e-mail message inviting prospects to visit your Web page.

QUALIFYING THE PROSPECT

One of the most important keys to success in personal selling is the ability to qualify prospects. **Qualifying** is the process of identifying prospects who should be contacted. Top salespeople use good research and analysis skills to qualify leads effectively.[24]

The qualification process is important for two reasons. First, a salesperson cannot afford to spend time calling on persons who are not legitimate prospects. Time conservation should always be a primary concern. Calling on *potential* customers is much more time consuming than calling on *established* customers. In terms of sales closings, a new customer can require several contacts. Second, a salesperson should identify prospects who can place an order large enough to cover sales expenses. The average sales call costs more than $200, so salespeople must try to avoid calling on prospects who have limited buying potential. Salespeople often rank prospects according to anticipated sales volume.

Every salesperson needs to establish qualifying criteria. The process involves finding answers to several basic questions.

1. *Does the prospect have a need for my product?* If you sell copy machines, it might appear that every business firm is a prospect. However, a firm that is outsourcing its copy work to FedEx Kinko's may not be a legitimate prospect.

   Qualifying involves probing for real needs. Let's assume you sell real estate for a large agency. You receive a call from someone who believes that owning a home is a good tax benefit. At this point it's important to find out what else makes owning a home important for that person. Get permission to ask questions and then determine the person's real needs. In the final analysis you may decide it would be a waste of your time and the prospect's time to visit several homes that are on the market.[25]
2. *Can the prospect make the buying decision?* Ideally you should talk to a person who has the authority to buy or can influence the buying decision. Talking to the right person within a large organization may involve collecting information from several sources. Some buying decisions are made by individuals and others are made by a committee. Expensive products often require the approval of a decision maker higher up in the organization.
3. *Can the prospect pay for the purchase?* It is usually not difficult to obtain credit information for consumer and business buyers. If you are selling products to a business, the *Dun & Bradstreet Reference Book* is an excellent source of credit information. A local credit bureau can provide credit information for a consumer buyer.

   Although the collection of credit information is not difficult, detecting financial instability can be much more complicated. In recent years we have seen a steady stream of corporate scandals involving accounting irregularities, inflated balance sheets, and outright fraud.[26] Salespeople must be aware of the possibility that a customer may provide incorrect or misleading information.
4. *Will anyone close the sale?* Rick Page, author of *Hope Is Not a Strategy*, reminds us that many prospects evaluate products but do not buy. When an evaluation stalls, the prospect may have determined that the problem is not of great enough magnitude or urgency to make the purchase. Also, in some cases there is not enough support within the company to reach closure. Rather than walk away from this situation, some salespeople move higher in the organization to determine the level of support for the purchase.[27]

   A large number of senior executives say they get involved in the sale early in the decision process, yet salespeople have difficulty meeting with high-level decision makers. Most senior executives will not meet with salespeople who are making cold calls. When appointments are granted, the time allocated may be very short; 5 to 10 minutes is not uncommon. How do you establish credibility for yourself and your company in a short time period? Be sure you know a great deal about the company before the appointment and be prepared to demonstrate your knowledge of the company and the industry it serves. Do not propose solutions until you fully understand the buyer's problems. Be sure to communicate value.[28]

This list of questions can be revised to meet the needs of many different types of salespeople. A sales representative for an industrial equipment dealer may see the qualifying process differently from the person who sells commercial real estate. The main consideration is providing accurate answers to each question.

ORGANIZING YOUR PROSPECT INFORMATION

When it comes to organizing prospect information, the salesperson has several choices. Some salespeople record prospect information on blank file cards (4×6 is the most popular), on preprinted file cards that have space for specific kinds of information, or in loose-leaf notebooks. At Nordstrom and some other department stores, salespeople

Well known author Harvey Mackay instructs his salespeople to develop a 66 question customer profile. This information helps you know the prospect both as an individual and as a business representative.

record information about each customer in a computerized "personal book." Successful salespeople use this information to provide personalized service to each customer. In addition to the customer's name, address, and account number, they record the person's sizes, style preferences, hobbies and interests, birthday, previous items purchased, and any other appropriate information. With this information available, each customer becomes a "prospect" for future purchases. Sales personnel often call their customers when new products arrive.

Harvey Mackay instructs his salespeople to develop a 66-question customer profile. The form is divided into categories such as education, family, business background, special interests, and lifestyle. In the process of collecting and analyzing this information, the salesperson gets to know the customer better than competing salespeople do. Harvey Mackay describes the benefits of developing a customer profile:

> If selling were just a matter of determining who's got the low bid, then the world wouldn't need salespeople. It could all be done on computers. The "Mackay 66" is designed to convert you from an adversary to a colleague of the people you're dealing with and to help you make sales.[29]

Mackay says that the 66-item customer profile helps the salesperson systematize information in a way that makes it more useful and accessible.

The use of file cards and notebooks is adequate for salespeople who deal with a small number of prospects and do not get involved in complex sales. The use of some type of computerized contact management system is more appropriate for salespeople who deal with large numbers of prospects, frequently get involved in complex sales, and must continually network with management and members of the sales support team. With the aid of

Global Business Etiquette

DOING BUSINESS IN GERMANY

Germany represents the world's third largest economy and is America's largest European trading partner. If you are a salesperson planning a business trip to Germany, keep in mind that there is greater formality in the German business community.

- Germany has been described as a "low-context" culture in which words carry most of the information. Messages tend to be explicit and direct. In this culture, negotiations (verbal or written) tend to be explicit in defining terms of the agreement. By comparison, China is a high-context culture in which exact phrasing and the verbal part of the messages tend to be less significant than your relationship with the other person.
- There is a strong emphasis on punctuality so avoid being late for appointments. Germans tend to make appointments far in advance.
- Lunch is the most common meal for business meetings. Dining etiquette in Germany involves eating continental style—holding the fork in the left hand continually and the knife in the right hand.
- The sales presentation should include data and empirical evidence that support your proposal. Brochures and other printed information should be serious and detailed, not flashy.[d]

modern technology, salespeople can retrieve data from various sources no matter where they are. Regardless of the system used, most salespeople need to collect and organize two kinds of prospect information: information about the prospect as an individual and information about the prospect as a business representative.

Prospect as an Individual

The foundation for a sales philosophy that emphasizes the building of partnerships is the belief that we should always treat the other person as an individual. Each prospect is a one-of-a-kind person with a number of unique characteristics. The only possible way we can treat the prospect as an individual is to learn as much as possible about the person. The starting point is to learn the correct spelling and pronunciation of the prospect's name. Then acquire information about the person's educational background, work experience, communication style, special interests, hobbies, and family status. In some cases you will need to interview industry people or employees at the company to acquire personal information.

A lasting business partnership is based in large part on a strong personal relationship. Dale Carnegie, a pioneer in the field of human relations training and author of *How to Win Friends and Influence People*, recognized the importance of taking a personal interest in others. He said, "You can make more friends in two months by becoming interested in other people than you can in two years by trying to get other people interested in you." John Maxwell, author of *Winning With People* and more than 30 other books on leadership and human relations, credits Dale Carnegie's teachings for his own success. He says, "... people will respond to you more favorably if you first let them know that they matter to you as individuals."[30]

Prospect as a Business Representative

In addition to personal information about the prospect, it is important to collect certain business-related facts. This is especially important in business-to-business selling. Before calling on the prospect it pays to review various aspects of the company operation.

Research starts with a Web search for information about the company and industry. What does the company manufacture or sell? How long has the firm been in business? Is the firm a leader in the field? What are the "Politics" of the customer's decision-making procedures?[31]

Most established firms have been doing business with one or more other suppliers. When possible, find out who the company buys from and why. It always helps to know in advance who the competition is. Salespeople who take time to study personal and business facts are in a stronger position to meet the prospect's needs.

John Maxwell, author of Winning With People, and more than 30 other books, credits Dale Carnegie's teaching for his own success. Maxwell sasys, ". . . people will respond to you more favorably if you first let tham know that they matter to you as individuals."

DEVELOPING A PROSPECTING AND SALES FORECASTING PLAN

A major barrier to prospecting is time. There never seems to be enough time for a salesperson to do everything that needs to be done. In many situations, less than half of the workweek is devoted to actual sales calls. The remainder of the time is spent identifying and screening prospects, travel, paperwork, planning, sales meetings, and servicing accounts. Time devoted to prospecting often means that less time is available for actual selling. Given a choice, salespeople would rather spend their time with established customers. Attrition, of course, gradually reduces the number of persons in this category, and prospecting may be necessary for survival.

Prospecting activities can be approached in a more orderly fashion with the aid of a plan. It is difficult to prescribe one plan that fits all selling situations; however, most situations require the following similar types of decisions:

1. *Prepare a list of prospects.* You may recall that the prospect base includes current customers and potential customers. The process of enlarging the prospect base to include potential customers varies from one industry to another. In the food service distribution industry, salespeople often start with a territorial audit.[32] This involves the collection and analysis of information about every food service operator (restaurants, hotels, colleges, etc.) in a given territory. Important information such as the name of the operation, name of owner or manager, type of menu, and so forth is recorded on a card or entered into a PC. When the audit is complete, the salesperson analyzes the information on each food service operator and selects those who should be contacted.

   A salesperson who sells hotel and convention services could use a variation of the territorial audit. The list of prospects might include local businesses, educational institutions, civic groups, and other organizations that need banquet or conference services.
2. *Forecast the potential sales volume that might be generated by each new account for each product.* A **sales forecast** outlines expected sales for a specific product to a specific target group over a specific period of time. With a sales forecast the salesperson is able to set goals, establish a sales budget, and allocate resources with greater accuracy.

Most salespeople use CRM software in the development of their prospecting and sales forecasting plan. This software allows the convenient preparation and management of prospect lists.

Top salespeople give special emphasis to prospects who are likely to drive future growth, not just current sales. They calculate the potential revenue of each customer and use this information to develop call lists and route schedules. The best prospects are given the highest priority. Top performers view prospecting as an investment in the future and often spend 10 to 15 percent of their time on this activity.[33]

3. *Anticipate prospect calls when planning the sales route; a systematic routing plan saves time and reduces travel expenses.* The procedure used to determine which customers and prospects are to be visited during a certain period of time is called **routing**. Consider calls on prospective customers in developing your route plan. This approach helps minimize the cost of developing new accounts.

If you are taking over an existing sales territory, you need to work fast to get acquainted with established customers. Send an e-mail that announces you are taking over the territory. Then schedule face-to-face meetings with each customer. In some cases your predecessor will discuss accounts with you and may be willing to introduce you to each customer. When you meet with a well-established customer, do not hesitate to ask for referrals. To make new contacts quickly, attend conferences, trade shows, and meetings in your area. Attending these events will give you a quick sense of who are the key suppliers and customers in your area.[34]

Summary

Prospect identification has been called the lifeblood of selling. A continuous supply of new customers must be found to replace those lost for various reasons. *Prospecting* is the systematic process of locating potential customers.

Analysis of both your product and your existing customers can help to identify, locate, and even profile your prospects. Important sources of new customers include *referrals* (both endless chain referrals and referral letters and cards); friends, family members, and centers of influence; directories; trade publications; trade shows and special events; telemarketing;

direct-response advertising and sales letters; Web sites; computer databases; cold calling; educational seminars; networking; and prospecting by nonsale employees.

These prospecting techniques produce a list of names that must be evaluated using criteria developed by each salesperson. The process of prospect evaluation is called *qualifying*. The qualifying process involves finding answers to several basic questions: Does the prospect have a need for my product? Can the prospect make the buying decision? Can the prospect pay for the purchase? Will anyone close the sale? An estimate of the amount of sales that could be generated from this prospect and the prospect's credit rating also should be determined.

Information about both customers and prospects should be recorded systematically, whether on a special form, in a notebook, on cards, or in a computerized database. Information that is important to include about customers as individuals includes the correct name, age and experience, education, family status, special interests and hobbies, and communication style. Information that is important to include about customers as representatives of their business include the authority to buy, the business's ability to pay, the company operations, and the company buying practices.

Development of a prospecting and sales forecasting plan requires preparing a list of prospects, creating a forecast of potential sales volume from each new account, and anticipating prospect calls when planning a sales route.

KEY TERMS

Prospecting
Prospect
Prospect base
Referral
Telemarketing
Web site
Cold calling
Networking
Qualifying
Sales forecast
Routing

REVIEW QUESTIONS

1. List and briefly explain the common causes of customer attrition.
2. During periods of economic uncertainty, the decision-making process often moves upward. What basic tips would you give a salesperson who is calling on senior executives?
3. Describe three steps progressive marketers are taking to improve the quality of the prospecting effort.
4. List the major sources of prospects.
5. Explain how the endless chain referral prospecting method works.
6. Discuss how direct-response advertising and sales letters can be used to identify prospects.
7. What are the most common methods of organizing prospect information?
8. What is *networking*? How might a real estate salesperson use networking to identify prospects?
9. What does the term *qualifying* mean? What are the four basic questions that should be answered during the qualifying process?
10. What is *routing*? How does this relate to the prospecting plan?

APPLICATION EXERCISES

1. Prior to getting involved in networking, it's a good idea to prepare an "elevator" presentation. This is a 30-second pitch that summarizes what you want people to know about you. You might think of yourself as a "product" to be sold to an employer who has a job opening. Make your presentation upbeat and brief. Who are you? What are you currently doing? What type of work are you looking for? Practice the presentation alone in front of a mirror and then present it to one or two class members.
2. You are a sales representative for the Xerox Corporation. Assuming Xerox has just designed a new, less expensive, and better-quality copying machine, make a list of 15 prospects you would plan to contact. From the material in this chapter, identify the sources you would use in developing your prospect list.
3. You are in the process of interviewing for a sales position with the CIGNA Insurance Company. In addition to filling out an application form and taking an aptitude test, one of the items the agency manager requests of you is to develop a list of prospects with whom you are acquainted. He informs you that this list includes the prospects you will be working with during the first few weeks of employment. The agency manager recommends that you list at least 50 names. Prepare a list of 10 acquaintances you have that would qualify as prospects.

4. Sales automation software is most commonly used in the prospecting phase of selling. New-product releases are continually being developed that provide additional features and benefits to salespeople. The software used in this book is marketed by a leader in the field. Access the ACT! (*www.act.com*) Web page and research the latest version of ACT! Click on and examine the latest demonstration copy of this popular sales automation software.
5. Locating companies to work for is a form of prospecting. Assuming you are interested in changing careers, develop a list of 10 companies for which you would like to work. Assign each company a priority according to your interest, from the most desirable (1) to the least (10). Organize your list in six columns showing the company name, telephone number, address, person in charge of hiring, prospect information, and priority. What sources did you use to get this information?

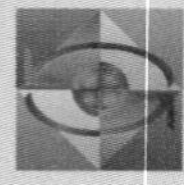

ROLE-PLAY EXERCISE

For this role-play, you will assume a sales position at a Lexus dealership. You have just completed a successful sale by signing the papers for the second new Lexus this customer has purchased in the past four years. Because you know your prospect has had a very successful experience with his first Lexus, you have decided to use the referral methods described in this chapter. Review the material on referrals and plan what you will say to your customer to build your prospect base. Pair off with another student who will assume the role of your customer. Explain that satisfied customers often know other people who would consider purchasing a Lexus. You might say, "Considering the positive experience you have had as a Lexus owner, you probably know others who appreciate fine automobiles. Is there anyone who comes to mind?" If, after probing, your customer doesn't recall someone immediately, ask permission to call him later to see if anyone has come to mind. Ask this person for actual names, addresses, and other qualifying information about prospective customers whom he knows. Also, ask the customer if he would write a referral note or letter that you could use.

CASE PROBLEM

Bill Coleman, general manager for ACT! contact software says, "Once you have a customer, maintaining the relationship is a lot cheaper than finding a new customer." A growing number of salespeople are using ACT! software or one of its competitors to improve service to customers. Shannon O'Connell, sales representative for 800-SOFTWARE Incorporated (one of the nation's largest resellers of microcomputer products), is giving her customers added value with ACT! contact software. Like most other salespeople, she is trying to cope with expanded duties, faster work pace, and customers with high expectations. ACT! software helps her in the following ways:

Customer profile. Complete information on each customer is available on screen at the touch of a key. In addition to name, phone number, and address, she has a complete record of all past contacts. The profile also includes important personal as well as business information about the customer.

Organization and planning. It is no longer necessary for Shannon to prepare a written "to do" list or a planning calendar. All this information can be entered easily into her portable computer. In the morning she simply clicks her Day At A Glance command where she is reminded of scheduled appointments, follow-up phone calls that need to be made, and other activities. If she needs to make a call at 2:00 P.M., she can press the Set Alarm button, which serves the same purpose as an alarm clock.

Correspondence. ACT! software features a built-in word processor that makes it easy to prepare memos, letters, and reports. To send a standard follow-up letter to a customer, she simply brings up the letter from storage, enters the customer's name, and presses the appropriate key. The word processor automatically prints the inside address and mailing label. With ACT! software you can even send and receive e-mail. Most salespeople are responsible for numerous reports. The ACT! software can be used to generate a wide range of reports with a minimum of effort. It features 30 predefined reports for use in a wide range of sales and sales support areas.

David Florence, a sales representative with Motorola-EMBARC, makes over 100 phone calls each day. He appreciates the ACT! feature that permits automatic telephone dialing. He simply identifies the customer's name and presses a key.

Questions

1. If your goal is to maintain long-term partnerships with each of your customers, what features of the ACT! contact software are most helpful?
2. Let us assume you are selling copy machines in a city with a population of 100,000 people. Your territory includes the entire city. What features of the ACT! software would you use most frequently?
3. Some salespeople who could benefit from use of ACT! software or a competing product continue to use a Rolodex or note cards to keep a record of the customers they call on. What are some barriers to the adoption of this type of technology?
4. Examine the first ACT! Contact Screen presented in Appendix 2.
   - **a.** What is Bradley Able's position within the company?
   - **b.** What is the "date expected" for the sale to close?
   - **c.** What is the forecasted dollar amount of this potential sale?

CRM CASE STUDY

Reviewing the Prospect Database

Becky Kemley is the sales manager in the Dallas, Texas, office of SimNet Systems, which sells network products and services. The productivity and the critical mission of Becky's customers can be considerably enhanced by selecting and using the correct LAN (local area network), WAN (wide area network), or VPN (virtual private network) systems. Becky's company is called a value-added reseller (VAR) because its people help customers maximize the value of the products bought through SimNet.

Becky's sales and technical support people may spend several months in the sales process (sales cycle). Salespeople telephone and call on prospects to determine if they qualify for SimNet's attention. Time is taken to study the customer's needs (needs discovery). The expert opinion of SimNet's technical people is incorporated into a sales proposal that is presented to the prospective customer. The presentation may be made to a number of decision makers in the prospect's firm. The final decision to purchase may follow weeks of consideration within the firm and negotiations with SimNet.

Once a decision is made by a customer to buy from SimNet, Becky's people begin the process of acquiring, assembling, and installing the network system and then follow through with appropriate training, integration, and support services.

Becky's company must carefully prospect for customers. SimNet may invest a significant amount of time helping a potential customer configure the right combination of products and services. This means that only the most serious prospects should be cultivated. Further, Becky's people must ascertain that if the investment of time is made in a prospective customer, the prospect will follow through with purchases from SimNet.

Becky is responsible for assuring that prospect information is collected and used effectively. The network salespeople use the ACT! CRM software to manage their prospect information. The system, which is the same as the software available for download, allows salespeople to document and manage their sales efforts with each prospect.

Becky has just hired you to sell for SimNet beginning December 1. Becky has given you the files of Pat Silva, a salesperson who just has been promoted to SimNet's corporate headquarters. Becky has asked you to review the status of Pat's 20 prospect accounts. Pat's customers have been notified that Pat is leaving and that a new salesperson, you, will be contacting them. Becky wants you to review each prospect's record. You are to meet with Becky next Monday and be prepared to answer the following questions.

Questions

1. Which contact can you ignore immediately *as a prospect* for making a potential purchase?
2. Referring only to the *date close* category, which four prospects would you call immediately?
3. Referring only to the *dollar amount* of sales forecasted category, which four accounts would you call first? Does the likelihood of closing percentage category have any influence on decisions concerning which prospects to call first? Why?
4. According to information on the records and Notes (View Notes) windows, which prospecting method did Pat Silva appear to use the most? Give examples.

DEVELOPING A CUSTOMER STRATEGY

Scenario

You are a sales representative employed by the Park Inn International hotel and convention center. One of your primary responsibilities is to identify prospects and make sales calls that result in the development of new accounts. During each of these calls you plan to build a relationship with the customer and describe selected value-added guest services and amenities offered by the Park Inn. You also try to learn as much as possible about the customer's buying process.

Customer Profile

Shannon Fordham is the founder and chief executive officer of USA Technologies, a growing high tech firm with over 300 employees. The company manufactures and sells security systems that can be used in residential homes, retail stores, and other commercial buildings. According to a recent article in the Wall Street Journal, USA Technologies is poised to grow very rapidly in the next year. The article described Shannon Fordham as a workaholic who usually puts in an 80 hour work week. Delegation does not come easy to this personable, hard charging entrepreneur.

Salesperson Profile

Jamie Julian has just completed the Park Inn sales training program and now wants to develop some new accounts. In addition to taking care of established customers, Julian plans to call on at least four new prospects every week.

Product

Park Inn International is a full-service hotel and convention center located in Rockport, Illinois. The hotel recently completed a $2.8 million renovation of its meeting and banquet rooms.

Instructions

For this role play activity you will meet with Shannon Fordham who appears to be a good prospect. During the first sales call plan to learn more about the prospect as an individual and acquire more information about USA Technologies. This meeting will provide you with the opportunity to begin building a long-term partnership.

During the first meeting with a prospect you like to present a limited amount of important product information. In this case the length of the appointment is 15 minutes, so you should not try to cover too much information. To prepare for the first sales call, read employment memorandum number 1 in Appendix 3. This memo describes the value-added guest services and amenities offered by the Park Inn. For the purpose of this role play Shannon Fordham should be considered a consultative process buyer. You can assume that the prospect will need help identifying and evaluating possible solutions. As you prepare for the first call, think about what may take place during future calls. Review the steps in the typical buying process (see Figure 8.3). Keep in mind that today's more demanding customers are seeking a cluster of satisfactions. Study the Product Selling Model (Figure 7.1) prior to meeting with the prospect.

To play any game well, you first have to learn the rules or principles of the game. And, second, you have to forget about them. That is, you have to learn to play without thinking about the rules. This is true whether the game is chess or golf or selling. Shortcuts won't work.

Al Ries and Jack Trout *Marketing Warfare*

PART 5

Developing a Presentation Strategy

➥ The chapters included in Part V review the basic principles used in the strategic/consultative sales presentation. This information is used as you prepare presentation objectives, develop a presentation plan that adds value, and identify ways to provide outstanding service after the sale.

Chapter Preview

When you finish reading this chapter, you should be able to

1. Describe the three prescriptions that are included in the presentation strategy

2. Describe the role of objectives in developing the presale presentation plan

3. Discuss the basic steps of the preapproach

4. Explain the merits of a planned presentation strategy

5. Describe the nature of team versus one-person presentation strategies

6. Describe the six main parts of the presentation plan

7. Explain how to effectively approach the customer

8. Describe seven ways to convert the prospect's attention and arouse interest

CHAPTER 10

Approaching the Customer

Some of the most difficult sales calls involve meeting with customers who do not know they have a need for your product. Michael Lotker, a sales consultant for Siemens Solar Industries headquartered in Camarillo, California, faces this challenge quite often. He frequently meets with officials who manage public utilities. They usually rely on oil or natural gas to generate electric power and may not have considered solar power. In most cases Lotker uses an informative sales presentation that explains modern solar thermal technology and the benefits it offers.

Sales representatives who work for Siemens Solar Industries must complete extensive training before they meet with prospects. They must be completely familiar with all types of power generating technologies including wind power, fuel cells, and the traditional oil- and gas-powered systems. One major objective of every sales presentation is to build credibility for solar thermal technology. During a typical sales call, Lotker is selling his company, his products, and himself. People working for a public utilities firm need ample assurances that he is well qualified to give sound professional advice concerning the application of complex solar technology.[1] As we noted in Chapter 1, the value added by salespeople today is increasingly derived from intangibles such as accurate information.

As noted in Chapter 2, there is a wide range of career options in the field of personal selling. How do you know if you have selected the most suitable sales position? If the position provides you with the new energy needed each day to be a true consultant to your customers, then you have probably made

Personal Selling Power, *a magazine with a circulation of over 200,000, understands the importance of value-added selling. This audio sales training program shows how a strategically planned presentation adds value when it is based on carefully developed call objectives and a presentation plan to meet these objectives.*

the right choice. Michael Lotker knows he made the right choice. Every day he gets to talk to prospects about the merits of using renewable energy as a power source. He truly believes that solar energy is a good business investment and a power source that is good for the environment.

DEVELOPING THE PRESENTATION STRATEGY

The presentation strategy combines elements of the relationship, product, and customer strategies. Each of the other three strategies must be developed before a salesperson can develop an effective presentation strategy.

FIGURE 10.1

The Strategic/Consultative Selling Model provides the foundation for a value added consultative presentation strategy.

STRATEGIC/CONSULTATIVE SELLING MODEL*

Strategic step	*Prescription*
Develop a Personal Selling Philosophy	☑ Adopt Marketing Concept ☑ Value Personal Selling ☑ Become a Problem Solver/Partner
Develop a Relationship Strategy	☑ Adopt Win-Win Philosophy ☑ Project Professional Image ☑ Maintain High Ethical Standards
Develop a Product Strategy	☑ Become a Product Expert ☑ Sell Benefits ☑ Configure Value-Added Solutions
Develop a Customer Strategy	☑ Understand the Buying Process ☑ Understand Buyer Behavior ☑ Develop Prospect Base
Develop a Presentation Strategy	☑ Prepare Objectives ☑ Develop Presentation Plan ☑ Provide Outstanding Service

*Strategic/consultative selling evolved in response to increased competition, more complex products, increased emphasis on customer needs, and growing importance of long-term relationships.

The **presentation strategy** is a well-conceived plan that includes three prescriptions: (1) establishing objectives for the sales presentation, (2) developing the presale presentation plan needed to meet these objectives, and (3) renewing one's commitment to providing outstanding customer service (Fig. 10.1, Strategic/Consultative Selling Model).

The first prescription reminds us that we need to establish one or more objectives for each sales call. High-performance salespeople like Michael Lotker understand that it is often possible to accomplish several goals during a single call. A common objective of sales calls is to collect information about the prospect's needs. Another common objective is to develop, build, or sustain a relationship with those who make the buying decision.

A carefully prepared presentation plan ensures that salespeople are well organized during the sales presentation and prepared to achieve their objectives. A six-step presentation plan is introduced later in this chapter.

Establishment of objectives for the sales presentation and preparation of the presentation plan must be guided by a strong desire to offer outstanding customer service. Achieving excellence is the result of careful needs analysis, correct product selection, clear presentations, informative demonstrations, win-win negotiations, and flawless service after the sale. Salespeople who are committed to doing their best in each of these areas are richly rewarded.

Presentation Strategy Adds Value

How does precall planning add value? Value is added when you position yourself as a resource—not just a vendor. You must prove that you have important ideas and advice to offer.[2] A well-planned presentation adds value when it is based on carefully developed sales call objectives and a presentation plan needed to meet these objectives. Good planning ensures that the presentation is customized to meet the needs and time constraints of the prospect.

Salespeople need to be aware of the changing needs of their customers or risk losing out to the competition. Some salespeople do not pay enough attention to how they conduct business with their established customers. Without a precall plan, it's easy to miss opportunities to increase your knowledge of the customer's business, sell new products, or discover ways to improve service.[3]

PLANNING THE PREAPPROACH

Preparation for the actual sales presentation is a two-part process. Part one is referred to as the **preapproach**. The preapproach involves preparing presale objectives and developing a presale presentation plan. Part two is called the **approach** and involves making a favorable first impression, securing the prospect's attention, and transitioning to need identification. (Fig. 10.2). The preapproach and approach, when handled correctly, establish a foundation for an effective sales presentation.

The preapproach should be viewed as a key step in preparing for each sales presentation. Professional salespeople complete the preapproach for every presentation whether it involves a new account or an established customer. Top salespeople often spend two or three hours planning for a 25-minute sales call. The preapproach includes the first two prescriptions for developing a presentation strategy: establishing objectives and creating a presale presentation plan.

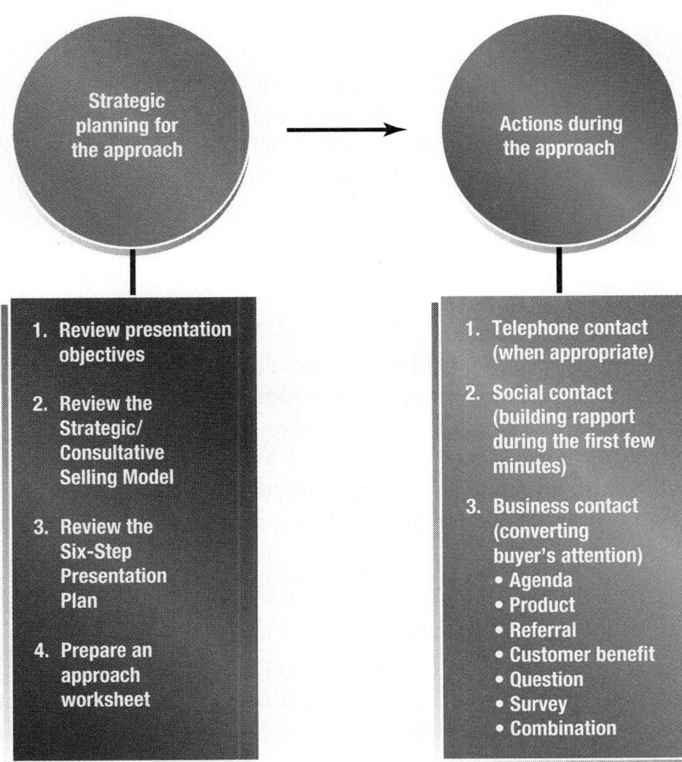

FIGURE 10.2

Preparing for the presentation involves planning for the activities that occur before meeting the prospect and for the first few minutes of actual contact with the prospect.

Establishing Presentation Objectives

Preparation for a sales call is part research, part planning, and part critical thinking. Sales representatives employed by Nalco Chemical Company prepare for each sales call by filling out a 13-point precall planner. One section of this form requires the salesperson to identify the objectives of the call. Nalco is a company that emphasizes professionalism, long-term partnerships, and staying focused on customer needs.[4]

In Chapter 8, we introduced the five stages of the typical buying process (see Figure 8.3). When you are calling on a *consultative* or *strategic alliance* buyer, you will usually not cover all of these stages during a single sales call. Multicall sales presentations are especially common in complex sales. Therefore, it's best to develop presentation objectives suitable for each stage of the buying process. During the first stage—need awareness—customers may or may not be aware of their needs and problems. The need awareness stage is the "investigation" stage. To uncover and clarify needs will require the use of appropriate questions (covered in detail in Chapter 11). The following presentation objectives would be appropriate during the first call on a new prospect:

- Establish rapport and begin building a relationship with the customer.
- Obtain permission to ask need identification questions.
- Obtain personal and business information to establish the customer's file.

During stage two of the buying process—evaluation of solutions—the customer is ready to consider possible problem solutions. In some cases, there may be several solutions that must be evaluated. Presentation objectives for stage two might include the following:

- Involve the customer in a product demonstration.
- Provide value justification in terms of cost reduction and increased revenues.
- Compare and contrast the features of, for example, a truck fleet lease plan with a fleet purchase plan.

Selecting presentation objectives with care can pay big dividends. When the sales presentation is guided by carefully established objectives, the sales cycle is usually shorter. In the business world where everyone subscribes to the belief that "time is money," efficient planning and execution of the sales process is greatly valued by customers.

Once you have an appointment with the prospect and the presentation objectives have been established, consider sending a fax or e-mail message that outlines the agenda for the meeting. This will confirm the appointment and clarify the topics to be discussed.[5]

Multicall sales presentations are common in many areas, including the retail field. The sale of expensive recreational vehicles, leased automobiles, boats, and quality sound systems for the home or business often requires more than one sales call. Some clothing stores and independent tailors make office calls to sell tailored clothing. One example is Mitchells/Richards with stores in Westport and Greenwich, Connecticut. This progressive retailer, with a reputation for superior customer service, will make office calls upon request. Working with a customer at their office usually requires more than one sales call.[6]

Team Selling Presentation Objectives

In today's ever-changing business environment, team selling has surfaced as a major development. Team selling is ideally suited to organizations that sell complex or customized products and services that require direct communication between customers and technical

We make solving your toughest marketing challenges this easy.

Build Customer Loyalty

Drive Retail Traffic

Generate Qualified Leads

Launch New Product

(well, almost) Call The Jackson Group and you'll be introduced to one of the Midwest's foremost integrated marketing communications firms. Long before it became an industry buzzword, The Jackson Group was providing integrated turnkey solutions to its clients. From strategic planning to creative services to database management, we can help you solve your most difficult marketing challenges. Which helps make your job a whole lot easier. To learn how we've helped other clients just like you, visit us at www.jacksongroup.com. Or, call us at 1-888-JACKSON.

THE JACKSON GROUP

Powerful thinking. Stellar results.

*Building customer loyalty, driving retail traffic, generating qualified leads, and launching new products are challenging objectives faced by sales and marketing people. The Jackson Group's Strategic Marketing Lab (*www.jacksongroup.com*) helps clients develop programs to meet and exceed their goals in these areas.*

experts. Sales teams can often uncover problems, solutions, and sales opportunities that no individual salesperson could discover working alone.[7] In some situations the involvement of technical experts can shorten the selling cycle. The team approach often results in more precise need identification, improved selection of the product, and more informative sales presentations.

Selling Is Everyone's Business

TECHNICAL STAFF ASSUME SALES ROLE

Reggie Daniel, CEO of Scientific & Engineering Solutions, says, "The company culture is to have every employee bringing in business." His three full-time salespeople and a selected group of 15 nonsales personnel get paid commissions or bonuses based on the profitability of sales they help close. Steve Newcomb, a technical staff member, helped close a sale that resulted in a $700,000 contract. He not only collected the commission on the sale, but he also received a trip to the Super Bowl. Daniel wants his technical staff to have access to the business world because sales opportunities often surface when they are involved in technical problem solving.[a]

Reggie Daniel, CEO of Scientific & Engineering Solutions.

Team sales presentations require a more detailed precall plan than individual sales calls. Each team member must have a clear understanding of the role he or she will play during the sales call. Sales presentation objectives should be clearly stated. Team members should be given detailed information about the customer, understand the basics of a consultative sales presentation, and be prepared to add value.[8]

As noted in Chapter 1, we are seeing the growth of strategic alliances. These long-term partnerships are especially common in business-to-business sales. Teams often are involved in forming the alliance and making purchase decisions after the alliance is established. When a customer's decision-making process is guided by a team, the seller is likely to use a team-selling approach.[9]

A variation of the team approach to selling is used by some marketers. Salespeople are trained to seek the assistance of another salesperson or actually turn the customer over to another salesperson when problems surface. The other salesperson may bring to the selling situation greater ability to identify the customer's needs or select the appropriate product. Salespeople who have well-prepared presale objectives know when to seek assistance from another professional.

Selling to a Buying Team

In some cases salespeople must address and satisfy both the individual and collective concerns of each participant in a multibuyer situation. The decision makers may be members of a well-trained buying team, a buying committee assembled for a one-time purchase, or a board of directors.

As in any type of selling situation, the salesperson should attempt to determine the various buying influences. When possible, the role of each decision maker, the amount of influence he exerts, and each decision maker's needs should be determined before the

Rick Page's best selling trade book Hope Is Not a Strategy *emphasizes the need for strategic planning during the preapproach. His six keys to winning the complex sale help salespeople move to the next higher level of selling in the age of information.*

presentation. Careful observation during the presentation can reveal who may use the product, who controls the finances, and who can provide the expertise necessary to make the correct buying decision.

When you make a group selling presentation, make sure all parties feel involved. Any member of the group who feels ignored could prevent you from closing the sale. Be sure to direct questions and comments to all potential decision makers in the group. As early as possible, identify the most powerful influences.

Find out if there are any silent team or committee members. A silent member is one who can influence the buying decision but does not attend the presentation. Silent members are usually senior managers who have a major influence on the buying decision. If a silent member does exist, you must find a way to communicate, directly or indirectly, with this person.[10]

A survey of 19,000 salespeople and sales managers found that about one-fourth of the people contacted use sales teams. A carefully conceived presentation strategy, with each particpant having a clear understanding of the role and value he or she will add during the sales call, is essential.

Informative, Persuasive, and Reminder Presentation Objectives

Although presentation objectives should be as precise as possible, a sales call is often focused on a general theme or purpose. The major purpose may be to inform, persuade, remind, or some combination of these objectives. The sale of highly technical products and services often begins with an informative sales presentation. The customer needs to be familiar with the product before making a buying decision. In another situation, where the customer's needs have been carefully identified and your product is obviously suited to these needs, a persuasive presentation would be appropriate. In the case of repeat customers, it is often necessary to remind them of the products and services you offer.

Selling in Action

NO TECH TO HIGH TECH

Account planning by the 70 sales representatives at Sebastiani Winery used to be a time-consuming process. Without the aid of modern technology, salespeople were forced to manually analyze two monthly reports that were inches thick. Preparing for a sales call was burdensome. Some salespeople said that they spent almost half their time analyzing reports. A major sales force automation (SFA) initiative was started in the late 1990s. The project had these four objectives:

- Improve communication through the use of e-mail, file sharing, and intranet technology
- Support needed development of multimedia presentations
- Provide data analysis capabilities
- Ease the administrative burden

Each member of the Sebastiani sales force received a laptop loaded with Windows, PowerPoint, e-mail, and Business Objects—the software needed for analyzing data. The new technology was introduced during a three-day training program. Today, salespeople have the ability to do account planning that is much more effective than in the past.[b]

Careful observation during a presentation to a group can reveal who may use the product, who controls the finances, and who can provide the expertise necessary to make the correct buying decision.

Informative Presentation

The objective of a presentation that involves a new or unique product is generally to inform customers of its features and explain how these features can benefit the customer. Informative presentations are usually more prevalent when the product is being first introduced to the market. A **detail salesperson** (introduced in Chapter 2) usually spends a great deal of time informing customers of new products and changes in existing products.

Persuasive Presentation

Some degree of persuasion is common to most sales presentations. **Persuasion**—the act of presenting product appeals so as to influence the prospect's beliefs, attitudes, or behavior—is a strategy designed to encourage the buyer to make a buying decision. Persuasion can be integrated into every phase of the sales presentation. A friendly greeting and a firm handshake at the time of initial customer contact represents a relationship-oriented form of persuasion. Additional forms of persuasion include positioning yourself to ask questions, gaining agreement at each stage of the buying process, and asking for the sale.

Reminder Presentation

In some selling situations, the primary objective of the sales call is to remind the customer of products and services offered by the company. Without this occasional reminder the person may forget information that is beneficial. Computer salespeople might periodically remind customers about special services—training classes, service contracts, and customized programming, for example—available from the company they represent. An occasional reminder can prevent the competition from capturing the business.

DEVELOPING THE SIX-STEP PRESENTATION PLAN

Once you have established objectives for the sales presentation, the next step (prescription) involves developing the presentation plan. This plan helps you achieve your objectives.

Today, with increased time constraints, fierce competition, and rising travel costs, the opportunity for a face-to-face meeting with customers may occur less frequently. The few minutes you have with your customers may be your only opportunity to win their business, so careful planning is more critical than ever.

Steve Schiffman, president of DEI Management Group, recalls meeting with a Yellow Pages sales representative who had failed to do even the most basic research prior to the sales call. The salesperson began the meeting with a question: "Are you happy with your advertising in the Yellow Pages?" DEI was not, at that time, listed in the Yellow Pages. A quick search of the Yellow Pages would have prevented this embarrassing experience.[11]

In preparation for development of the presentation strategy, it is helpful to review the three broad strategic areas that have been described in previous chapters: relationship strategy, product strategy, and customer strategy. Why is this review so critical? It is because today's dynamic sales presentations require consideration of the simultaneous influences of the relationship, product, and customer strategies. A careful review of these three areas sets the stage for flexible presentations that meet the needs of the customer.

Planning the Presentation

Once you have collected background information, you are ready to develop a "customized" presale presentation plan. Preparing a customized sales presentation can take a great deal of time and energy. Nevertheless, this attention to detail gives you added confidence and helps you avoid delivering unconvincing hit-or-miss sales talks. The plan is developed after a careful study of the **six-step presentation plan** (Fig. 10.3). In most cases, the sales process includes the following activities.

1. *Approach.* Preparation for the approach involves making decisions concerning effective ways to make a favorable first impression during the initial contact, securing the prospect's attention, and developing the prospect's interest in the product. The approach should set the stage for an effective sales presentation.
2. *Presentation.* The presentation is one of the most critical parts of the selling process. If the salesperson is unable to discover the prospect's buying needs, select a product solution, and present the product in a convincing manner, the sale may be lost. Chapter 11 covers all aspects of the sales presentation.
3. *Demonstration.* An effective sales demonstration helps verify parts of the sales presentation. Demonstrations are important because they provide the customer with a better understanding of product benefits. Chapter 12 is devoted exclusively to this topic.
4. *Negotiation.* Buyer resistance is a natural part of the selling/buying process. An objection, however, does present a barrier to closing the sale. For this reason, all salespeople should become skillful at negotiating resistance. Chapter 13 covers this topic.
5. *Close.* As the sales presentation progresses, there may be several opportunities to close the sale. Salespeople must learn to spot closing clues. Chapter 14 provides suggestions on how to close sales.
6. *Servicing the sale.* The importance of developing a long-term relationship with the prospect is noted earlier in this chapter. This rapport is often the outgrowth of postsale service. Learning to service the sale is an important aspect of selling. Chapter 15 deals with this topic.

THE SIX-STEP PRESENTATION PLAN

Step One: Approach	☐ Review Strategic/Consultative Selling Model ☐ Initiate customer contact
Step Two: Presentation	☐ Determine prospect needs ☐ Select solution ☐ Initiate sales presentation
Step Three: Demonstration	☐ Decide what to demonstrate ☐ Select selling tools ☐ Initiate demonstration
Step Four: Negotiation	☐ Anticipate buyer concerns ☐ Plan negotiating methods ☐ Initiate win-win negotiations
Step Five: Close	☐ Plan appropriate closing methods ☐ Recognize closing clues ☐ Initiate closing methods
Step Six: Servicing the Sale	☐ Follow through ☐ Follow-up calls ☐ Expansion selling

Service, retail, wholesale, and manufacturer selling

FIGURE | 10.3

The Six-Step Presentation Plan

A presale plan is a logical and an orderly outline that features a salesperson's thoughts from one step to the next in the presentation. Each step in this plan is explained in Chapters 10 to 15.

A truly valuable idea or concept is timeless. The six parts of the presale presentation plan checklist have been discussed in the sales training literature for many years; therefore, they might be described as fundamentals of personal selling. These steps are basic elements of most sales and frequently occur in the same sequence. However, the activities included in the six-step presentation plan must be selected with care. Prior to developing the sales call plan, the salesperson must answer one very important question: Do these activities relate to the customers buying process? Assume that the owner of a small manufacturing company visits a trade show and sees a demonstration of a new high tech water purification system developed by Water Tech, Inc. The system seems ideal for his production facility. The prospect's name is given to a Water Tech Inc. sales representative who later visits the prospect at his office. This sales call would probably not include a product demonstration. In addition, the approach and presentation steps would need to reflect the needs of a prospect who is already familiar with the product. Selling steps are of little value *unless* they are firmly rooted in your customer's buying process.[12]

THE APPROACH

After a great deal of preparation, it is time to communicate with the prospect, either by face-to-face contact, by telephone or some other appropriate method of communication. We refer to the initial contact with the customer as the *approach*. All the effort you have put into developing relationship, product, and customer strategies can now be applied to the presentation strategy. If the approach is effective, you may be given the opportunity to

Global Business Etiquette

DOING BUSINESS IN ENGLAND

Linda Phillips, codirector of Executive Etiquette Company, says, "First and foremost is the British attention to detail." English businesspeople also tend to be more formal in terms of dress and person-to-person communication. It's helpful to study English business customs before visiting that country.

- Introductions in England tend to be very formal. The British look for whose name is spoken first. If you are calling on a client named Robert Timmons, the introduction of your sales manager would be, "Mr. Timmons, I would like you to meet Raymond Hill, my sales manager." In this case the client's name is first because he is the more important person. Never address someone by his or her first name unless you are invited to do so.
- Making decisions is often a time-consuming process, so don't expect a quick close.
- Do not use aggressive sales techniques, such as the hard sell, and avoid criticism of competing products. Focus on objective facts and evidence during the presentation.
- It would be poor manners to discuss business after the business day in England. This is true even when you have drinks or a meal with a businessperson.[c]

make the sales presentation. If, however, the approach is not effective, the chance to present your sales story may be lost. You can be the best prepared salesperson in the business, but without a good approach there may be little chance for a sale.

The approach has three important objectives. First, you want to build rapport with the prospect. Second, you want to capture the person's full attention. Never begin your sales story if the prospect seems preoccupied and is not paying attention. Third, you want to transition to the need discovery stage of the sales presentation.

In some selling situations the first contact with the customer is a telephone call. The call is made to schedule a meeting or in some cases conduct the sales presentation. The face-to-face sales call starts with the social contact and is followed by the business contact. The telephone contact, social contact, and business contact are discussed in this section.

Establish Your Credibility Early

Thomas A. Freese, author of *Secrets of Question Based Selling*, says credibility is critical to your success in sales. Credibility is an impression that people form about you very early in the sales process.[13] Sometimes little things can erode your credibility before you have a chance to prove yourself. Arriving late for appointment, spending 45 minutes with the prospect when you said you would need only fifteen minutes, or failure to send the prospect information that was promised can quickly weaken a relationship. Failure to be well prepared for the sales call will also undermine your credibility. Credibility grows when the customer realizes you are a competent sales representative who can add value throughout the sales process.

The Telephone Contact

A telephone call provides a quick and inexpensive method of scheduling an appointment. Appointments are important because many busy prospects may not meet with a salesperson who drops in unannounced. When you schedule an appointment, the prospect knows about the sales call in advance and can, therefore, make the necessary advance preparation.

Some salespeople use the telephone exclusively to establish and maintain contact with the customer. As noted in Chapter 2, inside salespeople rely almost totally on the telephone for sales. **Telesales**, not to be confused with telemarketing, include many of the same

Capturing the customer's full attention is a major objective of the approach. Attention has become a very scarce resource in today's fastpaced world.

elements as traditional sales: gathering customer information, determining needs, prescribing solutions, negotiating objections, and closing sales. Telesales usually are not scripted, a practice widely used in telemarketing. In some situations, telesales are as dynamic and unpredictable as a face-to-face sales call.

In Chapter 3, we examined some of the factors that influence the meaning we attach to an oral message from another person. With the aid of this information we can see that communication via telephone is challenging. The person who receives the call cannot see our facial expression, gestures, or posture, and, therefore, must rely totally on the sound of our voice and the words used. The telephone caller has a definite handicap.

The telephone has some additional limitations. A salesperson accustomed to meeting prospects in person may find telephone contact impersonal. Some salespeople try to avoid using the telephone because they believe it is too easy for the prospect to say no. It should be noted that these drawbacks are more imagined than real. With proper training a salesperson can use the telephone effectively to schedule appointments. When you make an appointment by telephone, use the following practices:

Plan in advance what you will say. It helps to use a written presentation plan as a guide during the first few seconds of the conversation. What you say is determined by the objectives of the sales call. Have a calendar available to suggest and confirm a date, time, and place for the appointment. Be sure to write it down.

Politely identify yourself and the company you represent. Set yourself apart from other callers by using a friendly tone and impeccable phone manners. This approach helps you avoid being shut out by a wary gatekeeper (secretary or receptionist).

State the purpose of your call and explain how the prospect can benefit from a meeting. In some cases it is helpful to use a powerful benefits statement that gets the prospect's attention and whets the person's appetite for more information. Present only enough information to stimulate interest.

Show respect for the prospect's time by telling the person how much time the appointment may take. Once the prospect agrees to meet with you, say, "Do you have your appointment calendar handy?" Be prepared to suggest a specific time: "Is Monday at 9:00 a.m. okay?"

Confirm the appointment with a brief note, e-mail message, or letter with the date, time, and place of your appointment. Enclose your business card and any printed information that can be of interest to the prospect.[14]

You should anticipate resistance from some prospects. After all, most decision makers are very busy. Be persistent and persuasive if you genuinely believe a meeting with the prospect can be mutually beneficial.

Effective Use of Voice Mail

The growing popularity of voice mail presents a challenge to salespeople. What type of message sets the stage for a second call or stimulates a return call? It's important to anticipate voice mail and know exactly what to say if you reach a recording. The prospect's perception of you is based on what you say and voice quality. The following message almost guarantees that you will be ignored:

> Ms. Simpson, I am Paul Watson and I am with Elliott Property Management Services. I would like to visit with you about our services. Please call me at 862–1500.[15]

Note that this message provides no compelling reason for the prospect to call back. It offers no valid item that would stimulate interest. The voice mail message should be similar to the opening statement you would make if you had a face-to-face contact with the prospect:

> Miss Simpson, my name is Paul Watson and I represent Elliott Property Management Services. We specialize in working with property managers. We can help you reduce the paperwork associated with maintenance jobs and provide an easy way to track the progress of each job. I would like the opportunity to visit with you and will call back in the morning.[16]

During the telephone contact, CRM contact screens and note windows can be important sources of information for making effective value-added calls. The calendar function is being used by this salesperson to schedule and confirm the date, time, and place for the sales call.

Note that this message is brief and describes benefits that customers can receive. If Paul Watson wants a call back, then he needs to give the best time to reach him. He should give his phone number slowly and completely. It's usually best to repeat the number. If you are acting on a referral, be sure to say who referred you and why.

Effective Use of E-Mail

Many prospects and established customers like the convenience of e-mail correspondence and prefer it as an alternative to telephone contact. Your challenge is to make it easy for your correspondents to read and handle your e-mail. Always use a meaningful, specific subject line. People who receive large amounts of e-mail may selectively choose which ones to read by scanning the subject lines and deleting those of no interest. An e-mail with a subject line titled "Action Steps From Our 9/28 Meeting" is more likely to be read than a subject line like "Meeting Notes."[17]

The e-mail message should tell the reader what you want and then encourage a response unless you merely want to share information. Put the most important information upfront—within the first or second paragraphs. Format the e-mail so it's easy to read. This may require the use of headings (with capitals or boldface print) to identify the main elements of the memo.[18] Always use the grammar and spell check tools. Messages that contain errors may misrepresent your competence. Finally, use a signature file—a small block of text that automatically follows each e-mail you send. A typical signature file includes full name, title, affiliation, phone number, and in some cases a slogan.

The Social Contact

According to many image consultants, "First impressions are lasting impressions." This statement is essentially true, and some profitable business relationships never crystallize because some trait or characteristic of the salesperson repels the prospective customer. Sales personnel have only a few minutes to create a positive first impression. Susan Bixler, author of *The New Professional Image*, describes the importance of the first impression this way:

> Books are judged by their covers, houses are appraised by their curb appeal, and people are initially evaluated on how they choose to dress and behave. In a perfect world this is not fair, moral, or just. What's inside should count a great deal more. And eventually it usually does, but not right away. In the meantime, a lot of opportunities can be lost.[19]

Customer Relationship Management with Technology

PLANNING PERSONAL VISITS

Personally visiting prospects and customers helps build strong relationships, yet traveling is expensive and time consuming. A salesperson is challenged to plan visits that optimize the investment represented by each trip. Access to customer relationship management (CRM) prospect records helps salespeople quickly identify all the accounts in a given geographic area.

CRM empowers salespeople to rapidly review and compare an area's prospects on the basis of position in sales cycle, potential size of account or purchase, likelihood of sale, and contribution that the visit could make to information gathering and relationship building. A well-managed CRM database provides salespeople with appropriate business and social topics to discuss when calling selected prospects for an appointment. (See the exercise, Planning Personal Visits, on p. 261 for more information.)

Building a rapport leads to credibility, which leads to trust. Once trust is established, the customer is likely to open up and share information. This information will provide clues regarding ways to create value. To be certain your first impression is appropriate, review the material in Chapter 3. The information in this chapter is timeless and can serve you well today and in the future.

Developing Conversation

The brief, general conversation during the social contact should hold the prospect's attention and establish a relaxed and friendly atmosphere for the business contact that is to follow. As mentioned in Chapter 3, there are three areas of conversation that should be considered in developing a social contact:

1. *Comments on here-and-now observations.* These comments may include general observations about an article in the *Wall Street Journal*, the victory of a local athletic team, or specific comments about awards on display in the prospect's office. Janis Taylor, sales representative with Trugreen Chemlawn, likes to start each new appointment by seeking "common ground" with her prospects. She looks for such items as a picture of the prospect's children or a trophy.[20]
2. *Compliments.* Most customers react positively to sincere compliments. Personal items in the prospect's office, achievements, or efficient operation of the prospect's business provide examples of what can be praised. A salesperson might say, "I learned recently that your company is ranked number one in customer satisfaction by J. D. Power and Associates."
3. *Search for mutual acquaintances or interests.* The discovering of mutual friends or interests can serve as the foundation for a strong social contact. Most people enjoy talking about themselves, their hobbies, and their achievements. Debra Fine, author of *The Fine Art of Small Talk*, says, "Small talk isn't stupid. It's the appetizer for all relationships."[21]

Communication on a personal basis is often the first step in discovering a common language that can improve communication between the salesperson and the prospect. How much time should be devoted to the social contact? There is no easy answer to this question. The length of the conversation depends on the type of product or service sold, how busy the prospect appears to be, and your awareness of topics of mutual interest (see Selling in Action, on page 253).

In many cases the conversation will take place over lunch or dinner. Many successful sales have been closed during or after a meal. This explains why some companies enroll their sales staff and other customer contact personnel in dining etiquette classes.

The Business Contact

Converting the prospect's attention from the social contact to the business proposal is an important part of the approach. When you convert and hold your prospect's attention, you have fulfilled an important step in the selling process. Furthermore, without this step the door has been closed on completing the remaining steps of the sale.

Some salespeople use a carefully planned opening statement or a question to convert the customer's attention to the sales presentation. A statement or question that focuses on the prospect's dominant buying motive is, of course, more likely to achieve the desired results. Buyers must like what they see and hear and must be made to feel that it is worthwhile to hear more.

Throughout the years, salespeople have identified and used a number of effective ways to capture the prospect's attention and arouse interest in the presentation. Seven of the most common are explained in the following material:

Agenda approch
Product demonstration approach
Referral approach
Customer benefit approach
Question approach
Survey approach
Premium approach

We also discuss combining two or more of these approaches.

Agenda Approach

One of the most effective ways to move from the social contact to the business contact is to thank the customer for taking time to meet with you and then review your goals for the meeting. You might say "Thank you for meeting with me this morning. I would like to accomplish three things during the time you have given me." This statement shows you value the person's time and you have preplanned a specific agenda. Always be open to changing the agenda based on input from the customer.[22]

Product Demonstration Approach

This straightforward method of getting the prospect's attention is used by sales representatives who sell copy machines, photographic equipment, automobiles, construction equipment, office furniture, and many other products. If the actual product cannot be demonstrated,

Selling in Action

THE SOCIAL CONTACT

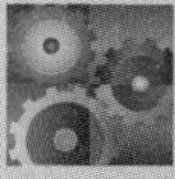

The social contact should be viewed as effective communication on a personal basis. This brief conversation establishes the foundation for the business contact, so it should never be viewed as an insignificant part of the presentation strategy. The following guidelines can help you develop the skills needed to make a good social contact.

1. *Prepare for the social contact.* Conduct a background check on topics of interest to the person you are contacting. This includes reviewing information in the prospect database, reading industry reports, and searching the Internet. Once you arrive at the customer's office, you will discover additional information about the person's interests. Most people communicate what is important to them in the way they personalize their work environment.
2. *Initiate social contact.* The most effective opening comments should be expressed in the form of an open-ended question, such as "I understand you have just been elected president of the United Way?" You can improve the possibility of a good response to your verbal question by applying nonverbal communication skills. Appropriate eye contact, voice inflections that communicate enthusiasm, and a warm smile will increase the customer's receptivity to your opening comments.
3. *Respond to the customer's conversations.* When the customer responds, it is imperative that you acknowledge the message both verbally and nonverbally. The verbal response might be "That is really interesting" or any other appropriate comment. Let the customer know you are listening and you want her to continue talking.
4. *Keep the social contact focused on the customer.* Because you cannot control where a conversation might go, you may be tempted to focus the conversation on topics with which you are familiar. A response such as, "Several years ago I was in charge of our company's United Way campaign and we had a difficult time meeting our goal," shifts the focus of the conversation back to you. Continue to focus the conversation on topics that are of interest to the customer. Dale Carnegie said that one of the best ways to build a relationship is to encourage others to talk about themselves.

salespeople can use appropriate audiovisual technology such as computer-generated graphics, slides, and videotapes. Trish Ormsby, a sales representative for Wells Fargo Alarm Services, uses her portable computer to create a visual image of security systems that meet the customer's security needs.[23]

Referral Approach

Research indicates that another person is far more impressed with your good points if these points are presented by a third party rather than by you. The referral approach is quite effective because a third party (a satisfied customer) believes the prospect can benefit from your product. This type of opening statement has universal appeal among salespeople from nearly every field.

A straightforward product demonstration method for getting the grocery store meat manager's attention would be the use of this ad from Cook's (www.cookshams.com), a division of ConAgra. The salesperson can explain the value of featuring meat products that are supported by a strong media promotion and point of sale merchandising program.

When you use the referral approach, your opening statement should include a direct reference to the third party. Here is an example: "Mrs. Follett, my name is Kurt Wheeler, and I represent the Cross Printing Company. We specialize in printing all types of business forms. Mr. Ameno—buyer for Raybale Products, Incorporated—is a regular customer of ours, and he suggested I mention his name to you."

Customer Benefit Approach

One of the most effective ways to gain a prospect's attention is to immediately point out one benefit of purchasing your product. Try to begin with the most important issue (or problem) facing the client. When using this approach, the most important buyer's benefit is included in the initial statement. For example, the salesperson selling a portable Sony projector might open with this statement:

> The Sony VPL-CS4 lightweight projector strikes a balance between cost, size, brightness, and convenience. It's a good choice for a quick business trip or for a work-at-home presentation.

Another example taken from the financial services field is:

> When you meet with a Charles Schwab investment specialist, you can obtain advice on over 1,200 no-load, no-transaction-fee mutual funds.

The key to achieving success with the customer benefit approach is advance preparation. Customers are annoyed when a salesperson cannot quickly communicate the benefits of meeting with them. Bruce Klassen, sales manager for Do All Industrial Supply, says, "Our salespeople begin the sales process by researching the prospect and the company. We need to be sure that our product line is going to benefit that prospect before we make even an initial sales approach."[24]

The survey approach offers many advantages. It is generally a nonthreatening way to open a sales call. You simply are asking permission to acquire information that can be used to determine the buyer's need for the product.

Question Approach

The question approach has two positive features. First, a question almost always triggers prospect involvement. Very few people avoid answering a direct question. Second, a question gets the prospect thinking about a problem that the salesperson may be prepared to solve.

Molly Hoover, a sales training consultant, conducts training classes for sales managers and car dealers who want to better understand the subtleties of selling to the new woman car buyer. She suggests an approach that includes a few basic questions such as:

> "Is the vehicle for business or pleasure?"
> "Will you be buying within the next week or so?"[25]

These opening questions are not difficult to answer, yet they get the customer mentally involved. Some of the best opening questions are carefully phrased to arouse attention. The authors of *The Sales Question Book* offer some good examples:

> "Are you aware that we just added three new services to our payroll and accounting package? Could I tell you about them?"
> "We are now offering all our customers a special auditing service that used to be reserved for our largest accounts. Would you be interested in hearing about it?"[26]

Once you ask the question, listen carefully to the response. If the answer is yes, proceed with an enthusiastic presentation of your product. If the answer is no, then you may have to gracefully try another approach or thank the prospect for her time and depart.

Survey Approach

Robert Hewitt, a Monterey, California, financial planner, has new clients fill out a detailed questionnaire before the first appointment. This procedure is part of his customer strategy. He studies the completed questionnaire and other documents before making any effort to find a solution to any of the customer's financial planning needs. The survey (data collection) is an important part of the problem-solving philosophy of selling. It often is used in selling office furniture, business security systems, insurance, and other products where the need cannot be established without careful study.

The survey approach offers many advantages. It is generally a nonthreatening way to open a sales call. You simply are asking permission to acquire information that can be used to determine the buyer's need for your product. Because the survey is tailor-made for a specific business, the buyer is given individual treatment. Finally, the survey approach helps avoid an early discussion of price. Price cannot be discussed until the survey is completed.

Premium Approach

The premium approach involves giving the customer a free sample or an inexpensive item. A financial services representative might give the customer a booklet that can be used to record expenses. Sales representatives for a large U.S. textbook publisher give faculty members a monthly planner. Product samples are frequently used by persons who sell cosmetics. Creative use of premiums is an effective way to get the customer's attention.

The agenda, product, referral, customer benefit, question, survey, and premium approaches offer the salesperson a variety of ways to set the stage for the presentation strategy. With experience, salespeople learn to select the most effective approach for each selling situation. Table 10.1 provides examples of how these approaches can be applied in real-world situations.

TABLE | 10.1 BUSINESS CONTACT WORKSHEET

This illustrates how to prepare effective real-world approaches that capture the customer's attention.

METHOD OF APPROACH	WHAT WILL YOU SAY?
1. Agenda	1. (Office supply) "Thank you for meeting with me. During the next 45 minutes, I plan to accomplish three things."
2. Product	2a. (Retail clothing) "We have just received a shipment of new fall sweaters from Braemar International."
	2b. (Business forms manufacturer) "Our plant has just purchased a $300,000 Harris Graphics composer, Mr. Reichart; I would like to show you a copy of your sales invoice with your logo printed on it."
3. Customer benefit	3. (Real estate) "Mr. and Mrs. Stuart, my company lists and sells more homes than any other company in the area where your home is located. Our past performance would lead me to believe we can sell your home within two weeks."
4. Referral	4. (Food wholesaler) "Paula Doeman, procurement manager for Mercy Medical Center, suggested that I provide you with information about our computerized 'Order It' system."
5. Question	5. (Hotel convention services) "Mrs. McClaughin, will your Annual Franchisee Meeting be held in April?"
6. Survey	6a. (Custom-designed computer software) "Mr. Vasquez, I would like the opportunity to learn about your accounts receivable and accounts payable procedures. We may be able to develop a customized program that will significantly improve your cash flow."
	6b. (Retail menswear) "May I ask you a few questions about your wardrobe? The information will help me better understand your clothing needs."
7. Premium	7. (Financial services) "I would like to give you a publication entitled *Guaranteed Growth Annuity.*"

Combination Approaches

A hallmark of consultative selling is flexibility. Therefore, a combination of approaches sometimes provides the best avenue to need identification. Sales personnel who have adopted the consultative style, of course, use the question and survey approaches most frequently. Some selling situations, however, require that one of the other approaches be used, either alone or in combination with the question and survey approaches (Fig. 10.4). An example of how a salesperson might use a referral and question approach combination follows:

Salesperson: Carl Hamilton at Simmons Modern Furniture suggested that I visit with you about our new line of compact furniture designed for smaller homes. He believes this line might complement the furniture you currently feature.

Customer: Yes, Carl called me yesterday and mentioned your name and company.

FIGURE 10.4

Combination approaches provide a smooth transition to the need discovery part of the consultative presentation.

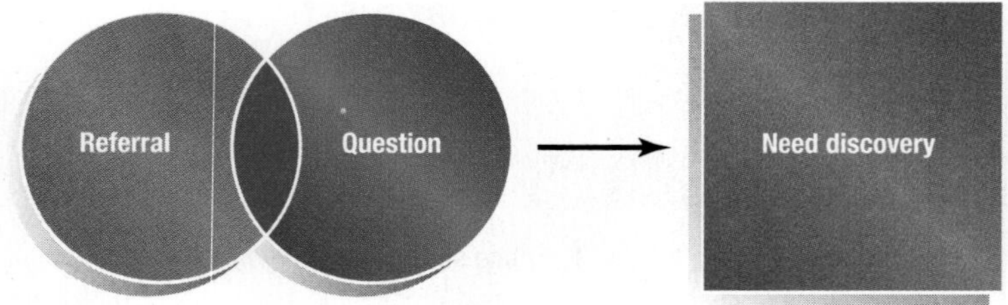

Salesperson: Before showing you our product lines, I would like to ask you some questions about your current product mix. First, what do you currently carry in the area of bedroom furniture?

Coping with Sales Call Reluctance

The transition from the preapproach to the approach is sometimes blocked by sales call reluctance. Fear of making the initial contact with the prospect is a problem for rookies and veterans in every selling field. For new salespeople, the problem can be career threatening. **Sales Call Reluctance** includes the thoughts, feelings and behavioral patterns that conspire to limit what a salesperson is able to accomplish. It is an internal, often emotional, barrier to sales success. Sales call reluctance can be caused by several different thought patterns:[27]

- Fear of taking risks
- Fear of group presentations
- Lack of self confidence
- Fear of rejection

Regardless of the reasons for sales call reluctance, you can learn to deal with it. These are some suggestions:

- *Be optimistic about the outcome of the initial contact.* It is better to anticipate success than to anticipate failure. Martin Seligman, professor of psychology at the University of Pennsylvania, and author of the best-selling book *Learned Optimism*, says that success in selling requires a healthy dose of optimism.[28] The anticipation of failure is a major barrier to making the initial contact.

In some cases, a secretary, assistant, or receptionist may screen incoming telephone calls. Be prepared to convince this person that your call is important. Always treat the gatekeeper with respect and courtesy.

"I don't think of myself as the Jenkins Doolittle & Bloom gatekeeper. I rather prefer lead blocker."

Source: *Wall Street Journal*, March 10, 1999, p. A-23. Reprinted by permission of Mark Litzler.

- *Practice your approach before making the initial contact.* A well-rehearsed effort to make the initial contact increases your self-confidence and reduces the possibility that you may handle the situation badly.
- *Recognize that it is normal to feel anxious about the initial contact.* Even the most experienced salespeople experience some degree of sales call reluctance and this reluctance can surface anywhere in the sales process.
- *Develop a deeper commitment to your goals.* Abraham Zaleznik, professor emeritus at Harvard Business School, says, "If your commitment is only in your mind, then you'll lose it when you encounter a big obstacle. If your commitment is in your heart *and* your mind, you'll create the power to break through the toughest obstacles."[29]

Selling to the Gatekeeper

Many decision makers have an assistant or secretary who manages their daily schedule. This person is often referred to as the "gatekeeper." If you want to reach the decision maker, work hard to align yourself with the person who schedules this person's appointments. Rule number one is to treat the gatekeeper with respect. Learn their name and what they do. Keep in mind this person can be an important source of information. For example, the gatekeeper can tell you how the buying process works and provide information regarding new developments in the company. This person may be able to help you make a preliminary qualification before you reach the decision maker. When you treat the person as an expert by soliciting their views, you establish a relationship that can pay big dividends today and in the future.[30]

When possible, use personal referrals from someone the prospect knows. If you have met the prospect previously, describe the meeting and tell the gatekeeper why you feel a second meeting would be beneficial.

Summary

As one sales consultant noted, "Organization multiplies the value of anything to which it is applied." This is especially true of precall planning. The well-prepared salesperson approaches the sales call with an attitude of confidence and expectancy.

Developing a presentation strategy involves preparing presale objectives, developing a *presale presentation* plan, and providing outstanding customer service. The presentation strategy combines elements of the relationship, product, and customer strategies.

Preparation for the sales presentation is a two-part process. Part one is referred to as the *preapproach* and involves preparing presale objectives and developing a presale presentation plan. Its best to develop presentation objectives for each stage of the buying process. Part two is called the *approach* and involves making a good first impression, securing the prospect's attention, and developing the prospect's interest in the product.

The nature of team versus one-person presentation strategies was discussed. In addition, the purpose of informative, persuasive, and reminder presentations was presented.

Over the years, salespeople have identified several ways to convert the prospect's attention and arouse interest in the presentation. Some of the most common ways include the agenda approach, product demonstration approach, referral approach, customer benefit approach, question approach, survey approach, and premium approach. This chapter also includes information on the social contact, the business contact, and how to cope with sales call reluctance.

KEY TERMS

Presentation strategy
Preapproach
Approach
Multicall sales presentations
Detail salesperson
Persuasion
Six-step presentation plan
Telesales
Sales call reluctance

REVIEW QUESTIONS

1. What is the purpose of the preapproach? What are the two prescriptions included in the preapproach?
2. Explain the role of objectives in developing the presale presentation plan.
3. Why should salespeople establish multiple-objective sales presentations? List four possible objectives that would be appropriate for stage one and stage two of the buying process.
4. Describe some common applications of telesales.
5. Describe the major purpose of the informative, persuasive, and reminder sales presentations.
6. What are the major objectives of the approach?
7. Review the Selling in Action box on p. 253. Briefly describe the four guidelines that can help you make a good social contact.
8. What are some rules to follow when leaving a message on voice mail? E-mail?
9. What methods can the salesperson use to convert the prospect's attention to the sales presentation?
10. Discuss why combination approaches are considered an important consultative-selling practice. Provide one example of a combination approach.

APPLICATION EXERCISES

1. Assume that you are a salesperson who calls on retailers. For some time you have been attempting to get an appointment with one of the best retailers in the city to carry your line. You have an appointment to see the head buyer in one and one half hours. You are sitting in your office. It will take you about 30 minutes to drive to your appointment. Outline what you should be doing between now and the time you leave to meet your prospect.
2. Tom Nelson has just graduated from Aspen College with a major in marketing. He has three years of experience in the retail grocery business and has decided he would like to go to work as a salesperson for the district office of Procter & Gamble. Tom has decided to telephone and set up an appointment for an interview. Write out exactly what Tom should *plan* to say during his telephone call.
3. Concepts from Dale Carnegie's *How to Win Friends and Influence People,* can help you prepare for the social contact. Access the Dale Carnegie Training home page (*www.dalecarnegie.com*) on the Internet and examine the courses offered. Click on the "Sales Advantage Course" and read the description. Note the books that are used with this course. Are enthusiasm and remembering names important parts of the approach?

ROLE-PLAY EXERCISE

Research the type of computer that you would like to purchase in the future or that you have just purchased. Strategically prepare to meet a potential customer who has been referred to you by a friend and who would like to purchase a similar computer. Using Table 10.1 on page 257, prepare four different business contact statements or questions you could use to approach your prospect. Review the material in this chapter and then pair off with another student who will assume the role of your customer. First, role-play the telephone contact and set up an appointment to get your customer into your store to meet with you and look at the computer. Second, role-play the approach you will use when the customer actually comes into the store. Review how well you made the approach.

CRM APPLICATION EXERCISE

Planning Personal Visits

CRM software allows trip planners to examine the status of prospects in the geographic area to be visited. Access your ACT! database. Assume that using the ACT! software you wish to visit prospects in the city of Bedford, Texas. The software permits a fast field search capability of selecting and sorting the records of prospects in that city: Lookup, City, type "Bedford," and press Enter. After arranging by phone to visit these people, the salesperson can print the information contained in these records and take them along: Report, Contact Report, Active Lookup, Printer, and Enter. You should now have printed information about all customers in Bedford. Salespeople today use the Internet to schedule trip transportation and lodging, and to check the weather forecast.

VIDEO CASE PROBLEM

The price and availability of energy can have a major impact on the U.S. economy. In the early 1970s the amount of imported oil dropped dramatically and, consequently, the price of gasoline and home heating oil increased sharply. It also cost more to generate energy for business and industry. At this point more people began to consider solar energy as an energy source. Siemens Solar Industries[1] (introduced at the beginning of this chapter) began to grow during this period. The company's growth from a 10-person firm in 1977 to the world's largest producer of solar technologies has been the result of a dedicated and optimistic staff.

Michael Lotker, a sales consultant for Siemens, is one of those optimistic employees. He is a strong believer in renewable energy and enjoys talking to audiences about solar technology. Most of his presentations are made to personnel working in the utilities industry, but he does set aside time for talks to consumer groups. Public support for solar energy is important. He must quickly determine how much his audience knows about solar thermal technology and then adjust his presentation accordingly. When talking to people who work

[1]Siemens Solar Industries was purchased by Shell Oil in 2002. The Company is now called Shell Solar.

for a utility company, he must be prepared to compare solar energy with other energy sources. At all times he must attempt to build support for solar energy and establish his own and his company's credibility.

To build interest in solar energy, Lotker feels it is important to discuss successful applications of solar technology. Siemens designed and constructed the world's first megawatt-scale power plant for Southern California Edison Company. This 20-acre unmanned power plant supplied enough power for 300 to 400 California homes. In the years that followed other plants were built using groundbreaking applications. Soon Siemens began building plants around the world.

Lotker must be prepared to discuss the advantages and the disadvantages of solar energy. Solar products work best in areas where sunshine is plentiful. Solar power is not the least expensive source of energy, but it can be a good long-term investment when the utility needs an additional power source during peak demand periods. In recent years, Siemens has reached new levels of product durability and now offers a 25-year warranty on power modules.

In the solar power industry, closing the sale is just the beginning. Well-trained product application specialists and project quotation personnel join Lotker to form a team committed to exceeding the customer's expectations.

Questions

1. Why should Michael Lotker adopt the three prescriptions for the presentation strategy?
2. Salespeople are encouraged to establish multiple-objective sales presentations. What are some objectives Michael Lotker should consider when he calls on personnel at a public utility?
3. What are some special challenges Michael Lotker faces when he talks to a community group about solar energy?
4. Put yourself in the position of a solar energy sales consultant. Can you envision a situation when you might combine the elements of an informative, persuasive, and reminder presentation? Explain.

CRM CASE STUDY

Establishing Your Approach

Becky Kemley, your sales manager at SimNet Systems, has notified Pat Silva's former prospects, by letter, that you will be calling on them soon. She wants to meet with you tomorrow to discuss your preapproach to your new prospects. Please review the records in the ACT! database.

Questions

1. Becky wants you to call on Robert Kelly. Describe what your call objectives would be with Mr. Kelly.
2. Describe a possible topic of your social contact with Mr. Kelly and how you would convert that to a buying contact.
3. Becky has given you a reprint of a new article about using networks for warehouse applications. Which of your prospects might have a strong interest in this kind of article? How would you use this article to make an approach to that prospect?

PARTNERSHIP SELLING: A ROLE-PLAY/SIMULATION

(see Appendix 3, pp. 500–501)

Developing a Relationship Strategy

Read *employment memorandum 2*, which announces your promotion to account executive. In your new position, you will be assigned by your instructor to one of the two major account categories in the convention center market. You will be assigned to either the *association accounts market* or the *corporate accounts market*. The association accounts market includes customers who have the responsibility for planning meetings for their association or group. The corporate accounts market includes customers who have the responsibility for planning meetings for the company they represent. (You will remain in the account category for the rest of the role-plays.)

Note the challenges you may have in your new position. Each of these challenges is represented in the future *sales memoranda* you receive from your sales manager.

Read *sales memorandum 1* for the account category you are assigned. (Note that the "A" means association and your customer is Erin Adkins, and "B" means corporate and your customer is Leigh Combs.) Follow the instructions in the sales memorandum and strategically prepare to approach your new customer. Your call objectives are to establish a relationship (social contact), share an appealing benefit, and find out if your customer is planning any future conventions (business contact).

You may be asked to assume the role of a customer in the account category to which you are not assigned as a salesperson. Your instructor will provide you with detailed instructions for correctly assuming this role.

Chapter Preview

When you finish reading this chapter, you should be able to

1 Describe the characteristics of the consultative sales presentation

2 Explain how to determine the prospect's needs

3 Discuss the use of questions to determine needs

4 Select products that match customer needs

5 List and describe three types of need-satisfaction presentation strategies

6 Present general guidelines for creating value-added presentations

CHAPTER 11

Creating the Consultative Sales Presentation

A pharmaceutical company that manufactures and distributes "miracle" drugs to health professionals really does not need a sales force, right? After all, if you are selling life-saving medical products, you should not need to worry about sales efforts. The truth is salespeople have played a key role in the success of Amgen (www.amgen.com), a pharmaceutical company that at one time had nothing to sell. Only after the Federal Drug Administration (FDA) approved a small number of drugs did Amgen evolve from a research and development (R&D) laboratory to a manufacturer to a marketer. A breakthrough by the Amgen R&D laboratory set the stage for the new company direction. The new drugs had to be manufactured and sold to the medical community. Today Amgen is one of the largest and most successful companies of its kind.

One of the first salespeople hired was Deborah Karish. She soon found that one of her greatest challenges was winning acceptance of her company, which was new to members of the medical community. Prospects were accustomed to buying products from well-established pharmaceutical companies. During a typical sales call, Deborah is selling her company, her products, and herself. Health care professionals need ample assurances that she is well qualified to give sound professional advice concerning the use of complex medical products.[1]

A growing number of salespeople, like Deborah Karish, have adopted the consultative sales presentation (Fig. 11.1). Consultative selling, as noted in Chapter 1, involves meeting customer needs by listening to customers, understanding—and caring about—their problems, selecting the appropriate solution,

THE SIX-STEP PRESENTATION PLAN

Step One: Approach	☑ Review Strategic/Consultative Selling Model ☑ Initiate customer contact
Step Two: Presentation	☐ Determine prospect needs ☐ Select solution ☐ Initiate sales presentation
Step Three: Demonstration	☐ Decide what to demonstrate ☐ Select selling tools ☐ Initiate demonstration
Step Four: Negotiation	☐ Anticipate buyer concerns ☐ Plan negotiating methods ☐ Initiate win-win negotiations
Step Five: Close	☐ Plan appropriate closing methods ☐ Recognize closing clues ☐ Initiate closing methods
Step Six: Servicing the Sale	☐ Follow through ☐ Follow-up calls ☐ Expansion selling

Service, retail, wholesale, and manufacturer selling

FIGURE | 11.1

Creating the Sales Presentation
A consultative sales presentation involves adding value by accurately determining the prospect's needs, selecting an appropriate product or service, and initiating an effective sales presentation.

and following through after the sale. Consultative selling focuses on identification of the customer's problem and finding a solution. This approach is very different than product-oriented selling. As one author noted, "Product-oriented selling can easily lapse into product evangelism …" Product-oriented selling is usually inefficient and ineffective.[2]

Figure 11.2 features key concepts related to creating the consultative sales presentation. This approach can be used effectively in the four major employment settings: service, retail, wholesale, and manufacturing. It results in increased customer satisfaction, more sales, fewer cancellations and returns, more repeat business, and more referrals.

CONSULTATIVE SALES PRESENTATION

As we note in Chapter 10, an effective approach sets the stage for the sales presentation. Once you have established rapport with the prospect, captured the prospect's full attention, you are ready to transition from the approach to need identification. There is no set formula to follow during the transition, but there are two tactics commonly used by salespeople. One is to state (or restate) the purpose of your sales call: "I want to determine if your company might benefit from an innovative truck leasing plan we have developed." The second tactic involves getting permission to ask questions. You might say, "Before I describe our leasing plan, would it be all right if I ask a few questions about your current truck fleet operation?"

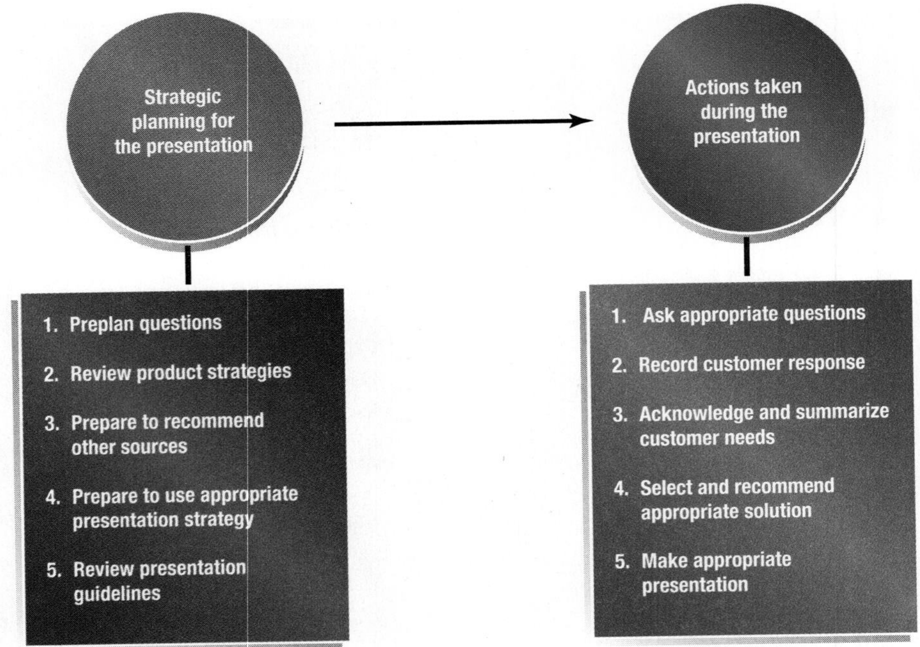

FIGURE | 11.2

Salespeople who truly represent value to their customers plan ahead strategically for the actions taken during the presentation.

To be most effective, the salesperson should think of the presentation as a four-part process. The Consultative Sales Presentation Guide (Fig. 11.3) features these four parts.

Part One—Need Discovery

A review of the behaviors displayed by high-performance salespeople helps us understand the importance of precise need discovery. They have learned how to skillfully diagnose and solve the customer's problems better than their competitors. This problem-solving capability translates into more repeat business and referrals and fewer order cancellations and returns.

Unless the selling situation requires mere order taking (customers know exactly what they want), need discovery is a standard part of the sales presentation. It may begin during the approach, if the salesperson uses questions or a survey during the initial contact with the customer. If neither of these two methods is used during the approach, need discovery begins immediately after you transition from the approach.

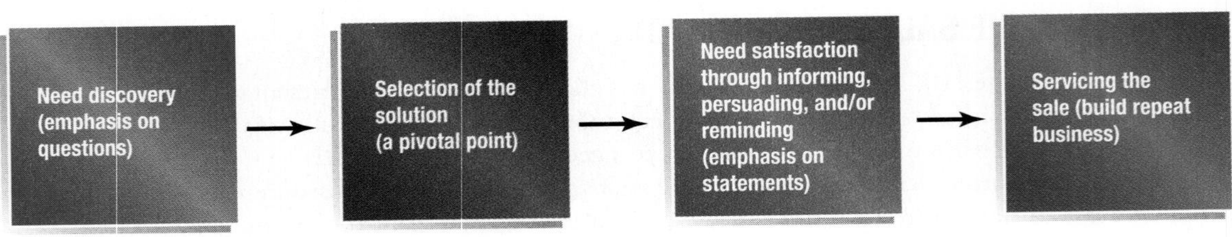

FIGURE | 11.3

The Consultative Sales Presentation Guide

To be most successful, the salesperson should think of the sales presentation as a four-part process.

The pace, scope, depth, and time allocated to inquiry depend on a variety of factors. Some of these include the sophistication of the product, the selling price, the customer's knowledge of the product, the product applications, and, of course, the time available for dialogue between the salesperson and the prospect. Each selling situation is different, so a standard set of guidelines for need discovery is not practical. Additional information on need discovery is presented later in the chapter.

Part Two—Selection of the Solution

The emphasis in sales and marketing today is on determining customer needs and then selecting or configuring custom-fitted solutions to satisfy these needs. Therefore, an important function of the salesperson is product selection and recommendation. The salesperson must choose the product or service that can provide maximum satisfaction. When making this decision, the salesperson must be aware of all product options, including those offered by the competition.

Salespeople who have the ability to conduct an effective value-added needs analysis achieve the status of trusted adviser. Mary Langston, personal shopper at Nordstrom's Michigan Avenue store in Chicago, helps customers update their wardrobes. When asked what her days are like she says, "It starts and ends with being a good listener." She promises her customers that she will never let them walk out of the store with clothing that does not look right.[3]

Part Three—Need Satisfaction Through Informing, Persuading, or Reminding

The third part of the consultative sales presentation consists of communicating to the customer, both verbally and nonverbally, the satisfaction that the product or service can provide. The salesperson places less emphasis on the use of questions and begins making

David Armstrong is an accounts manager for UPS in the San Francisco Bay area. He helps customers find the most effective way to ship products in the United States and around the world.

statements. These statements are organized into a presentation that informs, persuades, or reminds the customer of the most suitable product or service. Later in this chapter, and in several of the remaining chapters, we discuss specific strategies used in conjunction with the demonstration, negotiating buyer resistance, and closing the sale.

Part Four—Servicing the Sale

Servicing the sale is a major way to create value. These activities, which occur after closing the sale, ensure maximum customer satisfaction and set the stage for a long-term relationship. Service activities include suggestion selling, making credit arrangements, following through on assurances and promises, and dealing effectively with complaints. This topic is covered in detail in Chapter 15.

In those cases in which a sale is normally closed during a single sales call, the salesperson should be prepared to go through all four parts of the Consultative Sales Presentation Guide. However, when a salesperson uses a multicall approach, preparation for all the parts is usually not practical. The person selling computer systems or investments, for example, almost always uses a multicall sales presentation. Need discovery (part one) is the focus of the first call.

NEED DISCOVERY ACTIVITIES THAT CREATE VALUE

A lawyer does not give the client advice until the legal problem has been carefully studied and confirmed. A doctor does not prescribe medication until the patient's symptoms have been identified. In like manner, the salesperson should not recommend the purchase of a product without a thorough need identification. You start with the assumption that the client's problem is not known. The only way to determine and confirm the problem is to get the other person talking. You must obtain information to properly clarify the need.

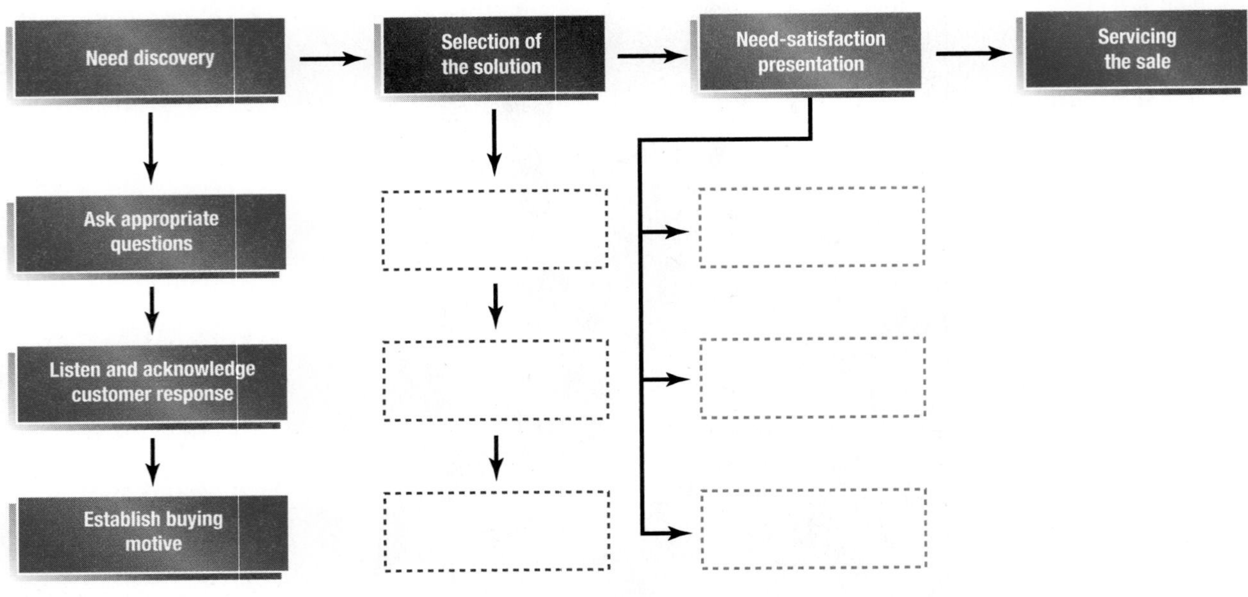

FIGURE | 11.4

Three Dimensions of Need Discovery

Customers may not realize that they actually have a problem. Even when they are aware of their need, they may not realize that an actual solution to their problem exists.

Need discovery (sometimes called need analysis) begins with precall preparation when the salesperson is acquiring background information on the prospect. It continues once the salesperson and the customer are engaged in a real dialogue. Through the process of need discovery, the salesperson establishes two-way communication by asking appropriate questions and listening carefully to the customer's responses. These responses usually provide clues concerning the customer's dominant buying motive (Fig. 11.4).

Asking Questions

The effective use of questions to achieve need identification and need satisfaction is the single greatest challenge facing most professional salespeople. The types of questions you ask, the timing of those questions, and how you pose them greatly impacts your ability to create customer value. Questions span the entire sales process, and today they are the tools salespeople use to gather information, probe, confirm, and persuade.

In every selling situation, you want the prospect to be actively thinking, sharing thoughts, and asking questions. Until the person begins to talk freely, the salesperson will have difficulty diagnosing and solving the customer's problems. A well-planned sales presentation includes a variety of preplanned questions (Table 11.1) and questions that are formulated spontaneously during the sales presentation. We describe the four most common types of questions used in the field of personal selling.

TABLE | 11.1 TYPES OF QUESTIONS USED IN CONJUNCTION WITH CONSULTATIVE SELLING

Salesperson selling fractional ownership of a jet aircraft to a well-known golf professional on the Professional Golf Association (PGA) Tour. The prospect is currently using commercial air travel.

TYPES OF QUESTION	DEFINITION	WHEN USED	EXAMPLES
Survey	Discovers basic facts about the buyer's existing situation and problem	Usually at the beginning of a sale	"Can you describe the problems you experience traveling to each of the pro golf tournaments?"
Probing	Designed to uncover and clarify the prospect's buying problem and the circumstances surrounding the problem	When you feel the need to obtain more specific information to fully understand the problem	"Are the travel problems affecting your concentration when you are preparing for the event?"
Confirmation	Used throughout the sales process to verify the accuracy and assure a mutual understanding of information exchanged by the salesperson and the buyer	After important information has been exchanged	"So you think the uncertainty associated with commercial air travel is having some affect on your game?"
Need-Satisfaction	Designed to move the sales process toward commitment and action	When you change the focus from the problem to a discussion of the solution	"With fractional ownership of your own jet, what personal benefits would this bring to your performance in the 30 tournaments you play each year?"

Survey Questions

At the beginning of most sales presentations, there is a need to collect basic facts about the buyer's existing situation and problem. **Survey questions**, or information gathering questions as they are sometimes called, are designed to obtain this knowledge. To accomplish this, there are two types of survey questions. **General Survey Questions** help the salesperson discover facts about the buyer's existing situation, and are often the first step in the partnership-building process. Here is a sampling of general survey questions that can be used in selected selling fields:

"Tell me about the new challenges you are facing in the area of data storage." (File Server)
"What is your current rate of employee turnover?" (Customer Service Training)
"Can you provide me with information on the kinds of meetings and conventions you plan for your clients and employees?" (Hotel Convention Services)
"Can you describe the style of home furnishings you prefer?" (Retail Home Furnishings)

In most selling situations, general survey questions are followed by specific survey questions.

Specific survey questions are designed to give prospects a chance to describe in more detail a problem, issue, or dissatisfaction from their point of view. These, **Specific survey questions**, sometimes referred to as problem questions give you an opportunity to delve more deeply into the customer's buying situation. Four examples of specific survey questions are:

"How do you feel about installing another server to your system?" (File Server)
"To what extent is employee turnover affecting your customer service?" (Customer Service Training)
"What meal function features are most important to your guests?" (Hotel Convention Services)
"Are you looking for an entertainment center that blends in with your existing furniture?" (Retail Home Furnishings)

Survey questions, general or specific, should not be used to collect factual information that can be acquired from other sources prior to the sales call. The pre-approach information gathering effort is especially important when the salesperson is involved in a large or complex sale. These buyers expect the salesperson to do their homework and not waste the buyer's time discussing basic factual information that is available from other sources.

Although survey questions are most often used at the beginning of the sales presentation, they can be used at other times. Information gathering may be necessary anytime during the sales presentation. We present the four types of questions in a sequence that has proven to be effective in most selling situations. However, it would be a mistake to view this sequence as a *rigid* plan for every sales presentation. High performing salespeople spend time strategically preparing tentative questions before they make the sales call. Table 11.2 provides some examples. Note that both open and closed questions are listed. **Open questions** require the prospect to go beyond a simple yes/no response. **Closed questions** can be answered with a yes or no, or a brief response.

Open questions are very effective in certain selling situations because they provoke thoughtful and insightful answers. The specific survey question, "What are the biggest challenges you face in the area of plant security?" focuses the prospect's attention on problems that need solutions. Closed questions however, can be equally effective when

TABLE | 11.2 NEED DISCOVERY WORKSHEET

Preplanned questions (sometimes used in conjunction with company supplied forms) are often used in service, retail, wholesale, and manufacturer selling. Salespeople who use the consultative approach frequently record answers to their questions and use this information to correctly select and recommend solutions that build repeat business and referrals. Open and closed questions used in the area of financial services appear in the following list.

PREPLANNED QUESTIONS TO DISCOVER BUYING MOTIVES	CUSTOMER RESPONSE
1. "Tell me a little bit about your investment portfolio?" (Open/General Survey)	
2. "What are your major concerns when managing your financial affairs?" (Open/Specific Survey)	
3. "Is providing for your children's college education a major concern at this time?" (Closed/Probing)	
4. "So, tax savings, growth in your portfolio, as well as providing for your children's college education are of primary importance, is that correct?" (Closed/Summary-Confirmation)	
5. "Are there any other benefits you see to converting your current real estate holdings to an IRS 1031 tax free exchange?" (Open/Need-Satisfaction)	
6.	
7.	
8.	

the sales conversation needs to be narrowed or focused on a specific issue. The general survey question, "Is your security concern primarily in the area of inventory control?" narrows the focus to a more specific problem.

Probing Questions

Early in the sales process the salesperson should make every effort to fully understand the buying problem and the consequences surrounding the problem. This clarification process will assure that the solution ultimately recommended and agreed upon will perform as intended.

Probing questions help you uncover and clarify the prospect's buying problem and the circumstances surrounding the problem. They are used more frequently in large, complex sales. These questions often uncover the current level of customer concern, fear, or frustration related to the problem. The following probing questions, sometimes referred to as *implication* or *pain* questions (see Selling in Action insert on page 274), are more focused than the survey questions presented earlier.

> "What would be the consequences if you choose to do nothing about your current server situation?" (File Server)
>
> "How does senior management feel about employee turnover and the related customer service problem?" (Customer Service Training)
>
> "Is poor service at the meal function negatively affecting the number of people returning to your seminar?" (Hotel Convention Services)
>
> "Is it important that you have easy access for connecting your DVD, TIVO, and your wireless LAN network?" (Retail Home Furnishings)

Neil Rackham conducted studies of 35,000 sales calls and from this research developed the material for his books SPIN SELLING and THE NEW SPIN SELLING FIELDBOOK. SPIN is an acronym for Situational, Problem, Implication, and Need-Payoff Questions. According to Rackham "more than half the Fortune 100 companies are using the SPIN *Selling Model to train their sales forces."*

Neil Rackham "The Spin Selling Fieldbook". Material reproduced with permission of The Mc-Graw Hill Companies.

Probing questions help the salesperson and customer gain a mutual understanding of *why* a problem is important. Asking effective probing questions requires extensive knowledge of your company's capabilities, much insight into your customer's buying problem, and a great deal of practice.

The best sales presentations are characterized by active dialogue. As the sales process progresses, the customer becomes more open and shares perceptions, ideas, and feelings freely. A series of appropriate probing questions stimulates the prospect to discover things that he had not considered before.

Confirmation Questions

Confirmation questions are used throughout the sales process to verify the accuracy and assure a mutual understanding of information exchanged by the salesperson and the buyer (see Table 11.1) These questions help determine if there is mutual understanding of the problems and circumstances the customer is experiencing. Throughout the sales process there is always the potential for a breakdown in communication. Perhaps the language used by the salesperson is too technical. Maybe the customer is preoccupied and has not listened closely to what has been said. Many confirmation questions are simple and to the point.

> "If I understand you correctly, the monitoring system for data storage must be set up for both your corporate headquarters and the manufacturing operation. Is that correct?" (File Server)
>
> "I want to be sure I am clear that you feel there is a direct relationship between employee turnover and the problems that exist in customer service?" (Customer Service Training)

"Did you say that your seminar attendance dropped twelve percent last year?" (Hotel Convention Services)

"So you want a new entertainment center that blends with your current light-colored oak furniture?" (Retail Home Furnishings)

The length of the sales process can vary from a few minutes during a single call presentation to weeks in a complex multicall sales presentation. As the sales process progresses, the amount of information available to the salesperson and the customer increases. As the need discovery progresses the customers buying criteria or buying conditions surface. **Buying conditions** are those qualifications that must be available or fulfilled before the sale can be closed. The customer may buy only if the product is available in a certain color or can be delivered by a certain date. In some selling situations, product installation or service after the sale are considered important buying conditions by the customer. In a large, complex sale, several buying conditions may surface. The salesperson has the responsibility of clarifying and confirming each condition.

One of the best ways to clarify and confirm several buying conditions is with a **summary-confirmation question**. To illustrate, let us consider a situation in which Tammy Rodriguez, sales manager at a major hotel, has interviewed a prospect who wants to schedule a large awards banquet. After a series of survey, probing, and confirmation questions. Tammy feels confident she has collected enough information to prepare a proposal. However, to be sure that she has all the facts and has clarified all important buying conditions, she asks the following *summary-confirmation question*:

"Let me summarize the major items you have mentioned. You want all of the banquet attendees served within an eight-minute time frame after the opening speaker has finished his speech?"

If the customer responds in the affirmative, Tammy continues with another summary confirmation questions:

"And, you need a room that will comfortably seat 60 persons banquet style and 10 of these persons will be seated at the head table. Is this correct?"

Once all the buying conditions are confirmed, Tammy can prepare a proposal that reflects the specific needs of her customer. The result is a win-win situation for the customer and the salesperson. The chances of closing the sale greatly improve. In multicall sales processes it is wise to begin subsequent calls with summary-confirmation questions that reestablish what was discussed in the previous call(s). This enables the salesperson to verify that the previously discovered buying conditions have remained the same and not changed since the last meeting.

Need-Satisfaction Questions

The fourth type of question used in the sales process is fundamentally different than the other three. **Need-satisfaction questions** are designed to move the sales process toward commitment and action. These are helpful questions that focus on the solution. The chances of closing the sale greatly improve because need-satisfaction, or as they are sometimes called Solution or Pleasure questions, focus on specific benefits and build desire for a solution.

Survey, probing and confirmation questions focus on understanding and clarifying the customer's problem. Need-satisfaction questions help the prospect see how your product or service provide a solution to the problem you have uncovered. The opportunity to close the sale greatly improves because you have cast the solution in a favorable light.

In most cases need-satisfaction questions are used after the salesperson has created awareness of the seriousness of the buyer's problem. The questions you ask will offer relief from their current levels of concern, fear, or frustration. The following examples provide insight into the use of need-satisfaction questions:

> "Tests on similar applications show a new file server can increase data storage by 30 to 40 per cent. How much of an increase do you feel you would achieve?" (File Server)

In many selling situations a product demonstration is an essential stage in the sales process. In this case, the salesperson might use the following need-satisfaction question:

> "What benefits do you see if we provided a demonstration of one of the training modules to senior management so they can understand what you and I have discovered about reducing employee turnover?" (Customer Service Training)

Once the prospect needs are clearly identified, need-satisfaction questions can be valuable closing tools. Consider this example:

> "Considering the benefits we have summarized and agreed on, and noting the fact that our staff will deliver an outstanding meal function, would you like to sign this confirmation so we can reserve the rooms and schedule the meals that you need?" (Hotel Convention Services)

Need-satisfaction questions, such as those above, are very powerful because they build desire for the solution and give ownership of the solution to the prospect. When the prospect understands which parts of the problem(s) your solution can solve, you are less likely to invite objections. In some cases you may identify problems that still need to be clarified. When this happens you can use survey, probing, or confirmation questions to obtain more information.

Selling in Action

SELLING IN ACTION

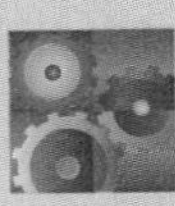

The use of questions to discover needs and present solutions is discussed in several popular personal selling books. For comparison purposes, the approximate equivalents to the four types of questions described in this chapter are listed.

Selling Today by Manning and Reece	The Spin Selling Fieldbook by Rackham	The New Solution Selling by Eades	The New Conceptual Selling by Heiman, Sanchez, with Tuleja	Secrets of Question Based Selling by Freese
SURVEY	SITUATION	OPEN	CONFIRMATION	STATUS
PROBING	PROBLEM	CONTROL	NEW INFORMATION	ISSUE
CONFIRMATION	IMPLICATION	CONFIRMING	ATTITUDE	IMPLICATION
NEED-SATISFACTION	NEED-PAYOFF		COMMITMENT	SOLUTION
			BASIC ISSUE	

The questions above are listed in the sequence presented by the authors. To determine the exact definition of each type of question, check the source.

Selling Is Everyone's Business

SELLING A PRODUCT THAT DOESN'T EXIST

Some creative entrepreneurs start selling their product before it even exists. Greg Gianforte wanted to start an Internet-software company in the late 1990s. He noted that no one seemed to be making a good product that would help companies respond to e-mail from customers. Armed with a product feature sheet, Gianforte started trying to sell a nonexistent product. He called customer-support managers at hundreds of companies. After reviewing the product features, he explained that the product would be ready in 90 days. Some of these potential customers mentioned features he had not thought of. This input helped him develop a better product. After two weeks of cold calls, he knew exactly what customers wanted and he began the development of RightNow software. It was ready for customer use in 90 days. He then hired his first three employees—all of them salespeople. Gianforte says, "Sales is really the most noble part of the business because it's the part that brings the solution together with the customer's need." Today, more than 1,200 organizations worldwide use RightNow solutions.[a]

At this point you have received only a basic introduction to the four most common types of questions used during the selling process. (For more insight into the application of questions to the sales process, view the three videos in the "Questions, Questions, Questions" series. Also refer to the Video Role-play Exercises on pages 288–289.) We will revisit these important sales tools later in this chapter and in Chapters 12, 13, 14, and 15.

Listening and Acknowledging the Customer's Response

To fully understand the customer, we must listen closely and acknowledge every response. The authors of *First Impressions* offer these words of advice to salespeople who use questions as part of the need identification process:

> "What you do after you ask a question can reveal even more about you than the questions you ask. You reveal your true level of interest in the way you listen."[4]

We are born with the ability to hear, but we have to learn how to listen. The starting point is developing a listening attitude. Always regard the customer as worthy of your respect and full attention. Once you have made a commitment to becoming a better listener, develop active listening skills.

Customer Relationship Management with Technology

REVIEWING ACCOUNT STATUS

Salespeople regularly review the status of their prospects' records in their customer relationship management (CRM) databases. In some cases, this is done on the computer screen. In other situations, a printed copy of the records can enhance the process.

Salespeople review their files to ascertain at what phase in the Consultative Sales Presentation Guide each prospect is in the sales cycle. Then they decide which action to take to help move the prospect to the next phase. Sales managers can be helpful with this process, especially for new salespeople. Managers can help salespeople evaluate the available information and suggest strategies designed to move to the next phase.

Even experienced salespeople count on their sales managers to help plan presentations. Managers can help salespeople evaluate their prospects' needs, select the best solution, and plan a presentation most likely to succeed. (See the exercise, Printing the Customer Database, on p. 291 for more information.)

Lisa Ciampi, account executive for Design Display Inc. in Birmingham, Alabama, believes consultative selling is about being a marketing advisor and problem solver. This approach creates value within the sales process.

Developing Active Listening Skills

Active listening is the process of sending back to the prospect what you as a listener think the person meant, both in terms of content and in terms of feelings. Active listening requires intense involvement as you concentrate on what you are hearing exhibit your listening attitude through your nonverbal messages (see Chapter 3), and feedback to the prospect what you think he or she meant.[5]

Developing active listening skills involves three practices that can be learned by any salesperson willing to make the commitment.

Source: Scot Ober, *Contemporary Business Communication*, 5th ed. (Boston: Houghton Mifflin, 2003), p. 62. Reprinted courtesy of Bunny Hoest.

Focus Your Full Attention This is not easy because the delivery of the messages we hear is often much slower than our capacity to listen. Thus, we have plenty of time to let our minds roam, to think ahead, and to plan what we are going to say next. Our senses are constantly feeding us new information while someone is trying to tell us something. Staying focused is often difficult and involves use of both verbal and nonverbal messages.[6] To show that you are paying attention, lean toward the prospect while saying "uh-huh," "okay", or "I understand" and nodding in agreement when appropriate. Avoid nodding rapidly or saying uh-huh rapidly because this will communicate impatience or a desire to turn the conversation back to yourself.[7]

Nash Finch salespeople create value-added product solutions based on their "performance driven" merchandising and advertising programs.

In many selling situations note taking will demonstrate a high level of professionalism.

Paraphrase the Customer's Meaning After the customer stops talking, pause for two or three seconds and then state in your own words with a confirmation question, what you think the person meant. This technique not only helps ensure understanding but also is an effective customer relations strategy. The customer feels good knowing that not only are you listening to what has been said but also you are making an effort to ensure accuracy.

In addition to paraphrasing the content, use questions to dig for full understanding of the customer's perceptions.[8] The use of survey or probing questions is appropriate anytime you need to clarify what is being said by the prospect.

Take Notes Although note taking is not necessary in every sales presentation, it is important in complex sales in which the information obtained from the customer is critical to the development of a buying solution. As a courtesy to the customer, it is usually best to request permission before you begin taking notes. Taking accurate notes is a good way to demonstrate to the customer that you are actively listening. When you take notes you increase your memory of what you heard. Your notes should be brief and to the point.[9]

Establishing Buying Motives

The primary goal of questioning, listening, and acknowledging is to uncover prospect needs and establish buying motives. Our efforts to discover prospect needs can be more effective if we focus our questioning on determining the prospect's primary reasons for buying. When a customer has a definite need, it is usually supported by specific buying motives.

The greatest time investment in personal selling is on the front end of the sales process. First you must plan the sales call and then, once you are face-to-face with the customer, you can begin the need discovery stage. It is during the early stage of the sales process that you can create the greatest value for the customer.[10]

SELECTING SOLUTIONS THAT ADD VALUE

The second part of the consultative sales presentation consists of selecting or creating a solution that satisfies the prospect's buying motives. After identifying the buying motives, the salesperson carefully reviews the available product options. At this point the

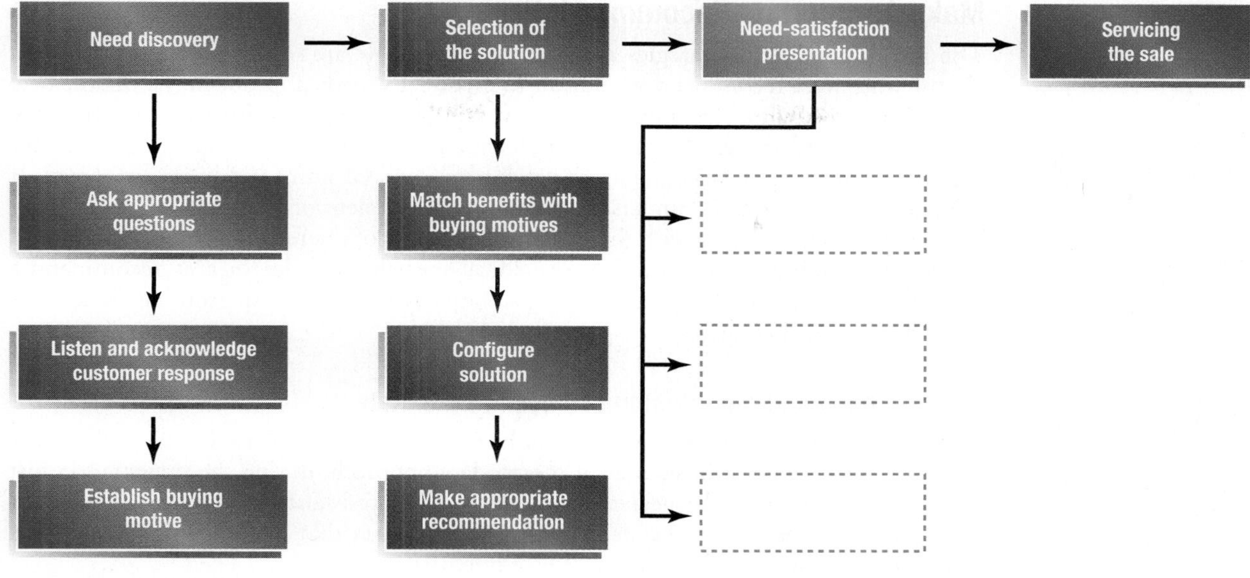

FIGURE | 11.5

Three Dimensions of Product Selection

salesperson is searching for a specific solution to satisfy the prospect's buying motives. Once the solution has been selected, the salesperson makes a recommendation to the prospect (Fig. 11.5).

If the sale involves several needs and the satisfaction of multiple buying motives, selection of the solution may take several days or even weeks and may involve the preparation of a detailed sales proposal. A company considering the purchase of automated production equipment would likely present this type of challenge to the salesperson. The problem needs careful analysis before a solution can be identified.

Match Specific Benefits with Buying Motives

As we note in Chapter 7, products and services represent problem-solving tools. People buy products when they perceive that they fulfill a need. We also note that today's more demanding customers seek a cluster of satisfactions that arise from the product itself, from the company that makes or distributes the product, and from the salesperson who sells and services the product (see Fig. 7.1). Tom Reilly, author of *Value-Added Selling*, says, "Value-added salespeople sell three things: the product, the company, and themselves. This is the three dimensional bundle of value."[11] When possible the salesperson should focus on benefits related to each dimension of value. Of course, it is a mistake to make benefit statements that do not relate to the specific needs of the customer.

Configure a Solution

Most salespeople bring to the sale a variety of products or services. Salespeople who represent food distributors can offer customers a mix of several hundred items. Most pharmaceutical sales representatives can offer the medical community a wide range of products. Best Buy, a large retailer of electronics, offers customers a wide range of audio and visual entertainment options. The customer who wants to purchase a sound system, for example, can choose from many combinations of receivers, speakers, and so on.

Make Appropriate Recommendations

The recommendation strategies available to salespeople are similar to those used by a doctor who must recommend a solution to a patient's medical problem. In the medical field, three possibilities for providing patient satisfaction exist. In situations in which the patient easily understands the medical problem and the appropriate treatment, the doctor can make a recommendation, and the patient can proceed immediately toward a cure. If the patient does not easily understand the medical problem or solution, the doctor may need to discuss thoroughly with the patient the benefits of the recommended treatment. If the medical problem is not within his medical specialty, the doctor may recommend a specialist to provide the treatment. In consultative selling the salesperson has these same three counseling alternatives.

Recommend solution—Customer Buys Immediately

The selection and recommendation of products to meet customer needs may occur at the beginning of the sales call, such as in the product approach; during the presentation just after the need discovery; or near the end, when minor resistance has been negotiated. At any of these three times, the presentation of products that are well matched to the prospect's needs may result in an immediate purchase.

Recommend solution—Salesperson Makes Need-Satisfaction Presentation

This alternative requires a presentation of product benefits including demonstrations and negotiating objections before the sale is closed. In this situation the customer may not be totally aware of a buying problem, and the solution may not be easily understood or apparent. Because of this, the salesperson needs to carefully define the problem and communicate a solution to the customer.

Recommend Another Source

Earlier in this book we indicated that professional salespeople may recommend that a prospect buy a product or service from another source, maybe even a competitor. If, after a careful needs assessment, the salesperson concludes that the products represented do not satisfy the customer's needs, the consultative salesperson should recommend another source.

Paul Roos, a sales representative for Hewlett-Packard, once met with a customer who wanted to buy a newly introduced HP product for an application that would not work. He explained why the application would not work and then took time to configure a

competing product to meet the customer's needs. He lost that sale to a competitor, but the assistance provided confirmed his integrity and made a lasting impression on the customer. That customer later became a high-value account.[12]

NEED SATISFACTION—SELECTING A PRESENTATION STRATEGY

Decisions concerning which presentation strategy to emphasize have become more complex. This is due to several factors discussed in previous chapters: longer sales cycles, multiple buying influences, emphasis on repeat sales and referrals, greater emphasis on custom fitting of products, and building of long-term partnerships.

Conducting business in the new economy, which is based on the assets of knowledge and information, requires that we think about ways to improve the sales presentation. This is how one author described this challenge:[13]

> As we move from the rutted byways of the Industrial Age to the electronic thorough-fares of the Information Age, business presentations become a measure of our ability to adapt to new surroundings. The most successful and forward-thinking companies already have assigned presentations a new, fundamental, and strategic importance.

The need-satisfaction strategy involves assessing the customer's needs; selecting the product; and deciding whether to use an informative, persuasive, or reminder presentation (Fig. 11.6).

Informative Presentation Strategy

To be informative, a message must be clearly understood by the customer. Of course, clarity is important in any presentation, but it needs special attention in a presentation whose primary purpose is to inform. The **informative presentation** emphasizes factual information

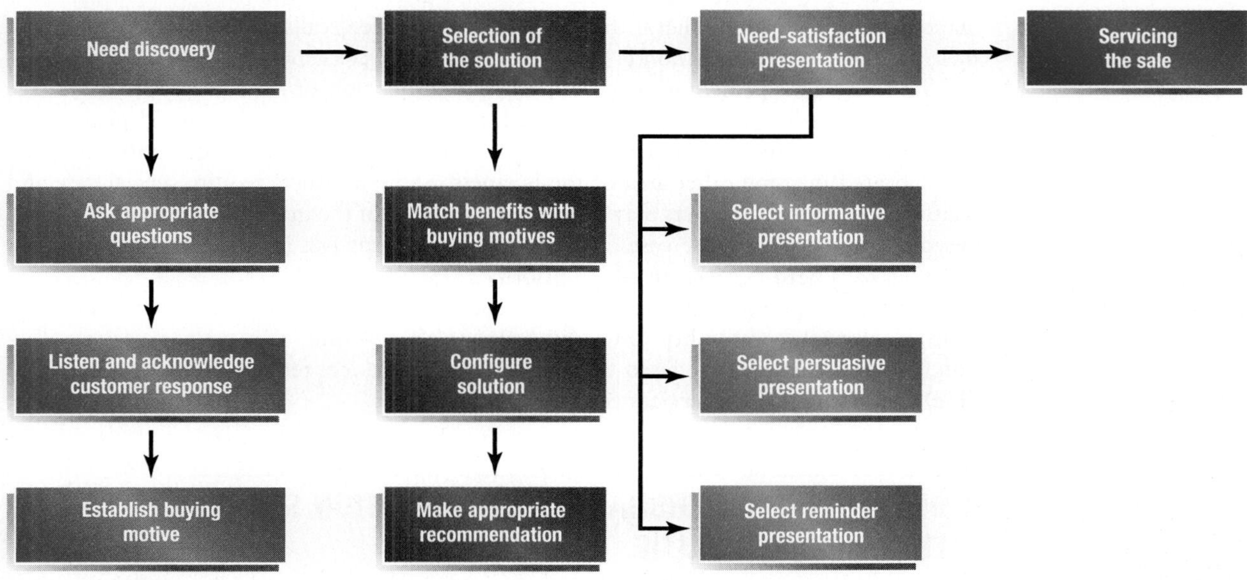

FIGURE | 11.6

The Three Strategies to Use in Developing an Effective Need-Satisfaction Presentation

often taken from technical reports, company-prepared sales literature, or written testimonials from persons who have used the product. This type of presentation is commonly used to introduce new products and services. This strategy emphasizes clarity, simplicity, and directness. Salespeople need to keep in mind the "less is more" concept. Too often the prospect is given far too much information and detail.[14]

Persuasive Presentation Strategy

Many salespeople believe that when a real need for their product exists, the stage is set for a persuasive presentation. The major goal of the **persuasive presentation** strategy is to influence the prospect's beliefs, attitudes, or behavior and to encourage buyer action. Persuasive sales presentations include a subtle transition stage where the dialogue shifts from an intellectual emphasis to an emotional appeal. Every buying decision is influenced by both reason and emotion, but the amount of weight given to each of these elements during the decision-making process can vary greatly depending on the prospect.[15]

In the field of personal selling, persuasion is an acceptable strategy once a need has been identified and a suitable product has been selected. When it is clear that the buyer can benefit from ownership of the product or service, an enthusiastic and persuasive sales presentation is usually appropriate.

The persuasive presentation strategy requires a high level of training and experience to be effective, because a poorly planned and delivered persuasive presentation may raise the prospect's anxiety level. The persuasive presentation, when handled improperly, can trigger fear or distrust.

Reminder Presentation Strategy

Studies show that awareness of a company's products and services declines as promotion is stopped. This problem represents one of the reasons many companies employ missionary salespeople to maintain an ongoing awareness and familiarity with their product lines. Other types of salespeople also use this presentation strategy. Route salespeople rely heavily on **reminder presentations** (sometimes called *reinforcement presentations*) to maintain their market share. They know that if they do not make frequent calls and remind customers of their products, the competition is likely to capture some customers.

The reminder presentation is sometimes a dimension of service after the sale (see Chapter 15). Sales personnel working with repeat customers are in a good position to remind them of products or services offered in their own department or another department located in some other area of the business. Some products require special care and maintenance. Busy customers may need to be reminded of the maintenance services offered by your company. In some cases, the service department is a major profit generator, so reminder calls need to be given a high priority.

Some customers get used to the great quality and service you provide and begin to view your product as a commodity. Once this happens, the customer may ask for a price reduction. To keep customers focused on value rather than price, remind them (from time to time) of the value-added services you provide.[16]

DEVELOPING A PERSUASIVE PRESENTATION STRATEGY THAT CREATES VALUE

There are many ways to incorporate persuasion into a sales presentation and most will create value for the customer. In this section we review a series of guidelines that should be followed during preparation of a persuasive presentation.

Global Business Etiquette

DOING BUSINESS IN JAPAN

Many American businesspeople travel to Japan because it is the United States' largest trading partner. Japan is the world's second largest economy so it helps to become familiar with the Japanese business culture.

- Courtesy is a major key to success in Japan. When you address someone, be sure to use titles such as Mr., Ms., or Dr. and wait to be invited before using first names.
- The Japanese are very hierarchical so the business card is an important source of information regarding the relative status of the other person. Accept the card with care and then examine it. Do not put it in your pocket or wallet. Place it in a card holder.
- In Japan the culture emphasizes the group over the individual. It would not be appropriate to praise one member of a group.
- Decision making in Japan is done very slowly. Be patient as the group reaches a consensus. Aggressive sales methods should be avoided.[b]

Place Special Emphasis on the Relationship

Throughout this book we emphasize the importance of the relationship strategy in selling. Good rapport between the salesperson and the prospect establishes a foundation for an open exchange of information. Robert Cialdini, writing in the *Harvard Business Review*, says the science of persuasion is built on the principle of liking: *People like those who like them*. Establish a bond with the customer early by uncovering areas of common interest, using praise when it's appropriate, and being completely trustworthy.[17] Always do what you say you will do.

Sell Specific Benefits and Obtain Customer Reactions

People do not buy things, they buy what the things can do for them. They do not buy an auto battery, they buy a sure start on a cold morning. Office managers do not buy laser printers, they buy better-looking letters and reports. Every product or service offers the customer certain benefits. The benefit might be greater comfort, security, feeling of confidence, or economy.

If you are selling Allstate insurance, for example, you should become familiar with the service features. One feature is well-trained employees and the convenient location of Allstate offices across the nation. The benefit to customers is greater peace of mind in knowing that they can receive good service at a nearby location. Allstate salespeople understand the importance of selling the company, the product, and themselves.

After you state the feature and convert it into a buyer benefit, obtain a reaction from the customer by using confirmation or need-satisfaction questions (refer to Table 11.1). You should always check to see if you are on the right track and your prospect is following the logic of your presentation. Some examples follow:

FEATURE	BENEFIT	QUESTION
Seven hour battery life*	Fewer work interuptions when traveling	"Battery life is important to you isn't it?" (confirmation question)
Automatic climate control system for automobile	Temperature in car not varying after initial setting	"Would you like the luxury of setting the temperature and then not worrying about it?" (need-satisfaction question)

*Feature of Fujitsu Lifebook laptop

The feature–benefit–reaction (FBR) approach is used by many high-performance salespeople. Involving the customer with appropriate questions helps you maintain two-way communication with the customer.

Minimize the Negative Impact of Change

As we noted earlier, salespeople are constantly threatening the status quo. They sell people the new, the different, and the untried. In nearly all selling situations the customer is being asked to consider change of some sort, and in some cases it is only natural for the person to resist change. Whenever possible, we should try to help the customer view change in a positive and realistic way. Change is more acceptable to people who understand the benefits of it and do not see it as a threat. Always anticipate the one question (spoken or unspoken) that every buyer asks: "How will this product benefit me?" To minimize the impact of change, be sure to personalize the benefit with a specific reference to the customer's need.

Place the Strongest Appeal at the Beginning or End

Research indicates that appeals made at the beginning or end of a presentation are more effective than those given in the middle. A strong appeal at the beginning of a presentation, of course, gets the prospect's attention and possibly develops interest. Made near the end of the presentation, the appeal sets the stage for closing the sale.

Target Emotional Links

Emotional links are the connectors between your messages and the internal emotions of the prospect.[18] Some common emotional links in the business community are quality improvement, on-time delivery, increased market share, innovation, customer service, and reduction of operating expenses. Targeting just a few emotional links can increase your chances of closing the sale. When you target emotional links, use persuasive words such as *proven, efficient, save, convenient, world-class, new*, and *improved*. Also, use the language to which your prospect is most attuned.

Do not hesitate to present important information in a dramatic way. In Chapter 4, we discussed the importance of communication style flexibility. To be more convincing and to compel your prospect to pay attention, you often need to communicate genuine enthusiasm for the product you represent.

Use Metaphors, Stories, and Testimonials

Metaphors, sometimes referred to as *figurative language*, are highly persuasive sales tools. Metaphors are words or phrases that suggest pictorial relationships between objects or ideas. With the aid of metaphors you can paint vivid, visual pictures for prospects that command their attention and keep their interest. The success of the metaphor rests on finding common ground (shared or well-known experiences) so that your message gets a free boost from a fact already known or believed to be true. A salesperson representing Cobalt boats, a line of high quality runabouts selling for $30,000 to $300,000 might refer to his products as "The Steinways of the runabout class."[19]

Donald J. Moine, noted speaker and sales trainer, says that stories not only help you sell more products but also help you enrich relationships with your customers. A good story focuses the customer's attention and can effectively communicate the value of a product or a service as well. The story should be appropriate to the customer's situation, short, and told with enthusiasm.[20]

Many salespeople find it beneficial to quote a specific third party. Third-party testimonials from satisfied clients can help a prospect feel confident about using your product.

GENERAL GUIDELINES FOR CREATING VALUE-ADDED PRESENTATIONS

There are many ways to make all three need-satisfaction presentation strategies more interesting and more valuable. A more effective presentation can be developed using the following general guidelines. Each of these guidelines are discussed in more detail in Chapters 12–15.

Strengthen the Presentation Strategy with an Effective Demonstration

The need-satisfaction presentation can be strengthened if the salesperson preplans effective demonstrations that clarify the product features and benefits. Many salespeople encounter doubt or skepticism during the sales presentation. The prospect often wants some kind of assurance or proof. If the demonstration is convincing and removes doubt from the customer's mind, you have created value. The following list of proof strategies is explained in detail in Chapter 12.

- Product itself
- Models
- Photos, illustrations and brochures
- Reprints
- Catalogs
- Graphs, charts, and test results
- Laptop computers and demonstration software
- Bound paper presentations
- Portfolios

Preplan Methods for Negotiating and Closing the Sale

Salespeople who make the most efficient use of time are adding value. To make your presentation as concise and to the point as possible, you should preplan methods for negotiating misunderstandings or resistance that often surfaces during the presentation. You need to bring some degree of urgency to the selling environment by presenting focused solutions. In most cases the focus of the negotiation is on one of the following areas:

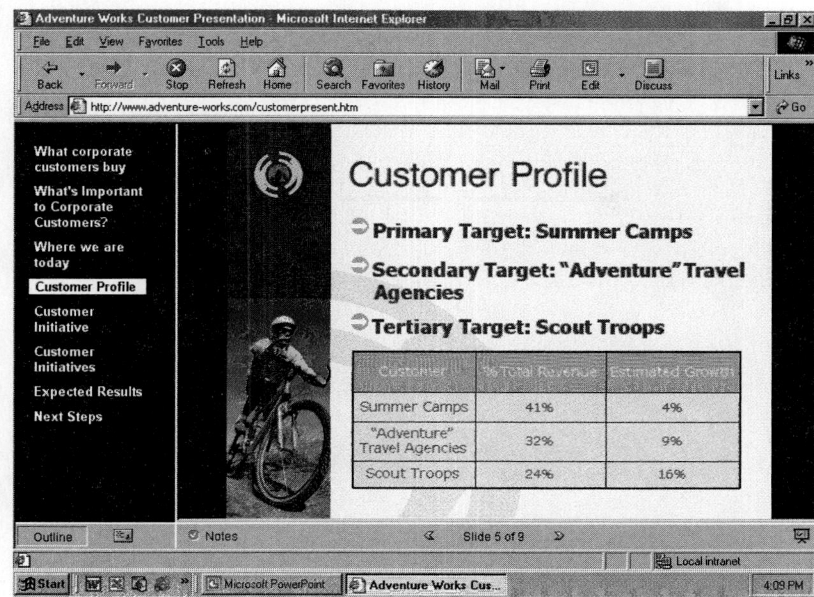

A well-developed Microsoft PowerPoint sales presentation strategy can add value. When using this software, keep the presentation simple and concise.

- *Need* awareness is vague or nonexistent.
- The *product* does not meet the buyer's perceived requirement.
- *Price* does not equal perceived value.
- The buyer is satisfied with present *source*.
- The *time* is not right.

Methods used to negotiate buyer resistance in each of these areas are introduced in Chapter 13. It also is important to preplan closing and confirming the sale. This planning should include a review of closing clues that may surface during the sales presentation and methods of closing the sale. These and other topics are discussed in Chapter 14.

Preplan Customer Service Methods That Add Value

Customer service, in its many forms, provides an opportunity to add value. Very often customers want a preview of the customer service options during the sales presentation. And, in some cases, customer service is the key to closing the sale. Consider the purchase that must be financed and the customer expects you to be familiar with various credit options. You can also add value with timely delivery of the product, proper installation, and follow-up to ensure customer satisfaction. Customer service will be discussed in detail in Chapter 15.

Keep Your Presentation Simple and Concise

The best way to achieve conciseness is to preplan your sales call. Think ahead of time about what you are going to say and do. Anticipate questions and objections the prospect may voice, and be prepared with accurate information and concise answers.

Preplanning also involves time allocation. Figure 11.7 illustrates an ideal breakdown of time allocation between the salesperson and the prospect during all three parts of the sales presentation. In terms of involvement the prospect assumes a greater role during the need-

FIGURE | 11.7

Time Used by Salesperson and Customer During Each Part of the Consultative Sales Presentation

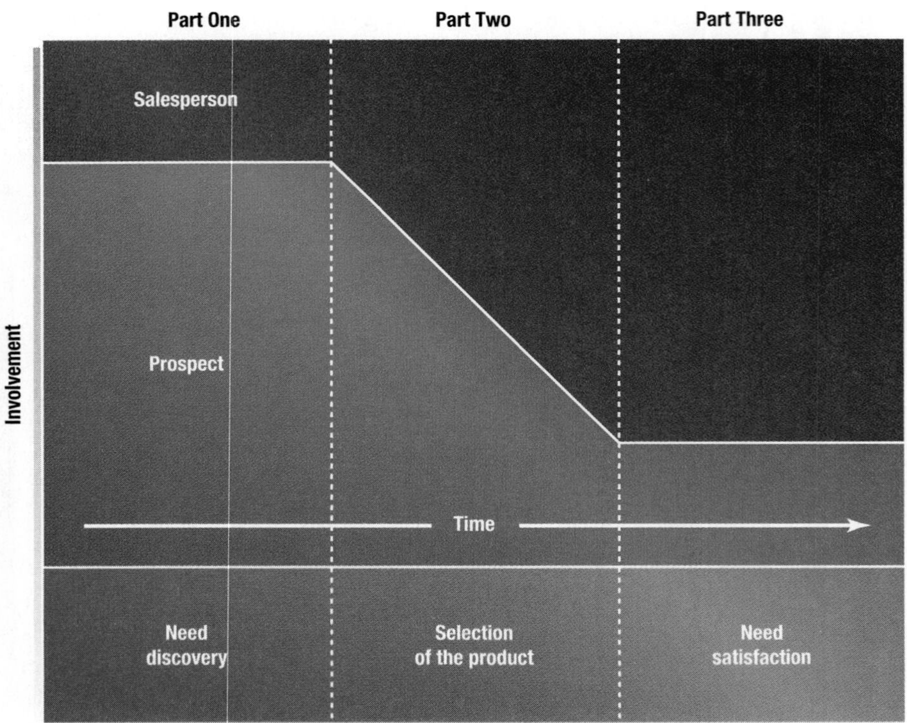

discovery stage. As the salesperson begins the product selection process, the prospect's involvement decreases. During the need-satisfaction stage, the salesperson is doing most of the talking, but note that the prospect is never excluded totally.

In addition to preplanning the sales presentation, consider a "dress rehearsal" in front of your colleagues. A less threatening approach might be to practice in front of your spouse or a close friend. Videotaping the rehearsal can help you see how you really look. Do you appear too stiff and motionless? Do you talk too fast or too slow? It's a good idea to practice presentations with specific customers in mind.[21]

The Consultative Sales Presentation and the Transactional Buyer

Throughout this chapter you have been given a comprehensive introduction to the consultative sales presentation. It is important to keep in mind that the fundamentals of consultative selling must be customized to meet the individual needs of the customer. For example, some of the guidelines for developing an effective presentation must be abandoned or greatly altered when you are working with a transactional buyer. In most cases transactional buyers understand what product they need and when they need it. The Internet has armed many transactional buyers with a great deal of information, so the salesperson who spends time asking survey questions or making a detailed informative presentation may be wasting the customer's time. Most of these buyers want the salesperson to configure a product solution that focuses on pricing and delivery issues.[22]

Summary

A well-planned and well-executed consultative sales presentation is an important key to success in personal selling. To be most effective, the presentation should be viewed as a four-part process: need discovery; selection of the product; need-satisfaction through informing, persuading, or reminding; and servicing the sale.

The most effective sales presentation is characterized by two-way communication. It should be a dialogue between the salesperson and the prospect, whose involvement should be encouraged with survey, probing, confirmation, summary-confirmation and need-satisfaction questions. Beware of assuming information about the prospect, and be sure the language of your presentation is clearly understood. Listen attentively as the prospect responds to your questions or volunteers information. Develop active listening skills.

After making a good first impression during the approach and getting the customer's full attention, the salesperson begins the presentation. The salesperson's ability is tested during this part of the sale, because this is where the prospect's buying motives are established. The salesperson's ability to verbalize specific product benefits also is being tested during this part of the sale.

Once you have selected a solution that matches the customer's needs, you must decide which presentation strategy to emphasize. Need satisfaction can be achieved through informing, persuading, or reminding. The salesperson can, of course, use a combination of these presentation strategies in some cases. An effective presentation is an important part of the sales call and often determines the ease or difficulty of proceeding through the rest of the steps to a successful sale. General guidelines for developing effective persuasive presentations were discussed.

KEY TERMS

Need Discovery
Survey questions
Probing questions
Confirmation questions
Need-satisfaction questions
Buying conditions
Summary–confirmation questions
Active listening
Informative presentation
Persuasive presentation
Reminder presentation
Emotional links
Open questions
Closed questions

REVIEW QUESTIONS

1. List and describe the four parts of the Consultative Sales Presentation Guide.
2. List and describe the four types of questions commonly used in the selling field.
3. Define the term *buying conditions*. What are some common buying conditions?
4. Describe the process of active listening, and explain how it can improve the listening efficiency rate.
5. Discuss the three dimensions of need discovery.
6. Distinguish between the three types of need-satisfaction presentations: informative, persuasive, and reminder.
7. What are the guidelines to be followed when developing a persuasive sales presentation?
8. What are some advantages of using the feature-benefit-reaction (FBR) approach?
9. What is a metaphor? Why is the use of metaphors considered a persuasive sales tool?
10. A friend of yours is planning to begin selling U.S.-made products in Japan. What tips can you give her that will improve her chances of achieving success?

ROLE-PLAY APPLICATION EXERCISES FOR "QUESTIONING" VIDEO SERIES

Most sales skill development exercises used in the classroom are product-oriented. As noted on page 265, "Product oriented selling can easily lapse into product evangelism." This three-part video series on questioning focuses on the customer's buying process, consultative selling, and building high quality partnerships.

The goal of this series is the identification and clarification of the customer's problem and finding a solution. The first video focuses on the appropriate use of survey and confirmation questions to identify the customer's problem. Video two introduces the use of probing and need-satisfaction questions. Probing questions examine and clarify the potential issues surrounding the customer's problem, while need-satisfaction questions focus the sales process on the appropriate solution. The third video demonstrates the use of these questions in a challenging, yet typical contemporary sales setting.

The role-play exercises presented below challenge the participant to understand, apply and integrate questioning skills presented in this chapter and in the video series. Product information needed for these exercises is found in Appendix III on pages 459 to 495. Customer information will be found in the B. H. Rivera Contact Report presented on page 459 (disregard any other information on this page). You will assume the role of a newly hired salesperson as described in the Position Description on page 462. Refer to the questioning material and examples presented on pages 465–278. Use a Need Discovery Worksheet like the one on page 271 for developing your questions.

After viewing the video **"Questions—Discovering and Confirming Customer Problems,"** study information presented in Appendix 3, pages 459 to 495. Refer to the Contact Report on page 459 (as noted, disregard any other information on this page). Assume you were assigned to this account and you are meeting B. H. Rivera to inquire about additional information regarding dates when the meeting will be held, and what audiovisual equipment might be needed. Prepare a list of general survey and specific survey questions that reveal when, during the next month, the meeting will be held and what, if any, audiovisual equipment (see page 487) might be needed. Plan to use a summary-confirmation question to verify the existing four items on the Contact Sheet. Using the questions you have created, role-play this part of the need discovery process.

After viewing the video **"Questions—Discovering Pain and Pleasure,"** and reviewing the information you prepared in the role-play above, prepare three probing questions. These questions should clarify and reveal a mutual understanding of issues and consequences regarding food service, facility design, and audiovisual equipment. Also, using the information of pages 459 to 491, prepare five need-satisfaction questions that reveal how the features of your convention center provide a solution to the buying situation. Select appropriate proof devices to demonstrate these specific benefits. Using these questions, meet again with B. H. Rivera, and role-play this part of the questioning process. Prepare and use confirmation questions as the need arises.

After viewing the video **"Questions Getting it Right,"** and using the information in the first two role-plays, prepare a need-satisfaction presentation to Cameron Rivera, a new meeting planner just hired at Graphic Forms. Cameron, a cousin of B. H., had been previously employed as a training coordinator at West College. Due to extensive growth in the company, B. H. has turned all meeting planning over to Cameron. Cameron will make the final selection of a facility for the meeting described on page 459, plus eleven more identical meetings to be scheduled in the next twelve months. You have also been informed that the Marriott and Sheraton Hotels will be making presentations (note the comparative room, parking, and transportation rates). You will travel to Graphic Forms to make your presentation. Prepare appropriate survey, probing, confirmation, and need-satisfaction questions and presentation strategies that will help secure this important account—then role-play this presentation.

CRM APPLICATION EXERCISE

Printing the Customer Database

Sales managers regularly help salespeople review the status of their accounts. These strategic account review meetings often involve examining all the information available on the salespeople's most promising prospects. Both the sales manager and the salesperson have a copy of all information currently available for the accounts either on their computer screens or on paper. To produce a paper record of the information contained in the ACT! database, select: Lookup, Everyone, Report, Contact Report, Active Group, Printer, and Enter. Approximately 40 pages of information will be printed.

VIDEO CASE PROBLEM

When Deborah Karish wakes up in the morning, she does not have to worry about a long commute to work. Her office is in her home. As an Amgen (*www.amgen.com*) pharmaceutical sales representative, Deborah spends most of her day visiting hospitals, medical clinics, and doctors' offices. She spends a large part of each day serving as a consultant to doctors, head nurses, pharmacists, and others who need information and advice about the complex medical products available from her company. As might be expected, she also spends a considerable amount of time conducting informative presentations designed to achieve a variety of objectives. In some situations she is introducing a new product and in other cases she is providing up-to-date information on an existing product. Some of her presentations are given to individual health care professionals, and others are given to a group. Each of these presentations must be carefully planned.

Deborah uses informative and reminder presentations almost daily in her work. Informative presentations are given to doctors who are in a position to prescribe her products. The verbal presentation often is supplemented with audiovisual aids and printed materials. Reprints of articles from leading medical journals are often used to explain the success of her products in treating patients. These articles give added credibility to her presentations. Some of her informative presentations are designed to give customers updates on the prescription drugs she sells. Reminder presentations are frequently given to pharmacists who must maintain an inventory of her products. She has found that it is necessary to periodically remind pharmacists of product delivery procedures and policies and special services available from Amgen. She knows that without an occasional reminder, a customer can forget information that is beneficial.

In some cases a careful needs analysis is needed to determine if her products can solve a specific medical problem. Every patient is different, so generalizations concerning the use of her products can be dangerous. When doctors talk about their patients, Deborah must listen carefully and take good notes. In some cases she must get additional information from company support staff. If a customer needs immediate help with a problem, she gives the person a toll-free 800 number to call for expert advice. This line is an important part of the Amgen customer service program.

Deborah's career in pharmaceutical sales has required continuous learning. In the beginning she had to learn the meaning of dozens of medical terms and become familiar with a large number of medical problems. If a doctor asks, "What is the bioavailability of Neutogen?" she must know the meaning of the medical term and be knowledgeable about this Amgen product.

Deborah also spends time learning about the people with whom she works. She recently said, "If I get along with the people I work with it makes my job a lot easier." When meeting someone for the first time, she takes time to assess his communication style and then adjusts her own style to meet his needs. She points out that in some cases the competition offers a similar product at a similar price. In these situations a good relationship with the customer can influence the purchase decision. (For more information refer to the opening paragraph on page 264.)

Questions

1. If you become a pharmaceutical sales representative, how important is it to adopt the three prescriptions for a presentation strategy? Explain.
2. Deborah Karish spends a great deal of time giving individual and group presentations. Why is it essential that she be well prepared for each presentation? Why would a "canned" presentation, one that is memorized and delivered almost word for word, be inappropriate in her type of selling?
3. Salespeople are encouraged to establish multiple-objective sales presentations. What are some objectives that Deborah Karish might achieve during a sales presentation to doctors who are not currently using her products?
4. What are some special challenges faced by Deborah Karish when she makes a group presentation? How might she enhance her group presentations?
5. Put yourself in the position of a pharmaceutical sales representative. Can you envision a situation when you might combine the elements of an informative, persuasive, and reminder presentation? Explain.

CRM CASE STUDY

Planning Presentations

Becky Kemley, your sales manager at SimNet Systems, wants to meet with you this afternoon to discuss the status of your accounts. It is common for prospects to have several contacts with SimNet before ordering a network system. These multicall contacts, or sales cycle phases, usually include getting acquainted and prequalifying, need discovery, proposal presentation, closing, and account maintenance. Becky wants to know what phase each account is in and, particularly, which accounts may be ready for a presentation.

Questions

1. Which five accounts already have had a need discovery? Which two accounts are scheduled for a need discovery? Which six accounts are likely to buy but have not yet had a need discovery?
2. Which two accounts have had a need discovery and now need a product solution configured?
3. Which three accounts do not now have a network and appear to be ready for your sales presentation?
4. For those accounts listed next that are ready for your sales presentation, which strategy would you use for each: informative, persuasive, or reminder?
   - **a.** Able Profit Machines
   - **b.** Big Tex Auto Sales
   - **c.** International Studios
   - **d.** Lakeside Clinic
5. Which accounts appear to be planning to buy without a need discovery or product configuration/proposal? What risks does this pose?

PARTNERSHIP SELLING: A ROLE-PLAY/SIMULATION

(see Appendix 3, pp. 504–505)

Understanding Your Customer's Buying Strategy

Read *sales memorandum 2* ("A" or "B" depending on the account category you were assigned in Chapter 10). Your customer has called you back because you made such a good approach in call 1 and wants to visit with you about a convention recently assigned. In this call you are to use the information gathered in sales call 1 to reestablish a good relationship, discover your customer's convention needs, and set an appointment to return and make a presentation.

Follow the instructions carefully and prepare information-gathering questions prior to your appointment. Keep your information-gathering questions general and attempt to get your customer to openly share information. Use probing questions later during the appointment to gain more insight. Be careful about doing too much of the talking. In the need discovery, your customer should do most of the talking, with you taking notes and using them to ask confirmation and summary-confirmation questions to check the accuracy of your perceptions concerning what the customer wants. After this meeting, you will be asked to prepare a sales proposal from the information you have gathered.

Your instructor may again ask you to assume the role of a customer in the account category that you are not assigned to as a salesperson. If so, you will receive detailed customer instructions that you should follow closely. This will provide you with an opportunity to experience the strategic/consultative/partnering style of selling from a customer's perspective.

Chapter Preview

When you finish reading this chapter you should be able to

1 Discuss how sales demonstrations add value

2 Explain the guidelines to be followed when planning a sales demonstration

3 Complete a demonstration worksheet

4 Develop selling tools that can add value to your sales presentation

5 Discuss how to use audiovisual presentations effectively

CHAPTER 12

Creating Value with the Sales Demonstration

SimGraphics Systems (*www.simgraphics.com*) headquartered in North Brunswick, New Jersey, specializes in the development of visual simulation systems based on virtual reality. These systems have application in such diverse areas as television programming, the training of medical doctors, and product design. At the University of North Carolina, for example, medical students use a virtual reality system to learn and practice eye surgery skills before working on real patients. The SimGraphics system animates virtual characters from the motion-captured performance of a human actor in real time—as the performance is taking place. Performance animation enjoys advantages in immediacy and cost-effectiveness that cannot be matched by a traditional animation system. Needless to say, it's not easy to explain this without a well-planned demonstration. SimGraphics recently opened a state-of-the art development facility in India to tap into the huge talent pool available in that country.[1]

IMPORTANCE OF THE SALES DEMONSTRATION

In today's fuzzy, complex, out-of-focus world, customers are desperately seeking help with decisions. The salesperson who can simplify things and who can communicate with clarity will be welcomed with open arms. Every effort that is made to uncomplicate the situation adds value.[2] Throughout this text, we have defined value-added selling as a series of creative improvements that enhance the customer experience. The perception of value is enhanced with a well-developed demonstration.

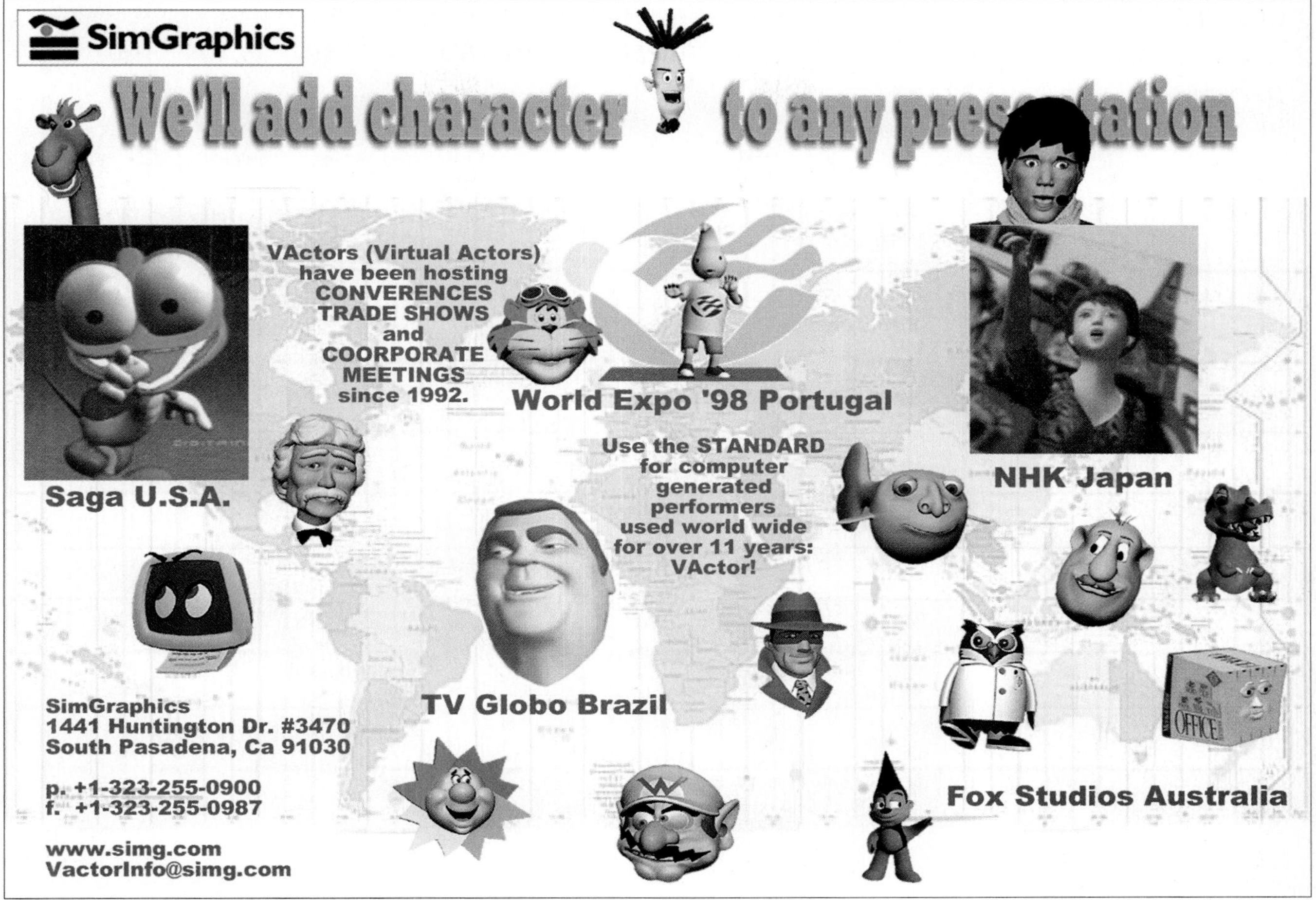

The sales force at SimGraphics must develop a well planned, value-added demonstration to explain their virtual reality based visual simulation systems. Customers with complex simulation training needs, such as a medical school, need custom-fitted demonstrations.

One of the scarcest resources today is people's attention. Some customers will be distracted and will have difficulty maintaining their concentration during the sales presentation. If the customer isn't paying attention, there is little chance of closing the sale. The increase in look-alike products and greater competition present additional challenges. The sales demonstration has become a more important communication tool. A well-planned **demonstration** adds sensory appeal to the product (Fig. 12.1). It attracts the customer's attention, stimulates interest, and creates desire. It usually is not possible to make this type of impression with words alone. The salesperson finds it easier to show what the product can do and how it can fit the customer's needs. Strategic planning, of course, sets the stage for an effective demonstration that adds value to the sale (Fig. 12.2). Some of the most important ways to create value with the demonstration are discussed next.

Improved Communication and Retention

In Chapter 3, we note the limitation of the verbal presentation; words provide only part of the meaning attached to messages that flow between the salesperson and the prospect. When we try to explain a point with words alone, people frequently do not understand our messages.

FIGURE 12.1

Conducting the Sales Demonstration

THE SIX-STEP PRESENTATION PLAN

Step One: Approach	☑ Review Strategic/Consultative Selling Model ☑ Initiate customer contact
Step Two: Presentation	☑ Determine prospect needs ☑ Select solution ☑ Initiate sales presentation
Step Three: Demonstration	☐ Decide what to demonstrate ☐ Select selling tools ☐ Initiate demonstration
Step Four: Negotiation	☐ Anticipate buyer concerns ☐ Plan negotiating methods ☐ Initiate win-win negotiations
Step Five: Close	☐ Plan appropriate closing methods ☐ Recognize closing clues ☐ Initiate closing methods
Step Six: Servicing the Sale	☐ Follow through ☐ Follow-up calls ☐ Expansion selling

Service, retail, wholesale, and manufacturer selling

Why is communication via the spoken word alone so difficult? One major reason is that we are visually oriented from birth. We grow up surrounded by the influence of movies, television, commercial advertising, Web-based messages, and other visual stimulation. People are accustomed to learning new concepts through the sense of sight or through a combination of seeing and hearing.

Many sales representatives recognize the limitations of the spoken word. When talking to prospects about the economic benefits of delivering training programs with a satellite system, a salesperson used a table (Table 12.1) to illustrate savings. With the aid of this table, prospects can visualize the economic benefits of the satellite delivery system compared with a competing system using high-bandwidth terrestrial lines.

When we rely on verbal messages alone to communicate, retention of information is minimal. A number of studies provide evidence to support this important point. Research conducted at Harvard and Columbia Universities found that retention increases from 14 to 38 percent when the spoken word is accompanied with effective visuals. In addition, the time needed to present a concept can be reduced by up to 40 percent with the use of appropriate visuals.[3]

Proof of Buyer Benefits

A well-planned and well-executed sales demonstration is one of the most convincing forms of proof. This is especially true if your product has dramatic points of superiority.

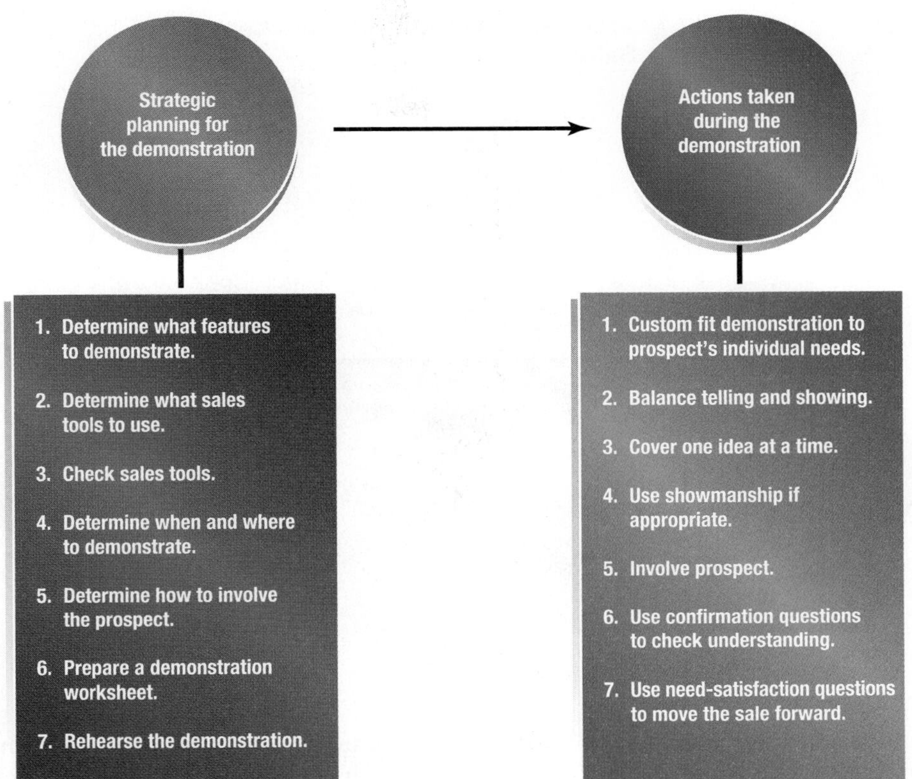

FIGURE | 12.2

Poorly conducted demonstrations usually result from a lack of strategic planning and preparation.

Salespeople representing Epson, Canon, Hewlett Packard, and other manufacturers can offer the customer a wide range of printers. What is the real difference between a $200 basic printer and a $400 high resolution laser printer? The laser equipment prints a neater and more attractive letter or report. The most effective way to provide proof of this buyer benefit is to show the customer material that has been printed on both printers. By letting the prospect compare the examples, the salesperson is converting product features to a buyer benefit. Be prepared to prove with tests, findings, and performance records every claim you make.

TABLE | 12.1 HOW MUCH CAN A SATELLITE SYSTEM SAVE YOU?

TYPE OF SYSTEM	PER PERSON COST 20 SITES	PER PERSON COST 30 SITES	PER PERSON COST 40 SITES	PER PERSON COST 50 SITES
Satellite delivery system	$7.80	$7.20	$6.60	$6.00
High-bandwidth terrestrial lines	$7.10	$7.40	$7.70	$8.00

These cost estimates are based on current satellite broadcast rates and rates for use of terrestrial lines. The per person cost is based on an audience size of 25 trainees at each site.

When salespeople use effective visual proof devices in their presentations, research indicates that retention increases from 14 to 38 percent; and the time needed to present a concept is reduced by up to 40 percent.

Proof Devices

We have noted that when trust is present, customers are more open to the sales presentation. One way to build trust is to use proof devices that enhance your credibility. **Proof devices** can take the form of a statement, a report, a testimonial, customer data, or a photograph. A salesperson selling conference services for a large hotel/conference center might use the following proof statement: "We were selected by *Training* magazine as one of the nation's top ten conference centers." Later the salesperson shows the customer photographs of the conference facilities and guest rooms. Then the customer is given a

Selling in Action

DO YOU NEED A VOICE COACH?

African Americans, Hispanics, Asians, Native Americans, and recent immigrants to America often face special challenges in verbal communication. New arrivals may have a unique accent because the phonetic habits of their native language are carried over to the new language. Many people born and raised in America have a strong regional accent. Should this uniqueness be viewed as a problem? Kim Radford, vice president of marketing at Wachovia Trust Company, had to answer this question soon after graduating from college. He took a position as a stockbroker in Charleston, West Virginia. Radford, an African American, conducted most of his business on the telephone and seldom met clients face-to-face. Early on, someone said, "Kim, you need to get that black accent out of your voice if you're going to be successful in this business." Radford faced a real dilemma: He wanted to be successful, but he did not want to compromise his personal integrity. He talked to several people, black and white, and the advice he received boiled down to this guideline:

> Stay honest to yourself, but communicate and be understood. There's no need to clean up the fact that you sound black as long as you're articulate and your diction's good and people can understand you.

It is a fact of life that people in every community are certain that the way they talk is the "natural" way. So if you believe that your accent and dialect need to be changed, or you want to improve pronunciation, consider seeking help from a voice coach.[a]

copy of a testimonial letter from a satisfied customer. The statement, photos, and letter help build the customer's confidence in the product. Later in this chapter we will examine proof devices in more detail.

Feeling of Ownership

Many effective sales demonstrations give the prospect a temporary feeling of ownership. This pleasant feeling builds desire to own the product. Let us consider the person who enters a men's clothing store and tries on an Oxxford suit which features the highest quality fabrics and hundreds of hand-stitched features that improve comfort and fit. The salesperson notes that there are 900 hand stitches in the collar alone. During the few minutes the customer is wearing the suit a feeling a pride is apt to develop, and desire to own an Oxxford suit will likely build.[4]

Many firms offer prospects an opportunity to enjoy products on a trial basis. This is done to give people a chance to assess the merits of the product in their own home or business. Some firms that sell office equipment and office furniture use this sales strategy.

Quantifying the Solution

In Chapter 6 we explained that the process of determining whether or not a sales proposal adds value is called *quantifying the solution*. If the cost of the proposal is offset by added value, closing the sale will be much easier. In business-to-business selling, quantifying the solution is very common. Let's assume you represent a manufacturing company that sells robots—a reprogrammable machine capable of performing a variety of tasks. The two primary benefits are (1) payroll cost savings and (2) vastly improved quality. One way to quantify the solution in this case is to use simple **cost–benefit analysis**. This involves listing the costs to the buyer and the savings to be achieved from the purchase of the robots.

Another way to quantify the solution is to calculate the net profits or savings, expressed as a percentage of the original investment. This is called **return on investment**. Using the following formula, you can determine the net profits or savings from a given investment.

$$\text{ROI} = \text{Net Profits (or Savings) divided by Investment} \times 100$$

If the robotic system costs $16,000 but saves the firm $4000, the ROI is 25 percent ($\$4000/\$16{,}000 \times 100 = 25\%$). Some companies set a minimum ROI for new products or cost-saving programs. Salespeople often acquire this information at the need assessment stage and then include it in the written proposal.

Space does not permit a review of the many methods of quantifying the solution. Some of the additional ways include payback period, opportunity cost, net present value, after-tax cash flow, turnover, and contribution margin.

The Value Proposition Revisited

Most customers are searching for the product that offers the most value. Salespeople who position their product with a value proposition (introduced in Chapter 7) are in a strong position to close the sale. The value proposition includes a mix of key benefits and values on which the product is positioned. Very often the sales demonstration is the vehicle used to present several, if not all, of the major benefits. Principal Financial Group has positioned itself as a leader in 401(k) retirement solutions. The company can customize a plan for both small and large business firms. Principal also works hard to provide excellent customer service. All of the major benefits offered by this company can be highlighted in the demonstration.

The value proposition includes a mix of key benefits to meet the needs of the customer. This ad illustrates the three parts of Durkee's value proposition: support, flavor, and performance.

Courtesy of Tone Brothers, Inc.

PLANNING DEMONSTRATIONS THAT ADD VALUE

A sales demonstration that adds value is the result of both planning and practice. Planning gives the salesperson a chance to review all the important details that should be considered in advance of the actual demonstration. Practice (or rehearsal) provides an opportunity for a trial run to uncover areas that need additional polish. For large, complex sales the salesperson should plan to spend several hours preparing for the sales presentation.[5] During the planning stage it helps to review a series of guidelines that has helped salespeople over the years to develop effective demonstrations.

Develop Creative Demonstrations

Presenting product features and buyer benefits in an interesting and appealing way requires some amount of creativity. Creativity is needed to develop a sales demonstration that can gain attention, increase desire, and add value. The ability to come up with problem-solving answers or different ways of looking at situations is greatly valued in today's fast-changing business environment. Creativity is enhanced by expertise in the field of endeavor. For salespeople, this means knowledge of the sales process, product knowledge, and an understanding of human behavior. Creativity is also enhanced by the capacity for divergent thinking and a willingness to take risks.[6]

Use Custom-Fitted Demonstrations

In nonmanipulative selling, each presentation is custom tailored because individual client problems and priorities are unique. In other words, every aspect of the sales presentation, including the demonstration, should relate to the needs or problems mutually identified by the prospect and the salesperson.

It is possible to develop a sales demonstration so structured and so mechanical that the prospect feels like a number. We must try to avoid what some veteran marketing people refer to as the *depersonalization* of the selling/buying process. If the demonstration is overly structured, it cannot be personalized to meet specific customer wants and needs.

Bell Helicopter (*www.bellhelicopter.com*) sells several models with countless custom options, and each option changes its price and performance. One customer may want a helicopter for emergency medical care and another may want one for electronic news gathering. Bell's sales force, all of whom are licensed helicopter pilots, can introduce the Bell product line with a video presentation and then follow up with a demonstration flight if necessary. Sales representatives also have access to a sales configuration system that supports the customization process. Price and performance

Selling in Action

TRACKING DOWN A SALE

Care Trak (*www.caretrak.com*) is a product designed to locate patients who suffer from the effects of brain injuries or Alzheimer's disease who may wander away from a care center and get lost. During a sales call at a New Jersey nursing home, a sales representative was explaining the benefits of Care Trak when a doubting staff member picked up the transmitter and asked the salesperson to wait 20 minutes and then try to find him. After a 20-minute wait, the salesperson began the search under the watchful eyes of the nursing home administrator and members of the nursing staff. After tracking the staff member to a specific location, the locater signal became very strong in spite of the fact that they were standing in the middle of an empty hallway. At that point the staff members began having doubts about the value of the equipment. Then the salesperson pointed the directional antenna straight up to the ceiling. He pushed aside a ceiling tile to reveal the nursing home employee in his hiding place. The nursing home placed an order for the product that day.[b]

Bell's 18-member sales force, all of whom are licensed helicopter pilots, can introduce the Bell product line with a video presentation and then follow up with a demonstration flight if necessary.

data can be quickly determined for each accessory needed by the customer. The software automatically provides answers to the numerous questions that can surface during the sales presentation.[7]

Choose the Right Setting

The location of the sales demonstration can make a difference. Some companies routinely rent space at a hotel, motel, or conference center so that the demonstration can be conducted in a controlled environment free of noise and other interruptions. Many organizations have conference rooms that can be reserved with advanced notice. In these busy times, prospects are often unwilling or unable to participate in a presentation held off premises.

Check Sales Tools

Be sure to check every item to be used in conjunction with the sales demonstration. If you are using audiovisual equipment, be certain that it is in good working condition. Always carry an extension cord and a spare bulb. If you are making a laptop presentation, be sure you can go online in front of the customer. If you plan to demonstrate a Web site, save it on a hard disk instead of going online. Be prepared for technological snags by having multiple backups. Always carry extra batteries for your laptop.[8]

Cover One Idea at a Time and Confirm Agreement

Pace the demonstration so that the customer does not become confused. Offer one idea at a time, and be sure the customer understands each point before moving on. When you neglect this practice, there is the danger that the customer's concentration may remain fixed on a previous point. Some demonstrations are ruined by a salesperson who moves too rapidly from one point to another. Consider using a confirmation question to get agreement on each key point before moving on to the next. One objective of the sales demonstration is to increase the customer's desire for a solution to their problem. Therefore, a *need-satisfaction question* (see Chapter 11) can help move the sale forward. During the demonstration of an animation publishing platform, the salesperson might say, "This program can help you produce a complex animation in a very short period of time. Do you often work on projects with tight deadlines?"

Appeal to All Senses

In conducting a sales demonstration it is a good idea to appeal to all appropriate senses. Each of the five senses—sight, hearing, smell, touch, and taste—represents an avenue by which the salesperson can attract the prospect's attention and build desire.

Although sight is considered the most powerful attention-attracting sense, it may not be the most important motivating force in every selling situation. When

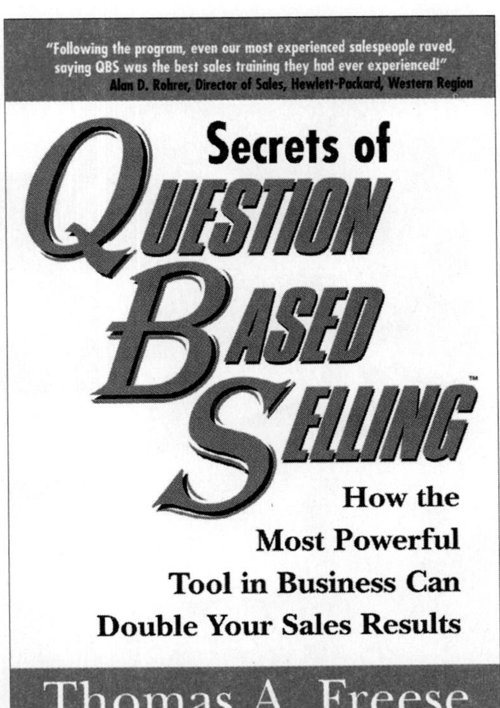

QUESTION BASED SELLING (www.qbsresearch.com)*, used in sales organizations around the world, focuses on asking the right questions that pique customer interest, build credibility, uncover greater needs, and solicit more accurate information.*

presenting a food product, the taste and aroma may be critical. Designers and decorators tell us that most furniture buyers still want to touch and feel the product before they buy it.

Gary Eberle, owner of Eberle Winery (*www.eberle.com*) located in San Luis Obispo County, California, understands the importance of reaching the prospect through as many senses as possible. He spends considerable time each year selling his wines to retailers and restaurant owners.[9] The sales presentation for a quality wine usually highlights four areas:

Consumer demand. The wine's sales potential is described in realistic terms.

Marketing strategies. Suggested ways to merchandise the wine are discussed.

Bouquet. The distinctive fragrance of the wine is introduced.

Taste. A sample of the wine is given to the prospect in a quality wineglass.

Note that a sales presentation featuring these appeals can reach the prospect through four of the five senses. Collectively, these appeals add value. When you involve more than one sense, the sales presentation is more informative and more persuasive.

Balance Telling, Showing, and Involvement

A Chinese proverb says "Tell me, I'll forget; show me, I may remember; but involve me and I'll understand."[10] Some of the most effective sales demonstrations combine telling, showing, and involvement of the prospect. To plan an effective demonstration, consider developing a demonstration worksheet. Simply divide a sheet of paper into four columns. Head the first column, "Feature to Be Demonstrated." Head the second column, "Proof Device to Be Used." Head the third column, "What I Will Say." Head the

In a complex sale, it is imperative to check every part of your demonstration prior to the presentation. During the presentation you should cover one idea at a time and secure agreement before moving on.

Dunbar's sales force can use a combination demonstration/premium approach by offering their "Tasting Kit." Dunbar knows that by appealing to the senses of taste, sight, hearing, and touch, they can add value to their presentation.

fourth column, "What I or the Customer Will Do." List the major features you plan to demonstrate in proper sequence in the first column. In the second column describe the proof devices you will use. In the third column, describe what you will say about the feature, converting the feature to a customer benefit. In the fourth column, describe what you (or the customer) will do at the time this benefit is discussed. A sample demonstration worksheet appears in Figure 12.3.

Prospects can be involved in many demonstrations. Two examples follow:

Furniture. To prove comfort or quality, have the buyer sit in a chair, lie on a mattress, or feel the highly polished finish of a coffee table.

Clothing. Have the customer try it on to highlight style, fit, and comfort features. This involvement is especially important in the sale of quality garments.

If it is not possible for the prospect to participate in the demonstration or handle the product, place sales literature, pictures, or brochures in the person's hands. After the sales call these items remind the prospect of not only who called but also why.

FIGURE | 12.3

The demonstration worksheet enables the salesperson to strategically plan and then rehearse demonstrations that strengthen the presentation.

Demonstration Worksheet			
Feature to Be Demonstrated	Proof Device to Be Used	What I Will Say (Include Benefit)	What I or the Customer Will Do
Special computer circuit board to accelerate drawing graphics on a color monitor screen.	Monitor and software	"This monitor is large enough to display multiple windows. You can easily compare several graphics."	Have the customer bring up several windows using computer keyboard.
Meeting room setup at a hotel and conference center.	Floor plan	"This setup will provide 3 feet of elbow space for each participant. For long meetings, the added space provides more comfort."	Give the customer a tour of the room and invite her to sit in a chair at one of the conference tables.

Rehearse the Demonstration

While you are actually putting on the demonstration, you need to be concentrating on a variety of details. The movements you make and what you say and do should be so familiar to you that each response is nearly automatic. To achieve this level of skill, you need to rehearse the demonstration.

Rehearse both what you are going to say and what you are going to do. Say the words aloud exactly as if the prospect were present. It is surprising how often a concept that seems quite clear as you think it over becomes hopelessly mixed up when you try to discuss it with a customer. Rehearsal is the best way to avoid this embarrassing situation. Whenever possible, have your presentation/demonstration videotaped before you give it. This is perhaps the best way to perfect what you say and do.

Plan for the Dynamic Nature of Selling

The sales presentation is a dynamic activity. From the moment the salesperson and the customer meet, the sales presentation is being altered and fine-tuned to reflect the new information available. The salesperson must be able to execute strategy instantaneously. In the movie *Top Gun*, Kelly McGillis asks Tom Cruise, "What were you thinking up there?" His reply was, "You don't have time to think. You take time to think up there, you're dead." By that he meant the response must be habit and reflex.[11]

During a typical presentation the salesperson asks numerous questions, discusses several product features, and demonstrates the appropriate product benefits. The customer also is asking questions and, in many cases, voicing concerns. The successful sales presentation is a good model of two-way communication. Because of the dynamic nature of the sales presentation, the salesperson must be prepared to apply several different selling skills to meet the variety of buyer responses. Figure 12.4 illustrates how the various selling skills can be applied during all parts of the sales presentation. In creating effective presentations the salesperson should be prepared to meet a wide range of buyer responses with effective questions, benefit statements, demonstrations, negotiating methods, and closing methods.

Consultative selling skills	Parts of the Sales Presentation			
	Need discovery	Selecting solution	Need–satisfaction presentation	Servicing the sale
Questioning skills	• As a question approach • To find needs and buying motives • To probe for buying motives • To confirm needs and buying motives	• To confirm selection	• To confirm benefits • To confirm mutual understanding • To increase desire for a solution	• To make suggestions • To confirm delivery and installation • To resolve complaints • To build goodwill • To secure credit arrangements
Presenting benefits	• As a benefit approach • To discover specific benefits	• To match up with buying motives	• To build support for the solution	• To make suggestions • To use credit as a close
Demonstrating skills	• As a product approach • To clarify need	• To clarify selection	• To strengthen product claims	• When making effective suggestions
Negotiating skills	• To overcome initial resistance to sales interview • To overcome need objection	• To overcome product objection	• To overcome source, price, and time objections	• In handling complaints • To overcome financing objection
Closing skills	• When customer has made buying decision	• When buyer immediately recognizes solutions	• Whenever buyer presents closing signals	• After suggestion • To secure repeats and referrals

FIGURE | 12.4

The Selling Dynamics Matrix

A sales demonstration that creates value increases the dynamic nature of personal selling.

PROOF DEVICES FOR EFFECTIVE DEMONSTRATIONS

Nearly every sales organization provides its staff with sales tools or proof devices of one kind or another. Many of these, when used correctly, add value to the sales effort. If the company does not provide these items, the creative salesperson secures or develops sales tools independently. In addition to technology-based presentations, sales personnel can utilize a wide range of other selling tools. Creative salespeople are continually developing new types of sales tools. The following section summarizes some of the most common tools used today.

Product and Plant Tours

Without a doubt the best-selling aid is often the product itself. As noted previously, Bell Helicopter uses an effective video to describe various products. However, some customers do not buy without a demonstration ride. In the growing market for ergonomic office chairs, ranging in price from $700 to $1,500, furniture makers know the best way to close the sale is to provide an opportunity for the customer to sit in the chair. With growing awareness of the hazards of poor sitting posture and bad ergonomics, more people are searching for a comfortable work chair.[12]

Doug Adams was the first salesperson hired by a major manufacturer of high-quality optical equipment. Although he was not a technician or an engineer, he quickly realized that the equipment had product superiority that physicians would recognize if they saw it demonstrated. During the first year he sold 28 machines, far surpassing the expectations of his employer.[13]

As noted in a previous chapter, plant tours provide an excellent source of product information. EMP (Engineered Machine Products) makes high-efficiency thermal management systems for cooling engines. Products are made at a state-of-the art manufacturing facility in Escanaba, Michigan. The company has learned that the key to closing many large, complex sales is a facility tour.[14]

Models

In some cases it is not practical to demonstrate the product itself because it is too big or immobile. It is easier to demonstrate a small-scale model or cross section of the original equipment. A working model, like the actual product, can give the prospect a clear picture of how a piece of equipment operates.

With the aid of modern technology it's possible to create a model in picture form. ClosetMaid (*www.closetmaid.com*), a manufacturer of ventilated wire for commercial closets and other storage products, uses desktop visualization software to create a three-dimensional presentation that allows customers to see exactly what the finished facility will look like. Sales representatives can print out a hard copy so the customer has a picture of the custom-designed model for future reference. With the aid of this visualization technology, ClosetMaid salespeople can modify closet layouts on screen and produce a detailed bill of materials for each project.[15]

Photos, Illustrations, and Brochures

The old proverb, "One picture is worth a thousand words," can be put into practical application by a creative salesperson. A great deal of valuable information can be given to the prospect with the aid of photos and illustrations. Chris Roberts, area manager for Downing Displays, a manufacturer of trade show displays, says that the photo presentation book is the most important item he takes on a first sales call. He says, "Because what we sell is very visual, it's important for the client to *see* the displays."[16]

Many companies develop brochures that visually reinforce specific need/benefit areas. Brochures can be effective during the initial discussion of needs when the salesperson wants to provide a brief overview of possible solutions. Someone planning to remodel a kitchen might be given a Colors of Corian brochure that features color photos of numerous countertop materials and kitchen design examples.[17]

Portfolio

A **portfolio** is a portable case or loose-leaf binder containing a wide variety of sales-supporting materials. The portfolio is used to add visual life to the sales message and to prove claims. A person who sells advertising might develop a portfolio including the following items:

Successful advertisements used in conjunction with previous campaigns

Selected illustrations that can be incorporated into advertisements

A selection of testimonial letters

One or more case histories of specific clients who have used the media with success

The portfolio has been used as a sales tool by people who sell interior design services, insurance, real estate, securities, and convention services. It is a flexible proof device that can be revised at any time to meet the needs of each customer.

Reprints

Leading magazines and journals sometimes feature articles that directly or indirectly support the salesperson's product. A reprint of the article can be a forceful selling tool. It is also an inexpensive selling tool. Pharmaceutical and medical sales representatives often use reprints from journals that report on research in the field of medicine. A few years ago Closure Medical Corporation received approval to sell Dermabond (*www.dermabond.com*), a surgical glue used to close cuts. This innovative product received national attention when the prestigious *Journal of the American Medical*

Global Business Etiquette

DOING BUSINESS IN ITALY

The majority of Italian Americans have roots in Sicily or southern Italy. American businesspeople tend to think that all Italians are like the Italian Americans whom they have had contact with in America. In reality, Italy is a very varied country where you will find all types of physical characteristics—fair, dark, short, tall, and varied accents and customs.

- Italian businesspeople tend to be quite formal in terms of introductions and dress. When you introduce yourself, say your last name only and then shake hands. Wait until invited to use your first name. Personal and professional titles are used almost all the time in business dealings.
- Entertaining clients should be done at restaurants, not in the home.
- Most Italian businesspeople are not in a hurry, so be patient and do not try to rush the sale.
- The practice of gift giving will vary. A nominal gift such as a bottle of wine at Christmas is quite common.[c]

Salespeople can add value to their presentation with the aid of photos and illustrations. This salesperson has balanced telling, showing, and involvement by getting the sales literature in the hands of the prospect.

Association concluded that gluing a wound could be just as effective as sewing it shut. Salespeople representing Dermabond used the article to help educate doctors on the product's merits and applications.[18]

In many cases prospects are far more impressed with the good points of your product if they are presented by a third party rather than you. A reprint from a respected journal can be very persuasive.

Catalogs

A well-designed catalog shows the range and comprehensiveness of your product line. It may include specifications needed for installation and current price information. If you plan to give customers a copy of your catalog, review the important features such as a comprehensive index or important appendix material.[19]

Graphs, Charts, and Test Results

Graphs and charts can be used to illustrate the change of some variable such as payroll expense, fuel consumption, or return on investment. For example, a bar graph might be used to illustrate the increase in fuel costs over a 10-year period.

Although graphs are usually quite descriptive, the layperson may misunderstand them. It is best to interpret the graph for the prospect. Do not move too fast because the full impact of the message may be lost.

Test results from a reliable agency often can be convincing. This is especially true when the test results are published by a respected independent agency such as J. D. Power and Associates.

Laptop Computers and Demonstration Software

A survey conducted by *Selling Power* magazine found that 87 percent of salespeople use laptops during their sales presentations.[20] Many salespeople will tell you that the laptop computer is the single most powerful sales tool they use. Many of the things needed during the demonstration can be stored in the computer. If the customer is interested in a specific product, pull up the appropriate brochure or videotape on your laptop screen. If the client wants a copy of printed material, you can either print the pages or send them via e-mail. If the customer raises a question regarding product availability, use your laptop to access the information. You can place an order and in some cases print an invoice.[21]

Thanks to modern computer technology it's possible to conduct impressive multiple, simultaneous product demonstrations without leaving your office. Let's assume you are presenting a new employee disability insurance plan to members of the DaimlerChrysler human resources staff. One key decision maker is based in Germany and the other in the United States. With the aid of Pixion PictureTalk software, or a similar product, you can use the Internet to conduct the demonstration for both persons in real time. Sales managers might use this same approach to train members of their sales team in remote offices.

Personal computers (PCs) with the support of online presentation technologies and presentation software have played an important role in increasing sales force productivity. Salespeople have instant access to customer data, so it is often easier to customize the sales presentation. Many salespeople report that PC-based presentations, using graphics software, are very effective. Today's PC can produce striking visuals and attractive printed material that can be given to the customer for future reference.

Enhancing Demonstrations with PowerPoint

The PowerPoint software program from Microsoft has been available to salespeople for almost 20 years. PowerPoint is so common that many prospects find the standard presentation graphics very familiar, even dull. Salespeople who want their demonstration

A growing number of salespeople are using laptop computers in conjunction with sales presentations. Graphics software can enhance the laptop presentation.

Graphs produced with Excel software can add value and be very persuasive in demonstrating key benefits of a sales presentation. This Excel graph also uses a PowerPoint background design to add more value. Go to www.prenhall.com/manning and click on Caxambas PowerPoint Presentation to view a PowerPoint sales presentation.

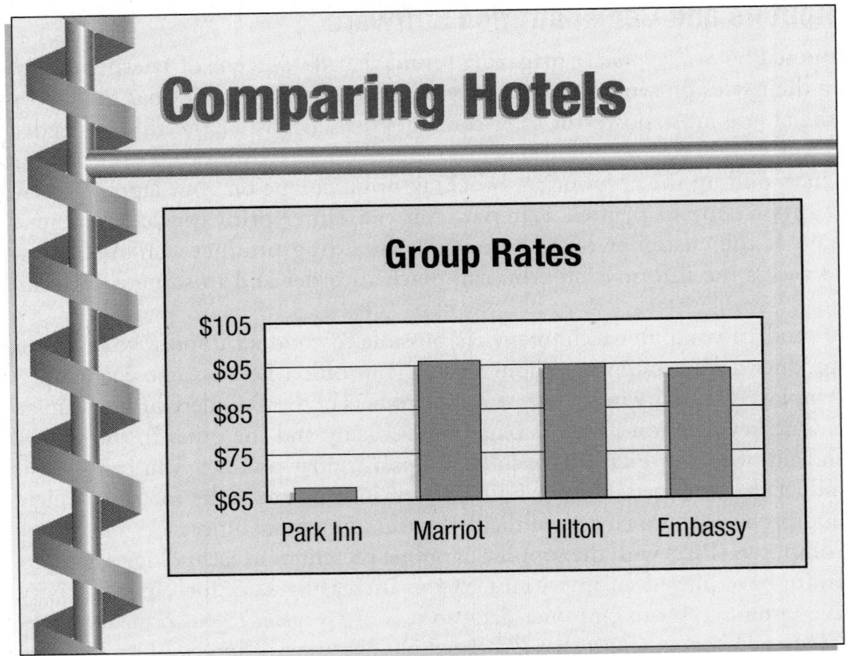

to look unique and different can create their own corporate template, animate their logo, or put video clips of their own company information into the PowerPoint presentation. When developing a PowerPoint presentation, use bold, simple and large fonts (such as Arial and Veranda) and put graphics on several slides. Limit the number of words to 15 or less per slide.[22]

Creating Electronic Spreadsheets

For many years, salespeople have been using electronic spreadsheets to prepare sales proposals. The electronic spreadsheet is an excellent tool to organize the numbers involved in preparing quotes, such as quantities, costs, and prices. The electronic spreadsheet allows the user to answer "what if" questions about the effects of lowering costs or raising prices. Once the preparation work is finished, the electronic spreadsheet itself can be printed and used to serve as the proposal or to accompany the proposal.[23] The spreadsheet data can also be converted to a chart or graph that can enhance the proposal.

Many computers sold today include an electronic spreadsheet program. The leading electronic spreadsheet, Excel, is part of Microsoft's Office Suite of products. If you have access to Excel, or any other electronic spreadsheet software, you can explore the power of this tool for preparing proposals.

Web-Based Demonstrations

Some salespeople create computerized demonstrations that are stored in a central library and accessed on demand. With a few clicks of a mouse, presenters can call up the information they wish to showcase using a Web browser. Salespeople can also use WebEx's Meeting Center to deliver interactive presentations to customers in various locations. Meeting

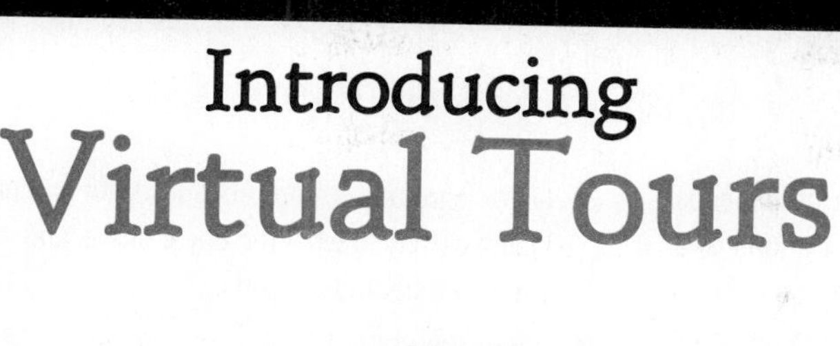

Virtual reality tours enable real estate salespeople to add value to the demonstration of the features of a home for sale. This technology should be carefully planned and integrated into the sales process. Of course, clients can also access this information on their own.

Center presentations integrate data, voice, and video with a standard Web browser. The salesperson can show PowerPoint presentations, present product features, and conduct question and answer sessions in real time.[24]

The WebEx Presentation Studio solution is available for added client convenience. Salespeople create the demonstration, record it, and then make it available to prospects. The prospect decides when and where to view the presentation.[25]

Bound Paper Presentations

Although many salespeople are using some type of presentation technology in conjunction with the sales demonstration, paper is still widely used. For many sales and marketing organizations, bound paper presentations continue to be a very popular medium.[26]

Selling Is Everyone's Business

LEARNING TO PLAY THE GAME

The survival of many small business firms depends on winning contracts with large corporations and government agencies. Many of the action steps needed to win contracts are the same as those steps taken by salespeople to win sales.

- Achieve exposure among procurement officers by attending conferences, trade shows, and business fairs. Make contacts and follow up.
- Listen carefully during meetings with procurement officers. Listen closely to what the buyer needs and then determine if you can meet those needs.
- Adopt the marketing concept, which means dedicating all policies, planning, and operation to the satisfaction of the customer.
- Never make promises you can't keep. Don't bid on a contract unless you can deliver the product on time.[d]

With the aid of computer-generated graphics, it is easy to print attractive graphs, charts, and other proof information. Product guarantees and warranties are sometimes included in a bound paper presentation. Some marketers use guarantees and warranties to differentiate their products from competing products. Customer testimonials represent another common element of bound paper presentations. A testimonial letter from a prominent satisfied customer provides persuasive evidence that the product has support in the industry. Prospects like bound paper presentations because the document is readily available for future reference.

Audiovisual Presentation Fundamentals

Many companies provide their salespeople with audiovisual aids such as videotapes or computer-based presentations. Unfortunately, they sometimes fail to explain how to use these tools in the most effective way. Here are some suggestions on how to use audiovisual presentations to achieve maximum impact.

1. Never rely too heavily on "bells and whistles" to sell your products. Audiovisual technology provides support for the major points in your presentation, but it does not replace an interactive sales demonstration.
2. Be sure the prospect knows the purpose of the presentation. Preview the material and describe a few highlights. Always try to build interest in advance of the audiovisual presentation.
3. Be prepared to stop the presentation to clarify a point or to allow the prospect to ask questions. Do not permit the audiovisual presentation to become a barrier to good two-way communication.
4. At the conclusion of the audiovisual presentation, review key points and allow the prospect an opportunity to ask questions.

Audiovisual technology can provide support for the major points in your presentation. No matter how exotic the sales tool, remember you are still the central figure in the selling situation.

Summary

In selling, the prospect is moving from a known quantity (the money in hand or an obligation for future payment) to something of an unknown quantity (amount of satisfaction to be gained from the potential purchase). With most people this produces anxiety and insecurity. The professional salesperson reduces prospect anxiety and insecurity by supplying proof of product performance. The objective of the *demonstration* is to supply this proof. The demonstration can also help the customer better understand the solution to their problem.

People perceive impressions through the five senses. In the presentation the salesperson communicates verbally to the prospect primarily through the sense of sound. In the demonstration the salesperson broadens communication strategy to include as many of the other senses as possible. Generally, the more senses we appeal to, the more effective our sales appeal becomes.

This chapter includes a series of guidelines to be followed when planning a sales demonstration. Completion of a demonstration worksheet is an important first step in preparing an effective sales demonstration.

Nearly every marketing-driven organization provides its salespeople with a variety of sales tools to use in the demonstration. A partial list of these tools includes the product itself, models, photos, reprints, portfolios, graphs, charts, test results, testimonials, audiovisual presentations via laptop computers, demonstration software, catalogs, and bound paper presentations.

KEY TERMS

Demonstration
Proof devices
Portfolio
Cost–benefit analysis
Return on investment

REVIEW QUESTIONS

1. List the benefits of using a sales demonstration during the presentation of a product or service.
2. Assume the role of a sales representative for a large newspaper. What type of portfolio would you use during a sales call?
3. Discuss the advantages of using the demonstration worksheet.
4. Explain why a salesperson should organize the sales presentation so that it appeals to as many of the five senses as possible.
5. List the guidelines to follow in planning an effective demonstration.
6. Develop a list of the sales tools that the salesperson should consider when planning a sales demonstration.
7. Describe the merits of a bound paper presentation. What can be done to strengthen the persuasive power of a bound paper presentation?
8. Explain how magazine and trade journal reprints can be used to assist the salesperson in a persuasive sales presentation.
9. Describe the audiovisual presentation fundamentals.
10. What are some of the common sales functions performed by small, laptop computers and demonstration software?

APPLICATION EXERCISES

1. In many selling situations it is difficult, if not impossible, to demonstrate the product itself. List means other than the product itself that can be used to demonstrate the product features and benefits.

2. Develop a list of sales tools you could use in a job interview situation. What tools could you use to demonstrate your skills and capabilities?
3. As noted in this chapter, demonstration software is becoming increasingly popular. Real estate salespeople are using this software to showcase homes to prospective buyers. Assume you are a salesperson for First Realty GMAC Real Estate, and you have a customer who wants a $250,000 to $300,000 home in the Des Moines suburb of Clive. Go to the *www.firstrealtyhomes.com* Web site and click on the "select a Des Moines Area City" button. Next select the suburb "Clive" and click on "Go." Input the data you have from your customer and request a search for homes in this category. From your search, select two homes and click on the "virtual tour" button. Examine the exterior and interior features of these two homes.

ROLE-PLAY EXERCISE

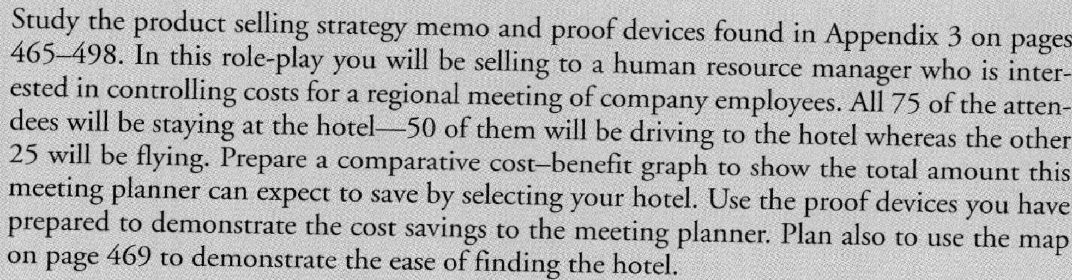
Study the product selling strategy memo and proof devices found in Appendix 3 on pages 465–498. In this role-play you will be selling to a human resource manager who is interested in controlling costs for a regional meeting of company employees. All 75 of the attendees will be staying at the hotel—50 of them will be driving to the hotel whereas the other 25 will be flying. Prepare a comparative cost–benefit graph to show the total amount this meeting planner can expect to save by selecting your hotel. Use the proof devices you have prepared to demonstrate the cost savings to the meeting planner. Plan also to use the map on page 469 to demonstrate the ease of finding the hotel.

VIDEO CASE PROBLEM

Simulation has proven to be a very cost-effective training method. Commercial airline pilots can practice takeoff and landing procedures over and over again without endangering the lives of passengers. Medical students can develop basic surgery skills with the aid of a virtual reality system. This practice precedes working on real patients. SimGraphics Engineering Corporation, based in South Pasadena, California, specializes in the development of visual simulation systems. Steve Tice, president, and Steve Glenn, vice president of new business development, are frequently involved in sales presentations. Prior to a sales call they try to answer several questions:

- *What is the customer's area of expertise?* Someone with an engineering background will usually want to know how the system was developed and may ask specific technical questions. In contrast, the customer who works primarily in entertainment or the design of training programs will be more focused on the creative applications of a particular system.
- *What type of demonstration is best for this client?* SimGraphics has developed a system that animates virtual characters from the motion-captured performance of a human actor in real time—as the performance is taking place. One option is to videotape the human actor who is preparing the performance animation. The video can be shown in the client's office or conference room. The other option is to let the customer see the actual performance animation process. Moving the equipment from the SimGraphics laboratory to a client's office is possible. The sales staff must also decide which finished products, developed for other clients, should be integrated into the demonstration.
- *What is the most effective way to quantify the solution?* Performance animation enjoys advantages in cost-effectiveness that traditional animation systems cannot match. The

sales staff must determine the best way to illustrate cost-effectiveness. This will usually require obtaining certain information from the customer.

- *Will it be necessary to develop a prototype visual simulation prior to the sales demonstration?* In some cases, the needs of the customer are so unique that no existing product is suitable for the demonstration. In this case, a prototype is required.

Questions

1. You have decided to prepare a value proposition for a customer who has indicated an interest in your product. What are some of the key benefits you would include in the proposition?
2. Assume that you are preparing a sales presentation for a customer who has spent several years as a movie director. Today he is developing training programs for a *Fortune* 500 company. Describe how you would organize the sales demonstration for this client.
3. How might you quantify the solution if the customer is a small manufacturing company with a need for a safety training program?

CRM CASE STUDY

Custom Fitting the Demonstrations

Your SimNet Systems sales manager, Becky Kemley, has asked you to meet with her to discuss demonstrations. She wants you to tell her if any of your accounts need a demonstration and, if so, what type of demonstration.

Questions

1. Which two accounts need a demonstration of the speed and power capabilities of the recommended network?
2. Which account needs to be shown that the recommended network product configuration can meet the account's specifications?
3. Which account with many sites needs a demonstration of SimNet's ability to put together a complex solution?
4. Which account seeking a low price needs a testimonial of SimNet's value-added ability to help customers maximize the power of their network?
5. Which account needs a demonstration of SimNet's financial stability?

PARTNERSHIP SELLING: A ROLE-PLAY/SIMULATION

(see Appendix 3, pp. 508–509, 512–517)

Developing a Sales Presentation Strategy—The Demonstration

Read *sales memorandum 3* ("A" or "B" depending on the category you were assigned in sales call 1). In this role-play your call objectives are to make a persuasive presentation, negotiate any customer concerns, and close and service the sale.

At this time you should complete item 1 of the presentation plan and prepare and price a product solution. This should include completing the sales proposal form. Also, you should obtain a three-ring binder with pockets in the front and back for the development of a portfolio presentation. In this binder you should prepare your presentation and demonstration, following the instructions in items 2a, 2b, 2c, and 2d under the presentation plan. The presentation and demonstration materials (use the product strategy materials, i.e., photos, price lists, menus, awards, etc., provided to you with employment memorandum 1) should be placed in the three-ring binder as a part of your portfolio presentation.

Using PowerPoint and Excel software, you may want to produce computer-generated presentation graphics to enhance your demonstrations. For instructions on how to produce computer-generated presentation graphics see Parts 2 and 3 in *Selling Today: Creating Value With Computers.*

You should also consider using presentation paper and sheet protectors. You may want to select a person as your customer and rehearse the use of these materials.

Chapter Preview

When you finish reading this chapter you should be able to

1 Describe negotiations as part of a win-win strategy

2 Describe common types of buyer concerns

3 Outline general strategies for negotiating buyer concerns

4 Discuss specific methods of negotiating buyer concerns

5 Describe ways to deal effectively with buyers who are trained in negotiating

CHAPTER 13

Negotiating Buyer Concerns

The Renaissance Esmeralda Resort and Spa, (*www.renaissanceesmeralda.com*) formerly the Stouffer Esmeralda, located in Indian Wells, California, is a world-class hotel that offers the guest almost every amenity except a view of the ocean. The resort is located in the desert. Business meeting planners, representing groups from 50 to 500 persons, frequently seek what is called a *water destination*, a meeting site near a lake or the ocean. Brian Moon, sales manager at the Renaissance Esmeralda Resort and Spa, has a ready response when customers raise concerns about a land-based location. He describes the exquisite swimming pools offered by the Esmeralda and the Oasis water park that can be used for water games. A wave machine is used at the water park to simulate ocean waves. He also describes the other recreation facilities that include a golf course, tennis courts, and a health spa. The Esmeralda boosts 100,000 square feet of truly unique indoor and outdoor function space and state-of-the-art conference facilities. Of course, some types of buyer concerns are not communicated openly to Brian and other members of the sales staff. He must often work hard to identify the resistance, clarify it, and then overcome it.[1]

1 NEGOTIATING BUYER CONCERNS AND PROBLEMS

Many sales professionals are very proficient in need discovery and selecting the right solution, but are weak in the area of negotiating an agreement that is favorable to the customer and the salesperson's firm. Some salespeople fail to

The Esmeralda Resort and Spa is a world class hotel and convention center. Brian Moon, sales manager, uses a win-win strategy to negotiate with professional meeting planners who are experienced negotiators. These planners press hard for concessions including lower room and meal rates, complimentary suites or complimentary events such as a themed party.

anticipate buyer concerns and plan negotiating methods (Fig. 13.1). A common mistake is making last minute concessions in order to close the sale.[2] In this chapter, we describe effective strategies for anticipating and negotiating buyer concerns.

We have noted previously that the heaviest time investment in value-added selling is on the front end of the sale. This is especially true for large, complex sales that require a long sales cycle. Identifying the customer's needs and developing the best solution can be very time consuming. However, when you do these things effectively, you are creating value in the eyes of the customer. When you build value on the front end of the sale, price becomes less of an issue on the back end of the sale.[3]

Negotiation—Part of the Win-Win Relationship Strategy

Frank Acuff, negotiations trainer and author of *How to Negotiate Anything with Anyone, Anywhere around the Globe*, says, "Life is a negotiation."[4] Negotiating skills have application almost daily in our personal and professional lives.

Some of the traditional personal selling books discussed how we should "handle" buyer objections. The message communicated to the reader was that personal selling is a "we versus they" process. Somebody wins, and somebody loses. The win-win solution, where both sides win, was not offered as an option.

The foundation for win-win negotiations is a relationship with the customer built on trust and rapport. Ron Willingham, author of two books on integrity selling, says:

> When trust and rapport are strong, negotiation becomes a partnership to work through customer concerns. But when trust and rapport are weak, almost any negotiation becomes too combative.[5]

FIGURE | 13.1

Negotiating Customer Concerns and Problems

THE SIX-STEP PRESENTATION PLAN

Step One: Approach	☑ Review Strategic/Consultative Selling Model ☑ Initiate customer contact
Step Two: Presentation	☑ Determine prospect needs ☑ Select solution ☑ Initiate sales presentation
Step Three: Demonstration	☑ Decide what to demonstrate ☑ Select selling tools ☑ Initiate demonstration
Step Four: Negotiation	☐ Anticipate buyer concerns ☐ Plan negotiating methods ☐ Initiate win-win negotiations
Step Five: Close	☐ Plan appropriate closing methods ☐ Recognize closing clues ☐ Initiate closing methods
Step Six: Servicing the Sale	☐ Follow through ☐ Follow-up calls ☐ Expansion selling

Service, retail, wholesale, and manufacturer selling

Trust and rapport must be established on the front end of the sale and maintained throughout the sales process. High performance salespeople take time to discover the customer's needs and try to recommend the best possible solution. And always keep in mind that any agreement that leaves one party dissatisfied will come back to hurt you later, sometimes in ways that you cannot predict.[6]

What is **negotiation**? One definition is "working to reach an agreement that is mutually satisfactory to both buyer and seller." It involves resolving the problems or concerns that prevent people from buying.[7] As we noted in Chapter 1, the salesperson increasingly serves as a consultant or resource and provides solutions to buyers' problems. The consultant seeks to establish and maintain long-term relationships with customers. The ability to negotiate problems or objections is one of the most effective ways to create value for the customer. Figure 13.2 outlines the steps a salesperson can take to anticipate and negotiate problems.

Negotiation Is a Process

Negotiations can take place before the sales call or at any time during the sales presentation. Early negotiations may involve the meeting location, who will attend the sales presentation, or the amount of time available for the first meeting. Salespeople sometimes make early concessions to improve the relationship. This approach may set a costly precedent for later in the sale.[8] Some concessions can have a negative influence on the sales presentation. If, for example, you need 40 minutes for an effective product demonstration, do not agree to a 20-minute meeting.

Negotiation is defined as "working to reach an agreement that is mutually satisfactory to both buyer and seller." It involves building relationships instead of making one-time deals.

In most cases you can anticipate that the most important negotiations will take place during stage three of the buying process (refer to Figure 8.3). Resolution of problems can sometimes be very time consuming. Establishing a strategic alliance, described in Chapter 1 as the highest form of partnering, requires lengthy negotiations. These negotiations may extend over several months. Once the alliance is finalized, negotiations continue when concerns voiced by one party or the other surface.

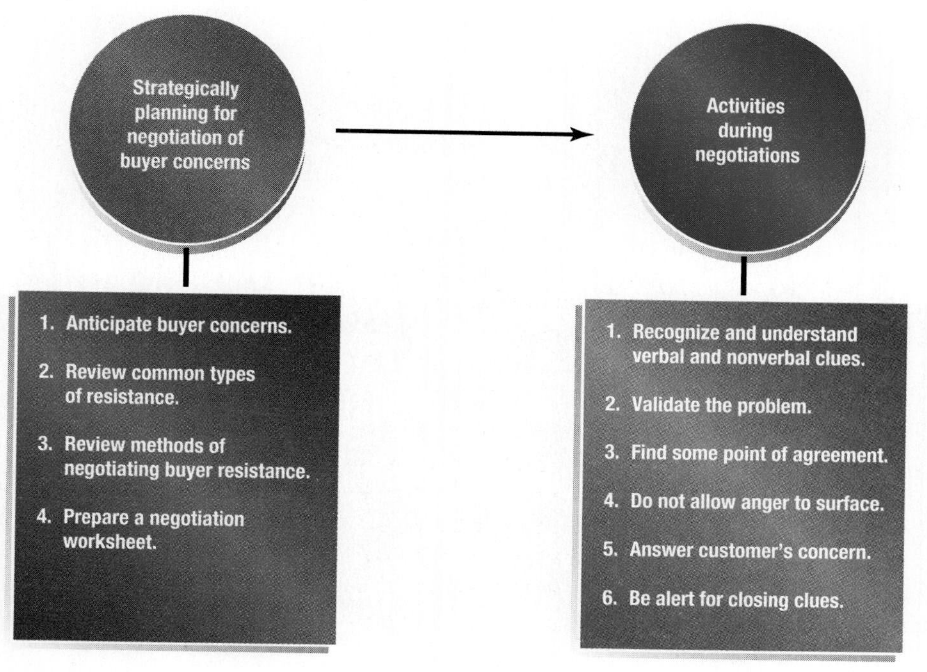

FIGURE | 13.2

Today salespeople must be prepared to anticipate and negotiate buyer concerns and problems.

COMMON TYPES OF BUYER CONCERNS

Salespeople learn that patterns of buyer resistance exist, and they, therefore, can anticipate that certain concerns may arise during the sales call. With this information it is possible to be better prepared for each meeting with a customer. The great majority of buyer concerns fall into five categories: need, product, source, price, and time.

Concerns Related to Need for the Product

If you have carefully completed your precall planning, then the prospect will likely have a need for your product. You still can expect, however, that the initial response may be, "I do not need your product." This might be a conditioned response that arises nearly every time the prospect meets with a sales representative. It also may be a cover-up for the real reason for not buying, which might be lack of funds, lack of time to examine your proposal carefully, or some other reason.

Sincere need resistance is one of the great challenges that faces a salesperson during the early part of the sales process. Think about it for a moment. Why would any customer want to purchase a product that does not seem to provide any real benefits? Unless we can create need awareness in the prospect's mind, there is no possible way to close the sale.

If you are calling on business prospects, the best way to overcome need resistance is to prove that your product is a good investment. Every business hopes to make a profit. Therefore, you must demonstrate how your product or service can contribute to that goal. Can your product increase sales volume? Can it reduce operating expenses? If the owner of a hardware store says, "I already carry a line of high-quality tools," point out how a second line of less expensive tools can appeal to another large segment of the buying public. With the addition of the new line the store can be in a better position to compete with other stores (discount merchandise stores and supermarkets) that sell inexpensive tools.

The desire to buy low is quite common. However, when buyers are faced with information overload, their decisions become more difficult. When concerns surface, salespeople need to explain the benefits that add value and use skillful negotiations to gain acceptance of the selling price. If the selling price is too low, profit margins may suffer.

Fast Company, December 1998.

In some selling situations you must help the prospect solve a problem before you have any chance of closing the sale. Suppose the prospect says, "I am already overstocked." If you call on wholesalers or retailers, expect to hear this objection quite frequently. Often the prospect is unwilling to buy additional merchandise until older stock is sold. If there is no demand for the older merchandise, then a real problem exists. In this situation your best bet is to offer the buyer one or more solutions to the problem. Some value-added tactics are

1. Suggest that the prospect hold a special sale to dispose of the unsold merchandise. It even may be necessary to sell the stock at a loss to recover at least part of the original investment. Closeouts can be painful, but it may be the best option.
2. Ask the prospect to accept a trial offer on a guaranteed sale or consignment basis. This option allows the customer to acquire new merchandise without an initial cash investment and opens the door for your product.
3. If company policy permits, consider negotiating the purchase of the prospect's inventory. Give the customer a credit against a minimum opening order.

The key to negotiating buyer concerns in many cases is creative problem solving. Work closely with the prospect to overcome the barrier that prevents closing the sale.

Concerns About the Product

You will recall from Chapter 8 that consultative process buyers may lack needs awareness or need help evaluating possible solutions. Therefore, the product (solution) often becomes the focal point of buyer resistance. When this happens, try to discover specific reasons why the prospect has doubts about your product. Often you may find that one of the following factors has influenced the buyer's attitude:

1. *The product is not well established.* This is a common buyer concern if you are selling a new or relatively new product. People do not like to take risks. They need plenty of assurance that the product is dependable. Use laboratory test results, third-party testimonials from satisfied users, or an effective demonstration to create value.
2. *The product will not be popular.* If the product is for resale, discuss sales results at other firms. Discuss the success other firms have had with your product. Also, discuss any efforts your company has taken to increase demand. For example, show the prospect sample advertisements that have appeared in the newspaper or commercials that have appeared on television.
3. *Friends or acquaintances did not like the product.* It is not easy to handle this buyer concern. After all, you cannot say, "Your friend is all wet—our product is the best on the market!" Move cautiously to acquire more information. Use questions to pinpoint the problem, and clarify any misinformation that the person may have concerning your product.
4. *The present product is satisfactory.* Change does not come easily to many people. Purchasing a new product may mean adopting new procedures or retraining employees. In the prospect's mind the advantages do not outweigh the disadvantages, so buyer resistance surfaces. To overcome this concern, you must build a greater amount of desire in the prospect's mind. Concentrate on a value proposition that gives your product a major advantage over the existing product, or reconfigure the product to better meet the customer's needs.

Concerns Related to Source

Concerns related to source can be especially challenging when the prospect is a strategic alliance buyer. The buyer may already have well established partnerships with other companies. If the prospect feels genuine loyalty to their present supplier, you will have to work harder to establish a relationship and begin the need discovery process.

When dealing with the loyalty problem, it is usually best to avoid direct criticism of the competing firm. Negative comments are apt to backfire because they damage your professional image. It is best to keep the sales presentation focused on the customer's problems and your solutions.

There are positive ways to cope with the loyalty objection. Some suggestions follow:

1. *Work harder to identify problems your company can solve with its products or services.* With the help of good questions, you may be able to understand the prospect's problems better than your competitors.
2. *Point out the superior benefits of your product and your company.* By doing this you hope the logic of your presentation can overcome the emotional ties that may exist between the prospect and the present supplier.
3. *Point out that the business may profit from the addition of a second line.* You do not expect the person to drop the present supplier, but you do want the person to try your product.
4. *Encourage the prospect to place a trial order, and then evaluate the merits of your product.* Again, you are not asking the person to quit the present supplier.
5. *Work on recruiting internal champions to build more support for your message.* Use referrals whenever possible.[9]
6. *Try to stay visible and connected.* Every contact with the prospect is one more step in building a relationship. Anthony Tringale, owner of Insurance Consulting Group in Fairfax, Virginia, says that he is involved with many potential clients in social and charitable events.[10]

Concerns Related to Price

There are two important points to keep in mind concerning price resistance. First, it is one of the most *common* buyer concerns in the field of selling. Therefore, you must learn to negotiate skillfully in this area. Secondly, price objections may be nothing more than an excuse. If you are selling a product or service to a transactional buyer, price may be the primary barrier to closing the sale. When people say, "Your price is too high," they probably mean, "You have not sold me yet." In the eyes of most customers, value is more important than price.

Always try to position your product with a convincing value proposition. Customers who perceive added value are less likely to choose a competing product simply on the basis of price.

Working with Buyers Who Are Trained in Negotiation

In recent years, we have seen an increase in the number of training programs developed for professional buyers. One such course is Fundamentals of Purchasing for the Newly Appointed Buyer, offered by the American Management Association. Enrollees learn how to negotiate with salespeople. Some salespeople also are returning to the classroom to learn negotiation skills. Acclivus Corporation (*www.acclivus.com*), a Dallas-based training company, offers the Acclivus Sales Negotiation System for salespeople who work in the business-to-business selling arena. Karrass Limited (*www.karrass.com*) offers the Effective Sales Negotiating seminar.

Professional buyers often learn to use specific tactics in dealing with salespeople. Homer Smith, author of *Selling through Negotiation*, provides these examples.

Selling in Action

APPLYING NEGOTIATION SKILLS IN THE JOB MARKET

Chester L. Karrass, creator of the Effective Negotiating seminar, says, "In business, you don't get what you deserve, you get what you negotiate." This is good advice for the job seeker. Most employers do not propose the highest wage possible at the beginning of the offer. If you want a higher starting wage, you must ask for it. Employers often have a predetermined range for each position and the highest salary is reserved for the applicant who brings something extra to the job. To prepare for a productive negotiation, you must know your own needs and you must know something about the worth of the position. Many employers tell you the salary range prior to the interview. The Internet can be a good source of salary information for certain types of jobs. In terms of your needs, try to determine what you care about the most: interesting work, future promotion, or flexible work schedule. If you are willing to negotiate, you can increase your pay by hundreds or even thousands of dollars. Be prepared to sell yourself, negotiate the salary you believe is appropriate, and achieve a win-win solution in the process.[a]

Budget Limitation Tactic[11]

The buyer may say, "We like your proposal, but our budget for the convention is only $8,500." Is the buyer telling the truth, or is the person testing your price? The best approach in this instance is to take the budget limitation seriously and use appropriate negotiation strategies. One strategy is to reduce the price by eliminating some items, sometimes described as **unbundling**. In the case of a fleet truck sale the salesperson might say, "We can deliver the trucks with a less powerful engine and, thus, meet your budget figure. Would you be willing to purchase trucks with less powerful engines?"

Take-It-or-Leave-It Tactic[12] How do you respond to a buyer who says, "My final offer is $3,300, take it or leave it?" A price concession is, of course, one option. However, this is likely to reduce profits for the company and lower your commission. An alternative strategy is to confidently review the superior benefits of your product and make another closing attempt. Appealing to the other person's sense of fairness also may move the discussion forward. If the final offer is totally without merit, consider calling a halt to the negotiation to allow the other party to back down from his position without losing face.[13]

Let-Us-Split-the-Difference Tactic[14] In some cases the salesperson may find this price concession acceptable. If the buyer's suggestion is not acceptable, then the salesperson might make a counteroffer.

These tactics represent only a sample of those used by professional buyers. To prepare for these and other tactics, salespeople need to plan their negotiating strategies in advance and have clear goals. Decide in advance on the terms you can (and cannot) accept. It is important that you have the authority to set prices. Buyers want to do business with someone who has decision-making authority.

THE PITFALLS OF PAYING TOO LITTLE

It's unwise to pay too much. But it's worse to pay too little.
When you pay too much, you lose a little money, that is all.
When you pay too little you sometimes lose everything, because the thing you bought was incapable of doing the thing it was bought to do.
The common law of business balances prohibits paying a little and getting a lot. It can't be done.
If you deal with the lowest bidder, it is well to add something for the risk you run.

John Ruskin, British Writer

Negotiating Price with a Low-Price Strategy

As noted in Chapter 7, some marketers have positioned their products with a price strategy. The goal is to earn a small profit margin on a large sales volume. Many of these companies have empowered their salespeople to use various low-price strategies such as quantity discounts, trade discounts, seasonal discounts, and promotional discounts. Some salespeople are given permission to match the price of any competitor. Transactional buyers will always give price a high priority during negotiations.

How to Deal with Price Concerns

As we have noted, price resistance is common, so we must prepare for it. There are some important "do's and don'ts" to keep in mind when the price concern surfaces.

Do Clarify Price Concerns with Questions When you are confronted with a price objection, determine what the customer is really saying. You will recall from Chapter 11 that *specific survey questions* encourage the customer to give you more details. The following questions might be used when price concerns surface:

> "When you say we are higher, could you be more specific, please?"
>
> "What did you anticipate the price to be?"

When the customer says budget is the primary reason for delaying the purchase, you might ask, "If you had the budget, would you buy?" Questions can help you determine what the customer is really thinking.[15]

Do Add Value with a Cluster of Satisfactions As noted in Chapter 7, a growing number of customers are seeking a cluster of satisfactions that includes a good product, a salesperson who is truly a partner, and a company that stands behind its products (see Fig. 7.1). Many business firms are at a competitive disadvantage when the price alone is considered. When you look beyond price, however, it may become obvious that your company offers more value for the dollar.

Stephen Smith, senior account manager for Bell Atlantic, says that price is like the tip of the iceberg—it is often the only feature the customer sees. Salespeople need to direct the customer's attention to the value-added features that make up the bulk of the iceberg that is below the surface (Figure 13.3).[16] Do not forget to sell yourself as a high-value element of the sales proposal. Emphasize your commitment to customer service after the sale.

Do Not Make Price the Focal Point of Your Sales Presentation You may need to discuss price, but do not bring it up too early. The best time to deal with price is after you have reviewed product features and discussed buyer benefits. You increase the chances for a win-win outcome by increasing the number of issues you can resolve. If you negotiate price along with delivery date, support services, or volume purchases, you increase the opportunities for a trade-off so you and the customer both win something of value.[17]

Do Not Apologize for the Price When you do mention price, do so in a confident and straightforward manner. Do not have even a hint of apology in your voice. Convey to the prospect that you believe your price is fair and make every effort to relate price to value. Many people fear paying too much for a product or service. If your company has adopted a value-added strategy, point this fact out to the prospect. Then discuss how you and your company add value.

Do Point Out the Relationship between Price and Quality In our highly competitive, free enterprise economy there are forces at work that tend to promote fair pricing. The highest quality can never be obtained at the lowest price. Quality comes from that Latin word

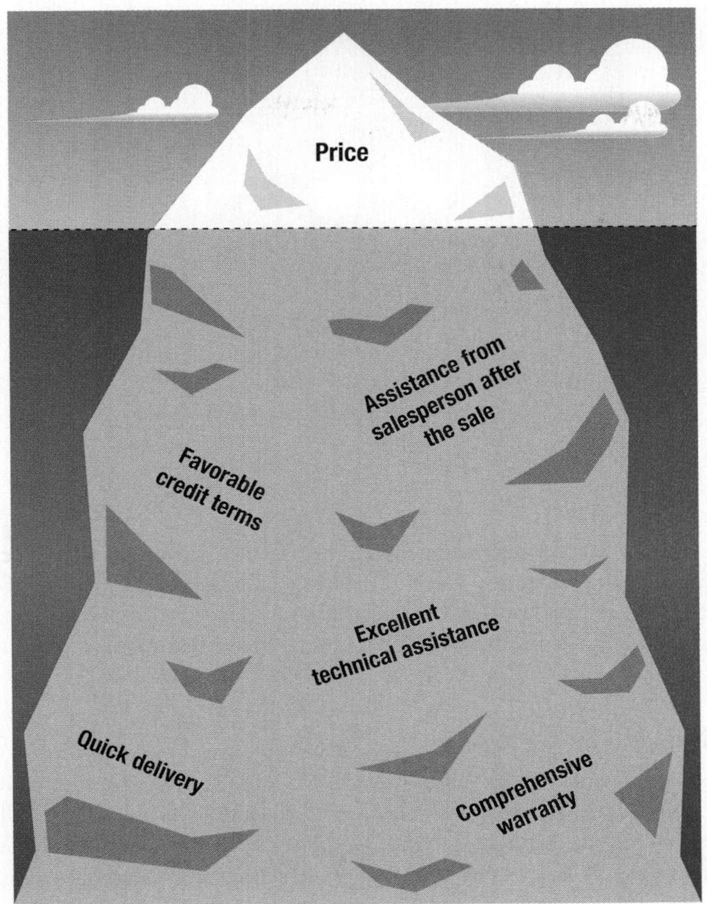

FIGURE | 13.3

A sales proposal is sometimes like an iceberg. The customer sees the tip of the iceberg (price) but does not see the value-added features below the surface.

qualitas, meaning, "What is the worth?" When you sell quality, price is more likely to be secondary in the prospect's mind. Always point out the value-added features that create the difference in price. Keep in mind that cheap products are built down to a price rather than up to a standard.[18]

Do Explain and Demonstrate the Difference between Price and Cost Price represents the initial amount the buyer pays for the product. Cost represents the amount the buyer pays for a product as it is used over a period of time. The price–cost comparison is particularly relevant with a product or service that lasts a long time or is particularly reliable. Today, airlines are comparing the price and cost of small regional jets manufactured by Bombardier of Canada and Embraer of Brazil with large jets sold by Boeing and Airbus. Figure 13.4 compares the CRJ200 offered by Bombardier with the A320 offered by Airbus. Sales representatives at Bombardier point out the fast speed (534 MPH) and low fuel consumption of the CRJ200.[19]

Do Not Make Concessions Too Quickly Give away concessions methodically and reluctantly, and always try to get something in return. A concession given too freely can diminish the value of your product. Also, giving a concession too easily may send the signal you are negotiating from a position of weakness. Neil Rackham, author of several books on SPIN selling, says, "Negotiate late, negotiate little and never let negotiation become a substitute for good selling."[20]

FIGURE | 13.4

The Winner in the Short Run
Airlines are comparing the price and cost of small regional jets with large jets sold by Boeing and Airbus. The cavernous Airbus leads on seat cost per mile, but the much lower price per trip of the CRJ200 makes it a winner in the minds of some buyers.

	CRJ200	A320
Passengers (seats)	50	150
Cost of aircraft	$21.0 million	$48.2 million
SHORT TRIP (575 miles)		
Cost per seat per mile	3.34¢	2.85¢
Total cost of trip	$961	$2,460
LONG TRIP (1,150 miles)		
Cost per seat per mile	2.79¢	2.16¢
Total cost of trip	$1,604	$3,722

Many *transactional buyers* are primarily interested in price and convenience, so consider eliminating (unbundling) features that contribute to a higher selling price. If the buyer is only interested in the lowest possible price, and you represent a marketer committed to a value-added sales strategy, consider withdrawing from negotiations.

Concerns Related to Time

If a prospect says, "I want time to think it over," you may be encountering concerns related to time. Resistance related to time is often referred to as the **stall**. A stall usually means the customer does not yet perceive the benefits of buying now. In most cases the stall indicates that the prospect has both positive and negative feelings about your product. Consider using *probing questions* to determine the negative feelings: "Is it my company that concerns you?" "Do you have any concerns about our warranty program?"

It is all right to be persuasive if the prospect can truly benefit from buying now. If the price may soon rise, or if the item may not be available in the future, then you should provide this information. You must, however, present this information sincerely and accurately. It is never proper to distort the truth in the hope of getting the order.

GENERAL STRATEGIES FOR NEGOTIATING BUYER CONCERNS

The successful negotiation of buyer concerns is based in large part on understanding human behavior. This knowledge, coupled with a good measure of common sense, helps us overcome most buyer concerns. It is also helpful to be aware of general methods for negotiating buyer resistance.

Know the Value of What You Are Offering

It is important that we know what is of real value to the customer and not consider value only in terms of purchase price. The real value of what you are offering may be a value-added intangible such as superior product knowledge, good credit terms, prompt delivery, or a reputation for honest dealings. An important aspect of the negotiation process is

TABLE | 13.1

Objections are often requests for more information to justify the buying decision. Objections can tell us a lot about the real source of hesitation and what type of information the customer is seeking.

OBJECTION	SOURCE OF HESITATION	REQUEST FOR . . .
"Price too high"	Perceived cost versus benefit	Value articulation
"Think about it"	Afraid to make a bad decision	Create comfort, provide proof
"Talk to boss"	Unable to justify decision	Risk reduction, benefit review
"Need more quotes"	Unsure you're their best option	Targeted solutions, value
"Set with current provider"	Doesn't see benefit of change	Differentiation
"Bad history"	Past experience is affecting current view	Offer proof of change

Adapted from "Hide-and-Seek," a table from Nancy J. Stephens, "Objections Are a 'Yes' About to Happen," *Selling*, November 1998, p. 3.

discovering what is of utmost importance to the buyer (see Table 13.1). The focus of personal selling today should be the mutual search for value. Some salespeople make the mistake of offering a lower price the moment buyer concerns surface. In the customer's mind, price may be of secondary importance compared with the quality of service after the sale. As noted previously, do not be in a hurry to make price concessions.

Prepare for Negotiations

It helps to classify possible resistance with the aid of a negotiations worksheet. To illustrate how this form works, let us review an example from the food industry. Mary Turner is a salesperson for Durkee Famous Foods. She represents more than 350 products. Mary calls on supermarkets daily and offers assistance in the areas of ordering and merchandising. Recently, her company decided to offer retail food stores an allowance of $1 per case of olives if the store purchased 15 or more cases. Prior to talking with her customers about this offer, Mary sat down and developed a negotiations

Selling Is Everyone's Business

SELLING SAVES FACTORY JOBS

The workers at the Parker Hannifin Corporation factory in Irwin, Pennsylvania, count on Ken Sweet to save their jobs. He is the general manager. When sales at this automation-equipment plant drop, there is pressure to cut the payroll. The pressure to cut costs through layoffs builds during a recession when sales typically decline. Fortunately, Mr. Sweet has an ace up his sleeve. As general manager he is responsible for sales as well as getting the product out the door. When manufacturing operations slow down, Mr. Sweet redoubles his sales efforts. He urges his equipment-development teams to focus on potential customers that offer the best chance for big contracts. Some production workers are recruited to help with the sales effort. Jim Manion, an assembler, calls prospects that have visited the company's Web site when work is scarce at the plant. These sales efforts help save jobs.[b]

FIGURE 13.5

Before the Presentation It Is Important To Prepare a Negotiations Worksheet.

Negotiations Worksheet		
Customer's concern	Type of concern	Possible response
"Fifteen cases of olives will take up valuable space in my receiving room. It is already crowded."	Need	Combination Direct denial/Superior benefit "You will not have to face that problem. With the aid of our merchandising plan you can display 10 cases immediately on the sales floor. Only five cases will become reserve stock. You should move all 15 cases in about two weeks."
"This is a poor time of the year to buy a large order of olives. People are not buying olives at this time."	Time	Combination Indirect denial/Third-party testimony "I agree that it has been a problem in the past, but consumer attitudes seem to be changing. We have found that olives sell well all year long if displayed properly. More people are using olives in the preparation of omelets, pizza, and other dishes. Of course, most relish trays feature olives. We will supply you with point-of-purchase material that provides kitchen-tested ways to use this high-profit item."
"I have to stay within my budget."	Price	Superior benefit "As you know, olives represent a high-profit item. The average margin is 26 percent. With the addition of our $1.00 per case allowance the margin will rise to about 30 percent. This order will give you a good return on your investment."
"I am very satisfied with my present supplier."	Source	Combination question/Trial order "What can I do to get you to take just a trial order?"

worksheet, shown in Fig. 13.5. We cannot anticipate every possible problem, but it is possible to identify the most common problems that are likely to arise. The negotiations worksheet can be a useful tool.

Understand the Problem

David Stiebel, author of *When Talking Makes Things Worse!*, says we need to understand the difference between a misunderstanding and a true disagreement. A *misunderstanding* is a failure to accurately understand the other person's point. For example, the salesperson believes the customer is primarily interested in price, but the customer's primary need is on-time delivery. A *disagreement*, in contrast, is a failure to agree that would persist despite

Many salespeople have learned to anticipate certain problems and forestall them with a well-planned and well-executed presentation.

the most accurate understanding.[21] Be certain that both you and the prospect are clear on the true nature of what needs to be negotiated. When the prospect begins talking, listen carefully and then listen some more. With *probing questions*, you can fine-tune your understanding of the problem.

Create Alternative Solutions

When the prospect finishes talking, it is a good practice to validate the problem, using a *confirmation question*. This helps to isolate the true problem and reduce the chance of misunderstanding. The confirmation question might sound like this: "I think I understand your concern. You feel the warranty does not provide you with sufficient protection. Is this correct?" By taking time to ask this question you accomplish two important objectives. First, you are giving personal attention to the problem, which pleases the customer. Second, you gain time to think about the best possible response.

The best possible response is very often an alternative solution. Many of today's customers do not want to hear that there is only one way or a single solution. In the age of information, people have less time to manage their work and their lives, so they expect new levels of flexibility.

Find Some Point of Agreement

Negotiating buying problems is a little like the art of diplomacy. It helps to know what points of agreement exist. This saves time and helps establish a closer bond between you and the prospect. At some point during the presentation, you might summarize by using a *summary-confirmation question*: "Let us see if I fully understand your position. You think our product is well constructed and will provide the reliability you are looking for. Also, you believe our price is fair. Am I correct on these two points?"

Once all the areas of agreement have been identified, there may be surprisingly few points of disagreement. The prospect suddenly sees that the advantages of ownership far outweigh the disadvantages. Now that the air is cleared, both the salesperson and the customer can give their full attention to any remaining points of disagreement.

Global Business Etiquette

NEGOTIATING ACROSS CULTURES

Negotiations in the international area vary from one country to another because of cultural differences. German buyers are more apt to look you in the eye and tell you what they do not like about your product. Japanese buyers, on the other hand, do not want to embarrass you and, therefore, bury their concerns beneath several layers of courtesy. In China, now the largest market in the world for American products, negotiations are more straightforward. People who have been doing business in China for many years suggest a very direct approach to negotiations. However, do not become antagonistic or discourteous. Do get involved in native business rituals that are intended to create a friendly atmosphere.

When you enter into negotiations in foreign countries, it is important to understand and accommodate the customer's culture. You may not get every detail exactly right, but you win respect by trying.

Selling in certain cultures often requires more time in bonding and building a rapport. Several meetings may be needed to lay the groundwork for the actual sale.[c]

Know When to Walk Away

For many reasons salespeople must sometimes walk away from a potential sale. If the customer's budget doesn't allow the purchase of your product, don't press the issue. If the customer's best offer is not favorable for your company, don't continue to waste your time. If you discover that the prospect is dishonest or fails to keep their word, discontinue negotiations. Be aware of how much flexibility you have in terms of price, specifications, delivery schedules, and so forth, and know when you have reached your "walk-away" point.[22]

SPECIFIC METHODS OF NEGOTIATING BUYER CONCERNS

There are seven specific methods of negotiating buyer concerns. In analyzing each buyer concern, we should try to determine which method can be most effective. In most cases we can use a combination of the following methods to negotiate buyer concerns.

Direct Denial

Direct denial involves refuting the opinion or belief of a prospect. The direct denial of a problem is considered a high-risk method of negotiating buyer concerns. Therefore, you should use it with care. People do not like to be told they are wrong. Even when the facts prove the prospect is wrong, resentment can build if we fail to handle the situation properly.

When a prospect offers buyer resistance that is not valid, we sometimes have no option other than to openly disagree. If the person is misinformed, we must provide accurate information. For example, if the customer questions the product's quality, meet the concern head-on with whatever proof seems appropriate. It is almost never proper to ignore misinformation. High-performance salespeople counter inaccurate responses from the prospect promptly and directly.

The manner in which you state the denial is of major importance. Use a win-win approach. Be firm and sincere in stating your beliefs, but do not be offensive. Above all, do not patronize the prospect. A "know-it-all" attitude can be irritating.

Indirect Denial

Sometimes the prospect's concern is completely valid or at least accurate to a large degree. This method is referred to as the **indirect denial**. The best approach is to bend a little and acknowledge that the prospect is at least partially correct. After all, if you offered a product that is objection proof, you would likely have no competitors. Every product has a shortcoming or limitation.[23] The success of this method is based in part on the need most people have to feel that their views are worthwhile. For this reason the indirect denial method is widely used. An exchange that features the use of this approach follows. The salesperson is a key account sales representative for Pacific Bell Directory.[24]

Salesperson: The total cost of placing your 6- by 8-inch ad in the yellow pages of five different Pacific Bell directories is $32,000.

Prospect: As a builder I want to reach people who are planning to build a home. I am afraid my ad will be lost among the hundreds of ads featured in your directories.

Salesperson: Yes, I agree the yellow pages in our directories do feature hundreds of ads, but the section for general contractors features less than 30 ads. Our design staff can prepare an ad that can be highly visible and can set your company apart from ads placed by other contractors.

Note that the salesperson used the words, "Yes, I agree . . . " to reduce the impact of denial. The prospect is less likely to feel her point of view has been totally disproved. One note of caution: Avoid the "Yes . . . but" response. When you use the word *but*, it invalidates anything preceding it. A more effective response would be, "I understand your concerns, Ms. Thomas, however there is another way to view this issue."[25]

Feel–Felt–Found

Successful salespeople are sensitive to clues that indicate the client feels something is wrong. One way to empathize with the client's concerns is to use the "feel–felt–found" strategy. Here is how it works. Assume the customer is concerned about the complexity of the new computer software, and says, "I do not think I will ever understand the process." Your response might be, "I understand how you *feel*, Mr. Pearson. Many of my customers *felt* the same way, until they started using the software and *found* it quite easy to master."

Questions

Throughout this chapter, we have described several situations where probing or confirmation questions can enhance the negotiation process. We must also keep in mind the important role of need-satisfaction questions. In Chapter 11, we noted that *need-satisfaction questions* are designed to move the sales process forward toward commitment and action. These questions focus on the solution.[26] Consider the following exchange that involves a price concern:

Buyer: It would be difficult for our Human Resources Department to absorb the cost of your psychological tests.

Seller: What would a 10 percent reduction in employee turnover save your company?

In these examples, the questions are designed to get the customer's attention focused on the solution. These questions also give ownership of the solution to the prospect. See Chapter 11 for more examples of the need-satisfaction question.

In their best selling THE NEW CONCEPTUAL SELLING authors Heiman, Sanchez and Tuleja recommend using the question "What are your concerns *with this proposal?" They also suggest you ask questions in a positive rather than negative manner, and that you "wait for answers."*

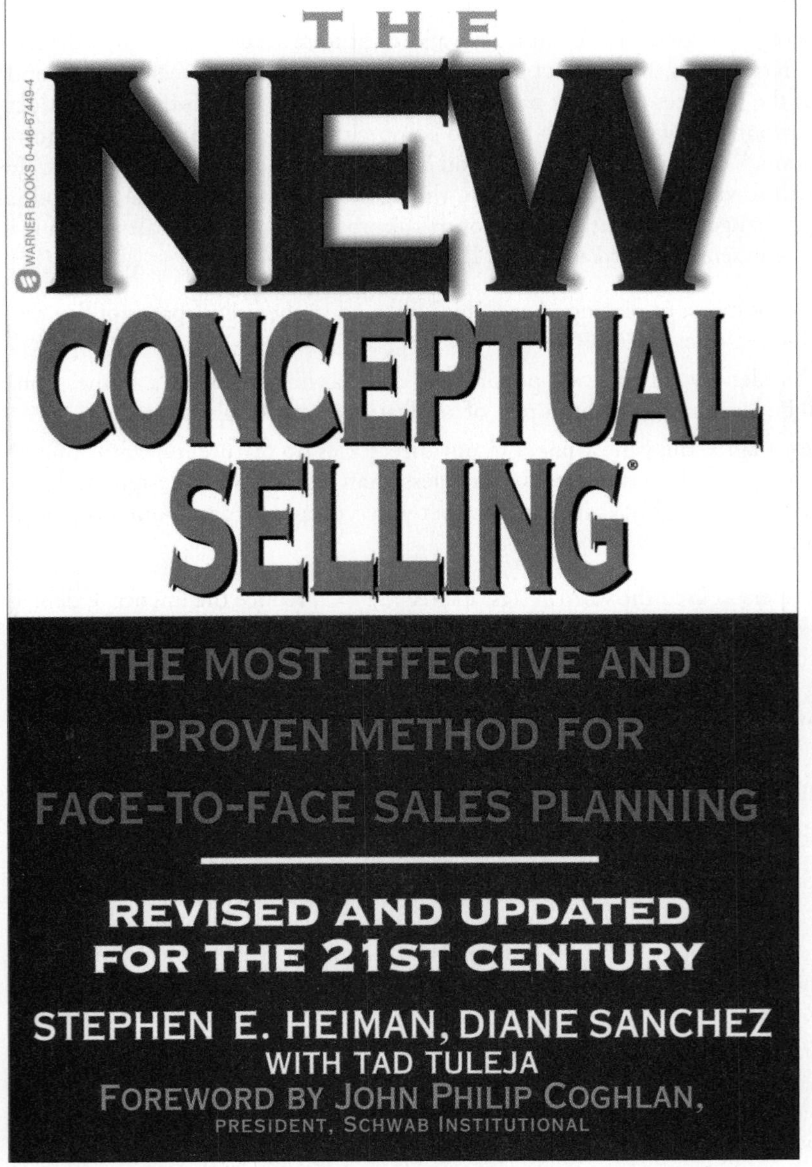

Superior Benefit

Sometimes the customer raises a problem that cannot be answered with a denial. For example: "Your television commercial proposal does not include payroll costs for actors who will be used during the shoot. This means we must cover this expense." You should acknowledge the valid objection and then discuss one or more superior benefits: "Yes, you are correct. We do conduct the talent search and coach the actors throughout the development of the commercial. In addition, if you are not happy with the performance of the actors, we will conduct a second search for new actors and remake the commercial at no additional cost to you." A **superior benefit** is a benefit that in most cases outweighs the customer's specific concern.

The focus of a presentation strategy should be a mutual search for value. With more knowledgeable customers today, it is important to keep the negotiations focused on the value proposition, with alternative solutions created ahead of time.

Demonstration

If you are familiar with your product as well as that of your competition, this method of negotiating buyer resistance is easy to use. You know the competitive advantages of your product and can discuss these features with confidence.

The product demonstration is one of the most convincing ways to overcome buyer skepticism. With the aid of an effective demonstration you can overcome specific concerns.

Sometimes a second demonstration is needed to overcome buyer skepticism. This demonstration can provide additional proof. High-achieving sales personnel know when and how to use proof devices to overcome buyer resistance.

Trial Offer

A **trial offer** involves giving the prospect an opportunity to try the product without making a purchase commitment. The trial offer (especially with new products) is popular with customers because they can get fully acquainted with your product without making a major commitment. Assume that a buyer for a large restaurant chain says, "I am sure you have a good cooking oil, but we are happy with our present brand. We have had no complaints from our managers." In response to this comment you might say, "I can understand your reluctance to try our product. However, I do believe our oil is the finest on the market. With your permission I would like to ship you 30 gallons of our oil at no cost. You can use our product at selected restaurants and evaluate the results. If our oil does not provide you with superior results, you are under no obligation to place an order."

Third-Party Testimony

Studies indicate that the favorable testimony of a neutral third party can be an effective method of responding to buyer resistance. Let us assume that the owner of a small business states that he can get along without the services of a professional landscaping service. The salesperson might respond in this manner: "Some business owners feel the way you do. However, once they contract for our service, they do not regret the decision." Mark Williams, owner of Williams

Customer Relationship Management with Technology

AUTOMATED SORTING AND PRODUCTIVITY

The notes of a busy salesperson soon can become extensive. Paper notes make it difficult, if not impossible, to cross-reference important information within those notes. The notes in a customer relationship management (CRM) system gives salespeople immediate access to records containing needed words or phrases. This offers users many advantages, including a method of quickly finding information about buyers with similar interests or concerns. (See the exercise, Finding Keywords in a CRM Database, on p. 338 for more information.)

Hardware, says our service completely changed the image his business projects to the public." Third-party testimony provides a positive way to solve certain types of buying problems. The positive experiences of a neutral third party almost never trigger an argument with the prospect.

Postpone Method

Today's customers are well informed and may want to engage in negotiations early in the sales process. The customer may raise concerns that you would prefer to respond to later in the presentation. Let's assume you are calling on an office manager who is interested in well-equipped cubicles for eight employees. Soon after you present some product information the customers says, "How much will eight well-equipped cubicles cost us?" Using the **postpone method**, your response might be, "I would prefer to answer that question in a few minutes. Once I learn what features you prefer, I can calculate a cost estimate." Every customer concern should be taken seriously. Always try to explain why you want to postpone the response.

Combination Methods

As noted previously, consultative selling is characterized by flexibility. A combination of methods sometimes proves to be the best way to deal with buyer resistance. For example, an indirect denial might be followed by a question: "The cost of our business security system is a little higher than the competition. The price I have quoted reflects the high-quality materials used to develop our system. Wouldn't you feel better entrusting your security needs to a firm with more than 25 years of experience in the business security field?" In this situation the salesperson also might consider combining the indirect denial with an offer to arrange a demonstration of the security system.

Summary

Sales resistance is natural and should be welcomed as an opportunity to learn more about how to satisfy the prospect's needs. Buyers' concerns often provide salespeople with precisely the information they need to close a sale.

Concerns may arise from a variety of reasons, some related to the content or manner of the presentation strategy and others related to the prospect's own concerns. Whatever the reasons, the salesperson should *negotiate* sales resistance with the proper attitude, never making too much or too little of the prospect's concerns.

General strategies for negotiating buyer concerns include, knowing the value of what you are offering, preparing for negotiations, understanding the problem, creating alternate solutions, finding some point of agreement, and knowing when to walk away.

The best strategy for negotiating sales resistance is to anticipate it and preplan methods to answer the prospect's concerns. If a salesperson uses a negotiations worksheet, then it can be much easier to deal with buyer concerns.

We discuss the various types of problems likely to surface during the sales presentation. Most objections can be placed in one of five categories: need, product, source, price, and time.

Specific methods and combinations of methods of negotiating resistance vary depending on the particular combination of salesperson, product, and prospect. We have described several common methods, but you should remember that practice in applying them is essential and that there is room for a great deal of creative imagination in developing variations or additional methods. With careful preparation and practice, negotiating the most common types of buyer concerns should become a stimulating challenge to each salesperson's professional growth.

KEY TERMS

Negotiation
Stall
Direct denial
Indirect denial
Superior benefit
Unbundling
Trial offer
Postpone method

REVIEW QUESTIONS

1. Explain why a salesperson should welcome buyer concerns.
2. List the common types of buyer resistance that might surface in a presentation.
3. How does the negotiations worksheet form help the salesperson prepare to negotiate buyer concerns?
4. Explain the value of using *probing* and *confirmation* questions when negotiating buyer concerns.
5. List eight specific strategies for negotiating buyer resistance.
6. John Ruskin (see p. 325) says that it is unwise to pay too much when making a purchase, but it is worse to pay too little. Do you agree or disagree with this statement? Explain.
7. What is usually the most common reason prospects give for not buying? How can salespeople deal effectively with this type of concern?
8. Professional buyers often learn to use specific negotiation tactics in dealing with salespeople. List and describe two tactics that are commonly used today.
9. When a customer says, "I want time to think it over," what type of resistance is the salesperson encountering? Suggest ways to overcome this type of buyer concern.
10. Discuss the merits of using need-satisfaction questions to negotiate buyer concerns.

APPLICATION EXERCISES

1. When conducting negotiations with a customer, take into consideration their communication style. Select two of the four communication styles (emotive, director, reflective, or supportive) and prepare guidelines for negotiating with each one. Review material in Chapter 4 before completing this exercise.
2. During an interview with a prospective employer the interviewer raises the objection that you are not qualified for the job for which you are applying. On the basis of your observation you do not believe the interviewer fully understands the amount of experience you have or that you really have the ability to perform the job requirements. Write how you would overcome the objection the interviewer has raised.
3. Assume you have decided to sell your own home. During an open house a prospect, whom you are showing through the house, begins to criticize major selling points about your home.
   a. You have taken excellent care of your home, believe it to be a good home, and have done a lot of special projects to make it more enjoyable. What will be your emotional reaction to this prospect's criticisms? Should you express this emotional reaction?
   b. Underneath this surface criticism you think this prospect is really interested in buying your home. How would you negotiate the sales resistance she is showing?

4. Acclivus Corporation (*www.acclivus.com*) is a leading supplier of sales training programs. As noted in this chapter, one of their most popular programs is the Acclivus Sales Negotiation course. Access the Acclivus home page on the Internet, and click on the "programs" link. Click on "negotiation" and review the information on the Acclivus Sales Negotiation course. Report your findings.

ROLE-PLAY EXERCISE

You have had two previous interviews for a career position that really interests you. You understand that with the hiring process in this company most interviewers want to "buy low." However, you want to "sell high." The vice president of sales indicated she really wants you to be a part of her department and has offered you a position. However, the first year's salary and benefits are $10,000 below what you feel you are worth. This salary is also several thousand dollars below what you will need to cover the kind of lifestyle you want. The only thing between you and the position is the difference in compensation. Using a negotiations worksheet, plan your response to the following statements made by the vice president: (1) Our salary budget limits us. (2) Can we split the difference? (3) Either take it or leave it. Decide at what point in the salary negotiations will you decide to turn down the offer or accept the offer. Role-play your response to each of these statements.

CRM APPLICATION EXERCISE

Finding Keywords in a CRM Database

During sales training this week, your sales manager, Becky Kemley, led a discussion about negotiating buyer resistance and managing objections. The discussion included methods of identifying and responding to price concerns. You wish to find those contacts who might have a price objection so that you can better prepare for working with them. Using the

ACT! software, access all records containing the word "price" by selecting Lookup, Keyword, type "price," and check Notes; and then press Enter. After searching, ACT! displays three records in which price is an issue. Print contact reports for these three records by selecting Report, Contact Report, Active Lookup, Printer, and OK.

VIDEO CASE PROBLEM

Each year public and private organizations send thousands of employees to meetings held at hotels, motels, convention centers, conference centers, and resorts. These meetings represent a multimillion-dollar business in the United States. Some of the largest providers of meeting space and related services are catering to clients in new and exciting ways. The Renaissance Esmeralda Resort and Spa (introduced at the beginning of this chapter) provides a good example of such a destination. The goal of this hotel is to provide guests with an experience they can talk about the rest of their lives. The hotel offers 560 deluxe guest rooms, several suites, soundproof meeting rooms with state-of-the-art audiovisual technology, and continuous break service that can accommodate any agenda. Lavish customized meal events are a specialty of the Renaissance Esmeralda Resort and Spa. Guests enjoy use of a championship golf course; tennis courts; swimming pools; and a fitness center complete with whirlpools, saunas, weight room, and aerobic classes. Several restaurants and lounges are available to guests.

In an ideal situation, Brian Moon, sales manager, likes to guide prospects on a site inspection of the property. This tour, in some ways, fulfills the function of a sales demonstration. Throughout the tour he describes special amenities and services offered by the hotel. He also uses this time to get better acquainted with the needs of the prospect. Once the tour is completed he escorts the prospect back to his office and completes the needs assessment. Next, he prepares a detailed sales proposal. In most cases the proposal is presented to the prospect at a second meeting. The proposal needs to contain accurate and complete facts because when signed, it becomes a legally enforceable sales contract.

Rarely is the sales proposal accepted without modification. Professional meeting planners are experienced negotiators and press hard for concessions. Some have completed training programs developed for professional buyers. The concessions requested may include a lower guest room rate, lower meal costs, complimentary suites, or a complimentary event such as a wine and cheese reception or a theme party.

Of course, some buyer resistance is not easily identified. Brian Moon says that he follows three steps in dealing with buyer concerns:

1. *Locate the resistance.* Some prospects are reluctant to accept a sales proposal, but the reason may be unclear. Brian has discovered in some cases that small groups are concerned about the sheer size of the Esmeralda. They wonder if a small group can receive the same personalized attention given to a large group. Once this perception is uncovered, Brian knows how to deal with it.
2. *Clarify the resistance.* If a prospect says, "I like your facilities, but your prices are a little high," then the salesperson must clarify the meaning of this objection. Is the prospect seeking a major price concession or a small price concession?
3. *Overcome the objection.* Brian says, "You must be prepared for negotiations and know the value of what you are offering." The resort must earn a profit, so concessions can be made only after careful consideration of the bottom line.

Brian has discovered that the best way to negotiate buyer concerns is to make sure both the prospect and the resort feel like winners once the negotiations are finalized. If either party feels like a loser, a long-term partnership will not be possible. Refer to the opening paragraph of this chapter for more information.

Questions

1. If you were selling convention services for a hotel located in a large city, what types of buyer concerns would you expect from a new prospect?
2. Let us assume that you are representing the Renaissance Esmeralda Resort and Spa and you are meeting with a new prospect in her office. She is a busy meeting planner who does not want to visit your property until she has a meeting with you. What are some tools that you might use during the sales presentation? What proof devices might you use to support your claims?
3. If you meet with a professional buyer who is trained in negotiation, what tactics can you expect the person to use? How would you respond to each of these tactics?

CRM CASE STUDY

Negotiating Resistance

Becky Kemley has asked you to review Pat Silva's former prospect accounts. She wants you to look for accounts with which you might anticipate objections during a presentation.

Questions

1. Which account might voice a time objection and say, "We want to put off our decision for now," and how would you propose dealing with this objection?
2. Which account is most likely to try to get you to agree to a lower price and how would you respond?
3. Which account might you anticipate would use the phrase "we want to shop around for a good solid supplier," and what would be your response?

PARTNERSHIP SELLING: A ROLE-PLAY/SIMULATION

(see Appendix 3, pp. 509–510, 518)

Developing a Presentation Strategy—Negotiating

Refer to *sales memorandum 3* and strategically plan to anticipate and negotiate any objections or concerns your customer may have to your presentation. You should prepare a negotiations worksheet to organize this part of your presentation.

The instructions for item 2e direct you to prepare negotiations for the time, price, source, and product objections. You note that your price is approximately $200 more than your customer budgeted for this meeting. You have to be very effective in negotiating a value-added strategy because your convention center is not a low-price supplier (see Chapter 2 on value-added product strategies).

During the presentation you should use proof devices from the product strategy materials provided in *employment memorandum 1* to negotiate concerns you anticipate. You also may want to use a calculator to negotiate any financial arrangements such as savings on parking, airport transportation, and so on. Using spreadsheet software you may want to prepare graphs to illustrate competitive pricing. Place these materials in the front pocket of your three-ring binder (portfolio) so that you can easily access them during your presentation. You may want to secure another person to be your customer, instructing him or her to voice the objections you have anticipated, and then you respond with your negotiation strategies. This experience can provide you with the opportunity to rehearse your negotiation strategies.

CHAPTER 14

Chapter Preview

When you finish reading this chapter you should be able to

1. Describe the proper attitude to display toward closing the sale
2. List and discuss selected guidelines for closing the sale
3. Explain how to recognize closing clues
4. Discuss selected methods of closing the sale
5. Explain what to do when the buyer says yes and what to do when the buyer says no

Closing the Sale and Confirming the Partnership

Gretchen Parr-Silver, director of special event sales at Universal Studios, looks at closing from the prospect's point of view. Although the special event plan she prepared may seem perfect, she realizes that the customer may have a different point of view. A special event in her department may be a corporate reception, a wedding, a bar mitzvah, or a class reunion. She must try to see the actual event through the eyes of the customer. Gretchen believes that relationship-building skills must be applied at every step of the sales process. If she is continuously adding value throughout the sales presentation, closing is much easier. This is especially true in those cases in which price might be a barrier to closing.[1]

CLOSING THE SALE—YESTERDAY AND TODAY

Throughout the evolution of personal selling, we have seen major changes in the way closing is perceived. Prior to the introduction of consultative selling and the partnering era, closing was often presented as the most important aspect of the sales process. The early sales training literature also presented closing methods that encouraged the manipulation of the customer. For example, some sales training programs included the *standing-room-only* close. The sales trainee was encouraged to emphasize the negative consequences of waiting: "If you don't place the order today, I can't guarantee delivery by June 1." If the salesperson's statement is true, this information should be given to the customer. However, this important deadline should have been discussed much earlier in the sales process. Use of any closing method that is perceived by the customer as pushy or manipulative will damage your chances of building a long-term partnership.

Some companies have taken steps to avoid the use of closing methods that might damage trust. Bill Goodwin, manager of training, sales, and marketing at the 3M Learning Center, says that closing methods are no longer included in 3M's sales training program. 3M wants salespeople to become more diagnostic and more responsive to feedback from the customer. Goodwin believes that thorough diagnostic efforts on the front end of the sales presentation will result in less buyer resistance on the back end of the sale.[2]

Closing the sale is easier if you review the value proposition effectively from the prospect's point of view.

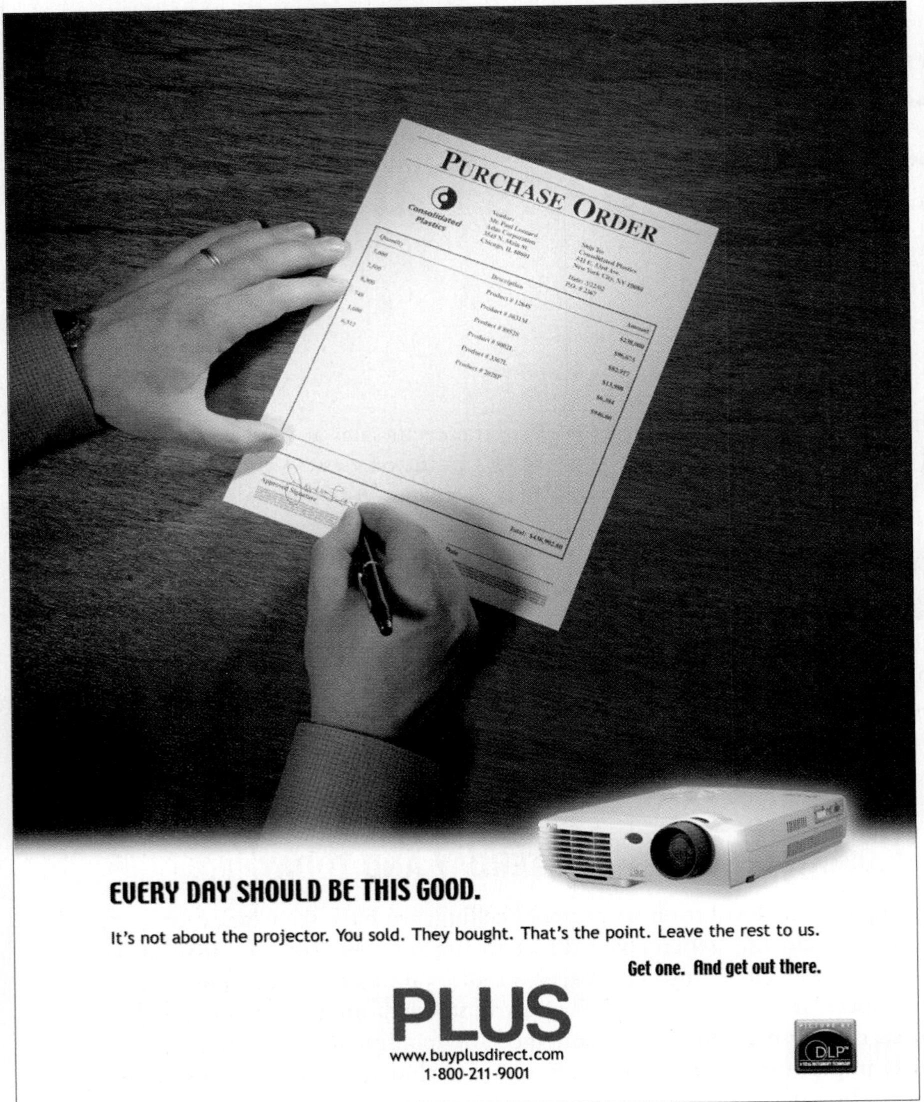

THE SIX-STEP PRESENTATION PLAN

Step One: Approach	☑ Review Strategic/Consultative Selling Model ☑ Initiate customer contact
Step Two: Presentation	☑ Determine prospect needs ☑ Select solution ☑ Initiate sales presentation
Step Three: Demonstration	☑ Decide what to demonstrate ☑ Select selling tools ☑ Initiate demonstration
Step Four: Negotiation	☑ Anticipate buyer concerns ☑ Plan negotiating methods ☑ Initiate win-win negotiations
Step Five: Close	☐ Plan appropriate closing methods ☐ Recognize closing clues ☐ Initiate closing methods
Step Six: Servicing the Sale	☐ Follow through ☐ Follow-up calls ☐ Expansion selling

Service, retail, wholesale, and manufacturer selling

FIGURE 14.1

Effective closing methods require careful planning.

We take the position that in many selling situations the salesperson needs to assume responsibility for obtaining commitment from the customer. Some closing methods can move the customer from indecision to commitment. When these methods are used effectively, the prospect will not feel pressured. In some cases, we need to simply replace defense-arousing language, such as, "This is the lowest price available anywhere," with a positive *need-satisfaction question* such as, "Wouldn't this new software help you achieve more efficient inventory control?"

Obtaining commitment is less difficult if the salesperson is strategically prepared for the close. Preparation for the close involves planning appropriate closing methods. Throughout the sales presentation the salesperson should recognize closing clues and be prepared to use effective closing methods (Fig. 14.1).

Review the Value Proposition from the Prospect's Point of View

Closing the sale is usually easier if you look at the *value proposition* from the prospect's point of view. Have you effectively summarized the mix of key benefits? Will your proposal provide a solution that solves the customer's problem? Is your proposal strong enough to win over a customer who is experiencing buying anxieties?

Noted author Gene Bedell reminds us that buying often causes emotional stress. A loss of options, fear of making a mistake, and/or social pressures can cause high levels of anxiety. Salespeople must be prepared to help the anxious customer make a decision.

Gene Bedell, author of *3 Steps to Yes*, reminds us that buying often causes emotional stress. The following buying anxieties help explain why some customers are reluctant to make a commitment to your proposal.[3]

Loss of options. If the customer agrees to purchase a $5,000 design proposal, then that money will not be available for other purchases or investments. Agreeing to purchase a product or service often means that some other purchase must be postponed. Anxiety and stress build as we think about allocating limited resources.

Fear of making a mistake. If the customer believes that agreeing with a closing request may be the wrong thing to do, he may back away just when the decision seems imminent. Fear of making a mistake can be caused by lack of trust in the salesperson.

Social or peer pressures. Some customers make buying decisions with an eye on the opinions and reactions of others. A business buyer may have to justify a purchase to her boss or employees who will actually use the product. Be prepared to deal with these anxieties as you get closer to closing the sale. Sometimes just a little gentle persuasion will help the anxious customer make a decision.

Closing the Sale—The Beginning of the Partnership

Tom Reilly, in his book *Value-Added Selling*, says " . . . you don't close sales; you build commitment to a course of action that brings value to the customer and profit to the seller."[4] There is a building process that begins with an interesting approach and need

Closing should be viewed as part of the selling process—the logical outcome of a well-planned presentation strategy.

discovery. It continues with effective product selection and presentation of benefits that build desire for the product. After a well-planned demonstration and after negotiating sales resistance, it is time to obtain commitment. Closing should be thought of as the beginning of a long-term partnership.

GUIDELINES FOR CLOSING THE SALE

A number of factors increase the odds that you will close the sale (Fig. 14.2). These guidelines for closing the sale have universal application in the field of selling.

Focus on Dominant Buying Motives

Most salespeople incorporate the outstanding benefits of their product into the sales presentation. This is only natural. However, be alert to the *one* specific benefit that generates the most excitement. The buying motive that is of greatest interest deserves special attention. Vince Peters, director of sales training and development for Wyeth-Ayerst International, tells his 8,000 pharmaceutical salespeople that the key to closing " . . . is to find out exactly what a prospect is looking for."[5]

Throughout the need discovery stage, pay close attention to the buyer's interests. Focus your closing efforts on the point of greatest interest and give the prospect a reason for buying.

Longer Selling Cycles Require Multiple Commitments

Longer, more complex selling cycles have become a fact of life. One reason for this change is that more decision makers are involved in purchasing some products. The purchase of highly technical products such as computer systems that serve an entire company, security equipment, and robotics may involve persons from many areas of the organization. In some cases the buyer has more options than in the past and will take more time to make a buying decision.

FIGURE | 14.2

The presentation strategy should include reviewing these guidelines for closing and confirming the sale.

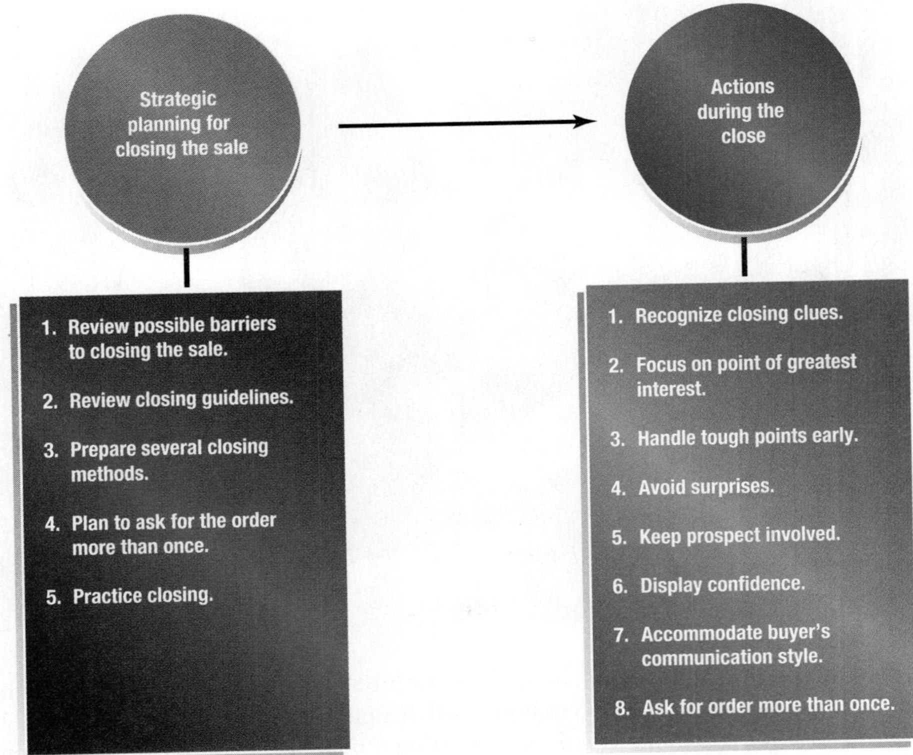

When you are working on a large, complex sale you should try to achieve **incremental commitment** throughout the sales process. Assume you are a sales representative for Guardsmark, a company that develops and implements high quality security systems. You have presented your security plan to the vice president of operations and she is committed to your proposal. However, this person cannot give final approval to the sale. In this case, you should request her help in arranging a meeting with the person who can approve your proposal. Some form of incremental commitment should be obtained during each step in a multicall sales presentation. Otherwise, you are not moving the sale forward toward obtaining a signed order.[6]

It is helpful to view each customer commitment as a "close." At the conclusion of the first sales call, you may need to obtain commitment to an agenda for the second call. Getting this commitment is essentially a form for closing.

Negotiating the Tough Points Before Attempting the Close

Many products have what might be thought of as an Achilles heel. In other words, the product is vulnerable, or appears to be vulnerable, in one or more areas. Negotiate a win-win solution to the tough points before you attempt to close the sale. Such factors can lose the sale if you ignore them. The close should be a positive phase of the sales presentation. This is not the time to deal with a controversial issue or problem.

In the case of Guardsmark security systems, Hickey-Freeman hand-tailored suits, Lexus automobiles, or Ritz-Carlton conference facilities, the Achilles heel may be price. Each of these products may seem expensive in comparison with competing ones. People who sell them find ways to establish the value of their product before attempting the close.

Avoid Surprises at the Close

Some salespeople make the mistake of waiting until the close to reveal information that may come as a surprise to the prospect. For example, the salesperson quotes a price but is not specific concerning what the price includes. Let us assume that the price of a central air-conditioning unit is $1,800. The prospect believes that the price is competitive in relation to similar units on the market and is ready to sign the order form. Then the salesperson mentions casually that the installation charge is an extra $225. The prospect had assumed that the $1,800 fee included installation. Suddenly, the extra fee looms as a major obstacle to closing the sale.

The surprise might come in the form of an accessory that costs extra, terms of the warranty, customer service limitations, or some other issue. Do not let a last-minute surprise damage the relationship and threaten the completion of a sale.

Display a High Degree of Self-Confidence at the Close

Do you believe in your product? Do you believe in your company? Do you believe in yourself? Have you identified a solution to the customer's problem? If you can answer yes to each of these questions, then there is no need to display timidity. Look the prospect in the eye and ask for the order. Do not be apologetic at this important point in the sales presentation. The salesperson who confidently asks for the sale is displaying the boldness that often is needed in personal selling.

Ask for the Order More Than Once

Too often, salespeople make the mistake of not asking for the order or asking just once. If the prospect says no, they give up. Michael LeBoeuf, author of *How to Win Customers and Keep Them for Life*, reports that almost two-thirds of all sales calls conclude without the salesperson asking for the order. He also says that a majority of all customers say no several times before saying yes.[7] Some of the most productive salespeople ask for the order three, four, or even five times. A surprising number of yes responses come on the fourth or fifth attempt. Of course, not all these closing attempts necessarily came during one call. Determination is a virtue if your product solution solves the customer's problem.

Recognize Closing Clues

As the sales presentation progresses, you need to be alert to closing clues (sometimes called buying signals). A **closing clue** is an indication, either verbal or nonverbal, that the prospect is preparing to make a buying decision. It is a form of feedback, which is so important in selling. When you detect a closing clue, it may be time to attempt a close.

Many closing clues are quite subtle and may be missed if you are not alert. This is especially true in the case of nonverbal buying signals. If you pay careful attention—with your eyes and your ears—many prospects will signal their degree of commitment.[8] As we have noted earlier in this text, one of the most important

Selling in Action

SELLING IN ACTION

Salespeople have the ultimate responsibility for bringing all of their selling activities to a close, but many do not ask for the order. This problem motivated Arthur R. Bauer and Gerald L. Manning, sales trainers, authors and consultants, to reproduce a video-based sales training course entitled *Ask for the Order* (www.iafto.com). Most customers expect the salesperson to ask for the order and will be puzzled when the salesperson fails to ask for their business. Fear of rejection is a major reason salespeople don't ask for the sale. Lack of discipline and determination can also serve as barriers to the use of closing attempts.[a] This new sales training video emphasizes the importance of securing incremental commitment throughout a multicall sales presentation.

ASK FOR THE ORDER

TRAINING LEADER'S GUIDE

Run an engaging, informative and fun training session!

Art Bauer

personality traits salespeople need is empathy, the ability to sense what the other person is feeling. In this section we review some of the most common verbal and non-verbal clues.

Verbal Clues

Closing clues come in many forms. Spoken words (verbal clues) are usually the easiest to perceive. These clues can be divided into three categories: (1) questions, (2) recognitions, and (3) requirements.

Questions One of the least subtle buying signals is the question. You might attempt a trial close after responding to one of the following questions:

"Do you have a credit plan to cover this purchase?"
"What type of warranty do you provide?"
"How soon can our company get delivery?"

Recognitions A recognition is any positive statement concerning your product or some factor related to the sale, such as credit terms or delivery date. Some examples follow:

"We like the quality control system you have recommended."
"I have always wanted to own a boat like this."
"Your delivery schedule fits our plans."

Requirements Sometimes, customers outline a condition that must be met before they can buy. If you are able to meet this requirement, it may be a good time to try a trial close. Some requirements that the prospect might voice are:

"We will need shipment within two weeks."
"Our staff will need to be trained in how to use this equipment."
"All our equipment must be certified by the plant safety officer."

In some cases, verbal buying clues do not jump out at you. Important buying signals may be interwoven into normal conversation. Listen closely whenever the prospect is talking.

Nonverbal Clues

Nonverbal buying clues are even more difficult to detect. Once detected, this type of signal is not easy to interpret. Nevertheless, you should be alert to body movement, facial expression, and tone of voice. Some actions follow that suggest the prospect may be prepared to purchase the product.[9]

The prospect's facial expression changes. Suddenly, the person's eyes widen, and genuine interest is clear in the facial expression.

The prospect begins showing agreement by nodding.

The prospect leans forward and appears to be intent on hearing your message.

The prospect begins to examine the product or study the sales literature intently.

When you observe or sense one of these nonverbal buying clues, do not hesitate to ask for commitment. There may be several opportunities to close throughout the sales presentation. Important buying signals may surface at any time. Do not miss them.

Selling Is Everyone's Business

BRAND DEVELOPMENT STARTS WITH PERSONAL SELLING

Building a brand name for a line of "unmentionables" (bras, underwear, and camisoles) can be a challenge. Alka and Mona Srivastava, sisters and business partners, readily agree that they didn't know what they were getting themselves into when they started Florentyna Intima, a lingerie company. The two economics majors knew very little about design, manufacturing, and marketing. Once they had a business plan and some money borrowed from their parents, Alka and Mona began the search for a designer and manufacturer. They needed prototypes to show to customers. Once the prototypes were completed by a firm in Bangkok, they tried to hire a sales representative to present the new line. Unfortunately, no one was willing to represent a line sold by an inexperienced manufacturer. That's when they decided to become salespeople. They hit the road, calling on owners of lingerie boutiques coast to coast and visiting trade shows. Soon buyers were calling with orders. Sales have grown about 30 percent each year.[b]

Alka and Mona Srivastava.

SPECIFIC METHODS FOR CLOSING THE SALE

The sales presentation is a process, not a single action. Each step during the process should create another layer of trust and move the customer closer to making the purchase. Throughout the sales process you are moving closer to the close by positioning yourself as a valued resource.[10]

There is no *best* closing method. Your best bet is to preplan several closing methods and use the ones that seem appropriate (Fig. 14.3). Given the complex nature of many sales, it is often a good idea to be prepared to use a combination of closing methods. Do keep in mind that your goal is not only to close the sale but also to develop a long-term partnership.

Trial Close

A **trial close** is a closing attempt made at an opportune time during the sales presentation to encourage the customer to reveal readiness or unwillingness to buy. When you are reasonably sure that the prospect is about to make a decision but is being held back by natural caution, the trial close may be appropriate. It is a good way to test the buyer's attitude toward the actual purchase. A trial close often is presented in the form of a confirmation question. Here are some examples:

"We can arrange an August first shipment. Would this date be satisfactory?"
"Would you rather begin this plan on July first or July fifteenth?"
"Will a $2,000 down payment be possible at this time?"

Closing Worksheet		
Closing clue (prospect)	Closing method	Closing statement (salesperson)
"That sounds fine." (Verbal recognition)	Direct appeal close	"Good, may I get your signature on this order form?"
"What kind of financing do you offer?" (Verbal question)	Multiple options close	"We have two financing methods available: 90-day open credit or two-year long-term financing. Which of these do you prefer?"
"Well, we don't have large amounts of cash available at this time." (Verbal requirement)	Assumptive close	"Based on your cash position, I would recommend you consider our lease–purchase plan. This plan allows you to pay a very small initial amount at this time and keep the cash you now have for your everyday business expenses. I will be happy to write up your order on the lease–purchase plan."
The prospect completes a careful reading of the proposal and communicates (nonverbal clue) a look of satisfaction. (Nonverbal message)	Combination summary-of-benefits/direct appeal close	"That solution surpasses your quality requirements, meets your time deadlines, and provides your accounting department with the details it requested. Can you get your chief financial officer's signature on the order?"

FIGURE | 14.3

Preparing for the close requires the preplanning of several closing methods. Research indicates that in many selling situations several closing attempts may be necessary.

Some salespeople use the trial close more than once during the sales presentation. After the salesperson presents a feature, converts that feature to a buyer benefit, and confirms the prospect's agreement that the benefit is important, it would be appropriate to use a trial close.

In broader terms, it would be appropriate to attempt a trial close after steps two, three, or four of the six-step presentation plan (Fig. 14.4).

Summary-of-Benefits Close

Let us assume that you have discussed and demonstrated the major benefits of your product and you detect considerable buyer interest. However, you have covered a great deal of material. There is a chance that the prospect is not able to put the entire picture together without your help. At this point you should provide a concise summary of the most important buyer benefits. Your goal in the **summary-of-benefits close** is to reemphasize the value-added benefits that can help bring about a favorable decision. This closing statement gives you the opportunity to restate how the benefits will outweigh the costs.[11]

Let us see how this closing method works in the hospitality industry. Terry Hall, sales manager of the Emory Hotel, recently called on Mr. Ray Busch, director of marketing for a large corporation. Near the end of the sales presentation, Terry

FIGURE | 14.4

The trial close should be attempted at an opportune time during the sales presentation. It is appropriate to initiate a trial close after steps two, three, or four of the six-step presentation plan.

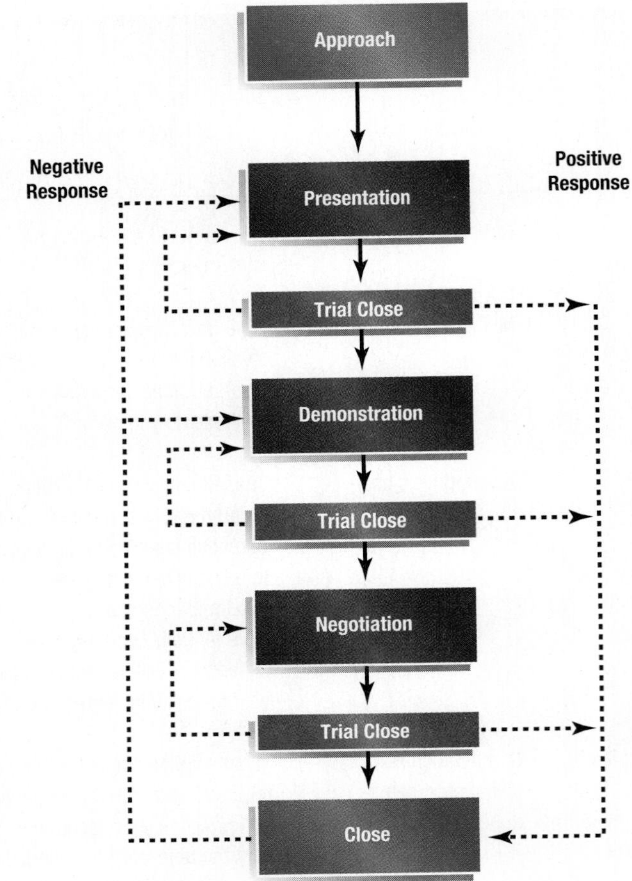

summarized the major benefits and buying conditions in this manner: "Mr. Busch, we can provide you with a conference room that will seat 200 people comfortably and four smaller rooms for the workshops you have planned. Our staff will serve a noon lunch, and the cost will be less than $11 per person. Finally, we will see that each of your employees receives a pad of paper, a pen, and a copy of the conference program. Today, I can reserve these facilities for November 24 which is your first preference for a meeting date. Can I go ahead and enter your reservation into our computer?" Notice that the salesperson has reviewed all the important elements of the value proposition and then asked a *need-satisfaction question.* This question is designed to move the sales process toward commitment and action.

Assumptive Close

The **assumptive close** asks for a minor decision, assuming that the customer has already decided to buy.[12] This closing approach comes near the end of the planned presentation. If you have identified a genuine need, presented your solutions in terms of buyer benefits, presented an effective sales demonstration, and negotiated buyer concerns satisfactorily, it may be natural to assume the person is ready to buy. The assumptive close usually takes the form of a question that focuses on a minor point. Some examples may include:

"If you feel the Model 211 gives you the major benefits you are looking for, let's schedule delivery for next Tuesday."

"Since our production system provides you with the order fulfillment flexibility you require, let's go ahead and place your order."

Most customers will view these statements as the natural conclusion of the events that preceded it. Assumptive closes often include a benefit with your request for action.[13]

This closing method provides a subtle way to ask for a decision when you are quite certain the customer has already decided to buy. You are only bringing the selling/buying process to a close.

Special Concession Close

The **special concession close** offers the buyer an extra incentive for acting immediately. A special inducement is offered if the prospect agrees to sign the order. The concession may be part of a low-price strategy, such as a sale price, a quantity discount, a more liberal credit plan, or an added feature that the prospect did not anticipate.

You should use this closing approach with care, because some customers are skeptical of concessions. This is especially true when the concession comes after the salesperson has made what appears to be the final offer.

Nicholas Graham, founder and chairman of Joe Boxer Corporation, spends considerable time presenting his novelty underwear line to retailers. Graham recalls that one of his most difficult sales involved Saks Fifth Avenue, the prestigious department store company. He wanted the company to carry Joe Boxer underwear and suggested a Daniel Boone–inspired boxer with a detachable raccoon tail. Graham says, "They had never seen anything so absurd in their life." To close the sale he let the store take 24 pairs on consignment. "They sold out in one hour," Graham says. Saks has been a committed customer ever since.[14]

The assumptive close asks for a minor decision, assuming that the customer has decided to buy.

Multiple Options Close

In many selling situations it is a good idea to provide the prospect with options regarding product configuration, delivery options, and price. This is especially true when you are dealing with the price-conscious *transactional* buyer. As noted in the previous chapter, today's customer expects new levels of flexibility. In the **multiple options close**, allow the person to examine several different options, and try to assess the degree of interest in each one. As you near the point at which a close seems appropriate, remove some of the options. This reduces confusion and indecision.

You often see the multiple options close used in office equipment sales. If a small business owner wants to purchase a copy machine, most vendors offer several models for consideration. Let us assume that the prospect has examined four models and seems to be uncertain about which one would be the best choice. The salesperson might determine which copier is least appealing and eliminate it as an option. Now the prospect can choose between three copiers. If the prospect seems to favor one copier, it would be appropriate to ask for the order.

When using the multiple options close, follow these simple steps:

1. Configure more than one product solution.
2. Cease presenting product options when it appears that the prospect has been given ample selection. Too many choices can result in confusion and indecision.
3. Remove products (or features) that the prospect does not seem genuinely interested in and concentrate on the options the prospect seems to be interested in.

Balance Sheet Close

The **balance sheet close** appeals to customers who are having difficulty making a decision even though they have been given plenty of information. Let's assume that the customer feels she has a choice: buy now or buy later. The salesperson draws a T on a sheet of paper and places the captions on each side of the crossbar.

REASONS FOR BUYING NOW	REASONS FOR NOT BUYING NOW
1.	1.
2.	2.
3.	3.
4.	4.

To get the process moving, the salesperson might say, "Let's see how many reasons we can list for buying now." On the left side of the T the salesperson lists some reasons for buying now. These should be benefits that the customer has already expressed an interest in. On the right side, reasons for not buying now are listed. Throughout the listing process, the salesperson and the customer must engage in a dialogue. This closing method will not be effective if the salesperson is doing all the talking.

Management Close

In previous chapters we have discussed the merits of involving the sales manager or senior executives in sales calls. To close a major account, salespeople sometimes call on top management for help. Ryan Hegman, who works for Hegman Machine Tool Inc., recalls a sale that involved a $1.5 million automated manufacturing system. During the sales process, he brought in the president of the company, the vice president of sales, and the lead engineer.

"Each added value in a separate way," Hegman explains. One important reason to involve management is to make prospects feel your whole company's resources will be available to support the customer.[15]

Direct Appeal Close

The **direct appeal close** has the advantages of clarity and simplicity. This close involves simply asking for the order in a straightforward manner. It is the most direct closing approach, and many buyers find it attractive. Realistically, most customers expect salespeople to ask for the sale.

The direct appeal should not, of course, come too early. It should not be used until the prospect has displayed a definite interest in the product or service. The salesperson also must gain the prospect's respect before initiating this appeal. Once you make the direct appeal, stop talking. John Livesay, West Coast Ad Director for *W* magazine, says being patient at the close is his "secret weapon." After asking the customer to buy he stays silent. He avoids asking more questions or making additional statements. This approach gives the customer time to think about the proposal.[16]

A variation of the direct appeal close involves use of a question to determine how close the customer is to making a buying decision. The question might be, "How close are we to closing the sale?" This direct question calls for a direct answer. The customer is encouraged to reflect on the progress of the sale.[17]

Combination Closes

In some cases the most effective close is one that combines two or more of the closing methods we have discussed. To illustrate, let us observe Colleen White as she attempts to close a sale in the office of a buyer for a large department store. Colleen represents a firm that manufactures a wide range of leather clothing and accessories. Near the end of her planned presentation she senses that the prospect is quite interested in her products but seems reluctant to make a decision.

This is how Colleen handles the close: "Ms. Taylor, I have described two benefits that seem especially important to you. First, you agree that this line will be popular with the fashion-conscious shoppers your store caters to. Second, you indicated that the prices I quoted will allow you excellent profit margins. If we process your order now, you will have the merchandise in time for the pre-Christmas buying period. We can guarantee the delivery at this point." Notice that this starts with a summary of benefits and ends with a special concession.

PRACTICE CLOSING

Your success in selling can depend in large part on learning how to make these eight closing methods work for you. You may not master these approaches in a few days or a few weeks, but you can speed up the learning process with preparation and practice. Role playing is one of the best ways to experience the feelings that accompany closing and to practice the skills needed to close sales. To prepare the role-play, anticipate various closing scenarios and then prepare a written script of the drama.[18] Find someone (your sales manager, friend, or spouse) to play the role of the customer and give that person a script to act out. Practice the role-plays in front of a video recorder, and then sit back and observe your performance. The video monitor provides excellent feedback. Use the closing worksheet (see Fig. 14.3) to prepare for practice sessions.

CONFIRMING THE PARTNERSHIP WHEN THE BUYER SAYS YES

Congratulations! You have closed the sale and have established the beginning of what you hope will be a long and satisfying partnership with the customer. Before preparing to leave, be sure that all the details related to the purchase agreement are completed. Check all particulars with the buyer, and then ask for a signature if necessary.

Once the sale has been closed, it is important to take time to reassure the customer. This is the **confirmation step** in closing the sale. Before you leave, reassure the customer by pointing out that she has made the correct decision, and describe the satisfaction that will come with ownership of the product. The reason for doing this is to resell the buyer and to prevent buyer's remorse. **Buyer's remorse** is an emotional response that can take various forms such as feelings of regret, fear, or anxiety.[19] It's common to wonder whether or not we have made the right decision. Compliment the person for making a wise decision. Once the sale is closed, the customer may be required to justify the purchase to others. Your words of reassurance can be helpful.

Before leaving, thank the customer for the order. This is very important. Everyone likes to think that a purchase is appreciated. No one should believe that a purchase is taken for granted. Even a small order deserves words of appreciation. In many cases a follow-up thank-you letter is appropriate.

In several previous chapters we note that a satisfied customer is one of the best sources of new prospects. Never hesitate to ask, "Do you know anyone else who might benefit from owning this product?" or a similar question. Some customers may even agree to write an introductory letter on your behalf.

What to Do When the Buyer Says No

High-performance salespeople learn to manage disappointment. A strong display of disappointment or resentment is likely to close the door to future sales. Losing a sale may be painful, but it can also be a valuable learning opportunity. Doing some analysis of what went wrong can help you change the outcome of future sales. Here are some things you should do after a lost sale.[20]

Before leaving, thank the customer for the order. This is very important. Everyone likes to think that a purchase is appreciated.

Beth Manning, Jody Sprock Interiors & Associates
119 19th Street, Suite 202
West Des Moines, Iowa 50265-4226
515-225-9253 Fax 515-225-9386

Letter of Agreement

Beth Manning Jody Sprock Interiors (BMJSI) is pleased to be of service to you in designing and beautifying the interior of your design project. Our design service is described in the following contract agreement.

DESIGN SERVICES: The designer may perform the following services for the client:
Schematic Design - Space Planning - Budget Estimates
Design Development - Product and Finish Specification
Procurement - Administration - Installation - Design Execution

A. DESIGN SERVICES - PURCHASING THROUGH *BMJSI* - RETAINER
Client shall pay in advance a retainer of $565.00. This is estimated to cover approximately 7 1/2 hours of design time (This includes driving time.). The $565.00 retainer will be applied to your final invoice as a credit, if procurement occurs through ***BMJSI*** as planned. When a minimum $2500.00 purchase is made within a three month period, the retainer will be credited to a final product invoice. If a minimum $2500.00 purchase is not made within a three month period, the retainer will be used as hourly compensation. In the event that specified products are purchased elsewhere or if a portion of the job that the designer has done research and development on is not completed, the designer will be compensated at an hourly rate ($75.00) for services/time rendered. A detailed account of the designer's hours will be charged and billed to client if the project does not proceed as planned. When a minimum sale of $2500.00 per project occurs, the hourly fee will be waived.

B. DESIGN/CONSULTATION SERVICES ONLY - NO PROCUREMENT THROUGH BMJSI
An advance retainer of $375.00 will be collected in order to begin work on the project. This covers approximately 5 hours of design research and development. Clients using design services only will be billed at an hourly rate of $75.00 (This includes driving time.). Billing will be after each appointment. Payment is due within 10 days or prior to the next appointment. ***Billable design services*** may include: SPACE PLANNING, DESIGN PLANNING, COLOR GUIDELINING, PHASE PLANNING, SHOPPING SERVICES, ACCESSORIZING, PROJECT MANAGEMENT, PRODUCT SPECIFICATION, BID PREPARATION.
OTHER: ____________________

C. TRIP CHARGE
A trip allowance will be billed for out of town job sites.

D. WARRANTIES AND WORKMANSHIP
We wish to inform you that by using a professional design firm you are guaranteed:
1. Professional coordination of fabrics and furnishings and concern for your needs first.
2. Prompt, professional follow-up if problems do arise.
3. Recommended resources that maintain the highest standards of workmanship.

BMJSI is not responsible for:
1. Work by third parties not engaged by ***BMJSI.***
2. Warranties not provided by our manufacturers and resources.

CLIENT: ____________________ **DATE:** ____________

DESIGNER: ____________________ **DATE:** ____________

"SPECIALIZING IN LIFE STYLE DESIGN"

After the buyer says yes, be sure that all details related to the purchase agreement are completed, and then ask for a signature. A signature is required on this "Letter of Agreement."

1. Make sure the deal is really dead. There is always a chance that the customer's decision can be changed. You might want to mount a last-ditch effort to reopen the presentation.
2. Review the chain of events. When you experience a no-sale call, try to benefit from the experience. If you were part of a sales team, get input from each member.

Global Business Etiquette

DOING BUSINESS IN SOUTH AMERICA

Although specific customs vary in the countries of South America, some generalizations can be made. For example, residents of Brazil, Argentina, and other countries have a different idea of what is appropriate personal space. They tend to stand closer to you during conversations. To step back may be viewed as impolite. You should expect more physical contact such as pats on the back and hugs. Lunch is the main meal of the day and it's not uncommon for a business meal to last several hours. Latin Americans often arrive late for appointments. Be patient with decision makers and do not use the hard-sell approach. Be aware of language preferences. Brazilians speak Portuguese; addressing them in Spanish would be insulting. Business associates in Argentina will likely speak English and Spanish. However, your business card should be translated into Spanish.[c]

Soon after the prospect says no, schedule a debriefing session. If you worked alone, engage in honest self-analysis. Look carefully at your performance during every aspect of the sales process, you may be able to identify weaknesses that can be corrected.

3. Interview the client. Obtaining feedback requires a delicate approach. If you probe too aggressively, you may appear argumentative. If your approach is too passive, and the client's comments are general, you will not know how to improve. The key is to couch your questions in neutral terms. Rather than asking, "Why didn't we get the order?" try this approach: "Thank you for considering our company. We hope to do business with you at some time in the future. Would you mind helping me understand any shortcomings in our sales proposal?"

Follow-up telephone calls can be used to provide the prospect with additional information needed to make a buying decision.

Customer Relationship Management with Technology

ADDING AND DELETING PROSPECTS

Prospect and customer databases are continually changing. Promotions, transfers, mergers, and many other events require additions and deletions in a salesperson's automated data. Most customer relationship management (CRM) software makes this an easy process and warns users against the inadvertent removal of an account. (See the exercise, Adding and Deleting Prospects, on p. 361 for more information.)

Always keep the door open for future sales. Tell the prospect you would love to work with her at some time in the future. Then, put this person back on your prospect list, record any new information you have learned about the prospect, and continue to keep in touch.

Prepare the Prospect for Contact with the Competition

Some prospects refuse to buy because they want to take a close look at the competing products. This response is not unusual in the field of selling. You should do everything possible to help the customer make an intelligent comparison.

It is always a good practice to review your product's strong points one more time. Give special emphasis to areas in which your product has a superior advantage over the competition. Make it easy for the person to buy your product at some future date.

Summary

Prior to the introduction of consultative selling and the partnering era, closing was often presented as the most important aspect of the sales process. Some of the early closing methods encouraged manipulation of the customer. Use of any closing method that is perceived by the customer as pushy or manipulative will damage your chances of building a long-term partnership.

Long sales cycles require multiple commitments. These commitments need to be obtained from the prospect throughout a multicall sales presentation. The salesperson must be alert to *closing clues* from the prospect. These clues fall into two categories: verbal and nonverbal. Verbal clues are the easiest to recognize, but they may be subtle as well. Again it is important to be an attentive listener. The recognition of nonverbal clues is more difficult, but careful observation helps in detecting them.

Several closing methods may be necessary to get the prospect to make a buying decision; therefore, it is wise for the salesperson to preplan several closes. These closing methods should be chosen from the list provided in this chapter and then customized to fit the product and the type of buyer with whom the salesperson is dealing. In some selling situations the use of *combination closes* is very effective.

The professional salesperson is not discouraged or offended if the sale is not closed. Every effort should be made to be of further assistance to the prospect—the sale might be closed on another call. Even if the sale is lost, the experience may be valuable if analyzed to learn from it.

KEY TERMS

Closing clue
Trial close
Summary-of-benefits close
Assumptive close
Incremental commitment
Special concession close
Multiple options close
Direct appeal close
Combination closes
Confirmation step
Buyer's remorse
Balance sheet close
Management close

REVIEW QUESTIONS

1. List some aspects of the sales presentation that can make closing and confirming the sale difficult to achieve.
2. Describe three buying anxieties that sometimes serve as barriers to closing the sale.
3. What guidelines should a salesperson follow for closing the sale?
4. Why is it important to review the value proposition from the prospect's point of view?
5. Define the term *incremental commitment.* Why is it important to achieve incremental commitments throughout the sale?
6. Explain how the multiple options close might be used in the sale of men's and women's suits.
7. Is there a best method to use in closing the sale? Explain.
8. What is meant by a trial close? When should a salesperson attempt a trial close?
9. Explain the summary-of-benefits close.
10. What confirming steps should a salesperson follow when the customer says yes? What should be done when the customer says no?

APPLICATION EXERCISES

1. Which of the following statements, often made by prospects, would you interpret as buying signals?
   a. "How much would the payments be?"
   b. "Tell me about your service department."
   c. "The company already has an older model that seems good enough."
   d. "We do not have enough cash flow right now."
   e. "How much would you allow me for my old model?"
   f. "I do not need one."
   g. "How does that switch work?"
   h. "When would I have to pay for it?"
2. You are an accountant who owns and operates an accounting service. You have been contacted by the president of an advertising agency about the possibility of your auditing his business on a regular basis. The president has indicated that he investigated other accounting firms and thinks they price their services too high. With the knowledge you have about the other firms you know you are in a strong competitive position. Also, you realize his account would be profitable for your firm. You really would like to capture this account. How will you close the deal? List and describe two closing methods you might use in this situation.

3. Zig Ziglar, Brian Tracy, and Tom Reilly are all well-known authors and speakers on the subject of closing the sale. Access each of their Web sites by using *www.(their name).com* and research the books, courses, and videos they have available for companies and individuals to purchase and learn more about closing the sale. Prepare a summary of what you find available. Does the material in this chapter parallel the kind of information these individuals present?

ROLE-PLAY EXERCISE

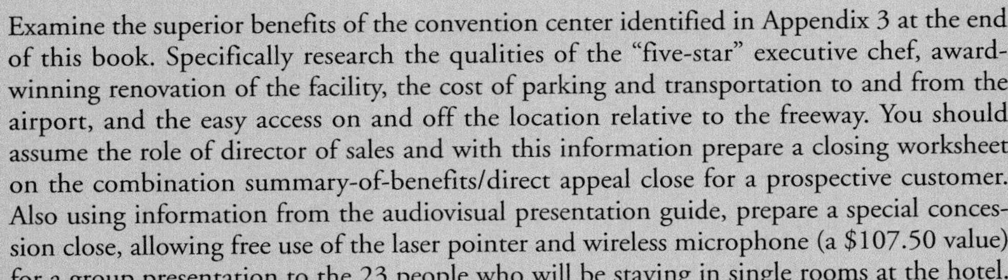

Examine the superior benefits of the convention center identified in Appendix 3 at the end of this book. Specifically research the qualities of the "five-star" executive chef, award-winning renovation of the facility, the cost of parking and transportation to and from the airport, and the easy access on and off the location relative to the freeway. You should assume the role of director of sales and with this information prepare a closing worksheet on the combination summary-of-benefits/direct appeal close for a prospective customer. Also using information from the audiovisual presentation guide, prepare a special concession close, allowing free use of the laser pointer and wireless microphone (a $107.50 value) for a group presentation to the 23 people who will be staying in single rooms at the hotel. Role-play the close of a sale using these closing methods to a propect who is also seriously considering using one of your competitors.

CRM APPLICATION EXERCISE

Adding and Deleting Prospects

Adding and deleting contacts is easy with the ACT! software, as it is with most CRM software. Create a Contact record for a B. H. Rivera by selecting Edit, New Contact or by pressing the Insert key (Ins on some keyboards). This displays a blank record that can be completed by selecting fields with the mouse or by using the Tab key to move from field to field. In the Company field, type "Graphic Forms" and type 3195556194 (no hyphens) into the Phone field. The address is "2134 Martin Luther King"; and Atlanta, GA, and 61740 are City, State, and Zip.

Most CRM software permits you to save time and avoid errors by selecting field data from menus. For example, point at the ID/Status field label and double-click with your mouse on the label, not the field. A menu of choices should appear. Another method to obtain this menu is to place the cursor in the field and press the F2 function key. From this menu, select Prospect as the ID/Status for the B. H. Rivera record.

You have just added a new record to the ACT! database. The demonstration version of the ACT! software version limits the number of contacts to 25. The full version of ACT! has no such limit. Do not enter more than 25 contacts into this demonstration version. Print this new record by selecting Report, Contact Report, Active Contact, Printer, and OK.

To remove a contact, select Edit, Delete Contact. The window is displayed with a box for Contact, Lookup, and Cancel. Picking Contact causes the individual record to be deleted, Lookup deletes all records currently being looked up, and Cancel terminates the procedure. Choosing to delete a record causes a warning window to be displayed. This window asks if you are sure that you wish to delete the contact. Caution is advised when deleting records or using the delete function. Pressing the F1 function key displays the appropriate help screen.

VIDEO CASE PROBLEM

The Special Event Sales Department at Universal Studios can make your dreams come true. The staff can help you plan a wedding reception that guests will be talking about for years. (How about a Jurassic Park theme?) If you want to show appreciation to your chief executive officer who is retiring, the staff will make sure the party is truly special. The staff can also help you plan a bar mitzvah, a class reunion, or any other special event.

Gretchen Parr-Silver, director of the Special Event Sales Department, enjoys working with customers. Her customers vary greatly in terms of age, education, income, and social class. The key to working effectively with all of these people is relationship building. Once she builds rapport with clients and establishes a foundation built on trust, they are more likely to open up and discuss their needs. Event planners have at their disposal a wide range of props, facilities, and production expertise, but customer needs guide the use of these resources.

Gretchen finds that if the sales presentation is well planned and delivered, closing the sale is easier. She believes that good listening skills and careful probing can help uncover dominant buying motives. For example, the client who wants a wedding reception with a special theme may have difficulty expressing her thoughts. Gretchen must probe and listen closely in order to understand the customer's desires. She must also create value throughout the presentation in order to set the stage for the close. A special event can cost several thousand dollars, so price can be a barrier to closing.

Questions

1. What closing clues should Gretchen Parr-Silver look for?
2. What trial closes would be appropriate?
3. What tough points should be negotiated before attempting to close?
4. Can you visualize a situation in which Gretchen Parr-Silver might use a multiple options close? Explain.
5. Assume that a large corporation wants to schedule a recognition party for 40 people. This event will begin with cocktails and appetizers and end with a served meal. Special entertainment will precede the meal. What items might be included in a summary-of-benefits close?

CRM CASE STUDY

Forecasting the Close

You are interested in discovering what your commissions may be for the next few months, just from Pat Silva's former accounts. To do this, you review the information on each Contact record. There are four fields on the first page of the Contact Screen from which you can forecast your expected sales: Network Need, Likelihood, Dollar Amount, and Date Close. When working with these accounts, Pat entered the information found in each of these fields. In the Network Need field, Pat entered the type of network that the prospect might order. In the Likelihood field, Pat estimated the percentage of possibility that the account might place an order (0.80 means 80%). The Dollar Amount field refers to how much Pat thought the account would spend and the month Pat believed the account would order is in the Date Close field (01/31 means January).

You can estimate each month's likely sales by multiplying the Dollar Amount field number times the Likelihood field percentage number. An 80 percent chance of a $100,000 sale is a forecast of $80,000 in sales. If the Date Close field for several accounts is 12/31, you can calculate the sales for that month (December) by totaling the forecasts for each account. For an estimate of your commission income, multiply each month's forecast by 10 percent.

Pat did not show that any forecasted sales were 100 percent. Pat recognized that the sales might not close, the amount anticipated (Dollar Amount) might not be achieved, and the close might not take place during the month projected. Pat knew that these prospects would not close themselves; certain steps would have to be taken to increase the possibility that the prospect would place an order. To collect your commissions, you have to discover the steps most likely to close these sales.

Questions

1. What would your commission income be for all Pat's accounts if you closed them as Pat forecasted?
2. What kind of special concession might be necessary to close the sale with Quality Builders?
3. What kind of close may be necessary to get an order from Computerized Labs?
4. What kind of close would be appropriate for the Lakeside Clinic?

PARTNERSHIP SELLING: A ROLE-PLAY/SIMULATION

(see Appendix 3, pp. 508–509, 519)

Developing a Presentation Strategy—Closing the Sale

Refer to *sales memorandum 3* and strategically plan to close the sale with your customer. To consider the sale closed you need to secure the signature of your customer on the sales proposal form. This guarantees your customer the accommodations listed on the form. These accommodations may change depending on the final number of people attending your customer's convention. This is an important point to keep in mind when closing the sale; however, you still must get the signature to guarantee the accommodations.

Follow the instructions carefully, and prepare a closing worksheet (See Strategic Planning Form C) listing at least four closes using the methods outlined in this chapter. Two of these methods should include the summary of the benefits and the direct appeal. Remember it is not the policy of your convention center to cut prices, so your methods should include value-added strategies.

Use proof devices to make your closes more convincing and place them in the front pocket of your three-ring binder/portfolio for easy access during your presentation. You may want to secure another person to be your customer, and practice the closing strategies you have developed.

Chapter Preview

When you finish reading this chapter, you should be able to

1. Explain how to build long-term partnerships with customer service
2. Describe current developments in customer service
3. List and describe the major customer service methods that add value to the partnership
4. Explain how to work effectively with customer support personnel
5. Explain how to deal effectively with complaints

CHAPTER 15

Servicing the Sale and Building the Partnership

Body Glove International (*www.bodyglove.com*), a leading manufacturer of wet suits for a variety of water sports, had a humble beginning. Bill and Randy Meistrell, founders of the company, were active in surfing and scuba diving in the early 1950s when good-quality wet suits were hard to find. They decided to turn this problem into an opportunity and developed their own wet suit design. The first suits were sold at a small dive shop in Redondo Beach, California. Today Body Glove International is a multimillion dollar global company that is recognized worldwide for its quality products and outstanding **customer service.**

Sales professionals who represent the Body Glove line of products embrace the company philosophy that is based on the belief that you never sacrifice quality in any area, including service after the sale. Servicing the sale is an important element of the presentation strategy. Body Glove has invested in a modern customer service center, which is equipped with the newest technology. With the aid of modern computers, staff members can check the status of any order. The customer service staff, working with salespeople, continue to add value after the sale is closed.[1]

Servicing the sale encompasses a variety of activities that take place during and after the implementation stage of the buying process (Fig. 8.3). In this chapter, we present servicing the sale as a three-part process: follow through on assurances and promises, follow up with ongoing communication after the sale, and expansion selling, which involves the identification of additional needs and providing solutions (Figure 15.1). Each of these strategies can add value and build the partnership.

Body Glove is an international company with a strong commitment to customer services. The company views customer service as a key element of partnership building.

BUILDING LONG-TERM PARTNERSHIPS WITH CUSTOMER SERVICE

In a world of increased global competition and narrowing profit margins, customer retention through value-based initiatives can mean the difference between increasing or eroding market share. Progressive marketers are searching for ways to differentiate their service from competitors and to build emotional loyalty through value.[2]

FIGURE | 15.1

Servicing the sale involves three steps: follow through, follow-up calls, and expansion selling.

THE SIX-STEP PRESENTATION PLAN

Step One: Approach	☑ Review Strategic/Consultative Selling Model ☑ Initiate customer contact
Step Two: Presentation	☑ Determine prospect needs ☑ Select solution ☑ Initiate sales presentation
Step Three: Demonstration	☑ Decide what to demonstrate ☑ Select selling tools ☑ Initiate demonstration
Step Four: Negotiation	☑ Anticipate buyer concerns ☑ Plan negotiating methods ☑ Initiate win-win negotiations
Step Five: Close	☑ Plan appropriate closing methods ☑ Recognize closing clues ☑ Initiate closing methods
Step Six: Servicing the Sale	☐ Follow through ☐ Follow-up calls ☐ Expansion selling

Service, retail, wholesale, and manufacturer selling

A sales organization that can develop a reputation for servicing each sale (Fig. 15.1) is sought out by customers who want a long-term partner to help them with their buying needs. Satisfied customers represent an "auxiliary" sales force—a group of people who recommend customer-driven organizations to others. If customers are pleased with the service that they receive after the sale, be assured that they will tell other people. Research shows that when someone has a good customer service experience, he tells an average of six people; when he has an outstanding experience, he tells twice as many.[3]

Achieving Successive Sales

In Chapter 1 we described *partnering* as a strategically developed, long-term relationship that solves the customer's problem. A successful partnering effort results in successive sales and referrals (Fig. 1.8).

Many of today's large companies want to partner with suppliers who sell and deliver quality products and services that continually improve their processes and profits. The first sale is only the beginning of the relationship—an opportunity to earn a repeat sale. Repeat sales come after the supplier demonstrates the ability to add value in various ways.[4] This value may take the form of timely delivery, superior installation, accurate invoicing, technical know-how, social contacts, or something else that is important to the customer. In business-to-business sales, the relationship should intensify as the supplier delivers extensive postsale support.

Responding to Increased Postsale Customer Expectations

People buy expectations, not products, according to Ted Levitt, author of *The Marketing Imagination.* They buy the expectations of benefits you promised. Once the customer buys your product, expectations increase. Levitt points out that after the sale is closed, the buyer's attitude changes. The customer expects the salesperson to remember the purchase as a favor bestowed on him by the buyer.

Nitin Nohria, Harvard Business School professor and co-author of *What Really Works: The 4+2 Formula for Sustained Business Success*, says, "Customers are enormously punishing when companies don't meet their expectations."[5]

Increased customer expectations, after the sale is closed, require a strategic plan for servicing the sale. Certain aspects of the relationship, product, and customer strategies can have a positive influence on the customer's heightened expectations. In most business-to-business sales, the salesperson cannot service the sale alone. To properly manage the account, the salesperson will need assistance from the shipping department, technical support, engineering, and other areas. Customer service is increasingly a team effort.

How do we respond to a customer who has increased expectations? First, we should be certain our customer strategy is on target. We must fully understand the needs and wants of the customer. What is the customer trying to accomplish and how can you help the person do it better?

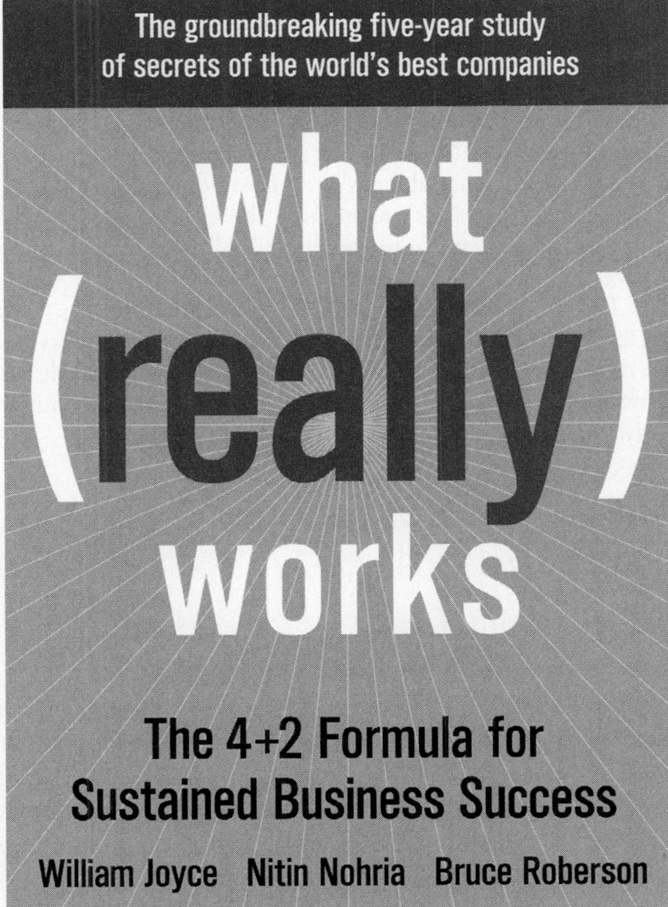

Nitin Nohria, Harvard Business School professor and co-author of What Really Works, *says "Customers are enormously punishing when companies don't meet their expectations."*

This salesperson is preparing a thank-you note that will strengthen the relationship with the customer.

Second, you should focus like a laser beam on follow-through and follow-up activities. Throughout every sales presentation the salesperson will offer assurances and make some promises. The salesperson's credibility will be tarnished if any of these commitments are ignored.

Third, we should reexamine our product strategy. In some cases we can enhance customer satisfaction by suggesting related products or services. If the product is expensive, we can follow through and offer assistance in making credit arrangements. If the product is complex, we can make suggestions concerning use and maintenance. Each of these forms of assistance may add value to the sale.

Selling Is Everyone's Business

JOB SEARCHES REQUIRE WIDENING THE NET

You have a good education but you don't have a job. This scenario is being played out in the lives of thousands of people across the nation. Before you send out another 1,000 résumés via the Internet or spend more time searching the Net for employment opportunities, consider the results of a study conducted by Drake Beam Morin (DBM) at www.dbm.com, a workplace-consulting firm. Networking is the top tactic for landing a job, outpacing other strategies such as the Internet and newspaper ads. The report indicates that 66 percent of DBM clients found new jobs via networking, whereas just 6 percent found employment through the Internet. Don't overlook the value of personal contact that gives you an opportunity to sell yourself.[a]

High Cost of Customer Attrition

Financial institutions, public utilities, airlines, retail stores, restaurants, manufacturers, and wholesalers face the problem of gaining and retaining the patronage of clients and customers. These companies realize that keeping a customer happy is a winning strategy. To regain a lost customer can be four to five times more expensive than keeping a current customer satisfied.[6]

There is no longer any doubt that poor service is the primary cause of customer attrition. A surprisingly small number of customers (12 to 15 percent) are lost due to product dissatisfaction. No more than 10 to 15 percent of lost customers leave due to price considerations. Some studies have found that from 50 to 70 percent of customer attrition is due to poor service.[7] A carefully developed strategic plan to reduce customer defection pays big dividends.

Carl Sewell, chairman of Sewell Automotive Companies with dealerships in Dallas, Fort Worth, New Orleans, and San Antonio, has fully embraced the customer-for-life philosophy of doing business. He lives, sleeps, eats, and breathes his obsession with customer service and the result is a family of dealerships that are the envy of almost everyone in the automobile business.[8]

Carl Sewell lives, sleeps, eats, and breathes his obsession with customer service and the result is a half-billion-dollar dealership that is the envy of almost everyone in the automobile business. (www.sewell.com)

CURRENT DEVELOPMENTS IN CUSTOMER SERVICE

Bill Gates, in his book *Business @ The Speed of Thought*, predicts that in the new millennium customer service may become the primary value-added function.[9] He recognizes that customer service is the primary method of building and extending the partnership. Customer service, in its many forms, nourishes the partnership and keeps it alive. The age of information has ushered in a series of customer service initiatives that affect the daily work of salespeople. We discuss three of these current developments.

- *Salespeople must spend more time monitoring customer satisfaction.* There is a growing trend in which companies rely on their salespeople to continually monitor their customers' needs, concerns, and future plans. In the past many salespeople would live or die by the number of sales closed and too little attention was given to service after the sale. Lost customer studies have found that benign neglect is a primary reason for defection. The salesperson did not keep in touch so it was easy for the customer to walk away.[10]

  Salespeople who have frequent contact with the customer are in an excellent position to assess the health of the partnership. Mack Hanan, author of *Consultative Selling*, encourages salespeople to seek answers to several questions:[11] Is the customer still growing because of your products and your expertise? How much more growth can take place in the future? How much is the partner growing you? In other words, is your company benefiting enough from the partnership? When the partnership involves a *strategic alliance*, answers to these questions are especially important.
- *Customer knowledge is viewed by sales and sales support personnel as an important key to improving customer service.* Bob Johnson, vice president of Information Technology Services Marketing Association, says that the ability to manage your customer knowledge is the number-one lesson for anyone who wants to build customer loyalty:[12]

  > If you can't capture, manage and leverage customer history (as well as information regarding current and future needs), you can forget about loyalty. Limited knowledge management capability fosters the sense that the company has no real interest in the customer—or his repeat patronage.

Bill Gates, author of Business @ The Speed of Thought, *predicts that in the new economy customer service may become the primary value-added function.*

Once you acquire knowledge about your customer, you can tailor your customer service initiatives to develop a more productive and cost-effective partnership. Sanwa Bank California, headquartered in Los Angeles, uses customer knowledge to determine what type of service may be beneficial for each customer. Customers use money in many different ways, and the bank offers a complex line of products and services. Sales representatives at Sanwa can access a computerized customer database for any bank customer in a matter of seconds.[13]

Selling in Action

THE MOMENT OF MAGIC

Tony Alessandra (www.alessandra.com) a well-known sales trainer and consultant, says that there are three possible outcomes when a customer does business with an organization.

The moment of truth. In these selling situations the customer's expectations were met. Nothing happened to disappoint the customer, and the salesperson did not do anything to surpass the customer's expectations. The customer is apt to have somewhat neutral feelings about her relationship with the salesperson. The moment of truth usually does not build customer loyalty.

The moment of misery. This is the outcome of a selling situation in which the customer's expectations were not met. The customer may feel a sense of disappointment or even anger. Many customers who experience the moment of misery may share their feelings with others and often make a decision to "fire" the salesperson.

The moment of magic. This is the outcome of a sale in which the customer received more than he expected. The salesperson surpassed the customer's expectations by going the extra mile and providing a level of service that added value to the customer–salesperson relationship. This extra effort is likely to establish a foundation for increased customer loyalty.[b]

The "moment of magic" is the outcome of a sale in which the customer receives more than he expected. Value-added customer service strategies often produce this outcome.

- *Customer-friendly, computer-based systems frequently are used to enhance customer service.* Computers give both the salesperson and the customer ready access to information and problem-solving alternatives. Nantucket Nectars provides a good example of a company that has enhanced customer service with computer-based systems. The 150 distributors can log on to (www.juiceguys.com) to place and check orders. Nantucket Nectars' 85 field salespeople can log on to NectarNet, a dedicated company web site, from their homes to check on the status of customer orders and determine inventory levels.[14]

The sales staff at Mitchells/Richards, the highly successful clothing stores introduced in a previous chapter, uses technology to establish a more personal relationship with the customer. In a matter of seconds salespeople can review a customer's complete buying history and personal information such as their birthday and anniversary, clothing sizes, favorite colors, names of their children, and even the name of their pet. With this information sales-people are better able to bond with their customers.[15]

CUSTOMER SERVICE METHODS THAT STRENGTHEN THE PARTNERSHIP

Customer service encompasses all activities that enhance or facilitate the sale and use of one's product or service. The skills required to service a sale are different from those required prior to the sale (Fig. 15.2). High-performance sales personnel do not abdicate responsibility for delivery, installation, warranty interpretation, or other customer service responsibilities. They continue to strengthen the partnership with follow-through, follow-up, and expansion selling.

Adding Value with Follow-Through

A major key to an effective customer service strategy is follow-through on assurances and promises that were part of the sales presentation. Did your sales presentation include claims for superior performance; promises of speedy delivery; assistance with credit arrangements; and guaranteed factory assistance with installation, training, and service?

Most sales presentations are made up of claims and promises that the company can fulfill. However, fulfillment of these claims depends to a large degree on after-sale action. Postsale follow-through is the key to holding that customer you worked so hard to develop.

Common Postsale Services

The first sale can be the beginning of a long-term partnership or it can be the last sale. The following services can help ensure a second sale and successive sales.

Make Credit Arrangements

Credit has become a common way to finance purchases. This is true of industrial products, real estate, automobiles, home appliances, and many other products. Closing the sale often

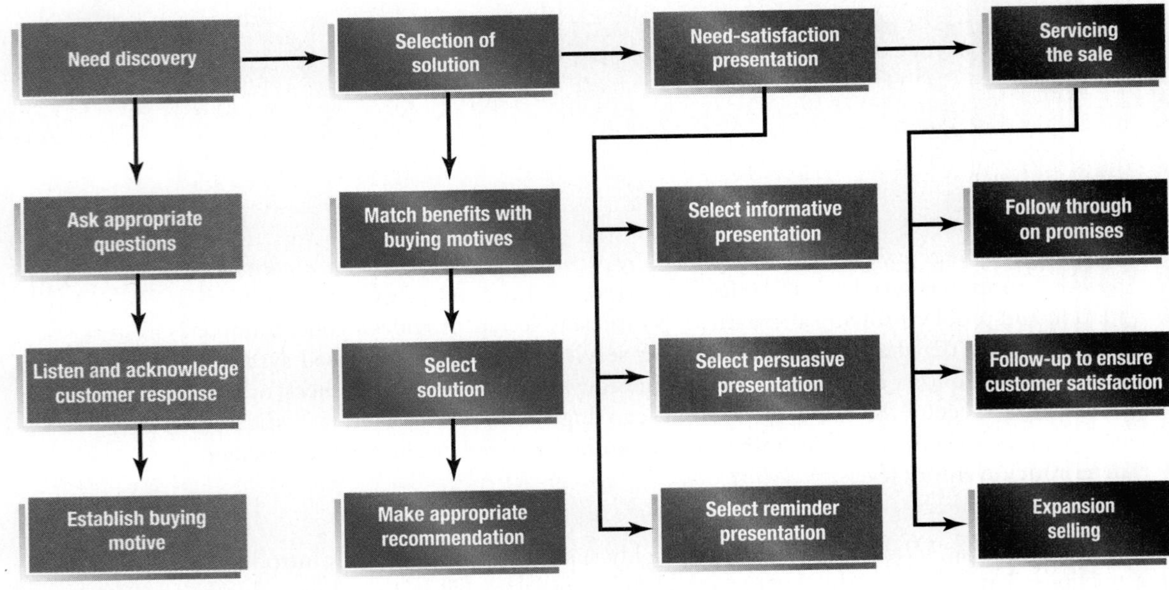

FIGURE | 15.2

The completed Consultative Sales Presentation Guide illustrates the ways in which high-performance salespeople use value-added strategies to service the sale and build repeat business and referrals. Customer service provides many opportunities to strengthen the partnership.

Global Business Etiquette

DOING BUSINESS IN RUSSIA

The cold war has ended and Russia has become an important American trading partner. In recent years Russia has changed politically, socially, and economically. Prior to doing business in the new Russia, get acquainted with the business etiquette and ethics of this important market for American products and services.

- Meetings may not start on time, but it's still a good idea to be punctual.
- The first meeting with your Russian counterparts may be just a formality. They will attempt to assess your credibility and relationship skills, so be warm and approachable.
- Presentations should be simple. Your counterparts would not expect computer-generated visuals or other frills.
- Most Russians enjoy having a drink and a good meal. Take this opportunity to establish goodwill. Some restaurants and bars do not accept credit cards, so bring cash.[c]

depends on your ability to develop and present attractive credit plans to the customer. Even if you do not get directly involved in the firm's credit and collection activities, you must be familiar with how the company handles these matters. Salespeople need to establish a relationship with the credit department and learn how credit analysts make their decisions.[16]

Making credit decisions gets a lot tougher when you are conducting business in foreign countries. Overseas transactions can be complex, and in some cases there is little recourse if a customer does not pay. Doron Weissman, president of Overseas Brokers, a freight forwarder and export brokerage firm in Great Neck, New York, says, "When I sell my services, I automatically qualify the account to make sure they're financially able to meet my demands. If not, I move on."[17]

Schedule Deliveries

Many organizations are adding value with on-time deliveries. A late delivery can be a problem for both the supplier and the customer. To illustrate, let us assume that the supplier is a manufacturer of small appliances and the customer is a department store chain. A late delivery may mean lost sales due to out-of-stock conditions, cancellation of the order by the department store, or loss of future sales.

The causes of late delivery may be beyond your control. It is your responsibility, however, to keep the customer informed of any delays. You also can take steps to prevent a delay. Check to be sure your order was processed correctly. Follow up to see if the order was shipped on time. Always remember: "Every time an order is handled, the customer is handled. Every time an order sits unattended, the customer sits unattended."[18]

Be Present During Delivery When the first delivery is made, be there to be sure the customer is comfortable with the purchase. Check to determine if the order is complete and be available to offer assistance.[19]

Monitor Installation Buyer satisfaction is often related to proper installation of the product. This is true of consumer products such as security systems, central air-conditioning, solar heating systems, and carpeting. It also is true of industrial products such as electronic data processing equipment and air quality control systems. Some salespeople believe it is to their advantage to supervise product installation. They then are able to spot installation problems. Others make it a practice to follow up on the installation to be sure no problems exist.

Offer Training in the Use or Care of the Product For certain industries it is essential that users be skilled in how to use the new product. This is true of factory equipment, electronic cash registers, farm implements, and many other products. Technology has become

CREATING THE LIFETIME CUSTOMER

When we build a plant or purchase a computer—when we acquire just about any new asset—by accounting conventions, it begins to depreciate on day one. But there is one asset that can appreciate over the years. That asset is the well-served customer, who becomes the most significant sustainer of the business, the lifetime customer. (*www.tompeters.com*)

Tom Peters

Tom Peters believes there is one asset that can appreciate over the years. That asset is the well-served customer, who becomes the most significant sustainer of the business, the lifetime customer.

so complex that many suppliers must provide training as part of the follow-up to ensure customer satisfaction. Most organizations that sell computers and other types of electronic equipment for office use now schedule training classes to ensure that customers can properly use and care for the products. These companies believe that users must be skilled in handling their equipment.

Provide Price Change Information Price changes do not need to be a serious problem if they are handled correctly. The salesperson is responsible for maintaining an up-to-date price list. As your company issues price changes, record them accurately. Customers expect you to quote the correct price the first time.

Preventing Postsale Problems There are ways to prevent postsale problems. The key is conscientious follow-up to be sure everything has been handled properly. Get to know the people who operate your shipping and installation department. They are responsible for getting the right products shipped and installed on time, and it is important that they understand your customers' needs.

Become acquainted with people in the credit department. Be sure that they maintain a good, businesslike relationship with your customers. This is a delicate area; even small

Zero Mountain (www.zeromtn.com) partners with its customers and has one of the best value-added, Web-enabled inventory tracking systems to assure timely deliveries and outstanding service after the sale.

mistakes (a "pay now" notice sent too early, for example) can cause hurt feelings. If your company uses a customer support staff to resolve postsale problems, be sure to get acquainted with people who provide this service.

Adding Value with Customer Follow-Up

Customer follow-up methods usually have two major objectives. One is to express appreciation for the purchase and, thus, enhance the relationship established during the sales presentation. You no doubt thanked the customer at the time the sale was closed, but appreciation should be expressed again a few days later. The second purpose of the follow-up is to determine if the customer is satisfied with the purchase. Both of these methods can strengthen the buyer–seller relationship and build a partnership that results in additional sales.

Source: *Wall Street Journal*, April 11, 2002, p. D-7

In survey after survey, poor service and lack of follow-up after the sale are given as primary reasons people stop buying from us. Most customers are sensitive to indifferent treatment by salespeople and sales support personnel. With this fact in mind you should approach follow-up in a systematic and businesslike way. There are five follow-up methods.

Personal Visit

This is usually the most costly follow-up method, but it may produce the best results. It is the only strategy that allows face-to-face, two-way communication. When you take time to make a personal visit, the customer knows that you really care.

Use the personal follow-up to keep the customer informed of new developments, new products, or new applications. This information may pave the way for additional sales. Use the personal visit to reassess where you stand with the account. The reassessment process should involve something more than a “How's it going?” question. If you want the customer to see you as a partner, ask the tough questions: “Are there any problems that I need to address?” “Can you suggest any ways we can better serve your business?” Tom Reilly, author and sales trainer, says “Your perception of your performance is meaningless. It's the customer's perceptions that count.”[20]

Personal visits provide a wonderful opportunity to engage in value reinforcement. **Value reinforcement** means getting credit for the value you create for the customer. You might review all of your follow-through activities so the customer realizes the many ways you have added value. Whenever possible, document your value added services and point out any benefits that the customer has received. In some cases, positive bragging is an effective value reinforcement technique.[21]

Telephone Call

The telephone provides a quick and efficient way to follow up a sale. A salesperson can easily make 10 or 12 phone calls in a single hour, and the cost can be minimal. If you plan to send a thank-you card or letter, follow it up with a thank-you call. The personal appeal of the phone call increases the effectiveness of the written correspondence. The telephone

At Eastern Shore Seafood, value is added by giving customers the opportunity to talk directly to the customer service staff.

call has one major advantage over written correspondence. It allows for a two-way exchange of information. Once an account is well established, you may be able to obtain repeat sales by telephone.

E-Mail Message

In many cases it is a lot quicker to send an e-mail message than to make a phone call. Salespeople report that they waste a lot of time playing "phone tag." Some customers prefer e-mail messages and may become irritated if you do not adhere to their wishes.

Customer Relationship Management with Technology

CONFIRMING IMMEDIATELY

Close-up and personal information sharing creates a core on which successful relationships may be built and sustained. Friends have long supplemented their personal visits with notes, letters, and telephone calls.

Contemporary technology offers new ways to save time in addition to enhancing and extending relationship-rich communications. Enlightened salespeople use the fax and computer modem as fast, thus effective, methods to give information to their customers. The fax function can be particularly useful to quickly convey temporary messages such as those that confirm, affirm, or verify. (See the exercise, Corresponding with CRM, on p. 386 for more information.)

If you know that a customer is not in the habit of checking her e-mail all that often, use the telephone as a back-up method. When in doubt, use parallel channels of communication.

Letter or Card

Written correspondence is an inexpensive and convenient form of customer follow-up. Letters and cards can be used to thank the customer for the order and to promise continued service. Some companies encourage their salespeople to use a formal letter typed on company stationery. Other companies have designed special thank-you cards, which are signed and sent routinely after a sale is closed. The salesperson may enclose a business card. These thank-you cards do have one major limitation: They are mass-produced and, therefore, lack the personal touch of handwritten cards and envelopes. Personalized notes, birthday cards, and anniversary cards can make a positive impression.

Call Report

The **call report** is a form that serves as a communications link with persons who can assist with customer service. The format varies, but generally it is a simple form with only four or five spaces. The sample call report form that appears in the text is used by a company that installs security systems at banks and other financial institutions.

A form such as this is one solution to the problem of communication between the company personnel and the customer. It is a method of follow-through that triggers the desired action. It is simple, yet businesslike.

Follow-up programs can be as creative or as ingenious as you wish. Every sales organization competes on value, so you must continually think of new ways to add value. Creative use of your interpersonal communication skills can keep your messages fresh and personalized. Keep in mind that people buy both from the head and the heart. Let customers know how much you care about their business.[22] You can use these five methods independently or in combination. Your main consideration should be some type of appropriate follow-up that (1) tells customers you appreciate their business and (2) determines if they are satisfied with the purchase.

Adding Value with Expansion Selling

Personal selling is the process of identifying and filling the customer's needs. As the salesperson learns more about the customer, and establishes a relationship based on trust

THE CALL REPORT

Date: October 26, 200_
To: Walt Higgins, service engineer
From: Diane Ray, sales representative

Action Promised: Visit the First National Bank of Middleberg within the next week to check on installation of our security system.

Assistance Needed: System B-420 was installed at the First National Bank of Middleberg on October 24. As per our agreement, you should make a follow-up call to check the installation of the system and provide bank personnel with a Form 82 certification checklist. The form should be given to Mr. Kurt Heller, president.

Copies to: Mr. Kurt Heller

and mutual respect, opportunities for expansion selling will arise. Expansion selling can take three forms: full-line selling, cross-selling, and upselling.

Full-Line Selling

Full-line selling, sometimes called suggestion selling, is the process of recommending products or services that are related to the main item sold to the customer. The recommendation is made when, in the salesperson's judgment, the product or service can provide additional satisfaction.

To illustrate, let us look at the sale of new homes by K B Home, a builder of large planned communities. Customers who want to differentiate their home from those down the block are offered an array of options such as marble in the entryway, granite countertops, gourmet kitchen appliances, or Jacuzzi-like tubs for the bathroom. Customization has proven to be a popular value-added service to customers.[23]

Full-line selling is no less important when selling services. For example, a travel agent has many opportunities to suggest related products. Let us assume that a customer purchases a two-week vacation in Germany. The agent can offer to book hotel reservations or schedule a guided tour. Another related product would be a rental car. Sometimes a new product is simply not "right" without related merchandise. A new business suit may not look right without a new shirt and tie. An executive training program held at a fine hotel can be enhanced with a refreshment break featuring a variety of soft drinks, fresh coffee, and freshly baked pastries.

Customers may view full-line selling as a form of value-added service when it is presented correctly. There is a right way and a wrong way to make recommendations. Some guidelines to follow include:

1. *Plan for full-line selling during the preapproach step.* Before meeting with the customer, develop a general plan that includes your objectives for this important dimension of selling. Full-line selling is easier when you are prepared.
2. *Make recommendations after you have first satisfied the customer's primary need.* Although there are some exceptions to this rule, it's usually best to meet the primary need first. In the case of a new home purchase from K B Home, the customer should first select the model home and then make decisions regarding the upgrades.
3. *Make your suggestions thoughtful and positive.* "We will deliver your new copy machine on Monday. Would you like us to deliver some copy paper?" Avoid questions such as, "Can we ship anything else?" This question invites a negative response.
4. *When appropriate, demonstrate the suggested item or use sales tools to build interest.* If you have suggested a shirt to go with a new suit, allow the customer to see it next to the suit. If you are calling on a commercial account, show the customer a sample or at least a picture if the actual product is not available.

Full line selling is a means of providing value-added service. When you use it correctly, customers thank you for your thoughtfulness and extra service. It is also a proven sales-building strategy.

Cross-Selling

We have seen an increase in the use of cross-selling to grow sales volume. **Cross-selling** involves selling products that are not directly associated with products that you have sold to an established customer. A bank customer who has a home equity loan might be contacted and asked to consider purchase of a mutual fund. The customer who has purchased a town house might be a candidate for a security service. Quick & Reilly, a nationwide financial services company, has trained its 600 customer service representatives to use cross-selling when customers call concerning their current investments. Representatives from 118 offices nationwide completed cross-selling training programs.

They learned how to assess the caller's financial goals and to develop a tailored proposal of products and services. Quick & Reilly achieved a 35 percent sales increase after developing the cross-selling program.[24]

A growing number of companies are using cross-selling to discover additional sources of business within established accounts. Buyers often welcome cross-selling efforts because they are searching for ways to consolidate purchases. They like the convenience of buying several items from the same source.[25]

Cross selling is most effective in those situations in which the salesperson and the customer enjoy a true partnership. Salespeople who have a good understanding of the customer's needs and have earned the customer's respect, will face less resistance when recommending a product or service. Prior to implementing a cross-selling program, salespeople must learn about products that might meet the customer's needs. Bank of the West, based in Walnut Creek, California, required all of its salespeople to complete special training before the cross-selling program was launched.[26]

Upselling

The effort to sell better-quality products is known as **upselling**. It is an important selling method that often adds customer value. Mike Weber, sales manager at Young Electric Sign Company, offers us two important tips on upselling. First, you need a well-established relationship with the customer—a relationship built on trust. Second, you need to

Rackham and DeVincentis in their best selling RETHINKING THE SALES FORCE say that success no longer depends on merely communicating the value of products and services, but rather success rests on the critical ability to create value. They state that value is created by making the purchase painless, convenient, hassle free; and that salespeople can create significant value by showing customers how to install and use the product.

continuously qualify the prospect throughout the buying process. As customers tell you more about their needs, you may see an opportunity to upsell. Weber says his salespeople often engage in upselling at the design stage. The customer is shown a rough sketch of the desired sign and another rendition of something better. The added value of the more expensive option will often become obvious to the customer.[27] In many selling situations such factors as durability, comfort, or economy help justify the higher-priced product. A professional salesperson explains to the customer why it is in his or her best interest to spend "just a little more" and get the best value for the dollar. Most customers are more concerned with making the right purchase than they are with making the least expensive purchase.[28]

Preplan Your Service Strategy

Servicing the sale is a very important dimension of personal selling, so a certain amount of preplanning is essential. It helps to preplan your service strategy for each of the three areas we have discussed: follow-through, follow-up and expansion selling. You cannot anticipate every aspect of the service, but you can preplan important ways to add value once the sale is implemented. Develop a servicing-the-sale worksheet, shown in Figure 15.3, prior to each sales presentation.

Servicing-the-Sale Worksheet

Method of Adding Value	What You Will Say or Do
Follow-Through	
Set up a secured Web site or extranet so client can track the production and delivery of the custom-engineered research equipment.	Set up the secured Web site in a timely manner and then contact the customer when it is operational. Explain how to access the Web site and review the benefits of using this source of assistance.
Schedule training for persons who will be using the new technology.	Send training schedule to customer and confirm the dates with a follow-up call.
Follow-Up	
Send a thank-you letter to each member of the team that made the purchase decision.	Express sincere appreciation for the purchase and explain the steps you will take to ensure a long-term partnership.
Check to be certain that the training was effective.	Visit the customer's research facility and talk with the employees who completed the training. Answer questions and provide additional assistance as needed.
Expansion Selling	
Suggest the purchase of global positioning system (GPS) technology to enhance use of seed research equipment.	"GPS technology will enable you to track all your research and plot the findings on your computer screen."

FIGURE 15.3

Follow-through on assurances and promises, customer follow-up and expansion selling must be carefully planned. Use of this worksheet can help you preplan ways to add value.

PARTNERSHIP-BUILDING STRATEGIES SHOULD ENCOMPASS ALL KEY PEOPLE

Some salespeople do a great job of communicating with the prospect but ignore other key people involved in the sale. To illustrate how serious this problem can be, let us look at the approach used by Jill Bisignano, a sales representative for a major restaurant supply firm. Jill had called on Bellino's Italian Restaurant for several years. Although she was always very friendly to Nick Bellino, she treated the other employees with nearly total indifference. One day she called on Nick and was surprised to learn that he was retiring and had decided to sell his restaurant to two longtime employees.

As you might expect, it did not take the new owners long to find another supplier. Jill lost a large account because she failed to develop a good personal relationship with other key employees. It pays to be nice to everyone.

Here is a partial list of people in your company and in the prospect's company who can influence both initial and repeat sales.

1. *Receptionist.* Some salespeople simply do not use common sense when dealing with the receptionist. This person has daily contact with your customer and may schedule most or all calls. To repeatedly forget this individual's name or display indifference in other ways may cost you dearly.
2. *Technical personnel.* Some products must be cleaned, lubricated, or adjusted on a regular basis. Take time to get acquainted with the people who perform these duties. Answer their questions, share technical information with them if necessary, and show appreciation for the work they are doing.
3. *Stock clerks or receiving clerks.* People working in the receiving room are often responsible for pricing incoming merchandise and making sure that these items are stored properly. They also may be responsible for stock rotation and processing damage claims.
4. *Management personnel.* Although you may be working closely with someone at the departmental or division level, do not forget the person who has the final authority and responsibility for this area. Spend time with management personnel occasionally and be alert to any concerns they may have.

This is not a complete list of the people you may need to depend on for support. There may well be other key people who influence sales. Always look beyond the customer to see who else might influence the sale.

PARTNERING WITH AN UNHAPPY CUSTOMER

We have learned that unhappy customers often do not initiate a verbal or written complaint. This means that postsale problems may not come to the attention of salespeople or other personnel within the organization. We also know that unhappy customers do share their negative experiences with other people. A dissatisfied customer often tells 8 to 10 people about his problem.[29] A double loss occurs when the customer stops buying our products and takes steps to discourage other people from buying our products. When complaints do surface, we should view the problem as an opportunity to strengthen the business relationship. To achieve this goal, follow these suggestions.

1. *Give customers every opportunity to disclose their feelings.* Companies noted for outstanding customer service rely heavily on telephone systems—like toll-free "hot lines" to ensure easy access. At Federal Express, Cadillac Division of General Motors, and IBM, to name a few companies, specially trained advisors answer the calls and offer assistance. When a

Selling in Action

EFFECTIVE DESIGN AND USE OF THE BUSINESS CARD

The business card continues to be a powerful tool for salespeople and sales support personnel. It provides a personal touch in our high-tech world. The business card is a convenient way to communicate important information to customers, sales support personnel, and others. When you develop your business card, keep these tips in mind.

- Use eye-catching items such as your company logo, raised letters, and textured paper. The card should be tasteful and pleasing to the eye. Do use a white background.
- The card should feature all current contact information such as your e-mail address, telephone numbers, and mailing address. List a home phone number only if there's a second line for business calls.
- Consider using both sides of the card. You might print your customer service philosophy on the back of the card or list the products you sell.

Give your cards generously to anyone who might need to contact you later. Always offer your business card when networking. The card is useful when the contact tells others about your products or services.[d] (See Exercise 3.3 in *Selling Today: Creating Customer Value with Computers* for instructions on creating your own business card.)

customer purchases a Ford vehicle, the salesperson introduces the customer to service staff who play a key role in providing postsale service. The goal is to personalize the relationship with another member of the service team. Ford has discovered that after-sale contact builds a perception of value.[30] When customers do complain, by telephone, or in person, encourage them to express all their anger and frustration. Do not interrupt. Do not become defensive. Do not make any judgments until you have heard all the facts as the customer sees them.[31] If the customer stops talking, try to get him or her to talk some more.

2. *As the customer is talking, listen carefully and attentively.* You need accurate information to solve the problem. One of the biggest barriers to effective listening is emotion. Do not become angry, and do not get into an argument. Once you feel the customer has fully vented, paraphrase what she said to prove you cared enough to listen.[32]
3. *Keep in mind that it does not really matter whether a complaint is real or perceived.* If the customer is upset, you should be polite and sympathetic. Do not yield to the temptation to say, "You do not really have a problem." Remember, problems exist when customers perceive they exist.[33]
4. *Do not alibi.* Avoid the temptation to blame the shipping department, the installation crew, or anyone else associated with your company. Never tear down the company you work for. The problem has been placed in your hands, and you must accept responsibility for handling it. "Passing the buck" only leaves the customer with a feeling of helplessness.
5. *Politely share with the customer your point of view concerning the problem's cause.* At least explain what you think happened. The customer deserves an explanation. At this point a sincere apology is usually appropriate.
6. *Decide what action must be taken to remedy the problem.* Take action quickly and offer a value-added atonement. Don't just do what is expected, but delight the customer by exceeding his expectations. Winning customer loyalty today means going beyond making it right.[34]

The value of customer complaints can emerge in two forms. First, complaints can be a source of important information that may be difficult to obtain by other means. Second, customer complaints provide unique opportunities for companies to *prove* their commitment to service. Loyalty builds in the customer's mind if you do a good job of solving her problem.[35]

A Word of Caution

When you are dealing with major or minor customer service problems and an apology is necessary, do not use e-mail. When a minor problem surfaces, call the customer personally. Do not delegate this task to someone else in your organization. If you need to apologize for a major problem that has occurred, meet with the customer in person. Schedule the meeting as soon as possible.[36]

Summary

Servicing the sale is a major dimension of the selling process, with the objectives of providing maximum customer satisfaction and establishing a long-term partnership. Good service ensures that the product meets the customer's current needs and builds a foundation for the future. A reputation for good service is essential in attracting new accounts and keeping old ones. The goal is to develop lifetime customers. We review several current developments in *customer service*. Salespeople must spend more time monitoring customer satisfaction. Customer knowledge is an important key to improving customer service, and computer-based systems are being used to enhance customer service.

The customer service strategy is made up of three activities: adding value with follow-through, adding value with customer follow-up, and adding value with expansion selling. These activities can create a positive impression of the salesperson and the company.

A salesperson depends on the support of many other people in servicing a sale. Maintaining good relationships with support staff members who help service your accounts is well worth the time and energy required. This chapter also includes information on ways to effectively solve the customer's problem. Regular and objective self-evaluation is also a valuable practice. Efficient performance of the functions involved in customer service is important to ensure continuing customer satisfaction and should be a matter of professional pride.

KEY TERMS

Customer service
Full-line selling
Cross-selling
Call report
Upselling
Value reinforcement

REVIEW QUESTIONS

1. You are currently a sales manager employed by a company that sells long-term care insurance. Tomorrow you will meet with five new sales trainees. Your major goal is to explain why it is important to service the sale. What important points will you cover?
2. Define customer service. List the three major activities associated with this phase of personal selling.
3. Explain how full-line selling fits into the definition of customer service. How does full-line selling differ from cross-selling?

4. List and describe three current developments in customer service.
5. Adding value with follow-through can involve several post sale services. List five possible services.
6. How does credit become a part of servicing the sale?
7. This chapter describes the value of the lifetime customer. Is it realistic to believe that people will become lifetime customers in our very competitive marketplace?
8. Define upselling and explain how it can add value.
9. What types of customer service problems might be prevented with the use of a call report?
10. Briefly describe the important design elements of an effective business card.

APPLICATION EXERCISES

1. You work as a wholesale salesperson for a plumbing supply company. One of your customers, a contractor, has an open line of credit with your company for $10,000 worth of products. He is currently at his limit; however, he is not overdue. He just received word that he has been awarded a $40,000 plumbing contract at the local airport. The contract requires that he supply $9,000 worth of plumbing products. Your customer does not have the cash to pay for the additional products. He informs you that unless you can provide him with some type of financing, he may lose the contract. He says that he can pay you when he finishes his next job in 60 days. Explain what you will do.
2. You have just interviewed for a job that you really would like to have. You have heard it is a good idea to follow up an interview with a thank-you note or letter and an indication of your enthusiasm for the position. Select the strategy you will use for your follow-up, and explain why you chose it.
3. Using your search engine, examine the Internet for information on customer satisfaction. Type in "customer satisfaction" + selling. Are you surprised by the number of queries on this subject? Examine some of the queries related to what customers have said about specific company's customer service programs.

ROLE-PLAY EXERCISE

An important aspect of personal selling is the need to add value with follow-up and follow-through. Both of these account management activities can be time consuming, especially if the salesperson is not skilled at setting up appointments that fit into a busy schedule. In this role-play, you are to set up three follow-through meetings with a customer who has just purchased convention services from the convention center you represent (see Appendix 3). First, you must contact your client three days from today to confirm the availability of the Revolving Platform Room (see p. 515) for a meeting of 300 people. Second, you must contact this same client a week from today to get approval on the number of servings of Chicken Wellington Banquet Style Dinners needed (see p. 475 and Guarantees on p. 493). And, third, because your client isn't sure about the need for a microphone (see p. 485), you need to call your client the day before the meeting (the meeting is scheduled four weeks from today) to verify whether you or your client will supply a microphone.

Equipped with a calendar, you should establish dates and times when your client will be available to talk or meet with you. Before you meet with your client, plan to recommend at least two times of the day that fit into your schedule for each of your meetings. If your client cannot meet at either of these times, ask your client to recommend a time. Do not start out by asking when your client is available because this could conflict with your busy schedule. Write the times and dates in your calendar, suggesting your client does the same, so there will be no misunderstandings. Because these dates are deadlines, suggest that your client call you back if for some reason the schedule changes. Inform your client that you will plan to be at the hotel when the client's meeting starts and that you will be available to make sure everything is properly scheduled. Tell your client to contact you (give your client your phone number and e-mail address) if there are any questions between now and the meeting date.

CRM APPLICATION EXERCISE

Corresponding with CRM

Waiting for a client who forgot an appointment can be very time consuming. The client who promptly receives a faxed reminder note is more likely to remember and honor a commitment to meet. Quickly confirming an agreement reached by telephone is easy for customer relationship management (CRM) systems such as ACT!. Look up the contact Ian Program, select Write, and Fax Cover. This displays the fax cover sheet that by itself may be used to convey a short confirmation message. Position the cursor at Subject and type "Lunch," and then press Enter twice and type "I look forward to lunch with you Friday noon at Jimmy's." Select File Print (Ctrl + P) to print the fax cover note. If your computer is running fax software, you could send the fax cover note directly to your client's fax machine.

VIDEO CASE PROBLEM

This chapter opens with an introduction to Body Glove International (*www.bodyglove.com*), a global company that manufactures a quality line of wet suits for persons who like water sports. Many of the consumers who are involved in water skiing, scuba diving, surfing, or jet skiing purchase Body Glove products because they represent both quality and value. The company was started in 1953 by Bill and Randy Meistrell, two persons who shared a passion for surfing and diving. The first suits were custom made for customers who responded to ads placed in local publications. As sales increased the Meistrell brothers developed a small manufacturing facility and began distributing their products through retail stores on the West Coast. Soon Body Glove became a national company and later an international company. The success of Body Glove can be traced to several factors:

- A company philosophy that is based on the belief that you never sacrifice quality. A product that is comfortable and well made attracts the customer who is willing to spend a little more to get the best product. The company used to manufacture its own products, but now it outsources all manufacturing. These companies must maintain high-quality standards established by Body Glove.
- A belief that brand management is very important. Today Body Glove International is placing more emphasis on brand management. The company wants to influence the perception of Body Glove products in the minds of customers. Company officials recognize that in a world of sensory overload caused by too much

information, brands are more important than ever. Customers think about what matters to them, analyze their choices, and usually select a brand that meets their needs.

- Innovations in sales and marketing strategies that enhance product distribution and sales. Body Glove International has developed over 30 partnerships with distributors. These distributors (called marketing intermediaries) employ salespeople who call on retail stores. At the present time distributors employ about 250 salespeople. The company now has a stronger global sales organization with special emphasis on South America, New Zealand, and Australia.
- Investment in a first-class customer service center. The people at Body Glove believe that excellent customer service adds value to the product. The staff makes sure that all orders are carefully processed. With the aid of modern computers, they can check on the status of any order. The staff can also process special orders quickly. The customer service employees work hard to build the strongest possible partnership with the customer.

Questions

1. The company officers have made a decision to develop partnerships with a group of distributors. Thes distributors will employ salespeople to call on retailers who sell Body Glove products. What steps can Body Glove take to ensure that retailers and retail customers receive excellent service?
2. How might a Body Glove salesperson add value with full-line selling? Cross-selling?
3. What types of follow through activities and follow-up calls should Body Glove sales representatives be prepared to initiate?
4. Assume that a large order sent to one of your best customers arrived very late. The products were not available for a major weekend sale. How might you partner with this unhappy customer?

CRM CASE STUDY

Servicing the Sale with CRM

You have taken over a number of accounts of another salesperson, Pat Silva. Most of these accounts are prospects, which means that they have not yet purchased from SimNet. Two accounts did purchase networks from Pat: Ms. Karen Murray of Murray D'Zines, and Ms. Judith Albright, owner of Piccadilly Studio. You now want to be sure that these sales are well serviced.

Questions

1. Whom should you speak with, within SimNet, before following through and contacting each of the customers? What would you need to discover?
2. What will be your follow-up strategy for each customer?
3. Does the fact that these customers initiated their orders (they were not sold the products, they bought them) influence your follow-up strategy?
4. Might other customers or prospects be affected by your service activities? How would this influence your activities? Could customer service be your competitive edge?
5. Do you see any expansion-selling opportunities with these two accounts? Which *suggestion*-selling methods should you consider?

PARTNERSHIP SELLING: A ROLE-PLAY/SIMULATION

(see Appendix 3, pp. 508–509, 520)

Developing a Presentation Strategy—Servicing the Sale

Refer to *sales memorandum 3* and strategically plan to service the sale with your customer. After closing the sale (getting the customer's signature), there are several steps to add value and build customer confidence and satisfaction. These steps are important to providing total quality customer service and should provide for repeat sales and a list of referred customers.

Follow the instructions in item 2g of your presentation plan. You need to schedule a future appointment to telephone or personally call and confirm the number of people attending the convention and final room and menu needs (see convention center policies). Also, during this conversation, you may suggest beverages for breaks, audiovisual needs, and any other items that can make this an outstanding convention for your customer.

You should have your calendar available to suggest and write down dates and times for this future contact. Any special materials such as a calendar can be placed in the back pocket of your portfolio. You may want to secure another person to be your customer and practice the customer service strategies you have prepared.

At this point you should be strategically prepared to make the presentation outlined in sales memorandum 3 to your customer. Your instructor will provide you with further instructions.

DEVELOPING A PRESENTATION STRATEGY

Scenario

This role play is a continuation of the Part 4 role play exercise. You recently met with Shannon Fordham, founder and chief executive officer of USA Technologies. The purpose of the first sales call was to begin the relationship building process and present selected value-added guest services and amenities offered by the Park Inn. You also obtained some information regarding the customer's buying process.

Customer Profile

Prior to starting USA Technologies, Shannon Fordham spent 12 years working in sales and sales management at General Electric Corporation. Working for General Electric, described by *Fortune* magazine as America's most admired company, was a great learning experience. Fordham is trying to apply the GE success formula to USA Technologies. Shannon Fordham is the classic extravert, a person who combines high sociability and high dominance.

Salesperson Profile

Jamie Julian is new to the field of sales, but he is a quick learner. The first visit with Shannon Fordham went well, and now it is time to prepare for the second sales call. Fordham is planning a large employee recognition banquet, but has not yet selected a location for this event. While working for GE, Fordham had attended more than 25 business conferences and many of these meetings were a big disappointment. Too often, according to Fordham, the meetings were held at look-alike hotels that served bland food. The food was often served by poorly trained waiters who displayed little enthusiasm for their work. Jamie took notes throughout the meeting and will address these concerns during the second sales call.

Product

The Park Inn International is a full-service hotel and convention center. After completion of a recent $2.8 million renovation, the Park Inn received the "Excellence in Renovation Design" award from the Illinois Architectural Association.

Instructions

The first sales call was basically an informative presentation. Near the end of the visit Shannon Fordham did disclose plans for a large recognition banquet to be held on October 25. This date marks the company's second anniversary. No other information was provided, but Fordham did agree to a second meeting to be held the following week. Based on the information collected during the first call, you are now planning a persuasive presentation that will involve the first three steps of the six-step presentation plan (see Figure 15.1). Upon arrival in Shannon Fordham's office, reestablish the relationship and then initiate the agenda approach (see Chapter 10). Begin the presentation with appropriate survey, probing, and confirmation questions. These questions should be preplanned using information found in Chapter 11. As the need discovery phase of the presentation progresses, the customer's buying criteria or buying conditions should surface. Prior to the second sales call you should also select and be prepared to demonstrate appropriate selling tools (proof devices). A variety of selling tools suitable for reproduction can be found in Appendix 3. Also, preplan feature/benefit selling statements that appeal to Shannon Fordham's needs. The importance of selling specific benefits and obtaining customer reactions cannot be overemphasized (see.Chapter 11).

A major objective of the second sales call is to move the sale forward by convincing Shannon Fordham that the Park Inn offers an outstanding combination of value-added guest services and amenities, and is prepared to meet the customer's needs. The sale will not be closed during the second call, bur Jamie Julian will try to obtain a commitment to prepare a formal sales proposal that will be presented to Fordham within 48 hours. See page 497 for a sample sales proposal form.

"The primary cause of success in life is the ability to set and achieve goals. That's why the people who do not have goals are doomed forever to work for those who do. You either work to achieve your own goals or you work to achieve someone else's goals."

Brian Tracy

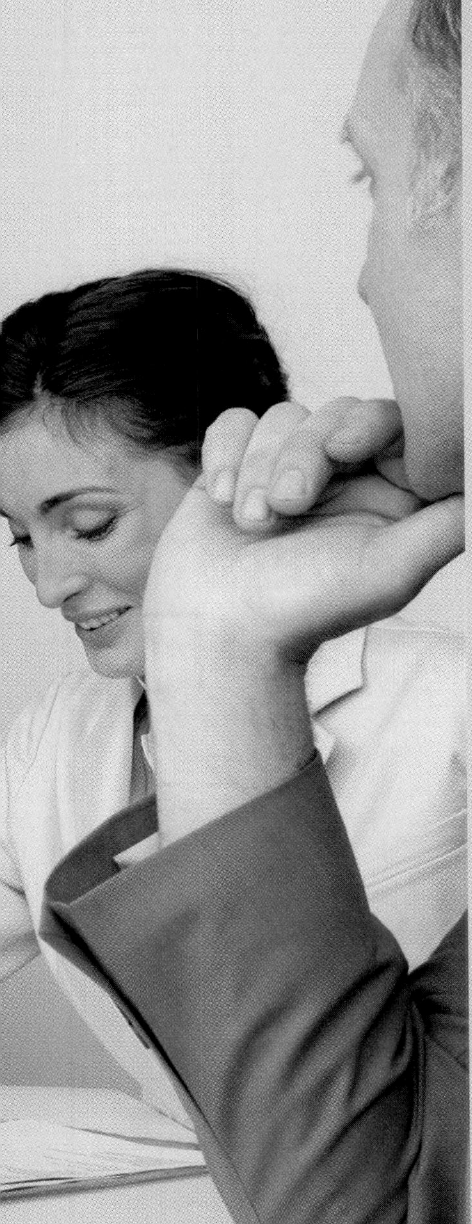

PART 6

Management of Self and Others

➥ Personal selling requires a great deal of self-discipline and self-direction. Chapter 16 examines the four dimensions of opportunity management. The final chapter examines the fundamentals of sales force management.

Chapter Preview

When you finish reading this chapter, you should be able to

1 Discuss the four dimensions of opportunity-management

2 List and describe time management strategies

3 Explain factors that contribute to improved territory management

4 Identify and discuss common elements of a records management system

5 Discuss stress management practices

CHAPTER 16

Opportunity Management: The Key to Greater Sales Productivity

Julio Melara, born to Honduran immigrant parents, made work the centerpiece of his life at an early age. Throughout high school he cut grass, worked as a busboy, delivered newspapers, and sold newspaper subscriptions. While attending college he worked as a courier with *New Orleans City Business*, a local business newspaper. By age 23 he was top producer and head of national sales. Later he left the newspaper and went into radio advertising sales. By age 28, Melara broke all sales records at WWL and became the radio's first million-dollar producer. He is a self-motivated person who says that he has learned a great deal from such books as *The Power of Positive Thinking* by Norman Vincent Peale. He is also someone who believes in management of self. Goal setting is the central theme of Melara's sales philosophy (*www.juliomelara.com*). He believes that written goals (personal and professional) facilitate growth and success.[1]

Today Julio Melara is sharing his no-nonsense steps for achieving success with audiences throughout America. *Selling Power* magazine has named him one of America's top motivational speakers. He is also president and co-owner of the *Greater Baton Rouge Business Report*.[2]

A salesperson is much like the individual who owns and operates a business. The successful sales representative, like the successful entrepreneur, depends on good self-management. Both of them must keep their own records, use self-discipline in scheduling their time, and analyze their own performance.

OPPORTUNITY MANAGEMENT—A FOUR-DIMENSIONAL PROCESS

What makes a salesperson successful? Some people believe the most important factor is hard work. This is only partly true. Some people work hard but do not accomplish much. They lack purpose and direction. This lack of organization results in wasted time and energy. Hard work must be preceded by careful planning. Every moment spent planning, according to some experts in self-management, saves three or four moments in execution.[3]

Wasting time and energy is the key to failure in the age of information. Many salespeople are drowning in information and the flood of messages each day leaves little time to think and reflect. Sales and sales support personnel, like most other knowledge workers, are working under tighter deadlines. The response time to customer inquiries has been shortened and customers are less tolerant of delays.

As pressures build, it's easy to overlook opportunities to identify prospects, make sales, and improve service to customers. The ability to perceive opportunities and seize them is an important characteristic of high-achieving salespeople.[4] **Opportunity management** should be viewed as a four-dimensional process consisting of the following components:

1. *Time management.* There are only about 250 business days per year. Within each day there is only so much time to devote to selling. Selling hours are extremely valuable. When salespeople are asked to evaluate the major challenges they face in their work, "Not enough time" is often rated number one. Dealing with information overload and achieving balance in their life are also major challenges.
2. *Territory management.* A sales territory is a group of customers and prospective customers assigned to a single salesperson. Every territory is unique. Some territories consist of one or two counties, whereas others encompass several states. The number of accounts within each territory also varies. Today, territory management is becoming less of an art and more of a science.
3. *Records management.* Every salesperson must maintain a certain number of records. These records help to "systematize" data collection and storage. A wise salesperson never relies on memory. Some of the most common records include planning calendars, prospect forms, call reports, summary reports, and expense reports.
4. *Stress management.* A certain amount of stress comes with many selling positions. Some salespeople have learned how to take stressful situations in stride. Others allow stress to trigger anger and frustration. Learning to cope with various stressors that surface in the daily life of a salesperson is an important part of the self-management process.

Goal setting is a major element of Julio Melara's opportunity management program. Today he is President and co-owner of the Greater Batton Rouge Business Report, and is one of America's top motivational speakers.

TIME MANAGEMENT

A salesperson can increase sales volume in two major ways. One is to improve selling effectiveness, and the other is to spend more time in face-to-face selling situations. The latter objective can be achieved best through improved time and territory management.

Improving the management of both time and territory is a high-priority concern in the field of selling. These two closely related functions represent major challenges for salespeople.

Let us first look closely at the area of time management. There is definitely a close relationship between sales volume and the number of customer contacts made by the salesperson. You have to make calls to get results.

Selling Is Everyone's Business

BILL BLASS CONNECTED WITH HIS CUSTOMERS

The late Bill Blass, American fashion designer, understood the power of personal contact. He also understood that he was working for his customers, not the other way around. Growing up in Fort Wayne, Indiana, during the depression, he often went to the movies to see Carole Lombard and other stars. He sold his first fashion drawings to New York manufacturers when he was 14. By 17, he had moved to New York and started to build relationships among the city's social elite. Although New York City became his home, he frequently traveled to places like St. Louis, Houston, and Detroit for trunk shows. Bill Blass was one of the first designers to travel with his collections and was generally regarded as the king of the trunk show. He felt it was important to connect with women who were willing to spend $3,500 for a suit. Thus, he built his global reputation one woman at a time.[a]

Most people who achieve success in selling have a strong work ethic. They are "self-starters" who are committed to achieving their personal and professional goals.

Time-Consuming Activities

Some salespeople who have kept careful records of how they spend their time each day are surprised to learn how little is spent in face-to-face selling situations. A national survey of 1,500 salespeople from 13 industries found that on average, salespeople spend 60 percent of their time on administrative duties or travel.[5] Administrative duties can include such things as completion of sales records and time spent on customer follow through and follow up. Salespeople need to carefully examine all of their activities and determine whether too much or too little time is spent in any area. One way to assess time use is to keep a time log. This involves recording, at the end of every hour, the activities in which they were engaged during that time.[6] At the end of the week, add up the number of minutes spent on the various activities and ask yourself, "Is this the best use of my time?"

Once you have tabulated the results of your time log, it should be easy to identify the "time wasters." Pick one or two of the most wasteful areas, and then make plans to correct the problem. Set realistic goals that can be achieved. Keep in mind that wasting time is usually a habit. To manage your time more effectively, you need to form new habits. Changing habits is hard work, but it can be done.[7]

Time Management Methods

Sound time management methods can pave the way to greater sales productivity. The starting point is forming a new attitude toward time conservation. You must view time as a scarce resource not to be wasted.[8] The timesaving strategies presented here are not new, nor are they unique. They are being used by time-conscious people in all walks of life.

Develop a Series of Personal Goals

According to Alan Lakein, author of *How to Get Control of Your Time and Your Life*, the most important aspect of time management is knowing what your goals are. He is referring to all goals—career goals, family goals, and life goals. People who cannot or do not

To manage your time more effectively you need to form new habits. Changing habits is hard work, but it can be done.

Reprinted by permission of *Agency Sales Magazine*, September 1997.

sit down and write out exactly what they want from life lack direction. Brian Tracy, who developed the "Law of Direction" says, "Your ability to set clear, specific goals will do more to guarantee you higher levels of success and achievement than any other single skill or quality."[9]

The goal-setting process requires that you be clear about what you want to accomplish. If your goal is too general or vague, progress toward achieving that goal is difficult to observe. Goals such as "I want to be a success" or "I desire good health" are much too general. The major principles that encompass goal setting are outlined in Table 16.1.

TABLE | 16.1 GOAL-SETTING PRINCIPLES

The following goal-setting principles give you the power to take control of the present and the future.

1. *Reflect on the things you want to change in your life.* Then prepare written goals that are specific, measurable, and realistic.
2. *Develop a written goal-setting plan that includes the steps necessary to achieve the goal.* Review your plan daily—repetition increases the probability of success.
3. *Modify your environment by changing the stimuli around you.* This may involve finding a mentor or spending less time with persons who are negative.
4. *Monitor your behavior, and reward your progress.* Reinforcement from yourself and/or others is necessary for change.

Source: Barry L. Reece and Rhonda Brandt, *Effective Human Relations: Personal and Organizational Applications*, Boston: Houghton Mifflin Company, 2005. Reprinted by permission of the publisher.

Heather Gardner, with the investment firm of William Blair & Company, uses her Blackberry and Microsoft Outlook calendar to record all of her planned activities.

Goals have a great deal of psychological value to people in selling. Sales goals, for example, can serve as a strong motivational force. To illustrate, let us assume that Mary Paulson, sales representative for a cosmetic manufacturer, decides to increase her sales by 15 percent over the previous year. She now has a clear goal to aim for and can begin identifying specific steps to achieve the new goal.

This salesperson is using a personal digital assistant (PDA). It serves as an electronic memo pad, calendar, expense log, address book, and more. It is invaluable to salespeople who want to add value with efficient time and territory management.

Mary Paulson has established a long-term goal as part of a yearly plan. Some goals require considerable time and should be part of a one-year plan. Next, Mary should set aside an hour or so at the end of each month to decide what she wants to accomplish during the coming month. Weekly planning is also important. Once a week—Friday is a good time—set goals for the next week and develop a plan for reaching them. Finally, Mary should develop a daily plan.[10]

Prepare a Daily "To Do" List

Sales professionals who complete the time management course offered by FranklinCovey are encouraged to engage in event control. This involves planning and prioritizing events every day.[11] Start each day by thinking about what you want to accomplish. Then write down the activities (Fig. 16.1). Putting your thoughts on paper (or in your computer) forces you to clarify your thinking. Heather Gardner, a Regional Director with the Chicago investment firm William Blair & Company, records her daily planned activities in her BlackBerry and Microsoft Outlook calendar. On a typical day the BlackBerry will show entries for every half hour. Gardner works through her detailed to-do list by adhering to one unshakable rule: avoid nonpaying activities during working hours.[12]

FIGURE 16.1

A daily list of activities can help us set priorities and save time. Today this list is recorded electronically in most CRM systems. The list is one of the first things salespeople see when they access the software each day.

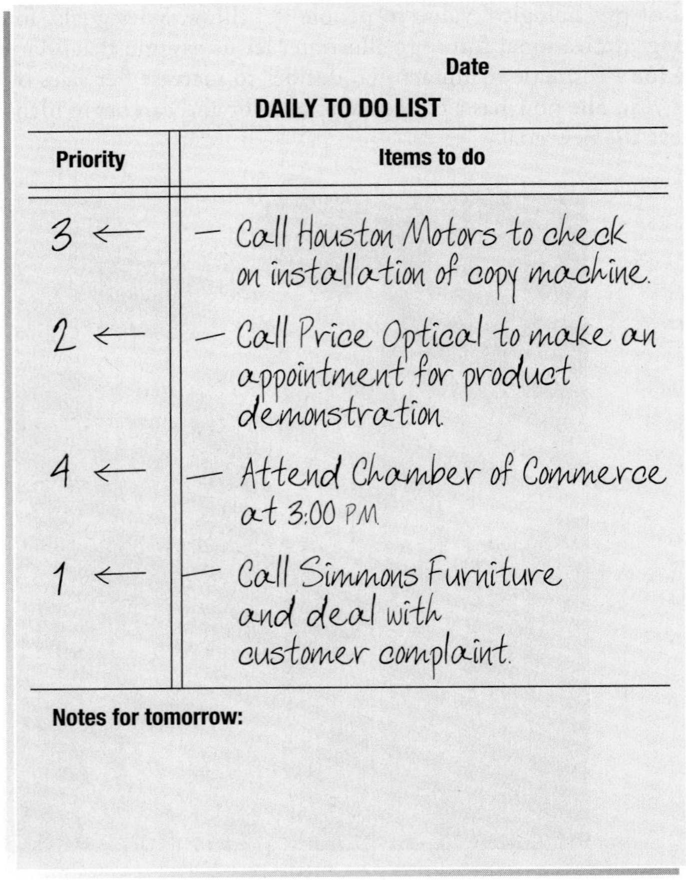

Date ________

DAILY TO DO LIST

Priority	Items to do
3 ←	— Call Houston Motors to check on installation of copy machine.
2 ←	— Call Price Optical to make an appointment for product demonstration.
4 ←	— Attend Chamber of Commerce at 3:00 PM
1 ←	— Call Simmons Furniture and deal with customer complaint.

Notes for tomorrow:

Now you should prioritize your "to do" list and do not let outside distractions interfere with your plan. Begin each day with the highest-priority task.

Maintain a Planning Calendar

Ideally, a salesperson needs a single place to record daily appointments (personal and business), deadlines, and tasks. Unfortunately, many salespeople write daily tasks on any slip of paper they can find—backs of envelopes, three-by-five cards, napkins, or Post-it notes. Hyrum W. Smith, author of *The 10 Natural Laws of Successful Time and Life Management*, calls these pieces of paper "floaters."

> They just float around until you either follow through on them or lose them. It's a terribly disorganized method for someone who wants to gain greater control of his or her life.[13]

The use of floaters often leads to the loss of critical information, missed appointments, and lack of focus. Select a planning calendar design (the FranklinCovey Day Planner is one option) that can bring efficiency to your daily planning efforts. You should be able to determine at a glance what is coming up in the days and weeks ahead (Fig. 16.2).

Many salespeople are using **personal digital assistants** (PDA) to organize information. Small, pocket size PDAs available from Palm or BlackBerry offer many of the features common to laptop computers. The salesperson can send and receive e-mails, and download important customer information. Salespeople can also input their customer notes immediately after a sales call. The PDA also serves as an electronic memo pad, calendar, expense log, address book, and more. These organizers can be used to keep track of appointments and serve as a perpetual calendar. You simply key in a birthday or anniversary, and a gentle beep jogs your memory on the appropriate date.

Organize Your Selling Tools

You can save valuable time by finding ways to organize sales literature, business cards, order blanks, samples, and other items needed during a sales call. You may waste time on a callback because some item was not available during your first call. You may even lose a sale because you forgot or misplaced a key selling tool.

If you have a great deal of paperwork, invest in one or more file systems. Some salespeople purchase small, lightweight cardboard file boxes to keep their materials organized. These boxes can be placed easily in your car trunk and moved from one sales call to another. The orderly arrangement of selling tools is just one more method of time conservation.

The key to regular use of the four timesaving tools described previously is *commitment*. Unless you are convinced that efficient time management is important, you will probably find it difficult to adopt these new habits. A salesperson who fully accepts the "time is money" philosophy uses these methods routinely.

Saving Time with Meetings in Cyberspace and Other Methods of Communication

As the cost of travel increases, more salespeople are asking the question, "Is this trip necessary?" Instead of traveling to a customer's office, some salespeople schedule a telephone conference call. A modern alternative to this type of conference call is a meeting

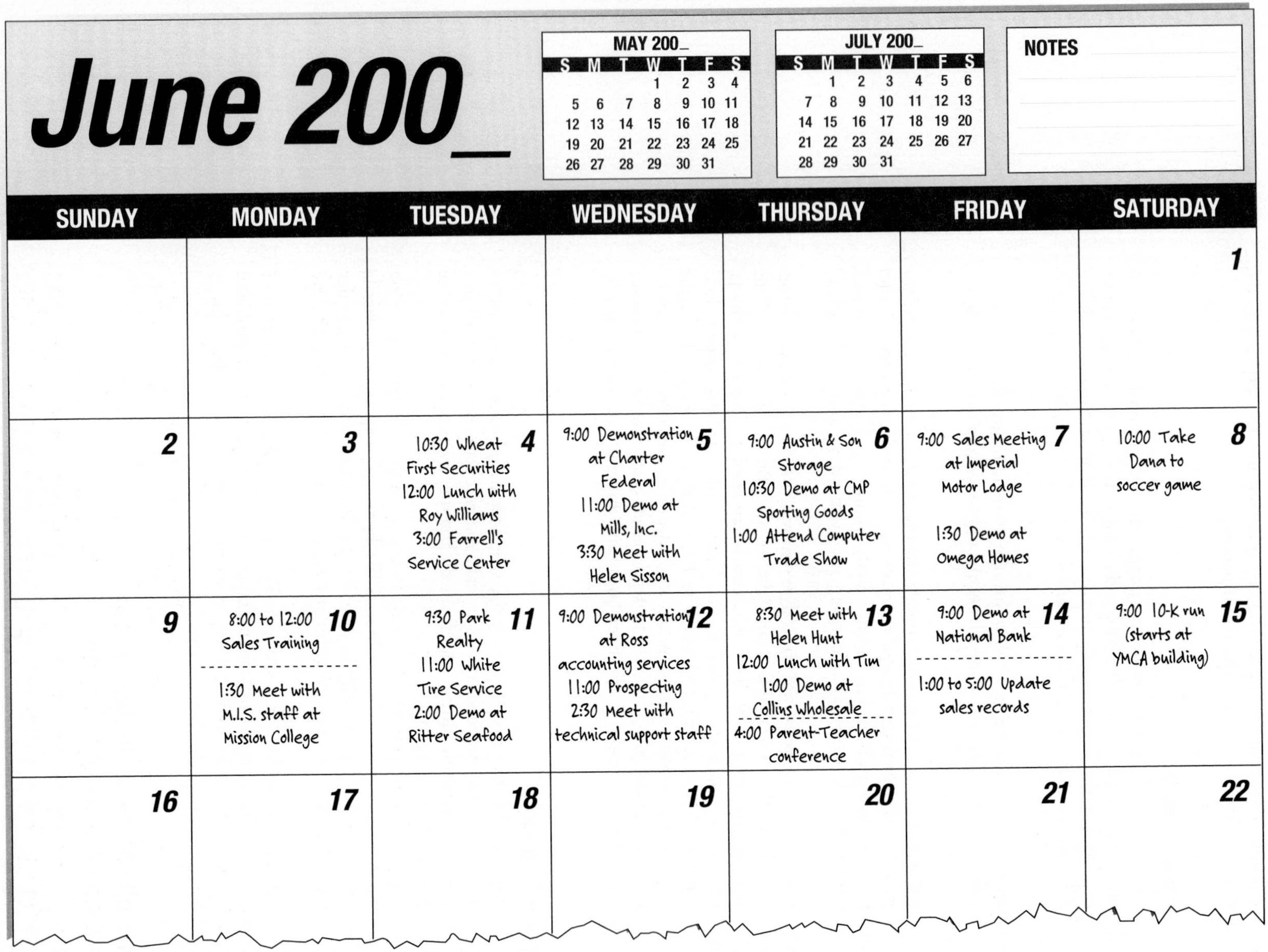

June 200_

MAY 200_						
S	M	T	W	T	F	S
			1	2	3	4
5	6	7	8	9	10	11
12	13	14	15	16	17	18
19	20	21	22	23	24	25
26	27	28	29	30	31	

JULY 200_						
S	M	T	W	T	F	S
	1	2	3	4	5	6
7	8	9	10	11	12	13
14	15	16	17	18	19	20
21	22	23	24	25	26	27
28	29	30	31			

NOTES

SUNDAY	MONDAY	TUESDAY	WEDNESDAY	THURSDAY	FRIDAY	SATURDAY
						1
2	3	4 10:30 Wheat First Securities 12:00 Lunch with Roy Williams 3:00 Farrell's Service Center	5 9:00 Demonstration at Charter Federal 11:00 Demo at Mills, Inc. 3:30 Meet with Helen Sisson	6 9:00 Austin & Son Storage 10:30 Demo at CMP Sporting Goods 1:00 Attend Computer Trade Show	7 9:00 Sales Meeting at Imperial Motor Lodge 1:30 Demo at Omega Homes	8 10:00 Take Dana to soccer game
9	10 8:00 to 12:00 Sales Training 1:30 Meet with M.I.S. staff at Mission College	11 9:30 Park Realty 11:00 White Tire Service 2:00 Demo at Ritter Seafood	12 9:00 Demonstration at Ross accounting services 11:00 Prospecting 2:30 Meet with technical support staff	13 8:30 Meet with Helen Hunt 12:00 Lunch with Tim 1:00 Demo at Collins Wholesale 4:00 Parent-Teacher conference	14 9:00 Demo at National Bank 1:00 to 5:00 Update sales records	15 9:00 10-K run (starts at YMCA building)
16	17	18	19	20	21	22

FIGURE | 16.2

Monthly Planning Calendar Sample

Shown are 11 days of a monthly planning calendar for a computer service sales representative. Monthly planning calendars such as this one are now a key function of most CRM systems.

in cyberspace. The voice of each meeting participant travels over a phone line and attendees view visuals—PowerPoint presentations—on their desktop computers. Nerac Inc., an information-services company, often schedules a Web conference for potential customers. The sales representative can bring online a Nerac researcher who presents an introduction to the company's closely guarded databases. Clients get to watch the researcher at work over the Internet.[14]

Some customers actually prefer telephone contact for certain types of business transactions. Some situations in which the phone call is appropriate follow:

Call the customer in advance to make an appointment. You save time, and the customer knows when to expect you.

Use the telephone to keep the customer informed. A phone call provides instant communication with customers at a low cost.

Build customer goodwill with a follow-up phone call. Make it a practice to call customers to thank them for buying your product and determine if the customer is satisfied with the purchase.

Some customers prefer to be contacted by e-mail and it would be a mistake to ignore their preference. Busy people often discourage telephone calls as a means of minimizing interruptions.

Voice mail automated telephone systems are now being used by companies of all sizes. These systems not only answer the phone and take messages but also provide information-retrieval systems that are accessible by telephone. This technology is especially useful for salespeople who need to exchange information with others. For many salespeople the cellular telephone has become a convenient and timesaving sales tool. A pager also can be used to facilitate communication with customers and the main office.

The cellular telephone has become a convenient and time saving sales tool. It is often used to conduct follow-up or follow-through activities.

Customer Relationship Management with Technology

ISLANDS OF INFORMATION

Companies often use many different software programs that contain information about customers. The firm may have customer purchase and payment history in its accounting system. Customer service problems may be recorded in the service department's software. A help desk program may be used by people in customer support.

The company's salespeople may be using one software program to manage their contacts with customer personnel, another program to prepare quotes, and yet another for correspondence with customers. To reduce these "islands" of customer information, more companies are finding ways to merge this information or to acquire software that performs more than one of these functions. Some customer relationship management (CRM) systems are combining a number of these functions into one integrated package.

Fax machines and computer scanning equipment takes telecommunications a step further. With this equipment salespeople can send and receive documents in seconds, using standard cable or telephone lines. Detailed designs, charts, and graphs can be transmitted across the nation or around the world.

TERRITORY MANAGEMENT

Many marketing organizations have found it helpful to break down the total market into manageable units called sales territories. A **sales territory** is the geographic area where prospects and customers reside. Although some firms have developed territories solely

With the aid of fax machines and computer scanning equipment, salespeople can send and receive documents in seconds. Hardcopy documents are often needed to move the sales process to a successful outcome.

on the basis of geographic considerations, a more common approach is to establish a territory on the basis of classes of customers. Territories are often classified according to sales potential. Some marketers assign sales representatives to key industries. The Ottawa *Citizen* newspaper divided the paper's customer base into major business lines such as real estate and automotive.[15] Regardless of how the sales territory is established, it is essentially a specific number of present and potential accounts that can be called on conveniently.

What Does Territory Management Involve?

To appreciate fully the many facets of territory management, it is helpful to examine a typical selling situation. Put yourself in the shoes of a salesperson who has just accepted a position with a firm that manufactures a line of high-quality tools. You are responsible for a territory that covers six counties. The territory includes 88 auto supply firms that carry your line of tools. It also includes 38 stores that do not carry your tools. On the basis of this limited information, how would you carry out your selling duties? To answer this question, it is necessary to follow these steps.

Step 1—Classify All Customers

If you classify customers according to potential sales volume, then you must answer two questions: What is the dollar amount of the firm's current purchases? What amount of additional sales might be developed with greater selling effort? Store A may be purchasing $3,000 worth of tools each year, but potential sales for this firm amount to $5,000. Store B currently purchases $2,000 worth of tools a year, and potential sales amount to $2,500. In this example, store A clearly deserves more time than store B.

It is important to realize that a small number of accounts may provide a majority of the sales volume. Many companies get 75 to 80 percent of their sales volume from 20 to 25 percent of their total number of customers. The problem lies in accurately identifying

Selling in Action

BALANCING CAREER AND FAMILY

Women today know that they will probably be working for pay for part or all of their adult lives. Most will also perform multiple roles that can be stressful and tiring. Many women who work full-time in sales also assume the responsibilities of wife and mother. Ellyn Foltz, vice president of sales and marketing for Dataline Incorporated, maintains a fully equipped personal computer (PC) and Internet hookup at her home. She gets up early and usually spends about 90 minutes on her work while family members are eating breakfast. In the evening, she logs on and completes two or three hours of work after her son is in bed. Foltz has structured her life so that she does not have to make "impossible choices" between work and family. She turned down a high-profile job that would have required constant travel.

Jill Doran, director of national accounts for National Car Rental, says that her employer gives her the tools and support she needs to maintain balance in her life. She received 10 weeks of maternity leave for each of her children and has the freedom to work from her home part of each week. When she is at home, Doran checks her phone mail and e-mail frequently to be sure she is responsive to each of her national accounts. She records everything in her Daytimer to avoid work–family conflicts.

As women struggle to balance career and family choices, many employers are doing more to help. Women, as well as men, who work in sales often have the option of spending part of every week working at home.[b]

which accounts and prospects fall into the top 20 to 25 percent category. Once this information is available, you can develop customer classification data that can be used to establish the frequency of calls.

The typical sales territory is constantly changing, so the realignment of territories from time to time is necessary. A division of AT&T based in Albany, New York, uses MapInfo ProAlign software to realign its sales territories. Accounts are segmented based on industry, size, dollar volume, and complexity. The sales manager enters a variety of account information and then produces maps that show accounts in different configurations.[16]

Step 2—Develop a Routing and Scheduling Plan

Many salespeople have found that travel is one of their most time-consuming nonselling activities. A great deal of time also can be wasted just waiting to see a customer. The primary objective of a sales routing and scheduling plan is to increase actual selling by reducing time spent traveling between accounts and time spent waiting to see customers.

If a salesperson called only on established accounts and spent the same amount of time with each customer, routing and scheduling would not be difficult. In most cases, however, you need to consider other variables. For example, you may be expected to develop new accounts on a regular basis. In this case, you must adjust your schedule to accommodate calls on prospects. Another variable involves customer service. Some salespeople devote considerable time to adjusting warranty claims, solving customer problems, and paying goodwill visits.

There are no precise rules to observe in establishing a sales routing and scheduling plan, but the following guiding principles apply to nearly all selling situations:

1. Obtain or create a map of your territory, and mark the location of present accounts with pins or marking pen. Each account might be color coded according to sales potential. This gives you a picture of the entire territory. Many companies are using mapping software to create a territory picture that can be viewed on the computer screen. With the aid of TerrAlign mapping software, salespeople can align sales territories by account size or geography, analyze sales information, generate maps and reports, and produce territory recommendations.[17]
2. If your territory is quite large, consider organizing it into smaller zones. Zip code zones provide one option. You can then plan work in terms of several zones that make up the entire territory.
3. Develop a routing plan for a specific period of time. This might be a one- or two-week period. Once the plan is firm, notify customers by telephone, letter, or e-mail of your anticipated arrival time.
4. Develop a schedule that accommodates your customers' needs. Some customers appreciate getting calls on a certain day of the week or at a certain hour of the day. Try to schedule your calls in accordance with their wishes.
5. Think ahead, and establish one or more tentative calls in case you have some extra time. If your sales calls take less time than expected or if there is an unexpected cancellation, you need optional calls to fill in the void.
6. Decide how frequently to call on the basis of sales potential. Give the greatest attention to the most profitable customers. Many salespeople use the 80/20 rule. They spend 80 percent of their time calling on the most productive customers and 20 percent calling on smaller accounts and prospects.[18]

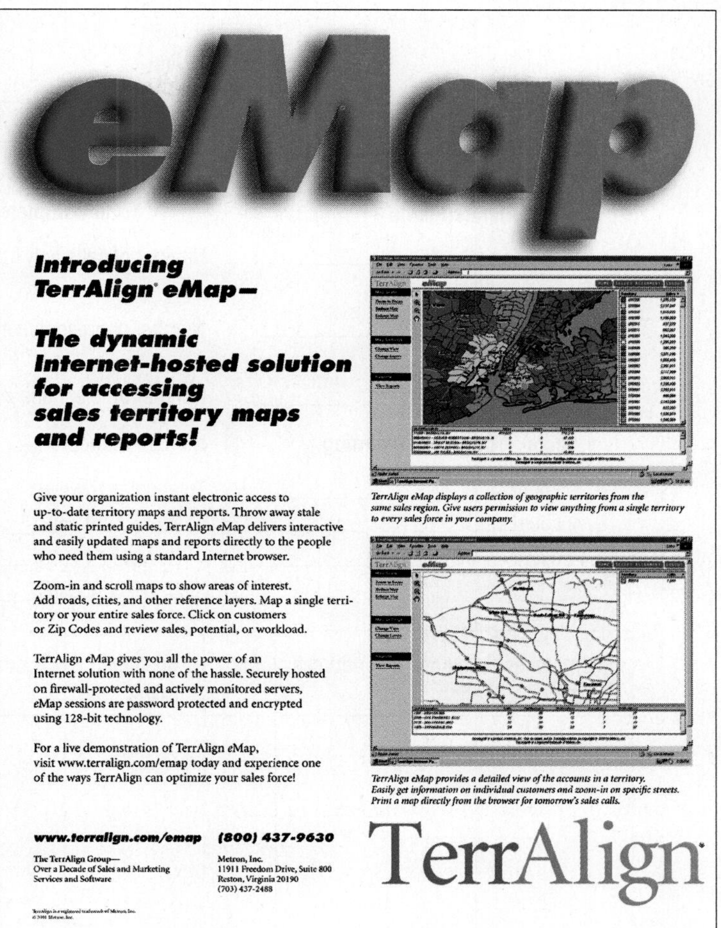

Today sales call planning is easier and more effective because salespeople can use software programs such as TerrAlign.

Sales Call Plans

You can use information from the routing and scheduling plan to develop a **sales call plan.** This proposal is a weekly action plan, often initiated by the sales manager. Its primary purpose is to ensure efficient and effective account coverage.

The form most sales managers use is similar to Figure 16.3. One section of the form is used to record planned calls. A parallel section is for completed calls. Additional space is provided for the names of firms called on.

The sales manager usually presents the sales call plan to individual members of the sales staff. The plan's success depends on how realistic the goals are in the eyes of the sales staff, how persuasive the sales manager is, and what type of training accompanies the plan's introduction. It is not unusual for members of the sales force to respond with comments such as, "My territory is different," "Do not put me in a procedural straitjacket," or "My territory cannot be organized." The sales manager must not only present the plan in a convincing manner but also provide training that helps each salesperson implement the plan successfully.

FIGURE 16.3

The sales call plan is part of most CRM systems and is sent electronically.

Sales Call Plan

Salesperson__________ For week ending __________

Territory __________ Days worked __________

Planned Calls

Number of planned calls __________

Number of planned presentations __________

Number of planned telephone calls __________

Account Category Planning

A. Account calls __________

B. Account calls __________

C. Account calls __________

Total Completed Calls

Number of calls only __________

Number of presentations __________

Number of telephone calls __________

Number of orders __________

Total miles traveled __________

A. Account calls __________

B. Account calls __________

C. Account calls __________

Companies called on	Address	Date	Customer rating	Comments about call

RECORDS MANAGEMENT

Although some salespeople complain that paperwork is too time consuming and reduces the amount of time available for actual selling, others recognize that accurate, up-to-date records are important. Their work is better organized, and quick accessibility to information often makes it possible to close more sales and improve customer service.

A good record-keeping system gives salespeople useful information with which to check their own progress. For instance, an examination of sales call plans at the end of the day provides a review of who was called on and what was accomplished. The company also benefits from complete and accurate records. Reports from the field help management make important decisions. A company with a large sales force operating throughout a wide geographic area relies heavily on information sent to the home office.

Global Business Etiquette

DOING BUSINESS IN BELGIUM

Belgium is a country of northwestern Europe on the North Sea. It has long been a strategic crossroads of Europe. The country is culturally divided into Dutch-speaking Flanders to the north of Brussels and French-speaking Wallonia to the south. A small population of German speakers is in the south. Avoid confusing the different languages and cultures. This mistake could come across as insulting. Be sure your business cards are printed in the appropriate language for the area you are visiting. Do not expect one selling strategy to work within its borders given the cultural differences.[c]

Common Records Kept by Salespeople

A good policy is never to require a record that is not absolutely necessary. The only records worth keeping are those that provide positive benefits to the customer, the salesperson, or the personnel who work in sales-supporting areas of the company. Each record should be brief, easy to complete, and free of requests for useless detail. Where possible the format should provide for the use of check marks as a substitute for written responses. Completing sales record forms should not be a major burden.

What records should you keep? The answer to this question varies depending on the type of selling position. Some of the most common records salespeople keep are described in this section.

Customer and Prospect Files

Most salespeople find it helpful to keep records of customers and prospects. Each of these files has space for name, address, and phone number. Other information recorded might be the buyer's personal characteristics, the names of people who might influence the purchase, or appropriate times to make calls. Most salespeople have replaced card files with computerized record systems.

Salespeople often use CRM systems to record handwritten notes taken during meetings with the customer.

Call Reports

The call report (also called activity report) is a variation of the sales call plan described earlier in this chapter. It is used to record information about the people you have called on and about what took place. The call report is one of the most basic records used in the field of

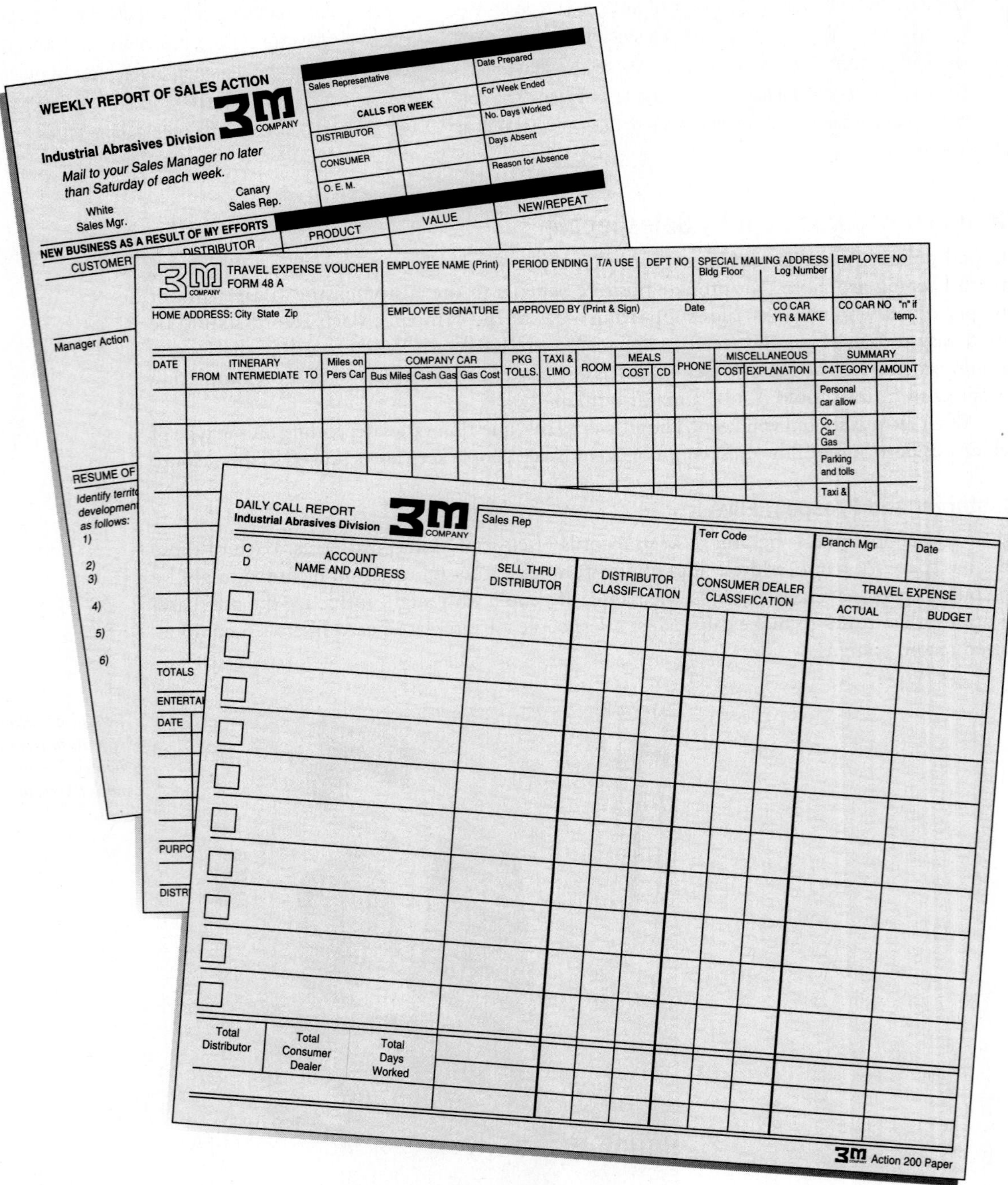

WEEKLY REPORT OF SALES ACTION
3M COMPANY
Industrial Abrasives Division
Mail to your Sales Manager no later than Saturday of each week.
White Sales Mgr.
Canary Sales Rep.
Sales Representative
Date Prepared
For Week Ended
CALLS FOR WEEK
DISTRIBUTOR
CONSUMER
O. E. M.
No. Days Worked
Days Absent
Reason for Absence
NEW BUSINESS AS A RESULT OF MY EFFORTS
CUSTOMER
DISTRIBUTOR
PRODUCT
VALUE
NEW/REPEAT
Manager Action
RESUME OF
Identify territ
developmen
as follows:
1)
2)
3)
4)
5)
6)

3M COMPANY TRAVEL EXPENSE VOUCHER FORM 48 A
EMPLOYEE NAME (Print)
PERIOD ENDING
T/A USE
DEPT NO
SPECIAL MAILING ADDRESS Bldg Floor Log Number
EMPLOYEE NO
HOME ADDRESS: City State Zip
EMPLOYEE SIGNATURE
APPROVED BY (Print & Sign) Date
CO CAR YR & MAKE
CO CAR NO "n" if temp.

DATE	ITINERARY FROM	INTERMEDIATE	TO	Miles on Pers Car	COMPANY CAR Bus Miles	Cash Gas	Gas Cost	PKG TOLLS.	TAXI & LIMO	ROOM	MEALS COST	CD	PHONE	MISCELLANEOUS COST	EXPLANATION	SUMMARY CATEGORY	AMOUNT
																Personal car allow	
																Co. Car Gas	
																Parking and tolls	
																Taxi &	

TOTALS
ENTERTA
DATE
PURPO
DISTR

DAILY CALL REPORT
Industrial Abrasives Division
3M COMPANY
Sales Rep
Terr Code
Branch Mgr
Date

C D	ACCOUNT NAME AND ADDRESS	SELL THRU DISTRIBUTOR	DISTRIBUTOR CLASSIFICATION	CONSUMER DEALER CLASSIFICATION	TRAVEL EXPENSE ACTUAL	BUDGET
☐						
☐						
☐						
☐						
☐						
☐						
☐						
☐						
☐						
☐						

Total Distributor
Total Consumer Dealer
Total Days Worked
3M Action 200 Paper

FIGURE | 16.4

Call Report, Expense Voucher, and Weekly Sales Report

These are three of the most common records kept by 3M salespeople. Many salespeople process these forms via electronic mail.

selling. It provides a summary of what happened during the call and an indication of what future action is required. The call report (daily and weekly) featured in Figure 16.4 is typical of those used in the field.

We are seeing less emphasis on call reports that require only numbers (calls made each day, number of proposals written, etc.). Companies that emphasize consultative selling are requesting more personal information on the customer (information that expands the customer profile) and more information on the customer's short- and long-range buying plans.

Expense Records

Both your company and the government agencies that monitor business expenses require a record of selling expenses. These usually include such items as meals, lodging, travel, and in some cases entertainment expenses. Several expense reporting software packages are now available to streamline the expense reporting process. Automated expense reports save the salesperson a great deal of time and allow them to get reimbursed while still on the road.

Sales Records

The records used to report sales vary greatly in design. Some companies require daily reports, others weekly ones. As you would expect, one primary use of the sales report is to analyze salespeople's performance.

You can take certain steps to improve a reporting system. Some records should be completed right away, while you can easily recall the information. Accuracy is always important. It can be embarrassing to have an order sent to the wrong address simply because you have transposed a figure. Take time to proofread forms and use a spell checker.

You should reexamine your territory management plan continually. Update it often so it reflects the current status of your various accounts. When possible, use a portable computer or PDA and appropriate software to improve your records management system. Mobile technology can help you achieve increased selling time and enhance customer service.

STRESS MANAGEMENT

Personal selling produces a certain amount of stress. This is due in part to the nonroutine nature of sales work. Each day brings a variety of new experiences, some of which may cause stress. Prospecting, for example, can be threatening to some salespeople. Long hours on the job, the loss of leisure time, and too little time for family members also can be stressful.

Although "variety is the spice of life," there is a limit to how much diversity one can cope with. One of the keys to success in selling is learning how to bring order to the many facets of the job. We also must be physically and mentally prepared to handle work-related stress.

Stress refers to two simultaneous events: an external stimulus called a stressor, and the physical and emotional responses to that stimulus (anxiety, fear, muscle tension, surging heart rate, and so on). Negative, threatening, or worrisome situations accumulated over time, can cause depression, and burnout, and make you sick.[19] In personal selling, too much negative stress hurts relationships and productivity. Some stress is beneficial because it helps keep us motivated, but too much stress can be unhealthy if left unchecked.

Stress might be caused by trying to figure out ways to meet a sales quota or schedule travel throughout a sales territory. Missed appointments, presentations before large groups, and lack of feedback concerning your performance also can create stress. Ironically, some of the timesaving tools used by salespeople (fax machines, cell phones, pagers, and e-mail) make it difficult for them to escape the pressures of their job. Many salespeople feel they are "on call" 24 hours a day.

As noted in Chapter 1, information surplus has replaced information scarcity as an important new problem in the age of information. A growing number of knowledge workers report tension with colleagues, loss of job satisfaction, and strained personal relationships as a result of information overload. Too much information also crowds out quiet moments needed to restore balance in our lives.[20]

It is not possible to eliminate stress from your life, but you can adopt stress management strategies that can help you cope with the stress in your life. Three stress management strategies are discussed next.

Develop a Stress-Free Home Office

Many salespeople maintain a home office. With a little effort, it's possible to create a less stressful home office environment. Install a business line (phone and fax) that rings only in the office. It's not professional to have other family members answering business calls. If your office is not an appropriate meeting space, meet with clients at their office or at a restaurant. Establish set hours. Try not to let work hours extend into evenings and weekends. Let your neighbors and friends know you keep office hours and cannot be disturbed during "working" hours.[21]

Maintain an Optimistic Outlook

Optimistic thoughts give rise to positive attitudes and effective relationships with customers. According to Martin Seligman, professor of psychology at the University of Pennsylvania and author of *Learned Optimism*, optimists are more likely to view problems as merely temporary setbacks. They focus on their potential success rather than on their failures. Pessimists, in contrast, tend to believe bad events will last a long time and tend to give up more easily when faced with a challenge.[22]

Seligman reminds us that optimism is a learned behavior. For example, you can spend more time visualizing yourself succeeding. If you want to succeed at something, picture yourself doing it successfully. The visualization process needs to be repeated over and over again.[23]

Practice Healthy Emotional Expression

When stress occurs, you may undergo physiological and psychological changes. The heartbeat quickens, the blood pressure rises, and tension builds. To relieve the pressure, you may choose a *fight* or *flight* response. Fighting the problem may mean unleashing an avalanche of harsh words or ignoring the other person. These reactions, of course, are not recommended. This behavior may damage relationships with team members, customers, or customer support personnel.

Increasingly, in the age of information, physical exercise is a very important part of a stress management program. Exercise also helps us maintain peak mental performance.

Flight is the act of running away from the problem. Instead of facing the issue squarely, you decide to turn your back on it. The flight response is usually not satisfactory; the problem seldom goes away by itself. If you feel stress from an impractical quota, talk to your sales manager and try to get the quota reduced. Don't just give in to the feeling of being overwhelmed. If you are spending too much time away from family and friends, take a close look at your territory management plan and try to develop a more efficient way to make sale calls. If you feel perpetually overwhelmed by job demands and you cannot negotiate a less demanding work schedule, then leaving this stressful environment may be the only solution. To achieve a more balanced life, consider a sales career in a less hectic industry.[24]

Maintain a Healthy Lifestyle

An effective exercise program—jogging, tennis, golf, racquetball, walking, or some other favorite exercise—can "burn off" the harmful chemicals that build up in your bloodstream after a prolonged period of stress. Salespeople at Owens Corning in Toledo, Ohio, formed a sales wellness advisory team (SWAT). The team organized a health screening for Owen's 600 salespeople and instituted an incentive program that rewarded those who reached exercise goals.[25] The food you eat can play a critical role in helping you manage stress. Health experts agree that the typical American diet—high in saturated fats, refined sugar, additives, caffeine, and too much sodium—is the wrong menu for coping with stress. Leisure time also can provide you with the opportunity to relax and get rid of work-related stress. Mike McGinnity, director of sales and marketing at the Excelsior Hotel in Little Rock, Arkansas, encourages his salespeople to take full advantage of vacations. He helps them organize their workload so they are able to fully enjoy their vacations.[26]

AN ACTION PLAN TO REDUCE STRESS

1. Take 15 minutes.
2. Make two columns on a piece of paper. Write "Work" at the top of one, "Personal" at the top of the other. Write down all the things that are driving you crazy.
3. Underline the most important items on the lists.
4. Separate them into "chronic" and "acute."
5. For each one, ask yourself: What do I need to do to reduce the stress arising from this factor *right now*? Some answers could be as simple as "Get a good night's sleep, or begin some form of meditation."
6. Take action.[d]

One additional way to handle stress is to come to work rested and relaxed. One of the most effective strategies for managing the negative aspects of stress is getting enough quality sleep. The number of hours of sleep required for good health varies from person to person, but seven or eight hours seem to be about right for most people. The critical test is if you feel rested in the morning and prepared to deal with the day's activities.

In many respects, salespeople must possess the same self-discipline as a professional athlete. Sales work can be physically demanding. Lack of proper rest, poor eating habits, excessive drinking, and failure to exercise properly can reduce one's ability to deal with stress and strain.

Selling in Action

FOUR MODERATORS OF STRESS

The stress-related tension that surfaces in our lives can be a barrier to effective interpersonal relations. The psychological problems that can result from too much stress are anxiety, depression, instability, and reduced interest in personal relationships. The authors of *The One-Minute Manager Gets Fit* have identified four moderators of stress. When these four are in good working order, they can help prevent stress from turning into strain.

1. *Autonomy* is a sense we get on weekends of being able to do what we want. Autonomy also can be working independently or having the necessary skills and qualifications to be able to move from one job to another.
2. *Connectedness* relates to the ties we have with those around us. People with a high sense of connectedness believe they have strong, positive relationships in all areas—at home, at work, and in the community.
3. *Perspective* has to do with the meaning of life—the direction, the purpose, the passion that you feel for what you are doing. It keeps you from letting little things get you down. Because you are looking at the big picture, normal strains of daily life do not get blown out of proportion.
4. *Tone* is your energy level, your physical well-being and appearance, and how you feel about your body. By having better tone a person can definitely improve self-esteem and, in doing so, help moderate stress.[e]

Summary

In this chapter we describe opportunity management as a four-dimensional process. It involves time management, territory management, records management, and stress management.

All salespeople can learn more about their products and improve their selling skills. However, there is no way to expand time. Our only option is to find ways to improve time and territory management. The four timesaving techniques discussed in this chapter should be used by every salesperson. When used on a regular basis, they can set the stage for more face-to-face selling time.

The first step in territory management is the classification of all customers according to sales volume or some other appropriate criteria. You normally should spend the most time with accounts that have the greatest sales potential. The second step requires developing a routing and scheduling plan. This plan should reduce time spent traveling between accounts. In some cases you can substitute telephone calls or e-mail messages for personal calls.

A good record-keeping system provides many advantages. Accurate, up-to-date records can actually save time because work is better organized. The company also benefits because sales reports provide an important communication link with members of the sales force. Today, computers are used to develop more efficient record-keeping systems.

There is a certain amount of stress associated with sales work. This is due in part to the nonroutine nature of personal selling. Salespeople must learn to cope with the factors that upset their equilibrium. Several stress management strategies are discussed.

KEY TERMS

Sales territory
Sales call plan
Stress
Opportunity management
Personal digital assistant

REVIEW QUESTIONS

1. Describe how a salesperson is much like the individual who owns and operates a business.
2. Opportunity management has been described as a four-dimensional process. Describe each dimension.
3. List and briefly describe the four goal-setting principles.
4. How can a salesperson use a time log to improve time management?
5. List four techniques the salesperson should use to make better use of valuable selling time.
6. Effective territory management involves two major steps. What are they?
7. What is a *sales call plan?* Explain how it is used.

8. Describe the most common records kept by salespeople.
9. What is the definition of *stress?* What are some indicators of stress?
10. The Selling in Action box on p. 412 describes four moderators of stress. Which of these four moderators do you think is most important for persons employed in the sales field? Explain.

APPLICATION EXERCISES

1. The key to successful time management lies in thinking and planning ahead. You must become conscious of yourself and decide what you want from your time. You can manage your time only when you have a clear picture of what is going on within and around you. To assess the quality of your working time, it is helpful to keep a careful record for a certain amount of time showing exactly how you have used your day. Over this period of time, write down everything you have done and how long it took. Next you can appraise your use of time and decide whether or not your time was put to good use. Some pertinent questions you might ask yourself in appraising your use of time are suggested by the following "time analysis questions":
   a. What items am I spending too much time on?
   b. What items am I spending too little time on?
   c. What items offer the most important opportunities for saving time?
   d. What am I doing that does not need to be done at all?
   e. How can I avoid overusing the time of others?
   f. What are some other suggestions?
2. Deciding on a goal can be the most crucial decision of your life. It is more damaging not to have a goal than it is not to reach a goal. It is generally agreed that the major cause of failure is the lack of a well-defined direction. A successful life results not from chance but from a succession of successful days. Prepare a list for the following categories:
   Career goals
   1.
   2.
   3.
   Family goals
   1.
   2.
   3.
   Educational goals
   1.
   2.
   3.
   Interpersonal relationship goals
   1.
   2.
   3.
3. Interview someone you know who uses a planning calendar. What kind is it—pocket, desk, or some other type? How long has the person been using it? How important is the calendar to daily, weekly, monthly, and yearly planning? Has the person ever considered discontinuing its use? What are the person's suggestions for someone who does not use one? Write your answer.

4. Time management is an important part of a successful salesperson's job. Using your search engine, examine the Internet for information on time management. Type in "time management"+selling. Examine the training products and services available on this topic.

ROLE-PLAY EXERCISE

Using the information in the Chapter 15 role-play, develop a contact plan regarding the future contacts you set up (see page 385–386). Your sales manager has scheduled a status report meeting to go over your activities with this account. With this information and with the information written into your calendar, plan to meet with your sales manager to talk about the account management meetings you have scheduled. Plan to cover how this schedule enhances both your time and territory management and adds value to the sale.

CASE PROBLEM

Julio Melara, introduced at the beginning of this chapter, has achieved success in several different sales and marketing positions in the fields of radio broadcasting and publishing. Today he is president and co-owner of the *Greater Baton Rouge Business Report* and is one of America's top motivational speakers. He is convinced that success comes to those who have the right attitude and the will to win. Now that he has proved himself in several competitive fields, Melara is ready to share the beliefs and success principles that made a difference in his own career. His success formula is made of five elements.

1. You have to believe you can achieve your dreams and desires. He likes to quote a verse from the book of Proverbs that says, "As a man thinketh, so he is." Put another way, "If you believe, you will achieve." Salespeople tend to behave in a way that supports their own ideas of how successful or unsuccessful they will be. Those who have serious doubts about their capabilities tend to reduce their efforts or give up altogether when faced with major challenges.
2. Put all your goals in writing. A written goal, reviewed daily, is much more likely to be achieved. Melara says that a written goal keeps the vision in front of you. Many salespeople avoid setting goals because they do not understand the importance of this self-improvement method. As we make and keep commitments to ourselves, we begin to establish a greater sense of self-confidence and self-control. For many salespeople, goals become an integral part of their plan to break old habits or form new ones.
3. Get all the education and information that you can. Melara is fond of saying, "You'll never earn more unless you learn more." In recent years, most salespeople have had to develop expertise in the area of customer relationship management. Knowledge of the customer's business is not an option if you want to build a strong partnership. Developing expertise in appropriate areas can result in increased self-confidence.
4. Commit to excellence in everything that you do. There is an interconnection among the many areas of work and family. Melara believes that salespeople must fulfill both work and family responsibilities. Many sales and marketing organizations have found that family problems are linked to employee problems such as tardiness, absenteeism, and low productivity. Of course, problems at work often have a negative influence on one's personal life.

5. Protect your enthusiasm. Melara says, "Watch the friends you hang out with, the people you associate with, and the television programs you watch." Enthusiasm for work and work-related activities is often fragile. The negative views of a co-worker or a friend can erode our enthusiasm. One of the best defenses against loss of enthusiasm is to maintain positive expectations about the future.

Questions

1. Which of these elements can make the most important contribution to a career in personal selling? Explain.
2. Reflect on your own approach to accomplishing tasks and select two of Melara's elements you would find easy to adopt. Then select two elements that you would find difficult to adopt. Explain your choices.
3. How might goal setting be used in conjunction with time management?
4. How might a commitment to excellence improve the processes of territory management and records management?
5. Do you agree or disagree that the people you associate with can influence your motivation?

CRM CASE STUDY

Managing Yourself with CRM

A key objective in managing your time is to confirm that, at any time, you are working on your highest priorities. Contacting prospective customers is the highest priority for most salespeople. The next challenge is to decide in which order prospects should be contacted. Many salespeople prioritize their accounts on the basis of their value, the amount that they are likely to spend with the sales organization.

Questions

1. On the basis of the dollar amount Pat Silva estimated that each account might spend, in what order would you contact the prospects in the ACT! database?
2. If you were to rank these prospects on the basis of your sales commission, would this priority list be different than the list developed in question 1? If so, why?
3. There are several ways that this list of prospects could be prioritized, for example, by date, dollar amount, or commission. Which of these rankings is best?

CHAPTER 17

Chapter Preview

When you finish reading this chapter, you should be able to

1. Describe the functions of a sales manager

2. List and discuss the qualities of an effective sales manager

3. Discuss recruitment and selection of salespeople

4. Describe effective orientation, training, and motivation practices

5. Develop an understanding of selected compensation plans

6. List and discuss criteria for evaluating sales performance

Management of the Sales Force

If you enter the field of personal selling and experience success, you may be given the opportunity to manage a sales force. Some salespeople are asked to accept the promotion but decline the offer. They do not want to give up a job they thoroughly enjoy. Many of the salespeople who do rise to management positions become exemplary leaders and advance to positions that offer even greater challenges.

Thanks to the efforts of James Kouzes and Barry Posner, we know a great deal about the practices of exemplary leaders. Many years of research on this topic have been summarized and reported in *The Leadership Challenge*, a best-selling book written by Kouzes and Posner. The book is based on countless interviews and observations conducted around the world.

Lindsay Levin, managing director of Whites Limited, was one of many exceptional leaders cited by the authors of *The Leadership Challenge*. Whites Limited, based in London, is an auto dealership built around three departments—sales, service, and parts. Soon after assuming her new management position, she began searching for answers to one important question: "What do our customers really think of us?" She visualized Whites as a company where every customer would say, "My experience at Whites was amazing." With input from customer focus groups she was able to identify some areas that needed improvement. She then asked employees to talk about changes they would like to implement and to form small voluntary teams to work on them.

Lindsay Levin also visualized a company where everyone is treated with respect, and feels involved and valued. She took the position that a leader can never have enough communication with their people. She never

The Leadership Challenge *by James Kouzes and Barry Posner provides many important insights into effective sales management practices. The book is based on research conducted around the world.*

hesitated to let the employees know what she was thinking and what she believed. She talked about her values often and listened attentively when employees expressed their views. Levin also recognized employee accomplishments with personal thanks and formal awards.[1]

APPLYING LEADERSHIP SKILLS TO SALES MANAGEMENT

People who rise to the position of sales manager must understand the difference between leadership and management. Leadership is the process of inspiring, influencing, and guiding employees to participate in a common effort.[2] Stephen Covey, author of *The 8th Habit* says, "Leadership is communicating people's worth and potential so clearly that

Samuel Palmisano, CEO of IBM, began his career in sales at IBM. After achieving success in sales, he quickly rose through the ranks.

they come to see it in themselves."[3] Leaders are made, not born. Leadership is a series of skills that can be acquired through study and practice. Lindsay Levin inspired the employees at Whites Limited by openly sharing her vision and enlisting support for her values. She fostered teamwork by promoting jointly shared goals and building trust. Levin was quick to recognize the contributions of her employees by showing appreciation for individual excellence.[4]

Sales Management is the process of planning, implementing, and controlling the personal selling function.[5] The sales manager typically performs such management functions as planning, recruiting, training, budgeting, development of compensation plans, and assessing sales force productivity. Managing the sales force is an external management function, focused on bringing in orders and revenue from outside the company. However, it also requires coordination and cooperation with almost every internal department including marketing, finance, and distribution.[6]

The true essence of sales management has been captured by Lisa Gschwandtner, editor-in-chief of *Selling Power* magazine. She described the sales manager as a leader, coach, mentor, facilitator, goal setter, motivator, number cruncher, and communicator.[7] Needless to say, it's a job that requires many qualities and skills. Today's sales manager is more likely to function in a virtual office environment. Sales force automation permits salespeople to receive data on their laptops or their home computers. The use of other technology—videoconferencing, teleconferencing, e-mail, and voice mail—reduces the need for frequent face-to-face contact with members of the sales team.[8]

Sales managers can have a dramatic influence on the salespeople they supervise. Depending on the leadership qualities adopted, sales managers can have an advantageous, neutral, or even detrimental effect on the performance of sales subordinates.[9]

Effective leadership has been discussed in hundreds of books and articles. A careful review of this material indicates that most successful supervisory management personnel have certain behaviors in common. Two of the most important dimensions of leadership—consideration and structure—have been identified in research studies

FIGURE | 17.1

Basic Leadership Styles from the Ohio State Study

This matrix is similar to the Leadership Grid (formerly called the Managerial Grid) developed by Robert Blake and Jane Mouton. The Leadership Grid is based on two leadership style dimensions: concern for people and concern for production.

Source: Robert *Kreitner*, *Management*, 9th Ed. (Boston: Houghton Mifflin Company 2004), p. 506. Reprinted by permission of the publisher.

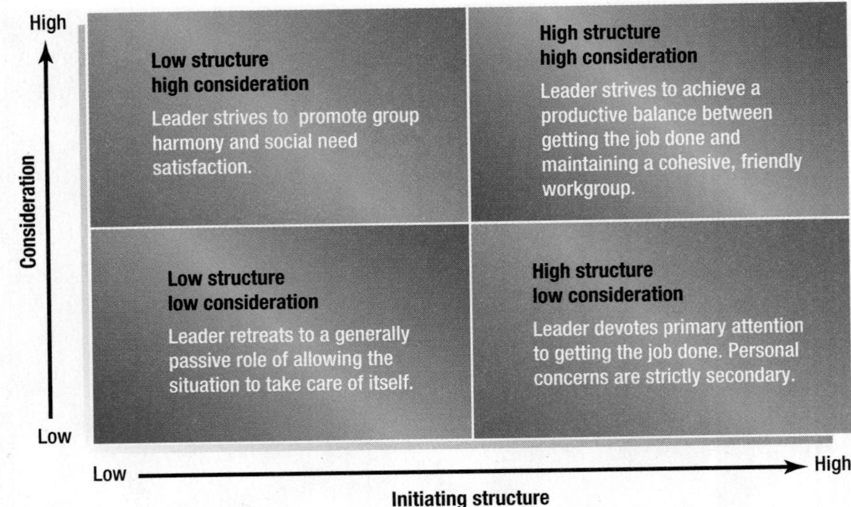

conducted by Ohio State University researchers.[10] By making a matrix out of these two independent dimensions of leadership, the researchers identified four styles of leadership (see Figure 17.1).

Structure

Sales managers who display **structure** clearly define their own duties and those of the sales staff. They assume an active role in directing their subordinates' work. Policies and procedures are clearly defined, and subordinates know what is expected of them.

Besides supervising the sales force, sales managers often are involved in establishing sales quotas, developing long-and short-term forecasts, and seeing that goals are achieved.

Salespeople also know how well they are doing because the structured supervisor evaluates their productivity and provides feedback. Members of the sales force usually appreciate the predictable nature of the highly structured sales manager. The following behaviors provide evidence of structure:

1. *Planning takes place on a regular basis.* The effective sales manager thinks ahead and decides what to do in the future. Strategic planning is the process of determining the company's current position in the market; determining where you want to be and when; and making decisions on how to secure the position you want. Strategic planning gives meaning and direction to the sales force.
2. *Expectations are clearly communicated.* The law of expectations, according to Brian Tracy, states, "Whatever you expect, with confidence, becomes your own self-fulfilling prophecy."[11] There is a strong connection between what you expect to accomplish and what you actually achieve. Sales managers must effectively formulate their expectations and then communicate them with conviction to the sales force.
3. *Decisions are made promptly and firmly.* An effective sales manager is willing and able to make decisions in a timely way. An ineffective manager often postpones important decisions, hoping the problem will go away. Of course, most decisions cannot be made until all the facts are available. A good sales manager keeps the lines of communication open and involves salespeople in making the important decisions.
4. *Performance of salespeople is appraised regularly.* All employees want to know "where they stand" with the manager. An effective sales manager provides regular feedback. When a salesperson is not performing up to established standards, the sales manager takes immediate action.

Although structure is an important aspect of sales management, too much structure can create problems. In an effort to become better organized and more systematized, some sales organizations have developed detailed policies and procedures that rob salespeople of time, energy and creativity. Filling out endless reports and forms, for example, can cause unnecessary frustration and may reduce productivity. Overcontrolling sales managers aren't just annoying, they are also inefficient.[12]

Consideration

A sales manager who displays the dimension of **consideration** is more likely to have relationships with salespeople that are characterized by mutual trust, respect for salespeoples' ideas, and consideration for their feelings. A climate of good two-way communication usually exists between the manager and members of the sales team. The following behaviors provide evidence of consideration:

1. *Regular and effective communication receives a high priority.* Whenever possible the sales manager engages in face-to-face communication with salespeople. They do not rely entirely on e-mail, letters, or sales reports for information sharing but arrange face-to-face meetings. John Morrone, vice president of sales for Pitney Bowes Management Services, frequently travels with his salespeople. He says, "My claim to fame is reaching out and touching people."[13] The effective sales manager is a good listener and creates an atmosphere of cooperation and understanding.
2. *Each salesperson is treated as an individual.* The sales manager takes a personal interest in each member of the sales force. No one is treated like a "number." The interest is genuine, not artificial. The effective sales manager does not endanger effectiveness by showing favoritism to anyone.

3. *Good performance is rewarded often.* Positive reinforcement is one of the strongest morale-building factors in the work environment. Ken Blanchard, coauthor of *The One Minute Manager*, says, "The key to developing people will always be to concentrate on catching them doing something right instead of blaming them for doing something wrong."[14] Recognition for a job well done is always appreciated.

Situational Leadership

Mastery of consideration and structure skills is an important first step toward achieving success in sales management. The next step is to match your leadership style to the various situations that surface among members of your sales force. Paul Hersey is credited with development of **situational leadership**. This leadership approach is based on the theory that the most successful leadership occurs when the leader's style matches the situation.[15]

Let's assume that a member of your sales team has almost totally abandoned customer service and follow-up activities. She is devoting nearly all of her attention to calls on new customers. Many of her regular customers have complained about poor service, and a crisis situation is developing. At this point, the leadership dimension of *structure* will require the most time and attention. This situation must be corrected immediately.

The Character Test

Sales managers who develop consideration and structure skills and the flexibility needed to be a situational leader must pass one additional test. If you fail the character test, you fail as a sales manager. Character is composed of your personal standards of behavior, including your honesty and integrity. If you are seen as an honest broker of advice and assistance, as someone who always tells the truth, trust and respect will build. But building trust is a slow process and it can be irreparably destroyed by a single lie or deception.[16]

Coaching for Peak Performance

Sales managers who develop a leadership style that combines structure and consideration behaviors possess the skills needed to be an effective coach. **Coaching** is an interpersonal process between the sales manager and the salesperson in which the manager helps the salesperson improve performance in a specific area. The coaching process has two primary areas of focus: helping the salesperson recognize the need to improve his or her performance and developing the salesperson's commitment to improve performance.[17]

Coaching is often used to correct a specific performance problem such as ineffective prospecting, poorly developed sales presentations, or failure to create value for the customer. An outline for a coaching strategy involves four steps. Step one in the coaching process involves documentation of performance problems. In some cases the best approach is to observe and assess performance during actual sales calls. Step two involves getting the salesperson to recognize and agree that there is a need to improve performance in a specific area. Sales managers should never assume the salesperson sees the problem in the same way they do. Step three involves exploring solutions. At this point it's often best to let the salesperson suggest ways to improve performance. Step four involves getting a commitment from the salesperson to take action. This step may involve development of a contract (written or verbal) that clarifies the coaching goals, approaches, and outcomes. A major goal of coaching meetings is to improve performance, while enabling sales managers and salespeople to maintain a relationship based on mutual respect and trust. Most salespeople welcome coaching, even when it involues constructive criticism.[18]

Selling Is Everyone's Business

HIRING INDEPENDENT SALESPEOPLE

Some companies hire independent sales representatives rather than establish a salaried sales force. These salespeople work for themselves, so the sales manager is really not the boss. In most cases, the independent sales agent will carry products from several companies. The challenge facing sales managers is motivating the independent seller to give their product enough attention. Successfully motivating the independent salesperson begins with solid communication and the establishment of goals. They must feel like they're part of the team. Dow Corning, Lucent Technologies, and other companies keep in touch with independent sellers via e-mail, conference calls, and face-to-face meetings.[a]

Cydcor is the largest outsourced face-to-face customer acquisition company in the world. Many Fortune 500 companies hire salespeople employed by Cydcor.

RECRUITMENT AND SELECTION OF SALESPEOPLE

Careful recruitment and selection of salespeople is very important. This is one of the most difficult tasks sales managers perform because sales organizations have been forced to become more sophisticated. The authors of *How to Hire and Develop Your Next Top Performer: The Five Qualities That Make Salespeople Great* say that about half of the people working in sales should be doing something else. In addition, they say that about 20 to 25 percent of the salespeople currently employed are selling products or services not suited to their personality.[19] If the research reported by these authors is accurate, then it appears that sales managers are frequently hiring the wrong people.

Successful salespeople are often difficult to identify. The selection of sales personnel today is, however, more of a "science" and less of an "art." Sales managers no longer need to rely on "gut feelings." The ability to identify sales aptitude accurately can be acquired. Many progressive sales organizations recognize the need to help sales managers develop the interviewing skills necessary to make profitable hiring decisions. It is impossible to avoid occasionally hiring a poor performer, but sales managers can improve their average by using some established recruitment and selection guidelines.

Determine Actual Job Requirements

To decide what type of applicant is needed, the manager should first outline the duties the person should perform. The sales manager must have a clear picture of the job requirements before beginning the recruitment process.

Some sales managers make every effort to discover the success factors that contribute to the achievements of their high-performance salespeople. Success factors are the skills, knowledge, abilities, and behaviors considered critical for successful performance. This information may be collected by use of interviews with salespeople or customers, by observing the salesperson during sales calls, or by some other method.

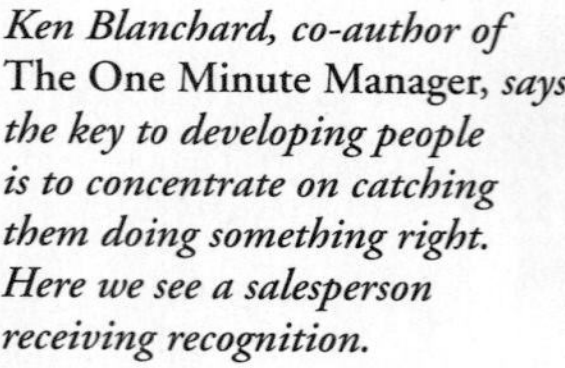

Ken Blanchard, co-author of The One Minute Manager, *says the key to developing people is to concentrate on catching them doing something right. Here we see a salesperson receiving recognition.*

After a careful study of the duties the salesperson should perform and identification of the success factors, a job description should be prepared. A job description is an explanation of what the salesperson will do and under what conditions the work will be performed. It is a good idea to spell out in as much detail as possible the abilities and qualities that the applicant needs to be successful. This can be accomplished by answering a few basic questions about the position.

1. Will the person be developing new sales territory or assuming responsibility for an established territory?
2. Is the product or service well established, or is it new to the marketplace?
3. Will the salesperson work under the sales manager's close supervision or independently?
4. What amount of travel is required? What are the likelihoods of eventual transfer and promotion?

Once the job description is prepared, the foundation has been established to determine the type of person to be hired. There is no substitute for knowing what the job requires.

Search Out Applicants from Several Sources

To identify the best possible person, it is usually best to seek applicants from more than one source. As a rule of thumb, try to interview three or more applicants for each opening. Some suggested sources of new employees follow:

1. *Candidates within the company.* One of the first places to look is within your own company. Is there someone in accounting, engineering, customer service, or some other area who aspires to a sales position? These people have the advantage of being familiar with the company's product offering, policies, operations, and what it takes to please the customer.
2. *College and university students.* Many business firms are turning to college and university campuses to recruit salespeople. As noted in Chapter 2, several colleges and universities have developed personal selling certificate and degree programs. Placement offices are usually cooperative and often publicize openings.
3. *Trade and newspaper advertisements.* A carefully prepared newspaper advertisement often attracts well-qualified job applicants. A well-written ad should describe the job requirements *and* spell out the opportunities. All information should be accurate. The ad should "sell" the position, but it should not exaggerate its benefits.
4. *Employment agencies and listings.* Nearly 2,000 public employment offices are located throughout the United States. These offices recruit applicants and screen them according to your specifications. There is no charge for this service. There are also many private employment agencies. These firms specialize in matching applicants to the job and usually do some initial screening for employers. A fee is assessed for the services these agencies provide.
5. *Internet.* Many companies are using the Internet to recruit for sales positions. Two popular Web sites are *Monster.com* and *JobBankUSA.com.*

Select the Best-Qualified Applicant

Once you have identified qualified applicants, the next step is to select the best person. This is becoming more difficult as products become more complex, customers become more sophisticated, and competitors become more aggressive. Selecting the best-qualified applicant is never easy, but there are some qualifications and characteristics that all sales managers should look for. One of the most important qualities is a high level of interest and enthusiasm for the job and high degree of self-motivation. Salespeople have to be self-starters.

At San Francisco's Get Real Girl (www.getrealgirl.com) *Co-CEOs Jana Machin (left) and Julia Chavez say, "Having the best salespeople is important." In the past year, 75 of these "best of class" salespeople have blazed their way into chains like Target, Toys R Us, Walmart, and Smyth's (Ireland's answer to Toys R Us), as well as hundreds of small independent retailers.*

Another very important quality is integrity. Dana Telford and Adrian Gostick, authors of *Integrity Works* say that managers spend about 90 percent of their time on capability related questions and almost no time on character-based questions. They suggest checking backgrounds and interviewing for character by asking ethics-based questions. Here are a few examples.[20]

"What are your three core values?"
"What does integrity mean to you?"
"Who are your role models and why?"
"What would your past manager say about you?"
"Tell me about a time when you were asked to compromise your integrity."

Bruce Diamond, vice president of sales for a large office equipment company, says, "Our salespeople now need to be much more professional, much more educated about the market, customers, products, and business in general."[21] His strategy for finding good salespeople includes discussions of business trends and developments. During the interview, he poses business situations and asks the candidate to come up with solutions. Diamond says he is impressed when a candidate displays an understanding of profitable revenues and finding the right customers to do business with.

One of the greatest challenges is hiring salespeople who can develop a close, trusting, long-term relationship with customers. As we have noted previously, the manner in which salespeople establish, build, and maintain relationships is no longer an incidental aspect of personal selling. Mike Mitchell, vice president of human resources for Tiffany & Company, says, "We look for people who feel a great sense of purpose in serving our customers. You can train people to be consultative in their approach to the point that they master the mechanics of the sales process, but you can't teach someone to care."[22]

Experts in the field of employment testing say that psychological tests can be helpful as an element of the hiring process. Psychological assessments can provide objective information about a candidate's skills and abilities. One example is the Sales Achievement Predictor developed by Western Psychological Services. This instrument assesses self-confidence, personal diplomacy, competitiveness, and other qualities deemed important in sales.[23] Caliper Corporation, a testing

Selling in Action

ARE YOU READY FOR THE SALES INTERVIEW?

The personal interview is an important part of the selection process when filling sales positions. When companies use a series of interviews, the first one often is used to eliminate unacceptable candidates—those who lack maturity, lack enthusiasm, or display poor appearance. Subsequent interviews are used to match people to job qualifications. At Hewlett Packard, candidates may have as many as six interviews with various people. At Smith Kline, a team approach is used so candidates do not learn the "right" answers from one interview to the next.

Although interviews vary from one company or interviewer to another, there are some popular questions and requests that you should be prepared to handle:

- Tell me about yourself.
- Describe the sales process as you understand it.
- What books have you read recently on selling or for personal development?
- What is your greatest weakness? Strength?
- What was the most boring job you ever had, and how did you handle it?
- How do you feel about your present (or previous) employer?
- What was the biggest contribution you made to your last employer?
- Sell me this pen (ashtray, laptop computer, lamp).
- Why should we hire you?

Some employers also ask you to complete a test to demonstrate your written communication skills, or your ability to handle "the numbers." These are both important skills for a sales professional.[b]

service with more than 40 years of experience, has developed the Caliper Profile, an instrument for personality assessment.[24] Test results always should be used *in conjunction* with information obtained from the interview with the candidate and the findings of reference checks.

ORIENTATION AND TRAINING

Once you have selected the best qualified salesperson, two steps should be taken to ensure that this person becomes a productive member of your staff. First, give the new employee a thorough orientation to your business operation. Provide the orientation *before* the person begins working. This should include a review of your company's history, philosophy of doing business, mission statement, business policies, compensation plan, and other important information.

Second, initiate a training program to help the person achieve success. Sales training that is carefully planned and executed can make a major contribution to the performance of every salesperson. Study results indicate that salespeople have a more positive view about their job situation, greater commitment, and improved performance when their sales managers clarify their job role, how to execute their tasks, and how their needs can be satisfied with successful job performance.[25]

Even salespeople with great potential are handicapped when the company fails to provide adequate training. Keep in mind that in the absence of formal training, employees develop their own approaches to performing tasks.

The size of the firm should not dictate the scope of the training program. Even the smallest marketing organization should have a formal sales training program. This program should have three dimensions:

1. Knowledge of the product line, company marketing strategies, territory information, and business trends
2. Attitude toward the company, the company's products and services, and the customers to be served

Selling Power magazine has some of the best hiring and training products available to assist sales managers. This publication often features articles that focus on recruitment, selection, orientation, and training of salespeople.

3. Skill in applying personal selling principles and practices—the "doing" part of the sales training program[26]

An important part of the sales training program is foundation level instruction. This aspect of sales training focuses on the *basics*. If salespeople are to plan and execute a sales call successfully, they must first master certain fundamental selling skills—the skills that form the foundation for everything salespeople do in their careers. The steps that make up the Six-Step Presentation Plan (approach, presentation, demonstration, negotiation, close, and servicing the sale) represent fundamental selling skills (see Fig. 15.1).

Sales training that is carefully planned and executed can make a major contribution to the performance of every salesperson.

SALES FORCE MOTIVATION

It is helpful to note the difference between internal and external motivation. An **internal motivation** is an intrinsic reward that occurs when a duty or task is performed. If a salesperson enjoys calling on customers and solving their problems, this activity is in itself rewarding, and the salesperson is likely to be self-motivated.[27] Internal motivation is likely to be triggered when sales positions provide an opportunity for achievement and individual growth. **External motivation** is an action taken by another person that involves rewards or other forms of reinforcement that cause the worker to behave in ways to ensure receipt of the award.[28] A cash bonus given to salespeople who achieve a sales goal provides an example of external motivation. Experts on motivation agree that organizations should attempt to provide a mix of external rewards and internal satisfaction.

Global Business Etiquette

DOING BUSINESS IN SWITZERLAND

Trudi Gallagher, a real estate sales associate with a U.S. firm, offers us some good advice on doing business in Switzerland. She was born and raised in that country.

- The Swiss are very private people, and it takes quite a while for them to get to know you and invite you to their home. They are more likely to entertain in restaurants and hotels.
- The Swiss are very punctual, very correct, and when they give their word, they mean it.
- Although four languages are spoken in Switzerland, businesspeople will almost always speak English.[c]

A basic contention among many sales managers has been that sales productivity can be improved by staging more elaborate sales contests, giving more expensive recognition awards, or picking truly exotic meeting locations. This point of view ignores two things we know for sure about the characteristics of motives. First, motives are individualistic. The desire for social standing (status) may be very strong for one salesperson, but not very important to another salesperson. What satisfies one person's needs may not be important to someone else. Second, motives change throughout our lives. What motivates us early in our career may not motivate us later in life.

Because people bring different interests, drives, and values to the workplace, they react differently to attempts at motivation. The owner of an incentive consulting company in Chicago rewarded one of his highly productive employees with an attractive mink coat. She thanked him sincerely, took the coat home, but never wore it. When he asked her why, she explained that she didn't wear fur.[29]

Very often intrinsic motivators (achievement, challenge, responsibility, advancement, growth, enjoyment of work itself, and involvement) have a longer-term effect on employees' attitudes and behaviors than extrinsic motivators (contests, prizes, quotas, and money). In many cases sales performance is linked directly to the appreciation the sales manager shows for a job well done. A salesperson who is intrinsically satisfied in the job will likely work willingly at high-performance levels.

Effective Use of External Rewards

Although criticisms of external rewards have a great deal of merit, the fact remains that large numbers of organizations continue to achieve positive results with carefully developed incentive programs. It is possible to design programs that have long-range benefits for both the organization and the individual employee if you follow these guidelines:

1. Design reward programs that focus on several important aspects of the salesperson's job such as developing new accounts, expanding sales of existing accounts, and improving customer service after the sale. Keep contest time frames short so more salespeople have an opportunity to win. However, don't use short-term motivation contests too often and don't use the same incentive plan over and over again.
2. Evaluate your incentive program often to determine what plan has the most impact. Is it cash bonuses? Travel? Merchandise? Bill Grassie, manager of compensation and business planning for Sprint, likes to use noncash incentives because he believes Sprint salespeople have a solid compensation package. He feels noncash incentives provide a lasting memory whereas a cash bonus is just one more way to earn money.[30] Of course, a salesperson who is not earning a lot of money in salary and commission might favor a cash incentive.
3. Avoid setting goals that are unrealistic. Some companies are under enormous pressure to meet sales and profit targets. In many cases sales targets increase while resources decline. A salesperson working for a company in Texas made President's Club for being 220 percent above quota and her whole team did well and was recognized as tops in the company. Her boss, the vice president for sales, immediately raised their overall quota by 65 percent for the next year. This was an impossible target and team morale plummeted.

Pressure to reach unrealistic sales goals can produce negative results. Employee loyalty and teamwork erode quickly, and in some cases so do business ethics. Salespeople who fear loss of their job if they do not meet established targets are more inclined to engage in unethical behavior.[31]

Should sales managers encourage their salespeople to *compete* or encourage them to *cooperate*? This is one of the dilemmas facing managers who want highly motivated salespeople, but they also want members of the sales team to share important information and become resources to each other. One answer is to develop a plan that rewards sales collaboration and the achievement of specific sales goals.[32]

Icelandic® offers a very attractive incentive program to its distribution sales representatives.

Recognition for success in sales can be an effective form of external motivation.

COMPENSATION PLANS

Compensation plans for salespeople combine direct monetary payments (salary and commissions) and indirect monetary payments such as paid vacations, pensions, and insurance plans. Compensation practices vary greatly throughout the field of selling. Furthermore, sales managers are constantly searching for the "perfect" sales force compensation plan. Of course, the perfect plan does not exist. Each plan must be chosen to suit the specific type of selling job, the objectives of the firm's marketing program, and the type of customer served.

As noted in Chapter 2, the highest amount of total compensation is earned by salespeople who are involved in value-added selling. Salespeople who use this approach realize that the solution to the customer's buying problem is more important than price. They are frequently involved in team selling and in some cases they are rewarded with a team compensation plan.

Customer Relationship Management with Technology

STAYING INFORMED

A key role of the sales manager is to provide a steady flow of information and advice to salespeople. Salespeople look to their managers for information about market trends, products, company policies, and assistance with their accounts. Customer relationship management (CRM) software improves and enhances the flow of information between managers and the sales force. The same features that are used to enrich communications with customers also support the sales organization's internal communications. With direct access to a shared CRM database, for example, a sales manager can review relationships with accounts in real time by examining a salesperson's notes at any time. This makes it possible for the manager to enter advice about an account directly into that account's record. (See the exercise, Receiving Advice Through CRM, on p. 437 for more information.)

A growing number of companies are abandoning compensation plans that are linked to a single target such as a sales quota. At Siebel Systems, an e-business software provider, 40 percent of each salesperson's incentive compensation is based on the customers' reported satisfaction with service and implementation of the products they have purchased. This plan encourages continuous customer follow-up, which generates repeat business.[33]

In the field of selling there are five basic compensation plans. Here is a description of each:

Straight commission plan. The only direct monetary compensation comes from sales. No sales, no income. Salespeople under this plan are very conscious of their sales. Lack of job security can be a strong inducement to produce results. However, these people also may concentrate more on immediate sales than on long-term customer development.

Commission plan with a draw provision or guaranteed salary. This plan has about the same impact on salespeople as the straight commission plan. However, it gives them more financial security.

Commission with a draw or guaranteed salary plus a bonus. This plan offers more direct financial security than the first two plans. Therefore, salespeople may adhere more to the company's objectives. The bonus may be based on sales or profits.

Fixed salary plus bonus. Salespeople functioning under this compensation plan tend to be more company centered and to have a fairly high degree of financial security if their salary is competitive. The bonus incentive helps motivate people under this plan.

Straight salary. Salespeople who work under this compensation plan are usually more company centered and have financial security.

According to the *Sales & Marketing Management* 2005 research study, most companies participating in the survey used some form of compensation plan that combined base salary and incentive.[34] The salary plus bonus and salary plus commission plans are both quite popular.

As might be expected, many companies are experimenting with some variation of these basic plans. In some situations, salespeople are rewarded for achieving a specific objective such as developing new accounts or account profitability. Awards in the form of cash or points that can be used to "purchase" prizes can be used. Award programs can be styled to suit a variety of sales objectives:

Specific product movement. Bonus points can be given for the sale of certain items during specified "push" selling periods.

Percentage sales increase. Sales levels can be established with points that are given only when those levels are reached.

Establish new accounts. A block of points can be awarded for opening a new account or for introducing new products through the existing outlets.

Increase sales activity. For each salesperson, points can be awarded based on the number of calls.[35]

There is no easy way to develop an effective compensation plan. There are, however, some important guidelines for your efforts to develop an effective plan. First, be sure that your sales and marketing objectives are defined in detail. The plan should complement these objectives. If sales and marketing objectives are in conflict with the compensation plan, problems surely arise.

Second, the compensation plan should be field tested before full implementation. Several questions should be answered: Is the new plan easy to administer? How does the proposed plan differ in terms of payout compared with the existing plan?

Third, explain the compensation plan carefully to the sales force. Misunderstanding may generate distrust of the plan. Keep in mind that some salespeople may see change as a threat.

Fourth, change the compensation plan when conditions in the marketplace warrant change. One reason for the poor showing of many plans is that firms fail to revise their plan as the business grows and market conditions change. Review the compensation plan at least annually to ensure that it's aligned with conditions in the marketplace and the company's overall marketing strategy.

ASSESSING SALES FORCE PRODUCTIVITY

As the cost of maintaining a sales force increases, sales managers must give more attention to measuring productivity. The goal is to analyze the profitability of each salesperson's sales volume. This task is complicated because sales territories, customers, and business conditions vary.

The problem of measuring sales force productivity is more complicated than it might appear at first glance. In most cases, sales volume alone does not tell you how much profit or loss you are making on the sales of each member of the sales force. A small manufacturer was losing money until he analyzed the profitability of sales generated by each person. He found that one salesperson created a loss on almost every order. This salesperson was concentrating on a market that had become so competitive that she had to reduce the markup to make sales.

Some sales managers view the frequency of calls as an indicator of success. This information is only helpful when compared with the profit earned on each account. The number of calls made on an account should bear some relationship to the sales and profit potential of that account. In some cases it is possible to maintain small accounts without making frequent personal calls.

To compare a salesperson's current productivity with the past also can be misleading. Changes in products, prices, competition, and assignments can make comparisons with the past unfair—sometimes to the salesperson, sometimes to the company. It is better to measure cumulative quarterly, semiannual, or annual results in relation to established goals.

Some sales managers use performance evaluation criteria that communicate to the sales force which elements of their jobs are most important and how they are doing in each area. Evaluating salespeople involves defining the bases on which they are to be evaluated, developing performance standards to determine the acceptable level of performance desired on each base, monitoring actual performance, and giving salespeople feedback on their performance.[36] Some of the most common criteria for assessing the productivity of salespeople are listed as follows:

Quantitative Criteria

Sales volume in dollars

Sales volume compared with previous year's sales

Sales volume by product or product line

Number of new accounts opened

Amount of new account sales

Net profit on each account

Number of customer calls

Qualitative Criteria

Attitude

Product knowledge

Communication skills

Personal appearance
Customer goodwill generated
Selling skills
Initiative
Team collaboration

In most cases it is best to emphasize assessment criteria that can be expressed in numbers (quantitative). The preceding quantitative items are especially significant when accompanied by target dates. For example, you might assess the number of new accounts opened during a six-month period. Of course, a sales manager should not ignore the other criteria listed here. The other items can affect a salesperson's productivity, and you do have to make judgments in these areas.

Some sales managers ask their salespeople to complete a self-evaluation as part of the overall evaluation process. Many salespeople believe that self-evaluation contributes to their personal development.[37]

Summary

Many capable salespeople have advanced to the position of *sales manager*. This job involves such diverse duties as recruiting, selecting, training, and supervising salespeople. Some sales managers are concerned solely with the management of salespeople; others have responsibility for additional marketing functions such as advertising and market research.

The sales manager is part of the management team and therefore must be concerned with leadership. An effective sales manager is an effective leader. Although the qualities of effective leaders are subject to debate, most research tells us that such people display two dimensions: *structure* and *consideration*. Sales managers who develop a leadership style that combines structure and consideration possess the skills needed to be an effective *coach*.

Many sales managers are involved directly or indirectly in recruiting and selecting salespeople. This is an important responsibility because mistakes can be costly. A portion of the company's profit picture and the firm's image can be influenced positively or negatively by each member of the sales force.

Training and motivating salespeople are almost daily concerns of the sales manager. Training should always be viewed as an investment in human resources. Training helps members of the sales force reach their fullest potential.

We discuss the difference between *internal* and *external motivation*. In many cases intrinsic motivators (achievement, challenge, responsibility, involvement, and enjoyment of work itself) have a longer-term effect on employee attitudes and behavior than extrinsic motivators (contests, prizes, and money). Sales managers need to discover the individual differences between salespeople to select the most effective motivation strategies.

The most common *compensation plans* are discussed. Compensation plans should be field tested before full implementation.

Assessing sales force productivity is a major responsibility of the sales manager. Sales managers use both quantitative and qualitative criteria.

KEY TERMS

Sales Management
Structure
Consideration
Coaching
Situational leadership
Internal motivation
External motivation
Compensation plans

REVIEW QUESTIONS

1. What is the difference between leadership and management?
2. Are all sales managers' duties the same? Explain.
3. What are the two main leadership qualities displayed by most successful sales managers? Define and explain each of these qualities.
4. List and describe the four basic steps involved in coaching.
5. What is a job description? Explain the importance of job descriptions in selecting salespeople.
6. What are four sources of recruiting new salespeople?
7. What should sales managers look for in selecting new salespeople? Describe at least three important qualities.
8. List and describe three guidelines that should be followed when you design a sales motivation program based on external rewards.
9. List and describe the five basic compensation plans for salespeople.
10. What are the *best* criteria for measuring a salesperson's performance? List additional criteria that should be considered in evaluating individual performance.

APPLICATION EXERCISES

1. Assume that you are a manager of a wholesale electrical supply business. Sales have increased to a level where you need to hire another salesperson. What sources can you use in recruiting a good professional salesperson? What criteria can you use in selecting the person you hire?
2. Carefully analyze the following types of selling positions:
   - **a.** A territory selling position for a national manufacturer that requires the salesperson to provide customer service to a large number of accounts plus open up several new accounts each month
   - **b.** A retail sales position in the cosmetics department of a department store
   - **c.** An automobile salesperson who sells and leases new and used cars
   - **d.** A real estate salesperson who sells residential real estate

   Assuming that each of the preceding positions is full time, identify the type of compensation plan you think is best for each. Supply an explanation for each of your answers.
3. Schedule an appointment with two sales managers. Interview each of them, using the following questions as a guide:
   - **a.** What are your functions as a sales manager?
   - **b.** How do the functions of a sales manager differ from those of a salesperson?
   - **c.** What criteria do you use in selecting salespeople?

d. What kinds of training programs do you have for new salespeople?
e. What method of compensation do you use for your salespeople?
f. How do you evaluate the performance of your salespeople?
g. What personal qualities are important for becoming a sales manager?

Write the answers to these questions. Summarize the similarities and differences of the sales managers' responses.

4. The Internet lists many sources of training in the field of sales management. Using your search engine, type in "sales management." How many queries did you find? Examine one or more of the training programs and list the topics that are covered. Compare this list of topics with the material presented in this chapter.

ROLE-PLAY EXERCISE

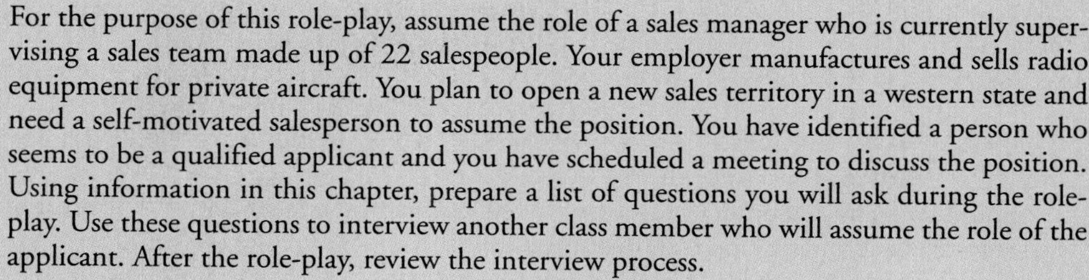

For the purpose of this role-play, assume the role of a sales manager who is currently supervising a sales team made up of 22 salespeople. Your employer manufactures and sells radio equipment for private aircraft. You plan to open a new sales territory in a western state and need a self-motivated salesperson to assume the position. You have identified a person who seems to be a qualified applicant and you have scheduled a meeting to discuss the position. Using information in this chapter, prepare a list of questions you will ask during the role-play. Use these questions to interview another class member who will assume the role of the applicant. After the role-play, review the interview process.

CRM APPLICATION EXERCISE

Receiving Advice Through CRM

Becky Kemley, your sales manager at SimNet Systems, regularly reviews your progress with accounts by examining your notes. She recently entered into one of your records a note about an account's debt problems. Find her note and the two accounts she refers to by selecting Lookup, Keyword, type "debt," check Notes, and press Enter. Print the information contained in these records by selecting Report, Contact Report, Active Lookup, Printer, and Enter.

CASE PROBLEM

One of the more interesting developments in sales force management is the use of customer feedback to improve the performance of salespeople. These programs go by a variety of names such as *360 degree feedback, customer-conscious compensation*, and *customer satisfaction rewards*. Organizations that have adopted this assessment strategy believe salespeople can benefit from feedback collected from the customers they serve. Also, the information collected can be used by the company to improve customer service.

The use of customer-driven evaluation programs is on the increase because of the rising regard for the role of sales at many companies. Tom Mott, a consultant with Hewitt Associates, says, "Salespeople who were volume pushers are now becoming the manager of their company's relationship with the customer." Mott points out that customer feedback is likely to reflect on the performance of the salesperson and the performance of the company. If problems surface in either area, customer dissatisfaction may need attention.

Data collection methodology is not uniform at this point. Some companies use telephone surveys while others use mailed questionnaires. IBM has experimented with a series of in-person meetings that bring together corporate customers, their IBM sales representatives, and the salesperson's boss.

Some salespeople have not welcomed the use of customer evaluations. Maryann Cirenza, senior account executive at Teleport Communications Group (TCG) of New York, said that she felt betrayed when she saw the questionnaire the company was sending to her customers. One of the questions asked, "Does your sales rep know your industry?" Cirenza said, "I thought the company was checking up on me." Later her anger subsided when she learned the survey was not simply a monitoring system but a trial run for a new compensation plan. After field testing the surveys, TCG used customer feedback to set bonuses. Cirenza was actually rewarded for good customer service by earning a bonus of about 20 percent of her base pay. Greg Buseman, a Chicago-based IBM salesman, believes the shift to compensation through customer feedback has improved personal selling at his company. He now spends more time understanding the customer's business and learning to be a problem solver for his clients.[38]

Questions

1. Should the customer be given a major voice in determining how salespeople are performing? Explain.
2. Should sales force compensation be linked to customer feedback? What are the advantages and disadvantages of this approach?
3. Assume you are a sales manager preparing to develop and implement a customer feedback system. How might you gain support for this system from members of your salespeople? What data collection method would you use?
4. Research indicates that customers rank "understanding of our business" as an important criterion used to evaluate salespeople. Why is this criterion ranked so high?

APPENDIX 1

Finding Employment: A Personalized Marketing Plan for the Age of Information

The principles of strategic/consultative selling can be used to prepare a personalized marketing plan to secure a high-paying, professional career position. In Chapter 1 we identified the marketing concept. This concept states that a good marketing program begins with research. After finding out the "what, where, when, why, and how much" during research, the marketing mix is developed (Fig. A.1). In designing a marketing mix, the elements of product, place, promotion, and pricing are coordinated to satisfy the job seeker's needs uncovered during the research phase. The following material describes the steps that should be followed to develop a personal marketing plan for securing a job.

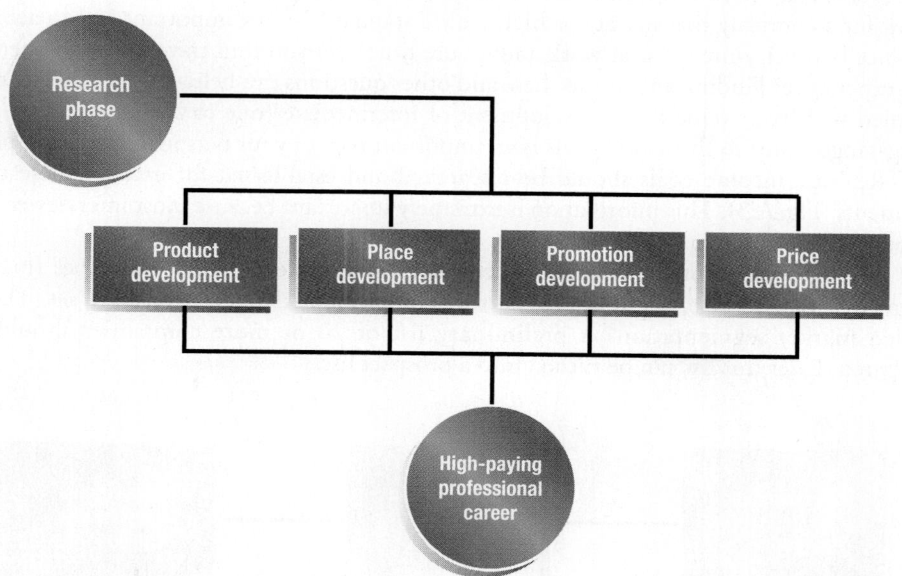

FIGURE | A.1

The Employment Marketing Mix

FIGURE | A.2

Research Conducted Before Designing a Job Marketing Mix

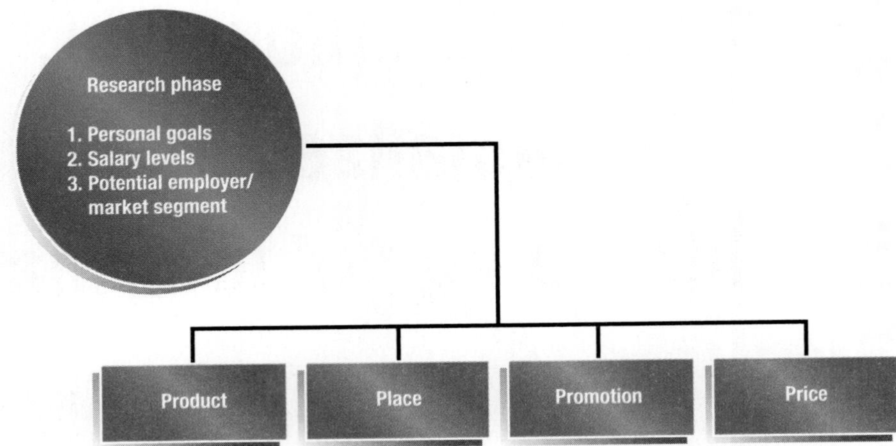

RESEARCH PHASE

During the research step of the personal marketing plan, the emphasis is on information gathering: (1) what type of career the individual is seeking, (2) what the market (in which that position exists) is looking for in applicants, and (3) what the market is willing to pay (Fig. A.2). This information is the starting point for the development of the rest of the personal marketing plan. Securing this basic information is fundamental to the personal marketing plan. Job seeking without this important first step is a waste of time. Many job seekers do not start with this first step and consequently fail to find a rewarding career position.

Deciding what you want to achieve in your career begins with a great deal of reflection on who you are and what you want to accomplish. Your future productivity and fulfillment depend on finding employment that matches your personal beliefs and preferences. How important is it for you to earn a great deal of money early in your career? Do you want to work for a company that maintains high ethical standards? How important is it to achieve balance between time spent at work and leisure time? Do you find travel to be an energizing experience? Finding answers to these and other questions can help you set goals that are aligned with your values. The development of intermediate (one to two years) goals and long-range (three to five years) goals is an important part of your personal marketing plan.

Realistic income goals should be researched and established for each of these time segments (Fig. A.3). This information is extremely important because most interviewers ask about income goals during the interview.

The next phase of the research process is to determine in which industries (market segments) the career opportunities exist that complement the goals you have set. This is called market segmentation. A preliminary list of 20 or more companies should be prepared. Later this list can be turned into a prospect list.

FIGURE | A.3

Setting Position and Salary Goals

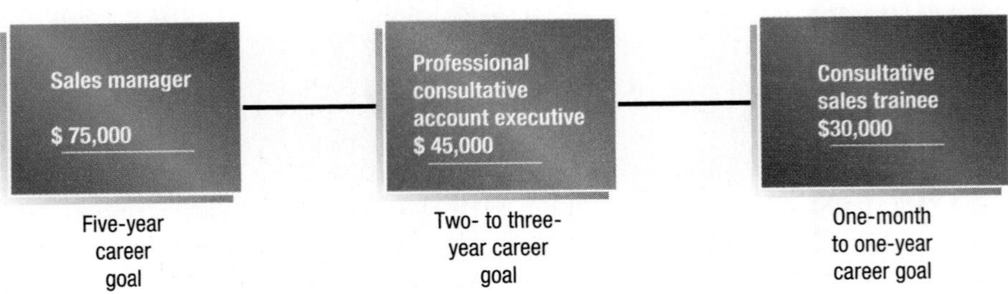

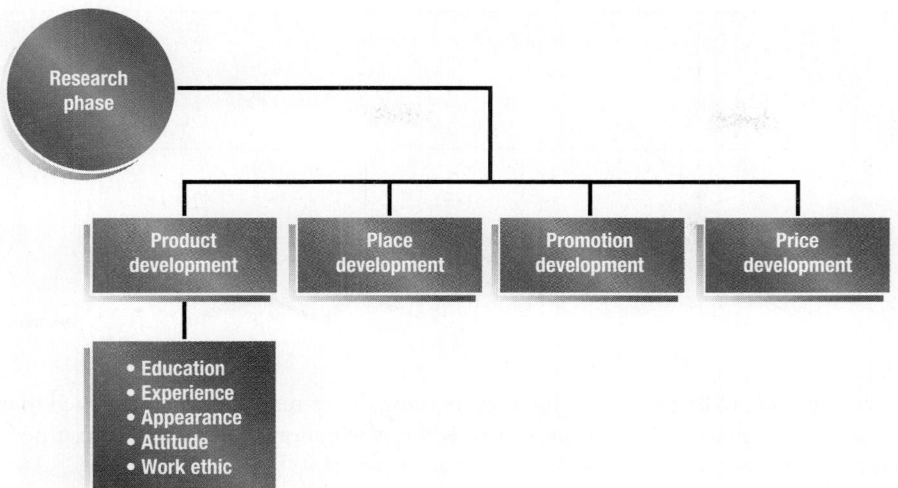

FIGURE | A.4

Product Development Activities Associated with Finding Employment

The final part of the research process is to determine what qualities the particular market segment wants in the people it selects for employees. In determining the hiring motives (see Chapter 8 on buying motives), does the market look for quantitative backgrounds, such as a minimum number of years of education or a minimum number of years of experience? Does it look for a qualitative background, such as a positive attitude (see Chapter 3), a professional image (see Chapter 3), or certain communication skills? During this stage it is important to find out which of these qualities or combination of qualities the potential employer (market segment) is looking for, because the design of the marketing mix is based on these findings.

PRODUCT DEVELOPMENT

After the research phase of the personal marketing plan is complete, the next step is the development of the marketing mix. This begins with a product development program—documenting the proper amount and kind of education and job experience, fostering an appropriate appearance (packaging) and attitude, and the work ethic (Fig. A.4).

It is important to take each of these areas of development and convert it into a benefit that helps the prospective employer or market segment achieve its objectives. For example, being elected an officer of a social or professional organization often means that the individual has a high-energy level, tends to get along well with people, and is respected by his peers (benefits). These are all important benefits that help a prospective employer meet quotas and profit objectives (see Chapters 6 and 7).

PLACE DEVELOPMENT

The next phase of the personal marketing mix consists of developing a sophisticated prospect base (see Chapter 9). The prospect base is made up of potential employers who offer career positions corresponding to the career goals set in the research phase. This prospect list should include the company name, address, telephone number, names and titles of individuals to be contacted concerning employment, and other background information on the company (Fig. A.5). The number of prospects depends on the desired

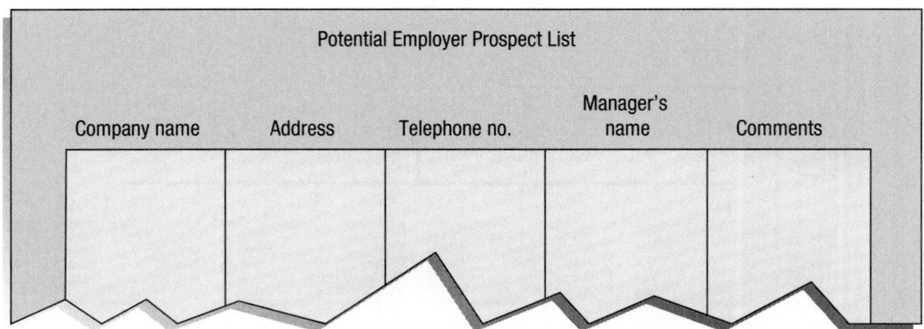

FIGURE | A.5

Place Development Through Using a Prospect List

size of the market to be contacted. Job seekers using direct-mail and internet-based marketing plans may contact up to 200 prospects, whereas telephone and direct-contact personal marketing plans begin with about 20 potential employers.

Source of Potential Employers

The easiest source of potential employers to add to the prospect list is probably the classified section of the newspaper; however, "seldom does anything good come easy," and the newspaper is generally not the best source of prospective employers. In many cases either the best positions advertised in the newspaper are informally filled before they are advertised or the competition for them is extremely keen. It is not uncommon for a company to receive from 100 to 150 résumés for jobs offering competitive salaries. In other cases, companies mass-merchandise jobs that are unattractive and difficult to fill. Although newspapers should not be overlooked in developing a prospect list, it is wise to use them with caution.

The Internet is an excellent place to start your search for job openings. More than half of the companies use the Internet for job postings. The use of online salary surveys can help you determine potential earnings. The Bureau of Labor Statistics (www.bls.gov) is a good source of Web-based salary data. JobStar California (www.jobstar.org) provides links to 300 salary surveys.[1] Consider starting your job search with a visit to the Web sites that follow:[2]

Careerbuilder.com This site links you to 25 online career centers. The site offers 80 job categories.

Jobsearch.org This site, a product of the U.S. Department of Labor, contains over a million job openings.

Monster.com Job seekers can find over 250,000 job listings and a database of 1 million résumés.

Hotjobs.com Job seekers can post their résumé on this site and then control which companies are allowed to view it.

In addition to these sites, most trade organizations and many companies have their own online list of job openings.

To build a good list of prospective employers, you should also use directories, referrals, friends, acquaintances, and cold calls (Fig. A.6). Most jobs can be found by visiting job fairs, talking to recruiters, networking with friends and acquaintances, and knocking on doors. (See Chapter 9, for information on these methods.)

Do not include in your list only companies with existing job vacancies. Research shows that companies frequently have openings that are not actively being recruited. Turnover also creates openings, and many firms go back into applicant files to fill these openings. In addition, many companies create openings, especially for trainees, when a well-qualified person applies for a career-oriented position.

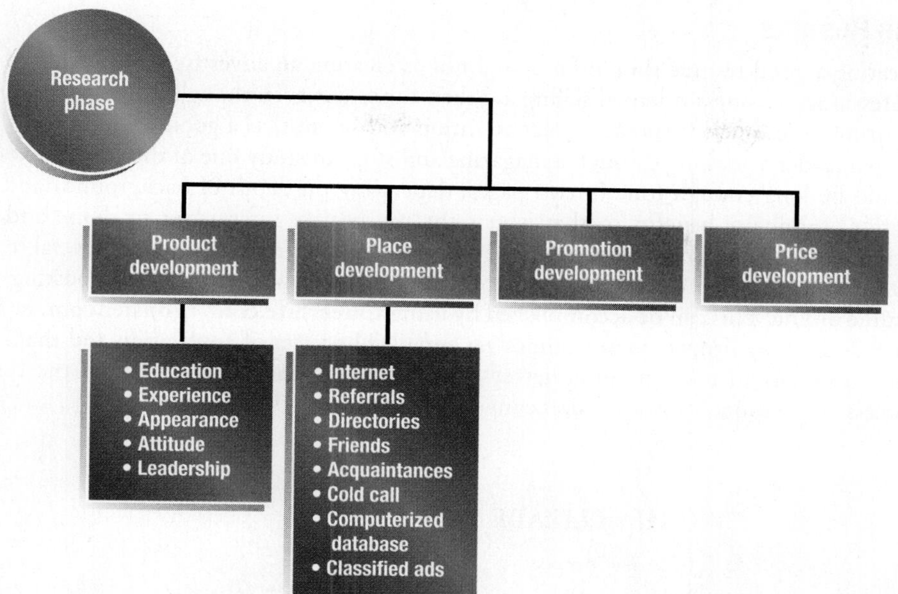

FIGURE | A.6

Sources for Developing a Prospective Employer List

PROMOTION DEVELOPMENT

Developing the promotional element of the personal marketing program consists of creating an effective résumé (advertisement), writing good application and thank-you letters (sales promotion), and conducting convincing job interviews (sales presentation) (Fig. A.7). The rules for developing each of these promotional concepts are much different at the professional-career level than at part-time and entry levels. They also tend to be different for acquiring a position in the private business sector than in public employment. The following promotional principles relate mainly to the professional-career level in private business, although many also apply to securing entry level, part-time, or public employment positions.

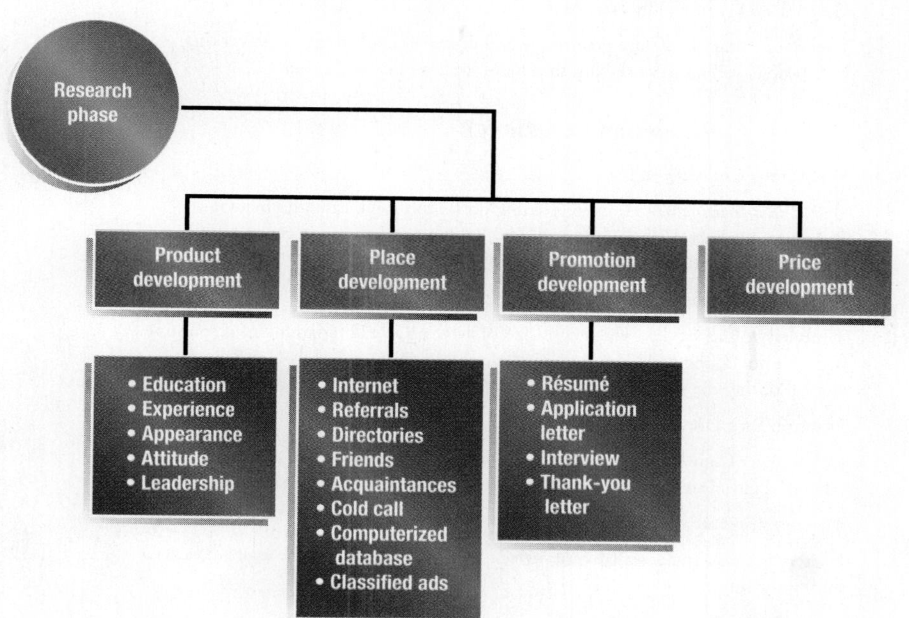

FIGURE | A.7

Promotional Elements Used to Market Yourself

The Résumé

Creating a good résumé should be thought of as creating an advertisement. It should be a professional, business-oriented selling aid that stands out even though it is part of a pile of 20 or more résumés. It should attract attention and interest, as a good advertisement does when a reader is looking through a magazine and stops to study one of the ads. The résumé should be long enough (one to two pages, depending on depth of background) and well written, supplying benefits so that it gets the prospective interviewer to desire and take action to set up a personal interview. The Microsoft Word program provides several résumé wizards to use when developing your résumé. You may want to consider posting your résumé online. This can be accomplished by using **CareerSite.com**, **Monster.com**, or some other site. Many firms request résumés via e-mail. The letter of application and thank-you letter also should take the interviewer's mind through the mental steps in the buying process—attention, interest, desire, conviction, and action (see Chapter 8).

CYNTHIA ELIZABETH SMITH

Current Address	**Permanent Address**
	cesmith @ mchi.com
1305 34th Street	**617 Hail Street**
Des Moines, Iowa 50311	**Rockport, Illinois 60202**
(515) 277–4753	**(312) 246–3872**

Objectives: To secure a growth-oriented sales position in the wholesale, service, or manufacturing industries

Primary Skills: Have acquired background skills in selling, buying computers, and management at Drake through classroom work and On the Job Training

Possess progressive work experience in retail, from a small specialty store to a large department store

Have the ability to understand and apply creative design concepts through my previous classroom experience

Have the ability to work effectively and harmoniously with a wide range of people

Have the ability to rapidly learn new techniques and concepts

Summary: Twenty-one-year-old college graduate with a degree in marketing; enjoy working with people; willing to work hard to achieve success in chosen career

WORK EXPERIENCE

2005–Present Von Maurs, Des Moines, Iowa

Started in a Management Trainee position; duties and responsibilities include Professional Selling, Visual Merchandising, Buying and Inventory; exposure to a broad variety of management and supervisory philosophies

2003 Temporary Manpower, Chicago, Illinois

Temporary office service, which consisted of working as a librarian for an accounting firm, Author Young and Company; also as a receptionist for Loyola Law School; worked during the summer while attending evening classes

2002–03 Evanston Park District, Glen Ellyn, Illinois

Park District Counselor, taught safety to young children, instructed crafts, and coached a girl's softball team; also worked as a receptionist at the main office

2001 Maloney's Restaurant, Lombard, Illinois

Hostess at a restaurant; seated customers, cleaned tables, and ran the register; worked during the summer

	EDUCATION
	Drake University, Des Moines, Iowa
	Graduated with a B.S.B.A. in Marketing and an emphasis in Art and Design; major areas of study include Selling, Sales and Promotion, Marketing, Marketing Management, Accounting, Economics, and Consumer Behavior; earned a G.P.A. of 3.3
	Completed an internship study program at Von Maurs, at Valley West Mall in Des Moines, Iowa; major emphasis included learning different store procedures
	Graduated from Glenbard West High School, in Glen Ellyn, Illinois
	ORGANIZATIONS, ACTIVITIES, AND INTERESTS
College:	Member of Kappa Kappa Gamma Social Sorority
	Vice President of Marketing Club—attended a large number of personal and professional development seminars
	Director of house Variety Show
	Registrar of Kappa Kappa Gamma
	Intramural Football
Honors and Awards:	Alpha Lambda Delta Freshman Honor Society
	Dean's list for three semesters

The Interview

The interview should be viewed as a strategic/consultative sales presentation (see Chapters 10–15). The applicant should be well prepared with preapproach information such as determination of goals, answers to challenging questions (negotiating objections), clear understanding of personal qualities and benefits, and knowledge of the interviewer and the company. When meeting the interviewer, a good first impression (good social contact) must be made. Transition from social contact to need discovery (finding out precisely what the company is looking for in an applicant) should be preplanned with well-chosen questions (see Chapter 11). Effective listening results in productive two-way communication that maintains positive impressions. Effective listening also helps determine which parts of the interviewee's background (specific benefits) should be stressed. If for some reason the interviewer has not seen the résumé, the interviewee should offer it at this point to review the selling points made so far. Closing questions should be preplanned by the interviewee. These might include questions such as, "When do you plan to fill this position?" or "May I call you back on Friday?" Courtesy closing statements, such as "Thank you very much for an informative interview" or "I appreciate the time you spent with me, and I enjoyed our visit very much," should be preplanned. It is important to follow up the interview with a thank-you letter. This letter can be sent via e-mail or through normal mail delivery.

PRICE DEVELOPMENT

Price development involves salary negotiations. Adequate preinterviewing preparation is important for effective salary negotiations (Fig. A.8). The following guidelines should be followed during salary negotiations:

1. Determine the amount of money you want to make during the first year of employment. Convert this to a range with a difference from \$3,000 to \$5,000 (*example:* from \$30,000 to \$35,000).

FIGURE | A.8

The Complete Marketing Program Used to Find a High-Paying Professional Career

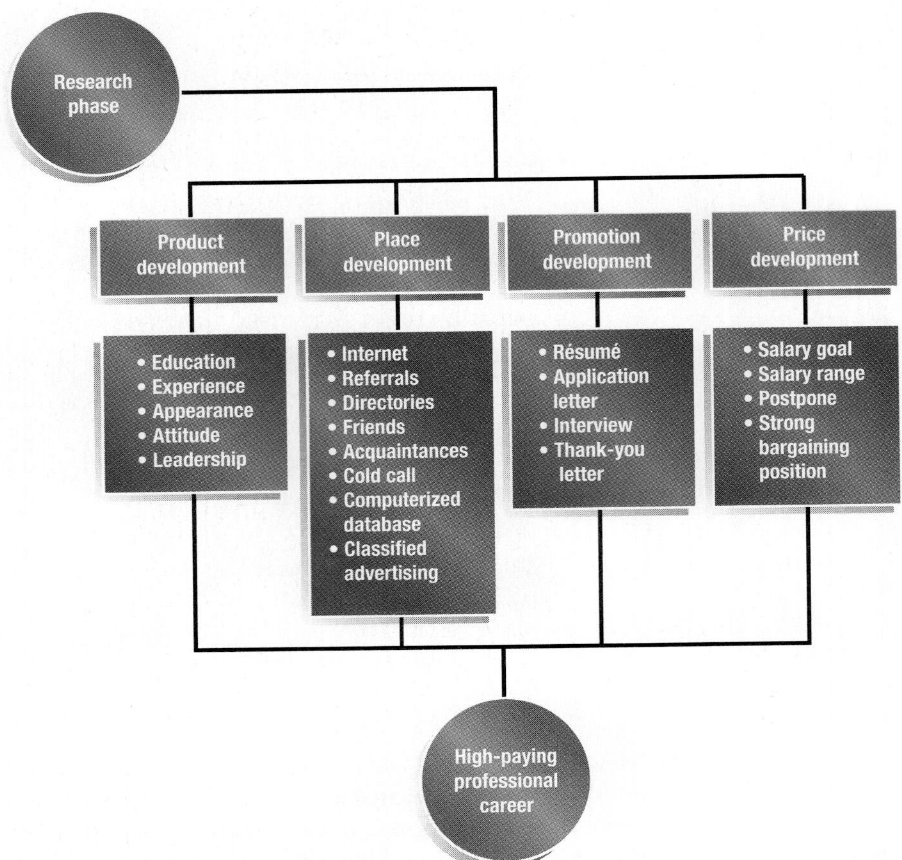

2. Try to find out what salary range the position pays before the interview. As noted previously, the Internet can be your link to a large number of salary surveys.
3. Plan to state that, while starting salary is important, it is more important to know what can be made during the first year, given an excellent review.
4. As a general rule, if possible, postpone salary discussions until a job offer is made. This maintains a better bargaining position.
5. Position yourself in a strong bargaining position with a good personal marketing program.
   - **a.** Have goals well thought out and be able to articulate them clearly.
   - **b.** Have outstanding references.
   - **c.** Have outstanding written materials that show achievement and accomplishment.
   - **d.** Possess good knowledge of industry, company, product, personnel, and salary ranges.
   - **e.** Be currently employed with no sense of urgency to leave.
   - **f.** Sell credentials first and discuss salary second.
   - **g.** Indicate your knowledge of how to get a job.
   - **h.** Become effective in face-to-face selling situations.

SUMMARY

From the employer's viewpoint, the decision to accept the personal marketing plan of a career-oriented job seeker is a major one. An employee who stays with a company five to seven years can be paid from $200,000 to $280,000 in salary (five to seven years times an average annual salary of $40,000). The $200,000–$280,000 salary plus the cost of benefits is the price the employer is paying for the marketing plan. When you make an analogy between the price of a human resource and the purchase of a piece of equipment, it becomes apparent that this is a large purchase. Therefore, a company is going to carefully examine all dimensions of the purchase.

A job seeker with knowledge of the hiring and employment process realizes the dollar value of the purchase an employer is making and designs a professional personal marketing plan with this in mind. The personal marketing plan emphasizes a high-quality professional approach to identifying the right product, positioning it in the right places with the right quality and quantity of promotion, and the right price.

APPENDIX 2

Use of Customer Relationship Management (CRM) Software (ACT!)

STUDENTS—A SPECIAL OPPORTUNITY

Selling Today now offers you a unique opportunity to learn the reason modern software is helping to redefine sales and marketing.

You can load from the CD included with this book a version of the popular ACT! software, which more than 4 million salespeople use to build relationships with their customers. The software is easy to use and includes information about more than 20 customers. You can experience firsthand how salespeople today gain the sales advantage with this category of software.

Beginning in Chapter 1, you will find the first ***Customer Relationship Management with Technology*** insight. These insights, along with the ***CRM APPLICATION EXCERCISE*** at the end of the chapter are simple, easy to follow, instructions on using this software to store and access a wide variety of business and personal information about your customers. You will discover the convenience of using this software to stay in touch with people.

The ACT! software includes important customer information that you will use in your ***CRM CASE STUDY*** assignments for Chapter 9 through 15. You will access the information in your ACT database to approach, present, demonstrate, negotiate, close, and service more than $1.2 million worth of sales.

Effectively using information technology, especially Customer Relationship Management software, will give you a career advantage in today's highly competitive workplace. After mastering the exercises provided, you can report your CRM experience on your résumé.

INSTRUCTIONS FOR USING THE CUSTOMER RELATIONSHIP MANAGEMENT (CRM) SOFTWARE

The software that you will be using is a demonstration version of ACT!, the leading CRM software. This demonstration version is limited to only 25 contacts that may be entered. Today's full version of the ACT! software is more robust and can manage thousands of contacts.

The software and data you need is on the CD included with this book. Place the CD in your drive and its menu will be displayed. Instructions on the CD will guide you through your selections.

Running the Software

Once the launch program has saved the SimNet.exe file on your hard disk drive, it is easy to run the software. An easy way to start the software is to click the Windows Start button, select Run, enter "c:\SimNet\actwin2.exe," and then click OK. The first screen that you see is your record in the SimNet database. It has Pat Silva's name displayed because Pat was the salesperson you are replacing.

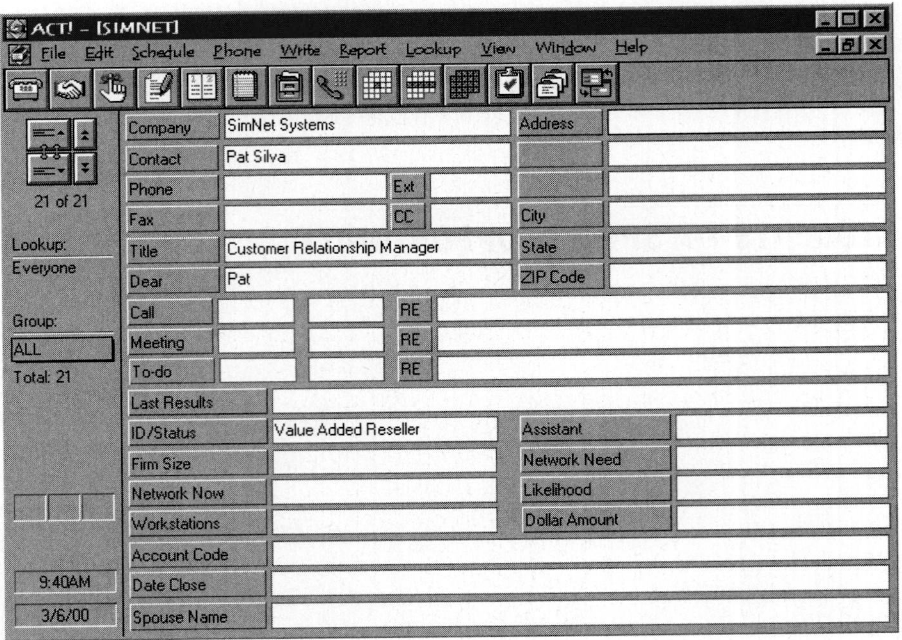

Software Status

The program on your hard disk drive can be run as many times as you need. After completing the case study, you may choose to leave the demonstration software on your hard disk drive or you may remove it. If you need another copy of the software, you may load it again from the CD.

Using the Software

ACT! is a Windows-based program and uses the standard Windows features. It is "menu driven," which means that you can operate the program by selecting from lists of choices. The main menu is displayed at the top of the screen as above displayed.

The screen that displays the information about a customer is referred to as the contact screen. ACT! has two contact screens that can be toggled by pressing the F6 function key.

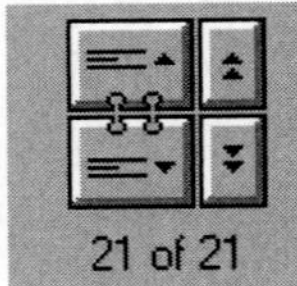

You can use the arrows on the Rolodex icon (see inset) to move among the records. A single arrow moves to the next record and a double arrow displays the first (up) or last (down) record in the database. You can also use the PageUp and PageDown keys to move between records. The records are in alphabetical order, by company name. The first record (double arrow up) in the database is for Able Profit Machines, Inc.

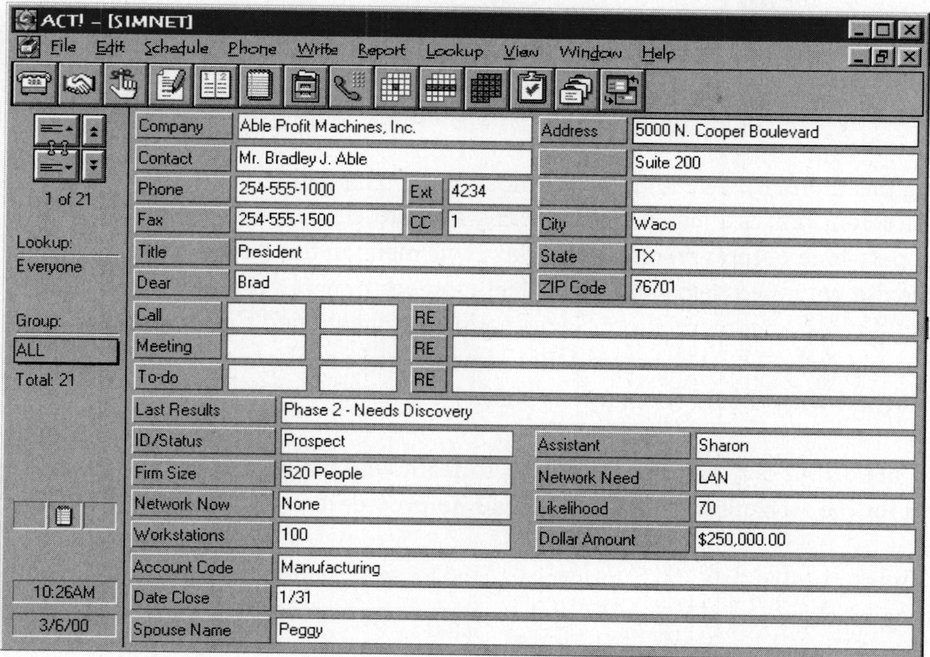

Most records contain notes taken by the previous salesperson, Pat Silva. To display these notes, press the F9 function key. When you are through examining a note, you can press the Escape key (to save changes, select File Close). The notes for the Able Profit Machines company are shown in figure on page 452.

The icons across the top of the screen can speed up the use of the database. The description of each icon can be found by selecting Help, Contents (or F1), and ACT! Screens. Clicking on each of the displayed icons will open a window that explains its use. Following is a list of icons and their uses.

ACT! - [SIMNET]

File Edit Schedule Phone Write Report Lookup View Window Help

1	2	3	4	5	6	7	8	9	10	11	12	13	14	15	16	17

1. Call Icon. Click this icon to schedule a phone contact.
2. Meeting Icon. Click this icon to schedule a meeting.
3. To-do Icon. Click this icon to schedule a task (To-do).
4. Letter Icon. Click this icon to write a letter to the current contact (Person shown on screen).
5. Activities Icon. Click this icon to view any activities you have scheduled with the current contact.
6. Notes Icon. Click this icon to view or record notes regarding the current contact.

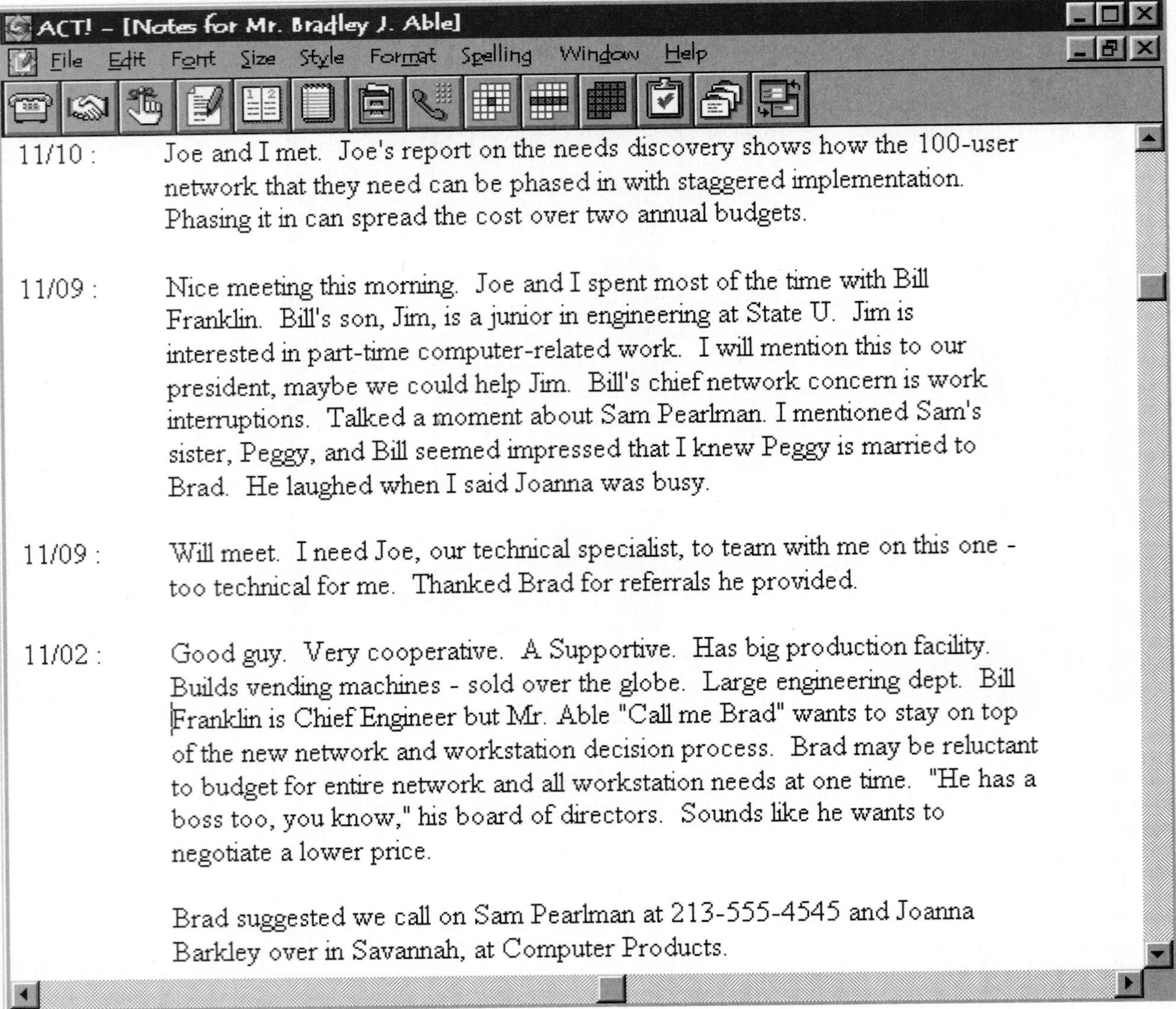

7. History Icon. Click this icon to view the history of activities with a contact.
8. Phone List Icon. Click this icon to use the Autodialer and view phone numbers for the current contact.
9. Day View Icon. Click this icon to display the activities scheduled for a specific day (day view calendar).
10. Week View Icon. Click this icon to display the activities scheduled for a specific week (week view calendar).
11. Month View Icon. Click this icon to display the activities scheduled for a specific month (month view calendar).
12. Task List Icon. Click this icon to view the list of tasks that are scheduled with all contacts.
13. Contact List Icon. Click this icon to view a list of all contacts or the current lookup of contacts.
14. Switch Layout Icon. Click this icon to toggle between screen layouts.

15. Create Message Icon. Click this icon to create new e-mail messages.
16. Inbox Icon. Click this icon to view the e-mail inbox.
17. Outbox Icon. Click this icon to view the e-mail outbox.

Software License Agreement

ACT! software is subject to the terms and conditions detailed in licensing agreements from the The Sage Group plc company. The terms of these licenses can be found on their Web site, www.act.com. You are bound by the terms and conditions of their licensing agreement. The software is the property of The Sage Group plc or its licensors and is protected by copyright law.

You may not sublicense, rent or lease any portion of the Software; or reverse engineer, decompile, disassemble, modify, translate, make any attempt to discover the source code of the Software, or create derivative works from the Software.

Warranty Disclaimer: NO REPRESENTATIONS OR WARRANTIES ARE MADE BY ANY PARTY ABOUT THE SUITABILITY OF THIS SOFTWARE FOR ANY PURPOSE. THE SOFTWARE IS PROVIDED "AS IS" WITHOUT EXPRESS OR IMPLIED WARRANTIES, INCLUDING WARRANTIES OF MERCHANTABILITY AND FITNESS FOR A PARTICULAR PURPOSE OR NONINFRINGEMENT. THIS SOFTWARE IS PROVIDED GRATUITOUSLY AND, ACCORDINGLY, NO PARTY SHALL BE LIABLE UNDER ANY THEORY OR ANY DAMAGES SUFFERED BY YOU OR ANY USER OF THE SOFTWARE.

Disclaimer of Damages: IN NO EVENT WILL ANY PARTY BE LIABLE TO YOU FOR ANY SPECIAL, CONSEQUENTIAL, INDIRECT OR SIMILAR DAMAGES, INCLUDING ANY LOST PROFITS OR LOST DATA ARISING OUT OF THE USE OR INABILITY TO USE THE SOFTWARE EVEN IF ANY PARTY HAS BEEN ADVISED OF THE POSSIBILITY OF SUCH DAMAGES.

Compliance With Applicable Law:

Your use of the ACT! software means that you agree to abide by the copyright law and all other applicable laws of the United States including, but not limited to, export control laws. You acknowledge that the Software in source code form remains a confidential trade secret of its owner and therefore you agree not to modify the Software or attempt to decipher, decompile, disassemble or reverse engineer the Software.

APPENDIX 3

Partnership Selling: A Role-Play/Simulation for Selling Today

Table of Contents

A SPECIAL NOTE TO THE STUDENT: USE OF THE ROLE-PLAY/SIMULATION APPENDIX

This role-play/simulation provides an opportunity to apply the principles that serve as a foundation for the four broad strategic areas of personal selling: relationship, product, customer, and presentation strategies. The activities are designed to take you from "learning about" selling to "learning to do" selling.

You will start as a convention center sales and marketing department trainee. Your sales manager will supply you with memos that will assist you in learning about your product, competition, customers, and presentations. You will be supplied many sales tools including photos, awards, schedules, menus, floor plans, references, company policies, electronic sales proposal/product configurators (see pp. 465–478) and sales planning worksheets.

The first memo on p. 459 provides background information about your product, company, industry, and competition. As a trainee your first sales and marketing assignment (see memo on p. 495) will be to create an electronic sales proposal and cover sales letter. This activity will give you an opportunity to apply information presented in Chapter 6.

After successfully communicating with your first customer and being promoted to account executive, you are instructed by your sales manager in memos on pp. 499–500 to plan and conduct your first face-to-face contact with another potential customer. The primary objective of this first contact is to establish a relationship with your customer.

The next memo from your sales manager on pp. 504–505 requests that you use your questioning skills to conduct a needs analysis involving the customer you previously contacted. Your customer, who was favorably impressed as a result of your first meeting, has called and requested a meeting to talk about an important convention being planned.

The last memo on pp. 508–509 assists you in creating and presenting a proposal that meets your customer's needs. You will create a portfolio presentation using the awards, photos, price lists, menus, references, floor plans, and schedules provided.

You can access digital images of the pictures in this simulation by clicking on the *www.prenhall.com/manning* Web site. You can also access an electronic sales proposal configuration to complete the customer service/sales memorandum 1 and sales memorandum 3 assignments.

INTRODUCTION

Salespeople today are working hard to become more effective in such important areas as person-to-person communications, needs analysis, interpersonal relations, and decision making. This role-play/simulation will help you develop these critical selling skills. You will assume the role of a new sales trainee employed by the Park Inn International Convention Center.

Part I

Developing a Sales-Oriented Product Strategy will challenge you to acquire the necessary product information needed to be an effective sales representative for the Park Inn (see Chapters 6 and 7). Your sales manager, T. J. McKee, will describe your new trainee position in an employment memorandum. Your instructions will include the study of materials featured on the following pages, viewing a video that describes the convention facilities and services provided by a competitor, and role-playing the request made in a T. J. McKee customer service/sales memorandum.

Part II

Developing a Relationship Strategy is another major challenge in personal selling. An employment memorandum will inform you of a promotion to an account executive position. A sales memorandum will inform you of your assignment to accounts in a specific market segment. Part II also involves a role-play on the development of a relationship with a new customer in your market segment (see Chapters 3 and 10). Your call objective will be to acquire background information on your new customer, who may have a need for your services.

Part III

Understanding Your Customer's Buying Strategy involves a needs analysis role-play (see Chapters 8 and 11). You will again meet with the customer who has indicated an interest in scheduling a business conference at your convention center. During this meeting, you will acquire information to complete Part IV, which involves preparation for the sales presentation.

Part IV

Developing a Presentation Strategy will involve preparation of a sales proposal and a *portfolio* presentation (see Chapters 11–15). This section also involves a third role-play with the customer. During the role-play, you will reestablish your relationship with the customer, present your proposal, negotiate customer's concerns, and attempt to close and service the sale.

Throughout completion of the role-play/simulation, you will be guided by the employment and sales memoranda (from the sales manager) and instructions and additional forms provided by your instructor.

As you complete this simulation activity, note that the principles and practices you are learning to use have application in nearly all personal selling situations.

GENERAL INSTRUCTIONS FOR ROLE-PLAYING

Overview

The primary goal of a simulation in personal selling should be to strike a balance between just enough detail to focus on the process of selling and not so much as to drown in an ocean of facts. Either too much detail or too little detail can develop anxiety in role-play participants. *Partnership Selling* is designed to minimize anxiety by including only the facts needed to focus on learning the processes involved in high-performance selling.

Some anxiety will occur, however, because you are asked to perform under pressure (in terms of building relationships, securing strategic information, changing people's thinking, and getting them to take action). Learning to perform in an environment full of genuine but nonthreatening pressure affords you the opportunity to practice your selling skills so you will be prepared for real-world selling anxiety.

The following suggestions for role-playing will help you develop the ability to perform under stress.

Instructions for Salesperson Role-Plays

1. Be well prepared with product knowledge.
2. Read information for each role-play ahead of time.
3. Follow specific instructions carefully.
4. Attempt to sense both the context and the facts of the situation presented.
5. Conduct a mental rehearsal. See yourself successfully conducting and completing the role-play.
6. Be prepared to take notes during the role-play.
7. After the role-play, take note of your feelings and mentally put them into the context of what just occurred.
8. Be prepared to discuss your reaction to what occurred during the role-play.

Instructions for Customer Role-Plays

1. Read the instructions carefully. Be sure to note both the role-play instructions and the information you are about to share.
2. Attempt to sense both the context of the buying situation and the individual facts presented in the instructions.
3. Let the salesperson initiate greetings, conversations, and concluding actions. React appropriately.
4. Supply only the customer information presented in the background description.
5. Supply customer information in a positive manner.
6. Do not attempt to throw the salesperson off track.

Part One: Developing a Sales-Oriented Product Strategy

PARK INN
INTERNATIONAL™

EMPLOYMENT MEMORANDUM 1

To: **New Convention Sales Center Trainees**
From: **T. J. McKee, Sales Manager**
Re: **Your New Sales Training Program—"Developing a Product Selling Strategy"**

I am extremely happy that you accepted our offer to join the Sales and Marketing Department. Enclosed is a copy of your new position description (see p. 462). Your first assignment as a trainee will be to learn about our product and what we have recently done to provide *total quality* customer service. *To apply what you are learning, I would like you to follow up on a customer service request I recently received. (See memo p. 495.)* You will use the following product information to complete the assignment:

AN AWARD-WINNING UPDATE (See pp. 465–467)

We have recently completed a *$2.8 million investment in our convention center.* This customer service investment included renovating all guest rooms and suites, lobby and front desk area, meeting rooms, restaurant and lounge, and enclosure of the swimming pool. Enclosed is a copy of the "Regional Architect's Award" that our facility won. We are the only facility in the Metro Area to have been presented with this award.

MEETING AND BANQUET ROOMS (See pp. 481–485)

The Park Inn offers convention planners just over *8,000 square feet of award-winning meeting space* in attractive, newly renovated meeting and banquet rooms. Our Central Park East and West rooms are conveniently located on the lobby level of the hotel. Each of these rooms can accommodate 180 people in a theater-style setting or 80 in a classroom-style setting. They also have a divider wall that can be retracted and, with the combined rooms, can accommodate up to 370 people.

The Top of the Park provides a spectacular view of the city through windows that surround that ballroom. This unique room, located on the top floor, can accommodate 225 classroom style, 350 banquet style, or 450 people theater style. Also located in the Top of the Park is a revolving platform area that slowly moves, giving guests a 360-degree panoramic view of the city. The Parkview Room, which is also located on the top floor of the hotel, can accommodate 150 people theater style and 80 people classroom style.

In addition for *groups booking 40 rooms or more, we provide one luxurious suite* ***free***. This suite features a meeting room, bedroom, wet bar with refrigerator, and jacuzzi.

Be sure your clients understand that our meeting rooms *need to be reserved*. The first organization to sign a sales proposal for a specific date has the designated rooms guaranteed.

GUEST ROOM DECOR AND RATES (See pp. 453 and 485)

Our recent renovation included complete redecoration of all 250 of our large and spacious guest rooms. This includes all new furniture, wallcoverings, drapes, bedspreads, and carpets. Our interior designer succeeded in creating a comfortable, attractive and restful atmosphere. *Seventy of our rooms are designated nonsmoking.*

(continued)

ROOM RATES *(continued)*

	REGULAR RATES	GROUP RATES	SAVINGS
Single	$88	$78	$10
Double	$98	$88	$10
Triple	$106	$96	$10
Quad	$114	$104	$10

A comparison of competitive room, parking, and transportation rates is presented on p. 461.

BANQUET MEALS (See pp. 471–475)

Our executive chef, Ricardo Guido, recently won the *National Restaurant Association's "Outstanding Chef of the Year" Award.* His winning entry consisted of the three chicken entrees featured on the enclosed menus. Ricardo served as Executive Chef at the five-star rated Williamsburg Inn in Williamsburg, Virginia, before we convinced him to join us six months ago. He personally oversees all our food and beverage operations. Ricardo, in my opinion, is one of the outstanding chefs in the country. His expertise and commitment to total quality customer service will help develop long-term relationships with our customers.

The enclosed dinner selections are only suggestions. We will design a special menu for your clients if they wish. A 16 percent gratuity or service charge is added to all group meal functions.

HOTEL/MOTEL AND SALES TAXES

All room rates are subject to the *local hotel/motel room tax, which is an additional 8 percent. In addition, all billings must have a 4 percent sales tax added. (The sales tax is not added to the hotel/motel tax and does not apply to gratuities.)*

LOCATION, TRANSPORTATION, AND PARKING (See map on p. 469)

We are located in a dynamic growing metropolitan area of over 400,000 people. With *convenient access, just off Interstate 237 at the downtown exits,* we are within a block of the nationally recognized, climate-controlled skywalk system. This five-mile system is connected to theaters, excellent shopping, the civic center, the metropolitan convention center, and a large selection of ethnic and fast-food restaurants. Our location offers guests the privacy they deserve during their meetings, and yet is close enough to downtown to enjoy all the excitement.

***Free** courtesy van transportation* (also known as limousine service) is provided for our overnight guests to and from the airport, as well as anywhere in the downtown area. This service saves our guests who arrive by plane from *$8.00 to $10.00 each way.*

Guests who will be driving to the hotel will find over *300 parking spaces* available to them at *no charge.* Unlike other downtown properties, our free parking saves guests up to *$6.00 per day* in parking fees. For security purposes, we have closed-circuit camera systems in the parking lot and underground parking areas.

VALUE-ADDED GUEST SERVICES AND AMENITIES

Our convention center owners have invested heavily in the facility to provide our clients with *total quality service,* unmatched by our competition. Additional value-added services and amenities include:

- A large *indoor pool, sundeck, sauna, whirlpool, and complimentary Nautilus exercise room* in an attractive tropical atmosphere (see p. 479)
- "Cafe in the Park" featuring 24-hour continental cuisine seven days a week
- "Pub in the Park" where friendly people meet, featuring *free hors d'oeuvres* Monday through Friday, 5 to 7 P.M.
- Cable television with HBO
- A.V. rental of most equipment in-house, at a nominal fee (see p. 487)
- *Free coffee and donuts or rolls* in the lobby each morning from 6 to 8 A.M.
- A team of *well-trained, dedicated, and friendly associates* providing total quality front desk, food, and guest services
- Express check in
- Electronic key entry system
- Hair dryer, iron, and ironing board in each room
- Data port capabilities for laptop computers in each room
- Desk in each room
- Video message retrieval
- Voice mail
- On-command video (choice of 50 new release movies)

SALES LITERATURE (See pp. 465–493)

Included in your product training materials are photos, references, letters, room schedules, sales proposals, and other information that you will use in your written proposals and verbal sales presentations. When you move into outside sales, you should use these tools to create effective sales portfolios.

TOTAL QUALITY COMMITMENT

Our convention center is committed to *total quality customer service. Our Partnership Style of Customer Service and Selling* is an extension of our total quality process. The Total Quality Customer Service Glossary provides definitions of terms that describe our total quality process (see p. 463).

The Hotel and Convention center industry is mature and well established. Our sales and customer service plan is to *establish strong relationships, focus on solving customer problems, provide total quality customer service, and become a long-term hotel and convention center partner with our clients.* By utilizing this type of selling and customer service, your compensation and our sales revenue will both increase substantially.

TJM:ESS

Enclosures

PARK INN
INTERNATIONAL™

POSITION DESCRIPTION—CONVENTION CENTER ACCOUNT EXECUTIVE

COMPANY DESCRIPTION

The Park Inn Convention Center is a total quality, full-service equal opportunity employment convention center that has recently made large investments in the physical facility, the food and beverage department, and sales department. Company culture includes an effective and enthusiastic team approach to creating *total quality*, value-added solutions for customers in a very competitive industry. The primary sales promotion tool is *Partnership Selling* with extensive marketing support in the form of photos, reference letters, team selling, etc. The company goal is to increase revenues 20 percent in the coming year by providing outstanding customer service.

SUCCESSFUL ACCOUNT EXECUTIVE WILL

1. Acquire necessary convention center company, product, industry, and competitive information through company training program
2. Be committed to a total quality customer service process
3. Develop a list of potential prospects in the assigned target market
4. Develop long-term, total quality selling relationships that focus on solving the meeting planner's convention center needs
5. Achieve a sales volume of $700,000 to $800,000 annually

WORKING RELATIONSHIPS

Reports to: Sales Manager
Works with: Internal Support Team including Food Service, Housekeeping and Operations, Customer Service and Front Desk; External Relationships including customers, professional associations, and industry personnel

SPECIFIC REQUIREMENTS

1. Must project a positive and professional sales image
2. Must be able to establish and maintain long-term relationships
3. Must be goal oriented with a plan for self-improvement
4. Must be flexible to deal effectively with a wide range of customers
5. Must be good at asking questions and listening effectively
6. Must be accurate and creative in developing customer's solutions
7. Must be clear and persuasive in communicating and negotiating solutions
8. Must be good at closing the sale
9. Must follow through on promises and assurances
10. Must have math skills necessary for figuring sales proposals

SPECIFIC REWARDS

1. Attractive compensation package that includes base salary, a commission of 10 percent of sales, bonuses, and an attractive fringe benefit package
2. Pride in working for an organization that practices total quality management in employee relations and customer service
3. Extensive sales and educational support
4. Opportunity for growth and advancement

EOE/AA/TQM

TOTAL QUALITY CUSTOMER SERVICE GLOSSARY

DIRFT—DO IT RIGHT THE FIRST TIME means being prepared, asking the right questions, selecting the right solutions, and making effective presentations. This creates repeats and referrals.

QIP—QUALITY IMPROVEMENT PROCESS means always striving to better serve our customers resulting in high-quality, long-term relationships.

TQM—TOTAL QUALITY MANAGEMENT means the commitment to support and empower people to deliver legendary customer service.

QIT—QUALITY IMPROVEMENT TEAM means a team approach to deliver outstanding customer service.

COQ—COST OF QUALITY means the ultimate lowering of cost by providing outstanding service the first time, so as to build a list of repeat and referred customers.

PONC—PRICE OF NONCONFORMANCE means the high cost of not meeting high standards. This results in correcting problems and losing customers. PONC also causes longer sales cycles and higher sales costs.

POC—PRICE OF CONFORMANCE means the lower costs of providing outstanding customer service and achieving a list of repeat or referred customers.

WIIFM—WHAT IS IN IT FOR ME means the psychic and monetary rewards in the form of personal enjoyment, higher salaries, commissions, or bonuses caused by delivering outstanding customer service.

QES—QUALITY EDUCATION SYSTEMS means internal and external educational activities designed to improve the quality of customer service.

YOU—THE MOST IMPORTANT PART OF QUALITY means the ongoing program of self-improvement that results in outstanding customer service and personal and financial growth.

THE ALL NEW PARK INN

(With an award winning 2.8 million dollar renovation)

➥ Use the sales information on the reverse side of this page to position your convention center and the $2.8 million renovation in the mind of your customer.

REGIONAL ARCHITECTS ASSOCIATION

"EXCELLENCE IN RENOVATION DESIGN"

PRESENTED TO:

Park Inn International

WITH SPECIAL RECOGNITION FOR CREATING AN OUTSTANDING CONVENTION ENVIRONMENT.

PRESENTED ON THE ELEVENTH DAY OF MARCH, 200_.

Patricia Bennett
PRESIDENT, REGIONAL ARCHITECTS ASSOCIATION

Allen Rogge
CHAIRPERSON, DESIGN SELECTION COMMITTEE

➡ Use the sales information on the reverse side of this page to demonstrate and describe the award for "Creating an Outstanding Convention Environment" and explain that it was given with regard to the quality of the meeting rooms, guest rooms, ambiance of lobby and restaurant, and the pool area.

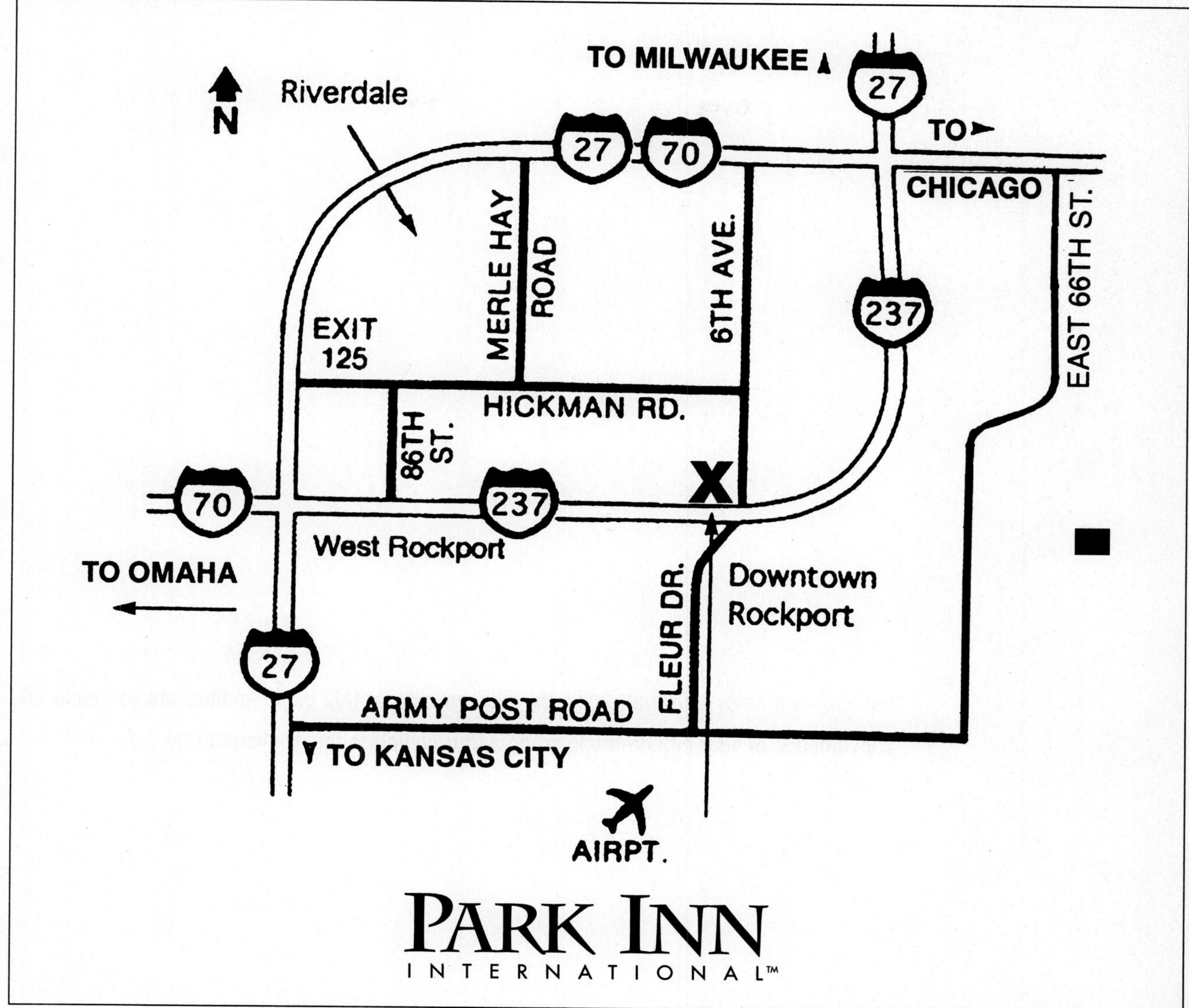

CONVENIENT, EASY TO FIND LOCATION WITH "FREE" PARKING

Conveniently located at I-237 and 6th Ave.

Just 8 miles from Rockport International Airport

➡ Use the sales information on the reverse side of this page to illustrate the ease and convenience of your customers locating and traveling to the Convention Center.

OUTSTANDING FOOD SERVICE

Personally Supervised by Award-Winning "Executive Chef of the Year" Ricardo Guido

➡ Use the sales information on the reverse side of this page to introduce and explain the "outstanding food service" that will be personally supervised by Executive Chef of the Year Ricardo Guido.

NATIONAL RESTAURANT ASSOCIATION

EXECUTIVE CHEF OF THE YEAR

AWARDED TO:

Ricardo Guido

PRESENTED ON THE ELEVENTH DAY OF APRIL, 200_.

Patricia Reed
PRESIDENT, NATIONAL RESTAURANT ASSOCIATION

Ella Reed
CONFERENCE CHAIRPERSON

➡ Use the sales information on the reverse side of this page to explain the benefits of having an award-winning executive chef and describe his background.

BANQUET STYLE MENU SELECTIONS

All selections include tossed greens with choice of dressing, choice of potato (baked, oven browned, au gratin, or mashed), rice or buttered noodles, rolls with butter, coffee, decaffeinated coffee, tea, or iced tea.

ENTREES

CHICKEN WELLINGTON—Boneless breast of chicken topped with a mushroom mixture, wrapped in puff pastry shell and baked to a golden brown $17.95

CHICKEN BREAST TERIYAKI—Marinated boneless breast of chicken grilled and topped with our *special* teriyaki sauce. $17.95

CHICKEN BREAST NEW ORLEANS—Baked boneless breast of chicken, garnished with peppers, mushrooms, onions, and Monterey Jack cheese $17.95

BROILED NEW YORK STRIP STEAK—Center cut New York strip steak broiled to perfection, topped with our own seasoned herb butter $23.50

BROILED FILET MIGNON—A steak from the center cut tenderloin, broiled and served with a rich red wine sauce $24.50

SLICED PORK LOIN WITH MUSTARD SAUCE—Boneless loin of pork oven roasted and sliced, served with a mustard sauce. $18.95

GRILLED PORK CHOP—A thick cut of pork grilled to juicy perfection $18.95

BROILED ORANGE ROUGHY—A filet of orange roughy broiled and covered with basil-lemon sauce $18.95

BROILED HALIBUT STEAK—Tender flaky halibut cut into steaks and broiled in lemon-butter served with fresh lemon slices $19.95

* BUFFET STYLE meals are available. Approval of pricing on Buffet Style servings must be made by the Executive Chef.

Prices do not include 16 percent service charge or sales tax.

➡ Use the sales information on the reverse side of this page to explain and configure the menus available for banquet-style meals.

ATTRACTIVE, COMFORTABLE GUEST ROOMS

(All new furnishings, HBO in every room, free *USA Today* weekday delivery, no telephone access charges for 800 and credit card calls, and data port capabilities for laptop computers)

➡ Use the sales information on the reverse side of this page to explain and illustrate the attractive and comfortable guest rooms. Remind customers that the rooms were a major factor in receiving the Architect's Award.

A TROPICAL PARADISE

**For relaxation after a day's work—
attractive pool, sauna, whirlpool, sundeck,
and Nautilus fitness center**

➡ Use the sales information on the reverse side of this page to explain and illustrate the benefits of the totally renovated and redesigned pool, with the sauna, whirlpool, sundeck, and Nautilus fitness center.

BRIGHT, COMFORTABLE, AND STRATEGICALLY ARRANGED MEETING ROOMS

Everything you need for outstanding meetings

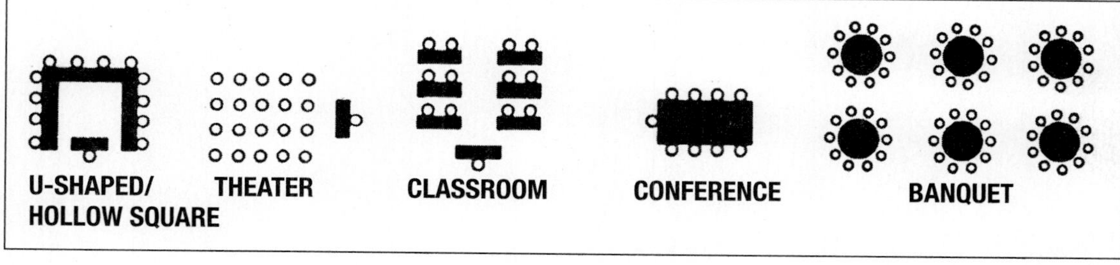

➡ Use the sales information on the reverse side of this page to illustrate the attractiveness of the newly remodeled meeting rooms, which were another important factor in receiving the Architect's Award. Also, use this form to explain and illustrate the various seating arrrangements for meeting rooms.

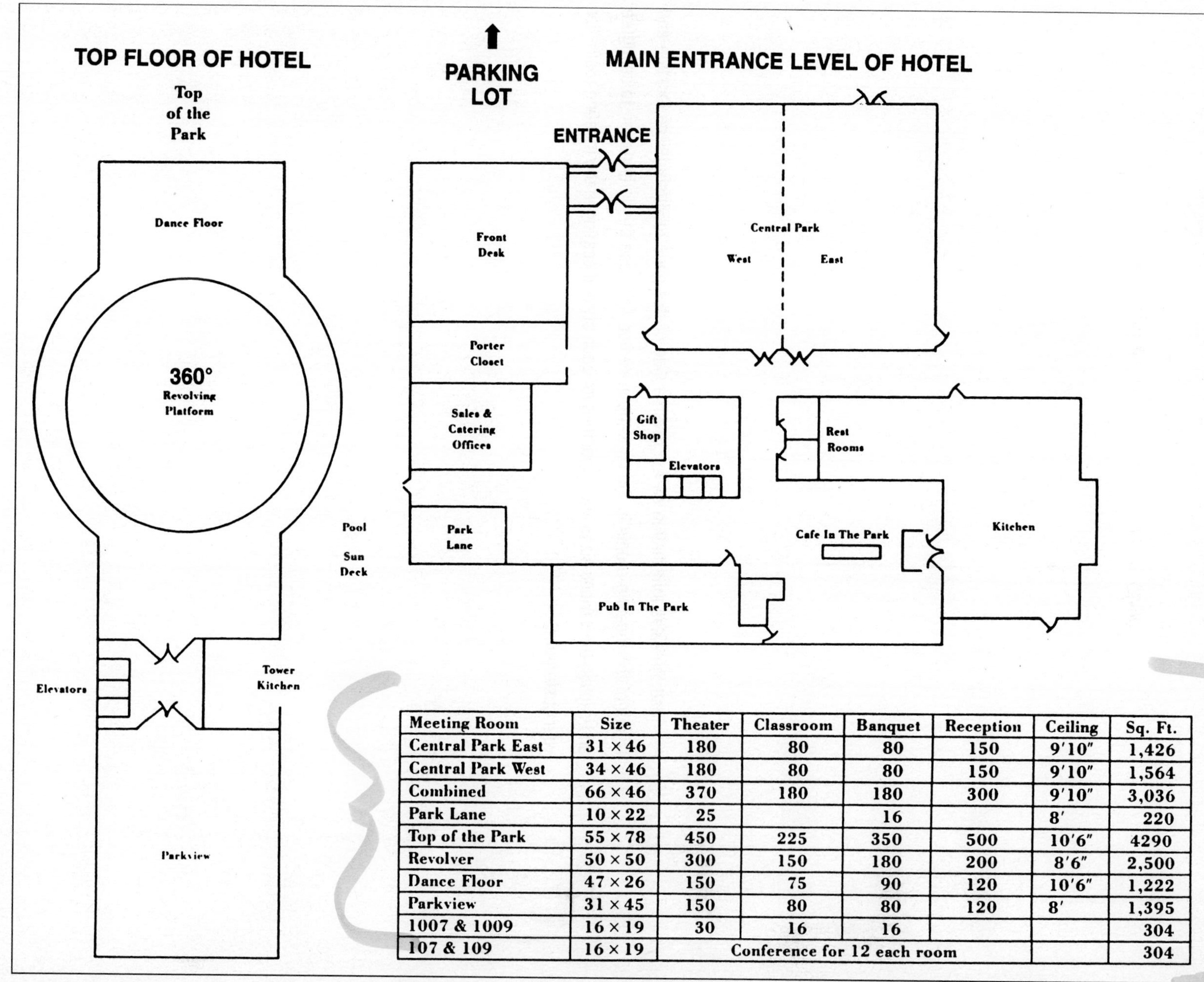

Meeting Room	Size	Theater	Classroom	Banquet	Reception	Ceiling	Sq. Ft.
Central Park East	31 × 46	180	80	80	150	9'10"	1,426
Central Park West	34 × 46	180	80	80	150	9'10"	1,564
Combined	66 × 46	370	180	180	300	9'10"	3,036
Park Lane	10 × 22	25		16		8'	220
Top of the Park	55 × 78	450	225	350	500	10'6"	4290
Revolver	50 × 50	300	150	180	200	8'6"	2,500
Dance Floor	47 × 26	150	75	90	120	10'6"	1,222
Parkview	31 × 45	150	80	80	120	8'	1,395
1007 & 1009	16 × 19	30	16	16			304
107 & 109	16 × 19	Conference for 12 each room					304

➡ Use the sales information on the reverse side of this page to illustrate the location and layout of the meeting rooms in the convention center. Also, use this information to configure and explain the various sizes and capacities for each style of seating in the meeting rooms for your customers.

METRO AREA COMPETITIVE SURVEY

QUOTED GROUP RATES (IN DOLLARS) FOR HOTEL/MOTEL GUEST ROOMS

HOTEL/MOTEL	*SINGLE*	*DOUBLE*	*DAILY PARKING*	*AIRPORT TRANS.*
Park Inn	**78**	**88**	**Free**	**Free**
Marriott	80	90	6	10 each way
Sheraton	85	105	6	12 each way
Hilton	80	100	7	9 each way
Embassy	82	103	6	8 each way
Guest Quarters	84	104	Free	8 each way
Carlton	75	95	8	3 each way
Saboe	75	85	Free	12 each way
Chesterfield	70	80	Free	13 each way
Best Western	65	70	Free	15 each way
Days Inn	60	65	Free	12 each way
Sunset Inn	55	n/a	Free	12 each way

MEETING ROOM RATES

SQUARE FEET	*MEETING ROOM*	*4 HOURS*	*8 HOURS*	*24 HOURS*
4,290	**Top of the Park**	**$400**	**$600**	**$900**
1,426	**Central Park East**	**$150**	**$200**	**$300**
1,564	**Central Park West**	**$160**	**$200**	**$300**
3,036	**Combined Central Park**	**$300**	**$400**	**$500**
220	**Park Lane**	**$ 25**	**$ 40**	**$ 60**
2,500	**Revolver**	**$300**	**$500**	**$700**
1,222	**Dance Floor**	**$100**	**$175**	**$275**
$1,395	**Park View**	**$110**	**$185**	**$300**
304	**1,007 and 1,009**	**$ 40**	**$ 60**	**$ 80**
304	**107 and 109**	**$ 40**	**$ 60**	**$ 80**

- Meeting room rental charges based on set changes at 12:00 noon, 5:00 P.M., or 10:00 P.M.
- For groups of 20 or more who are reserving 20 or more guest rooms or scheduling 20 or more banquet meals, rental rates will be waived for rooms up to 1,600 square feet for up to 8 hours of use per day.
- For groups of 50 or more who are reserving 50 or more guest rooms or scheduling 50 or more banquet meals, rental rates will be waived for all rooms for up to 24 hours of use.

➡ Use the sales information on the reverse side of this page to configure and demonstrate the prices for the convention center as well as the competing convention centers in the Rockport area. Note the pricing for daily parking and transportation to and from the Rockport Airport. These prices are collected weekly and distributed to all sales and marketing personnel.

➡ Also, use the sales information at the bottom of the page to configure and explain the pricing and policies with regard to charges for use of the meeting rooms. Explain that the convention center's policies with regard to pricing and the use of meeting rooms are very competitive with the charges of other centers in the Rockport area.

AUDIOVISUAL PRESENTATIONS GUIDE

These are the most popular audiovisual equipment items. If you require special equipment and services not listed, please let us know. We'll do the rest!

AUDIOVISUAL EQUIPMENT PACKAGES

Saves Money • Saves Time

35mm Slides

Kodak Ektagraphic III 35mm Slide projector package features a projection stand or cart, 4″ to 8″ zoom lens, wireless remote control, spare 80 slide tray, all extension AC cords safely taped. Select Screens Below. 35mm Slide Projector Package $45.00

Recommended by Professional Meeting Planners:

Complete speaker freedom with
Laser Pointer $27.50
Wireless Microphone $80.00
Groups over 75 people:
Special Zoom Lens $11.00

Video VCR/Monitor

VHS 1/2″ or U-MATIC 3/4″ Player/Recorder package features a roll-around 54″ projection cart, a 27″ full-function color video monitor/receiver. All cable connections. AC extension cords safely taped.
*VHS 1/2″ $150.00
3/4″ U-MATIC $185.00

Recommended by Professional Meeting Planners:

More visibility for large groups with additional 27″ video, monitor and cart, includes cables and connectors. Each....$90.00
Full House Sound $27.50

LCD Video Projection

LCD* Proxima Video Projector $500.00
Color Video Projector Projects Full Color Video or Computer Images up to SVGA. Recommended for larger groups. Select Screen Below.

Overhead Projectors

Popular overhead projector package with superwide overhead projector featuring automatic spare lamp changer. All AC extension cords safely taped. Select Screens Below.

Overhead Projector Package....$40.00

Recommended by Professional Meeting Planners:

Complete speaker freedom with
Laser Pointer $27.50
Wireless Microphone $80.00

LCD Panel Projection

Color Computer Data Panel....$325.00
Full Color Panel Projects Computer Images on a 6′–10′ Projection Screen with Hi-Intensity Overhead Projector. Select Screen Below.

Full-Motion Video Projection

CRT Projector with VCR....$550.00
Color video projector projects full-motion video on screen. Recommended for larger groups. Select Screen Below.

AUDIO VISUAL EQUIPMENT Á LA CARTE

Motion Picture Projection

16mm Autoload projector w/2″ prime lens with stand....$40.00

Hi-Intensity Overhead Projector

4000 Lumen projector for LCD computer
Data panel or larger groups $65.00

Meeting Accessories

Laser Pointer....$27.50
Flip Chart Easel (No Pen) $14.00
Flip Chart Rental w/Markers $22.00
Projection carts and stands $16.50
Meeting accessories such as acetate rolls and sheets are available on request.

Video Equipment

Camcorder with tripod....$120.00
VCR....$60.00

Audio Equipment

Cassette Player/Recorder $40.00
CD Player $40.00
Portable CD/Cassette Player $40.00

AV Technician Services

AV Tech is on site for installation and dismantle. Requirements for exclusive event management will be charged these hourly rates:
Monday through Friday, 7am–5pm $30.00
Evenings, Weekdays, and Holidays....$40.00

Microphones

Microphone, wired $22.00
Lavaliere, wired....$22.00
Wireless microphone (Hand held or Lavaliere)....$80.00
Sound patch to house system....$27.50
4 Channel mixer $27.50

Screens

6′ × 6′ Tripod $22.00
8′ × 8′ Tripod $27.50
10′ × 10′ Cradle....$55.00
*7 1/2′ × 10′ Fast Fold $80.00
*9′ × 12′ Fast Fold....$110.00
*(Front or rear projection)
Fast fold drape kits included.

➥ Use the sales information on the reverse side of this page to sell, configure, and explain the availability of audiovisual equipment to customers scheduling meetings in the convention center. This equipment must be reserved in advance of the scheduled date to guarantee availability.

THE PRINCIPAL COMPANY

1900 Grand Avenue
Rockport, IL 50322
www.prencom.com

December 15, 200_

Carroll Parez, General Manager
The Park Inn
555 West Side Street
Rockport, IL 50310

Dear Carroll:

On behalf of our employees I thank you and your associates for the wonderful time we had at the Park Inn during our convention last month. Enclosed is a check for $22,991.23 to pay the invoice for the meeting costs.

The hospitality that we received during our time there was unparalleled. The friendliness and dedication of the staff simply made our time so enjoyable we hated to leave.

The Chicken New Orleans was superb. Our *heartfelt thanks to Chef Ricardo Guido* for creating the best meals we have ever had at a convention.

Without reservation I will direct anyone looking for convention space to your award-winning property. The group that gave you the award certainly knew what was important to convention planners. You may count on us to return in the future.

Sincerely,

Reggie Regan

Reggie Regan, Vice President
Field Sales Division

Enclosures:
Schedule for our next eight convention dates
Check
Service Evaluation

ss

➡ Use this reference letter with customers to support the outstanding service we strive to provide to ALL of our convention center customers. Note the friendliness and dedication of the center staff, the quality of the food service, the reference to the award, and the enclosures regarding repeat business involving eight more meeting dates and the check in the amount of $22,991.23.

REFERENCES

COMPANY/ADDRESS	*TELEPHONE NO.*	*DATE OF BOOKING*
Association of Business and Industry 2425 Hubbell Mr. James Warner (Director)	265–8181	July 1–2
Acme Supply Company 2531 Dean Linn Compiano (Training Manager)	265–9831	July 14
Rotary International 1230 Executive Towers Mr. Roger Shannon (Executive Director)	792–4616	July 28–29
Archway Cookie Company Boone Industrial Park Mr. Bill Sorenson (Sales Manager)	432–4084	August 9
West College 4821 College Parkway Toni Bush (Athletic Director)	283–4142	September 9–11
Travelers Insurance Company 1452 29th Mr. Richard Wiese (Training Manager)	223–7500	November 14
Meredith Corporation 1716 Locust Mrs. Carol Rains (Public Relations)	284–2654	November 23–24
Pioneer Hi-Bred Incorporated 5700 Merle Highway Mrs. Sheri Sitterly (Administrative Services)	272–3660	December 12–13

➡ Use the sales information on the reverse side of this page to supply a list of successful businesspeople who can be contacted regarding the quality of food and service they received at previous meetings they have scheduled at the convention center.

CONVENTION CENTER POLICIES AND GENERAL INFORMATION

FOOD AND BEVERAGE

- A 16 percent gratuity or service charge and applicable sales tax will be added to all food and beverage purchases. Any group requesting a tax exemption must submit their Certificate of Exemption prior to the event.
- There is a $25 setup fee for each meal function of 25 persons or less.

GUARANTEES

- The Convention Center will require your menus and meeting room requirements no later than two weeks before your meeting or food function.
- Convention Center facilities are guaranteed on a "first confirmed, first served" basis.
- A meal guarantee is required 48 hours prior to your function. This guarantee is the minimum your group will be charged for the function. If no guarantee is received by the Catering Office, we will then consider your last number of attendees as the guarantee. We will be prepared to serve 5 percent over your guaranteed number.

BANQUET AND MEETING ROOMS

- As other groups may be utilizing the same room prior to or following your function, please adhere to the times agreed on. Should your time schedule change, please contact the Catering Office, and every effort will be made to accommodate you.
- Function rooms are assigned by the room number of people anticipated. If attendance drops or increases, please contact the Catering Office to ensure proper assignment of rooms.

AUDIOVISUAL SERVICES

- A wide selection of audiovisual equipment and services is available on a rental basis. See audiovisual presentation guide for details.

➡ Use the sales information on the reverse side of this page to carefully explain the policies and general information on the operation of the convention center. Please note the 16 percent gratuity and the $25 setup fee for certain meals. Also, note the policies and guarantees that are required for menus, meeting rooms, and meals.

PARK INN
INTERNATIONAL™

CUSTOMER SERVICE/SALES MEMORANDUM 1

To: Convention Sales Trainee
From: T. J. McKee, Sales Manager
Re: Assistance with a Customer Request

A new prospect called and requested that we immediately submit a proposal for a planned Rockport meeting. Please review the profile in our automated database (printed as follows).

CONTACT REPORT

Name:	Graphic Forms	Address:	2134 Martin Luther King
Contact:	B. H. Rivera	:	
Phone:	314-619-4879	:	
Title:	President	City:	Atlanta
Sec:		State:	GA
Dear:	B. H. Rivera	ZIP:	61740

(McKee) Visited with B. H. Rivera on the phone. Seemed very interested. Nice emotive person. Has a son, Matt, attending West College. Also knew Toni Bush of West, who is an excellent account of ours. B. H. wants a proposal ASAP to cover the following buying conditions:

1. Ten single guest rooms for two nights—Friday and Saturday
2. A meeting room for 20 people, classroom style, Friday and Saturday from 2 to 6 P.M.
3. Dinner for 20, banquet style, at 6 P.M. each night
   Friday: Grilled Pork Chops
   Saturday: Broiled Orange Roughy
4. A swimming pool

◄ CONTACT SCREEN

◄ NOTES WINDOW

Complete the following customer service/sales assignment using the material in your product sales training program (pp. 459–474) and the forms on the next two pages. (See Chapters 6 and 7 on Developing a Product Strategy.)

1. *Complete the sales proposal worksheet (p. 497).*
   Our sales proposal needs to contain accurate and complete facts because, when signed, it becomes a legally enforceable sales contract. All the product and pricing guidelines have been supplied in your sales training materials. You should sign your name with your new job title "Account Executive" in the lower left-hand corner of the form. You can access an Electronic Sales Proposal Writer at www.selling-today.com.
2. *Write a sales letter (p. 498).*
   Prepare a letter that custom fits and positions the benefits that will appeal to B. H. Rivera. Be sure to list any sales literature you will be sending under the Enclosure section of your letter. (Use business letter format on p. 489 and rules on page 137.)

Make file copies of everything you prepare so our food and beverage, housekeeping, and accounting departments will have them available.

We should send or fax the proposal, cover letter, and sales literature by tomorrow afternoon.

Thank you.

Enclosures

PARK INN
INTERNATIONAL™

SALES PROPOSAL

Customer Name: ______________________ Title: ______________________
Organization Name: ______________________ Telephone: ______________________
Address: ______________________
Date(s) of Meetings: ______________________
Kind of Meetings: ______________________
Buying Conditions (What the customer needs—be specific): ______________________

____

____

A. Meal Functions Needed

	Time	Description	Quantity	Price	Total
Meal 1 Meal 2 Other		(Beverages, setup fees, etc.)			

Total ______________
Sales Tax ______________
Service Charge ______________
Total Meal Cost ______________

B. Meeting and Banquet Rooms and Equipment Needed (describe time, date, and cost)

Total ______________
Sales Tax ______________
Total Meeting/Banquet Rooms and Equipment Charges ______________

C. Guest Rooms Needed

Number of Rooms Needed	Description (dates, locations, special conditions)	Group Rate Per Room	Total Cost

Total ______________
Room Tax ______________
Sales Tax ______________
Total Guest Room Charges ______________

D. Total Customer Costs (from above)
A. $__________ plus **B.** $__________ plus **C.** $__________ equals **Total Charges** $ ______________

______________________ ______________________
Authorized Signature Date Customer Signature Date

______________________ ______________________
Title Title

PARK INN
INTERNATIONAL™

555 West Side Street, Rockport, IL 50322
618-225-0925 Fax 618-225-9386

PARTS II to IV

PARK INN
INTERNATIONAL™

EMPLOYMENT MEMORANDUM 2

To: **New Convention Center Account Executives**
From: **T. J. McKee, Sales Manager**
Re: **Your New Sales Assignment**

Congratulations on successfully completing your training program and receiving your new appointment. You will find three challenges as you work with your customer's buying process.

Your *first challenge will be establishing relationships* with your customers. This will require that you do strategic planning before you can call on your client for the first time. Make sure your initial meetings focus on subjects of interest to your customer. Remember, "Customers don't care how much you know until they know how much you care."

Your *second major challenge will be to gain a complete and accurate understanding of your customer's needs.* You should prepare to ask good questions, take detailed and accurate notes, and confirm your customer's and your own understanding of their need. This process is a part of our total quality management program, which strives to provide total quality customer service. "To be an effective consultative salesperson you need to seek first to understand."

Your *third challenge as an account executive will be to make good presentations.* Our industry, as most others these days, is competitive and is characterized by many look-alike products and some price cutting. Always *organize and deliver good presentations* that focus on (1) providing solutions to immediate and long-term customer's needs, (2) negotiating win-win solutions to customer's concerns, and (3) closing sales that keep our facility full. This approach will give you a competitive edge and help you maintain high-quality, long-term profitable relationships.

Attached you will find a memorandum on an account I would like you to develop. Please follow the instructions included and provide me with appropriate feedback on your progress. I look forward to working with you on this account.

P.S. I want to compliment you on your excellent work on the B. H. Rivera account. B. H. called while you were attending a training meeting and said that your proposal and letter looked very good. Their organization was impressed with our facility, the apparent quality of our food, and your letter. Their organization will be scheduling a total of *11 more meetings* at our convention center during the next 12 months if everything works the way you describe it. Each of these sales will be reflected in your *commission checks.* Great work.

Part Two: Developing a Relationship Strategy for Selling

PARK INN
INTERNATIONAL™

SALES MEMORANDUM 1A

To: Association Account Sales
From: T. J. McKee, Sales Manager
Re: Developing the Erin Adkins YWCA Account (Call 1, Establishing a Relationship Strategy)

My sales assistant has called Erin Adkins, chairperson of the YWCA Physical Fitness Week program (see following contact report), and set up an appointment for you on Monday at 1:00 P.M. in Erin's office. During your first sales call with Erin, your call objectives will be to (1) establish a strong relationship, (2) share an appealing benefit of our property to create customer's interest, and (3) find out if your customer is planning any conventions in the future.

As we discussed during your training class, using Erin Adkins's prospect information presented below and the sales tools in your product strategy materials, your presentation plan should be to (see Chapters 3 and 10):

1. Use compliments, comments on observations, or search for mutual acquaintances to determine which topics Erin wants to talk about (Erin will only want to talk about three of these topics). This should set the stage for a good relationship.
2. Take notes on the topics of interest to Erin so we can add them to our customer information data bank for future calls. (Erin will share three new items of information on each topic of interest, if you acknowledge interest.)
3. Show and describe an appealing and unique benefit of our facility so we will be considered for Erin's future convention needs. (Consider using the Architect's Award, p. 467.)
4. Discuss any conventions Erin may be planning.
5. Schedule a call back appointment.

Name: YWCA | Address: 16 Ruan Center
Contact: Erin Adkins | :
Phone: 515-555-3740 | :
Title: Chairperson, Physical Fitness Programs | City: Rockport
Sec: | State: IL
Dear: Erin | ZIP: 50322

← CONTACT SCREEN

(McKee) Toni Bush, the Athletic Director of West College, supplied the following information about Erin Adkins:
1. Toni and Erin have a close relationship.
2. Erin just designed and built a new home.
3. Erin appears in local TV advertising about the YWCA.
Toni reports that in Erin's office you will observe the following:
4. An autographed picture of Tiger Woods
5. A Schwinn Air-dyne Fitness Cycle

← NOTES WINDOW

Comments, Compliments, and Questions	Notes on New Items of Interest to Customer
(Toni Bush suggested you mention his name.)	1. (Example) Toni Bush is my cousin 2. 3.
	1. 2. 3.
	1. 2. 3.

PARK INN
INTERNATIONAL™

SALES MEMORANDUM 1B

To: **Corporate Account Sales**
From: **T. J. McKee, Sales Manager**
Re: **Developing the Leigh Combs, Epic Design Systems Account (Call 1, Establishing a Relationship Strategy)**

My sales assistant has called Epic Design Systems (see following contact report) and set up an appointment for you on Monday at 1:00 P.M. in Leigh's office. During your first sales call with Leigh, your call objectives will be to (1) establish a strong relationship, (2) share an appealing benefit of our property to create customer's interest, and (3) find out if your customer is planning any conventions in the future.

As we discussed during your training class, using Leigh Combs's prospect information presented below and the sales tools in your product strategy materials, your presentation plan should be to (see Chapters 3 and 10):

1. Use compliments, comments on observations, or search for mutual acquaintances to determine which topics Leigh wants to talk about (Leigh will only want to talk about three of these topics). This should set the stage for a good relationship.
2. Take notes on the topics of interest to Leigh so we can add them to our customer information data bank for future calls. (Leigh will share three new items of information on each topic of interest, if you verbally or nonverbally acknowledge interest.)
3. Show and describe an appealing and unique benefit of our facility so we will be considered for Leigh's future convention needs. (Consider using the Executive Chef's Award, p. 473.)
4. Discuss any conventions Leigh may be planning.
5. Schedule a call back appointment.

Name:	Epic Design Systems	Address:	2401 West Towers
Contact:	Leigh Combs	:	Suite 200
Phone:	416-555-1000 X: CC:	:	
Title:	Customer Service Manager	City:	West Rockport
Sec:	Rhiannon	State:	IL
Dear:	Leigh	ZIP:	50265

◄ CONTACT SCREEN

(McKee) Linn Compiano, the Training Manager at Acme Supply Company, provided the following information about Leigh Combs:
1. Leigh has been on vacation.
2. Leigh is Linn Compiano's cousin.

Linn reports that in Leigh's office you will observe the following:
3. A large picture of Napoleon Bonaparte
4. A degree from our state university
5. An extra-large bookcase containing many business books

◄ NOTES WINDOW

Comments, Compliments, and Questions	Notes on New Items of Interest to Customer
(Linn Compiano mentioned that Leigh Combs just returned from a very enjoyable vacation.)	1. (Example) Spent one week in California 2. 3.
	1. 2. 3.
	1. 2. 3.

ASSESSMENT FORM 1

RELATIONSHIP STRATEGY

Salesperson's Name: ____________________
Date: ____________________

Assessment Item	Excellent		Average		Poor	Did Not Do
1. Conducted good verbal introductions (shared full name, title, and company name)	10	9	8	7	6	0
2. Made good nonverbal introduction (good entrance, carriage, handshake, and seating posture)	10	9	8	7	6	0
3. Communicated call objectives (shared why salesperson was calling)	10	9	8	7	6	0
4. Verbalized effective comments and compliments (sincerely made comments and compliments on five relationship topics)	10	9	8	7	6	0
5. Kept conversation focused on customer topics (acknowledged new information provided by customer)	10	9	8	7	6	0
6. Took effective nondistractive notes (was organized and prepared to take notes)	10	9	8	7	6	0
7. Attractively showed material on convention center (was well prepared with a proof device)	10	9	8	7	6	0
8. Made specific benefit statement (made a benefit statement that appealed to customer)	10	9	8	7	6	0
9. Effectively inquired about convention needs (asked good questions about future needs)	10	9	8	7	6	0
10. Effectively thanked customer (communicated appreciation, said thank-you, indicated interest in prospect future business)	10	9	8	7	6	0

Relationship Presentation: ____________________
Total Points

Your Name: ____________________

Return this form to salesperson and discuss your reaction to this presentation!

Part Three
Understanding Your Customer's Buying Strategy

PARK INN
INTERNATIONAL™

SALES MEMORANDUM 2A

To: **Association Account Salesperson**
From: **T. J. McKee, Sales Manager**
Re: **Erin Adkins Account—phone call from customer**
(Call 2, Discovering a Customer's Buying Strategy)

Erin Adkins from the YWCA, whom you called on recently, left a message for you to stop in about a program they are planning. Congratulations on making that first call so effectively. Apparently, you established a good relationship.

As we discussed in your training program, your *call objectives* for this sales call should be to:

1. Reestablish your relationship
2. Discover specific information about Erin's buying conditions (the what, why, who, when, and what price needs), so we can custom fit a program for them
3. Set up an appointment to present your solution

Also, as we discussed, your *presentation plan* for this call should include (see Chapters 8 and 11)

1. In advance of your meeting, prepare *general survey questions* to gather facts about your customer's buying situation and to achieve your call objectives.
2. During your meeting, use *confirmation questions* to clarify and confirm Erin's and your own perception of each buying condition. Later, use *specific survey questions* to discover any special buying problems.
3. During your sales meeting, write down each of Erin's buying conditions.
4. To end your first meeting, use your notes to construct a *summary-confirmation question* to clarify and confirm all six of Erin's buying conditions.
5. Schedule a call back appointment to make your presentation and present your proposal.

Good luck!

GENERAL SURVEY QUESTIONS	NOTES ON BUYING CONDITIONS
(Example: Can you share with me what you had in mind?)	(Example: Needs a small meeting room)
	1.
	2.
	3.
	4.
	5.
	6.

PARK INN
INTERNATIONAL™

SALES MEMORANDUM 2B

To: **Association Account Salesperson**
From: **T. J. McKee, Sales Manager**
Re: **Leigh Combs Account—phone call from customer (Call 2, Discovering a Customer's Buying Strategy)**

Leigh Combs from Epic Design Systems, whom you called on recently, left a message for you to stop in about a program they are planning. Congratulations on making that first call so effectively. Apparently, you established a good relationship.

As we discussed in your training program, your *call objectives* should be to

1. Reestablish your relationship
2. Discover the facts about Leigh's buying conditions (the what, why, who, when, and what price needs), so we can custom fit a program for them
3. Set up an appointment to present your solution

Also, as we discussed, your *presentation plan* for this call should include (see Chapters 8 and 11)

1. In advance of your meeting, prepare *general survey questions* to gather facts about your customer's buying situation and to achieve your call objectives.
2. During your meeting, use *confirmation questions* to clarify and confirm Leigh's and your own perceptions of each buying condition. Later, use *specific survey questions* to discover any special buying problems.
3. During your sales meeting, write down each of Leigh's buying conditions.
4. To end your first meeting, use your notes to construct a *summary-confirmatiom question* to clarify and confirm all six of Leigh's buying conditions.
5. Schedule a call back appointment to make your presentation and present your proposal.

Good luck!

GENERAL SURVEY QUESTIONS	**NOTES ON BUYING CONDITIONS**
(Example: Can you share with me what you had in mind?)	(Example: Needs a small meeting room)
	1.
	2.
	3.
	4.
	5.
	6.

ASSESSMENT FORM 2

CUSTOMER STRATEGY

Salesperson's Name: ______________________

Date: ______________________

Assessment Item	Excellent		Average		Poor	Did Not Do
1. Effectively reestablished relationship (made enthusiastic comments about information from first meeting)	10	9	8	7	6	0
2. Communicated positive body language (entrance, carriage, handshake, and seating)	10	9	8	7	6	0
3. Communicated positive verbal language (used positive words, showed enthusiasm with well-modulated voice)	10	9	8	7	6	0
4. Used customer's name effectively (used name at least three times)	10	9	8	7	6	0
5. Asked general survey questions to secure facts (seemed prepared, questions were general and open ended)	10	9	8	7	6	0
6. Verified customer needs with good confirmation questions (wanted to becorrect in interpreting customer needs)	10	9	8	7	6	0
7. Asked specific survey questions to discover special problems (followed up to secure all details)	10	9	8	7	6	0
8. Appeared to take effective notes (was organized and nondistracting, used notes in confirming needs)	10	9	8	7	6	0
9. Effectively set up next appointment (requested another meeting; suggested and wrote down date, time, and place)	10	9	8	7	6	0
10. Effectively thanked customer (communicated appreciation, said thank you, indicated enthusiasm for next meeting)	10	9	8	7	6	0

Discovering Customer Needs Presentation: ______________________
Total Points

Your Name: ______________________

Return this form to salesperson and discuss your reaction to this presentation!

Part Four
Developing a Sales Presentation Strategy

PARK INN
INTERNATIONAL™

SALES MEMORANDUM 3A

To: **Association Account Sales**
From: **T. J. McKee, Sales Manager**
Re: **Your recent meeting on the Erin Adkins Account (Call 3, Developing a Presentation Strategy)**

Congratulations on doing such a thorough job of discovering Erin's buying conditions. I found that your list of buying conditions includes the kind of customer information important to increasing our sales and partnering with our clients. I would like to see a copy of Erin's proposal when you complete it.

Reviewing what we discussed during your training, your next call objectives are:

1. Make a persuasive sales presentation that custom fits your proposal to Erin's needs
2. Negotiate any concerns Erin may have
3. Close and confirm the sale
4. Build repeat and referral business

Also, as we discussed, your *presentation plan* for this call should be to:

1. Prepare and price a product solution that meets Erin's needs. *Complete the Sales Proposal Worksheet* (p. 513).
2. Before your sales call, prepare a *portfolio* presentation (see model on p. 512) that follows these guidelines. Also, view the PowerPoint presentation at *www.prenhall.com/manning*.
   - **a.** Review the relationship information and prepare for those topics you will discuss.
   - **b.** Prepare a summary *confirmation* question that verifies the buying conditions secured in your second call. Prepare *Probing* questions to discover any pain your customer may be experiencing.
   - **c.** Select sales tools (proof devices), and create feature/benefit selling statements and *need-satisfaction questions* that appeal to Erin's buying conditions (see Chapter 12).
   - **d.** Plan summary confirmation questions that verify Erin's acceptance of your solution to each buying condition. *Complete Strategic Planning Form A* (p. 517) for items b, c, and d.
   - **e.** Prepare to negotiate the time, price, source, and product objections. *Complete Strategic Planning Form B* (p. 518) (see Chapter 13).
   - **f.** Prepare at least four closing methods in addition to the summary of benefits. *Complete Strategic Planning Form C* (p. 519) (see Chapter 14).
   - **g.** Plan methods to service the sale. Follow up by scheduling an appointment between now and the convention date (telephone call or personal visit) to follow through on guarantees concerning rooms and meals, suggestions about audiovisual needs, and any possible changes in the convention schedule. *Complete Strategic Planning Form D* (p. 520) (see Chapter 15).
3. During the sales call reestablish the relationship and, using your portfolio presentation,
   - **a.** Confirm all of Erin's previous buying conditions, and explore any pain being experienced
   - **b.** Match a proof device and feature/benefit selling statement with each buying condition
   - **c.** Confirm Erin's acceptance to each of your proposed benefit statements and need-satisfaction questions
   - **d.** Negotiate any sales resistance
   - **e.** Close the sale
   - **f.** Service the sale to get repeats and referrals

Good luck!

PARK INN
INTERNATIONAL™

SALES MEMORANDUM 3B

To: **Corporate Account Sales**
From: **T. J. McKee, Sales Manager**
Re: **Your recent meeting on the Leigh Combs Account (Call 3, Developing a Presentation Strategy)**

Congratulations on doing such a thorough job of discovering Leigh's buying conditions. I found that your list of buying conditions includes the kind of customer information important to increasing our sales and partnering with our clients. I would like to see a copy of Leigh's proposal when you complete it.

Reviewing what we discussed during your training, your next *call objectives* are:

1. Make a persuasive sales presentation that custom fits your proposal to Leigh's needs
2. Negotiate any concerns Leigh may have
3. Close and confirm the sale
4. Build repeat and referral business

Also, as we discussed, your *presentation plan* for this call should be to:

1. Prepare and price a product solution that meets Leigh's needs. *Complete the Sales Proposal Worksheet* (p. 513).
2. Before your sales call, prepare a *portfolio* presentation (see model on p. 512) that follows these guidelines. Also, view the PowerPoint presentation at *www.prenhall.com / manning*.
   a. Review the relationship information and prepare for those topics you will discuss.
   b. Prepare a summary *confirmation* question that verifies the buying conditions secured in your second call. Prepare *Probing* questions to discover any pain your customer may be experiencing.
   c. Select sales tools (proof devices) and create feature/benefit selling statements and *need-satisfaction questions* that appeal to Leigh's buying conditions (see Chapter 12).
   d. Plan confirmation questions that verify Leigh's acceptance of your solution to each buying condition. *Complete Strategic Planning Form A* (p. 517) for items b, c, and d.
   e. Prepare to negotiate the time, price, source, and product objections. *Complete Strategic Planning Form B* (p. 518) (see Chapter 13).
   f. Prepare at least four closing methods in addition to the summary-of-benefits close. *Complete Strategic Planning Form C* (p. 519) (see Chapter 14).
   g. Plan methods to service the sale. Follow up by scheduling an appointment between now and the convention date (telephone call or personal visit) to follow through on guarantees concerning rooms and meals, suggestions about audiovisual needs, and any possible changes in the convention schedule. *Complete Strategic Planning Form D* (p. 520) (see Chapter 15).
3. During the sales call reestablish the relationship and, using your portfolio presentation,
   a. Confirm all of Leigh's previous buying conditions, and explore any pain being experienced
   b. Match a proof device and feature/benefit selling statement with each buying condition
   c. Confirm Leigh's acceptance to each of your proposed benefit statements and *need-satisfaction* questions
   d. Negotiate any sales resistance
   e. Close the sale
   f. Service the sale to get repeats and referrals

Good luck!

ASSESSMENT FORM 3

PRESENTATION STRATEGY

Salesperson's Name: ____________________

Date:________________

Assessment Item	Excellent		Average		Poor	Did Not Do
1. Reestablished a good relationship (talked sincerely and enthusiastically about topics of interest to customer) Comments:	10	9	8	7	6	0
2. Confirmed needs from previous meeting Comments:	10	9	8	7	6	0
3. Made solution sound appealing (used nontechnical, customer-oriented benefit statements) Comments:	10	9	8	7	6	0
4. Used proof devices to prove sales appeals (made product sound appealing) Comments:	10	9	8	7	6	0
5. Verified customer's understanding of solution Comments:	10	9	8	7	6	0
6. Negotiated price objection (established high value to price impression) Comments:	10	9	8	7	6	0
7. Negotiated time objection (created need to sign now using empathy) Comments:	10	9	8	7	6	0
8. Negotiated source objection (knew the competition well) Comments:	10	9	8	7	6	0
9. Asked for the order, closed sale (attempted to close after each objection) Comments:	10	9	8	7	6	0
10. Serviced the sale (established relationship that would result in referrals or repeat sales opportunities) Comments:	10	9	8	7	6	0

____
Presentation Points

Overall quality of sales portfolio and proof devices — 25 20 15 0 5 0

Comments:

____
Total Points

Return this form to salesperson and discuss your reaction to this presentation!

Your Name: ____________________

PORTFOLIO PRESENTATION MODEL

THREE-RING BINDER WITH POCKETS RECOMMENDED

PAGE 1 Summary of Customer's Buying Conditions 1. 2. 3. 4. 5. 6. (confirmation question)	**PAGE 2** Buying Condition 1	**PAGE 3** Proof Devices (could be more than one) (state benefits, ask confirmation question)	**PAGE 4** Buying Condition 2
PAGE 5 Proof Devices (state benefits, ask confirmation question)	**PAGE 6** Buying Condition 3	**PAGE 7** Proof Devices (state benefits, ask confirmation question)	**PAGE 8** Buying Condition 4
PAGE 9 Proof Devices (state benefits, ask confirmation question)	**PAGE 10** Buying Condition 5	**PAGE 11** Proof Devices (state benefits, ask confirmation question)	**PAGE 12** Buying Condition 6
PAGE 13 Proof Devices (state benefits, ask confirmation question)	**PAGE 14** Summary of Benefits 1. 2. 3. 4. 5. 6. (trial close)	**FRONT POCKET MATERIALS** Additional value-added pages as needed to overcome sales resistance and close the sale	**BACK POCKET MATERIALS** Additional value-added pages as needed to service the sale

PARK INN
INTERNATIONAL™

SALES PROPOSAL FORM

Customer Name: ______________________________ Title: ______________________
Organization Name: ___________________________ Telephone: __________________
Address: ____
Date(s) of Meetings: ____
Kind of Meetings: ____
Buying Conditions (What the customer needs—be specific): _______________________
____
____

A. Meal Functions Needed

	Time	Description	Quantity	Price	Total
Meal 1 Meal 2 Other		(Beverages, setup fees, etc.)			

Total ____________
Sales Tax ____________
Service Charge ____________
Total Meal Cost ____________

B. Meeting and Banquet Rooms and Equipment Needed (describe time, date, and cost)

Total ____________
Sales Tax ____________
Total Meeting/Banquet Rooms and Equipment Charges ____________

C. Guest Rooms Needed

Number of Rooms Needed	Description (dates, locations, special conditions)	Group Rate Per Room	Total Cost

Total ____________
Room Tax ____________
Sales Tax ____________
Total Guest Room Charges ____________

D. Total Customer Costs (from above)
A. $__________ plus **B.** $__________ plus **C.** $__________ equals **Total Charges** $ __________

______________________________ ______________________________
Authorized Signature Date Customer Signature Date

______________________________ ______________________________
Title Title

PARK INN
INTERNATIONAL™

555 West Side Street, Rockport, IL 50322
618-225-0925 Fax 618-225-9386

MEETING AND BANQUET ROOM SCHEDULE OF EVENTS

1ST THURSDAY OF NEXT MONTH

Central Park East
Open—Expect confirmation tomorrow

Central Park West
Open—Expect confirmation tomorrow

Park Lane
10:00 A.M. C of C Membership Committee
2:00 P.M. County Central Planning Committee

Top of the Park
Open—Expect confirmation tomorrow

Revolver
Open

Dance Floor
7:00 P.M. IBM Dinner and Dance

Parkview
Open—Expect confirmation tomorrow

1007 and 1009
11:00 A.M. Advertising Prof's Luncheon
7:00 P.M. IBM Communication Seminar

107 and 109
10:00 A.M.—Expect confirmation tomorrow

ATTENTION: Phone 225-0925, ext. 8512 immediately to confirm reservations.

➡ Use the scheduling information on the reverse of this page to illustrate to your customers that reservations for rooms must be scheduled as soon as possible. All guest and meeting room reservations are guaranteed on a "first come, first signed" basis with the customer's signature on a sales proposal. Once a room has been reserved on a signed sales form, it is no longer available. Upon receiving a signature, sales and marketing personnel should immediately phone, fax, or e-mail this information to the reservations department. Noting that a possible meeting may be confirmed does not constitute a signed reservation.

STRATEGIC SALES PLANNING FORM A

MATCHING BUYING CONDITIONS WITH PROOF DEVICES AND FEATURE/BENEFITS

BUYING CONDITION *You indicated you wanted…*	PROOF DEVICE *Here is…*	FEATURE *which has (have)…*	SPECIFIC BENEFIT *which means to you…*	CONFIRMATION QUESTION *What do you think?*
1. ____ (number) guest rooms	A picture of one of our guest rooms (see p. 479)	Just been remodeled	Your people will enjoy clean, comfortable, spacious, and attractive surroundings	Is that what you had in mind?
2.				
3.				
4.				
5.				
6.				

Optional Role-Play 3-A Instructions (see Chapters 11 and 12)

Step 1 Prepare your presentation plan by completing the above form.

Step 2 Organize your presentation plan by placing the above information on $8\frac{1}{2}" \times 11"$ sheets of paper according to the portfolio presentation plan on page 512. Select proof devices from the product strategy materials presented on pages 465–498 and the completed proposal on page 513.

Step 3 Using the portfolio materials you have prepared, pair off with another student who will play the role of your customer. Review your customer's buying conditions, present your solutions with benefit statements, prove your sales appeals with demonstrations, secure your customer's reactions, and summarize the benefits presented. Discuss your customer's reactions to your presentation. This exercise will help you prepare for call 3.

STRATEGIC SALES PLANNING FORM B

ANTICIPATING AND NEGOTIATING SALES RESISTANCE WORKSHEET

PART I	ANTICIPATING SALES RESISTANCE	PART II	NEGOTIATING SALES RESISTANCE
Type	What Customer Might Say	Methods*	What You Will Say (include proof devices you will use)
Time	"I would like to take a day to think over your proposal."	Indirect denial	"I understand, however" (Show p. 515, Schedule of Events.)
Price	"That price is way over my budget."		
Source	"I'm going to check with the Marriott."		
Product	"I'm concerned about the size of your meeting rooms."		

Optional Role-Play 3-B Instructions

Using the preceding material you have prepared, pair off with another student who will play the role of your customer. Provide your customer with the material in Part I and instruct her to raise sales resistance in any order she chooses. Playing the role of the salesperson, you will respond with the material you prepared in Part II. Continue the dialogue until all the types of sales resistance have been successfully negotiated. Discuss with your customer her reaction to your methods of successfully negotiating the different types of sales resistance. This exercise will help you prepare for Sales Call 3.

* **Method of Negotiating Sales Resistance** (see Chapter 13)

- Direct denial
- Indirect denial
- Question
- Third party
- Superior benefit
- Demonstration
- Trial offer
- Feel, felt, found
- Postponement

STRATEGIC SALES PLANNING FORM C

CLOSING AND CONFIRMING THE SALE WORKSHEET

PART I	PART II	
Verbal and Nonverbal Closing Clues	Method of Closing*	What You Will Say (include proof devices you will use)
Agrees with each benefit	Summary of the benefits and direct appeal	"Let me review what we have talked about…. May I get your signature?" (Use p. 513, Sales Proposal.)
Agrees after an objection to price, time, or source	Assumption	
Appears enthusiastic and impatient	Trial close and assumption	
Agrees with all benefits but will not under any circumstances go over budget	Special concession	

Optional Role-Play 3-C Instructions

Using the preceding material you have prepared, pair off with another student who will play the role of your customer. Provide your customer with the appropriate closing clues from Part I and instruct him to provide verbal or nonverbal closing clues in any order he chooses. Playing the role of the salesperson, you will respond with the material you prepared in Part II. Continue the dialogue until you have responded to all the anticipated closing clues. Discuss with your customer his reaction to your methods of successfully closing and confirming the sale. This exercise will help you prepare for Sales Call 3.

* **Method of Closing the Sale** (see Chapter 14)

- Trial close
- Summary of the benefits
- Assumption
- Special concession
- Multiple option
- Direct appeal
- Balance sheet
- Management

STRATEGIC SALES PLANNING FORM D

SERVICING THE SALE WORKSHEET

PART I	PART II
What You Will Do to Add Value to the Sale	What You Will Say or Write to Add Value to the Sale
1. Schedule appointments to confirm rooms and final counts on meals. Dates 1 ________ 2 ________ Time 1 ________ 2 ________	"I would like to call to confirm. . . ." (Show p. 493, Convention Center Policies, and write date and time on your calendar.)
2. Make suggestions during next meeting about audiovisual equipment, beverages for breaks, etc.	
3. Provide personal assurances concerning your continuing efforts to make the meeting an outstanding success.	
4. Prepare thank-you letter concerning call 3.	

Optional Role-Play 3-D Instructions

Using the preceding material you have prepared, pair off with another student who will play the role of your customer. Using the topics identified in Part I, verbally present what you have prepared in Part II on this form. Discuss with your customer her reaction to your methods of servicing the sale. This exercise will help you prepare for Sales Call 3.

Method of Servicing the Sale (see Chapter 15)

- Follow through on promises and obligations
- Follow up to ensure customer satisfaction
- Expansion selling

ENDNOTES

Chapter 1

1. *The Big Picture: Sales Environments* (Pasadena, CA: Intelecom). "Pure and Simple," Cited January 14, 2005, www.altadenadairy.com.
2. *The Big Picture: Sales Environments* (Pasadena, CA: Intelecom). "About Us," Cited January 14, 2005, www.amgen.com.
3. Lucy McCauley, "Voices: The State of the New Economy," *Fast Company*, September 1999, p. 124.
4. Stan Davis and Christopher Meyer, *Blur: The Speed of Change in the Connected Economy* (New York: Addison-Wesley, 1998), p. 9.
5. David Shenk, *Data Smog: Surviving the Information Glut* (New York: HarperEdge, 1997), pp. 27–29.
6. Michael Hammer, *The Agenda* (New York: Random House, 2001), p. 6.
7. Greg Ip, "Why High-Fliers, Built on Big Ideas, Are Such Fast Fallers," *Wall Street Journal*, April 4, 2002, p. A–1.
8. Louis E. Boone and David L. Kurtz, *Contemporary Marketing*, 11th Ed. (Mason, Ohio: Southwestern Publishing, 2004), p. 11.
9. Norihiko Shirouzu, Gregory L. White, and Joseph B. White, "Beyond Explorer Woes, Ford Misses Key Turns in Buyers, Technology," *Wall Street Journal*, January 14, 2002, p. A–1.
10. Malcolm Fleschner, "World Wide Winner—The UPS Success Story," *Selling Power*, November/December 2001. p. 58, "50 Best Companies to Sell For," *Selling Power*, November/December 2004, pp. 94–95.
11. "America's 25 Best Sales Forces," *Sales & Marketing Management*, July 2000, p. 59, "The 25 Best Service Companies to Sell For," *Selling Power*, November/ December 2004, p. 95.
12. Gary Armstrong and Philip Kotler, *Marketing—An Introduction*, 7th Ed. (Upper Saddle River, NJ: Prentice Hall, 2005), p. 57.
13. Gerhard Gschwandtner, "The Power of the Selling Profession," *Selling Power*, October 2003, p. 10; Gerhard Gschwandtner, "SP 500 Salespeople Drive the Economy," *Selling Power*, October 2004, p. 59.
14. Robert M. Peterson, George H. Lucas, and Patrick L. Schul, "Forming Consultative Trade Alliances: Walking the Walk in the New Selling Environment," *NAMA Journal*, Spring 1998, p.11; Beth Belton, "Technology Is Changing Face of U.S. Sales Force," *USA Today*, February 9, 1999, p. 2A.
15. Charles Gottenkieny, "Proper Training Can Result in Positive ROI," *Selling*, August 2003, p. 9.
16. Michael R. Solomon, Greg W. Marshall, Elnora W. Stuart, *Marketing—Real People, Real Choices*, 4th Ed. (Upper Saddle River: New Jersey, Prentice Hall, 2006), p. 35.
17. Robert B. Miller and Stephen E. Heiman, *Strategic Selling* (New York: Warren Books, 1985), p. 26.
18. Jack Snader, "Is It Consultative Selling or Detailing?" *Newspost*, Fall 1999, pp. 21–32; Patricia Seybold, *The Customer Revolution* (New York: Random House, 2001), p. 1.
19. Keith M. Eades, *The New Solutions Selling*, (New York: McGraw-Hill, 2004), pp. ix-x.
20. Ibid, pp. 102–104.
21. Patricia Seybold, *The Customer Revolution* (New York: Random House, 2001), p. 1.
22. Francy Blackwood, "Equal, But Not Separate," *Selling*, June 1996, pp. 74–75; "Books & Videos," *Training*, February 1996, p. 62. "Doing Business with Baxter" (Cited April 8, 2002) www.baxter.com/doingbusiness.
23. William M. Pride, Robert J. Hughes, and Jack R. Kapoor, *Business*, 8th Ed. (Boston: Houghton Mifflin Company, 2005), p. 108.
24. Erin Strout, "Fast Forward," *Sales & Marketing Management*, December 2001, pp. 37–38.
25. Geoffrey Brewer, "The Customer Stops Here," *Sales & Marketing Management*, March 1998, pp. 31–32.
26. Gary Armstrong and Philip Kotler, *Marketing—An Introduction*, 7th Ed. (Upper Saddle River: NJ Prentice Hall, 2005), p. 23.
27. Lorrie Grant, "Radio Shack Uses Strategic Alliances to Spark Recovery," *USA Today*, January 26, 2001, p. 3–B.
28. See Cy Charney, "Choose Your Partners," *Value-Added Selling 21*, December 16, 2003, p. 3.
29. Gary Armstrong and Philip Kotler, *Marketing: An Introduction*, 7th Ed. (Upper Saddle River, NJ: Prentice Hall, 2005), p. 16.
30. Michael Hammer, *The Agenda* (New York: Random House, 2001), pp. 38–39.

Sources for Boxed Features

a Barbara Pachter and Marjorie Brody, *Complete Business Etiquette Handbook* (Upper Saddle River, NJ: Prentice Hall, 1995), pp. 279–280.

b Robert Kreitner, *Management*, 8th ed. (Boston: Houghton Mifflin, 2001), pp. 3–4.

Chapter 2

1. Julia Chang, "Faker or Deal Maker," *Sales & Marketing Management*, December 2003, p. 30; Kris Maher, "A Job Where Golf Comes to the Fore," *Wall Street Journal*, June 29, 2004, p. B6; Kris Maher, "Sales Chief is Called For," *Wall Street Journal*, May 20, 2003, p. B 10.
2. Stanley Marcus, "Sales School," *Fast Company*, November 1998, p. 105.
3. Thomas A. Stewart, "Knowledge, the Appreciating Commodity," *Fortune*, October 12, 1998, p. 18.
4. Christopher Caggiano, "Sign of the Cross-Training Times," *Inc.*, December 1998, pp. 122–123.
5. Julie Gordon, "Teaching Selling Skills to the Financial World," *The Denver Business Journal*, November 3–9, 2000, p. 10B; Henry Canady, "How Did You Become a Sales Manager," *Selling Power*, June 2004, p. 5.
6. Harry Beckwith, *Selling the Invisible* (New York: Warner Books, 1997), p. 38; See Norm Brodsky, "Street Smarts," *Inc.*, June 2004, pp. 53–54.
7. Linda Corman, "Look Who's Selling Now," *Selling*, July–August 1996, pp. 46–53; "Everyone's a Seller," *Sales & Marketing Management*, March 2003, p. 12
8. Ibid., p. 53.
9. Gerry Khermouch, "Keeping the Froth on Sam Adams," *Business Week*, September 1, 2003, pp. 54–56.
10. Beth Belton, "Technology Is Changing Face of U.S. Sales Force," *USA Today*, February 9, 1999, p. A2.

11. Brian Tracy, *The 100 Absolutely Unbreakable Laws of Business Success* (San Francisco: Berrett-Koehler Publishers, Inc., 2000), p. 192.
12. "The Major Sales Forces in America," *Selling Power*, October 2005, pp. 58–60.
13. Gabrielle Birkner, "Who Says Titles Don't Matter?" *Sales & Marketing Management*, July 2001, p. 14.
14. Christine Galea, "The 2004 Compensation Survey," Sales & Marketing Management, May 2004, pp. 28–34.
15. Michele Marchetti, "What a Sales Call Costs," *Sales & Marketing Management*, September 2000, pp. 80–81.
16. Carol Hymowitz, "Women Put Noses to the Grindstone, and Miss Opportunities," *Wall Street Journal*, February 3, 2004, p. B1.
17. Eli Jones, Jesse N. Moore, Andrea J. S. Stanaland, and Rosalind A. J. Wyatt, "Salesperson Race and Gender and the Access and Legitimacy Paradigm: Does Difference Make a Difference," *The Journal of Personal Selling & Sales Management*, Fall 1998, p. 71.
18. "Job Market Thaw," *Sales & Marketing Management*, February 2004, p. 28.
19. Mary Umberger, "Expert Advice," *Chicago Tribune*, June 1, 2003, p. W1.
20. "History of Julian's," (Cited April 17, 2002). www.julianstyle.com. Information was also obtained by personal interviews with employees.
21. Donna Harris, "Asbury Sells College Graduates on Auto Retail," *Automotive News*, January 26, 2004, p. 26.
22. Erika Rasmusson, "The Death of Retail?" *Sales & Marketing Management*, March 1999, p. 17.
23. Jenny McCune, "Listen, and Watch Sales Fall into Place," *Selling*, September 2003, p.15.
24. Gabrielle Birkner, "Who Says Titles Don't Matter," *Sales & Marketing Management*, July 2001, p. 14.
25. Michael R. Solomon, Greg W. Marshall, Elnora W. Stuart, *Marketing: Real People, Real Choices*, 4th ed. (Upper Saddle River, NJ: Prentice Hall, 2006), p. 438.
26. Gary Armstrong and Philip Kotler, *Marketing: An Introduction*, 7th ed. (Upper Saddle River, NJ: Prentice Hall, 2005), pp. 445–446.
27. Louis E. Boone and David L. Kurtz, *Contemporary Marketing*, 11th ed. (Mason, Ohio: Southwestern Publishing, 2004), p. 572.
28. Gary Armstrong and Philip Kotler, *Marketing: An Introduction*, 7th ed. (Upper Saddle River, NJ: Prentice Hall, 2005), p. 446.
29. Heather Johnson, "Field of Sales," *Training*, July 2004, p. 34.
30. Gerhard Gschwandtner, "Rendezvous with a Rainmaker," *Selling Power*, May 2001, pp. 98–100.
31. Kristine Ellis, "Deal Maker or Breaker?" *Training*, April 2002, pp. 34–37; Michele Marchetti, "Sales Training Even a Rep Could Love," *Sales & Marketing Management*, June 1998, p. 70.

Sources for Boxed Features

[a]Peter Elkind, "The Man Who Sold Silicon Valley on Giving," *Fortune*, November 27, 2000, pp. 182–190.

[b] Gene Koretz, "Women Swell the Workforce." *Business Week*, November 4, 1996, p. 32; Naomi Freundlich, "Maybe Working Women Can't Have It All," *Business Week*, September 15, 1997, pp. 19–22; Keith H. Hammonds, "She Works Hard for the Money," *Business Week*, May 22, 1995, p. 54; Anne Fisher, "Overseas, U.S. Businesswomen May Have the Edge," *Fortune*, September 28, 1998, p. 304; Carol Hymowitz, "Women Put Noses to the Grindstone, and Miss Opportunities," *Wall Street Journal*, February 3, 2004, p. B1.

[c] Betsy Cummings, "Selling Around the World," *Sales & Marketing Management*, May 2001, p. 70; Jan Yager, *Business Protocol*, 2nd ed. (Stamford, CT: Hannacroix Books, Inc., 2001), pp. 120–121.

Chapter 3

1. Information in the opening vignette and the case problem was taken from the video entitled "Sales Talk: Communication Styles" produced by Intelecom, Pasadena, California, and an interview with Steve Murphy, a Caldwell Banker franchise broker (May 6, 2002). In 2000 Cendant Corporation, parent company of Caldwell Banker Real Estate Services, purchased most of the Fred Sands corporate-owned offices and franchises. These units became Caldwell Banker real estate offices; Also see Mary Umberger, "Expert Advice," *Chicago Tribune*, June 1, 2003, p. W1.
2. Daniel Goleman, *Working with Emotional Intelligence* (New York: Bantam Books, 1998), pp. 24–28, 317; Geoffrey James, "Use Emotional Intelligence to Improve Sales," *Selling Power*, January/February 2005, p. 43–45.
3. Daniel Goleman, *Emotional Intelligence* (New York: Bantam Books, 1995), p. 34; Cary Cherniss and Daniel Goleman (eds.), *The Emotionally Intelligent Workplace* (San Francisco: Jossey-Bass, 2001), pp. 22–24. For more information on social competence, see Daniel Goleman, *Working With Emotional Intelligence* (New York: Bantam Books, 1998), pp. 24–28.
4. L. B. Gschwandtner and Gerhard Gschwandtner, "Balancing Act," *Selling Power*, June 1996, p. 24.
5. Ron Willingham, *Integrity Selling For The 21st Century* (New York: Currency Doubleday, 2003), p. 11.
6. Ilan Mochari, "In a Former Life," *Inc.*, April 2001, p. 100.
7. J. D. Power Consumer Center (Cited May 4, 2002) www.jdpower.com.
8. *Partnering: The Heart of Selling Today* (Des Moines, IA: American Media Incorproated, 1990).
9. Paul S. Goldner, "How to Set the Playing Field," *Selling*, April 1998, p. 9.
10. Larry Wilson, *Selling in the 90s* (Chicago: Nightingale Conant, 1988), p. 35.
11. William Keenan Jr., "Customer Satisfaction Builds Business," *Selling*, March 1998, p. 12.
12. Tim Sanders, *Love Is the Killer App* (New York: Crown Business, 2002), p. 23.
13. Malcolm Fleschner, "World Wide Winner—The UPS Story," *Selling Power*, November/December 2001, p. 58.
14. Neil Rackham and John R. DeVincentis, *Rethinking the Sales Force* (New York: McGraw-Hill, 1999), pp. 79–83.
15. Maxwell Maltz, *Psycho-Cybernetics* (Upper Saddle River, NJ: Prentice-Hall, 1960), p.2.
16. Phillip C. McGraw, "Dr. Phil: Know Your Goal, Make a Plan, and Pull the Trigger," *The Oprah Magazine*, September 2001, pp. 60–61; See Barry L. Reece and Rhonda Brandt, *Effective Human Relations—Personal and Organizational Applications* (Boston: Houghton Mifflin Company, 2005), pp. 95–102.
17. Stephen E. Heiman and Diane Sanchez, *The New Conceptual Selling* (New York: Warner Books, 1999), pp. 48–49.
18. Shoshana Zuboff, "A Starter Kit for Business Ethics," *Fast Company*, January 2005, p. 91.
19. Carol Hymowitz, "Management Missteps in '04 Hurt Companies, Endangered Customers," *Wall Street Journal*, December 21, 2004, p. B1; "Edward Jones Agrees to Settle Host of Charges," *Wall Street Journal*, December 21, 2004, p. C1; John

Hechinger, "Putmam May Owe $100 million," *Wall Street Journal*, February 2, 2005, p. C1; Erin McClam, "Witness Tells of Coverup," *News & Observer*, January 29, 2005, p. 3D.

20. Nathaniel Branden, *Self-Esteem at Work* (San Francisco: Jossey-Bass, 1998), p. 35.
21. Eli Jones, Jesse N. Moore, Andrea J. S. Stanaland, and Rosalind A. J. Wyatt, "Salesperson Race and Gender and the Access and Legitimacy Paradigm: Does Difference Make a Difference," *Journal of Personal Selling and Sales Management*, Fall 1998, p. 74; "Danielle Sacks, The Accidental Guru," *Fast Company*, January 2005, pp. 65–71.
22. Barry L. Reece and Rhonda Brandt, *Effective Human Relations—Personal and Organizational Application* 9th Ed. (Boston Houghton Mifflin Company, 2005), pp. 35–37.
23. Roy M. Berko, Andrew D. Wolvin, and Darlyn R. Wolvin, *Communicating*, 8th ed. (Boston: Houghton Mifflin Company, 2001), p. 45.
24. Ibid, p. 50
25. Susan Bixler, *The Professional Image* (New York: Putnam Publishing Group, 1984), p. 216.
26. Barbara Pachter and Marjorie Brody, *Complete Business Etiquette Handbook* (New York: Prentice-Hall, 1995), p. 14.
27. Adapted from Leonard Zunin, *Contact: The First Four Minutes* (New York: Nash Publishing, Ballantine Books, 1972), p. 109; and Jerry La Martina, "Shake It, Don't Crush It," *San Jose Mercury News*, June 25, 2000, p. 4PC.
28. "Name That Customer," *Personal Selling Power*, January–February 1993, p. 48.
29. Deborah Blum, "Face It!" *Psychology Today*, September–October 1998, pp. 32–69; See Julia Chang, "Selling in Acting," *Sales & Marketing Management*, May 2004, p. 22.
30. Barbara Pachter and Mary Brody, *Complete Business Etiquette Handbook* (Englewood Cliffs, NJ: Prentice Hall, 1995), p. 27; and "The Eyes Have It," *Sales & Marketing Management*, January 2002, p. 20.
31. Anne M. Phaneuf, "Decoding Dress Codes," *Sales & Marketing Management*, September 1995, p. 139.
32. Melinda Ligos, "Does Image Matter?" *Sales & Marketing Management*, March 2001, p. 52–55.
33. Margaret Webb Pressler, "Camouflage for the Cubicles," *News & Observer*, April 25, 2004, p. 4-E.
34. Susan Bixler and Nancy Nix-Rice, *The New Professional Image* (Adams Media Corporation, 1997), pp. 11–15; Barbara Pachter and Marjorie Brody, *Complete Business Etiquette Handbook* (New York: Prentice-Hall, 1995), p. 72.
35. Paul Galanti, "Talking Motivates—Communication Makes Things Happen," *Personal Selling Power*, November–December 1995, p. 88.
36. Susan Berkley, "Hone Your Sharpest Sales Weapon," *Sales & Field Force Automation*, July 1997, p. 24.
37. Barry L. Reece and Rhonda Brandt, *Effective Human Relations in Organizations*, 7th ed. (Boston: Houghton Mifflin, 1999), p. 293.
38. Joann S, Lublin, "To Win Advancement, You Need to Clean up Any Bad Speech Habits," *Wall Street Journal*, October 5, 2004, p. B.1.
39. David E. Weliver, "My Fair CEO," *Inc.*, October 30, 2001, p. 112.
40. "Is Etiquette a Core Value?" *Inc.*, May 2004, p. 22.
41. Tim Sanders, *Love Is the Killer App* (New York: Crown Business, 2002), p. 18.
42. Stephen Covey, *The Seven Habits of Highly Effective People* (New York: Simon & Schuster, 1989), pp. 240–241.
43. Robert Epstein, "Waiting," *Psychology Today*, September/October 2001, p. 5.
44. L. B. Gschwandtner, "Mary Lou Retton," *Personal Selling Power*, 15th Anniversary Issue, 1995, p. 99.
45. Jack Canfield, *The Success Principles* (New York: Harper Collins, 2005), pp. 342–343.
46. Colleen DeBaise, "Offbeat Hobbies May Help Build Relationships with Some Clients," *Wall Street Journal*, February 9, 2005, p. B2.
47. Anne Murphy Paul, "Self-Help: Shattering the Myths," *Psychology Today*, March/April 2001, p. 64; Arnold A. Lazarus and Clifford N. Lazarus, *The 60-Second Shrink* (San Luis Obispo, CA: Impact Publishers), 1997 pp. 3–4.
48. Phillip C. Mc Graw, *Self Matters* (New York: Simon & Shuster, 2001), pp. 69–76
49. Rick Saulle, "Honor Diversity," *Selling Power*, May 2004, p.54.

Sources for Boxed Features

[a] Ernest Beck, "How I Did It," *Inc.*, October 2004, pp. 120–122.

[b] Betsy Cummings, "Selling Around the World," *Sales & Marketing Management*, May 2001, p. 70.

[c] Andrew S. Gallan, "Bringing CARE to Your Customers," *Sales & Marketing Management*, May 2004, p. 72.

Chapter 4

1. Mike McNamee and Christopher Schmitt, "The Chainsaw Al Massacre," *Business Week*, May 28, 2001, p. 48; Dennis K. Berman and Joann S. Lublin, "Restructuring, Personality Clashes Led to Lucent Executive's Exit," *Wall Street Journal*, May 17, 2001, p. B1; Charles Fishmann, "Jeff Bezos," *Fast Company*, February 2001, pp. 80–82.
2. Douglas A. Bernstein, Louis A. Penner, Alison Clarke-Stewart, and Edward J. Roy, *Personality*, 6th ed. (Boston: Houghton Mifflin, 2003), p. 518.
3. Robert Bolton and Dorothy Grover Bolton, *People Styles at Work* (New York: AMACOM, 1996), p. 10.
4. David W. Merrill and Roger H. Reid, *Personal Styles and Effective Performance* (Radnor, PA: Chilton Book, 1981), p. 1.
5. For a more complete description of *The Versatile Salesperson* training program visit the Wilson Learning Corporation Web page. Accessed at www.wilsonlearning.com, January 20, 2005.
6. Robert J. Sternberg, *Thinking Styles* (New York: Cambridge University Press, 1997), p. 8.
7. Robert Bolton and Dorothy Grover Bolton, *People Styles at Work* (New York: AMACOM, 1996)
8. Geoff James, "Inside The Psychology of Selling," *Selling Power*, January/February 2004, pp. 25–28.
9. The dominance factor was described in an early book by William M. Marston, *The Emotions of Normal People* (New York: Harcourt, 1928). Research conducted by Rolfe LaForge and Robert F. Suczek resulted in the development of the Interpersonal Checklist (ICL) that features a dominant--submissive scale. A person who receives a high score on the ICL tends to lead, persuade, and control others. The Interpersonal Identity Profile, developed by David W. Merrill and James W. Taylor, features a factor called "assertiveness." Persons classified as being high in assertiveness tend to have strong opinions, make quick decisions, and be directive when dealing with people. Persons classified as being low in assertiveness tend to voice moderate opinions, make thoughtful decisions, and be supportive when dealing with others.
10. David W. Johnson, *Reaching Out—Interpersonal Effectiveness and Self-Actualization*, 8th ed. (Boston: Allyn and Bacon, 2003), p. 83.

11. The research conducted by LaForge and Suczek resulted in identification of the hostile–loving continuum, which is similar to the sociability continuum. Their Interpersonal Checklist features this scale. L. L. Thurstone and T. G. Thurstone developed the Thurstone Temperament Schedule, which provides an assessment of a "sociable" factor. Persons with high scores in this area enjoy the company of others and make friends easily. The Interpersonal Identity Profile developed by Merrill and Taylor contains an objectivity continuum. A person with low objectivity is seen as attention seeking, involved with the feelings of others, informal, and casual in social relationships. A person who is high in objectivity appears to be somewhat indifferent toward the feeling of others. This person is formal in social relationships.
12. Pierce J. Howard and Jane M. Howard, "Buddy, Can You Paradigm?" *Training & Development*, September 1995, p. 31.
13. Sam Deep and Lyle Sussman, *Close the Deal* (Reading, MA: Perseus Books, 1999), p. 157.
14. Len D'innocenzo and Jack Cullen, "Chameleon Management," *Personal Selling Power*, January–February 1995, p. 61.
15. Ron Willingham, *Integrity Selling for the 21st Century* (New York: Currency Doubleday, 2003), pp. 20–21.
16. Stuart Atkins, *How to Get the Most from Styles-Based Training* (Beverly Hills, CA: Stuart Atkins, 1996), p. 1.
17. Gary A. Williams and Robert B. Miller, "Change the Way You Persuade," *Harvard Business Review*, May 2002, p. 65.
18. Robert Bolton and Dorothy Groves Bolton, *People Styles at Work* (New York: AMACOM, 1996), p. 65.
19. David Merrill and Roger Reid, *Personal Styles and Effective Performance* (Radnor, PA: Chilton Books, 1981), p. 2.
20. Roger Wenschlag, *The Versatile Salesperson* (New York: John Wiley & Sons, 1989), pp. 165–171.
21. Nina Munk, "How Levi's Trashed a Great American Brand," *Fortune*, April 12, 1999, p. 85.
22. "The Top 25 Managers of the Year," *Business Week*, January 14, 2002, p. 65.
23. Stuart Atkins, *How to Get the Most from Styles-Based Training* (Beverly Hills, CA: Stuart Atkins, 1996), p. 3.
24. Ron Willingham, *Integrity Selling* (New York: Doubleday, 1987), pp. 21–23.
25. Eric F. Douglas, *Straight Talk* (Palo Alto, CA: Davies-Black Publishing, 1998), p. 92.
26. Ron Willingham, *Integrity Selling For the 21st Century* (New York: Currency Doubleday, 2003), p. 37.
27. David W. Merrill and Roger H. Reid, *Personal Styles and Effective Performance* (Radnor, PA: Chilton Book, 1981), pp. 134, 135.
28. Stuart Atkins, *The Name of the Game* (Beverly Hills, CA: Ellis & Stewart, 1981), pp. 49–50.

Sources for Boxed Features

a Andy Cohen, "Is This Guy for Real?" *Sales & Marketing Management*, May 2001, pp. 36–44.

b Christopher Caggiano, "Psychopath," *Inc.*, July 1998, p. 83.

c "Selling in Canada," *Sales & Marketing Management*, May 2002, p. 64; Jan Yager, *Business Protocol*, 2nd ed. (Stamford, CT: Hannacroix Creek Books, 2001), p. 112.

Chapter 5

1. Laura Johannes and John Hechinger, "SEC Divulges Details of How Edward Jones Pushed Mutual Funds," *Wall Street Journal*, December 23, 2004, p. C1; Susanne Craig and John Hechinger, "Regulators Find Problem Trading at Edward Jones," *Wall Street Journal*, December 29, 2004, p. C1.
2. Susanne Craig and John Hechinger, "Regulators Find Problem Trading at Edward Jones," *Wall Street Journal*, December 29, 2004, p. C.1.
3. O. C. Ferrell, John Fraedrich and Linda Ferrell, *Business Ethics*, 5th ed. (Boston: Houghton Mifflin Company, 2002), p. 6.
4. NASP Membership Information (Cited May 9, 2002). www.nasp.com.
5. Stephen R. Covey, *The Seven Habits of Highly Effective People* (New York: Simon & Schuster, 1989), pp. 18, 92. See Adam Hanft, "The New Lust for Integrity," *Inc.*, February 2004, p. 104.
6. Jan Yager, *Business Protocol* (Stamford, CT: Hannacroix Creek Books, Inc., 2001), pp. 199–200.
7. Sharon Begley, "A World of Their Own," *Newsweek*, May 8, 2000, pp. 53–56.
8. John A. Byrne, "How to Fix Corporate Governance," *Business Week*, May 6, 2002, pp. 69–78.
9. Josh Freed, "Investigators: Drug Salesman Foiled Pharmacist," *The News & Observer*, August 26, 2001, p. 12A.
10. Robert Simons, Henry Mintzburg, and Kunal Basu, "Memo to: CEOs," *Fast Company*, June 2002, pp. 117–121.
11. Marjorie Kelly, "Waving Goodbye to the Invisible Hand," *Business Ethics*, March/April 2002, p. 4. For a somewhat different point of view, see George Stalk, "Warm and Fuzzy Doesn't Cut It," *Wall Street Journal*, February 15, 2005, p. B2.
12. Yochi J. Dreazen, "Pressure for Sales Fostered Abuses at WorldCom," *Wall Street Journal*, May 16, 2002, p. B-1.
13. Robert Simons, Henry Mintzburg, and Kunal Basu, "Memo to: CEOs," *Fast Company*, June 2002 pp. 120–121.
14. Patrick Smith, "You Have a Job, But How About a Life?" *Business Week*, November 16, 1998, p. 30.
15. Mitchell Pacelle, "Citigroup Works on Reputation," *Wall Street Journal*, February 17, 2005, p. C3.
16. Ibid; "Survey Reveals What Motivates Loyalty," *Selling*, September 2000, p. 2.
17. Alan M. Webber, "Are All Consultants Corrupt?" *Fast Company*, May 2002, pp. 130–134.
18. Mary Ellen Egan, "Old Enough to Know Better," *Business Ethics*, January-February 1995, p. 19; "Our Mission and Values," (cited May 17, 2002). www.minnesota-mutual.com.
19. Gary Armstrong and Philip Kotler, *Marketing*, 6th ed. (Upper Saddle River, NJ: Prentice Hall, 2003), p. 619.
20. Betsy Cummings, "Ethical Breach," *Sales & Marketing Management*, July 2004, p. 10.
21. O. C. Ferrell, John Fraedrich and Linda Ferrell, *Business Ethics*, 5th ed. (Boston: Houghton Mifflin Company, 2002), p. 128.
22. Michele Krebs, "All the Marketing Men," *Autoweek*, February 16, 1998, p. 11.
23. Ken Brown and Gee L. Lee, "Lucent Fires Top China Executives," *Wall Street Journal*, April 7, 2004, p. A 8.
24. Steve Sack, "Watch the Words," *Sales & Marketing Management*, July 1, 1985, p. 56.
25. Patricia S. Eyres, "Steps for Staying Out of Court and Trouble," *Selling*, April 2002, p. 10.
26. Michael Schrage, "Internet: Internal Threat?" *Fortune*, July 9, 2001, p. 184.
27. Rob Zeiger, "Sex, Sales & Stereotypes," *Sales & Marketing Management*, July 1995, pp. 52–53.
28. Barry L. Reece and Rhonda Brandr, *Effective Human Relations—Personal and Organizational Applications*,

9th ed. (Boston: Houghton Mifflin. 2005), p. 113.

29. Betsy Cummings, "Do Customers Hate Salespeople?" *Sales & Marketing Management*, June 2001, pp. 50–51.
30. Ron Willingham, *Integrity Selling for the 21st Century* (New York: Currency Doubleday, 2003), p. 1.
31. Ron Willingham, "Four Traits All Highly Successful Salespeople Have in Common," Phoenix, AZ, 1998 (audiotape presentation).
32. Price Pritchett, *The Ethics of Excellence* (Dallas, TX: Pritchett & Associates, Inc., n.d.), p. 14.
33. Robert Kreitner, Barry Reece, and James P. O'Grady, *Business*, 2nd ed. (Boston: Houghton Mifflin Company, 1990), pp. 647–648.
34. Karin Schill Rives, "Workers Find Clause Has Teeth," *News & Observer*, July 29, 2001, p. E-1.
35. Dawn Marie Driscoll, "Don't Confuse Legal and Ethical Standards," *Business Week*, July–August 1996, p. 44.
36. Carol Wheeler, "Getting the Edge on Ethics," *Executive Female*, May–June 1996, p. 47.
37. Ron Willingham, *Integrity Selling for the 21st Century* (New York: Currency Doubleday, 2003), p. 11.
38. Sharon Drew Morgan, *Selling with Integrity* (San Francisco, Berrett-Koehler, 1997), pp. 25–27.
39. Ibid., pp. 27–28.
40. Tom Peters, *Thriving on Chaos* (New York: Alfred A. Knopf, 1988), p. 521.
41. Gerhard Gschwandtner, "Lies and Deception in Selling," *Personal Selling Power*, 15th Anniversary Issue, 1995, p. 62.
42. Price Pritchett, *The Ethics of Excellence* (Dallas, TX: Pritchett & Associates, Inc., no copyright), p. 18.
43. Neil Rackham and John R. DeVincentis, *Rethinking the Sales Force* (New York: McGraw-Hill, 1999), pp. 83–84.
44. Geoffrey Colvin, "The Verdict on Business: Presumed Guilty," *Fortune*, November 15, 2004, p. 78.

Sources for Boxed Features

a Jack Kemp, "Rules to Live by on and off the Field," *Imprimis*, July 1998, p. 3.

b Hilary Stout, "Couple Let Go by Enron Get Mad, Then Get Busy Building New Careers," *Wall Street Journal*, March 6, 2002, p. B-1.

c Michael T. Kenny, "Research, Observe Chinese Protocol to Land Sale," *Selling*, May 2001, p. 10; Jan Yager, *Business Protocol*, 2nd ed. (Stamford, CT: Hannacroix Books, Inc., 2001), p. 113.

Chapter 6

1. *In the Know: Acquiring Product Knowledge* (Pasadena, CA: Intelecom).
2. Keith M. Eades, *The New Solution Selling* (New York: McGraw-Hill, 2004), pp 4–5.
3. Michael R. Solomon and Elnora W. Stuart, *Marketing: Real People, Real Choices*, 2nd ed. (Upper Saddle River, NJ: Prentice Hall, 2000), p. 561.
4. Noel M. Tichy, "No Ordinary Boot Camp," *Harvard Business Review*, April 2001, p. 6.
5. Dana Hedgpeth, "The Changing Role of the Travel Agent," *The Roanoke Times*. May 26, 2002, pp. B1 and B2.
6. Neil Rackham and John R. DeVincentis, *Rethinking the Sales Force* (New York: McGraw-Hill, 1999), p. 79.
7. Emily Nelson, "Too Many Choices," *Wall Street Journal*, April 20, 2001, p. B.1; "Monthly Review of Mutual Funds," *Wall Street Journal*, June 3, 2002, pp. R1–R16.
8. Karen E. Starr, "Simple Solutions," *Selling Power*, July/August 2001, p. 22.
9. John Fellows, "A Decent Proposal," *Personal Selling Power*, November–December 1995, p. 56.
10. Adapted from John Fellows, "A Decent Proposal," *Personal Selling Power*, November–December 1995, p. 56. See Neil Rackham, "Seven Rules for Creating Winning Sales Proposal's," *Value-Added Selling* 21, December 16, 2003, p. 20.
11. "Feeling Under the Gun? Check Your Proposal," *Selling*, October 2001, p. 3.
12. Neil Rackam, "Seven Rules for Creating Winning Sales Proposals," *Value Added Selling* 20, December 16, 2003, p. 20.
13. "What Kind of Rep Is Most Trustworthy?" *Sales & Marketing Management*, February 2001, p. 90.
14. Tom Peters, *Re-Imagine! Business Excellence in a Disruptive Age* (London: Dording Kindersley Limited, 2003), p. 224.
15. "Extended Family," www.patagonia.com/culture/extended-family.shtml, Accessed 2/25/2005.
16. "Sea Ray," *Fortune*, April 5, 2004, p. S8.
17. Betsy Cummings, "Welcome to the Real World," *Sales & Marketing Management*, February 2001, pp. 87–88.
18. Ian Gelenter, "Build Satisfaction with a Service Contract," *Selling*, May 1998, p. 7.
19. Tom Reilly, "Should You Set Prices," *Selling*, August 2000, pp. 1 and 14.
20. Gerhard Gschwandtner, "ROI Selling," *Selling Power*, November/December 2004, p. 10
21. William M. Pride, Robert J. Hughes, and Jack R. Kapoor, *Business*, 8th ed. (Boston: Houghton Mifflin Company, 2005), pp. 456–457.
22. Robert Levering and Milton Moskowitz, "The 100 Best Companies to Work For," *Fortune*, January 24, 2005, pp. 73–74.
23. Michael R. Williams and Jill S. Attaway, "Exploring Salespersons' Customer Orientation as a Mediator of Organizational Culture's Influence on Buyer–Seller Relationships," *Journal of Personal Selling & Sales Management*, Fall 1996, pp. 33–52.
24. "Dealer Merchandising Portfolio," *Views: The Inner Circle News*, Winter 2000, p. 10.
25. "Grassroots Problem Solving," *Inc.*, March 1996, p. 92.
26. See Brian Tracy, "Analyzing the Competition," *Value Added Selling 21*, September 16, 2003, p.2.
27. Jim Dickie, "Lowest Price Isn't the Answer," *Selling*, August 2000, p. 14.
28. Bob Mundson, "A Personal Blend," *Training*, February 2004, p. 11.
29. "Extended Family," www.patagonia.com, Accessed 2/25/2005.
30. Jill Rosenfeld, "Unit of One," *Fast Company*, April 2000, p. 98.
31. Neil Rackham, *The SPIN Selling Fieldbook* (New York:McGraw-Hill, 1996), pp. 149–152.
32. Gary Hamil, *Leading the Revolution* (Boston: Harvard Business School Press, 2000), p. 87; Neil Rackham, "Improve This Skill and Boost Sales Up to 27%," *Value-Added Selling* 21, March 2, 2004, p. 1.
33. Jerry Vass, "Ten Expensive Selling Errors," *Agency Sales Magazine*, July 1998, pp. 38–39. Stephen E. Heiman and Diane Sanchez, *The New Conceptual Selling* (New York: Warner Books), 1987, pp. 83–85.

Sources for Boxed Features

a "A Living or a Life," *Fast Company*, January/February 2000, p. 264.

b "International Snapshot," *Sales & Marketing Management*, March 2000, p. 72: Jan Yager, *Business Protocol*, 2nd ed. (Stamford, CT: Hannacroix Books, Inc., 2001), p. 111.

Chapter 7

1. Peter Egan, "The Best of All Worlds Bunch," *Road & Track*, July 2002, pp. 52–78. "2005 Geneva: Lexus Finesses Next IS Sport Sedan," http://www.autoweek.com, Accessed March 1, 2005.
2. Neal E. Boudette, "The Luxury-Car Market Gets More Crowded," *Wall Street Journal*, March 3, 2005, p. Dl; J. P. Vettraino, "2006 BMW 3 Series: Technology Update," http://www.autoweek.com, Accessed March 1, 2005.
3. Michael R. Solomon, Grey W, Marshall, and Elnora W. Stuart, *Marketing: Real People, Real Choices*, 4th ed. (Upper Saddle River, NJ: Pearson Education, 2006), p. 212.
4. D. Lee Carpenter, "Return on Innovation—the Power of Being Different," *Retailing Issues Letter*, May 1998, p. 3.
5. Brian Tracy, "Keeping the Customers You Make," *Selling*, November 2003, pp. 1 and 4.
6. Tom Reilly, "You Must Differentiate to Win," *Selling*, April 2001, pp. 1 and 10.
7. Gary Armstrong and Philip Kotler, *Marketing: An Introduction*, 7th ed. (Upper Saddle River, NJ: Prentice Hall, 2005), p. 12.
8. Tom Leverton, "Five Questions," *Sales & Marketing Management*, July 2004, p. 13.
9. Carl K. Clayton, "Sell Quality, Service, Your Company, Yourself," *Personal Selling Power*, January–February 1990, p. 47.
10. Elaine Parker, "How I Made the Sale," *Value Added Selling 21*, June 17, 2003, pp. 1–2.
11. Suein L. Hwang, "It Was a WOMBAT for the Meatware, But It Was a Good Sell," *Wall Street Journal*, May 15, 2002, p. B-1.
12. J. Thomas Russell and W. Ronald Lane, *Kleppner's Advertising Procedure* (Upper Saddle River, NJ: Prentice Hall, 1996), pp. 46–47.
13. Jess McCuan, "Reeling In the Big One" *Inc.*, August 2004, pp. 43–44; "What Is IntraLinks?" http://www.intralinks.com, Accessed March 2, 2005.
14. Information was taken from *Report to Policyholders 2004*. This 24 page report was published by New York Life in 2005.
15. Michael R. Solomon and Elnora W. Stuart, *Marketing: Real People, Real Choices*, 4th ed. (Upper Saddle River, NJ: Prentice Hall, 2006), pp 347–348.
16. Carlos Tejada, "The Allure of Bundling," *Wall Street Journal*, October 7, 2003, p. B 1.
17. Michael Treacy, "You Need a Value Discipline—But Which One?" *Fortune*, April 17, 1995, p. 195.
18. Robert Shulman and Richard Miniter, "Discounting Is No Bargain," *Wall Street Journal*, December 7, 1998, p. A-30.
19. Andy Cohen, "Survey Says: Service Beats Price Online," *Sales & Marketing Management*, July 2002, p. 18.
20. Adopted from a model described in "Marketing Success through Differentiation—of Anything," *Harvard Business Review*, January–February 1980.
21. Joanna Johnson, "A New Perspective on Marketing," *Construction Dimensions*, April 1990, p. 14.
22. Ted Levitt, *Marketing Imagination* (New York: Free Press, 1983), p. 80.
23. Neil Rackham, "Boost Your Sales 20% by Improving This Skill," *Value-Added Selling 21*, June 17, 2003, pp. 1–2.
24. Thomas A. Stewart, "A Satisfied Customer Isn't Enough," *Fortune*, July 21, 1997, pp. 112–113.
25. "Business Bulletin," *Wall Street Journal*, September 24, 1998, p. A-1.
26. Chuck Salter, "On the Road Again," *Fast Company*, January 2002, pp. 50–58.
27. Ted Levitt, *Marketing Imagination* (New York: Free Press, 1983), p. 84.
28. Rebecca Smith, "Beyond Reycling: Manufacturers Embrace 'C2C' Design," *Wall Street Journal*, March 3, 2005, p. B1.
29. Neil Rackham and John R. DeVincentis, *Rethinking The Sales Force* (New York: McGraw-Hill, 1999), p. 89.
30. Ibid, pp. 89–90.
31. Ibid, p. 90.

Case Credits

Francy Blackwood, "The Concept That Sells," *Selling*, March 1995, pp. 34–36; *Systems Furniture Overview*, Steelcase Incorporated, November 1995, pp. 48–50. Rebecca Smith, "Beyond Recycling: Manufacturers Embrace 'C2' Design," *Wall Street Journal*, March 3, 2005, p. B1.

Sources for Boxed Features

[a] Malcolm Fleschner, "Chief Sales Executives," *Selling Power*, April 2002, pp. 58–59.

[b] Adapted from discussion in Leonard L. Berry, A. Parasuraman, and Valerie A. Zeithaml, "The Service-Quality Puzzle," *Business Horizons*, September–October 1988, pp. 35–43; Robert Kreitner, *Management*, 5th ed. (Boston: Houghton Mifflin, 1992), pp. 613–614.

[c] Charles Kozoll, "East Indian Customers Retain Buying Habits in U.S.," *Selling*, August 2000, p. 4; Jan Yager, *Business Protocol*, 2nd ed. (Stamford, CT: Hannacroix Books, Inc., 2001), p. 118.

[d] Rhonda M. Abrams, "Problem for Pros: Knowing How Much to Charge," *The Des Moines Register*, January 26, 1998, p. 2-B.

Chapter 8

1. Tom Peters, *Re-Imagine! Business Excellence in a Disruptive Age* (London: Dording Kindersley Limited, 2003), pp. 309–310.
2. *Step by Step: The Buying Process*, Pasadena, CA: Intelecom.
3. Michael Hammer and James Champy, *Reengineering the Corporation: A Manifest for Business Revolution* (New York: Harper Business, 1993), p. 18.
4. Keith M. Eades, *The New Solution Selling* (New York: McGraw-Hill, 2004), pp. 32–33.
5. Tom Peters and Nancy Austin, *A Passion for Excellence* (New York: Random House, 1985), p. 71.
6. "How Well Do You Know Your Customers?" *Sales & Field Force Automation*, January 1999, p. 141.
7. Gary Armstrong and Philip Kotler, *Marketing: An Introduction*, 6th ed. (Upper Saddle River, NJ: Prentice Hall, 2003), pp. 191–192 and 215.
8. Ibid., p. 215.
9. Michael R. Solomon and Elnora W. Stuart, *Marketing: Real People, Real Choices*, 3rd Ed. (Upper Saddle River, NJ: Prentice Hall, 2003), pp. 200–202.
10. Gary Armstrong and Philip Kotler, *Marketing: An Introduction*, 7th Ed. (Upper Saddle River, NJ: Prentice Hall, 2005), p. 169.
11. Ibid.
12. www.fedex.com, Accessed 12/16/2004.
13. Philip Kotler and Gary Armstrong, *Principles of Marketing*, 10th Ed. (Upper Saddle River, NJ: Prentice Hall, 2004), p. 198.
14. Ibid, p. 198.
15. Ibid, p. 197.
16. Keith M. Eades, *The New Solution Selling* (New York: McGraw-Hill, 2004), pp. 32–33.
17. Ibid, p. 31.
18. Stephen E. Heiman and Diane Sanchez, *The New Conceptual Selling* (New York: Warner Books, 1999), pp. 190–191.
19. Gary Armstrong and Philip Kotler, *Marketing: An Introduction*, 7th Ed.

(Upper Saddle River, NJ: Prentice Hall, 2005), p. 160.

20. Neil Rackham and John R. DeVincentis, *Rethinking the Sales Force* (New York: McGraw-Hill, 1999), p. 66.
21. Bill Stinnett, "Reverse-Engineer the Buying Process," *Selling*, December, 2004, p. 16.
22. Neil Rackham and John R. DeVincentis, *Rethinking the Sales Force* (New York: McGraw-Hill, 1999), p. 68.
23. Ibid, p. 69.
24. Neil Rackham and John DeVincentis, provide extensive coverage of these three selling modes in *Rethinking the Sales Force*. Also see "Let the Customer Define Value—and Sales Will Rise" by Neil Rackham and John DeVincentis, *Value-Added Selling 21*, January 13, 2004, pp. 1–2.
25. Neil Rackham and John DeVincentis, *Value-Added Selling* 21, January 13, 2004, pp. 1–2.
26. Ken Brown, "Little-Known Avaya Tackles Cisco in Internet Calling Gear," *Wall Street Journal*, October 26, 2004, P. B-1.
27. Neil Rackham and John R. DeVincentis, *Rethinking the Sales Force* (New York: McGraw-Hill, 1999), p. 74.
28. Philip Kotler and Gary Armstrong, *Principles of Marketing*, 10th Ed. (Upper Saddle River, NJ: Prentice Hall, 2004), p. 28.
29. Stan Davis and Christopher Meyer, *Blur: The Speed of Change in the Connected Economy* (New York: Addison-Wesley, 1998), p. 16.
30. William M. Pride and O. C. Ferrell, *Marketing*, 10th ed. (Boston: Houghton Mifflin, 1997), pp. 143–148.
31. Douglas A. Bernstein, Alison Clark-Stewart, Edward J. Roy, and *Psychology*, 6th ed. (Boston: Houghton Mifflin, 2003), p. 648.
32. Gary Armstrong and Philip Kotler, *Marketing: An Introduction*, 7th ed. (Upper Saddle River, NJ: Prentice Hall, 2005), pp. 147–148.
33. Douglas A. Bernstein, Alison Clark-Stewart, Louis A. Penner, Edward J. Roy, *Psychology*, 6th ed. (Boston: Houghton Mifflin, 2003), p. 21.
34. Gary Armstrong and Philip Kotler, *Marketing: An Introduction* 7th Ed. (Upper Saddle River, NJ: Prentice Hall, 2005), p. 145.
35. Louis E. Boone and David L. Kurtz, *Contemporary Marketing*, 11 Ed. (Mason, Ohio: Southwestern Publishing, 2004), p. 267.
36. Roger Hart, "Luxury, VW's Way," *Autoweek*, December 27, 2004, pp. 18–19; Tom Reilly, "All Sales Decisions are Emotional for the Buyer," *Selling*, July 2003, p. 13.
37. Phil Kline, "Dominant Buying Motive Is the Result of Strong Emotions," *Marketing News*, May 24, 1993, p. 4.
38. Stan Davis and Christopher Meyer, *Blur: The Speed of Change in the Connected Economy* (New York: Addison-Wesley, 1998), p. 52.
39. Hal Lancaster, "It's Time to Stop Promoting Yourself and Start Listening," *Wall Street Journal*, June, 1997, p. B-1.
40. Gary Armstrong and Philip Kotler, *Marketing: An Introduction*, 6th ed. (Upper Saddle River, NJ: Prentice Hall, 2003), p. 216; Sid Chadwick, "New Twists in Price vs. Perceived Value," *Sales and Marketing Advisory Magazine*, July/August 2001, p. 6.

Sources for Boxed Features

[a] Adopted from Jeffery Ball, "But How Does It Make You Feel?" *Wall Street Journal*, May 3, 1999, pp. B-1 and B-4; Joseph E. DeMatio, "2001 Chrysler PT Cruiser," *Automobile Magazine*, June 1999, pp. 76–82.

[b] Sam Walker, "Can Nascar Take Manhattan?" *Wall Street Journal*, March 8, 2002, p. W-6.

[c] "International Snapshot," *Sales & Marketing Management*, May 2001, p. 74; Jan Yager, *Business Protocol*, 2nd ed. (Stamford, CT: Hannacroix Books, Inc., 2001), p. 116

Chapter 9

1. ACT! Demonstration video, Symantec Corporation, Cupertino, CA, 1994; Stephen H. Wildstrom, "Can Your Rolodex Do This?" *Business Week*, May 27, 1966, p. 18; "SalesLogix Products Overview," cited July 10, 2002. www.saleslogix.com.
2. Don Peppers, Martha Rogers, and Bob Dorf, "Is Your Company Ready for One-to-One Marketing?" *Harvard Business Review*, January–February 1999, pp. 151–154.
3. Gerhard Gschwandtner, "Thoughts to Sell By," *Personal Selling Power*, 15th Anniversary Issue, 1995, p. 122.
4. Dorothy Leeds, "Where Are the Real Decision Makers?" *Personal Selling Power*, March 1993, p. 62; Gerhard Gschwandtner, "Getting Squeezed," *Selling Power*, May 2002, p. 10.
5. Gerhard Gschwandtner, "The Funnel Concept," *Personal Selling Power*, 15th Anniversary Issue, 1995, p. 23.
6. Joel R. Pecoraro, "Panning for Gold," *Sales & Marketing Management*, November 2004, p. 56.
7. "Skills Workshop," *Selling Power*, October 2000, p. 54.
8. Geoffrey James, "How to Earn Customer Referrals," *Selling Power*, July/August 2004, pp. 25–28.
9. "BNI-International Website," www.bni.com, Accessed February 14, 2005.
10. Thomas Petzinger Jr., "Selling a 'Killer App' Is a Far Tougher Job Than Dreaming It Up," *Wall Street Journal*, April 3, 1998, p. B-1.
11. Daniel Tynan,, "Tricks of the Trade Show," *Sales & Marketing Management*, January 2004, p. 27.
12. Ron Donoho, "Steering New Sales," *Sales & Marketing Management*, November 2001, pp. 31–35.
13. Trish Rintels, "Use Avatars to Enhance Your Sales Message Online," *Selling*, September 2001, p. 3.
14. Henry Canaday, "Lifeblood of Sales," *Selling Power*, March 2004, p. 84.
15. Andy Cohen, "Man About Town," *Sales & Marketing Management*, June 2000, p. 29.
16. Nicole Gull, "Warming Up to Cold Calls," *Inc.*, November 2004, pp. 41–43.
17. Maxwell Maltz, Dan S. Kennedy, William T. Brooks, Matt Oechsli, Jeff Paul, and Pamela Yellen, *Zero-Resistance Selling* (Paramus, NJ: Prentice-Hall, 1998), p. 167.
18. Stacy L. Bradford, "Ten Job-Networking Tips," *The News & Observer*, January 30, 2005, p. 7 E.
19. Michele Marchetti, "Do You Have the Knack for Networking?" *Sales & Marketing Management*, January 1996, p. 30; Deb Haggerty, "Successful Networking Begins as a State of Mind," *Selling*, December 2004, p. 13.
20. Maxwell Maltz, Dan S. Kennedy, William T. Brooks, Matt Oechsli, Jeff Paul, and Pamela Yellen, *Zero-Resistance Selling* (Paramus, NJ: Prentice-Hall, 1998), pp. 179–180.
21. "Hitting It Out of the Ballpark," *Inc.*, February 1996, p. 93.
22. Chad Kaydo, "Teach Your Clients Well," *Sales & Marketing Management*, April 1998, p. 83.
23. Steve Atlas, "Trouble Connecting?" *Selling Power*, September 2001, p. 27.

24. "Are You Generating and Using Quality Leads?" *Value-Added Selling 21*, September 16, 2003, p. 4.
25. This example was adopted from "Skills Workshop" by William F. Kendy, *Selling Power*, January/February 2000, p. 26.
26. Mitchell Pacelle, "Former SEC Chairman Levitt Decries Business Ethics in U.S.," *Wall Street Journal*, June 17, 2002, p. C7; Shoshana Zuboff, "A Starter Kit for Business Ethics," *Fast Company*, January 2005, p. 91.
27. Rick Page, *Hope Is Not a Strategy* (Atlanta, GA: Nautilus Press, 2002), pp. 69–71.
28. "Senior Execs Share Insider Tips," *Selling*, March 2000, pp. 1, 14; Tom Reilly, "Selling to Mr. Big Is Tough, But . . . " *Selling*, February 2001, pp. 1, 12.
29. Harvey Mackay, *Swim with the Sharks* (New York: William Morrow, 1988), pp. 43, 44; "Mackay 66," www.mackay.com Accessed March 18, 2005.
30. John C. Maxwell, *Winning With People* (Nashville, TN: Nelson Books, 2004), pp. 90–91.
31. Tom Peters, *Re-Imagine! Business Excellence in a Disruptive Age* (London: Dording Kindersley Limited, 2003), pp. 309–310.
32. "Prospecting Is Where the Gold Is," *Institutional Distribution*, May 15, 1990, pp. 70–72.
33. Chris Bogan, "Study: Four Ways Top Sellers Get Their Results," *Value-Added Selling 21*, March 16, 2004, p. 1.
34. Steve Atlas, "Up to Speed," *Selling Power*, January/February 2005, pp. 17–18; Carolee Bogles, "Touch All the Bases," *Selling Power*, January/February 2005, p. 25.

Sources for Boxed Features

a Sarah Lorge, "The Best Way to Prospect," *Sales & Marketing Management*, January 1998, p. 80.

b Chad Kaydo, "Becoming the Face of the Brand," *Sales & Marketing Management*, February 2000, p. 14.

c Barbara Siskind, *Seminars to Build Your Business* (North Vancouver, BC: Self-Counsel Press, 1998), pp. 9–12; Sheldon Gordon, "Punch Up Your Profits," *Profit*, May 1999, pp. 17–22.

d Barbara Pachter and Marjorie Brody, *Complete Business Etiquette Handbook* (Upper Saddle River, NJ: Prentice Hall, 1995), p. 278; "International Snapshot," *Sales & Marketing Management*, August 2001, p. 64; Jan Yager, *Business Protocol*, 2nd ed. (Stamford, CT: Hannacroix Books, Inc., 2001), pp. 116–117.

Chapter 10

1. A telephone interview with Mary Cathay on July 2, 2002 confirmed that Siemens Solar Industries was purchased by Shell Oil on April 18, 2002. The company is now called Shell Solar. *Plan of Action: Approaching the Customer* (Pasadena, CA: Intelecom).
2. Malcolm Fleschner, "Too Busy to Buy," *Selling Power*, March 1999, p. 36.
3. Bradford Agry, "Every Client Meeting Provides a Dynamic New Opportunity," *Selling*, April 2002, pp. 1, 4.
4. Malcolm Fleschner, "Anatomy of a Sale," *Selling Power*, April 1998, p. 76. Gina Rollins, "Prepare for the Unknown," *Selling Power*, July/August 2003, pp. 26–30.
5. "Set the Agenda," *Personal Selling Power*, May–June 1995, p. 79.
6. Donna Fenn, "Because His Family Business Makes An Art of Customer Service," *Inc.*, April 2005, p. 94; Telephone interview with Pamela Miles, staff member at Mitchells/Richards, March 22, 2005.
7. Philip Kotler and Gary Armstrong, *Principles of Marketing*, 10th ed (Upper Saddle River: NJ, 2004), p. 531.
8. Rick Page, *Hope Is Not a Strategy* (Atlanta, GA: Nautilus Press, 2002), p. 25.
9. Henry Canaday, "Teaming with Sales," *Selling Power*, May 1998, pp. 94–102.
10. James F. O'Hara, "Successful Selling to Buying Committees," *Selling*, February 1998, p. 8.
11. Betty Cummings, "Do Customers Hate Salespeople?" *Sales & Marketing Management*, June 2001, p. 46.
12. Neil Rackham and John R. Vincentis, *Rethinking the Sales Force* (New York: McGraw-Hill, 1999), p. 217.
13. Thomas A. Freese, *Secrets of Question Based Selling* (Naperville, Illinois, 2003), p. 114.
14. John Fellows, "Your Foot in the Door," *Selling Power*, March 1996, pp. 64–65.
15. Adapted from Art Sobczak, "Please, Call Me Back!" *Selling*, March 1999, p. 12.
16. Ibid.
17. Deborah Dumaine, "Managing Customers with E-Mail," *Selling Power*, March 2004, p. 94.
18. Ibid.
19. Susan Bixler and Nancy Nix-Rice, *The New Professional Image* (Holbrook, MA: Adams Media Corporation, 1997), p. 3.
20. Steve Atlas, "How to Cultivate New Turf," *Selling Power*, January/February 2003, p. 26.
21. Maxine Clayton, "60 Seconds on Small Talk," *Fast Company*, November 2004, p. 43.
22. Dean A Goettsch, "Make Your First Meeting Count," *Selling*, July 2004, pp. 1 and 4.
23. Melissa Campanelli, "Sound the Alarm," *Sales & Marketing Management*, December 1994, pp. 20–25.
24. Carolee Boyles, "Prewarm Cold Calls," *Selling Power*, July/August 2001, p. 30.
25. Abner Littel, "Selling to Women Revs up Car Sales," *Personal Selling Power*, July–August 1990, p. 50.
26. "Six Great Upselling Questions," *Personal Selling Power*, April 1993, p. 44.
27. Theodore Kinni, "How to Identify and Remove the Problems Underlying Call Reluctance," *Selling Power*, November/December 2004, pp. 69–71.
28. Alan Farnham, "Are You Smart Enough to Keep Your Job?" *Fortune*, January 15, 1996, pp. 34–42.
29. "The Disappointment Trap," *Selling Power*, January–February 1999, p. 14.
30. Roy Chitwood, "Still Trying to Slip Past Gatekeepers? Forget It." *Value-Added Selling 21*, December 16, 2003, pp. 1–2.

Sources for Boxed Features

a Susan Creco, "Sales: What Works Now," *Inc.*, February 2001, p. 56.

b Jay Winchester, "Ripe for Change," *Sales & Marketing Management*, August 1998, p. 81.

c "International Snapshot," *Sales & Marketing Management*, February 2001, p. 92; Jan Yager. *Business Protocol*, 2nd ed. (Stamford, CT: Hannacroix Books, Inc., 2001), pp. 114–115.

Chapter 11

1. *Going the Distance: The Consultative Sales Presentation* (Pasadena, CA: Intelecom). "The Amgen Difference," (Cited July 23, 2002). www.amgen.com.
2. Louise E. Boone and David L. Kurtz, *Contemporary Marketing*, 11th Ed. (Mason, Ohio: Southwestern Publishing, 2004), p. 576. Geoffrey James, "Consultative Selling Strategies," *Selling Power*, April 2004, pp. 17–20.
3. Rose A. Spinelli, "Listening A Priority In Shopping For Others," *Chicago Tribune*, November 30, 2003, p.55.

4. Ann Demarais and Valerie White, *First Impressions—What You Don't Know About How Other See You* (New York: Bantam Books, 2004), pp. 68–69.
5. Barry L Reece and Rhonda Brandt, *Effective Human Relations: Personal and Organizational Applications* (Boston: Houghton Mufflin Company, 2005), pp. 38–40.
6. Ibid, p. 40.
7. Demarais and White, *First Impressions*, p. 70.
8. Matthew McKay, Martha Davis, and Patrick Fanning; *Message: The Communication Skills Book* (Oakland CA: New Harbringer, 1995), p. 15; Susan Scott, *Fierce Conversation* (NY: Viking 2002), p. 157.
9. William F. Kendy, "How to Be a Good Listener," *Selling Power*, April 2004, p. 43.
10. Tom Reilly, *Value-Added Selling* (New York: McGraw-Hill, 2003), p. 130.
11. Ibid, pp. 17 and 167.
12. Paul F. Roos, "Just Say No," *Selling Power*, October 2003, p. 50.
13. "Presentation-Wise, We've Lost Our Tails," *Sales & Field Force Automation*, July 1999, p. 4.
14. Dean A. Goettsch, "Guidelines for Rethinking Sales Presentions," *Selling*, October 2001, p. 14.
15. Gary A. Williams and Robert B. Miller, "Change the Way You Persuade," *Harvard Business Review*, May 2002, p. 6.
16. Mike Coyne, "How I Made the Sale," *Value-Added Selling 21*, August 12, 2003, pp. 1 and 4.
17. Robert B. Cialdini, "Harnessing the Science of Persuasion," *Harvard Business Review*, October 2001, p. 74.
18. Stephanie G. Sherman and V. Clayton Sherman, *Make Yourself Memorable* (New York: AMACOM, 1996), pp. 58–59.
19. John Grossmann, "Location, Location, Location," *Inc.*, August 2004, p. 83.
20. Thomas A. Stewart, "The Cunning Plots of Leadership," *Fortune*, September 7, 1998, pp. 165–166; Lisa Ferrari, "How to Use Stories to Sell Anything and Everything," *Selling Power*, June 2001, pp. 60–64.
21. Chad Kaydo, "Lights! Camera! Sales!" *Sales & Marketing Management*, February 1998, p. 111.
22. Neil Racham and John DeVincentis, *Rethinking the Sales Force* (New York: McGraw-Hill, 1999), p. 17.

Sources for Boxed Features

[a] Emily Barker, "Start with . . . Nothing," Inc. February 2002, pp. 67–73. "About RightNow Technologies," www.rightnow.com Accessed April 4, 2005.
[b] "International Snapshot," *Sales & Marketing Management*, November 2001, p. 63; Jan Yager, *Business Protocol*, 2nd ed. (Stamford, CT: Hannacroix Books, 2001), pp. 120–121.

Chapter 12

1. *Show and Tell: Custom Fitting the Demonstration* (Pasadena, CA: Intelecom); "SimGraphic Systems." Accessed April 11, 2005, www.simgraphics.com.
2. Larry Tuck, "Presentations That Cut through the Information Clutter," *Sales & Field Force Automation*, June 1999, p. 86; Price Pritchett, *Carpe Manana* (Plano, TX: Pritchett, Rummler-Brache, 2000), p. 3.
3. Ken Taylor, "Help Your Audience Visualize Your Message." *Selling*, April 1998, p. 10, "Visual Aids Close Sales," *Value-Added Selling 21*, December 16, 2003, p. 4.
4. Karen Alberg Grossman, "Well Suited," *Apparel Forum*, Spring 2005, p. 90.
5. Lisa Gschwandtner, "Persuasive Presentation," *Selling Power*, July/August 2001, p. 92.
6. Douglas A. Bernstein, Alison Clarke-Stewart, Edward J. Roy, and Louis A. Penner, *Psychology*, 6th ed. (Boston: Houghton Mifflin, 2003), p. 373–374.
7. Lambeth Hochwald, "Simplify," *Sales & Marketing Management*, June 1998, pp. 66–67; "Company Information." Accessed April 13, 2005, www.bellhelicopter.textron.com.
8. Corbin Ball, "Avoiding Death by PowerPoint" Accessed April 12, 2005, www.corbinball.com.
9. Steve Heimoff, "Taking the Road Less Traveled," *Wine Spectator*, October 31, 1990, pp. 67–70; Jeff Morgan, "Geyser Peak's Turnaround," *Wine Spectator*, November 15, 1995, pp. 37–40. "Eberle Winery," Accessed April 13, 2005, www.eberlewinery.com.
10. Cindy Waxer, "The Lighter Side," *Selling Power*, January/February, 2005, p. 91.
11. Rick Page, *Hope Is Not a Strategy* (Atlanta, GA: Nautilus Press, 2002), pp. 114–115.
12. Joseph B. White, "New Ergonomic Chairs Battle to Save the Backs of Workers, for Big Bucks," *Wall Street Journal*, June 8, 1999, p. B-4B.
13. Rick Page, *Hope Is Not a Strategy* (Atlanta, GA: Nautilus Press, 2000), p. 126.
14. Geoffrey James, "Flight to Profit," *Selling Power*, September 2004, p. 74.
15. Lambeth Hochwald, "Simplify," *Sales & Marketing Management*, June 1998, pp. 65–66.
16. Ginger Trumfio, "Ready! Set! Sell!" *Sales & Marketing Management*, February 1995, pp. 82–84.
17. Landy Chase, "Master the Art of Brochure Selling," *Selling*, March 2005, pp. 8–9; "Colors of Corian," E.I. du Pont de Nemours and Company, 2002.
18. David Ranii, "Dermabond's Debut Disappoints," *News & Observer*, July 31, 1999, p. D-1.
19. "Three Guides to Using Your Catalog as a Sales Tool," *Value-Added Selling 21*, June 17, 2003, p. 4.
20. Heather Baldwin, "Star Light Star Bright," *Selling Power Source Book*, 2002, p. 55.
21. Heather Baldwin, "Up Your Powers," *Selling Power*, October 2001, pp. 88–92.
22. Kevin Ferguson, "Reinventing the PowerPoint," *Inc.* March 2004, p. 42, "Avoiding Death by PowerPoint," Corbin Ball Associates. Accessed April 12, 2005, www.corbinball.com.
23. Gerald L. Manning and Jack W. Linge, *Selling-Today.Com* (Upper Saddle River, NJ: Prentice-Hall, 2004), pp. 26–30
24. Cindy Waxer, "Presenting the Power," *Selling Power*, (Source book) 2005, p. 70–71.
25. Ibid, p. 71.
26. "The Presentation Paper Trail," *Sales & Marketing Management*, March 1995, p. 49.

Sources for Boxed Features

[a] Marc Hequet, "Giving Good Feedback," *Training*, September 1994, p. 74; Molly McGinn, "On Your Own," *News & Observer*, June 27, 1999" Polly Labarre, "Unit of One," *Fast Company*, June 1999, p. 103.
[b] Michael Chylewski, "Memorable Sale," Selling Power, January–February 1999, p. 22.
[c] "International Snapshot," *Sales & Marketing Management*, April 2000, p. 70; Jan Yager, *Business Protocol*, 2nd ed. (Stamford, CT: Hannacroix Books, 2001), p.120.
[d] Jan Norman, "Contracts Go to the People Who Play Game," *Des Moines Register*, June 17, 2002, p. D-1

Chapter 13

1. *Breaking Through: Dealing with Buyer Resistance* (Pasadena, CA: Intelecom). The Stouffer Esmeralda Resort was acquired by Marriott in 1997 and renamed Renaissance Esmeralda Resort. (Interview with Barbara Pierce on July 6, 2002.) "Meetings and Events," Accessed April 21, 2005, www.renaissanceesmeralda.com.
2. Geoff James, "The Art of Sales Negotiation," *Selling Power*, March 2004, pp. 25–28.
3. Tom Reilly, *Value-Added Selling*, (New York: McGraw-Hill, 2003), p. 17.
4. Hal Lancaster, "You Have to Negotiate for Everything in Life, So Get Good at It," *Wall Street Journal*, January 27, 1998, p. B-1.
5. Ron Willingham, *Integrity Selling for the 21st Century*, (New York: Currency Doubleday, 2003), p. 154.
6. Brain Tracy, *The 100 Absolutely Unbreakable Laws of Business Success*, (San Francisco: Berrett-Koehler Publishers, Inc., 2000), p. 235.
7. Ron Willingham, *Integrity Selling for the 21st Century*, p. 153.
8. Gregg Crawford, "Let's Negotiate," *Sales & Marketing Management*, November 1995, pp. 28–29.
9. William F. Kendy, "Solving the 'Friendship Buying' Problem," *Selling Power*, November/December 2001, pp. 40–44.
10. Sarah Mahoney, "Competing against a Long-Term Supplier," *Selling*, June 1998, p. 10.
11. Homer Smith, "How to Cope with Buyers Who Are Trained in Negotiation," *Personal Selling Power*, September 1988, p. 37.
12. Ibid.
13. Robert Adler, Benson Rosen, and Elliot Silverstein, "Thrust and Parry," *Training & Development*, March 1996, p. 47.
14. Homer Smith, "How to Cope with Buyers Who Are Trained in Negotiation," *Personal Selling Power*, September 1988, p. 37.
15. Tom Reilly, *Value-Added Selling* (New York: McGraw-Hill, 2003), pp. 191–192.
16. Joseph Conlin, "Negotiating Their Way to the Top," *Sales & Marketing Management*, April 1996, p. 58.
17. Sam Deep and Lyle Sussman, *Close the Deal: Smart Moves for Selling* (Reading, MA: Perseus Books, 1999), p. 225.
18. Roland M. Sandell, "Five Sure-Fire Methods to Overcome Objections to Price," *American Salesman*, October 1976, p. 38.
19. Alex Taylor, "Little Jets Are Huge," *Fortune*. September 4, 2000, pp. 275–278.
20. Joseph Conlin, "Negotiating Their Way to the Top," *Sales & Marketing Management*, April 1996, p. 62; Neil Rackham, "Winning the Price War," *Sales & Marketing Management*, November 2001, p. 26.
21. David Stiebel, *When Talking Makes Things Worse*! (Dallas: Whitehall & Nolton, 1997), p. 17.
22. Lain Ehman, "Not a Done Deal," *Selling Power*, November/December 2003, pp. 42–44; "Negotiate the Right Price Despite Customer Pressure," *Selling*, July 2004, p. 2.
23. Jeff Keller, "Objections? No Problem," *Selling Power*, September 1996, pp. 44–45.
24. Adapted from Nanci McCann, "Irate over Rates," *Selling*, July—August 1996, p. 25.
25. Tom Reilly, *Value-Added Selling* (New York: McGraw-Hill, 2003), p. 189.
26. See Neil Rackham, *The SPIN Selling Fieldbook* (New York: McGraw-Hill, 1996), pp. 127–145.

Sources for Boxed Features

[a] Hal Lancaster, "You Have to Negotiate for Everything in Life, So Get Good at It," *Wall Street Journal*, January 27, 1998, p. B-1; Amy Lindgren, "Want a Raise? Don't Daydream; Polish Your Negotiating Skills," *Des Moines Register*, April 26, 1998, p. IL. "The Karrass Story," Accessed April 24, 2005, www.Karrass.com.

[b] Timothy Aeppel, "A Factory Manager Improvises to Save Jobs in a Downturn," *Will Street Journal*, December 27, 2001, pp. A-1, A-14.

[c] "Getting to Yes, Chinese Style," *Sales & Marketing Management*, July 1996, pp. 44–45; Sam Deep and Lyle Sussman, *Close the Deal* (Reading, MA: Perseus Books, 1999), pp. 279–281; James K. Sebenius, "Six Habits of Merely Effective Negotiators," *Harvard Business Review*, April 2001, p. 90.

Chapter 14

1. *On the Dotted Line: Closing the Sale*, Pasadena, CA: Intelecom. "Special Events and Meetings," (Cited August 1, 2002). http://themeparks. universal-studios.com.
2. Kristine Ellis, "Deal Maker or Breaker?" *Training*, April 2002, p. 37.
3. Gene Bedell, *3 Steps to Yes* (New York: Crown Business, 2000), pp. 72–80.
4. Tom Reilly, *Value-Added Selling* (New York: McGraw Hill, 2003), p. 176.
5. Andy Cohen, "Are Your Reps Afraid to Close?" *Sales & Marketing Management*, March 1996, p. 43.
6. See Stephen E. Heiman and Dianne Sanchez, *The New Conceptual Selling*, (New York: Warner Books 1999), pp. 117–129.
7. Graham Denton, "The Single Biggest Closing Mistake," Graham Denton Skills Center (Web page) May 4, 1999, p. 1.
8. Ray Dreyfock, "Is the Buyer Ready?" *Selling Power*, January/February 2002, p. 52.
9. "The Closing Moment," *Personal Selling*, October 1995, p. 48; Lain Ehman, "How to Read Hidden Signals," *Selling Power*, June 2004, pp. 36–38.
10. Ron Karr, "Expert Advice—The Titan Principle." *Selling Power*, October 2001, p. 32.
11. Ron Willingham, *Integrity Selling For the 21st Century* (New York: Currency Doubleday, 2003), p. 184.
12. Ron Willingham, *Integrity Selling* (New York: Doubleday, 1987), p. 133.
13. Tom Reilly, *Value-Added Selling*, p. 179.
14. Jenny C. McCune, "The Brief Story of _____ Underwear's Stupendous Success," *Selling*, March 2000, p. 15.
15. Joan Leotta, "The Management Close," *Selling Power*, November/December 2001, pp. 26–28. See Megan Sweas, "Heavyweights on call," *Sales & Marketing Management*, December 2003, p. 14.
16. Jenny McCune, "Closing Sales with a Splash," *Selling*, September 2004, p. 15.
17. "Selling Tips," *Selling*, May 1999, p. 13.
18. Mel Silberman, *Active Training* (New York: Maxwell Macmillan Canada, 1990), pp. 96–99.
19. T. J. Becker, "That Queasy Feeling," *Chicago Tribune*, July 21, 2002, p. W1.
20. Betsy Wiesendanger, "When a Sale Goes South," *Selling Power*, November/December 2003, pp. 65–67.

Sources for Boxed Features

[a] "Ask for the Order," West Des Moines, 1A: Video Learning, LLC, 2004.

[b] Barbara Hagenbough, "Economics Majors Build Brand Name with Unmentionables," *USA Today*, May 20, 2002, p.3-B.

[c] "International Snapshot," *Sales & Marketing Management*, October 2001, p. 70; Jan Yager, *Business Protocol*, 2nd ed. (Stamford, CT: Hannacroix Books, 2001), pp. 116–117.

Chapter 15

1. *The Sales Engine: At the Heart of Economic Development* (Pasadena, CA: Intelecom). "The American Dream," Accessed May 9, 2005. www.bodyglove.com.
2. Bob Johnson, "Loyalty Lessons from the Pros," *Customer Support Management*, July-August 1999, p. 115. Ranjay Gulati and James B. Oldroyd, "The Quest for Customer Focus," *Harvard Business Review*, April 2005, pp. 92–97.
3. Ibid.
4. Gary Armstrong and Philip Kotler, *Marketing—An Introduction*, 6th ed. (Upper Saddle River, NJ: Prentice Hall, 2003), p. 533.
5. Theodore Levitt, *The Marketing Imagination* (New York: Macmillan, 1983), pp. 117–118. Tahl Raz, "The '4 + 2 Formula' for Success," *Inc.*, August 2003, p. 42.
6. Geoffrey Brewer, "The Customer Stops Here," *Sales & Marketing Management*, March 1998, pp. 31–32. See Ron Zemke and Chip Bell, *Service Magic* (Chicago: IL: Dearborn Trade Publishing, 2004).
7. "Why Customers Leave," *Sales & Marketing Management*, May 1998, p. 86; Tom Peters, *The Circle of Innovation* (New York: Vintage Books, 1997), pp. 138–139.
8. Tom Peters, *The Circle of Innovation* (New York: Vintage Books, 1997), p. 464. "Customers for Life" Accessed May 10, 2005, www.sewell.com.
9. Bill Gates, *Business @ The Speed of Thought* (New York: Warner Books, 1999), p. 67.
10. Jill Griffin and Michael Lowenstein, "Winning Back Lost Customers," *Retailing Issues Letter*, March 2001, p. 1.
11. Mack Hanan, *Consultative Selling*, 3rd ed. (New York: AMACOM, 1985), pp. 121–122.
12. Bob Johnson, "Loyalty Lesson from the Pros," *Customer Support Management*, July–August 1999, p. 116.
13. Jim Dey, "Who Is Your Customer?" *Customer Support Management*, July–August 1999, pp. 63–70.
14. Steve Ham, "Oracle—Why It's Cool Again," *Business Week*, May 8, 2000, pp. 115–119.
15. Jack Mitchell, *Hug Your Customers*, (New York: Hyperion 2003), pp. 129–132.
16. Chad Kaydo, "An Unlikely Sales Ally," *Sales & Marketing Management*, January 1999, p. 69.
17. Sally J. Silberman, "An Eye for Finance," *Sales & Marketing Management*, April 1996, p. 26.
18. Benson P. Shapiro, V. Kasturi Rangon, and John J. Sviokla, *Harvard Business Review*. July–August 2004, p. 162.
19. Daryl Allen, "Relationship Selling Is Key to Success," *Selling*, March 2002, p. 12.
20. Tom Reilly, "Create Satisfied Customers: Always Be Sure to Exceed Their Expectations," *Selling*, January 2001, p. 3. Mary Salafia. "Reassessment Planning," *Selling Power*, May 2004, p. 56.
21. Tom Reilly, *Value-Added Selling* (New York: McGraw Hill, 2003), p. 117.
22. Andrea Nierenberg, "Eight Ways to Stay Top of Mind," *Selling*, April 1998, p. 7.
23. Queena Sook Kim, "For Sale: Super-Model Home," *Wall Street Journal*, August 6, 2002, p. D-1.
24. Melinda Ligos, "The Joys of Cross-Selling," *Sales & Marketing Management*, August 1998, p. 75.
25. Tom Reilly, *Value Added Selling*, pp. 124–125.
26. Sara Calabro, "Service First," *Sales & Marketing Management*, November 2004, p. 16.
27. William F. Kendy, "Skills Workshop," *Selling Power*, June 2000, pp. 33–34.
28. Jo Ann Brezette, "Smart Answers to Client's Questions," *Window Fashions Design & Education Magazine*, September 2001, p. 120. Lain Ehman, "Upsell, Don't Oversell," *Selling Power*, January–February 2004, pp. 30–32.
29. "Inspirations from Michele," *Inspiring Solutions*, February 1999, p. 3.
30. Bob Johnson, "Loyalty Lessons from the Pros," *Customer Support Management*, July–August 1999, p. 115.
31. Bradley E. Wesner, "From Complaint to Opportunity," *Selling Power*, May 1996, p. 62.
32. Sam Deep and Lyle Sussman, *Close the Deal: Smart Moves for Selling* (Reading, MA: Perseus Books, 1999), p. 252.
33. Bradley E. Wesner, "From Complaint to Opportunity," *Selling Power*, May 1996, p. 62.
34. Gerald A. Michaelson, "When Things Go Wrong, Make It Right," *Selling*, March 1997, p. 12.
35. Michael Abrams and Matthew Paese, "Wining and Dining the Whiners," *Sales & Marketing Management*, February 1993, p. 73.
36. "How to Diffuse a Customer Problem," *Sales & Marketing Management*, May 2000, p. 14.

Sources for Boxed Features

[a] Jeff Barbian, "It's Who You Know," *Training*, December 2001, p. 22.

[b] "Relationships with Customers Must Be Job Number 1," *Food-Service Distributor*, July 1989, p. 74; Joan O. Fredericks and James M. Salter II, "Beyond Customer Satisfaction," *Management Review*, May 1995, pp. 29–32.

[c] Jan Yager, *Business Protocol*, 2nd ed. (Stamford, CT: Hannacroix Books, 2001), p. 123; "Selling in Russia," *Sales & Marketing Management*, March 2002, p. 60.

[d] Byran Ziegler, "Your Business Card Can Be Powerful Tool," *The Des Moines Register*, August 2, 1999, p. 17-B; Kemba J. Dunham, "Here's My Card," *Wall Street Journal*, May 14, 2002, p. B-12.

Chapter 16

1. Dana Ray, "The Secret of Success," *Personal Selling Power*, November-December 1995, pp. 80–83.
2. Julio Melara, "Time for Action," www.juliomelara.com, Accessed May 16, 2005.
3. Renee Houston Zemanski, "A Matter of Time," *Selling Power*, October 2001, p. 82.
4. Eugene Greissman, "Seven Characteristics of High-Achieving Salespeople," *Value-Added Selling* 21, March 16, 2004, p. 4.
5. Betty Cummings, "Increasing Face Time," *Sales & Marketing Management*, January 2004, p. 12.
6. Barry J. Farber, "Not Enough Hours in the Day," *Sales & Marketing Management*, July 1995, pp. 28–29.
7. If you are interested in how to break bad habits and form good ones, see James Claiborn and Cherry Pedrick, *The Habit Change Workbook* (Oakland, CA: New Harbinger Publications, 2001).
8. See Alison Stein Wellner, "The Time Trap," *Inc.*, June 2004, pp. 42–44.
9. Brian Tracy, *The 100 Absolutely Unbreakable Laws of Business Success* (San Francisco: Berrett-Koehler Publishers, Inc., 2000), pp. 40–47.

10. Charles R. Hall, "Create Excitement, Get Motivated Through Planning," *Selling*, February 2000, p. 13.
11. Ed Brown, "Stephen Covey's New One-Day Seminar," *Fortune*, January 1999, p. 138.
12. Besty Wiesendanger, "Time to Spend," *Selling Power*, November/December 2003, pp. 28. 28–32.
13. Hyrum W. Smith, *The 10 Natural Laws of Successful Time and Life Management* (New York: Warner Books, 1994), p. 108.
14. Thomas E. Weber, "Meetings in Cyberspace May Soon Be as Routine as the Conference Call," *Wall Street Journal*, June 4, 2001, p. B1.
15. Michele Marchetti, "Territories: For Optimal Performance, Segment Your Customer Base by Industry," *Sales & Marketing Management*, December 1998, p. 35.
16. Ken Liebeskind, "Where Is Everyone?" *Selling Power*, March 1998, p. 35; Marie Warner, "Take Careful Steps When Redefining Territories," *Selling*, June 2001, p. 10.
17. Alison Smith, "Plan Your Territory," *Selling Power*, March 2003, pp. 37–38.
18. Daryl Allen, "Maximize Your Territory Coverage, Increased Sales and Higher Profits Will Follow," *Selling*, June 2001, p. 10.
19. Bruce Cryer, Rollin McCraty, and Doc Childre, "Pull the Plug On Stress," *Harvard Business Review*, July 2003, pp. 1–2.
20. David Shenk, "Data Smog," *Perdid*, Spring 1999, pp. 5–7.
21. "More Useful Tips for Running Your Home Office," *Selling*, January 2001, p. 11; "Home Office Etiquette," *Sales & Marketing Management*, January 2000, p. 74.
22. Patricia Sellers, "Now Bounce Back," *Fortune*, May 1, 1995, p. 57.
23. Martin Seligman, *Learned Optimism*, New York: Knoph, 2001, p. 4. Annie Murphy Paul, "Self-Help: Shattering the Myths," *Psychology Today*, March/April 2001, p. 64; Arnold A. Lazarus and Clifford N. Lazarus. *The 60-Second Shrink* (San Luis, Obispo CA: Impact Publishers, 1997), pp. 3, 4.
24. Betsy Cummings, "Sales Ruined My Personal Life," *Sales & Marketing Management*, November 2001, pp. 45–50.
25. Sandra Lotz Fisher, "Stress—Will You Cope or Crack?" *Selling*, May 1996, p. 31.
26. Geoffrey Brewer, "Person-to-Person," *Sales & Marketing Management*, December 1995, p. 29.

Sources for Boxed Features

[a] Amy Finnerty, "Bill Blass, A Designer with Class," *Wall Street Journal*, June 18, 2002, p. D–9; Susan Orlean, *The Bullfighter Checks Her Makeup* (New York: Random House, 2002), pp. 177–187.

[b] Michael Adams, "Family Matters," *Sales & Marketing Management*, March 1998, pp. 61–65.

[c] "Selling in Belgium," *Sales & Marketing Management*, August 2002, p. 58.

[d] Sandra Lotz Fisher, "Stress—Will You Cope or Crack?" *Selling*, May 1996, p. 29.

[e] Kenneth Blanchard, D. W. Edington, and Marjorie Blanchard, *The One-Minute Manager Gets Fit* (New York: William Morrow, 1986), pp. 25–28.

Chapter 17

1. James M. Kouzes and Barry Z. Posner, *The Leadership Challenge*, 3rd ed. (San Francisco: CA, Jossey-Bass 2002), pp. 3–12.
2. Robert Kreitner, *Management* 9th ed. (Boston: Houghton Mifflin Company, 2004), p. 503.
3. "Stephen Covey Talks About the 8th Habit: Effective Is No Longer Enough," *Training*, February 2005, pp.17–19.
4. James M. Kouzes and Barry Z. Posner, *The Leadership Challenge*, pp. 13–20. The difference between leadership and management is discussed in Michael Feiner, *The Feiner Points of Leadership* (New York: Warner Business Books 2004), pp. 16–30.
5. Michael R. Solomon, Greg W. Marshall, and Elnora W. Stuart, *Marketing—Real People, Real Choices*, 4th ed. (Upper Saddle River, NJ, 2006), p. 444.
6. Jack Falvey, "Fly by Night, Sell by Day," *Wall Street Journal*, June 9, 1997, p. A-18.
7. Lisa Gschwandtner, "What Makes an Ideal Sales Manager," *Selling Power*, June 2001, p. 54.
8. William Keenan Jr., "Death of the Sales Manager," *Sales & Marketing Management*, April 1998, pp. 72–79.
9. Alan J. Dubinsky, Francis J. Yammarino, Marvin A. Jolson, and William D. Spangler, "Transformational Leadership: An Initial Investigation in Sales Management," *Journal of Personal Selling & Sales Management*, Spring 1995, pp. 17–29.
10. These dimensions are described in Edwin A. Fleischman, *Manual for Leadership Opinion Questionnaire* (Chicago: Science Research Associates, 1960), p. 3. The dimensions of consideration and structure are also described in Robert Kreitner, *Management*, 9th ed. (Boston: Houghton Mifflin Company, 2004), p. 506.
11. Brian Tracy, *The 100 Absolutely Unbreakable Laws of Business Success* (San Francisco: Berrett-Koehler Publishers, 2000), pp. 19–20.
12. Jared Sandberg, "Overcontrolling Bosses Aren't Just Annoying; They're Also Inefficient," *Wall Street Journal*, March 30, 2005, p. B1.
13. Sarah Lorge, "In the Box," *Sales & Marketing Management*, April 1998, p. 15.
14. Ken Blanchard, "3 Secrets of the One Minute Manager," *Personal Selling Power*, March 1993, p. 48.
15. Robert Kreitner, *Management*, 9th ed., (Boston: Houghton Mifflin, 2004), p. 508, Paul Hersey, *The Situational Leader* (Escondido, CA: Center for Leadership Studies, 1984), pp. 29–30.
16. Ron Zemke, "Trust Inspires Trust," *Training*, January 2002, p. 10; William F. Kendy, "Build Trust—Don't Destroy It," *Selling Power*, July/August 2001, p. 56.
17. Kenneth R. Phillips, "The Achilles' Heel of Coaching," *Training & Development*, March 1998, p. 41.
18. Anne Fisher, "In Praise of Micromanaging," *Fortune*, August 23, 2004, p. 40.
19. Anne fisher, "Essential Employees Called Up to Serve," *Fortune*, October 2000, p. 210.
20. Dana Telford and Adrian Gostick, "Hiring Character," *Sales and Marketing Management*, June 2005, pp. 39–42.
21. Andy Cohen, "What Keeps You Up at Night?" *Sales & Marketing Management*, February 2000, pp. 44–52.
22. Gerhard Gschwandtner, "A Jewel of a Company," *Personal Selling Power*, March 1995, p. 17.
23. "Sales Achievement Predictor," www.wpspublish.com, Accessed June 8, 2005.
24. "Hiring & Selection," www.calipercorp.com. Accessed June 8, 2005.
25. Alan J. Dubinsky, Francis J. Yammarino, Marvin A. Jolson, and William D. Spangler, "Transformational Leadership: An Initial Investigation in Sales

Management," *Journal of Personal Selling & Sales Management*, Spring 1995, p. 27.
26. Skip Corsini, "The Great (Sales) Training Robbery," *Training*, February 2005, p. 14.
27. Barry L. Reece and Rhonda Brandt, *Effective Human Relations: Personal and Organizational Applications*, 9th ed. (Boston: Houghton Mifflin, 2005), p. 161–162.
28. Ibid., p. 162.
29. Audrey Bottjen, "Incentives Gone Awry," *Sales & Marketing Management*, May 2001, p. 72.
30. Julie Chang, "Trophy Value," *Sales & Marketing Management*, October 2004, p. 26.
31. Carol Hymorwitz, "When Meeting Targets Becomes the Strategy, CEO Is on Wrong Path," *Wall Street Journal*, March 8, 2005, p. B1. Carol Hymorwitz, "Readers Share Tales of Jobs Where Strategy Became Meeting Target," *Wall Street Journal*, March 22, 2005, p. B1.
32. Michael Schrage, "A Lesson in Perversity," *Sales and Marketing Management*, January 2004, p. 28.
33. Eilene Zimmerman, "Quota Busters," *Sales & Marketing Management*, January 2001, pp. 59–63.
34. Christine Galea, "2005 Compensation Survey," *Sales & Marketing Management*, May 2005, pp. 24–29.
35. "Point Incentive Sales Programs," *SBR Update*, Vol. I, No. 4.
36. Donald W. Jackson Jr., John L. Schlacter, and William G. Wolfe, "Examining the Bases Utilized for Evaluating Salespeople's Performance," *Journal of Personal Selling & Sales Management*, February 1995, p. 57.
37. "Survey of Sales Evaluation Process—What Works, What Doesn't," *Selling Power*, September 1999, p. 115.
38. Lisa Holton, "Look Who's in on Your Performance Review," *Selling*, January–February 1995, pp. 47–55: Barry L. Reece and Rhonda Brandt, *Effective Human Relations: Personal and Organizational Applications* (Boston: Houghton Mifflin, 2005), p. 195; "Customer Ratings Are Misleading," *Selling*, November 1996, p. 1.

Sources for Boxed Features

[a] Dan Hanover, "Independents Day," *Sales & Marketing Management*, April 2000, pp. 65–68.
[b] Douglas J. Dalrymple and William L. Cron, *Sales Management: Concepts and Cases* (New York: John Wiley & Sons, 1998), pp. 344–347; William Keenan, "Time Is Everything," *Sales & Management*, August 1993, p. 61.
[c] Jan Yager, *Business Protocol*, 2nd ed., (Stamford, CT: Hannocroix Creek Books. 2000), p. 124.

GLOSSARY

A

active listening The process of sending back to the person what you as a listener think the individual meant, both in terms of content and in terms of feelings. It involves taking into consideration both verbal and nonverbal signals.

adaptive selling Used to describe sales training programs that encourage salespeople to adjust their communication style to accommodate the communication style of the customer.

added-value negotiating A negotiating process where both the seller and the customer search for mutual value so both feel more comfortable after a sale.

approach The first contact with the prospect, either face-to-face or by telephone. The approach has three objectives: to build rapport with the prospect, to capture the person's full attention, and to generate interest in the product you are selling.

assumptive close After the salesperson identifies a genuine need, presents solutions in terms of buyer benefits, conducts an effective sales demonstration, and negotiates buyer resistance satisfactorily, the assumption is that the prospect has already bought the product. The closing activity is based on the assumption that a buying decision has already been made.

B

balance sheet close A closing method that appeals to customers who are having difficulty making a decision. The salesperson draws a T on a sheet of paper and places captions on each side of the crossbar: reasons for buying now (left) and reasons for not buying now (right).

benefit A feature that provides the customer with personal advantage or gain. This usually answers the question, "How will the customer benefit from owning or using the product?"

body language A form of nonverbal communication that has been defined as "messages without words" and "silent messages."

bridge statement A transitional phrase that connects a statement of features with a statement of benefits. This method permits customers to connect the features of your product to the benefits they will receive.

business buyer behavior Refers to the organizations that buy goods and services for use in the production of other products and services that are sold, rented, or supplied to others.

business casual Clothing that allows you to feel comfortable at work but looks neat and professional.

business ethics Comprises principles and standards that guide behavior in the world of business.

buyer's remorse Feelings of regret, fear, or anxiety that a buyer may feel after placing an order.

buyer resolution theory A selling theory that recognizes a purchase will be made only after the prospect has made five buying decisions involving specific affirmative responses to the following items: need, product, source, price, and time.

buying conditions Those circumstances that must be available or fulfilled before the sale can be closed.

buying motives An aroused need, drive, or desire that initiates the sequence of events that may lead to a purchase.

buying process A systematic series of actions, or a series of defined, repeatable steps intended to achieve a result.

C

call report A written summary that provides information on a sales call to people in the sales organization so that follow-up action will be taken when necessary.

caveat emptor A philosophy that states, "Let the buyer beware." The buyer is expected to examine the product and presentation carefully. Once the transaction is concluded, the business relationship ends for all practical purposes.

character Your personal standards of behavior, including your honesty and integrity. Your character is based on your internal values and the resulting judgments you make about what is right and what is wrong.

closed questions These questions can be answered with a yes or no, or a brief response.

closing clue An indication, either verbal or nonverbal, that the prospect is preparing to make a buying decision.

coaching An interpersonal process between a sales manager and a salesperson in which the manager helps the salesperson improve performance in a specific area.

cold calling A method of prospecting in which the salesperson selects a group of people who may or may not be actual prospects and then calls on each one.

combination close With the combination close, the salesperson tries to use two or more closing methods at the same time.

commodity A product that is nearly identical or appears to be the same as competing products in the customer's mind.

communication-style bias A state of mind we often experience when we have contact with another person whose communication style is different from our own.

communication style The patterns of behavior that others observe.

compensation plans Pay plans for salespeople that combine direct monetary pay and indirect monetary payments such as paid vacations, pensions, and insurance plans.

complex buying decision These decisions are characterized by a high degree of involvement by the consumer.

confirmation questions A type of question used throughout the sales presentation to find out if the message is getting through to the prospect. It checks both the prospect's level of understanding and the prospect's agreement with the presentation's claims.

confirmation step Reassuring the customer after the sale has been closed, pointing out that he has made the correct decision. This may involve describing the satisfaction of owning the product.

consideration Sales managers displaying consideration are more likely to have relationships with salespeople that are characterized by mutual trust, respect for the salesperson's ideas, and consideration for their feelings.

consultative selling An approach to personal selling that is an extension of the marketing concept. Emphasis is placed on need identification, need satisfaction, and the building of a relationship that results in repeat business.

consumer buyer behavior The buying behavior of individuals and households who buy goods and services for personal consumption.

contract A promise or promises that the courts will enforce.

cooling-off laws The primary purpose of these laws is to give customers an opportunity to reconsider a buying decision.

cost-benefit analysis This involves listing the costs to the buyer and the savings to be achieved. A common approach to quantifying the solution.

cross selling Selling products to an established customer that are not directly related to products the customer has already bought.

culture The arts, beliefs, institutions, transmitted behavior patterns, and thoughts of a community or population.

customer relationship management (CRM) The process of building and maintaining strong customer relationships by providing customer value. A modern CRM program relies on a variety of technologies to enhance customer responsiveness.

customer service All those activities enhancing or facilitating the sale and use of a product or service, including suggestion selling, delivery and installation, assistance with warranty or service contract, securing credit arrangements, and making postsale courtesy calls.

customer service representative These people process reservations, accept orders by phone or by other means, deliver products, handle customer complaints, provide technical assistance, and assist salespeople.

customer strategy A carefully conceived plan that will result in maximum responsiveness to the customer's needs. The salesperson should develop an understanding of customer's buying process, understand buyer behavior, and develop a prospect base.

D

demonstration A sales technique that adds sensory appeal to the product. It attracts the customer's attention, stimulates interest, and creates desire.

detail salesperson A salesperson representing a manufacturer, whose primary goal is to develop goodwill and stimulate demand for a product or product line. This person usually assists the customer by improving the customer's ability to sell the product.

differentiation Refers to your ability to separate yourself and your product from that of your competitors.

direct appeal close Involves simply asking for the order in a straightforward manner. It is the most direct closing approach.

direct denial Involves refuting prospect's opinion or belief. The direct denial of a problem is considered a high-risk method of negotiating buyer resistance.

Director style A communication style that displays the following characteristics: appears to be businesslike, displays a serious attitude, and voices strong opinions.

dominant buying motive The buying motive that has the greatest influence on a customer's buying decision.

dominance Reflects the tendency to influence or exert one's will over others in a relationship. Each of us falls somewhere on this continuum.

double win The view that "if I help you win, I win too."

E

electronic business Involves the use of intranets, extranets, and the Internet to conduct a company's business. Customer relation management (CRM) software is an important element of electronic business.

electronic commerce A specific form of e-business such as buying and selling activities conducted on Internet.

emotional buying motives Those motives that prompt the prospect to act as a result of an appeal to some sentiment or passion.

emotional intelligence The capacity for recognizing our own feelings and those of others, for motivating ourselves, and for managing emotions well in ourselves and in our relationships.

emotional links The connectors that link the salesperson's message to the customer's internal emotions and increase the chance of closing a sale—for example, quality improvement, on-time delivery, service, and innovation.

Emotive style A communication style that displays the following characteristics: appears to be quite active, takes the social initiative in most cases, likes to encourage informality, and expresses emotional opinions.

entry-level sales representative Anyone who is learning about the company's products, services, and policies, as well as proven sales techniques, in preparation for a sales assignment.

esteem needs The desire to feel worthy in the eyes of others, to develop a sense of personal worth and adequacy or a feeling of competence and importance.

ethics Rules of conduct used to determine what is good or bad. They are moral principles or values concerned with what ought to be done—a person's adherence to honesty and fairness.

expected product Everything that represents the customer's minimal expectations.

external motivation Action (taken by another person) that involves rewards or other forms of reinforcement that cause the worker to behave in ways to ensure receipt of the reward.

extranet This is a private Internet site that enables several companies to securely share information and conduct business.

F

feature Anything that a customer can feel, see, taste, smell, or measure to answer the question, "What is it?" Features include technical facts about such aspects as craftsmanship, durability, design, and economy of operation.

field salesperson A salesperson employed by a manufacturer who handles well-established products that require a minimum of creative selling. The position usually does not require a high degree of technical knowledge.

full-line selling This selling approach, sometimes called suggestion selling, is the process of recommending products or services that are related to the main item sold to the customer.

G

generic product Describes only the basic substantive product being sold.

group influences Buyer behavior is influenced by the people around us. Group influences are the forces that other people exert on buying behavior.

H

habitual buying decisions These decisions usually require very little consumer involvement and brand differences are usually insignificant.

I

incremental commitment When working on a large, complex sale, some form of commitment should be obtained during each step in the multicall sales presentation.

indirect denial Often used when the prospect's concern is completely valid, or at least accurate to a large degree. The salesperson bends a little and acknowledges that the prospect is at least partially correct.

information-gathering questions Questions used to collect certain basic information from the prospect. These questions help the salesperson to acquire facts about the prospect that may reveal the person's need for the product or service.

informative presentation Emphasizes factual information that is often taken from technical reports, company-prepared sales literature, or written testimonials from people who have used the product.

inside salesperson A salesperson employed by a wholesaler who solicits orders over the telephone. In addition to extensive product knowledge, the inside salesperson must be skilled in customer relations, merchandising, and suggestion selling.

integrity Part of your character. It is what you have when your behavior is in accordance with your professed standards and personal code of moral values.

intermediate sales representative A salesperson who has broad knowledge of the company's products and services and sells in a specifically assigned territory. She maintains contact with established customers and develops new prospects.

internal motivation An intrinsic reward that occurs when a duty or task is performed.

interpersonal value Win-win relationship building with the customer that results from keeping that person's best interest always at the forefront.

M

management close Involving the sales manager or a senior executive to assist with the close.

marketing concept A belief that the business firm should dedicate all its policies, planning, and operation to the satisfaction of the customer; a belief that the final result of all business activity should be to earn a profit by satisfying the customer.

marketing mix The combination of elements (product, promotion, place, and price) that creates continuing customer satisfaction for a business.

modified rebuy A situation where the customer wishes to modify product specifications, change delivery schedules, or renegotiate prices.

multicall sales presentations A standard practice in some industries where products are complex and buying decisions are made by more than one person. The purpose of the first call is to collect and analyze certain basic information that is used to develop a specific proposal.

multiple options close With the multiple options close, the salesperson gives the prospect several options to consider and tries to assess the prospect's degree of interest in each.

N

need discovery The salesperson establishes two-way communication by asking appropriate questions and listening carefully to the customer's responses.

need-satisfaction questions Designed to move the sales process toward commitment and action. These are questions that focus on the solution.

negotiation Working to reach an agreement that is mutually satisfactory to both buyer and seller.

networking Networking is the practice of making and using contacts. It involves people meeting people and profiting from the connection.

new-task buy A first time purchase of a product or service.

nonverbal messages These are "messages without words" or "silent messages." These are messages we communicate through facial expressions, voice tone, gestures, appearance, and posture.

O

open questions These questions require the prospect to go beyond a simple yes/no response.

opportunity management It should be viewed as a four-dimensional process consisting of time management, territory management, records management, and stress management.

organizational culture A collection of beliefs, behaviors, and work patterns held in common by people employed by a specific firm.

outside salesperson A salesperson, employed by a wholesaler, who must have knowledge of many products and be able to serve as a consultant to the customer on product or service applications. This position usually requires an in-depth understanding of the customer's operation.

P

partnering A strategically developed, high-quality relationship that focuses on solving the customer's buying problem.

patronage buying motives A motive that causes the prospect to buy a product from one particular company rather than another. Typical patronage buying motives include superior service, attractive decor, product selection, and competence of the salesperson.

perception A process whereby we receive stimuli (information) through our five senses and then assign meaning to them.

personal digital assistants These small pocket size organizers offer many features common to laptop computers.

personality The thoughts, feelings, and actions that characterize someone.

personal selling Involves person-to-person communication with a prospect. It is a process of developing relationships; discovering customer's needs; matching appropriate products with these needs; and communicating benefits through informing, reminding, or persuading.

personal selling philosophy Involves three things: full acceptance of the marketing concept, developing an appreciation for the expanding role of personal selling in our competitive national and international markets, and assuming the role of problem solver or partner in helping customers to make complex buying decisions.

persuasion The act of presenting product appeals so as to influence the prospect's beliefs, attitudes, or behavior.

persuasive presentation A sales strategy that influences the prospect's beliefs, attitudes, or behavior, and encourages buyer's action.

physiological needs Primary needs or physical needs, including the need for food, water, sleep, clothing, and shelter.

portfolio A portable case or loose-leaf binder containing a wide variety of sales-supporting materials. It is used to add visual life to the sales message and to prove claims.

positioning Refers to decisions, activities, and communication strategies that are directed toward trying to create and maintain a firm's intended product concept in the customer's mind.

postpone method When selling a complex product, it is often necessary to postpone negotiations until you can complete the needs assessment or acquire additional information regarding such things as final price or delivery dates.

potential product Refers to what may remain to be done, that is, what is possible.

preapproach Activities that precede the actual sales call and set the stage for a personalized sales approach, tailored to the specific needs of the prospect. This involves the planning necessary for the actual meeting with a prospect.

premium approach Involves giving the customer a free sample or an inexpensive item. This is an effective way to get the customer's attention.

presentation strategy A well-conceived plan that includes three prescriptions: establishing objectives for the sales presentation; preparing the presale presentation plan needed to meet these objectives; and renewing one's commitment to providing outstanding customer service.

probing questions Helps you uncover and clarify the prospects buying problem and the circumstances surrounding the problem.

product One element of the marketing mix. The term *product* should be broadly interpreted to encompass goods, services, and ideas.

product buying motives Reasons that cause the prospect to buy one particular product brand or label over another. Typical product buying motives include brand preference, quality preference, price preference, and design or engineering preference.

product configuration If the customer has complex buying needs, then the salesperson may have to bring together many different parts of the company's product mix in order to develop a custom-fitted solution. The product selection process is often referred to as product configuration.

product development Testing, modifying, and retesting an idea for a product several times before offering it to the customer.

product life cycle Stages of a product from the time it is first introduced to the market until it is taken off the market, including the stages of introduction, growth, maturity, and decline.

product strategy A well-conceived plan that emphasizes acquiring extensive product knowledge, learning to select and communicate appropriate product benefits that will appeal to the customer, and configuring value-added solutions.

promotional allowance A price reduction given to a customer who participates in an advertising or sales support program.

proof devices A proof device can take the form of a statement, a report, a testimonial, customer data, or a photograph.

prospect Someone who has three basic qualifications. First, the person must have a need for the product or service. Second, the individual must be able to afford the purchase. Third, the person must be authorized to purchase the product.

prospect base A list of current customers and potential customers.

prospecting A systematic process of identifying potential customers.

psychic income Consists of factors that provide psychological rewards; helps to satisfy these needs and motivates us to achieve higher levels of performance.

Q

qualifying Examining the prospect list to identify the people who are most apt to buy a product.

quality control The evaluation or testing of products against established standards. This has important sales appeal when used by the salesperson to convince a prospect of a product's quality.

quantifying the solution The process of determining if a sales proposal adds value. Quantifying the solution is especially important in situations where the purchase represents a major buying decision.

quantity discount A price reduction made to encourage a larger volume purchase than would otherwise be expected.

R

rational buying motives Prompt the prospect to act because of an appeal to the prospect's reason or better judgment; include profit potential, quality, and availability of technical assistance. Generally these result from an objective review of available information.

reciprocity A mutual exchange of benefits, as when a firm buys products from its own customers.

reference group Two or more people who have well-established interpersonal communications and tend to influence the values, attitudes, and buying behaviors of one another. They act as a point of comparison and a source of information for a prospective buyer.

referral A prospect who has been recommended by a current customer or by someone who is familiar with the product.

Reflective style A communication style that displays the following characteristics: controls emotional expression, displays a preference for orderliness, tends to express measured opinions, and seems difficult to get to know.

relationship selling Salespeople who have adopted relationship selling work hard to build and nourish long-term partnerships. They rely on a personal, customized approach to each customer.

relationship strategy A well-thought-out plan for establishing, building, and maintaining quality relationships.

reminder presentation Sometimes called the reinforcement presentation. This assumes that the prospect has already been involved in an informative or persuasive presentation. The customer understands at least the basic product features and buyer benefits.

retail salesperson Salesperson who is employed at the retail level to help prospects solve buying problems. This person is usually involved in selling higher priced, technical, and specialty retail products.

return on investment A formula used to determine the net profits or savings from a given investment. It is a common way to quantify the solution.

role A set of characteristics and expected social behaviors based on the expectations of others. All the roles we assume may influence our buying behavior.

routing The procedure used to determine which customers and prospects will be visited during a certain period of time.

S

sales automation A term used to describe those technologies used to improve communications in a sales organization and improve customer responsiveness. These activities are used to improve the productivity of the sales force and the sales support personnel.

sales call plan A plan developed with information taken from the routing and scheduling plan. The primary purpose of the plan is to ensure efficient and effective account coverage.

sales call reluctance Includes the thoughts, feelings, and behavioral patterns that conspire to limit what a salesperson can accomplish.

sales engineer A person who must have detailed and precise technical knowledge and the ability to discuss the technical aspects of his products. He sometimes introduces new products that represent a breakthrough in technology.

sales forecast Outlines expected sales for a specific product or service to a specific target group over a specific period of time.

sales management The process of planning, implementing, and controlling the personal selling function.

sales territory A geographic area where prospects and customers reside.

satisfactions The positive benefits that customers seek when making a purchase.

Satisfactions arise from the product itself, from the company that makes or distributes the product, and from the salesperson who sells and services the product.

seasonal discount Adjusting prices up or down during specific times to spur or acknowledge changes in demand.

security needs These needs represent our desire to be free from danger and uncertainty.

self-actualization The need for self-fulfillment; a full tapping of one's potential to meet a goal; the need to be everything one is capable of being. This is one of the needs in Maslow's hierarchy.

self-image A set of ideas, attitudes, and feelings you have about yourself that influences the way you relate to others.

self-talk An effort to override past negative mental programming by erasing or replacing it with conscious, positive new directions. It is one way to get rid of barriers to goal achievement.

senior sales representative A salesperson at the highest nonsupervisory level of selling responsibility. She is completely familiar with the company's products, services, and policies; usually has years of experience; and is assigned to major accounts and territories.

situational leadership This leadership approach is based on the theory that the most successful leadership occurs when the leader's style matches the situation.

six-step presentation plan Preparation involving consideration of those activities that will take place during the sales presentation.

sociability Reflects the amount of control one exerts over emotional expressiveness. People who are high in sociability tend to express their feelings freely, while people who are low on this continuum tend to control their feelings.

social class A group of people who are similar in income, wealth, educational background, and occupational prestige.

social needs Needs that reflect a person's desire for affection, identification with a group, and approval from others.

solution A mutually shared answer to a recognized customer problem. In many selling situations, a solution is more encompassing than a specific product.

special concession close Offers the buyer something extra for acting immediately.

stall Resistance related to time. A stall usually means the customer does not yet perceive the benefits of buying now.

straight rebuy A routine purchase of items needed by a business-to-business customer.

strategic alliance These alliances are achieved by teaming up with another company whose products or services fit well with your own.

strategic planning A managerial process that matches the firms resources to its market opportunities. It takes into consideration the various functional areas of the business that must be coordinated such as financial assets, workforce, production capabilities, and marketing.

strategies The things that salespeople do as the result of pre-call planning to ensure they call on the right people, at the right time, and with the right tactics to achieve positive results.

stress The response of the body or mind to demands on it, in the form of either physiological or psychological strain.

structure Sales managers clearly defining their own duties and those of the sales staff. They assume an active role in directing their subordinates.

style flexing The deliberate attempt to adjust one's communication style to accommodate the needs of the other person.

subculture Within many cultures the groups whose members share ideals and beliefs that differ from those held by the wider society of which they are a part.

suggestion selling The process of suggesting merchandise or services that are related to the main item being sold to the customer. This is an important form of customer service.

summary-confirmation questions Questions used to clarify and confirm buying conditions.

summary-of-benefits close Involves summarizing the most important buyer benefits, reemphasizing the benefits that will help bring about a favorable decision.

superior benefit A benefit that will, in most cases, outweigh the customer's specific concern.

Supportive style A communication style that displays the following characteristics: appears quiet and reserved, listens attentively to other people, tends to avoid the use of power, and makes decisions in a thoughtful and deliberate manner.

survey questions Questions used to collect information about the buyer's exiting situation and problem.

systems selling A form of strategic alliance that appeals to buyers who prefer to purchase a packaged solution to a problem from a single seller, thus avoiding all the separate decisions involved in a complex buying situation.

T

tactics Techniques, practices, or methods salespeople use during face-to-face interactions with customers.

target market A well-defined set of present and potential customers that an organization attempts to serve.

telemarketing The practice of marketing goods and services through telephone contact.

telesales The process of using the telephone to acquire information about the customer, determine needs, suggest solutions, negotiate buyer resistance, close the sale, and service the sale.

territory The geographic area where prospects and customers reside.

trade discount This discount covers the cost of services (credit, storage, or transportation) offered by channel intermediaries such as wholesalers.

transactional selling A type of selling that most effectively matches the needs of the value-conscious buyer who is primarily interested in price and convenience.

trial close A closing attempt made at an opportune time during the sales presentation to encourage the customer to reveal readiness or unwillingness to buy.

trial offer Involves giving the prospect an opportunity to try the product without making a purchase commitment.

U

unconscious expectations Certain views concerning appropriate dress.

upselling An effort to sell better quality products that will, in many cases, add value.

unbundling A strategy used to reduce the price by eliminating some items.

V

values Deep personal beliefs and preferences that influence your behavior.

value-added strategies Adding value to a product with a cluster of intangibles such as better trained salespeople, increased levels of courtesy, dependable product deliveries, better service after the sale, and innovations that truly improve the product's value in the customer's eyes.

value-added product Product that exists when salespeople offer the customers more than they expect.

value proposition A value proposition is the set of benefits and values the company promises to deliver to customers to satisfy their needs.

value reinforcement This strategy involves getting credit for the value you create for the customer.

variety-seeking buying decisions These are characterized by low customer involvement, but important perceived brand differences.

versatility Describes our ability to minimize communication style bias.

visualize To form a mental image of something you want to succeed at.

W

wardrobe engineering Combining the elements of psychology, fashion, sociology, and art into clothing selection.

Web site A collection of Web pages maintained by a single person or organization. It is accessible to anyone with a computer and a modem.

written proposals A specific plan of action based on the facts, assumptions, and supporting documentation included in the sales presentation. Written proposals vary in terms of format and content.

CREDITS

Chapter 3

Fig. 3.5: Source: Moravian Study of Nonverbal Communications, p. 66.

Chapter 6

Fig. 6.3: Courtesy of GEAR For Sports, p. 143.

Chapter 9

Fig. 9.2: Courtesy of Dun & Bradstreet, p. 222.

Chapter 13

Fig. 13.3: Reprinted by permission of Warner Books, p. 334.

Fig. 13-4: © 2004 Time Inc. All rights reserved, p. 328.

Chapter 14

Fig. 14.4: Courtesy of Beth Manning, Jody Sprock Interiors & Associates, p. 357.

Chapter 17

Fig. 17.1: Courtesy of Houghton Mifflin, p. 420.

Advertisement Credits:

p. 20: Courtesy of Campbell's Soup Company. **p. 21:** Courtesy of Cushman & Wakefield, Inc. **p. 23:** Courtesy of Sales Logix Corporation. **p. 24:** Courtesy of Wisconsin Milk Marketing Board, Inc. **p. 46:** Courtesy of CMR Institute. **p. 58:** Courtesy of Brakebush Brothers, Inc. **p. 72:** Used by permission of HarperCollins Publishers. **p. 73:** Courtesy of Pivotal. **p. 96:** Copyright © 1987. Reprinted with permission of John Wiley & Sons, Inc. **p. 113:** Courtesy of The Saint Paul. **p. 118:** Used by permission of Doubleday, a devision of Random House, Inc. **p. 131:** Copyright © 2004. Reprinted by permission of The McGraw-Hill Companies, Inc. **p. 133:** Courtesy of Mclhenny Company. **p. 135:** Courtesy of Busch Inc. **p. 139:** Reprinted by permission of Sea Ray. **p. 140:** Courtesy of BOC. **p. 144:** Courtesy of Bar-S. **p. 165:** Courtesy of FMC FoodTech. **p. 171:** Copyright © 2004. Reprinted by permission of The McGraw-Hill Companies, Inc. **p. 172:** Courtesy of Parametric Technology Corporation. **p. 174:** Courtesy of LEXUS. **p. 186:** Reprinted by permission of Christina B. Bliss. **p. 188:** Courtesy of Yerecic Label. **p. 192:** Reprinted by permission of Avaya. **p. 198:** Courtesy of DaimlerChrysler Motor Company. **p. 201:** Courtesy of Formax Inc. **p. 211:** Courtesy of Hancock Information Group. **p. 216:** Courtesy of Thomas Register. **p. 220:** Courtesy of InfoUSA. **p. 225:** Reprinted by permission of Ballantine Books, a Division of Random House Inc. Used by permission of Ballantine Books, a division of Random House, Inc. **p. 237:** Courtesy of Personal Selling Power. **p. 241:** Courtesy of The Jackson Group. **p. 243:** Courtesy of Complex Sale, Inc. **p. 244:** Microsoft product screen shot(s) screen shot reprinted with permission from Microsoft Corporation. **p. 254:** Courtesy of ConAgra Foods, Inc. **p. 272:** Copyright © 1996. Reprinted by permission of The McGraw-Hill Companies, Inc. **p. 277:** Courtesy of Nash Finch Company. **p. 293:** Courtesy of SIMS Graphic. **p. 298:** Courtesy of Tone Brother. **p. 300:** Courtesy of Bell Helicopter Textron. **p. 301:** Reprinted by permission of QBS Publishing (May 17, 2001). **p. 303:** Courtesy of Moody Dunbar, Inc. **p. 310:** Microsoft product screen shot(s) screen shot reprinted with permission from Microsoft Corporation. **p. 311:** Courtesy of Iowa Realty. **p. 313:** Courtesy of InFocus Corporation. **p. 322:** Fast Company, December 1998. **p. 342:** Courtesy of PLUS. **p. 344:** Copyright © 2000 by Gene Bedell. Used by permission of Crown Publishers, a division of Random House, Inc. **p. 348:** Courtesy of IAFTO. **p. 365:** Courtesy of Body Glove Wetsuites. **p. 367:** Reprinted by permission of Harper Collins. **p. 369:** Courtesy of The Sewell Family of Dealership. **p. 375:** Courtesy of Zero Mountain Inc. **p. 377:** Courtesy of Eastern Shore Seafood. **p. 380:** Copyright © 1999. Reprinted by permission of The McGraw-Hill Companies, Inc. **p. 405:** Courtesy of TerrAlign Group. **p. 418:** Copyright © 1995 John Wiley & Sons, Inc. Reprinted with permission of John Wiley & Sons, Inc. **p. 423:** Courtesy of CYDCOR. **p. 428:** Courtesy of Selling Power. **p. 431:** Courtesy of Icelandic.

Photo Credits:

p. 2: Lonny Kalfus/Stone/Getty Images. **p. 7:** Hammer & Company. **p. 8:** RON CHAPPLE/ Getty Images, Inc. – Taxi. **p. 11:** AP Wide World Photos. **p. 12:** Jon Feingersh/Masterfile Corporation. **p. 14:** Andrew Wakeford/Getty Images, Inc. – Photodisc./PhotoDisc/Getty Images Inc. **p. 16:** Sigrid Estrada/Photo Credit – Sigrid Estrada. **p. 17:** Patricia Seybold Group. **p. 32 top:** Todd Hido. **p. 32 bottom:** The Speakers Group. **p. 33:** Brian Tracy International/Brian Tracy International. **p. 37:** SuperStock, Inc. **p. 41:** Jose Luis Pelaez/Corbis/Bettmann. **p. 52:** Getty Images, Inc. – Taxi. **p. 55:** Frank Ward. **p. 56:** Rob Levine/Corbis/Bettmann. **p. 57 top:** Getty Images/Digital Vision. **p. 57 bottom:** Carol Kaplan. **p. 62:** Franklin Covey. **p. 64:** SuperStock, Inc. **p. 65:** Coxe's Enterprises/ Courtesy of Gary Coxe. **p. 68:** David P. Hall/ Masterfile Corporation. **p. 71:** arnoldadler.com. **p. 74:** Getty Images, Inc. – Taxi. **p. 81:** Stan Honda/Stan Honda/Agence France Presse/Getty Images. **p. 83:** Bruce Ayres/Getty Images Inc. – Stone Allstock. **p. 84:** AFP/ Paul Buck/Agence France Presse/Getty Images. **p. 88:** Harpo Production/AP Wide World Photos. **p. 89:** AP Wide World Photos. **p. 93 top:** Tim Graham Picture Library/AP Wide World Photos. **p. 93 bottom:** SuperStock, Inc. **p. 97:** AP Wide World Photos. **p. 99:** Charles Thatcher/Getty Images Inc. – Stone Allstock. **p. 109 top:** Matt Campbell/Getty Images, Inc. **p. 109 bottom:** Jose Luis Pelaez/Corbis/Bettmann. **p. 115:** Steve Niedorf/Getty Images Inc. – Image Bank. **p. 117:** Jim Craigmyle/Masterfile Corporation. **p. 122:** Getty Images, Inc. – Taxi. **p. 128:** Rommilly Lockyer/Getty Images, Inc. **p. 134:** Steve Robb/Cynthia Cunningham. **p. 136:** LWA – Dann Tardif/Corbis/Bettmann. **p. 142:** James T. Havey/Index Stock Imagery, Inc. **p. 146:** Eric Audras/PhotoAlto/ Photodisc/Getty Images. **p. 148:** Michael Rosenfield/Getty Images Inc. – Stone Allstock. **p. 157 top left:** Reuters/Pascal Lauener/ Corbis/Bettmann. **p. 157 top right:** REUTERS/ARC/Jean Bernard Sieber/Landov LLC. **p. 157 bottom left:** AP Wide World Photos. **p. 157 bottom right:** Copyright General Motors Corp. Used with permission of GM Media Archives. **p. 158:** Dell/Getty Images/Getty Images, Inc. **p. 180:** Neil Farrin/Getty Images, Inc. **p. 190:** SuperStock, Inc. **p. 200:** CORBIS – NY. **p. 203:** Jose Luis Pelaez/Corbis/Bettmann. **p. 217: top** David Barber/PhotoEdit. **p. 217 bottom:** Kyodo/Landov LLC. **p. 218:** E.J Gallo Winery/E&J Gallo. **p. 219:** Jose L. Pelaez/Corbis/Stock Market. **p. 227:** Courtesy Maximum Impact. **p. 228:** Govin-Sorel/Getty Images Inc. – Stone Allstock. **p. 234:** Getty Images – Digital Vision. **p. 242:** Peter Ross/ Peter Ross. **p. 244:** Julian Hirshowitz/ Ronnie Kaufman/Corbis/Bettmann. **p. 245:** Masterfile Corporation. **p. 249:** Kevin Radford/

SuperStock, Inc. **p. 250:** MTPA Stock/Masterfile Corporation. **p. 255:** Rhoda Sidney/Rhoda Sidney. **p. 267:** Leslie Flores Photography. **p. 276:** Edward Badham Photography, Inc. **p. 278:** Jose L Pelaez/Corbis/Stock Market. **p. 296:** © 2003 SMART Technologies Inc. Used with permission. **p. 302:** SuperStock, Inc. **p. 308:** SuperStock, Inc. **p. 309:** Joseph Giannetti/Index Stock Imagery, Inc. **p. 319:** Mark Milroy/Milroy & McAleer Photography. **p. 321:** SuperStock, Inc. **p. 331:** Tony May/Getty Images Inc. – Stone Allstock. **p. 335:** Jeff Scheid/Getty Images, Inc – Liaison. **p. 345:** Reid Ken/Getty Images, Inc. – Taxi. **p. 348:** Art Bauer, President of EIC Incorporated. **p. 350:** Robert Hanashiro/Copyright 2002, USA TODAY. Reprinted with permission. **p. 353:** Tim Pannell/Corbis Sharpshooters. **p. 356:** Timothy Shonnard/Getty Images Inc. – Stone Allstock. **p. 358:** Kevin Altman. **p. 368:** Tom & DeeAnn McCarthy/Corbis/Bettmann. **p. 370:** Kazuhiro Nogi/AFP/Getty Images, Inc. **p. 371:** Alessandra & Associates. **p. 374:** Toby Talbot/AP Wide World Photos. **p. 391:** Louis Moses/zefa/CORBIS – NY. **p. 393:** Donn Young Photography, Inc. **p. 394:** AP Wide World Photos. **p. 395:** SuperStock, Inc. **p. 397 top:** Cynthia Howe/Cynthia Howe. **p. 397 bottom:** Michael Keller/Corbis/Bettmann. **p. 401:** Mark Bolster/ImageState/International Stock Photography Ltd. **p. 402:** Jose Luis Pelaez/Corbis/Bettmann. **p. 407:** Masterfile Corporation. **p. 411:** David Mautson/Getty Images Inc. – Stone Allstock. **p. 419:** Jeff Geissler/Bloomberg/Jeff Geissler/Bloomberg/Landov. **p. 420:** Getty Images, Inc. – Taxi. **p. 424:** Masterfile Corporation. **p. 426:** Peter Ross/© 2002 Peter Ross. **p. 429:** Fisher/Thatcher/Getty Images Inc. – Stone Allstock. **p. 432:** Tom and DeeAnn McCarthy/Corbis/Bettmann. **p. 465:** Park Plaza International. **p. 471:** H. Armstrong Roberts/Bavaria/Robertstock.com. **p. 477:** The Westin Philippine Plaza. **p. 479:** Sheraton Suites on the Hudson, Weehawken, NJ. **p. 481:** Tom Vano/Index Stock Imagery, Inc.

NAME INDEX

SUBJECT INDEX

D

E

SINGLE PC LICENSE AGREEMENT AND LIMITED WARRANTY

READ THIS LICENSE CAREFULLY BEFORE USING THIS PACKAGE. BY USING THIS PACKAGE, YOU ARE AGREEING TO THE TERMS AND CONDITIONS OF THIS LICENSE. IF YOU DO NOT AGREE, DO NOT USE THE PACKAGE. PROMPTLY RETURN THE UNUSED PACKAGE AND ALL ACCOMPANYING ITEMS TO THE PLACE YOU OBTAINED THEM FOR A FULL REFUND OF ANY SUMS YOU HAVE PAID FOR THE SOFTWARE. ***THESE TERMS APPLY TO ALL LICENSED SOFTWARE ON THE DISK EXCEPT THAT THE TERMS FOR USE OF ANY SHAREWARE OR FREEWARE ON THE DISKETTES ARE AS SET FORTH IN THE ELECTRONIC LICENSE LOCATED ON THE DISK:***

1. GRANT OF LICENSE and OWNERSHIP: The enclosed computer programs and data ("Software") are licensed, not sold, to you by Pearson Education, Inc. publishing as Prentice-Hall, Inc. ("We" or the "Company") and in consideration of the license fee, which is part of the price you paid and your agreement to these terms. We reserve any rights not granted to you. You own only the disk(s) but we and/or our licensors own the Software itself. This license allows you to use and display your copy of the Software on a single computer (i.e., with a single CPU) at a single location for academic use only, so long as you comply with the terms of this Agreement. You may make one copy for back up, or transfer your copy to another CPU, provided that the Software is usable on only one computer.

2. RESTRICTIONS: You may not transfer or distribute the Software or documentation to anyone else. Except for backup, you may not copy the documentation or the Software. You may not network the Software or otherwise use it on more than one computer or computer terminal at the same time. You may not reverse engineer, disassemble, decompile, modify, adapt, translate, or create derivative works based on the Software or the Documentation. You may be held legally responsible for any copying or copyright infringement that is caused by your failure to abide by the terms of these restrictions.

3. TERMINATION: This license is effective until terminated. This license will terminate automatically without notice from the Company if you fail to comply with any provisions or limitations of this license. Upon termination, you shall destroy the Documentation and all copies of the Software. All provisions of this Agreement as to limitation and disclaimer of warranties, limitation of liability, remedies or damages, and our ownership rights shall survive termination.

4. LIMITED WARRANTY AND DISCLAIMER OF WARRANTY: Company warrants that for a period of 60 days from the date you purchase this SOFTWARE (or purchase or adopt the accompanying textbook), the Software, when properly installed and used in accordance with the Documentation, will operate in substantial conformity with the description of the Software set forth in the Documentation, and that for a period of 30 days the disk(s) on which the Software is delivered shall be free from defects in materials and workmanship under normal use. The Company does not warrant that the Software will meet your requirements or that the operation of the Software will be uninterrupted or error-free. Your only remedy and the Company's only obligation under these limited warranties is, at the Company's option, return of the disk for a refund of any amounts paid for it by you or replacement of the disk. THIS LIMITED WARRANTY IS THE ONLY WARRANTY PROVIDED BY THE COMPANY AND ITS LICENSORS, AND THE COMPANY AND ITS LICENSORS DISCLAIM ALL OTHER WARRANTIES, EXPRESS OR IMPLIED, INCLUDING WITHOUT LIMITATION, THE IMPLIED WARRANTIES OF MERCHANTABILITY AND FITNESS FOR A PARTICULAR PURPOSE. THE COMPANY DOES NOT WARRANT, GUARANTEE OR MAKE ANY REPRESENTATION REGARDING THE ACCURACY, RELIABILITY, CURRENTNESS, USE, OR RESULTS OF USE, OF THE SOFTWARE.

5. LIMITATION OF REMEDIES AND DAMAGES: IN NO EVENT, SHALL THE COMPANY OR ITS EMPLOYEES, AGENTS, LICENSORS, OR CONTRACTORS BE LIABLE FOR ANY INCIDENTAL, INDIRECT, SPECIAL, OR CONSEQUENTIAL DAMAGES ARISING OUT OF OR IN CONNECTION WITH THIS LICENSE OR THE SOFTWARE, INCLUDING FOR LOSS OF USE, LOSS OF DATA, LOSS OF INCOME OR PROFIT, OR OTHER LOSSES, SUSTAINED AS A RESULT OF INJURY TO ANY PERSON, OR LOSS OF OR DAMAGE TO PROPERTY, OR CLAIMS OF THIRD PARTIES, EVEN IF THE COMPANY OR AN AUTHORIZED REPRESENTATIVE OF THE COMPANY HAS BEEN ADVISED OF THE POSSIBILITY OF SUCH DAMAGES. IN NO EVENT SHALL THE LIABILITY OF THE COMPANY FOR DAMAGES WITH RESPECT TO THE SOFTWARE EXCEED THE AMOUNTS ACTUALLY PAID BY YOU, IF ANY, FOR THE SOFTWARE OR THE ACCOMPANYING TEXTBOOK. BECAUSE SOME JURISDICTIONS DO NOT ALLOW THE LIMITATION OF LIABILITY IN CERTAIN CIRCUMSTANCES, THE ABOVE LIMITATIONS MAY NOT ALWAYS APPLY TO YOU.

6. GENERAL: THIS AGREEMENT SHALL BE CONSTRUED IN ACCORDANCE WITH THE LAWS OF THE UNITED STATES OF AMERICA AND THE STATE OF NEW YORK, APPLICABLE TO CONTRACTS MADE IN NEW YORK, AND SHALL BENEFIT THE COMPANY, ITS AFFILIATES AND ASSIGNEES. HIS AGREEMENT IS THE COMPLETE AND EXCLUSIVE STATEMENT OF THE AGREEMENT BETWEEN YOU AND THE COMPANY AND SUPERSEDES ALL PROPOSALS OR PRIOR AGREEMENTS, ORAL, OR WRITTEN, AND ANY OTHER COMMUNICATIONS BETWEEN YOU AND THE COMPANY OR ANY REPRESENTATIVE OF THE COMPANY RELATING TO THE SUBJECT MATTER OF THIS AGREEMENT. If you are a U.S. Government user, this Software is licensed with "restricted rights" as set forth in subparagraphs (a)-(d) of the Commercial Computer-Restricted Rights clause at FAR 52.227-19 or in subparagraphs (c)(1)(ii) of the Rights in Technical Data and Computer Software clause at DFARS 252.227-7013, and similar clauses, as applicable.

Should you have any questions concerning this agreement or if you wish to contact the Company for any reason, please contact in writing:

Director of New Media
Higher Education Division
Prentice Hall, Inc.
1 Lake Street
Upper Saddle River, NJ 07458